Adventuring in Southern Africa

The Sierra Club Adventure Travel Guides

Adventuring in Southern Africa

BOTSWANA

ZIMBABWE

ZAMBIA

MALAWI

NAMIBIA

SOUTH AFRICA

SWAZILAND

LESOTHO

ALLEN BECHKY

SIERRA CLUB BOOKS • SAN FRANCISCO

The Sierra Club, founded in 1892 by John Muir, has devoted itself to the study and protection of the earth's scenic and ecological resources—mountains, wetlands, woodlands, wild shores and rivers, deserts and plains. The publishing program of the Sierra Club offers books to the public as a nonprofit educational service in the hope that they may enlarge the public's understanding of the Club's basic concerns. The point of view expressed in each book, however, does not necessarily represent that of the Club. The Sierra Club has some sixty chapters coast to coast, in Canada, Hawaii, and Alaska. For information about how you may participate in its programs to preserve wilderness and the quality of life, please address inquiries to Sierra Club, 85 Second Street, San Francisco, CA 94105.
http://www.sierraclub.org/books

LIBRARY OF CONGRESS CATALOGING-IN-PUBLICATION DATA
Bechky, Allen, 1947 –
    Adventuring in Southern Africa : Botswana, Zimbabwe, Zambia, Namibia, South Africa, Makawi, Lesotho, and Swaziland / by Allen Bechky.
        p.   cm.
    Includes bibliographical references and index.
    ISBN 0-87156-593-5 (alk. paper)
    1. Africa, Southern — Guidebooks.   2. Safaris — Africa, Southern — Guidebooks.   3. Wildlife watching — Africa, Southern — Guidebooks. I. Title.
    DT1017.B43   1997
    916.804'65 — dc21   97–8048

Production by Susan Ristow · Cover design by Bonnie Smetts Design
Book design by Amy Evans · Maps by Duncan Butchart
Composition by David Peattie

Printed in the United States on acid-free paper containing a minimum of 50% recovered waste paper of which at least 10% of the fiber content is post-consumer waste.

10 9 8 7 6 5 4 3 2 1

Contents

Maps

Preface

I have long had a love affair with Africa. As a kid, I was crazy about wild animals and often day-dreamed about going on safari. In 1971, the dream was realized when I spent six months hitchhiking around the game parks of East Africa. At trip's end, I was truly hooked on safaris, so I found a niche in the travel industry and began organizing and leading African safari tours.

I have guided safaris in all the great wildlife paradises of the continent and have mounted expeditions everywhere from Tanzania's Serengeti Plains to the deserts of Namibia. My preference has always been for camping safaris, and a taste for hiking has led me on unusual foot safaris in big game country and on treks in Africa's highest mountain ranges. I have been very fortunate to see the best the continent has to offer. I am also proud that I could share the benefit of my experiences through my first guidebook, *Adventuring in East Africa*. After more than two decades of safaris, my passion for Africa's wildlife and wild places has not diminished one bit. I hope that some of that enthusiasm comes through in the pages of this guidebook.

The book has been many years in the making. Even before the publication of *Adventuring in East Africa*, I was planning a companion volume that would cover the gamelands of the southern part of the continent. Although I had already traveled extensively in that region, I felt that I needed even more personal familiarity with the south before I could properly write about it, so, over the next few years, I set about further explorations in southern Africa.

In the course of those explorations, I revisited Botswana's glorious Okavango Delta, gliding over its waterways in a dugout canoe, then flew to remote private safari camps. I camped in the "desert" of the Central Kalahari Game Reserve and watched massive elephant herds drink from the Chobe River. I savored purple sunsets over the Zambezi at Mana

Pools in Zimbabwe, and I hiked among the bouldered koppies of the Matobo Hills in search of hidden galleries of Bushman rock paintings. I tracked black rhinos through thick jesse bush in Matusadona National Park, and I bumped into a pride of lions in the sandy bed of Chizarira's isolated Busi River. A portered foot safari in the wilds of Zambia's North Luangwa National Park was a great complement to the superb game viewing I enjoyed in South Luangwa. The discovery of Zambia's game-rich Busanga Plains was unexpected, as was a long swim through big Zambezi rapids that woke me up to the full adrenaline-rush potential of whitewater rafting. In South Africa, I drove around Kruger National Park and visited Africa's most famous private game reserves. I hiked below the imposing wall of KwaZulu-Natal's Drakensberg Mountains and swam among the coral gardens along its wild Maputaland coast. The pounding surf and seal colonies of Namibia's cold Skeleton Coast and the dune-choked sand rivers of its far away Kaokoveld—the haunt of a hardy race of desert elephants—provided a unique African experience. So, too, did snorkeling in the waters of Lake Malawi. All these experiences and more await you in southern Africa.

In writing this book, my object is to cover the whole range of safari activities in southern Africa from the perspective of someone who is devoted to nature and conservation. Naturally, there is a heavy emphasis on exploring the game parks. I include information about fascinating wild places that are remote and relatively unknown, as well as the most celebrated national parks and private game reserves. I also discuss wilderness areas outside park boundaries and cover those places that can only be explored by the trekker or hiker. Throughout the book, pride of place is given to wildlife, which is, after all, the subject of prime interest on most African safaris. My object is to facilitate a greater understanding of *what* to look for in each area and *how* to find it, as well as to answer the basic questions of *where* to go. Perhaps most importantly, I try to explain what makes each place unique from the naturalist's point of view. In so doing, I address the all-important issue of *why* to go.

This book is meant to be both trip planner and traveling companion. The "Into Africa: Planning Your Trip" chapter focuses on vital pretrip information. Part of this chapter is devoted to the relative merits of various styles of African travel, with the aim of helping you decide whether independent or group touring most suits you. The same chapter also reviews the preparations necessary for any trip to Africa: considerations of health, safety, etiquette, and equipment are treated with more than ordinary attention to detail. A separate section deals extensively with the specialized requirements of camping, walking, and living in the bush.

The chapter called "Africa: The Land and Its People" outlines the geography, history, and peoples of the continent with a view to putting a safari to southern Africa into its larger context. Another chapter, "The African Realm: Tips on Watching Wildlife," is presented as a primer on natural history. It offers a great deal of information on African fauna, flora, ecology, and conservation, along with practical hints on how to maximize field opportunities to find and observe African wildlife.

The book covers the six countries where game viewing safaris take place in southern Africa: Botswana, Zimbabwe, Zambia, Malawi, Namibia, and South Africa. Mozambique is not included because it is just beginning to recover from its long civil war, and tourism is currently limited to a few islands along its tropical coast.

In the country chapters, each park and wilderness region is introduced by an overview of its natural and human history and relevant conservation issues. Access and accommodation information follows, including the locations of many out-of-the-way lodges and special campsites. Attention is also paid to remote and often overlooked regions of each park. Plants and animals likely to be encountered in each particular area are pointed out; birds, reptiles, and small mammals are discussed as well as the larger animals.

Keep in mind that this volume is no starry-eyed account of the safari scene: I try to point out the problems as well as the appeal of the various locales.

This book is about safaris. Relatively scant space is given to Africa's diverse peoples and cultures, or cities, towns, and highly populated regions that do not have much interest as destinations for natural history safaris. I do present an overview of the history and politics of the six countries as a background for visiting their wilderness areas. Although some might wish for a more in-depth treatment of nightlife, dining, hotels, and urban culture, such information is available elsewhere, and I have preferred to devote more space to the wild places that are the focus of the book.

In Africa, as elsewhere, nothing changes as fast as prices, and most of the costs quoted in guidebooks are outdated by the time they see print. For that reason, I have not listed prices for hotels or services other than national park fees (which generally have more stability, although even those can rise sharply and suddenly). Nor have I created formal classifications for hotels and lodges. Instead, I have chosen to describe them in everyday language, using such terms as budget, moderate, or luxury. The reader will know which facilities will best suit his or her needs.

I would be happy to receive any comments from travelers that will be useful for future editions of this book. I am also available to answer

questions or assist anyone who is interested in going on an African safari. I can be reached at (510) 524-7587 or E-mailed at abechky@pac-
bell.net.

I hope that my book will add to the enjoyment of your African experience and, especially, that it will stimulate you to aid the cause of conservation. The beauty of the African realm makes the best case for its
preservation. See it soon, and do what you can to help. Have a great safari!

Allen Bechky, January 1997

Acknowledgments

If, as they say in Africa, it takes a village to raise a child, it takes an army to gather all the information needed to produce a guidebook. I am grateful to the many people who made this volume possible. Some provided me with assistance, hospitality, or information; others contributed in less tangible but equally important ways—lending inspiration, companionship, and moral support.

I am especially indebted to those of my colleagues in Africa who were kind enough to read various portions of the manuscript; their expertise made an invaluable contribution to the final product. Special thanks to Colin Bell of Wilderness Safaris, who reviewed the chapters on Botswana, Namibia, and South Africa and kept me constantly up to date on new developments all over the region (thanks also to his wife, Margot, for putting me up whenever I passed through Johannesburg). Judy Helmholtz of Zambezi Nkuku was always a most helpful (and funny) correspondent from Livingstone, Zambia (I can only wish Judy and Arthur Sonnenberg the best of luck with all those chickens). Phil Berry of Chinzombo Safari Lodge provided corrections for the Zambia chapter, while Babette Alfieri of Chinzombo kept me abreast of the myriad changes constantly taking place in the Zambian tourism industry. Thanks to Garth Thompson of Safari Consultants, Zimbabwe, for his comments on elephant conservation in that country, and to Pam Badger of Central African Wilderness Safaris for her review of the Malawi material. Special thanks goes to Duncan Butchart not only for his useful criticisms of the natural history and South Africa chapters, but also for producing the fine maps that appear in this book.

Many thanks go to all of the following for their help in marshaling the facts or for their hospitality in Africa:

In Botswana, special thanks to my friend Alan Wolframm of Okavango Wilderness Safaris for looking over that country chapter and for sending me numerous updates. Much gratitude goes to guides Dave van Smeerdjik, Heidi Dednam, and Matt Grimley for putting up with me on various expeditions (and to Heidi for her *babotie* recipe). Thanks also to Brian and Janice Graham of Linyanti Explorations.

In Zambia, I'd like to thank Charlie Ross of Sobek Expeditions; Norman Carr, Nick and Jessica Aslin of Kapani Lodge; Will Ruck-Keene and Ben Parker of Tongabezi; F. E. C. Munyenyembe of the L.I.R.D.P.; Edson Tembo of the Zambia National Tourist Board (New York); John Coppinger of Remote Africa Safaris; John Tolmay of Across Africa Safaris; M. A. P. Patel of Busanga Trails; Mark Harvey of Shiwa Ngandu; Jo Pope of Robin Pope Safaris; Wilderness Trails Ltd. (Chibembe Lodge and Nsefu Camp); Chinzombo Safari Lodge; Clive Kelly and Iain MacDonald (who accompanied me on a wonderful walking safari in North Luangwa); and to river guides Conrad Fourney, Jeannette Smith, Greg Findley, and Heidi White (for a most eventful raft trip on the Zambezi).

In Zimbabwe, special thanks to Brian and Lindi Worsley of Wilderness Safaris Zimbabwe for their generosity and assistance; it was a great delight to accompany them in the field. Thanks also to Mike Haines and Justin White for their hospitality and companionship on safari. I extend my gratitude to Mary Hatendi of the Zimbabwe Tourist Board (New York); Tom Muller of the National Botanical Gardens in Harare; Russell Pumfrey of Black Rhino Safaris; Victoria Nash of Landela Safaris, and the good folk at Ilala Lodge in Victoria Falls (who always seem to find room at the inn). Thanks also to professional guides John Stevens, Ivan Carter, and Dave Bennett (of Londemela Safaris) for helpful information.

In Namibia, I'd like to thank Louw and Bertus Schoeman of Skeleton Coast Safaris; Denis Liebenberg of Edenteka Wilderness Camp; Wayne Hanssen and Lisa Conradie of Okanjima Lodge; Dennis and Ros Rundle of Wilderness Safaris Namibia; Alan Cilliers of !Ha N!Jore Safaris; Jan Joubert of Ecotour; and the Kalahari Sands Hotel.

In South Africa, many thanks to Tim Farrell of the MalaMala/Rattray Reserves, Hugh Marshal of Londolozi, and the staff at MalaMala, Londolozi, and Inyati camps for their hospitality on various visits to the Sabi Sand Game Reserve; also to Rocktail Bay Lodge for a delightful base on the Maputaland coast. Many thanks also to Ric Wilmot of Honeyguide Camp; Roland and Roxy Geiger of Motswari/M'Bali in Timbavati; Steve Hirst of Battlefield Safaris; Peter Ruddle of Mkuze Trails; Brian Paterson of Trans Africa Safaris; Rob Deane of Bushlands Game Lodge; Francois Meyer of Shakaland; John and Meryn Turner of Babanango Lodge; David Hibbs of the Natal Parks Board; Peter Lawson of Lawson's Tours; and to both Imperial Car Rental and Avis. I also want to thank Yvonne Hormasji and Phil Westernoff of South African Airlines (Los Angeles), Pamela Nicholson of SATOUR (Los Angeles) for their kind assistance, and Richard McConnell of the Adventure Center.

A special thank you to my friends at Wilderness Safaris, South Africa, for giving me a place from which to organize various forays around the country and the subcontinent. I am especially grateful to Ginger Hill for her long-suffering correspondence and to Patrick Boddam-Whetham for his friendship, comments, and encouragement.

There are many people who helped on this side of the Atlantic, too:

I particularly want to thank Pam Shandrick for editing the manuscript. Pam is a great editor and a delight to work with.

I'd like to acknowledge my many friends and co-workers at Mountain Travel/Sobek for their patience and support while I took time off to write. My best wishes go to Dave Parker, Dena Bartolome, Nicole Peelle, Kerston Edgerton, Sandy Olson (who always undertook the unenviable task of getting my last-minute flight schedule in order), Nadia LeBon, Gayle Price, Nancy Griffin, Perry Robertson, Alicia Zablocki, Paul Vesper, Narendra Gurung, Lisa Broughton, Mia Pearson, Teresa Hotchkin, Tom Stanley, Jean Pulley, Janet Williams, Sandy Jonas, Wendy Dobras, Paul Schicke, Elizabeth Burrell, Cathy Ann Taylor, Ping Tian, Stephanie Trinh, Peggy Day, Anna Bezzola, Buffy Murphy, Chris Dunham, Olaf Malver, Massimo Prioreschi (the computer guru), Peter Ourusoff, Lou Gibbs, Jim Ahern, Tom McCormack, Richard Weiss, and Jennifer Crook. Thanks also to Jennifer for helping out with map corrections, and to Christine and Bret Furnas for their input on Lesotho.

My deep appreciation goes to those close friends who light up my life and, in doing so, make a long book project bearable. Great affection and gratitude go to my zany long-time companion, Michele Swide (the self-confessed most beautiful woman in the world); to my Bay Area family, Judy, Mark, Willy, Tom, Annie, and Bo Decker; to Dave Parker and Judy Hartman (and Mike); to my life-long buddy Jay Rasumny; and to my other California family, Hans Schnelle, Nancy Miyamoto, Andreas, and Keiko, who provide a refuge for the mind in the north woods. Very special thanks also to Iain Allan and Lu Contemesa (who always welcome me into their home in Nairobi) and to my friends Dick and Louise McGowan, Penny Stewart, Wendy and Mike Russo, Sara Steck and Steve White, Volker Schnelle, Paul Noble, Pete Moacanon, Gary Hassan, Frank Edwards, Mark Friedman, Phil Rasori, Marilyn Simons, Howie Stark, Amy Schectman, Sue Siegal, Betty Noble, and John Rissman, each of whom has given me needed encouragement at one time or another over the years. I literally owe my life to an exceptionally fine physician, Dr. Mario Corona, for pulling me through a very tight spot.

I am very grateful for all the love and cheerleading that only a family can give: to my mom, Ruth Bechky, my brothers Ron and Stan and sister Gail and their ever-growing families, to cousins Lisa Teiger and Andy Alexander-Crossan (and my godchild Benjamin), and to cousin Carole Teiger. To my sorrow, two loved ones to whom I would like to express my debt are no longer here: my aunts, Rose and Ella.

I dedicate this book to the wild animals and wild places of Africa.

CHAPTER ONE

Africa:
The Land and Its People

SOME 1,500 MILES separate the headwaters of the Zambezi River in northern Zambia from South Africa's Cape of Good Hope, and it is roughly the same distance again between the Zambezi's mouth on the Indian Ocean and the Atlantic beaches of Namibia's Skeleton Coast. This southern third of Africa is one of the great natural regions of the continent — and the world. Here are found some of Africa's finest wildlife reserves.

Big game still abounds in the wild bushlands of the Zambezi drainage, the sandy thirstlands of the Kalahari, the lush marshes of the Okavango Delta, and the Lowveld savannas of South Africa. To these premier gamelands must be added the potpourri of mountain ranges, deserts, and wilderness coastlines that make southern Africa a paradise for nature lovers and safari adventurers.

Before you start planning your trip, it's useful to take a look at the geography and history of this southern region while placing it into the context of the continent as a whole.

An Overview of the Geography of Southern Africa

Geologically, Africa is a very old continent. Two hundred forty million years ago, it was lumped together with South America, Australia, India, and Antarctica in a supercontinent — the ancient Gondwanaland. When that huge southern land mass completed its breakup some 65 million years ago, Africa was left pretty much with the familiar shape it has today. About 15 million years ago, a new series of violent geologic upheavals began to fissure eastern Africa, creating the long chain of lakes, escarpments, and volcanoes that we see today throughout the Great Rift Valley system. But unlike the northern continents, Africa was neither submerged by ancient seas nor scoured by late Ice Age glaciers. The diverse habitats and life forms of its Pleistocene landscape were allowed to evolve almost intact into the modern era.

Almost 12 million square miles in area, Africa is the world's second largest continent. With the equator running through its middle, most of it lies squarely in the tropics. But it is not a jungle continent, for aside from a zone of equatorial rainforest found along the Atlantic coast and in the Congo Basin, most regions receive fewer than 40 inches of rain a year. Since rainfall is concentrated in distinct wet seasons, most months are entirely dry. Even where annual precipitation is high, a tremendous amount of rainwater is lost immediately in heavy runoff, with later loss through evaporation over the long dry seasons. By far the greater part of the continent is covered by zones of vegetation adapted to varying degrees of aridity — savanna and desert.

The Sahara, the largest desert in the world, stretches across the breadth of the northern third of the continent from the Atlantic to the Red Sea. This brutal region receives fewer than 5 inches of rain per year throughout its 1,000-mile-wide east-west belt. Even that precipitation is extraordinarily variable, for interior regions may go years without a drop. Rock paintings tell us that the Sahara has not always been a desert, but has been undergoing a dramatic drying-out process within recent times. Portraits of giraffes and elephants in the waterless heart of its Tassili region are sure signs that the Sahara enjoyed a much wetter climate only 7,000 years ago. Later paintings show that the Sahara was inhabited by cattle-herding peoples until roughly 1200 B.C. Generations of gradual desiccation eventually forced most of the Sahara's peoples and animals to emigrate.

Along the southern edge of the Sahara runs the Sahel, a semidesert transition zone to the savannas of black Africa. Here rainfall is very erratic, yet averages between 10 and 20 inches per year. Increasing human population and overgrazing are quickening the process of desertification in the Sahel: each year, the true desert, the Sahara, continues to advance a few miles further southward.

Below the Sahel, rainfall increases markedly (to between 20 and 40 inches per year), and the country greens up into the wooded grasslands broadly known as tropical savannas. Like the Sahara, the northern savanna zone stretches across Africa in an unbroken east-west band. In West Africa, this savanna belt merges into the zone of the equatorial rainforest. In the drier east, savannas dominate the high East African plateau, then spread deep into southern Africa. There are many different types of savanna country: some are pure grasslands, while others are dominated by various woodland communities. Most of Africa's people live in the savanna zone, but its wilderness areas remain Africa's classic big game country. It is within the savanna reserves of East Africa and southern Africa that the greatest concentrations of wild animals are found.

The mile-high grassy plains of East Africa along the border of Kenya and Tanzania are probably the most game-rich savannas left on the continent. This is primarily due to modern human activities in the analogous open plains habitats of southern Africa — particularly in the Kalahari and parts of South Africa — where unfenced rangeland has been eliminated or greatly reduced, causing catastrophic harm to the huge herds of migratory animals that formerly lived there. Most of the remaining wilderness areas in southern Africa are more densely wooded environments which, though less favorable to massive herds of grazing animals, still teem with game. The transition to more heavily wooded country begins in southern Tanzania, where wide-open grasslands are replaced by miombo woodlands, a type of savanna vegetation that occurs in areas above 3,000 feet. Miombo dominates the central African plateau that covers most of Zambia and Malawi, and is found as far south as Zimbabwe.

The high plains of East Africa are close to the equator and have two rainy seasons annually. The weather pattern shifts in southern Africa, where there is only one long rainy season, between November and April, with the rest of the year remaining dry. Rainfall in southern Africa is heaviest in the northeastern part of the subcontinent, which is influenced by warm, moist air coming off the Indian Ocean. Rain decreases steadily to the west and south — while the coastal lowlands along the Indian Ocean receive more than 40 inches a year and Luangwa Valley in Zambia gets about 37 inches, Maun, in the northern Kalahari, receives only 20 inches. Namibia's Skeleton Coast averages less than an inch — and that irregularly! In southern Africa, the rainy season coincides with summer. Vegetation during the hot summer months is therefore lush and green, while most of the woodland trees lose their leaves during the dry season.

Deciduous "dry woodlands" predominate in the low-lying parts of Zambia and Zimbabwe (such as the valley of the Zambezi River), as well as in northern Botswana. Mopane woodlands are a widespread component of the dry woodlands zone, and they are a very game-rich savanna habitat. Although elephants are by no means restricted to mopane areas, Africa's largest remaining elephant herds are concentrated in the

wildlife reserves of this region. Mopane and other dry woodlands vegetation reach down as far as the northern part of South Africa's Kruger
National Park. Further south, they are replaced by "mixed woodlands"
composed of acacias and a wide variety of broad-leafed trees. Mixed
woodlands prevail at lower altitudes throughout eastern South Africa,
where this type of savanna vegetation is commonly called bushveld. The
bushveld parks of South Africa include Kruger and its satellite reserves
in the eastern Transvaal, as well as the parks of Natal. They are the richest wildlife areas in the country.

Africa's Great Rift Valley makes a dramatic entry into southern
Africa, cutting into the region in the long, deep, trench filled by Lake
Malawi, southernmost of the great African lakes. Other fractures in the
Rift Valley system spread deeper into the region — notably Zambia's long
Luangwa Valley, which is one of the most prolific game areas on the continent. Indeed, the escarpments that frame the valley of the Zambezi
River are also the result of Rift Valley faulting. Further southward, such
dramatic escarpments disappear, but the effects of Rift Valley faulting in
shaping the landscape have been no less profound. Subtle shifts along
underground faults have altered the courses of the great river networks
of southern Africa, leading to the creation of features as spectacular and
diverse as the Victoria Falls, the Makgadikgadi Pans, and the Okavango
Delta.

The Makgadikgadi Pans are the remains of an ancient lakebed. Although a shallow lake may form in the pans during rainy years, the pans
remain vast flats of shimmering white salt most of the time. The Delta is
a true oasis, where the Okavango River spreads out into a paradise of
waterways and marshes that are one of Africa's most celebrated wetlands.

Both the Makgadikgadi Pans and the Okavango Delta are found in
the northern Kalahari, that vast and famous territory at the geographic
center of southern Africa. Although commonly referred to as a desert,
the Kalahari does not technically qualify as such. True enough, it is a
harsh thirstland without surface water, save that which collects in shallow pans after summer rain showers. But, though dry, the Kalahari is
wide-open savanna country covered by grassland with scattered acacia
trees and bushes. Beneath its surface are unimaginably deep deposits of
ancient sand. Sparsely inhabited by humans, the Kalahari is one of
Africa's unique wildlife regions.

The Tropic of Capricorn marks the northern edge of a distinctly temperate region. From there southward, the tropical savanna, with its typical baobabs and umbrella-shaped acacia trees, gradually gives way to
communities of vegetation that can tolerate a definite period of cool

Pristine African wilderness on the lower Zambesi River at Mana Pools National Park, Zimbabwe. Photo: Allen Bechky.

winter weather. Temperate grasslands appear on the Highveld plains of South Africa, while the mountains of Natal and Lesotho are seasonally dusted with snow. The climate gets progressively drier toward the south Atlantic coast, as the semidesert savanna grasslands of the Kalahari merge into the true desert conditions of the Namib. Southward, in the interior of western South Africa, the Kalahari melds into another semi-desert region known as the Karoo. The Indian Ocean warms the land on the eastern coast, so a semitropical climate persists almost to the Cape of Good Hope. The Cape marks the very southern tip of Africa. It has a Mediterranean climate with a cool winter season and supports a unique type of vegetation known as fynbos.

Humankind in Africa

Human history in Africa goes back to the very roots of our species. Fossil evidence suggests a line of development stretching from the appearance of the first primate, *Aegyptopithecus* ("the dawn ape"), some 33 million years ago, to the presence of *Homo sapiens*. While current research is focused on the East African Rift Valley, important discoveries of early hominids (bipedal primates in the human family) have also been made in South Africa. Both *Australopithecus africanus*, an apelike creature that walked the plains perhaps as long as 3 million years ago, and its larger successor, *Australopithecus robustus*, were unearthed in limestone caves in the eastern Transvaal. Neither is regarded as being in the direct line of human ancestors. A more likely candidate for the position of human progenitor is *Australopithecus afarensis*, of which a 3-million-year-old specimen (the celebrated "Lucy") was discovered in Ethiopia. The more recent fossil record goes on to reveal larger-brained species: the first tool users, *Homo habilis* ("able man") and the more refined *Homo erectus* ("erect man"). They lived at least 1.6 million years ago at both Tanzania's Olduvai Gorge and at Lake Turkana in Kenya. The earliest *Homo sapiens* are believed to have made their debut no more than half a million years ago. Although controversy among anthropologists swirls around the exact relationship of the various specimens unearthed, the betting is heavy that our species was born in Africa. The artifacts of human cultures stretching from the Stone Age to historic times are found all over the continent.

The most ancient of Africa's present-day ethnic groups are the Pygmies and the Bushmen. Bushmen are more properly known as the San, and, along with the Xoi (or Hottentots), form a racially and linguistically distinct group known as the Xoisan. While the Pygmies still live in the equatorial forests of the Congo Basin, the Bushmen were exterminated or pushed out of the richer savannas of southern Africa and are now found only in the Kalahari desert. Both groups traditionally lived as hunter-gatherers, completely adapted to their respective environments. For millennia, they survived in small bands, wandering as the seasons and food sources required.

Of course, black people are the dominant ethnic group in sub-Saharan Africa today. Their geographic origins are obscure; very possibly they came from North African regions that are now abandoned to the Sahara. The hunters who appear in the Saharan rock paintings of some 5,000 years B.C. were negroid, as were the cattle herders who replaced them. It seems likely that with the great drying out of the Sahara, those prehistoric peoples moved southward.

The ancient tribes spoke many languages, but one linguistic group in particular — the Bantu — was spectacularly successful in its expansion throughout sub-Saharan Africa. Bantu-speaking peoples spread through the West African savannas and the tropical forest zone and eventually reached the high plateaus of East Africa, from which they moved southward, almost to the Cape. The Bantu herded cattle where they could (in regions not infested with tsetse flies), but were generally more dependent on farming for their survival.

After the collapse of the Roman Empire and the rise of Islam, European contact with Africa was limited by centuries of warfare with the Arabs of the Mediterranean coast. Geographic knowledge was reduced to what could be gleaned from the works of classical Greco-Roman texts. Meanwhile, the Arabs were learning about the continent and peoples to their south — throughout the Middle Ages, they carried on a brisk trade with the tribes of the Horn of Africa and sent maritime expeditions down the eastern coast. By the 10th century, they had founded a string of towns along the Indian Ocean. These trading outposts eventually developed into the lively city-states from which the Swahili culture of East Africa evolved, and from which the European explorers later set off to "discover" the African hinterland. The southernmost of these Arab coastal towns was Sofala, near present-day Beira in Mozambique. Sofala's merchants established strong links with the Shona founders of Great Zimbabwe, the hub of a commercial empire that reached its heyday in the early 15th century. Today, the ruins of Great Zimbabwe's stone towers and enclosures remain one of Africa's most dramatic archaeological sites.

The European discovery of Africa began with the voyages of the seafaring Portuguese during the 14th and 15th centuries. Slowly, the Iberian mariners extended their voyages down the Atlantic coast until Bartholomeu Dias finally rounded the Cape of Good Hope in 1488. He was soon followed by Vasco da Gama's exploration of the Indian Ocean coast as far north as the Arab towns of Mombasa and Malindi in present-day Kenya. Throughout Europe's age of exploration, while sailors from a half-dozen nations were charting the world's oceans and opening up new lands for colonization, European ships plied the coasts of Africa. Offshore islands were colonized and a few fortified towns were founded on the mainland. These were meant to supply the fleets cruising to their lucrative East Indian possessions. The African hinterland was deemed too dangerous to explore and not worth the risk. Its wealth — ivory and, especially, slaves — was exploited by proxy. Only a few missionaries and explorers bothered to penetrate the interior. With the exception of the establishment of the Dutch colony at Cape Town in 1652, no real attempts were made to colonize Africa until the 19th century.

Yet the age of exploration, with its discoveries and exploitation of new lands, had profound effects on the African continent. The colonization of the New World, particularly the development of plantation agriculture in the American tropics, required the importation of huge numbers of slaves. As the Indians of the Caribbean died off wholesale from European-imported epidemics of smallpox and measles, they were replaced by Africans, whose bodies already had some immune resistance to those killers. Blacks soon became the only source of slave labor. Over a period spanning almost four centuries, an estimated 10 million Africans were carried into bondage in the Americas. The social disruption and suffering caused in Africa by the constant depredations of slaving expeditions are incalculable.

Most slaving took place in West Africa. Rather than venture into the dangerous interior, white traders preferred to buy slaves at coastal enclaves. The business of catching slaves was left primarily to African allies, who received European firearms to make their jobs easier. On Africa's east coast, Arab slavers organized their own slave-catching expeditions. They forged a system of inland caravan routes that were later to become the highways of the European explorers.

The founding of the Dutch colony at Cape Town in 1652 was to have lasting significance for the history of the continent. The colony at Table Bay was originally established merely as a supply and "refreshment" station for Dutch ships. But independent-minded *boers* ("farmers") soon spread to the fertile valleys of the temperate Cape region, from which the cattle-herding Hottentots and the Bushmen were easily displaced. By the 1770s, the edge of Boer settlement had reached the Great Fish River, some 500 miles east of Cape Town, where it first collided with the vanguard of the Bantu wave that had been lapping southward across the continent for centuries. The Bantus were not so easily pushed aside as the Hottentots, and frontier warfare flared up sporadically ever after.

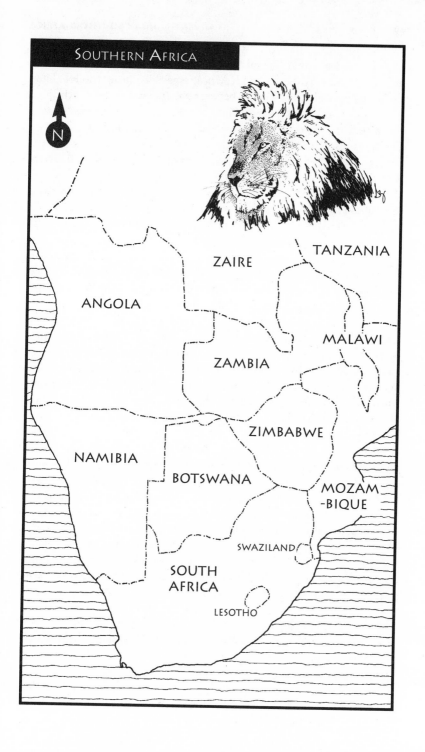

SOUTHERN AFRICA

N

ZAIRE

TANZANIA

ANGOLA

ZAMBIA

MALAWI

ZIMBABWE

NAMIBIA

BOTSWANA

MOZAM
-BIQUE

SWAZILAND

SOUTH
AFRICA

LESOTHO

The advance of the Boers stopped the southward drift of Bantu migration. Within a half century, the bottleneck was causing crowding among the Nguni tribes of South Africa, especially those who inhabited the fertile coastal strip of Natal between the Indian Ocean and the high mountains of the Drakensberg. In the 1820s, that region erupted in warfare associated with the rise of King Shaka and his Zulu nation. Defeated rivals, dispossessed of their cattle and fleeing for their lives, crossed the barrier of the Drakensberg to fall on the tribes of the interior Highveld. A chain reaction of destruction followed: as each tribe was attacked and chased from its lands, the starving refugees had little choice but to raid their weaker neighbors for food and cattle. The central plateau became a place of horror and starvation. Between 1822 and 1828, an estimated 1 to 2 million people died.

This catastrophe, known as the *mfecane* ("the crushing"), was crucial to subsequent historical developments in southern Africa. The depopulation of the Highveld greatly facilitated the advance of the Boers in their Great Trek of 1835–1839, when they moved out of the Cape to establish their own republics in the Orange Free State and the Transvaal. The Boers encountered little opposition until they met the Zulus and their breakaway offshoots, the Matabele. Both those warlike tribes fought and were defeated by the Boer *voortrekkers* ("pioneers"), but the Zulus maintained the power and independence of their kingdom until 1879, when they were finally subjugated by the British. The Matabele chief, Mzilikaze, who had played a key role in unleashing the *mfecane*, took his people northwards to establish his own powerful kingdom in western Zimbabwe. In the wake of the *mfecane* chaos, the Sutu tribes of the Highveld coalesced in the mountainous kingdom that became Lesotho.

The British became players on the southern African stage when they took over the Cape colony in 1806. Simmering resentment against the newcomers' meddling with their way of life (and the abolition of slavery within the British Empire) led the Boers to undertake their Great Trek. But the British initially showed little concern about what went on in the African interior. Their colony was, however, a good springboard for exploration, and they acquired it just at the time when European geographers were becoming interested in unraveling the mysteries of Africa. Until then, British maps delineated only the outlines of the continent with any degree of certainty; the interior was left "dark," signifying *terra incognita* (unknown territory). Ironically, it was the new-fledged passion for the suppression of the slave trade that spurred Africa's most celebrated explorer to his greatest discoveries.

Dr. David Livingstone went out to Africa in 1841 at the behest of the London Missionary Society. He was posted to Kuruman in the northern

Cape colony, on the fringe of the great Kalahari, where he wooed and won his wife Mary, the daughter of pioneering missionary Robert Moffatt. But Livingstone never showed much enthusiasm for the routines of missionary work, preferring instead to roam the unknown lands beyond the mission's bounds. In 1849, he made his first big expedition, crossing the Kalahari to discover Lake Ngami at the southern tip of the Okavango Delta. In 1851, he again crossed the Kalahari, this time penetrating all the way to the Zambezi River. His joy at finding such a great river was tempered by a more sobering discovery: unbeknown to the outside world, a revitalized slave trade was flourishing in the uncharted African wilderness. From that time on, his passion for exploration was justified by a personal crusade against the slave trade. He believed the best means to end that trade in human chattel was to open Africa up to the "three Cs": Commerce, Christianity, and Civilization. He again returned to the Zambezi in 1853. This time he traveled upriver to its headwaters before starting west to cross the whole of Angola and arrive at the Portuguese colonial city of Luanda on the Atlantic. Then, turning back to the interior, he retraced his path to the Zambezi and followed most of its course downstream, arriving at its mouth in 1856. When he emerged, he stunned the world with the news of his discovery of Victoria Falls.

The celebrity brought on by that journey enabled him to get funding for his next expedition. Livingstone was convinced that the Zambezi could be opened up to navigation and used as a highway to bring civilization to the interior. He returned to the Zambezi in 1858, equipped with a riverboat on which he proposed to steam upriver. He was stopped by the impassable rapids of the Cahora Bassa Gorge. Frustrated on the Zambezi, and with his wife dead from malaria, Livingstone and his expedition accomplished little save for the discovery of Lake Malawi. Between 1866 and 1873, Livingstone undertook his last expedition, wandering around eastern and central Africa, getting "lost" and found by Stanley, and finally succumbing to fever in the Bangweulu Swamps of northern Zambia.

Although he was certainly the giant among explorers in southern Africa, Livingstone's legacy is impressive not so much for his many "first" discoveries as for the wide interest he generated about an unknown continent. The publicity that attended his wanderings attracted support for the expeditions of Burton, Speke, and Grant in search of the source of the Nile, and of Henry Morton Stanley's later transcontinental journey that culminated in his descent of the Congo River.

As the dark spots on the map of Africa were filled in, the scramble for colonies began in earnest. British interest in its Cape colony grew enormously after the discovery of diamonds in 1867. Within five years, thou-

Victoria Falls, also known as Mosi-oa-Tunya, *"the smoke that thunders."* Photo: Allen Bechky.

sands of Englishmen had run off to Africa to seek their fortunes in the diamond fields at Kimberly. One man was spectacularly successful: Cecil Rhodes amassed tremendous wealth by gaining control of the diamond mines, and thereafter vigorously pursued his dream of creating a British domain to stretch from the Cape to Cairo. All over the continent, French and British authorities began to exert control over interior regions far from their coastal enclaves. Newcomers were also getting into the act: King Leopold of Belgium hired Stanley to carve an empire out of the Congo, while Germany began to look for unclaimed territory it could call its own. Rivalries among the European nations played no small part in the final division of the continent. When Bismarck suddenly declared German protectorates in Africa, he did so more to obtain bargaining chips against his military rivals in Europe than out of genuine interest in empire building. At the Berlin Conference of 1884–1885, the great powers began the process of formally parceling out Africa among themselves. The colonial era had arrived.

The British already possessed the lion's share of southern Africa and were soon to get more. In the late 1870s, the British government planned to federate its colonies in the Cape and Natal with the independent Boer republics of the Orange Free State and the Transvaal. The Boers and the Zulus were thought to be minor impediments to the scheme, but both proved otherwise. In 1879, the Zulu army inflicted a stinging defeat on the British at Isandlwana, wiping out an entire column that included more than 800 of England's finest troops. This Custer-style disaster was so embarrassing to the British Crown that the Disraeli government immediately fell. Later that year, the Zulus were duly crushed, but the British were soon to experience further indignities. They had already announced the annexation of the Transvaal in 1877 and did not expect any serious opposition. But the Boers reasserted their independence in 1880 and quickly defeated the British forces sent against them. Afraid of an expensive war, the British government once again recognized the Transvaal's independence.

In 1884, the Germans asserted a claim to South-West Africa (later to become Namibia), while freebooting Boers from the Transvaal were stirring up trouble by stealing the lands of the Tswana tribes on the northern frontier of the Cape colony. To forestall any further land grabs from under their noses, the British annexed the territory of the southern Tswana and established a protectorate over the huge desert wilderness in northern Bechuanaland (later to become Botswana). Soon thereafter, gold was discovered in the Transvaal, bringing a flood of English immigration into that Boer republic and a new fortune to Cecil Rhodes.

Rhodes was already planning his great coup: to leapfrog the Boers in the Transvaal with a northward advance into central Africa. His agents tricked the Matabele king, Lobengula, into giving his British South Africa Company a "concession" to operate in the king's territory. In 1890, the Pioneer Column of the British South Africa Company occupied Mashonaland, establishing Fort Salisbury (now Harare). By 1896, revolts by the Shona and Matabele tribes had been quelled, and the British flag was flying over a new colony — Rhodesia — which encompassed all of present-day Zimbabwe and Zambia. Nyasaland, the territory to the west of the Great Rift Valley lake, had already been annexed by the British in 1883.

Rhodes's controlling interests in the gold mines around Johannesburg and his schemes to extend British political control led to further problems with the Boers. In 1896, he orchestrated an attempt to seize the Transvaal — the infamous and unsuccessful Jameson Raid. That event and subsequent efforts by the British government to subvert the independence of the Boer republics led to the outbreak of hostilities in 1899. It took almost three years of bitter warfare to force the Boers to concede defeat, but the British finally attained hegemony over the entire heartland of southern Africa. Only the thinly populated German colony in South-West Africa and the huge but unthreatening outposts of the moribund Portuguese Empire (Angola and Mozambique) remained beyond British control.

The colonial partition of the continent was to have lasting effects on Africa's political and economic development. The lines drawn on the new map of Africa reflected little ethnographic or economic rationale for the creation of future nations. Arbitrary borders divided some tribal groups from their closest relatives, while throwing others together with traditionally bitter enemies. Unified regions were sundered, migration and trade routes cut off. Later, these whimsical colonial boundaries were to harden into the inviolable borders of sovereign nations, setting the stage for the political and economic fragmentation that is a major stumbling block in Africa today.

The theory and practice of colonial administration differed under each of the European powers. In their protectorates, the British established a system of indirect rule: local rulers were made representatives of the Crown and remained in nominal control as long as they did what they were told. Colonies such as South Africa and Rhodesia, where good farmland, valuable minerals, and a pleasant climate attracted white immigrants, were given much higher degrees of true self-rule. France and Portugal ruled their colonies as overseas parts of the mother country.

The European governments that established colonies in Africa did so with economic as well as political motives. They desired minerals, agricultural products, and markets. Naturally, the justification for empire building was more high-minded: the Africans were to be brought out of savagery through economic development and the spread of Christianity. For the supposed beneficiaries of colonialism, the cost proved high. The Africans not only bore the psychological pains of cultural upheaval and racial discrimination, they also had to endure the physical suffering of forced labor and the horrors of war when they dared to resist. And there was plenty of resistance, as attested by the bloody military campaigns of the British against the Zulu and Matabele, as well as that of the Germans against the Herrero in South-West Africa. But resistance always proved futile against the superiority of modern firearms.

The Europeans soon turned their sophisticated weaponry on each other, and Africa became a battleground during the First World War. When the smoke cleared in 1918, Germany had lost all of its colonies. Those were parceled out among the victors; South-West Africa was given to the British Commonwealth's newly created Union of South Africa to be administered as a Mandated Territory under the aegis of the League of Nations. The period of peace that followed was one of quiet colonial development. Roads were built, cash crop economies instituted, public health conditions improved, and, in some areas, educational opportunities for Africans expanded. But de facto and legal racial discrimination was universal, and the budding demands of Africans for self-rule were temporarily ignored.

The renewal of European fratricide in the Second World War sounded the death knell of colonialism. The seeds of education and development that colonial activities had planted bloomed into national independence movements on all sides. At the war's end, the European countries attempted to resume business as usual in their colonies, but African leaders like Kwame Nkrumah and Jomo Kenyatta voiced the cry of freedom. They were jailed for their efforts, but even from inside prison, they raised the expectations of ordinary Africans that freedom would come. The Europeans were too exhausted to contest militarily all the national movements that confronted them. Nor was there public support at home to fight to keep the colonies. There was some violence — notably the Mau Mau Emergency in Kenya and, much more bloodily, the Algerian War of Independence — but for most British and French colonies, freedom was granted without protracted bloodshed. In 1957, Ghana became the first black African nation to be given its independence. The next decade saw a flood of new nations, and by 1967, only Portugal's African empire remained intact. In 1975, after protracted guerrilla wars, Portugal granted independence to its possessions, Angola and Mozambique.

The blacks in Rhodesia and South-West Africa had to wait longer for political power. Rather than allow native Africans to vote, the white settlers of Rhodesia proclaimed unilateral independence from Britain in 1965 while they confronted black guerrilla forces on the battlefield. It took more than a decade of bloodshed before the white government agreed to free elections. With the attainment of black majority rule in 1980, Rhodesia became Zimbabwe. South Africa still refused to give up its hold on what was then called South-West Africa/Namibia. Throughout the 1980s, a desultory bush war sputtered along that territory's northern frontier, complicated by South African involvement in the much bloodier civil war in Angola. With the withdrawal of the South African army from the Angolan conflict and the sudden end of the Cold War, the stage was finally set for Namibian independence, which was granted in 1990. Paradoxically, the tardiness of their independence may have been a blessing in disguise for Zimbabwe and Namibia, for it gave them the opportunity to learn from the mistakes of others.

The early decades of Africa's post-independence era were very troubled. The first years were filled with an optimistic idealism that looked toward a bright future of self-determination and economic development. In reaction to the century of foreign domination, a wave of anti-European feeling swept over the African intellectuals who became the leaders of the new nations. The appeal of Marxism, with its call for the rapid development of egalitarian economic systems to benefit the masses, was irresistible on a continent on which most people eked out a life of subsistence agriculture. The Soviet and, particularly, Chinese socialist models attracted many African leaders. Some countries, notably Ghana and Tanzania, became extremely anti-Western and looked to the communist world for assistance. Most of the new nations, however, while jealously guarding their nationalist prerogatives and often anti-Western in political rhetoric, turned to the West to fund their economic growth.

To the leaders of the new nations, rapid development meant the creation of large-scale modern industries, and massive projects involving the building of dams and factory complexes were begun. These grand schemes required huge influxes of foreign capital. Many programs looked impressive, but were ill-conceived or mismanaged, and did little good for the overall economy. A continual need for further funding started the drift toward permanent debt and dependence on Western aid.

The African elites who became national leaders were often idealistic but inexperienced. Although mismanagement of development schemes became commonplace, it was in the political sphere that inexperience had its most disastrous effects. The tendency throughout the New Africa was for the creation of one-party states in which no serious opposition to the government was tolerated. Inept officials or economic managers were protected from criticism or replacement, while poorly planned or mismanaged development projects became institutionalized white elephants. As some economies foundered through stagnation, others were flooded with foreign aid money. The temptation for corruption was often overwhelming; in many countries, bribery became a standard for doing business and black marketeering a way of life.

One-party rule usually resulted in one-man rule. The leader and his loyal followers often enriched themselves at the expense of the nation, sending huge sums of money into the safety of Swiss bank accounts. As political power became the road to wealth, and as constitutional change was impossible, the coup d'état became the principal means of changing the government. Although the leaders of each coup could point to the excesses and failures of their predecessors as they announced high-minded goals for reform, too often they fell into the same habits of self-enrichment. The cycle of coup and counter-coup became a regular feature of African politics.

Two factors that delayed the march of Zimbabwe and Namibia to independence also played lively negative tunes on the wider African stage: the struggle with white-ruled South Africa and the Cold War. Now that the Cold War is over and the apartheid state dead, it is to be hoped that all African nations will get on with the business of development without diverting so much of their resources to the bottomless hole of military security.

South Africa's peaceful transition from its oppressive apartheid system into a nonracial constitutional democracy has been nothing short of amazing. By adopting a constitution that enshrines human rights and the due process of law, South Africa offers the best hope that a fully functional democratic system of government will bloom on African soil. Given the country's racial history, some of the processes of democracy are likely to be messy. But, with good will, the needs and hopes of all of South Africa's ethnic groups may be realized while keeping the nation's economy going full blast. By dint of South Africa's wealth and preeminent position as a trading partner with black Africa, the emergence of the new South Africa should act as a spur to stability and economic development for the entire continent.

Such stability is much needed, for much of Africa remains in a state of chronic economic despair. Many of its people are desperately poor, and black Africa's goods and services total less than 5 percent of the world's gross production. The continent remains economically fragmented, with most countries looking to the outside world for trade rather than developing cooperative markets and meshing economies. The cycle of aid and foreign debt has become a crushing problem. The political horizon is not rosy either: internally, most countries still have no mechanisms for peaceful political transitions. While governments preoccupied with maintaining their own power continue to throttle opposition, the continent remains generally unstable.

Pointing to the mistakes and failures of the last decades, some would argue that independence came too soon, that Africans in the 1960s were not ready for nationhood because they had neither the institutions nor the expertise to govern themselves efficiently. On the other side are those who excuse every problem by placing all blame on Africa's colonial history. Although neither point of view holds a monopoly on truth, few black Africans would argue that the gains of dignity and self-determination do not overshadow the record of political excess and economic woe. In most African countries, there have been marked improvements in public education and a general increase in services due to the construction of roads, hospitals, water projects, and the like. Overall, the material quality of life for the average African has probably brightened over the years of independence. The prospects for a brighter future depend on the willingness of both the African governments and the international community to tackle the continent's serious economic and environmental problems.

Ironically, one major accomplishment of the colonial and independence eras is fueling a severe environmental crisis. The introduction of mass vaccinations against childhood disease and the creation of basic health care systems have sparked a tremendous population explosion: Africa's population is growing at an astronomical 3.5 percent each year. For cultural and religious reasons, little headway is being made in implementing birth control programs. Meanwhile, spiraling populations are compounding the problems of economic underdevelopment. In some places, arable land has absorbed all the human beings it can support. Huge numbers of people are streaming into the capital cities looking for employment that simply does not exist. Many African countries regularly fail to grow enough to feed themselves; when natural disaster strikes, the magnitude of famine is staggering. The extent of the hunger problem goes far beyond the simple solution of putting more land into cultivation. Although untamed wilderness still exists, much of it is fragile land, dry and unsuited to heavy agricultural use, or — like the tropical rainforest — lush only so long as the natural vegetation remains. Agricultural projects and settlement schemes may cause severe and irreparable damage to such environments. Human pressure is already closing in on the lands remaining to African wildlife, while poor agricultural practices and overgrazing are turning whole regions into dust bowls. The population bomb is a threat to the stability of African governments, which find it increasingly difficult to cope with the demands of additional millions for food, shelter, employment, and a decent life. This explosion may be the biggest problem Africa faces.

The AIDS epidemic is another pall on the African horizon. The combination of limited financial resources, poor sanitary conditions, lack of education, and increased mobility of its people have all contributed to the spread of HIV in Africa. It is suggested that more than a quarter of the population in some countries is infected with HIV, and the numbers are no doubt growing. If anywhere near that percentage of people develop full-blown AIDS, there is a very real possibility that Africa's already insufficient public health services may be completely overwhelmed. The potential consequences for African society and the world community are horrifying.

Understanding the Africans

Colonial domination by European civilization had a tremendous impact on Africa's materially primitive societies. From the first contact, Africans started to adopt the technical innovations that were to revolutionize their lives. Fancy trinkets and better tools were the first irresistible lures. Later, the forced introduction of monetary economies advanced modern institutions at the expense of traditional values and customs. But the habits of generations were not easily shed, especially among the uneducated. Native culture adapted and endured, synthesizing technological methods with ancient social structures. It is not surprising that the result is a society fraught with contradiction and paradox.

Today, Africans live with this awkward synthesis of old and new cultures. While leaders strive for rapid technological development and the masses readily accept the material benefits of modernity, African society nevertheless remains essentially conservative and traditional. Within the framework of national identity, Africans are bound by tribal loyalties that determine the social fabric of their lives. The family, extending far beyond Western concepts to include distant relatives within the larger clan and tribe, is the center of the individual's existence. Through family and tribe, a complex web of social obligations gives the individual identity and security from birth to death. While governments struggle to develop modern economies, the vast majority of Africans remain subsistence farmers, tied to tribal homelands that they divide and farm according to the customs of their forebears. A man's wealth is often measured by the number of wives or head of cattle he possesses; a woman's status, by the size of her dowry and the number of her offspring. Although the strength of traditional religions (often condescendingly referred to as "animist") continues to be eroded by Christianity and Islam, the evangelical religions are often grafted onto the old. This allows Africans to retain customary practices, such as sorcery and polygamy, which would otherwise be considered unorthodox or heretical.

Africa's contradictions are reflected in the lives of its people. You could meet a modern Zimbabwean and readily learn that he is an educated Christian, holding high degrees and an important government post. But you might fail to discern that he also regards himself as a Matabele, that he has several wives at his home kraal, and that he derives as much status from his tribal land holdings as from his modern business enterprises. Although he would not be the "typical" African, his position with roots in two worlds would not be at all unusual.

African women have a much harder time straddling the line between the traditional and the modern. A country woman who goes to the city to find work, but gets pregnant, may not be welcomed back to the parental home if her potential to bring in a bride price has evaporated. In addition to native cultural barriers, well-educated women must deal with the same workplace biases and role conflicts experienced by their Western counterparts.

Of course, the pace of social change in Africa is accelerating rapidly. The growth of the state is supplanting tribal identification with national loyalties. Political and state ideologies challenge and exploit both ancient customs and modern churches. Most importantly, changing economies threaten the security of the extended family system as Africans migrate by the millions into cities. They trade the boredom of rural life, which offers little but the security of strong family ties in an environment of hard-working poverty, for the excitement of the city and the hope of better economic conditions. Such hopes are more often frustrated than realized, but the life of the village — slow, traditional, and dull — is ridiculed by the growing class of city dwellers.

It would be a mistake to think of Africans as a homogeneous mass. Tribal, religious, and class differences factionalize the population of each country, not to mention that of the continent at large. Nor should we forget that all Africans are not black. The continent's other racial groups are relatively few in number, but have tremendous influence on their societies. Generally higher on the economic ladder and better educated, the nonblack Africans form distinct subcultures that are interesting both for their unique life styles and points of view.

Many white people call Africa home. In Africa, "Europeans" — the generic term for white people — are divided into two distinct groups: the colonial remnants and the expatriates. In most of the former colonies of southern Africa, many whites stayed on after independence. Those who could not accept black rule immediately packed up for their mother countries or moved to South Africa (where they now have to face a similar choice). In socialist countries, later attrition was caused by the breakup of private landholdings and the strangling restrictions of controlled economies. But in countries like Zambia and Zimbabwe, the whites who remained did very well. Their efficient farms became the mainstays of domestic food production and the chief earners of foreign exchange through export crops. Whites also came to dominate the tourist industry as hoteliers, tour operators, and guides.

The old colonials and their heirs are an interesting group. They speak the native languages fluently and are often well versed in local customs and lore. Among them are individuals with an extraordinary knowledge of the African wilds. While a few may long for the good old days, most have adjusted to black rule and have deep affection for their countries. They have lost all political power, but have by and large maintained their economic well-being.

The other European group — the expatriates — arrived in the wake of independence. Sponsored by the United Nations and various private or governmental agencies, they continue to flock into Africa to lend technical assistance for development. Where foreign companies are allowed in, they also bring managers and technical experts to see that their subsidiaries are well run. Most expatriates come on two-year contracts, signing on for perhaps one renewal. They are generally well paid, and often receive free housing, cars, and other special privileges. It is not an unattractive life, because the salary and perks allow a standard of living (including servants and child care) that would be beyond their means in their home countries. Yet most of them remain outsiders, cloistered in a country club existence, removed from interest in either the local people or the land. The more adaptable among them become permanent residents in their adopted countries, and those with a keen appreciation for the bush often find their way into the safari business.

The community of wildlife researchers comprises a small but distinct subculture that is sometimes encountered in the most out-of-the-way places. Researchers are not always friendly to tourists, however, and justifiably resent disturbance to their work; some are hostile enough to treat all visitors (except financial backers) as idiotic interlopers into their private domain. It's best for travelers to avoid research facilities unless they are invited or know that the facilities are open to the public.

Missionaries are still active in Africa, too. It is not rare to find white clerics or missionary doctors working in extremely remote outposts. Although they do not much concern themselves with tourist activities, some missions sponsor crafts shops or rent accommodations to visitors.

CHAPTER TWO

Into Africa:
Planning Your Trip

For most of us, an African safari is no light undertaking. But although the continent is distant and unfamiliar, it is not nearly as peril-filled as you might imagine. Good planning can ensure a rewarding journey. In this chapter, we consider what preparation you need for a happy and healthy safari, and we examine the conditions you will actually encounter on the road in Africa. Some of the information covered will be useful if you are extending your travels beyond southern Africa.

To get the most out of your African experience, first think about your objectives. Is your trip to focus on wildlife viewing or on cultural contact? Are you looking for a relaxing holiday or a real wilderness experience? Do you want your trip to include activities such as hiking or climbing? Getting a clear fix on your goals can be crucial in determining whether you should travel independently or with a group. For travel in many parts of the world, that decision usually boils down to simple preference. In Africa, the question is not so clear-cut. Although you may feel perfectly confident touring the cities of Europe or trekking the Himalayas on your own, independent travel in Africa may not be the best way to satisfy your goals for an African journey. If you crave wilderness and wildlife observation, independent travel can even prove frustrating. A good three-week safari tour often provides more deep-bush experience than half a year of poking around on your own. Let's consider the varieties of travel available in Africa.

Independent Travel

Even if you're a seasoned traveler, Africa can be a tough place to explore on your own. Its size, its poverty, and its political fragmentation make transcontinental journeys more difficult in Africa than on just about any other continent. This is particularly true for travel in western and central Africa, where problems with air connections, ground transportation, language (if you can't speak French), poor roads, visas, border closings, and political instability abound.

Fortunately, the situation is much brighter in southern Africa, where a decent network of roads and air services makes travel a reasonably easy proposition. South Africa, for example, is a modern country with excellent roads and air, rail, bus, and car rental services. The other countries of southern Africa (with the exception of Zambia) have fairly good air and road connections between major cities and even to a few principal game parks, but when you get off the main routes, roads are often poor, and distances great. Public transport in these southern African countries is also distinctly Third World: overcrowded buses compete with trucks or minivans carrying loads of packed-in people. While you'll find the same situation in the Andes or Asia, in Africa there is often *nothing* available to take you to the places you want to go, assuming you are hoping to visit parks and wilderness destinations. While you will have no trouble traveling from one town to another, you will find limited access to the game reserves or national parks. Almost universally in these countries, vehicles are required for entering and touring the wildlife parks. As an independent traveler, you'll have no choice but to book local tours, rent vehicles, or fly into safari camps that provide game viewing as well as accommodation, and these services can be expensive.

Although it is not too bad within the southern African region, airline travel between countries in Africa can present annoying problems. Airline connections between African cities are generally poor; daily flights are more the exception than the rule. If you are planning a trip that includes East Africa or other places outside the southern African region, direct service between the countries you want to visit may not exist. The situation is made worse by government regulations intended to protect each country's national airline. Sometimes conveniently scheduled flights exist, but government regulations forbid the airline to pick up passengers, even though the national carrier may have service only once a week. The result can be several extra days spent waiting for a flight, or expensive and time-consuming travel through intermediate countries that you don't want to visit. Misconnections, extra overnights, and complicated air itineraries are the norm.

Whatever the extra difficulties, if you have the right spirit, there are tremendous benefits to independent travel. For maximizing personal contact with local people, you can't beat going on your own. Fending for yourself, you will certainly meet all sorts of people you would miss if you were on a guided tour. Your freedom enables you to take advantage of unexpected opportunities: invitations to stay in people's homes, to team up with new friends for cooperative adventures, or to stay on in places you especially like. You can focus your energies on attaining the objectives you had when you set out, or pursue new interests that develop. You are completely free to do as you wish.

But freedom has its price. Although it is often possible to team up with other voyagers, such liaisons are usually temporary. You travel together for a spell, or accomplish a specific objective, and then go your own separate ways. You must be prepared to deal with being alone during those times when you are sick or depressed, and that can feel really lonely. Constant planning and organization will be required for you to attain your specific travel goals, and you'll be responsible for many decisions regarding both travel and your personal security. In short, you must be a very self-reliant person.

The monetary cost of going on your own presents a paradox: you can do it at a fraction of the cost of an organized tour, yet it can also be much more expensive indeed. Costs depend largely on your objectives and the amount of money you have to spend. If you want to have the classic safari experience — a catered, four-wheel-drive expedition in the company of an expert guide — it is going to cost you dearly. On the other hand, if you will be content with a quick peek into the parks on a standard local tour package, or are willing to participate in a bare-bones camping trip, you will unquestionably save money.

The Budget Traveler

Not everyone can throw on a backpack and take off on a footloose adventure, living by wit and without schedule. If you have the personality for it, this kind of travel has some great advantages. A little money can be stretched into a long journey, and you have maximum flexibility in where you concentrate your time. You can expect to meet lots of people, for the world of the budget traveler is exceptionally open and dynamic. Budget travelers (who in Africa are often generically called "backpackers") tend to congregate at strategic places where they exchange experiences and information. They generally travel the same routes, and naturally enough, often stay at the same cheap "backpacker" hotels and campsites. Faces become familiar and there is a tremendous amount of camaraderie on the circuit.

As a budget traveler, you must expect to immerse yourself in Africa.

The only cheap way to get around is to do as the inhabitants do. You'll be squeezing into packed buses or pickup trucks, sharing rides in makeshift taxis, negotiating lifts from lorry drivers, and lugging your pack on foot when all other transport fails. Budget hotels in Africa do not usually win any gold stars, nor do the occasional mission shelters at which you might stay. Colonial ambiance is not their forte. The cheapest hotels are pretty basic: a dingy room, a bed, possibly a sink and private bath. Standards of cleanliness vary considerably: some hotels and missions are meticulously clean, others offer recently used sheets. Fleas, bedbugs, and mosquitoes will be at least occasional companions.

Africa has few of the amenities that exist for budget travelers on other continents. Almost absent are the first-class buses and great hotel deals found in southeast Asia. Unlike Asia, there is no great volume of middle-class business travelers in Africa. Consequently, there are few moderately priced hotels to serve them. The few that exist are often packed with government officials, and although cheaper than first-class tourist hotels, they may still cost in the range of US$20–$30 per night, which is well above the backpacker's budget.

Also missing is the great food. Although prices in local restaurants are very cheap, the quality of the food is only so-so. With few exceptions, local African cuisine is nothing to write home about. In big towns, restaurants serve basic foods — steak, eggs, fried potatoes, and a few local dishes. In upcountry villages and bush towns, you will be lucky to have a choice between rice or cornmeal mush with a meat sauce (which can be very good) and a selection of deep-fried snacks — meatballs, Indian-style munchies, and greasy pastries. You'll probably be cooking for yourself a lot. In markets, you'll find good basic foods. In most places, you'll be able to feast on a variety of delectable tropical fruits. They will be your salvation. So will the occasional splurge at a fancy big-city restaurant or game lodge.

The toughest problems facing the budget traveler are the logistics of getting into the bush. Without a car of your own, you are limited to traveling the main roads. They can lead you into very remote areas and wonderful cultural experiences, and sometimes they pass through game reserves. But a drive through game country on a main highway is not the ideal way to see Africa's wildlife, and with few exceptions, Africa's national parks are closed to exploration by people without vehicles.

Hitchhiking is possible, but far from ideal. Most parks do not allow hitchhikers to enter, and they frown on anyone soliciting rides at entry gates. Most cars you see entering the park will belong to groups of people who have paid considerable sums for the privilege and comfort a car offers: window space is at a premium, so car travelers rarely pick up riders. Other vehicles will be full to capacity with passengers or camping gear. Even if you do find a ride, you are at the mercy of the car's owners — a prisoner of their interests or their *lack* of interests! After traveling thousands of miles and waiting hours for a ride, you may wind up driving at breakneck speed past exciting animals as you are driven to the lodge. On the other hand, you might luck out with a ride with an engaging warden or researcher, and be invited along on an extraordinary safari. That's always the charm of hitchhiking — wonderful things do happen (but don't count on it).

To visit the parks, you'll probably have to find a cheap, locally organized tour or some other travelers who want to share a car rental. Car rentals are fairly straightforward, where you can get them. (Try to make sure that your personality and goals jive with those of your companions: it's rough when you want to be up at five every morning to start your game drive, and your companions prefer to sleep in.) Budget tours are not always available, and the quality is not always great. Because lodges are usually fairly expensive, most budget tours are camping trips. On such tours, you can expect to be crowded into a Land Rover or a converted army truck, to share in food preparation and camp chores, and to set up your own tent. Budget tours often cover a lot of ground fast, so shop around for operators that allow enough time to adequately explore. They may not be the most satisfactory safaris, but they will get you around the parks, where you can't help but see some great things.

For some adventures, particularly hiking adventures, you won't have to hire a vehicle. National parks that feature mountain walking don't require a car for entry. Access to trekking areas can still be difficult, but the regular modes of transportation, plus determination, will get you to the roadhead. If you are thinking of doing any trekking in game country, it's a good idea to check out commercial walking safaris. They can be found in some countries — notably in Zimbabwe, South Africa, and Zambia — but are generally not cheap. Excellent and reasonably priced Walking Trails (ranger-led foot safaris) are operated by park authorities in South Africa and Namibia.

The Affluent Traveler

Travel is often a compromise between time and money: if you have the resources for a dream safari, you probably don't have the time. If you are fortunate enough to have both time and money, traveling on your own in southern Africa may exactly suit your needs.

It is possible to fly to Africa and organize a safari program locally, making arrangements in each locale. There are plenty of tour operators waiting to serve affluent travelers, and you can realize considerable savings by booking locally instead of prebooking with a US tour operator. If you have time for a really extended trip, you'll be able to pick and choose among a whole range of activities of which you may have been unaware before you left.

The key to a successful safari of this sort is research. You should have a pretty good idea which parks and regions you want to visit, and a very good knowledge of seasons, both climatic and touristic. Commercial safari seasons tend to coincide with the dry seasons, when it's easier to get around. All camps and safari operators are then quite busy. If you arrive without having made arrangements in advance, you may not be able to book any kind of tour, and certainly won't be able to organize a quality customized experience. In some areas, safari camps even shut down completely during the wet months. Those camps that do remain open in the wet season offer cheaper rates, but the range of available activities is smaller. Seasons are critical for specific activities. For example, there is not much point in visiting Botswana in January if you want to see huge herds of elephants, for it is unlikely that you will find big concentrations at that time of year. It would be even more futile to arrive for a safari in South Africa at Christmas time without firm reservations: every game lodge and campsite in the country would be fully booked. Likewise, don't count on doing a walking safari in Zambia's Luangwa Valley from November through May: walking safaris are not permitted in the rainy season.

Major safari centers such as Victoria Falls and Johannesburg are the headquarters for numerous outfitters, game lodges, and rental car agencies. A little shopping around in such areas will reveal a large selection of bush activities. Easiest to book are seats on regularly departing local tours. These are usually of short duration (one week would be a long tour) and they include visits to the better known parks and accommodation at lodges. These local tours provide the same experience that you'd get on a Holiday Safari (for more information on Holiday Safaris, see the Lodge Safaris section of this chapter). Seats on longer, overland camping safaris may be available locally. In addition, there are many luxury safari camps that can be reached by plane and you may be lucky enough to get in on short notice. These camps usually feature all-inclusive safari services, including game drives.

As a rule, the cost of joining scheduled local safaris is quite reasonable. It is when you want to get off the beaten track that costs really mount up, especially if you are traveling alone or as a couple. Throughout Africa, the expense of importing and maintaining vehicles is quite high, and this is reflected in the costs of rentals and charters. In some countries, self-drive car rentals are readily available. In South Africa, you can even rent campers or four-wheel-drive vehicles complete with camping equipment (although roads and services are so good that a regular car is all that is needed for travel within the country). In other countries, such as Zambia, self-drive is not possible and you have to charter (at prohibitive cost) a car with driver. If there are many lodges and good roads in a park, a do-it-yourself safari is relatively easy to organize. Travel to truly remote bush areas, however, should only be undertaken by people used to self-sufficiency in true wilderness country. Careful organization is essential, and a good knowledge of auto mechanics is highly recommended.

If you are an affluent traveler, you should also consider hiring a guide, because visiting a national park is not like going to a museum: the things you've come to see are not guaranteed to be there. Game spotting is an acquired skill. If you are green and without a guide, you are sure to miss lots of things that an experienced guide would notice. Top guides do not come cheap and are heavily in demand. If you want to have the benefit of an expert guide on a private safari, you must count on expenses well above those of the highest quality group tours, and it is essential that you arrange your safari well in advance of your arrival. On the tours you can book on short notice, the quality of guides is notoriously variable.

In the main tourist capitals, the affluent traveler should be able to book safari arrangements within a few days of arrival (except during peak holiday periods). Keep a flexible schedule to allow adequate time for checking around. Your task will be a lot easier if you have done your research in advance (reading this book is a good start). Write to the tourist offices of the countries you will visit and get brochures from various local tour operators. Local wildlife magazines also contain advertisements for numerous safari outfitters and lodges. That will give you a start on whom to see and what kind of trips are available.

Still, it must be emphasized that the kind of safaris available on short notice include only the most standard itineraries. If you want the ultimate safari, custom outfitted for your party, you will have to arrange it in advance. Although you can book such a trip directly with a local safari operator, the vagaries of communications can make it a difficult process. Even with the advent of the fax machine and E-mail, it may turn out better to let a good American safari company handle the arrangements for you. It will save you a lot of work, for it is a time-consuming process to explore itineraries, fix workable dates, and negotiate prices. US tour companies represent all the better safari outfitters. They have quick access to them and a good understanding of the logistics of safari planning. You will find it much more convenient to pick up the phone to discuss your questions with a US agent than to wait for answers from a correspondent in Africa. It will certainly cost more, but the convenience and certainty of satisfaction make it worthwhile.

Walking safaris in big game areas are exciting, but require an armed professional guide. Matusadona National Park, Zimbabwe. Photo: Allen Bechky.

Traveling with Your Own Vehicle

Few adventures in Africa are beyond you if you are traveling with your own four-wheel-drive vehicle. You can penetrate the heart of the Kalahari, splash through the muddy tracks of the equatorial forest region, and roam game parks at will. It requires a large investment to start, and you'll need to have a big chunk of time to make it worthwhile. The reward is that you will have total freedom of access, even to the most remote areas. For serious projects, such as wildlife studies or photographic work, a private vehicle is absolutely essential.

IMPORTING A SAFARI VEHICLE: Getting a car into Africa is the first serious problem. Almost all African nations have very severe customs duties on imported vehicles — often more than 100 percent of the value of a new model of that car. To enter or pass through most African countries without paying these duties, you will have to obtain a *carnet de passage* for your vehicle. A *carnet* is essentially a document issued by a national motoring club (such as the American Automobile Association in the US) which attests that a bond equal to the value of the duties has been posted by a bank or insurance company. If you bring your car into a country and fail to reexport it (through sale or loss), the bond will be paid to the national customs office. Premiums for these bonds are high, and if you lose or sell the car without the bond being properly canceled, you may be responsible for paying back the full amount. This bond is necessary, because a common rationale for bringing a car to Africa, particularly for those who are driving across from Europe, is the idea of selling it at the end of the journey. As long as the sale is properly concluded, with all duties paid to the country in which the vehicle is sold, the bond will be properly canceled and you will receive your deposit back, less premiums. If it sounds complicated to sell a car in Africa, it is. It can be done, however — good vehicles are always in demand.

Although it's possible to have your car shipped to a coastal African country and pick it up there, it is more common for travelers to buy a vehicle in Europe and drive across the Sahara. The trans-Africa drive is surely the best way to get a sense of the size and ethnic dimensions of the continent. Obviously, it takes a great amount of preparation and planning for such an expedition. You must be an able mechanic and carry all manner of spare parts with you. Even so, you may be stuck in the depths of the Central African Republic for weeks, waiting for the spare part that you *didn't* bring. That's part of the adventure.

If you plan to restrict your travel to the southern African region, getting a vehicle organized is a lot easier. In South Africa, aside from the normal payment of sales taxes and registration, there are no restrictions on the purchase or resale of cars, making it an easy place to buy a vehicle and resell it at the end of your journey. A good supply and assortment of vehicles is always available, and there are innumerable workshops for service or customizing. Furthermore, a *carnet de passage* is not required for entry into the other countries of the southern African region (with the exception of Zambia), so the paperwork and expense of a bond is not necessary.

Even if you plan to concentrate your motoring in a single country or region, you will need special equipment and self-reliant mechanical skills to undertake backcountry expeditions. Sand ladders, a heavy-duty jack, a complete puncture-repair kit, and a healthy supply of spares are essential. African drivers and mechanics can perform miracles of automotive repair — they keep relic vehicles running for years after they would have been condemned to the junkyard elsewhere, and African mechanics have a flair for substitutions when the needed part is unavailable. They can be counted on to assist if you have a problem, assuming that you are in an area where anyone is going to find you. When you bring your car into a shop for repairs, even routine maintenance, however, you must be on your guard. Quality parts are expensive and sometimes rare. It's possible to bring your car in for a tune-up and later discover that good parts have been taken out and replaced with old ones. You should stay in the shop while work is done and take an active interest in what is going on.

That hazard illustrates the main drawback of having your own car: your life will revolve largely around your vehicle. Care and maintenance, security, and red tape — permits, insurance, road taxes — can become major preoccupations. If you are not prepared for a comfortable marriage to your machine, better consider a tour or a local rental.

RENTING A SAFARI VEHICLE: Where rentals are possible, they allow you the freedom and fun of complete mobility while relieving you of the many burdens of importing a car. You'll still have to be prepared to be self-reliant in the bush, but you'll worry less. Some countries, notably South Africa, offer rentals of well-equipped, four-wheel-drive safari vehicles or campers. Packages sometimes include camping equipment. Regular two-wheel-drive cars are cheaper. They can be used for safaris to the more popular parks, where you can even stay at permanent camps and lodges.

Group Travel
Group tours are a convenient way to adventure in Africa. Not only do

they offer security and access to the wild — they also often present the best solution to the time and budget conundrum.

Most visitors to Africa are participants on some sort of group tour. Given the difficulties of individual travel, groups are attractive even to those who would not choose to join a tour when visiting other continents. Groups offer the security of prepared itineraries and companionship, and groups solve the problems of transport and accessibility to the wildlife parks. Group travel also provides direction and assurance that you will get to the places of particular interest — a big step toward reaching your personal travel goals. Moreover, "adventure" group tours, such as river rafting expeditions, may allow you to take part in activities which would be difficult or impossible to do on your own.

Not everybody is suited to group travel. Before you join a tour, you should consider, first and foremost, your suitability for participation in a group. On any tour, you will have much less independence than you are used to. If you look upon any kind of schedule as a straitjacket, you'll find yourself constantly struggling against the constraints of an itinerary. Group dynamics require some tolerance for personalities or interests different from your own. You may be thrown together with a birdwatcher who will want to stop for a look at every winged creature in Africa, and with a barfly intent only on getting to the next lodge selling cold beer. Such mismatches are more likely to occur on general interest tours. Tours organized around more specialized goals — mountain climbing, birding, or photography — tend to reduce conflict among members because group goals and personal interests coincide. But personality differences are inevitable. Most people are able to deal with group dynamics effectively enough to attain their personal goals for the trip, have a good time, and develop good — even lasting — friendships.

Safari Guides

One of the chief advantages of group travel is the presence of a guide. It's the guide's job to see that your trip runs smoothly as well as to find wildlife and inform you about the country. The quality of guides varies enormously. Experience, knowledge, and an engaging personality are the necessary ingredients. If these ingredients are mixed right, you wind up with a guide who will ensure that you have a meaningful and pleasant safari. Let's look at the different kinds of guides that you can expect to encounter on the various types of safari tours.

Although not necessarily an expert in all fields, a safari guide will have special areas of expertise that can really enrich your trip. A professional guide's knowledge of natural history is usually excellent: some are highly trained naturalists, others work on the strength of years of bush experience as campers or hunters. You will be strongly influenced by

Open vehicles are one of the great attractions of safaris in southern Africa. Mombo, Moremi Game Reserve, Botswana. Photo: Allen Bechky.

your guide's point of view on all African matters. Clients tend to accept their guide's words as written in stone, but you should keep them in perspective: all guides are not truly expert naturalists, and more than one has been known to pass along mythical wildlife lore as fact. Also, the overwhelming majority of professional guides are white, and their perspective on the country's politics and people is quite different from that of black Africans. Carry a few grains of salt.

In southern Africa, many professional guides got their start working as "rangers" or guides in private game reserves in South Africa. The training they receive at the better reserves is often excellent, and with experience, such guides become formidably knowledgeable. Zimbabwe has a strict grading system for licensing guides: the top safari guides have passed rigorous academic and practical field courses in all aspects of wildlife conservation. Zimbabwe's professional guides are skilled trackers and they make superb guides on walking safaris.

In East Africa, an African driver doubles as guide on most tours. This is not true in southern Africa, where driver-guides are usually white. This is changing as more black Africans are trained. Africans are employed as driver-guides or safari drivers mostly by the larger safari hotels and standard tour companies rather than by the small deluxe camps, although even those camps are now integrating their guiding staff. Many

African guides are outstanding and may possess great knowledge of the animals' habits and the ability to identify creatures great and small, including the more colorful birds. Their skills at spotting animals can be amazing, and they often regale visitors with a fascinating repertoire of bush stories. Other African guides are able to do little more than dash around the usual spots looking for sleeping lions. Generally, African driver-guides can show you a full variety of game and a good time. Unfortunately, few have the education to provide you with deep background on natural history or conservation. On the other hand, they can be a great resource for learning about the country. For most visitors, their driver is the main cultural link to black Africans. You should take full advantage of the opportunity to talk with him. Your discussions will reveal much about the lives and attitudes of typical Africans.

Choosing a Safari

A tremendous number of companies offer group tours in Africa. Destinations, itineraries, and travel styles are as varied as you could want, ranging from standard holiday safaris to the most esoteric adventures. Your satisfaction from any particular tour will depend largely on your expectations for the experience. If you are seeking a total immersion in the wilds of the African bush, don't expect to find it on a brief tour that rambles to a few game lodges and luxurious country clubs. On the other hand, that kind of itinerary would provide a wonderful vacation if your aim is to enjoy African scenery and wildlife on a relaxed schedule with all the modern comforts. To help you make the right choice, we'll discuss the various types of safaris available in the following sections of this chapter.

Trans-Africa Overland Expeditions

For the comprehensive trip across the African continent, overland tours are by far the most popular. The appeal of such a trip is obvious: how better to appreciate Africa's size and ethnic diversity, to experience the subtle shifts of climates and cultures on a continental scale, to get a feel for the whole of Africa? Overland tours make that kind of journey accessible.

Companies that organize overland expeditions use large, four-wheel-drive trucks designed for military use and specially converted to carry passengers on the long trip across Africa. These expedition trucks usually carry 15 to 20 passengers, sometimes more. Most have one driver/leader, although some companies also provide a second driver or cook. All community camping equipment is provided: tents, stretcher cots, chairs, and cooking gear. Everything is done expeditionary style. Participants buy and prepare food communally, sharing cleanup and camp chores. The driver takes care of the mechanical side of things, but members should be prepared to help with digging, pushing, cutting bush, and repairing bridges as required to keep the expedition moving.

Transcontinental overland tours are organized in two segments: a long leg across the Sahara and down to Nairobi, and a shorter, easier trip across eastern Africa and down to Johannesburg. Members may buy on to either segment. Naturally, most operators run back-to-back departures, so trips also head north from Johannesburg or Nairobi. Expeditions vary in length. Most companies allow three months for the northern leg of the trip, and about a month for the journey from Nairobi to South Africa. A few companies put on special departures that take about twice that time, allowing a lot more stops and side trips. Considering their duration, transcontinental overland expeditions are incredibly cheap. This is to some extent due to the operators' penchant for fiddling with the black markets along the way. Veteran operators know all the tricks of currency exchange, and are able to cut costs appreciably.

Overland tours are cheap, not comfortable. Travel and camping conditions are rough. The trucks are outfitted with a canvas roof over the rear passenger section, which affords much needed shade. The canvas, fitted with plastic windows, can be unfurled down the sides to provide rain protection, but usually remains rolled up to allow maximum ventilation and visibility to the sides. Forward views are somewhat blocked by the truck cabin, but passengers often ride on top of the cab for a bird's-eye view. Seating configurations on trucks vary considerably, but most are pretty weird. Most commonly, two rows of seats run the length of the vehicle, along the open sides or down a central column. Consequently, passengers sit in lines, either facing inward toward each other or back to back, facing outward. Very few trucks are outfitted with more sensible forward-facing seats. Trucks are slow; bouncy on wet, mudholed roads, dusty in dry conditions. Distances are great, and the country is sometimes monotonous. When the landscape assumes a sameness for days on end and the dust forms choking clouds, participants take on a glazed, shell-shocked look. Cleanup facilities are not always available, so clothes tend to stay dirty. Camps are efficiently organized, but not elegant. The tents provided are durable, but they are not generally top quality, well-ventilated pieces of equipment. It *is* an expedition, and you have to roll with the punches. You must be willing to accept repeated coatings of desert dust and annoying attacks by jungle insects.

As you might expect, overland trips attract a predominantly young crowd. Some operators have an age limit of forty. Others have no absolute age limit, but screen older applicants for suitability. Still, there are adventurous people in their sixties who have fulfilled a life's dream by taking an overland journey.

It is very hard to judge overland tour itineraries. The brochures usually detail a proposed route, or several alternative routes, but the actual route taken depends on the political and economic situations in the various African countries. Outbreaks of warfare, border closings, or currency crises periodically cause the route to be altered. All overland companies tend to use similar routes and alter their itineraries in the same way.

The classic overland route enters Africa in Morocco, crossing the Sahara through Algeria to Niger or Mali. The route skirts the northern edge of the West Africa region, passing through the Sahel in Burkina Faso or southern Niger to Lake Chad and Cameroon, where it breaks into savanna country. After crossing the desert and western savannas, the route enters the equatorial forests of the Central African Republic and Congo. The route then passes into Kenya through Uganda, although sometimes overlanders will dip down to Rwanda and Tanzania before doubling back to Nairobi. (A second major route follows the Nile directly to East Africa via Egypt and the Sudan but is not currently favored. Due to the civil war in the southern Sudan, it's necessary to complete the Sudan segment of the journey by air.)

Beginning in Morocco, the classic overland route encompasses quite an interesting chunk of Africa. It's a long, tough journey through some very fascinating regions. It presents a very good representation of desert, forest, and savanna country, and a fabulous mix of peoples: Arabs and Africans, English-speaking and Francophone, nations formerly English, French, Belgian, and German. From Kenya southward, the journey is easier and faster because the roads are better in East Africa. After passing through Tanzania and Malawi into Zambia, the trucks are on tar all the way to "Jo'burg," unless they detour into Botswana's game country.

Although changes in routing are occasionally abrupt, conditions are usually stable enough for the itinerary's published route to work. But there is another destabilizing factor: breakdown. When mechanical failures occur, as they often do, time is lost in making repairs. A reasonable number of days for maintenance and repair are built into every itinerary, but when major problems pop up, there can be serious delays. If a truck is stuck for three weeks in Bangui (capital of the Central African Republic) waiting for spare parts to be flown in, cleared by customs, and installed, that lost time has to made up somewhere else. All too frequently, many of the interesting side trips — the days supposed to be devoted to cultural and wildlife pursuits — have to be passed up to make up lost time.

Transcontinental overland trips, while providing a fascinating view of the continent, do not usually rate highly for wildlife experiences. Although the brochures describe all the game reserves along the way, they are often passed up or visited only briefly. After enjoying excellent wildlife viewing in one game park, chalking up lions and elephants and all the major species, it's common to rush through other reserves on the route, or to avoid them altogether. Major attractions are sometimes ignored. I have known overland trips to pass up the opportunity to view the Serengeti migration when they could easily have done so, to fail to descend into the Ngorongoro Crater after camping on the crater rim, and to divert from scheduled visits to Botswana's reserves in favor of the short cut to Johannesburg.

Even more than on other tours, the leader-driver is the critical determinant in the nature of the overland experience. The leader may be terrific: totally knowledgeable, and enthusiastic to a fault. Or he may be little more than a skilled mechanic, interested only in reaching the next town where cold beer is available. The leader not only drives the truck and coordinates expedition logistics, he also sets the tone for all the group's activities. Although expeditions require teamwork, they are not democratic: the leader is paramount. He can manipulate a majority-rule situation; divisive situations are not uncommon.

On trips of such long duration, it should be no surprise that close quarters almost inevitably lead to personality conflicts. Although some lucky expeditions generate terrific camaraderie, other groups degenerate into warring factions where members are no longer on speaking terms. It is very difficult to live with the same 15 people for weeks on end. You must carefully consider your adaptability to such a situation before you go. If you are not a "group person," overlanding is the wrong adventure for you.

Budget Camping Safaris

The budget traveler can realize many of the benefits of group travel by choosing a budget camping safari. Budget-oriented safari operators have sprung up in a number of areas in southern Africa, offering access to the bush at reasonable prices. Trips range from as short as a week to as long as a minioverland expedition of up to six weeks.

Less geographically ambitious than trans-Africa overland expeditions, regional tours have several advantages. Itineraries are more clearcut, so major attractions are not likely to be missed. Importantly, the focus of each trip is sharpened. Incidences of group burn-out and serious personality conflict are also greatly reduced. Travelers who have the time can take a combination of shorter tours in different areas, focusing their resources on activities of particular interest. Budget camping safari operators now run regular group departures in Kenya, Tanzania, and all the countries of southern Africa. Some minioverland itineraries combine Namibia, Botswana, and Zimbabwe, and may even include South Africa or Zambia as well. Budget travelers can shop around for those tours locally, though most reputable companies have representatives in the US or London, so it's possible to plan and book before departure.

Although a few nights in hotels may be included, budget safaris are by nature primarily camping trips. The minioverland operations have the same logistical organization as their lengthier cousins, based around the expedition truck. Many local operators use smaller four-wheel-drive vehicles. In southern Africa, the forward-control Land Rover is very popular. It is a small truck that is usually customized to carry eight or ten passengers. Other budget camping safari operators use standard-sized Land Rovers to run groups of no more than six clients. The small-sized vehicle can be a mixed blessing, as a small vehicle crammed to capacity with passengers and gear is neither comfortable nor ideal for game viewing. Solutions to the space problem vary: some vehicles carry roof racks for gear, others tow trailers. On the very cheapest tours, the vehicle is inevitably crowded and staff is limited to the leader-driver. Cooking and camp chores are participatory. A few budget safari outfitters specially design their own safari vehicles to comfortably accommodate up to eight passengers, and include the services of a cook. Typically, the higher priced trips are more comfortable, and more attention has been paid to the details of the itinerary.

Since most of these budget safaris emphasize the national parks, game viewing is usually very good. Some viewing time is inevitably eaten up by the necessity to set up camp or cook meals, but most itineraries allow for a pretty decent look around each park.

The question often arises as to whether trucks or smaller four-wheel-drive vehicles, such as Land Rovers or Land Cruisers, are superior for game viewing. Trucks are noisier, but I have never seen any evidence that the animals in the well-visited parks are more scared by trucks than smaller vehicles. Land Rovers are superior for negotiating broken, off-road ground, which is useful for following prowling cats or checking into gullies where something interesting may be hiding. But increased safari traffic has led to mounting environmental damage, so off-road driving within parks is now largely a thing of the past. The advantage of a truck's height is balanced by the open roof hatches featured on Land Rovers. In southern Africa, most of the private reserves and a few national parks allow "open vehicles" on which the roofs and sides have been completely removed. This permits extraordinary visibility, but such vehicles are rarely used on budget safaris. Clearly, small vehicles are superior for quick and quiet communications between driver and passengers. This is important for maneuvering into the best photographic position without scaring animals away. Easy communication with the driver is also a clear advantage in game spotting. It's difficult for passengers atop a truck to get the driver to stop if they see an animal that he has missed. Some trucks are outfitted with a buzzer system; when the passengers spot something, they signal a stop. On balance, either type of vehicle permits satisfactory game viewing, provided that group members remain quiet and that the driver switches off the engine when observing animals. The noise and fumes of idling engines can really spoil the natural beauty of the bush.

Budget camping safaris are good value for the experience they provide. They are not ideal from the standpoint of comfort. Like the transcontinental overland expeditions, some budget safari outfitters have age limits and all emphasize that the experience is for the young at heart. But if money is a prime consideration, this is the way to go for the adventurer interested primarily in game viewing.

Lodge Safaris

Over the last 20 years, hotels have sprung up all over Africa. Today, most game parks have some kind of lodge facility, be it a luxury modern hotel or a permanent tented camp. These facilities have really opened up the African bush to those who wish to enjoy its beauty without sacrificing the comforts of home. That means most of us: overwhelmingly, the most popular type of African adventure is the lodge safari.

HOTEL-LIKE LODGES: Lodges come in many shapes and sizes. Large, hotel-like lodges are found in most well known parks and reserves. Their quality of comfort, cleanliness, and service is generally very high. Each facility has its own ambiance. The newer safari lodges are modern hotels designed for harmony with the natural setting. Spacious verandahs in bars and dining rooms look out over game-viewing areas. Attractive grounds mix native vegetation with brilliantly flowering tropical plants. Rooms are comfortably cool, pleasantly furnished, and faultlessly clean. For a break from game viewing, guests can relax at the lodge swimming pool. Food is excellent—the buffet tables fairly groan under the weight of platters of delectable fruits, cold-cut meats, hot dishes, and sweets.

PERMANENT SAFARI CAMPS: Another form of lodge accommodation is the permanent safari camp. Although some are fairly large, these safari camps are generally smaller than the hotel-like lodges. In southern Africa, permanent safari camps tend to be quite small, taking an average of only about 16 guests. Such camps can be super-deluxe or more simple, but the standard is almost universally high. Accommodation can be in chalets or in luxury safari tents. Most feature private baths and toilets, although some have shared "ablution" facilities. Permanent safari camps are a great concept because guests enjoy all the comforts of a hotel, including excellent food, but generally have a quieter atmosphere with more personalized service. All activities are usually included in the daily cost. Game drives are normally conducted by professional guides using four-wheel-drive vehicles.

Permanent tented camps are romantic and they are fun. You can have unforgettable animal experiences not possible in the lodges: an elephant may nibble on a tree growing right next to your tent. The night sounds, whether the roars of distant lions or the nearby rustlings of some unknown animal, inspire all kinds of imaginings — philosophical, romantic, or fearful. It's all quite safe as long as you remain inside. Luxury tents are really quite elegant and will fulfill your Hemingway fantasies for safari accommodation. The tents are large canvas pavilions, erected on sturdy concrete foundations. They are fully insect-proof: the walls join to a tough plastic floor, while zippered doors and netted windows afford security and good ventilation. Above the tent, a thatched covering provides cooling shade and extra rain protection. Each tent has its own verandah. A rear door leads to an attached bath area, which includes a shower, sink, and toilet.

Most permanent tented camps have clever hot water systems: water is often heated in a 50-gallon drum mounted over a wood-burning furnace. This "Rhodesia boiler" is primitive (and consumes a lot of wood) but provides the same luxurious cleanup you would get in a hotel. Tent furnishings include twin camp beds, tables, and chairs. Some camps run generators to provide electric light, others depend on kerosene lamps. The most up-to-date camps have switched to environmentally friendly solar power, eliminating noisy, fuel-burning generators and the overconsumption of local woodland resources.

In southern Africa, many permanent safari camps are located on "private reserves" or hunting concession areas on the fringes of the national parks. This gives them the ability to operate without the restrictions that govern safaris within the parks. They can use "open vehicles," drive offroad at will, run nighttime game drives, and offer walking safaris. By operating on private land, the number of visitors and vehicles is limited, so game viewing is relatively private. Vehicles are usually linked by radio, so that all camp visitors have a good crack at seeing any big cats or other animals that are discovered on the property. All these advantages result in excellent close-up game viewing, and camps offering these features have become the most desirable safari lodges in Africa. Indeed, the concept of the private game reserve has become so successful that such "reserves" are springing up all over southern Africa and particularly in

South Africa. Many farms are being converted into game reserves, with wild animal stock bought and translocated from the national parks. While this is a positive development in many ways, it sometimes goes overboard, with exotic species that are not native to a locale being moved in, while other animals that should be there are absent. Also, although game viewing in these private reserves is undoubtedly extraordinary because you can see so much in so little time, the radio control makes the experience seem too contrived. After initially being wowed by the viewing, you may start to yearn for the feeling of a real safari on which you have to search for game, rather than just drive right up to it.

GOVERNMENT-RUN REST CAMPS: Many of the parks in southern Africa, notably those in Zimbabwe, Namibia, and South Africa, offer accommodation within their boundaries at government-run rest camps. Lodging is usually in detached chalets or "rondavels" (circular thatched huts that imitate traditional African houses) of various sizes and degrees of comfort. Most have their own bath, toilet, and kitchen facilities, and many feature air-conditioning. In the more popular parks, rest camps are large villages that include a public restaurant and store, a ranger station, and public campsites. Originally designed for local patronage, these camps offer very reasonably priced accommodation to independent travelers who have their own vehicles, and are often used by tour groups in Namibia and South Africa. On weekends and during local holiday seasons, independent travelers will have difficulty getting into the rest camps without advance bookings.

Many lodges and safari camps have been situated in fantastic locations, overlooking stunning landscapes, well visited by game. Some have been so well placed, usually at strategic watering points, that animals can be seen at any time. For those tired of beating the bush, an afternoon spent relaxing at the lodge can be just as productive as a drive: you need only sit at the bar and wait.

HOLIDAY SAFARIS: The majority of lodge-based tours can be classified as Holiday Safaris. These are meant to showcase the wonders of the bush in a relaxing style, without the inconveniences of outdoor living. Generally, Holiday Safaris are of short duration — ten days to two weeks in Africa is the norm — and reasonable cost. Accommodation tends to be at the bigger lodges or national park rest camps, rather than the more exclusive small safari camps. Such tours are typically all inclusive: members have merely to step off the plane to be shuttled through Africa with hardly a moment to fend for themselves. Participants enjoy a round of game drives, relaxation at lodge swimming pools, sumptuous buffets, and more game drives. Such a safari is not everyone's dream of African adventure, but it is a terrific vacation.

Transport for most Holiday Safaris is provided in vans. These vans have become almost as ubiquitous to the African scene as the zebra, whose stripes they sometimes imitate. Although often the butt of derisive comment, safari vans are actually excellent vehicles. They have to be, for the rutted tracks they ply daily take a terrible toll on automobiles. When all is said and done, safari vans carry people in relative comfort, even into very remote country. Many of the newer van models are four-wheel-drive, and even the older types are quite capable of getting through on really muddy roads and standing up to the mechanical rigors of long safaris. They may lack the off-road mystique of Land Rovers, but cross-country travel is now banned in most game parks, and vans are generally more comfortable. Late-model vans seat up to eight passengers, although seven should be considered maximum for comfort. Roof hatches permit passengers to pop out the top for game viewing or photo taking. Safari vans are reliable vehicles, perfectly suited for mobile lodge safaris.

Holiday Safaris allow adequate — rather than superlative — game viewing. Short itineraries are not comprehensive, and several days are usually eaten up in towns or country clubs. Game viewing is concentrated in the most popular wildlife reserves, where the animals tend to get used to vehicles. The lodges and rest camps used are strategically situated in areas where there is usually an abundance of resident game, ideal for short game drives. The regimen is generally fixed: wake-up coffee and an early morning game drive, with return to the lodge for breakfast. A later morning game drive returns in time for lunch, after which the mid-afternoon is spent relaxing and digesting before another drive from about 4:00 P.M. to sunset. For most visitors, this is plenty of game viewing, especially if the drives are productive, and such a schedule fits well with the conventional rhythm of safari life.

There are some disadvantages. The game tracks near lodges are regularly crowded by tour vehicles. The thrill of discovery and the rewards of undisturbed observation get lost in a herd of minibuses jostling for position around a lion pride. Lodge schedules must be met: when the choice is to sit tight with the chance to witness a lion hunt or to go without breakfast, you'll most likely be at the buffet table at the time of the kill. If game concentrations near the lodge are poor, the preset schedule probably won't permit you to travel to other areas. The logistics of Holiday Safaris do not leave much room for flexibility.

Most lodge tours are set up to be short and cheap, so as to appeal to the widest possible market. Driver-leaders are the rule, so detailed natural history interpretation may be lacking. But your driver will show you the animals, and probably a very good time, which is what a Holiday Safari is all about.

NATURAL HISTORY SAFARIS: More serious natural history tours also use the lodge safari format. Generally of longer duration and more comprehensive itinerary, they are escorted by expert guides. Guides lend not only expertise but flexibility, as they can decide when conditions warrant a longer drive with a picnic in the bush or arrange a late breakfast at the lodge. Properly organized and led, a lodge trip can be a very satisfying safari experience. Although the bush ambiance is somewhat dimmed by the large numbers of tourists at the lodges, where people-watching may take precedence over wild animal study, the lodges are a very pleasant base for forays into the wild.

FLYING SAFARIS: Flying safaris are a very popular alternative in southern Africa. In some countries, "wing safaris" work with scheduled flights into some of the most famous parks, including Hwange in Zimbabwe, Luangwa Valley in Zambia, and Kruger in South Africa. Elsewhere, and especially in Botswana, light aircraft are used to connect safari camps on a regular basis or can readily be chartered. Obviously, flying takes a lot of the wear and tear out of African travel, and saves a lot of time. Although some flying safaris use the larger lodges, many use the more exclusive safari camps. If you are willing to pay a premium, you can work out your own itinerary, subject only to the availability of camps in the areas you wish to visit.

First-Class and Luxury Camping Safaris

Camping safaris in Africa do not have to be rough participatory affairs. They can be quite luxurious by the standards most of us are used to for camping at home. If you want an authentic bush experience of the sort you've seen in the movies, a high-quality camping safari — either first class or luxury (the two top standards) — is the way to go.

FIRST-CLASS CAMPING SAFARIS: First-class camping safaris carry you into the bush in Land Rovers or similar four-wheel-drive vehicles. Your baggage, camping equipment, and camp staff go in a support vehicle, which travels ahead separately. Your party roams the bush at will, and when you pull into the campsite at the end of the day, everything is prepared and waiting: tents up, dinner cooking, hot water ready for a wash. The level of comfort is high. Tents are large and well ventilated. Passengers sleep on cots with foam pads; in most cases bedding is supplied, although some operators require participants to bring along a sleeping bag. Passengers dine in a special mess tent, which also serves as social center when rain forces the group away from the campfire. The staff sees to the setup of toilet and shower tents, and does all camp chores. A professional guide is always in attendance. For logistical purposes, and to provide a break from camping, a few nights at lodges are usually included on first-class camping safaris, and some sections of travel may be accomplished by air.

First-class camping safaris have a lot of advantages. You get the real ambiance of living in the bush, while doing so comfortably. Your time is not eaten up by camp chores beyond packing up your personal gear on travel days. You will have more time for exploring the bush, and for pursuing your own interests around camp. The efficiency of camp staff and the quality of guides is generally top standard, so you can expect the trip to be both enjoyable and informative. Of course, you can also expect to pay top dollar for all this professional pampering.

It may surprise you that a first-class camping safari is more expensive than a typical lodge safari. Consider that in addition to the costs of transport and accommodation, the expense of the support vehicle, the staff, and an expert guide must be borne by the group. Also, four-wheel-drive vehicles are more expensive to operate and have less seating capacity than safari vans. Group size is an important cost factor: many first-class safari operators in southern Africa run trips for seven to eight clients aboard a single vehicle; smaller groups get prohibitive in price, while groups of ten to fifteen people (using several vehicles) are more economical, with fifteen being about the logistical limit on this type of trip.

While bearing all this expense, participants on first-class camping safaris must still accept that camping will not be as comfortable as staying in a lodge. Camping safaris are complicated logistical operations; things can and do go wrong. If a breakdown delays the support vehicle, camp will be far from ready when you arrive. Instead of the expected warm washing water and a cold drink awaiting, you may drop into the organized chaos of a camp going up in the dark. Camp showers are available, but it takes time for water to be heated on the fire and transferred to the shower bucket for each individual's use: you may have to wait before your turn in the shower tent rolls around. Refrigeration and ice for cold drinks are not always available. At night, the toilet will seem an intimidating distance from your zippered tent. No matter how you cut it, you are still camping in the wilderness, and minor inconveniences must be taken with a sense of humor and adventure.

One additional feature of a first-class camping safari is too often overlooked by participants: the opportunity to get to know other members of the staff besides the guide and drivers. Talking with them is always interesting and sometimes a revelation. It's a real chance to learn directly about the home lives and concerns of modern Africans.

LUXURY CAMPING SAFARIS: Luxury safaris are operated in a similar format to first-class camping safaris, with more elegant frills thrown in a la Martha Stewart. Camp accommodation consists of walk-in canvas tents large enough for twin camp beds and a small table. They are similar to the tents used in permanent tented camps and like them usually have attached shower and toilet at the rear. Canvas mess tents are the rule, sturdy camp furnishings will be of the highest quality, and ice will not be absent. A few extra touches include white cloths on the table, uniformed waiters, and the regular appearance of wine and liquors at meals. The staff is apt to be larger and the service more polished. Indeed, the entire tone of the safari is more formal. Your guide will fulfill your expectations of the Great White Hunter, as he is likely to have been one, for many hunters have turned their attentions to this lucrative end of the tourist trade.

The logistics of luxury safaris make them available only to small groups. Eight persons is the maximum that can be properly looked after. Consequently, luxury trips are usually organized by special request, rather than offered as tours to the general public. Itineraries can be created according to your level of interest and expertise. If you are keen on going to special areas or seeing particular animals or tribes, that can be arranged. But for general interest trips and for first timers, you are likely to go to some of the same parks that regular lodge tours do, though you may well spend your time exploring remoter parts of the parks or adjacent private game reserves. Due to the logistics of moving and setting up the heavier equipment of a luxury camp, you are likely to visit fewer areas and spend more time in each locale.

The quality of every aspect of a luxury safari will be high, and so is the cost. If you require the highest standards possible and want to have the added benefit of enjoying complete control of your own trip, a chartered luxury safari is for you.

Special Interest Tours

Tours focusing on a special interest, such as birdwatching or African arts, have definite advantages. By their nature, group dynamics on these tours have a better chance of running smoothly, as everyone's interest is riveted on the same activities. Itineraries are custom designed to include places that ordinary groups would miss, and special activities are arranged to suit the group interest. In the case of birding groups, micro-habitats in little-known forest or mountain reserves will be investigated, and there will probably be excursions by boat to search swamps or lakes for hard-to-see species. The well-known parks will also be visited so that the large African mammals will not be missed. Indeed, birders tend to see more varieties of mammals as well as birds, for they tend to be sharp-eyed and constantly alert.

At the same time, specialized groups can have too narrow a focus to be enjoyed by all. It is sheer torture for someone who is not interested in birds to spend a half hour swatting flies while the rest of the group attempts to sort out the identity of an undistinguished little brown bird. Make sure your interest is really there before you get involved with such a tour.

Some groups come together through organizational identity rather than special interest. This is especially true of tours for professionals, such as doctors or lawyers, which are designed to give participants a tax write-off for their vacation. A few technical activities are included, such as visits to health clinics or law courts, to meet the tax requirements. The safari portions of the tours tend to be poorer for the time lost; unless the technical portions are of genuine interest, these trips are not worthwhile.

A great number of museums and zoos organize their own safaris. These trips not only build a feeling of participation among members, they also help raise money for the institutions. It is standard for a staff member from the institution to escort each group. This can be a real plus, as the escort is often an expert in some African specialty and may have spent a lifetime doing research in that field. These groups tend toward the lodge safari format. Most itineraries are fairly standardized, but occasionally, really terrific specialized tour plans are developed. Quality depends largely on the interest and degree of knowledge of the escort, as he or she may be in charge of planning the tour from the start. These trips are generally quite expensive, for aside from extra charges in the form of a donation to the sponsoring organization, the costs of the escort also have to be borne.

Family Safaris

It is becoming increasingly popular to take kids to Africa, and many safari operators now offer special group tours for people with children. Such tours make great vacations that combine recreation with education while affording a wonderful opportunity for family bonding. Family safaris have other advantages as well: discounts are often given to children, and kids will enjoy the presence of peers on a tour. In addition, parents won't feel that their children's behavior is disturbing to other people, as may occur if they are traveling with a nonfamily safari group.

Family safari itineraries usually follow the lodge or first-class camping formats: kids often crave the amenities more than their parents, even in the depths of the African bush. Small children tend to do very well in the early stages of a safari, when every type of animal is a major source of fascination. The novelty usually wanes after a few days, however, and young children are then likely to begin getting cranky about being cooped up in vehicles, and to start asking to be left behind in camp. If you are organizing a customized safari for your family, keep your itinerary relatively short. Also note that some of the smaller and more exclusive safari camps do not accept small children.

Adventure Safaris

Africa is one area where adventurers who focus on classic outdoor activities — such as hiking, trekking, and rafting — would do well to investigate group travel. Although it may go against the do-it-yourself instincts of many wilderness buffs, the peculiarities of the African outdoors frequently justify the security of group travel. Indeed, unless one is truly a master of wilderness self-sufficiency and has studiously planned for the trip, some outdoor adventures in Africa could be foolhardy and others simply impossible.

Adventure safaris allow you to participate on bush adventures without having to tackle a myriad of logistical problems. While a few adventures, such as Kilimanjaro climbs, are relatively easy to organize on your own, organizing the logistics for foot safaris in big game country or rafting expeditions on African rivers would be next to impossible on your own. These adventures require detailed planning and considerable expense. For adventures in national parks, special permits must be obtained, and the participation of professional guides or official personnel may be mandatory. When you join an organized adventure tour, all these arrangements have been worked out in advance.

Adventure tours also provide professional guides, who are essential for any serious African adventure to be attempted safely. The key here is experience. A guide knows the minutiae of the bush: how to handle contacts with potentially dangerous animals, where to find water, which potential swimming holes are crocodile- or bilharzia-free. The African bush is no place to learn the ropes by trial and error.

By their nature, adventure tours are participatory: if you are on a mountain trek, you have no choice but to walk. Still, adventure tours are usually fully catered, with porters on hand to carry the heavy loads and a trained staff to handle camp cookery. Such tours are never cheap, but are good value considering the costs and difficulties of doing it on your own.

Hunting Safaris

Until quite recently, safari was synonymous with big game hunting. Although most tourists now do their shooting with a camera, Africa remains the Mecca of the hunting fraternity. After all, the world's largest and most dangerous quarry are found in Africa, as is a wide variety of other trophy animals. Sport hunting is still permitted in most African countries. The ethics of trophy hunting and its effects on conservation are endlessly debatable, but the benefit to the countries involved is clear: cold cash. Many African nations have plenty of wild animals and a desperate shortage of foreign exchange. They readily welcome overseas hunters who, although fewer in number than camera-toting tourists, make a significant additional contribution to national revenues. For today, big game hunting is big business.

A modern hunting safari is a fantastically expensive proposition. In every African country, a nonresident must hire a locally licensed professional hunter to organize and accompany the safari, and their fees tend to be exceptionally high. To the expenses of guiding and outfitting must be added the costs of licenses, guns, ammunition, and taxidermy of trophies. When all these items are tallied, the cost of a hunting safari may total $1,500 a day or more per person. The typical safari lasts at least three weeks. Hunting companies generally lease blocks of land from the local game department on which they have exclusive rights to hunt. In season, they set up small but luxurious permanent camps to which they rotate their clients. Camp capacity is usually no more than two hunters, plus their wives or companions (four hunters would probably be a maximum). Many hunting safari companies have several camps set up in different regions or reserves. Clients shuttle from one reserve to the next. In one area, the client goes after lion and buffalo; in another, leopard and elephant; in a third, trophy antelopes. Many additional animals will be shot for the pot.

Hunting safaris are heavily taxed and closely controlled (at least theoretically) by the various African game departments. Licensing rules vary in each country. In some places, a hunter pays an expensive flat fee for a particular grade of license that enables him to shoot one or two of each animal on a long list of allowable species. In other countries, the permit is relatively cheap but the hunter pays an additional fee for each animal killed. Either way, the permits provide the game departments with revenues and clearly limit the numbers and species of animals which the hunter may take.

Hunting safaris are highly specialized affairs, and the details of out-fitting such safaris are beyond the scope of this book. They are not ca-sually arranged and generally have to be booked long in advance. The most select of the African hunting companies attend big game hunting shows and conventions held annually in the US, most often in Las Vegas. Many companies have US representatives.

Thoughts Before You Go

No matter what travel style you ultimately choose, you should consider such things as seasonal factors that may affect the timing of your trip and the types of official documentation that will be required.

Seasons

In most areas, the safari season coincides with the dry months — mainly because it is just plain easier to get around when roads are dry. During the rains, tracks dissolve into a series of slippery pools, which even four-wheel-drive vehicles get through with difficulty. Lodges and bush camps may close down because neither guests nor supplies can reach them. Game viewing during the rainy season may also be affected as high grass and thick foliage make spotting game difficult. Because waterholes are to be found throughout the bush, animals tend to disperse over wide areas in the rainy season, making them harder to find in big herds. Many re-serves are at their most spectacular at the height of the dry season, when animals concentrate in huge numbers around the few remaining water sources.

Rainy-season safaris do have their virtues. The scenery is at its most glorious: the land is swathed in a riot of fresh greenery and the cloud-flecked skies seem immense. Although game is more dispersed, many species give birth to their young during the rains. Bird life is particularly brilliant, as resident birds put on their most colorful mating plumage. Some parks, notably those in the Serengeti and the Kalahari, are at their best in the rainy months, the time when migrating herds swarm over grasslands that are completely waterless in the dry seasons. Where all-weather roads make park visits worthwhile, rainy-season safaris can be done at some savings because hotels and tour operators offer lower rates. This is not so in South Africa, however, where roads are excellent and the rainy season coincides with summer vacation time. With a large population of car-owning outdoor enthusiasts, South Africa's parks and private reserves are kept very full in the rainy season.

In East Africa, there are two rainy seasons, although neither is ab-solutely reliable as to arrival or duration. The heavier "long rains" occur in April and May, while the "short rains" take place around November.

Safaris run throughout the rest of the year, although showers may occur during the hot period between December and March. The coolest months run from June to August.

In southern Africa, the weather pattern is quite different. There is one long wet season that lasts throughout the hot "summer" months (keep in mind that in the Southern Hemisphere, the seasons are the opposite of ours): showers usually start to fall in November and continue until March or April. Rain usually falls in brief, heavy thunderstorms. The rest of the year is generally bone dry.

Southern Africa has a distinct "winter," a cold season that runs from May through August. Days are sunny and warm but nights are cold. Highs reach into the upper 70 degrees Fahrenheit, and lows reach down into the 30s and 40s. Cold snaps can bring nights down below freezing. Desert areas can be very cold at this time of year, and it can snow in the higher mountain ranges of South Africa. If you have problems dealing with hot weather, the winter months of May through August would be the best time to visit.

Southern Africa's weather warms up considerably by September, and most of the game areas are broiling hot by October, when daytime temperatures regularly get up into the 90s and 100s. During this period, skies are often hazy because of dust and smoke from bush fires, but game viewing is excellent. The remaining summer months — November through April — are generally hot and humid, with daytime temperatures in the 80s and 90s, and even above 100 degrees in the Kalahari, the valley of the lower Zambezi River between Zambia and Zimbabwe, and the Lowveld of Zimbabwe and South Africa.

The Cape region at the southern tip of Africa has a unique climate. Its rains fall mostly between May and September. Daytime highs during these months are then about 65 degrees Fahrenheit, with nights falling down below 50 degrees. It still rains a bit as it warms up in October, but is delightfully sunny from November to March, when temperatures range from a high of about 80 to a low of 60 degrees.

Of course, temperatures vary considerably with altitude and local climatic influences, such as proximity to the warm Indian Ocean or the cold Atlantic. On a typical safari, you will spend most of your time in low- or mid-elevation game country, but you may have a few days scheduled in higher areas, like Johannesburg, or in the cooler marine climate of the southern Cape.

Languages

English is the only language you need for comfortable travel in southern Africa as well as East Africa. It is spoken by all educated people in those regions and widely understood by many others.

While it is fun to be able to converse with local people in their own languages, and certainly worthwhile to learn the native tongue if you will be staying in one area for a long time, it is not necessary for ordinary travel purposes. It is also virtually impossible to prepare yourself to speak even a fraction of the tribal dialects that you could encounter in a single country. It is useful to learn the polite forms of address and expression in the local language of whatever region you will concentrate your visit: it always brightens faces when a foreigner is able to respond to greetings. Phrase books in local languages are generally available in capital cities. The only African language dictionaries and phrase books widely available in the United States are for Swahili. Swahili is widely spoken only in East Africa and Congo, where it enjoys official status among the dozens of local languages. It is not spoken in southern Africa.

Documents and Visas

You will need a valid passport. Make sure that its validity extends six months beyond the end of your trip, as some nations refuse entry if there are fewer than six months remaining before expiration. Most countries in southern Africa do not require any vaccinations for entry purposes, but if you will be traveling to Zambia or any countries to the north, you must have an International Vaccination Certificate showing you've had shots against yellow fever. (For more information on health matters, see the Staying Healthy section in this chapter.)

With the exception of Zambia, no countries in southern Africa require US citizens to have a visa for entry. This is quite the reverse from the rest of the continent, where visas are normally mandatory. It is important that you check the visa requirements of each country you plan to visit before you start your trip. For the major tourist-oriented countries of East Africa, the visa process is reasonably straightforward. For many of the West African countries, the paper shuffle is appalling. If you are going on an organized tour, the tour operator will probably give you detailed instructions on how to get visas.

If you are traveling on your own, you may be asked to provide proof of means or airline tickets that show ongoing transportation. Be sure to request single- or multiple-entry visas as needed, and find out the *validity* of the visa before you order it. Some countries require that you enter within three months of the date the visa is issued: this is inconvenient for long-term travelers, but the only solution is to pick up the needed visas at national embassies within Africa.

If you are planning an extended independent trip, take along a supply of extra passport photos in case you need an unexpected visa along the way.

Equipment and Clothing

Whether you are on a tour or traveling independently, the first and best rule for travelers is "go light." Safaris are basically informal; even on luxury trips, you can get by with less clothing than you think. Limit yourself to one piece of luggage and a small bag for carrying those items you will need with you during the day. It's important to be aware of size and weight limitations on baggage, especially if your trip includes flights on light aircraft, which often have maximum baggage-weight allowances as low as 26 pounds total, including hand luggage. Also remember that although international airlines allow two bags of virtually unlimited weight on departure from the United States, the maximum on return flights or flights within Africa is 44 pounds. Overweight baggage charges are expensive. Unless you are planning to bring over specialized equipment (for professional photography, hunting, and so on), there should be no reason for your checked baggage to approach anywhere near the maximum allowance. Leave room for souvenirs you will pick up along the way.

Clothing should be chosen for practicality and versatility. Cotton (or fast-drying synthetic) safari-style clothing, comfortable and in subdued color, is ideal for day wear in the bush. The necessity for khaki colors is dubious, unless you will be on a foot safari. But subdued safari colors are fun, and lend the traditional atmosphere. They also lend themselves to color coordination so you can create a varied wardrobe around a few basic pieces. Still, there's no need to buy the latest safari gear; T-shirts and shorts will do just as well.

You must be prepared for cool (even cold) as well as warm weather, especially if you will be traveling in southern Africa's dry season — May through August. Many African cities and game parks are located at mid-elevations where nights are cold. Dawn and sunset game drives in open vehicles can turn quite chilly. Bring a sweater and windproof parka shell on such drives, and layer your clothes as comfort requires. You may start a game drive in darkness, wearing the whole kit, then gradually peel off until you return for a late breakfast wearing only a T-shirt and shorts.

EQUIPMENT LIST FOR GROUP TRAVEL: If you are on a group tour, the tour operator will send a recommended list of clothing and equipment specific to your trip. For lodge safaris and high-quality camping trips, the following list is a recommended guideline, using *maximum* numbers for each item (you can probably get by with half the number of each recommended item, and will have to if your trip includes flights on light aircraft). The actual number of any particular item will vary according to your taste, space available, and weight restrictions that apply to transport on your trip. Take less if you can get away with it. Keep in mind that you can have laundry done at every lodge where you will be staying for two or more nights. Camp staff on safaris often do daily washing as well. (Note: Due to cultural taboos, African camp staff, who are normally all males, sometimes decline to wash ladies panties or briefs.) A number of cold-weather items are indicated for travel during southern Africa's colder season (between May and August) but are not needed at other times of the year. It's a great packing idea to organize your clothes in large self-sealing plastic bags (such as Zip-Lok). Also see the equipment list for independent travelers in this chapter for items that may be of use to you.

Duffle Bag or Suitcase. Your bag should be rugged and medium sized (large is okay, if you also have to include a sleeping bag). An additional bag or suitcase can usually be left in your hotel at the gateway city while you are out on safari. If you have any dressy city clothes for ongoing travel, leave them at the hotel. (Note: Most camping safari operators do not allow hard luggage like suitcases to be used on safari.)

Underwear. Five or six cotton pairs of underwear. In the cool season, also bring along lightweight polypropylene (or other insulating synthetic fabric) long underwear for nightwear; lodges may not provide that extra blanket you'd like, and your sleeping bag may not be up to snuff. A cotton warm-up suit can be used for the same purpose, and doubles nicely as evening wear around the campfire.

Shirts. Four or five short-sleeved shirts or T-shirts. At least one long-sleeved shirt should be brought along for sun protection or cool weather.

Pants. Two pairs of durable cotton or quick-drying, cotton-synthetic blend; one dressier pair for lodges and the other for use in the bush. Jeans are not recommended, as they are uncomfortable in hot weather and take too long to dry.

Shorts. Two pairs of hiking-type shorts should be sufficient.

Sweater. One light- to medium-weight sweater, depending on season. A polypropylene or acrylic pile jacket is also very welcome in the cold months.

Skirts. Although skirts are optional and not needed in the bush, they are appropriate for wear for women travelers in African cities. Pants are also acceptable everywhere, but few African women wear them, so you may feel more comfortable wearing a skirt when you are in towns.

Jacket. One windproof parka shell. Gore-Tex or other breathable fabric is ideal because it is waterproof as well as windproof. Canvas jackets are fine, too, but they are heavy. Safari jackets look good but do not provide practical wind protection.

Socks. Five to six pairs in cotton. One pair of polypropylene socks for cold weather is optional.

Footwear. One pair of comfortable walking shoes with traction soles. Lightweight hiking boots are best. An additional pair of walking shoes is useful on walking safaris or on rainy season trips. Also, bring a pair of rubber sandals (such as Tevas) to use in the shower, hotel rooms, or on game drives; this type of shoe is really useful if you are doing any boating activities.

Hats. Essential; preferably wide-brimmed. If your hat doesn't come with a drawstring, you should rig up a system for securing it on your head. If not, you'll be holding your hat or chasing it every time you pop your head out of a moving safari vehicle. In colder seasons, also bring a polypropylene cap that you can roll down over your ears.

Gloves. One lightweight pair for the colder season.

Rainwear. A poncho can be useful to protect your daypack from rain on walking trips, even if you have a waterproof jacket. A small, folding umbrella is optional for lodge trips. Check the likelihood of rain during your visit.

Bathing Suit. Bring one for hotel pools and other swimming opportunities.

Optional Clothing. Bandannas, sleepwear.

Daypack or Camera Bag. A daypack is preferable to a camera bag and essential if you are going to participate on any foot safaris. Some type of small bag is needed to tote camera equipment, a sweater, field guides, water bottle, and miscellany you bring along on game drives.

Miscellaneous. Sunglasses, sunscreen, insect repellent, medical kit, water purification kit (see the Staying Healthy section of this chapter), water bottle (essential because dehydration is a common problem), toiletries, sturdy flashlight with a good beam plus extra bulb and batteries, and a Swiss Army–type knife with scissors (optional but perennially useful).

Binoculars. These are *essential* for good game viewing. Do not plan to share a pair; each safari member should have his or her own.

Optional Miscellaneous Items. Cameras and photographic equipment, reference books, self-sealing plastic bags, stuff sack for dirty clothes, wash-up towelettes (useful), a roll of toilet paper, plastic spade, traveler's alarm clock, shoulder pouch or money belt, pocket calculator, and a collapsible nylon bag with zipper for packing souvenirs. Also see the equipment list for independent travelers in this chapter for other items.

Giveaways. Indiscriminate gift giving is not recommended, but you may meet people to whom you wish to give something. Clothing, especially T-shirts, is a useful gift as you can wear it, then give it to someone at the end of the trip. Other useful items for adults include sturdy fish hooks and fishing line for men in riverine areas, and sewing needles for women. Frisbees and balls are great friend-makers. Postcards, magazines, or books from your home town or country are also great items: Africans are keen to learn about your life, too. Many well-meaning people bring candy or balloons to give to children; these items are always a hit, but balloons spread disease from mouth to mouth, and candy is very destructive to teeth. It is better for the kids to give them pencils, pens, crayons, or notebooks. Gift giving has its negative side (for more information, see the Traveler's Etiquette section in this chapter).

Sleeping Bag. On some camping tours, you may have to provide your own sleeping bag. Unless you are doing a real mountain trip, a lightweight summer bag (usually rated down to 40 degrees Fahrenheit) will do fine in most situations, although you will want to wear something extra while you sleep if you are camping out during colder seasons. Also bring along a cotton *sleeping bag liner* or small *flannel sheet*; that is all you will need on those tropical nights when you would roast inside even the lightest sleeping bag.

EQUIPMENT LIST FOR INDEPENDENT TRAVEL: The Equipment List for Group Travel, listed above, would suit the affluent traveler, too. With a little judicious packing and paring (cut down the numbers of each item of clothing by half), the entire list can be squeezed into a manageable duffle and a daypack. Look over the following list for the odd item you might find useful: I'd particularly recommend the shoulder pouch, money belt, and pocket calculator.

If you are a budget traveler, you will want to carry far less. You won't have the aid of taxis, porters, or tour leaders. You'll be carrying your own load wherever you go, so every item you bring must be carefully weighed for its overall utility. It would be impossible to carry everything on the list above. The paradox is that you may need even more items, especially if you plan on camping and hiking. You must be ready for varying conditions of hot weather and cold, and even more prepared to be self-sufficient. The only solution is to cut down radically on the number of clothing items, eliminating every item that is not *absolutely* essential. Also, for ease of carrying (possibly for long distances), you will want to use a backpack instead of a duffle bag.

Backpack. A rugged pack with an internal frame is best. It will take quite a beating on top of buses and trucks (not to mention airplanes). It should be large enough to pack your sleeping bag and all other gear inside. Loops and slots for tying things on the outside are handy for treks but not so practical for use on public transport. Also, take a large flour sack to put the pack in when you are traveling on buses and planes; it hides your gear from prying eyes and helps prevent damage to buckles and straps.

Foam Pad. Needed for warmth on cold ground as well as for sleeping comfort.

Tent. See the Camping Equipment List in this chapter for a description.

Stove and Fuel Bottle. See the Camping Equipment List in this chapter for a description.

Cook Kit, Tableware, Scrubbers. See the Camping Equipment List in this chapter for a description.

Skirt. Recommended for women travelers. A long skirt is best if you will visit Muslim countries.

Rainwear. A poncho is best for protecting not only you but also your pack.

Footwear. If you are planning on serious mountain walking, you'll want to bring a pair of light hiking boots.

Money Belt. Since you will often be exposed to public situations where pickpockets thrive, a money belt is essential. Keep your invaluable documents (passport, International Vaccination Certificate, air tickets) as well as money and traveler's checks in it during bus trips and other high-risk situations. Some experienced travelers prefer to sew special secret pockets into their trousers.

Shoulder Pouch. A handy item for carrying documents and traveler's checks. It should have a tough strap that will resist slashing, and should not be carried conspicuously in dubious situations. Useful to all travelers for taking valuables on game drives or to meals, rather than leaving them in hotel rooms.

Pocket Calculator. I highly recommend a model that converts metric measurements automatically.

Miscellaneous. Towel, gloves (see the Camping Equipment List in this chapter), sewing kit, sink stopper (flat), clothesline and pins, safety pins, can opener, various-sized plastic bags, combination lock for hotel rooms.

Camping Equipment List

It's best to purchase quality camping equipment before you go, with the exception of plastic jerry cans, lamps, and cleanup items, which you can purchase in Africa.

Tent. Bring a good, lightweight tent, even if it is expensive. Good ventilation is important, and sturdiness is critical. Before you go, test that your tent will stay up and stay dry in a storm. Fully zippable doors and floors will add security against crawlies.

Stove. A kerosene-burning stove is best because kerosene is the most commonly available fuel in Africa. These stoves require a flammable starter, such as alcohol paste, which is a hassle, but you will always be able to find fuel. White gas is hard to find, as are butane gas containers (Bluet Camping Gaz cartridges are notably available in Nairobi, Kenya; Kigali, Rwanda; and in Bujumbura, Burundi; other types of propane stoves and containers are available in South Africa). Investigate stoves that can burn a variety of fuels, such as the Mountain Safety Research (MSR) stove.

Fuel Bottle. The Sigg brand of aluminum fuel bottles is ideal. Note: It is illegal and dangerous to carry any fuels aboard airplane flights.

Cook Kit, Tableware, Utensils. Get good quality, lightweight space savers.

Leather Gloves. Useful for handling thorny wood for camp fires.

Flashlight. If you have space, bring a powerful six-volt light. Its beam will pick up any animals around camp before you step out of your tent at night. I also recommend this kind of light to serious game watchers, even on lodge safaris, as one often finds interesting nocturnal animals on the edges of camps and lodges.

Lamps. Again, kerosene is the easiest to find in Africa.

Miscellaneous. Washing basin, dish scrubbers, plastic jerry cans (five gallon) or collapsible water containers, utility cord.

NOTES FOR WOMEN: In the most popular safari countries, you can feel free to wear whatever you want. In big cities, lodges, and beach resorts, the local people have been thoroughly exposed to modern fashions. In Muslim countries, modest dress is in order to conform to local custom and to avoid sexual harassment. Some countries may have official dress codes prohibiting miniskirts and other skimpy attire. Tour group members are never bothered about these matters but independent travelers may be.

Except in South Africa, tampons and sanitary pads are hard to find outside of major cities (and then they are expensive), so bring an adequate supply.

NOTES FOR CONTACT LENS WEARERS: Contact lens wearers always have extra problems when they travel. This is particularly so in Africa where dust can be a real problem, especially during the dry seasons. Bring plenty of lubricant and bring a pair of glasses as a backup. You should rely on a chemical system of cleaning contact lenses, rather than an electrical cooker.

Electricity

Hotels in capital cities usually have 24-hour electricity; game lodges run on generators, which are turned off at night to conserve fuel. Voltage is generally 220 AC, but socket systems vary around the continent. If you will need power, bring a 110–220-volt converter kit and a variety of plug adapters.

On camping safaris, the only electrical power may be the 12-volt battery of your vehicle. If you are bringing rechargeable battery packs, buy a kit that permits recharging from a car battery, and test the kit before the trip. Many vehicles allow access to the battery through the dashboard (usually through cigarette lighters), but all vehicles are not so equipped. If they are not, you will have to rely on the driver's ingenuity in cutting and splicing wires directly to the battery.

Photography

Some Africans living in remote areas must consider cameras regular pieces of the tourist's everyday dress, just like their own beaded jewelry. They could be right. Almost every tourist sports a camera. We all want a photographic record of our safari. Here are a few hints on how to make the most of your opportunities.

For the casual photographer, there is no need to run out to buy a complete new camera system. If it's a personal remembrance you are after, any of the new automatic cameras will yield satisfactory results. Scenery, companions, hotels, and people are easy subjects, while satisfactory wildlife shots can be taken in the game parks where animals let you come close. Use print film, in 100 or 200 ASA, for best color results. Faster ASA film is preferable for stop-action shots, but may produce overexposed photos.

Animals are challenging subjects for even the most experienced photographers. Those revealing wildlife shots we see in *National Geographic* are not taken on casual safaris. They are the result of months of patient work by professionals shooting with sophisticated equipment from the privacy of their own vehicles. And the shots you see are culled from thousands. That's not to say that you can't get great shots on your safari. The opportunities are there — you should come home with lots of good pictures, and a handful of great ones.

Serious photographers will carry a 35mm SLR camera with interchangeable lenses. A good zoom lens is indispensable for speed and versatility in framing. A 100mm–300mm zoom can get good wildlife pictures, even portraits, of most of the larger park animals. Lenses of 300mm or longer are needed for quality bird pictures and for shots of the many small or shy mammals. A wide-angle lens is fun for creative shots and for getting close subjects in the context of their surroundings, while a standard 50mm lens is useful for scenery and portraits. (A zoom lens in the low 28mm–150mm range could serve for all those purposes.) A macro lens is recommended for flower and insect subjects. It's helpful to have two camera bodies so that you won't be constantly changing lenses.

For speed and convenient operation from a vehicle, it's best to rely on lenses that can be hand-held. Telephoto lenses with a fixed focal length produce great full-frame shots at considerable distances, but require the stability of a tripod for good results. Long lenses are also heavy and are a major problem to transport. Easier to carry are mirror lenses, which at

500mm, give great magnification. But they have disadvantages: fixed at F8, they can be used only in situations where there is high light, and they are difficult to focus. They have an extremely shallow depth of field. In general, it's impossible to get sharp images while hand-holding any lens over 300mm. Vehicles are unsteady shooting platforms unless all passengers are motionless and the engine is turned off. A small tripod or bean bag that can be quickly set up on the roof of the car is essential for powerful telephoto work. A motor drive is a crucial accessory for game photography because animals are constantly moving and subtly changing their expressions; when the subject is good and the light is right, you will want to be able to fire rapidly.

Be prepared to use a lot of film: good animal shots demand it. The excitement of the first few days will carry you away. You will shoot everything you see, even when the light is poor and the subject far away. Afterwards, you will become more selective and won't need a shot of every distant giraffe and warthog. It's axiomatic that the best time to shoot is in the early morning and late afternoon. The sun is then low, bathing every subject in a perfect, soft, golden light. Midday tends to be too bright; pictures come out with a washed-out, overexposed look. It's useful to routinely stop down a half or even a full stop, except during those brief daily periods when the light is perfect. Travelers on extended trips have the luxury of shooting exclusively at those hours, but if you'll be in the bush for only two weeks, you'll have to shoot at the less favorable times of day, too.

A flash is useful, not only for night shots, but for daytime filler. Africans are particularly hard to photograph: their dark skins contrast strongly with the bright sunlight. Daytime flash can correct this sometimes insurmountable exposure problem.

It is best to shoot slides. It's much cheaper to cull slides and select the good ones for reproduction than to shoot a lot of similar exposures with print film. When the subject matter is there, and especially when the light is good, you should feel free to shoot with abandon, even if you previously have taken pictures of the same animal. You won't regret the multiple exposures when you cull your slides. Often the dream shot you thought you took will be ruined by the flick of an ear or an unnoticed tuft of grass, while others prove spectacularly expressive and well exposed.

Telephoto lenses require fast film to permit shooting at speeds high enough to result in sharp images. However, Africa is rich in color, and the faster-speed films do not give good color saturation. ASA 50, ASA 64, and ASA 100 films produce vivid color shots; many professionals try to shoot with nothing else. New ASA 200 films are also yielding good results. You should also bring some of this faster film (and possibly even a few rolls of ASA 400 or higher), or there will be times when you will be unable to shoot. Bring more film than you think you will need: it may not be available locally and, if available, would be more expensive than at home. Do not overworry about your film going bad in the heat. Keep your reserve and exposed rolls buried deep in your luggage, and they will survive nicely on a trip of a few weeks duration.

You do have to worry about your equipment. The bouncing and dust of safari travel is hard on photo gear, particularly delicate, high-tech electronic cameras. Once these cameras have a problem, they are likely to be useless for the rest of the trip. A backup camera, possibly a manual model, can suddenly become more than just a convenience. It's wise to keep your cameras and lenses packed when not in use. Some people suggest keeping them inside plastic bags for dust protection. However, keep in mind that if the camera is not easily accessible and ready to use, you are going to miss many of the best shots. It's really common for a perfect shot to disappear while a photographer fumbles to organize gear. Be ready, not overprotective.

More and more visitors are coming equipped with video cameras. Safari really lends itself to video: the immediacy of the experience really comes through. Buy a quality half-inch recorder so that you can edit your work when you get home; unedited videos lose viewers' interest really fast. Video cameras require a rechargeable power pack (for more information, see the Electricity section of this chapter).

Whether you are bringing a camera or a video recorder, learn how to use it properly before leaving home. Finally, don't let photography detract from your experience! Some people see Africa exclusively through a lens. They miss a lot.

Binoculars

On safari, a good pair of binoculars is more important than a credit card: don't leave home without one. Binoculars yield better views of big game animals, and allow you to see small creatures that would otherwise remain invisible. In the bush, you will be using them constantly, so do not count on sharing binoculars with companions; every visitor should have his or her own.

Binoculars range from tiny opera glasses to huge military models. They are classified as 7 x 35, 8 x 30, and so on. The first number refers to the power of magnification, the second to the diameter (in millimeters) of the main lens. The larger the diameter, the greater the light-gathering capability of the binoculars. This is important in low-light situations: a large-diameter lens renders better visibility at dawn or dusk or in deep forest shade. Choose a model with 7- to 10-power magnification (anything more powerful shakes as you look through them).

Many models in this range come in compact sizes, which are light and therefore very convenient. Top-of-the-line brands include Leica and Zeiss (both very expensive); other reputable brands include Nikon and Bushnell. Each company produces one line of expensive "custom" models in addition to cheaper types. The more expensive models offer better quality glass optics that reduce eyestrain (which can become a problem with prolonged use).

Staying Healthy

As a tropical and semitropical continent, Africa is beset by health problems almost unknown in the West. Here we review the vaccinations needed for an African journey, examine the most serious endemic diseases (and assess your risk of infection), and discuss insurance and the quality of local medical care. Also considered are the contents of your personal medical kit and ways to reduce the health risks associated with food and drink, heat and sun, and the bites of insects or snakes.

Vaccinations

All Africa-bound travelers should carry an International Vaccination Certificate detailing a complete record of inoculations received. This is important not only for meeting entry regulations at borders, but also for keeping yourself informed on your current status of protection.

Yellow Fever. Yellow fever is an often-fatal disease borne by the *Aedes aegypti* mosquito. It is endemic in many low-elevation areas of Africa's tropical zone. Many African nations *require* vaccination against yellow fever, and anyone planning to visit East, West, or central Africa should have the vaccination. It is not officially required for entry to any of the countries in southern Africa *unless* you are traveling from one of the nations in the endemic zone to the north. The vaccination is effective for 10 years. If you are going to be traveling in Africa, it is worth getting.

Cholera. Cholera is a great epidemic killer that breaks out in the wake of disasters such as famine, floods, or war. Since you won't be tarrying in areas suffering those hardships, you are unlikely to come in contact with it. It is treatable with antibiotics, but since intravenous fluids are needed to keep the patient alive, it's easier to stay away from epidemic zones. The medical community does not regard the cholera vaccination as highly effective and no longer recommends it for travelers. In spite of this, a few countries in West and central Africa continue to demand proof of this vaccination for entry. This is somewhat of a problem as many doctors and health clinics in the US refuse to give the shots. (A two-shot series is needed with a booster every six months.) If you will be traveling to countries that require cholera vaccination, you'll just have to explain to your physician why you need it: the doctor may give you a note stating that the shots are contraindicated for you or, better, give you a subcutaneous dose and sign your vaccination card. An alternative is merely to enter the notation in your International Vaccination Certificate, stamp in some official-looking numbers, and be done with it.

Several other immunizations are recommended, especially for overland and independent travelers, and they should also be recorded in your health certificate:

Tetanus. You should have a tetanus shot even for outdoor adventures in your own country. It is good for five years.

Polio. Get a polio booster if you haven't had one since childhood.

Typhoid. This disease is spread through contaminated food and water. Although your chances of contracting it are slight (less than 1 in 25,000) and vaccination is only 70 to 90 percent effective, most physicians recommend it. The typhoid vaccination is now an oral medication (four doses of tablets, taken over the course of seven days).

Meningococcal Meningitis. Outbreaks of this potentially deadly disease occur in sub-Saharan Africa. Although it is an illness to which few tourists are exposed, a single-dose vaccination (good for three years) is recommended if you are traveling to East Africa between December and June. It is not needed if you are traveling solely in southern Africa.

Hepatitis A. This viral infection of the liver is very widespread in Africa and other parts of the world where sanitation is poor. It is spread by contaminated food or water, as well as by direct person to person contact. An effective vaccine is available in the US and is recommended for long-term or frequent travelers. A gamma globulin shot confers only short-term protection: it is effective for three to six months, depending on the dose received.

Further information can be obtained from *Health Information for International Travelers* (US government publication #CDC 86-8280), a pamphlet available from the Public Health Service, Centers for Disease Control, Atlanta, Georgia 30333. You can also call the CDC for the most up-to-date information. For vaccination information, call (404) 639-3534. For malaria prevention information, call (404) 639-1610.

To have information faxed, call (404) 332-4565 and follow the prompts.

Malaria

Malaria is a parasitic disease spread by anopheles mosquitoes. There are several strains, the most common of which is caused by *Plasmodium vivax*. This form is not generally lethal, but recurs repeatedly if not treated. The organism has a dormant stage when it resides in the liver; it erupts periodically to attack red blood corpuscles, causing the classic symptoms of high fever, severe headache, chills, and aching joints. A weekly dose of chloroquine will help prevent the disease. However, a chloroquine-resistant form of malaria is now widespread in Africa. This *Plasmodium falciparum* type causes the so-called cerebral malaria that is responsible for most malaria fatalities.

Current guidelines from the World Health Organization (WHO) for malaria prophylaxis suggest the following drugs:

Larium (Meflaquine), 250 mg. Weekly. Start taking these tablets one week before departure for Africa, and continue for four weeks after leaving Africa. Larium is the drug of choice of both the WHO and the CDC. It is a costly prescription drug, effective against both *vivax* and *falciparum* malaria. It is contraindicated for pregnant women, young children, people with heart conditions, or those with a history of epilepsy or psychiatric disorders. Some people have unpleasant side effects when taking Larium: make sure to start taking it at least a week before departure so you can discontinue in favor of another drug if it makes you feel ill.

Chloroquine, 500 mg. Weekly. Start taking these tablets one week before departure for Africa and continue for four to six weeks after leaving Africa.

Paludrine (Proguanil), 200 mg. Daily. Begin one week before departure for Africa and continue for four weeks after leaving Africa. This drug is fairly effective against the dangerous *falciparum* malaria, but has not been approved for sale in the US. It should be taken along with chloroquine to afford protection against both forms of malaria. Paludrine is available over the counter in Europe, as well as in Nairobi and many other African capitals.

Fansidar. Bring at least one adult dose (three tablets) on safari, to be taken if you come down with severe fever and have no access to medical care. Fansidar provides effective protection against *falciparum* malaria, but is not recommended for prophylactic use because it can cause severe side effects, particularly in those allergic to sulfa drugs. If you are sulfa-sensitive, consult a physician about using doxycycline (100 mg daily) for malaria protection.

Many other types of antimalarials are sold over the counter in South Africa that are not available in the US. These include *Dapsone* and *Daraclor*, which are mixtures of chloroquine and pyrimethamine. These are locally regarded as the best prophylactics, but are not as effective against *falciparum* malaria as Larium; they should not be taken if you are allergic to sulfa drugs. *Maloprim*, *Deltaprim*, and *Malasone* are also available in South Africa.

Recommendations for malaria prophylaxis change frequently, so be sure to check with the CDC or your local health department for the latest information.

In addition to chemical prophylaxis, you should try to reduce your exposure to mosquito bites while in the field. As the malaria-carrying anopheles mosquitoes are active at night, there is no need to smear yourself with insect repellent or wear protective clothing during the day. At dawn or dusk, cover up with trousers and a long-sleeved shirt, and apply insect repellent when outdoors; sleep under a mosquito net or in a zipped tent. Many lodges spray rooms at dusk and provide insecticide coils to burn during the night (these are pyrethrum based and supposedly harmless to humans). Be sensible about your precautions: in the dry season, most areas will have no mosquitoes at all; take extra care during and just after the rains.

Malaria is responsible for an estimated 1 million deaths per year in Africa, and millions more suffer from chronic infection. The victims are mostly rural Africans who have no access to prophylactic drugs or medical care. Tourists are not immune, however; every year a few visitors come down with the disease. If you are one of the unlucky ones, seek medical attention and you will live to tell the tale. You need no longer fear life-long recurrences, as there are now drugs to cleanse the liver of dormant parasites.

Other Tropical Diseases

Parts of Africa, especially the steamy forest regions, used to be known as "the white man's grave." Modern drugs have made travel much more hospitable, although the tropical forests still harbor more than their share of exotic maladies. Ebola fever is great for paranoid fantasies, but it is extremely unlikely that you will encounter an epidemic of that rare disease, much less contract anything as gruesome as Guinea worm, elephantiasis, or leprosy. The following illnesses are of some real concern, although they, too, are unlikely to be caught by visitors.

BILHARZIA: Bilharzia, or schistosomiasis, is contracted by contact with infected water. The parasite takes many forms during its life cycle, living first in certain specific species of snail, then briefly as a free-floating microorganism, and finally as a fluke inside the human body (in the blood vessels of the intestines or bladder). It enters the body directly through the pores of the skin. Human wastes complete the cycle by putting the organism back into the waters they pollute. In this way, it has been widely spread around the continent. Bilharzia is found in standing and sluggish waters, especially those in inhabited districts.

The oft-heard rule to avoid bilharzia is an injunction *never* to enter any bodies of fresh water in Africa, except the few lakes supposed to be free of infection. This is a good rule *if* you are on your own and have no knowledge of the area you are in. But don't let it scare you into missing out on bathing opportunities when conditions are safe. I've had several clients who were suffering from intense heat exhaustion, but refused to take a cooling dip in the waters of a perfectly safe river that I've bathed in dozens of times, because they were overly paranoid about bilharzia. Fast-flowing rivers in uninhabited areas can be considered safe, or at least low risk. Camping in remote wilderness areas would be impossible without using river water for washing; even some rustic lodges may pump their shower water out of nearby wild rivers. Obviously, all river-running trips (and many walking safaris) would be out of the question if the water injunction were strictly kept. If you are with professional guides, trust their judgment: they don't want to be infected either. Nonetheless, on certain trips, particularly river journeys, there is a certain amount of risk. If you are not prepared to deal psychologically with reasonable risks, avoid such expeditions.

Bilharzia was formerly difficult to cure (the side effects of treatment were nearly as unpleasant as the disease), but a new drug — *Biltricide* (praziquantel) — clears it up with a single dose of oral medication. If symptoms develop — flu-like illness sometimes accompanied by a skin rash, or especially blood in the urine or stool — call the CDC and get a test immediately. Unfortunately, the parasite can live inside you asymptomatically, and is difficult to diagnose. In South Africa, many river rafters and canoers periodically dose themselves with Biltricide just to clear out any possible parasites. Few US physicians know anything about the organism or the disease, so if you have been on an African river journey (or may have been otherwise exposed) and you want to get a precautionary test, it is best to contact the CDC or ask your doctor to do so.

SLEEPING SICKNESS: Sleeping sickness is spread by the celebrated tsetse fly. Although you may visit parks where tsetse flies are amply present, you have little to fear. The worst zones for sleeping sickness are in tropical West Africa and central Africa (as usual), not the game parks of the east and south. Many tsetse-infested areas are completely free of human sleeping sickness. It has been estimated that only 1 in 100,000 tsetses in the infected zones carries the trypanosome that causes the disease. Risk of exposure is therefore relatively low for the short-term visitor. The disease is fatal if untreated, but is rare among tourists; it is rarer still for them to let it go unattended.

AIDS: Evidence seems to point to tropical Africa as the original home of the AIDS virus. It is estimated that millions of Africans, both men and woman, have been exposed to this deadly disease. AIDS is transmitted through intimate sexual contact or the use of contaminated needles and blood products. You can practically eliminate the possibility of catching it by practicing sexual abstinence or "safe sex" techniques (the use of condoms is recommended). If you have to get shots while in Africa, make sure that the needle has been sterilized (or bring your own disposable syringes). If you must have a blood transfusion in a remote area, you will have to take your chances or hope that someone in your party will be able to donate the needed plasma. You should know your blood group and type, and record it, in case of emergency. Blood supplies are screened in South Africa and in the best private hospitals in the more modern African capitals, but are not necessarily reliable elsewhere.

Insurance and Medical Care In Africa

With the exception of South Africa, African medical facilities are generally poor by Western standards. Most countries are able to deliver only rudimentary medical care to their own citizens; many people in remote areas simply have to do without. You probably won't have to go unattended if you need a doctor, but you should be aware of the quality of care you can expect.

Capital cities are the best places to seek care, as the governmental and diplomatic communities have to be served by the best. A fully modern private hospital staffed by European professionals is likely to be found in capital cities. Many countries have public hospitals and clinics where care is very low cost or free. Doctors may be highly qualified, but you can expect long waits and marginal sanitary conditions, and basic medical supplies may be in short supply. These public hospitals and clinics are suitable to visit for minor complaints, but if anything is seriously wrong, try to seek out a private hospital or physician, if available. There are also many missionary hospitals and clinics in Africa. Conditions are likely to be as crowded and chaotic as in the government-run public hospitals, but they are often staffed by highly qualified foreign doctors.

Virtually all of the above-mentioned facilities are capable of handling routine travelers' complaints, including serious bouts of malaria. But except in the direst emergency, you should avoid hospitalization, especially surgery, in most African countries. From any African capital, you are only a few hours flying time from Europe. Most expatriates in the region go to Johannesburg in South Africa for emergency medical treatment. Many tour operators in southern Africa provide insurance to their clients for emergency evacuation to Johannesburg by air ambulance.

Be sure to get your own medical insurance coverage for the length of your trip. Check your regular health insurance to see what is covered and if you can get a supplementary policy through them. Various insurance companies sell travelers' medical policies through travel agents. You must expect to pay any medical costs on the spot in Africa and be reimbursed by your insurance company after you present it with documentation of your bills.

Water and Food

Food and drink are the commonest sources of travelers' illnesses, from serious diseases like hepatitis to that familiar bugaboo, diarrhea. The basic rule for shunning illness is to watch what you eat or drink. Rigidly applied, this means avoiding all uncooked vegetables or unpeeled fruits and drinking only purified water. The problem is that it is difficult to apply these standards rigorously. Tour members, whether at lodges or private camps, will be confronted with a parade of tempting goodies, including fresh salads. Although standards of cleanliness are likely to be high on tours, there are no guarantees. Budget travelers, living on the local economy, will often be exposed to situations where there is no choice but to accept some risk. In the end, all travelers have to decide for themselves what constitutes reasonable risk.

We have to consider our individual differences in tolerance for new foods and resistance to gastrointestinal problems. The most common cause of tourist diarrhea is the *E. choli* bacterium, which is already present in each of our systems. The introduction of local strains may cause one person's intestines to go completely berserk, while another's adapt with ease. Someone who knows that he always gets sick when he travels should be totally strict about dietary rules. The experienced traveler, whose gut has been exposed to every bug in the world, is allowed a lot more discretion. If you are on a short tour, it's worth considering whether a tasty treat is going to cause three or four days of unpleasantness. That caution is not meant to encourage food paranoia — just decide how you will deal with food risks and accept your luck.

No discretion should be allowed when it comes to drinking water. Most lodges and camps claim to provide potable drinking water (either boiled and filtered or from deep underground boreholes) and use it to make their ice. Nonetheless, it does not hurt to be too careful. Every traveler should have a water purification kit of some kind. Halizone or Potable Agua tablets are acceptable; supernatant iodine solutions are better (they kill giardia and amoebic cysts). All of these purification methods discolor water and give it an unpleasant taste, so you might want to bring along a supply of powdered fruit drinks to make it more palatable. Charcoal-chemical filtration systems work well and do not affect the taste, but are probably too cumbersome for most travelers. Bring your own water bottle and keep a supply of purified water on hand. Use your own water to brush your teeth as well as for drinking.

Milk products in lodges and most cities are safe; the milk has been boiled, if not pasteurized. In the bush, it's wise to look for the skin floating on top of the milk to be sure it has been boiled.

Medical Kit

Every traveler should have a medical kit for minor emergencies (cuts, blisters, and so on) and should have medications to cover a fairly wide range of problems. The following items are recommended:

Tape and Sterile Gauze Pads. Breathable medical tape is useful not only for dressings but also for covering possible blister sites before they develop. Moleskin is also excellent for that purpose.

Band-Aids. A few assorted sizes.

Betadine. A germicidal solution for cleaning wounds. Available in convenient swabs.

Antibiotic Ointment.

Scissors.

Tweezers.

Thermometer.

Needle. For removing splinters.

The following items are useful options to include, especially for long-term travelers:

Ace Bandage.

Temporary Tooth Filling (Cavity). Oil of clove and a cotton ball will serve the same purpose if you lose a filling.

Eyecup. Very useful for washing foreign objects out of the eye. Dust or tiny flies in the eye are common, painful problems. Washing removes them faster and more safely than rubbing.

Cortisone Cream. For insect bites.

Safety Pins.

Many recommended medications require a doctor's prescription. Consult your doctor about dosages, side effects, and possible allergic reactions. Consider including the following medications in your medical kit:

Antibiotics. A wide-spectrum antibiotic can do wonders against serious cases of diarrhea. *Bactrim* or *Septra* (brand names for sulfamethoxazole) are highly favored. They are sulfa-based drugs, so beware of allergic reactions. *Doxycycline* is a mild form of the wide-spectrum antibiotic tetracycline. Taken prophylactically, it can effectively prevent traveler's diarrhea. However, it makes the skin more sensitive to sunburn — a real concern in Africa. *Cipro* is another wide-spectrum antibiotic that is particularly effective against staph infections caused by cuts and other wounds.

Lomotil (Diphenoxylate and Atropine) or Imodium (Loperamide). Either of these medications is effective for stopping diarrhea symptoms. They are plugs, not cures. They are very helpful on those sad days when you have the runs but must face hard travel.

Tylenol (Acetaminophen) with Codeine. Codeine can be used as a plug for the runs, or for serious pain.

Halcion (Triazolam). Good on those nights when you *must* sleep, and for overnight airplane flights.

Benadryl (Dophenhydramine). A life saver if you suffer terrible itching from insect bites.

Antihistamine. For colds and nasal allergies.

Aspirin.

Contraceptives. It's best to bring a supply that will last for the duration of your trip. Condoms may be available in big cities. Birth control pills and spermicides would be more difficult to find, and possibly of dubious quality.

Sun and Heat

Africa is generally hot — sometimes ferociously so. It is very important to keep up your fluid intake. Dehydration can lead to serious heat exhaustion, and in combination with antimalarial drugs, it may cause painful kidney stones. Carry your water bottle with you on game drives as well as walks, and drink frequently. Avail yourself of the opportunities to quaff soft drinks, coffee, tea, or beers.

The latter three are diuretics, so you'll lose fluid about as quickly as you gain it, but that's okay as long as you keep drinking.

The African sun should not be underestimated — it can be a real killer, especially during the hot seasons. You should worry more about sunstroke than suntan. When in the sun, wear your hat. If it's really hot, follow the animals' example: take advantage of shade at every opportunity. Avoid sunburn: use sunscreen or even wear long sleeves if you are particularly photosensitive.

Insects

Insect fear is a common pretrip paranoia of Africa-bound travelers. These fears are mostly groundless. Except within the steamy tropical zones, insects are no more a problem in safari country than in many parts of the US, and for the most part even less so.

In certain places and during certain seasons, mosquitoes are abundant, but they are more likely to be completely absent from most places on your itinerary. African mosquitoes are generally active only at night. They never occur in the daytime swarms that plague hikers in Alaska or California's Sierra Nevada. Where they are numerous, long sleeves or insect repellent can be worn outdoors, while mosquito nets or a fully netted tent assure comfort while you sleep.

Flies are an occasional nuisance. Tsetse flies are voracious biters, and many people suffer extreme itchiness as a reaction. In tsetse country, long sleeves and strong repellent are the way to go (repellent has variable results: sometimes it's effective, other times, seemingly useless). Tsetses seem to be attracted to dark colors, so wear light-colored, earth-toned fabrics. Fortunately, tsetses are largely absent from the more popular game parks. Where they do occur, their distribution tends to be spotty, although some bush-covered parks are more heavily infested. Although tsetses are responsible for the transmission of sleeping sickness, the incidence is so low that it is not worth worrying about for the short-term visitor. Other flies are occasionally abundant, but are annoying for their numbers rather than their bites. Sporadically, local conditions may be just right for ordinary housefly-type insects to be present in massive numbers. They are often attracted to the warmth and moisture of exposed human skin. It's unpleasant to have carpets of flies sitting on you, even though they don't bite. Long sleeves and repellent effectively prevent this uncomfortable circumstance. Flies are more of an aesthetic problem. It horrifies us to see African children sitting indifferently while flies crawl around their eyes (yes, this is unhealthy because it spreads eye disease), but they have tired of the impossible task of shooing away infinite numbers. You will never get accustomed to that, but you may have to accommodate yourself to the presence of flies.

"Killer bees" are the cause of some concern due to hysterical stories in the press chronicling their invasion of the Americas. The African honey bee does occasionally attack in dangerous swarms, but this is a very rare circumstance. Care should be taken not to provoke attack, particularly by inundating nesting holes with fumes, which sometimes inadvertently occurs when safarists happen to top up their gas tank while beneath the wrong tree. Baobabs are favorite nesting trees for bees because of the number of hollow nesting sites they offer. If a swarm attacks, it does so with great fury. Bee toxins are proportionately among the strongest animal poisons known. Massive numbers of stings can be fatal, but most often the result is swelling and extreme discomfort. Those persons most at risk are naturally those allergic to bee stings. Such people may suffer severe anaphylactic shock (swelling of the throat that cuts off breathing) from even a few stings, just as they might from bees at home. If you are severely allergic to bees, you may want to carry injectable adrenaline (available as EpiPen with a doctor's prescription) just in case. Chances are, you'll never use it. Antihistamines such as Benadryl are effective in reducing the pain and itching of bee stings as well as scorpion stings and insect bites.

Scorpions are common enough, particularly in hot country. Being secretive and largely nocturnal, they are rarely encountered on lodge safaris. Campers sometimes find them underneath tents when packing up camp. Stings may be sickeningly painful, but only the superallergic are in any danger. It's best to keep door and floor zips shut whenever you enter or leave your tent, and to keep your duffle zipped as well. This is an effective defense against all discomforting visitors.

Ticks climb aboard animals as they move through brush or long grass. Participants on foot safaris should check their bodies for them, especially on the legs and torso. Remove embedded ticks as soon as possible because they are potential carriers of febrile diseases. Tiny "pepper ticks" look like grains of spice. Itchy rather than dangerous, they can be picked up by the dozens as you walk through wet grass.

Snakebite

Snakes are common throughout much of Africa. For the most part, they are small and secretive. Many are poisonous, among them a few notably large and dangerous species. These species generate exaggerated fear, but are in fact not much of a threat to tourists. The burden of exposure to snakebite is borne by indigenous Africans who come into accidental contact with the reptiles during the normal course of their lives: cutting bush, gathering firewood, walking in nighttime darkness. Snakes avoid humans when they can, and you will be lucky even to see one during the course of a two-week game viewing safari. Campers and hikers are more likely to come into the proximity of snakes and should follow a few commonsense rules to stay out of trouble:

Use a flashlight when walking at night. This is the best protection against the puff adder, the bane of barefooted rural Africans. It is a common but sluggish snake that freezes motionless when approached, in the hope of going unnoticed. It most often succeeds, but will bite if stepped on.

Think snake! In cool weather, snakes are apt to lie in exposed places, warming themselves in the morning sun. At other times, they usually hide themselves in holes and rock crevices, or under logs. Consider where snakes are likely to be and take extra care in high-risk areas.

Be careful in long grass. Most snakes flee when ground vibrations warn them of approaching danger, so tread hard and they'll get off your path. (This is not a recommended procedure when stalking game.)

If you encounter a snake, back off. Give the snake a chance to escape. Do not attempt to kill or annoy it. Once it is seen, a snake is no longer a danger unless provoked.

The oft-quoted admonition to wear high boots and long pants whenever walking in the bush is pure nonsense. This rule is applicable to herpetologists who go actively searching for snakes. If you are planning on turning over logs and poking into holes, by all means take these extra precautions and more. Although boots and long pants do effectively protect the legs, they are cumbersome and uncomfortable. Few bush walkers consider the bother worth the extra margin of protection.

In the rare event of an actual snakebite, do not panic. Try to kill the animal for positive identification (but not at the risk of further bites). Do not make incisions to suck poisons (cutting should *never* be done as it substantially increases the risk of limb loss). Do not apply tourniquets unless the snake is positively identified as a cobra or mamba. The recommended first aid is to wrap the entire bitten limb snugly with bandage and apply a splint to immobilize it. The idea is to prevent the poison from spreading through the lymphatic system. Stay calm: sudden death from even the most poisonous snakebites is rare, while shock from non-poisonous bites is a common reaction. Get to medical attention as soon as possible. Antivenin serums are available for all the common poisonous snakes. Several species of cobras spit venom at the eyes of perceived attackers. Venom in the eye causes severe burning and temporary blindness. It should be flushed out thoroughly with any available liquid (water, Coke, even urine) to prevent any risk of permanent damage.

Personal Safety

Perhaps more than other continents, Africa seems tinged with an aura of danger. To routine concerns about the incidence of violent crime (which must be considered wherever we travel) are added worries about wars and political upheavals, as well as fears about wild animals. Here we examine each of these issues and put them into a proper perspective.

Political Stability

Africa has a reputation for coups and bush wars. Although there is plenty of conflict on the continent, the news media sometimes blow stories out of proportion. The true danger for visitors is often hard to assess; while news pundits discourse on guerrilla wars and diplomatic negotiations, tourists may be visiting peaceful game parks in another part of the same country. True hot spots — places where full-fledged wars are in progress and society has broken down — should definitely be avoided. These include the southern Sudan, and possibly Rwanda, eastern Congo, and Angola. There is always the possibility of random acts of terrorism, but that is the price of travel anywhere these days.

Coups in the countries that are major safari destinations have been rare. In the event of a coup, do what everyone else does: stay out of sight. Violence during these upheavals is usually confined to rival factions. Tourists should stay indoors until the smoke clears, then make their presence known to their embassy as soon as possible. During political crises, nervous police or army personnel have been known to accuse tourists of being spies. This may be scary, but will come out all right if you observe the usual rules governing ridiculous arrest: keep your cool, be patient, identify yourself, and insist (politely) on seeing higher-ranking officers.

Tourists occasionally find themselves in trouble for breaching local security regulations — usually by taking photos of forbidden places.

These may include bridges, railroads, dams, airports, police stations, and army bases. Such cases can result in protracted negotiations, the confiscation of film, or even detention. When No Photo signs are posted, take them seriously.

Crime

Lawlessness is no worse in Africa than other parts of the world, and the same commonsense rules apply. Cities are the highest crime areas, as the urban poor are the most desperate. Petty thievery is the biggest problem. In crowded situations, be extra alert for pickpockets. Use your money belt around town and when using public transport. When walking on city streets, keep a good grip on your purse or shoulder bag. Purse snatchers are fast: they sometimes slash the strap from behind. Hustlers, often with very good raps, have various schemes to part you from your money (usually voluntarily). Politely ignore them. Armed robberies and muggings are common in big towns. Avoid walking the streets after dark.

Money, not rape, is the usual object of violent encounters, and tourists are seldom sexually assaulted. However, women are advised not to stroll or sunbathe alone on deserted beaches. In major cities and tourist resorts, some men are not shy about approaching foreign women, but for the most part, their come-ons are strictly verbal. Unaccompanied women will find the level of sexual harassment in Africa not nearly as bad as it is in some other parts of the world.

The independent traveler will have the toughest time with security. Make sure that hotel room doors lock properly, and even check for access through the window. Your gear has to be constantly watched. You'll find yourself teaming up with other travelers to keep an eye out for each other's possessions.

Theft is not unknown even in the finest hotels or while on safari. Camera equipment can safely be left in your room in tourist-class hotels, or inside your safari vehicle during the day (it's part of your driver's job to look after your gear). But don't leave money or traveler's checks in your room or tent. It's a common technique for hotel personnel to remove only a few checks from the back of the book so that the theft is not discovered immediately. The best rule is not to put temptation in anyone's path. Avail yourself of the hotel safe, or carry your money with you at all times.

Wild Animals

One has to admit that it's partly the old hunter's mystique of the "dangerous game" that draws us to safari. African animals are not only beautiful — many of them are also large and dangerous. How dangerous? What are your chances of being killed or injured?

Many wild animals have the potential to be harmful to humans, but in fact the chances of them bothering with you are extremely low. Wildlife has been on the losing end of a very long war with humanity. By the process of natural selection, the animals have learned to fear us as their chief natural enemy. An animal's first inclination on contact with humans is almost inevitably to run away. There are situations where this is not so, but "accidents" involving tourists are rare. As usual, the brunt of wildlife danger falls mostly on indigenous Africans who come into contact and conflict with animals in the course of their normal lives. Elephants raid crop fields and the farmer gets hurt trying to chase them away. A woman gathering firewood in the forest meets a testy buffalo. The fisherman's dugout gets overturned by an angry hippo. The herdsman tries to protect his cattle from a hungry lion, but his spear is not aimed true. Poachers wound an animal, and it kills the hapless next person it meets. These are the typical situations where humans run into trouble with animals.

Most visitors come into contact with wildlife only while touring game parks from the safety of vehicles. Although it is not unknown for large animals to attack cars, it is an extremely rare event and usually takes some extraordinary provocation. Most parks have rules against getting out of the vehicle. Although these regulations are sometimes overrigorous, they are designed to protect naive people from themselves. Even with such rules, the occasional tourist does something stupid — like getting out of a car to take a better picture of lions. People have problems when they forget that the animals are truly wild. If a human gets too close, the instinct for fight overpowers the instinct for flight.

You are most likely to get into trouble with animals at lodges or campsites where certain individual animals lose all fear of humans. Troops of monkeys or baboons often forage on lodge grounds, stealing food from dining verandahs. The occasional bull elephant becomes a lodge regular, too. These animals are cute — the delight of guests — but should not to be taken for granted. Tourists often feed the baboons, and sometimes get bitten for their kindness (if it is kindness, for feeding reinforces pesky habits for which these animals eventually may "have to be shot"). Guests also routinely ignore warnings not to approach seemingly tame elephants. This is a mistake, for no matter how tame they seem, elephants are irascible, unpredictable, and capable of mayhem.

To a large extent, whether or not you have problems with wild animals is up to you. As long as you treat them with proper respect for their capabilities, you can enjoy them without incident. In fact, you are much less likely to be injured or killed by a wild animal in a park than killed by an automobile on one of Africa's main highways.

Special precautions govern animal safety on camping and walking safaris. (For more information, see the Living in the Bush section of this chapter.)

Living in the Bush

Even highly experienced outdoorsfolk need to be extra cautious when getting acquainted with the conditions they encounter in the African bush. Animal dangers may be exaggerated by pop traditions in literature and film, but the animals are there, and so is the potential for serious accident. You will have to learn to live with the presence of large wild animals. You may also find yourself adventuring in populated areas, which means being aware of camp security.

Camping

Camping is surely the best way to appreciate the full magic of Africa's outdoor experience. Pristine natural surroundings, balmy weather, and the proximity of wildlife are surefire ingredients for excitement and pleasure. That said, be aware of a few flies in the ointment.

Within parks, it is often forbidden to camp outside of designated public campgrounds. Facilities vary: in South Africa, campsites may include restaurants and swimming pools; in other countries, nothing more than a signpost may be in evidence. Most official campsites at least provide a water source and a latrine. Water is a prime advantage of formal camping sites, especially where shower facilities are available. Unfortunately, public campsites have disadvantages too, not the least of which is company. Crowding is a growing problem, particularly in the well-known parks. While neighbors don't necessarily spoil the fun, they are intrusive on the wilderness experience. More concretely, public campsites tend to get trashed out. Not all campers are circumspect in handling refuse, and park maintenance crews may be entirely absent. In some reserves, special private campsites are available. Considerably higher fees are charged, and they are generally difficult to reserve. The better commercial safaris feature private sites when they can, but even they are sometimes forced into public campgrounds.

In some wilderness areas, you can camp wherever you like. In choosing a wilderness site, water is usually key. If you are traveling with your own vehicle, bring along plenty of water just in case no water supply can be found. Shade is another consideration. Also note animal paths, particularly if camp is located near a river or lakeshore. It's ideal to situate your camp on a rise where animals can be observed in the daytime as they come to drink, rather than in a gully where animals pass during the night. Check the availability of firewood, and clear the ground of thorns before setting up your tent.

Collecting firewood is generally easy because downed wood abounds in most types of bushland and it dries out quickly in the African sun. Fires are comforting to us humans, but there is some question as to whether they effectively scare off lions and other camp marauders. One school of thought has it that the light actually attracts curious animals. Try to judge your need for a night-long bonfire by the local supply of wood, keeping in mind the heavy pressure of camping parties on the local environment. Also take care to prevent fires from getting away.

The proximity of wildlife is certainly one of the greatest thrills in African camping. Animals can and will come into your campsite, especially at night. Most are incidental visitors — elephants or antelopes seeking browse. Some are purposeful intruders intent on stealing your food. These latter are mostly small — porcupines or civets looking for scraps — but hyenas are frequent camp scavengers, too. Their mournful whooping cries are a typical nighttime sound, and a good flashlight often reveals their eyes in the darkness beyond the campfire. Lions also patrol campsites on occasion. All this is pretty disturbing to the newcomer, but there is actually little to fear. Animals tend to ignore tents. Elephants, for example, are remarkably conscious of where they place their feet. They don't trip over tent lines or inadvertently crush sleeping campers. A lion's claw can easily slice open a nylon tent, but he won't bother. As scary as the various noises emanating from the darkness may be (and the imagination works overtime when the rustlings of unknown animals seem to come from next to your tent), you are quite safe as long as you remain inside. It may be that the animals sense that camps are human territory and they retain their natural fear, or that they are simply timid about messing around with unfamiliar objects. The fact remains that animal attacks on tents are extremely rare.

There have been reports of attacks on campers who slept with their tents open, however, so it is mandatory to keep the door zipped shut. You will want ventilation, but keep windows zipped to a reasonable level. You will not feel too comfortable if you wake up to see a lion peering into your tent.

In southern Africa, it is somewhat the fashion to sleep out in the open, with camp cots circling around a good fire. This technique should only be used by groups accompanied by armed professional guides. Hunting parties often bivouac this way, and the practice has given rise to great campfire stories. One can hardly safari in Botswana or Zimbabwe without hearing about the poor chap who, while sleeping in the open "just the other night," had his arm carried off by a hyena. Either there are a hell of a lot of limbless hunters down there or the "Farewell to Arms" story must rank as one of the classic safari myths. Tall tales not withstanding, sleeping under the stars in big game country is risky.

Groups of hyenas will not hesitate to attack a sleeping human. Lions are opportunists, too — don't tempt them.

Lions in camp are worrisome, particularly if they include curious youngsters. If you are on an organized camping tour, your guide will probably use a car to chase intrusive lions away. If you are on your own and want to be prepared to do this, you should park your car immediately in front of your tent, leaving the car door unlocked for quick access.

Normally, after the camp has quieted and the fire has died to embers, you should remain in your tent (and sleep like a log). If you have to come out of the tent at night, have a good look around with a flashlight. To urinate, don't bother going far. For bowel emergencies, you might want to go nearby rather than wander any distance to the toilet. If so, be sure to clean up waste thoroughly in the morning.

Food and dishes should be properly secured for the night, preferably inside a vehicle rather than a tent. Don't leave shoes, towels, or anything portable lying around outside: hyenas are fond of carrying off odd items and chewing them up.

In true wilderness campsites, you may have to draw your water from a river. Rivers should be approached with care, especially if crocodiles are present. Crocs are usually afraid of people, but large specimens are opportunists. They make their living partly by keeping an eye on places where animals come down to the water regularly to drink, grabbing the occasional unwary victim. Tourists can fall into this category. Don't hang around the water's edge, wash, or bathe unless the water is clear with a sandy bottom that affords good visibility. Avoid these activities at dawn and dusk, and don't go near the water at night when crocs are most active.

During daylight and early evening hours, most animals will stay out of your camp area because they easily sense human activity. The exceptions are monkeys and baboons, the smarties who have learned that tourists don't bite. Without much fear of humans, they regularly forage at camp refuse dumps and are adept at darting in to pinch untended supplies. They have even learned to unzip and enter unguarded tents in which food has been stored. It is not pleasant to return to camp to find your provisions gone and your possessions a shambles.

Monkeys are not the only hazard to unguarded camps. Theft is an increasing problem, too. Campsites are often located on park boundaries and are regularly visited by local people. Even campsites deep within a park can be reached by knowledgeable thieves. Tour groups will have staff who can guard the camp against both monkeys and people, but individual travelers have to consider the risks of leaving their camp unattended. In proximity to villages, it is wise to pack up your gear and bring it with you. Alternatively, you may be able to hire someone to look after your camp, especially if regular park personnel are present.

Camp security is even a bigger headache outside parks. If you are visiting remote inhabited areas, throngs of curious locals may visit your camp. This is probably just the experience you want, but you have to be wary about sticky fingers. Again, on group tours, vigilant camp staff are useful, but even members of guided tours have to be responsible for their own goods in these situations. Security can fail: thieves sometimes cut through the rear walls of tents and enter unseen. Don't leave articles of clothing or other possessions lying around camp. It's best to keep your tent closed tight, and keep your most valuable items locked in a car (or in the case of money and important documents, on your person). If you are camping on your own in towns and populated areas, you may be allowed to camp in police or church compounds if there is no regular campground. These offer a little more privacy and security.

Trekking and Bush Walking

Areas accessible to wilderness trekking are limited in Africa. Although wilderness bush abounds, the vastness of the countryside and the hot climate make it inhospitable to all but the most hardy trekkers. Unlike other parts of the world, walking is prohibited in most national parks in Africa. Where walking is permitted, special permits or the participation of licensed guides is often required.

Despite all the difficulties, walking safaris are highly recommended. Foot safaris offer the excitement of meeting the animals on their own ground, which is a very different perspective than one gets from game drives. One gets a much clearer impression of the animals' senses and a heightened respect for their capabilities. There is also the chance to learn bushcraft: to recognize scats and learn how to stalk or avoid contacts with wildlife. More, there's a feeling of closeness to the environment that you can only get from hiking. You'll notice tracks and puzzle out which animals live in the many burrows you discover. You'll pay a lot more attention to the vegetation, too. It will certainly have more effect on you: nasty thorns will hold up your progress, while sharp grasses scratch your legs and riverine trees beckon welcome respite from the sun. You can expect to see less game on walking safaris — you cover a lot less ground on foot, and many of the animals will slip away unnoticed. Those animals you do see will not usually permit you to get as close as you would in a vehicle. Generally, wildlife observation and photography are more rewarding on game drives. But for a genuine feel for the bush, walking safaris are unbeatable. They are an enlightening supplement to the vehicular safari.

The chief obstacle to walking in big game areas is, obviously, the danger posed by wild animals. How real is this danger? Although animals are afraid of humans and most often run away at the first hint of their presence, wild animals can and do attack people. Walkers are at the most risk. In places where animals tolerate close human proximity, such as around camps and lodges, it is by their choice. An individual animal in these situations learns to feel enough confidence to considerably reduce the approach distance it tolerates before it feels threatened. In the bush, however, an animal's security zone is much larger, and its sensitivity to humans as enemies much greater. Still, an animal's instincts will most often lead to flight. But not always. It may stand its ground, concealed, until provoked into a charge by unsuspecting people who are approaching. Or it may not sense approaching danger until the humans blunder too close, resulting in a violent display. Obviously, the risk to walkers is greatly heightened in thick bush.

The presence of an experienced guide reduces the likelihood of aggressive incidents. The guide will know which patches of bush need extra caution to negotiate, or should be avoided altogether. Experience will have taught him (or her!) to read spore; fresh tracks or dung will tell him what animals may be up the trail. The guide will also be sensitive to the wind direction. But even professionals can be attacked. That's why foot safaris in big game country really do require the accompaniment of an armed guide. On most foot safaris, a gun is brought but not used. Bushcraft and the animals' instincts for avoidance see to that. But once initiated, aggressive incidents are highly unpredictable situations. Correct behavior is essential. To run can invite attack. If a firm stand and shouts don't scare a threatening animal off, a shot in the air is usually enough to send it on its way. If an actual charge is made, it may be necessary to shoot to kill.

Extensive foot safaris require an armed guard for your security, but that does not mean you can never walk in the bush on your own. In many situations, it is reasonably safe. If you are camping on your own, you will probably have to do some bush walking, if only to gather firewood. If you are on a mountain hike, you will likely walk through forest areas lightly inhabited by dangerous game. Experience will make you bolder, but always keep in mind a few commonsense rules:

Stick to open country when you can. Good visibility allows you to spot trouble a long way off. Thick bush invites sudden encounters of the dangerous kind.

To stalk game, it's necessary to proceed quietly. Walk lightly, speaking only in whispers or not at all. Heavy footsteps and loud, laughter-filled conversation practically guarantee that you will see no animal life. However, use the noisy method on forest walks: it warns animals of your approach so they can avoid you.

Stay alert. Keep your eyes and ears open. Even aggressive animals tend to warn intruders away before they charge. A growl, a snort, or a shaking in the bushes is an invitation for you to retreat or look for a tree to climb.

Pay attention to wind direction. If you are walking into the wind, you are much more likely to encounter animals ahead.

Stay cool. Psychologically, discouraging wild animals from attack is not unlike handling aggressive dogs. They can be bluffed out. Showing your fear emboldens them; running may invite attack. Give an animal plenty of room to escape, while you back off slowly. If you are in a group, stay together.

In extremis, climb a tree to evade buffalo. A steep embankment is the most effective barrier to an elephant.

Several species are notably dangerous: elephant, Cape buffalo, lion, and rhino. All are large and should not be approached without respect for their capabilities.

Elephants have no natural enemies except man, who persecutes them assiduously. As a result, they become extremely nervous when they sense humans in their vicinity. Bull elephants, which are often found alone or in small groups, are not as dangerous as females. The cows live in tight-knit family groups, which defend their calves very energetically. An encounter with an alarmed group of females is a hair-raising experience. The calves run underneath and behind the enraged mothers, who circle the young, trumpeting discontent. With trunks raised to pinpoint the enemy scent, the females present a wall of pachyderm fury.

While elephants are obviously highly dangerous, they get by mostly on bluster. A charge is frequently only a bluff and can be turned by shouts or a warning shot. Without firearms, however, it's very tough to escape from a determined charge. An elephant is faster than the average human and can plow right through thorny vegetation that would be an impenetrable barrier to a human. Climbing a tree is obviously problematical; a steep embankment, if it were handy, would give a little breathing space. A better strategy is to avoid too-close contact; circle wide around elephants or give them your scent at a long distance, so that they run off and out of your way.

The Cape buffalo (*Syncerus caffer*) has the reputation as the baddie of the bush. In big herds, which include cows, calves, and bulls, they are extremely skittish and are no threat. They will stand, staring balefully, until one of them bolts. Then the entire herd will follow suit in a retreating storm of thundering hooves and dust. Old bulls are solitary or live in groups of two or three. They are extremely wary and aggressive, and quite capable of defending themselves — even against lions. Unlike other dangerous animals, which may be content to let up on the attack once an enemy has been scared off, the buffalo means business. If he charges, he means to kill you and will press his attack with determination. While a rifle shot may turn his charge, shouting is not terribly effective. A good tree is a handy escape.

Lions are mostly bluff. Even if disturbed on a kill or while courting, lions are more likely to run than attack. They may make fearsome aggressive displays, however. Don't run: you don't want to encourage their instinct to chase running prey. Back off slowly, and be prepared to brazen it out with shouts, hand claps, and waved sticks. Like so many other animals, female lions are valiant in defense of their young, so it is bad news if you inadvertently approach a female with small cubs.

It is said that a rhino's charge can be escaped by stepping aside just before it hits you: it will continue straight on and disappear, too blind to find you for a second chance. I'm not sure I'd want to test that theory, but it's a moot point, for the testy black rhino is now too rarely encountered to be considered much of a danger. It's certain that your guide would be loath to shoot one if it did charge, so keep an eye out for a tree to climb. The white rhino is both more common and more mild-mannered; it can often be approached closely on foot in private game reserves.

It should be noted that animal attacks are universally described as "accidents." This implies that they are not routine calamities, and that they are, to a large extent, preventable. When they do occur, the victim inevitably takes the blame from local pundits: the circumstances always reveal that he or she (or the guide) made some "stupid" mistake. This judgment is harsh, for there is room for just plain bad luck. But there is one cardinal "stupid mistake": taking a wild animal for granted. In dealing with wildlife, judge an animal's capabilities, not its intentions.

Mountain Safaris

As in other parts of the world, mountains in Africa are the most attractive regions for trekkers. The highest ranges in Africa have trail or hut systems to encourage mountain walkers. Some have porters and guides available, too. Mountain habitats support low densities of dangerous game, so walking with armed guards while in mountain terrain is not required. The dangers of African mountains are the same as those encountered by trekkers on other mountains of the world: hypothermia, traumatic injury, and high-altitude illnesses.

On any mountain trek, hikers should be prepared for cold and wet weather, especially at elevations where frost occurs. Subfreezing weather (which you can expect nightly above about 12,000 feet at the equator and at much lower altitudes in South Africa) is not necessary to produce hypothermia: any exposure to cold and wet for enough time to lower the body's vital core temperature is sufficient. Good equipment, a respect for mountain weather, and common sense are the best protection. Falls that result in broken bones or twisted ankles are a risk on any hiking trip. They are more serious in Africa because of the difficulty of rescue. Porters or park rangers will have to carry you down. This is an uncomfortable process, but most of Africa (South Africa being a major exception) is still not in the age of helicopter evacuation. Even after you are down from the mountain itself, your transport problems may not be over unless you are traveling with a vehicle. Make sure to inform local park authorities of your route plan so that they can check up on you if you don't reappear on time. Porters and local guides are useful in such emergencies: they know where to get help as quickly as possible and can also carry you down in a pinch.

High-altitude problems can be experienced well below the icy mountain summits of Africa's highest mountains. The shortness of breath, headaches, and nausea of acute mountain sickness (AMS) is a familiar discomfort to many who climb too high, too fast (at altitudes above 8,000 feet). Acclimatization to altitude by hiking in slow stages is the best way to avoid problems. Unfortunately, considerations of time and money often lead trekkers in foreign lands to attempt too much, too quickly. They wind up suffering for their haste. High-altitude pulmonary edema (HAPE) and high-altitude cerebral edema (HACE) are both life-threatening conditions that can occur on Africa's highest equatorial mountain ranges but are not a major consideration in southern Africa's mountains.

Mountain hikers are well advised to carry plenty of water and drink much more than they normally do. Dehydration through vapor loss from normal breathing is considerable at high altitudes. Forcing fluids will help prevent the discomforts of AMS.

Several weather conditions are peculiar to the mountains of southern Africa and add to the risks of trekking there. In the summer months, blinding mists can reduce visibility to near zero: if you are lost in such fog, it's better to stay put and keep warm rather than wander around, which only increases the likelihood of adding injury to your woes. Lightning is also a considerable danger in summer, when violent thunderstorms occur almost every afternoon in upland regions. In the mountains of South Africa, hikers must be aware of berg winds, which can occur during the dry winter months (from May to September). These strong, desiccating winds (which actually presage a coming cold front) heat up as they sweep down the mountainsides and vastly increase the potential of dangerous bush fires.

A number of official hiking trails are available to self-reliant backpackers in southern Africa. South Africa has a well-developed system of trails and huts in mountainous regions throughout the country. Similar trails exist in the high mountain ranges of Zimbabwe and Malawi, and in several wilderness areas of Namibia. In most cases, the number of hikers is strictly regulated according to the capacity of huts and campsites, and the more popular treks must be prebooked long in advance. Huts and campsites have very basic facilities, and porters or guides are not generally available (except in Malawi), but the trails offer great walking to self-sufficient backpackers.

River Trips

African river trips are risky business. The normal perils of white water are not so much a problem as the less familiar dangers of hippos and crocodiles, and the possibility of infection with bilharzia. Experience is needed to keep these hazards down to the level of acceptable risk: there is little choice but to go with professionals. Commercial trips are operated in a few places — most notably, whitewater rafting and canoe safaris on the Zambezi River between Zambia and Zimbabwe, and *mokoro* (dugout canoe) safaris in Botswana's Okavango Delta.

One wouldn't think it to look at them, but hippos are one of the most dangerous African animals. They can be a threat to humans both in the water and on land. Highly territorial, aggressive bulls can attack rafts or canoes that venture too close. Their huge bulk can overturn boats; the long tusks that they so often reveal in their threatening "yawn" display are razor sharp and capable of cutting a person in two. When a boat approaches, a herd of hippos will splash from their resting place, where they have been lying half submerged, into the security of deeper water. Normally, they stay there, snorting and blowing as they break the surface for a quick peek between dives. Occasionally, an aggressive male will make a determined, purposeful attack. Another danger comes from stragglers, cut off from the main herd, who make sudden late dashes to the river: even an accidental collision with a hippo spells disaster. The technique for running boats past hippos is to alert animals downstream with the noise of paddles tapped on gunwales. This sends them splashing for deep water, and allows you to keep an eye on their positions as you glide by. The boats then hug the shallow water, letting the hippos have the security of the deep. Real attacks are rare, but in the course of a river trip, you may pass hundreds of these high-strung "river horses."

Hippos are also dangerous on land. They emerge from the water at night, walking long distances to graze. They are skittish and, notwithstanding their bulky shape and short legs, can run with remarkable speed. A human who unknowingly cuts a hippo off from its line of retreat to the water may be suddenly confronted with a fleeing hippo coming right at him or her. Whether you get run down or bitten, the effect is the same — lethal! Care must be taken not to camp on the hippos' regular trails. Also stay alert when walking around river banks in the early morning: the animals may still be moving about on land.

We are all familiar with the scenes in Tarzan movies where huge crocodiles slide swiftly into the water in pursuit of unlucky adventurers. More than likely, those films were taken of reptiles that were actually escaping. And that's the way you are most likely to see crocodiles. They lie basking on sunny banks until they sense a boat approaching. Then they vanish swiftly into the muddy water, not to be seen again. Although crocodiles attain dinosaur size, deliberate assaults by crocodiles on boats are almost nonexistent, for they fear humans and only attack with the opportunity of surprise. But they are dangerous to swimmers, and a boat overturned by hippos or by rapids puts overboard passengers at risk if large crocs are present.

All in all, the chances of hippo or crocodile attacks are slim if experienced hands are there to guide you. Aside from the thrills, river trips in Africa are attractive because they offer the peace of unspoiled wilderness: the waterways take you far off the beaten tracks of the heavily visited parks. Like foot safaris, however, they do not provide the best game viewing. Although a good variety of animals may be seen along the water's edge, it is hard to get close enough to photograph and observe them. A moving boat is also an unsteady platform for using binoculars or cameras to maximum advantage.

Traveler's Etiquette

No one consciously wants to play the part of the boorish tourist. Yet some travelers do as they please, without ever giving any thought to local standards of conduct or assessing their own responsibility for things that take place. In this section, we consider some of the thorny issues of personal behavior that you are likely to encounter during your trip to Africa.

Cultural Impact and Exchange

Whatever style of adventure you embark upon, you are guaranteed to come up against the cultural differences between our supermodern, superrich society and that of Africa. Africans think differently and do things differently than we do. By our standards, many things in Africa are done inefficiently or at least peculiarly. Attitudes toward time, business, or politics are governed by different traditions and philosophies. Some of those traditions are very old indeed. At the same time, no country or continent is an island now, and Western influences abound. Africans clamor after the trappings of consumer society. Government officials and nouveau riche have taken readily to the symbols of conspicuous consumption — the Mercedes car and bottles of imported foreign liquors are badges of success. For ordinary people, higher status can come in the form of a wristwatch or a good pair of shoes.

Approach Africans with an attitude of respect. By and large, they are hospitable people, ready with a smile and a greeting. Most tourists respond with genuine warmth, but some fall prey to treating Africans as curiosities, not as people. This rudeness naturally creates distance if not hostility. Africans are extremely sensitive to condescending attitudes. Traditional people are proud of their tribal attire. Poor Africans do not mean to horrify you with the raggedness of their clothes. Avoid giving inadvertent offense through thoughtless condescension.

Nothing will try your diplomatic skills more than negotiating the shoals of African paperwork and bureaucracy. What might be a simple task in the US — cashing a traveler's check at a bank or reconfirming an airline ticket, for example — can turn into a major test of patience. Long waiting lines, consultations with managers, and unexpected problems are routine in some quarters. Handling paperwork becomes a maddeningly slow process, especially if you are under time pressure. Generally, well-mannered patience and perseverance are your only recourse. A raised voice or bullying tone is inevitably met by a stony wall of resistance. All further entreaties and conversation may be ignored. Apologies may save the day, but just as likely, your cause is dead unless you can get to a higher official.

There are situations where any traveler's patience would fail. Scenario: you arrive at the airport to find that the record of your confirmed reservation has disappeared and you are now waitlisted for an obviously overbooked flight. Of course, it's best to keep your cool and remain polite, but in such truly do-or-die situations, dogged perseverance has to be combined with the right combination of humility and bluster. Where entreaty and threat fail, bribes may see you through, but this requires great discretion. When bumped from the flight roster, resubmitting your ticket with a US bank note tucked behind the coupon and a polite suggestion that there may have been some mistake is more effective than flashing a US$100 bill in full view of lookers-on. Bribery is always ethically questionable, but sometimes it works, and in some countries (like Congo or

Mozambique), it is all too necessary. You should resist deliberate shake-downs for bribes when possible.

Politics is another area where you must remain a diplomat. African political systems are almost universally one-party states governed with varying degrees of authoritarian control. Few countries have any strong tradition of a free press, so where outright repression doesn't inhibit political discussion, indifference or ignorance do. Sources of information for Africans are basically limited to the national media, which are absorbed in local trivia (sometimes interesting!), official pronouncements, and ideological rhetoric. Consequently, most Africans are not given to an interest in deep political discussions. But while conversations may be short on sophisticated analysis, they reveal a lot about the way the country is run and the ordinary citizen's attitudes toward the powers that be. There is generally a strong traditional respect for the authority of the presidential figure. Whoever is in charge of the country you are in, his face will smile down at you in countless shops and offices. Africans are often shocked by foreigners' candid criticisms of their own leaders; no matter how readily they may discuss their country's problems, they would rarely think to voice disapproval of their president or party.

Shopping is different in Africa, too. While modern shops tend to set fixed prices for their goods, local marketeers and craftsmen are ever ready to bargain. Where appropriate, you should not be put off by bargaining. It can be fun, and as in so many parts of the world, it is the traditional way to do business. You'll have to sharpen your negotiating skills or you may wind up paying twice as much as you need to spend. The standard formula is to offer about a quarter of what the vendor asks, and settle in between. (Be careful, though — you can as easily start at a tenth the asking price.) It helps to shop around without expressing too much interest. Prices often come tumbling down if you are willing to walk away. At the same time, there is no use beating a vendor down to a giveaway price — they do have to make a living and are entitled to a profit. Don't make offers on items you don't really want. You may find your price accepted and feel obligated to buy. Trading for Western goods, such as watches, calculators, and clothing, is an acceptable part of marketing. Many travelers bring items especially for this purpose. If you do, try to bring decent goods rather than junk.

Most Africans are cash poor but self-sufficient. The extended family system takes care of the sick and elderly, but some unfortunates are always left out. The desperate resort to begging. It doesn't hurt to give something to obviously handicapped or destitute people. But it may be harmful to make random gifts to perfectly healthy children. Many tourists like to give away candy or balloons. The kids love it, and it's certainly fun to watch the children enjoying the treat. But the long-term effect is to encourage them to demand gifts of every tourist they see, which is not a good habit. This is one of travel's moral dilemmas: do we cause more harm than good through our well-intentioned interactions with indigenous peoples? There really is no answer. If you'd like to bring giveaways, I'd suggest pencils, pens, or notebooks instead of candy. Such school supplies are always in demand, for adults as well as children.

The Black Market

Where economies are tightly controlled, black markets thrive. They are nowhere healthier than in Africa, where official currency exchange rates are often laughably low when compared to the actual purchasing power of the dollar in the local economy.

The black market is a reflection of the vicious circle of many African economies. Governments try to maximize their imports of foreign exchange ("hard" currencies like the US dollar, British pound, and so on) by arbitrarily setting their own exchange rates for their currencies. In a free market, these currencies would be valued much lower. By controlling the rates, the Africans force Western companies to pay higher prices for exported commodities. That's good for the African countries. But the system goes wrong because the governments are unable, or unwilling, to squelch the free market. Many people — businessmen, expatriate contract workers, and corrupt government officials — have an interest in getting foreign exchange out of the country. They may need the dollars (which they are forbidden to buy or export) to finance business ventures, foreign travel, education for their children, or the purchase of consumer items unavailable in Africa. Many people, especially government officials, want to amass assets outside their own country as security against an uncertain future. For an official in a coup-prone nation, a Swiss bank account is not an undesirable thing. Although the majority of African citizens see little of it, the wealthier classes have plenty of local currency and frequently nothing to spend it on. They can afford to buy dollars at two, three, five, or even twenty times the official exchange rate, creating the black market. None of the dollars exchanged on the black market do the African country any good. They are all smuggled out and do nothing to help the national treasury with its desperate foreign exchange deficit.

The black market presents the traveler with another moral dilemma. It enables you to stretch your travel dollars — often just a little, sometimes enormously. It also does incontestable harm to the African host economy. It is easy to rationalize black market trading: the exchange rate does reflect the real purchasing power of your money, while the official rate may be blatantly ridiculous. And everyone does it, often including the top political leaders of the country. Whether to participate or not is dictated by each traveler's circumstances. Many budget travelers would be hard put to get along in Africa without it. Tourists on prepaid tours usually have little contact with it. (Their tour companies have presumably paid for the arrangements through official bank channels. In this wicked world, however, that is no guarantee that all of the money will see its way to the proper African national treasury.) For group travelers, the black market is a lesser temptation, something that can stretch pocket money for souvenirs. For most, it is not worth bothering with.

Needless to say, the black market is illegal. Many countries have liberalized their economies in recent years and allow a free market exchange of currencies. Others officially maintain stringent currency-control regulations. On entry, you must make a written declaration of all cash and traveler's checks. All subsequent currency exchanges (made only with officially authorized institutions, such as banks, hotels, and airlines) should be recorded on your declaration form. On leaving the country, you have to surrender your currency form to customs. If they count your money going out, and the amount doesn't jive with the figures on your currency form, you are theoretically in trouble. However, it is very rare for customs officials to count a traveler's money, or even check the forms closely. And even if the figures don't measure up, the lamest excuses are almost invariably accepted. When travelers do wind up in trouble through black market dealings, it is usually through entrapment by undercover police. It is inadvisable to change money with people on the street: it is high risk for a rip-off, shakedown, or arrest. It's safest to exchange with shopkeepers.

Photographing People

Africans are touchy about having their pictures taken. The roots of this sensitivity may or may not lie with superstitions concerning the camera stealing the soul. Today, it is official discouragement and economic considerations that make Africans reluctant to smile for the camera.

In post-independence Africa, government officials spread the view that tourists took pictures of Africans only to mock them as curiosities, "just like the animals in the game parks." Officials took a particularly dim view of photos of bare-breasted or spear-toting natives. They were anxious to project a modern image for their countries, not to be seen as "primitives." In some places, it became illegal to take pictures of colorful tribespeople. Generally, the word was put out that Africans shouldn't allow themselves to be photographed. That view mellowed with the increasing influx of tourists. Once it became clear that tourists were willing to pay for pictures, photo privileges became an economic resource. Now it's standard to pay people if you want to take their picture. Many visitors take umbrage at having payment demanded for photos, but you can hardly blame the Africans for asking. They know that foreigners are wealthy by African standards and can easily afford a small payment. They also know that pictures are potentially valuable — that they can be sold to magazines for a great deal of money, none of which they will see. They have no way of knowing what shots will end up in a private photo album and which on the cover of *National Geographic*. It really is not unreasonable to pay them a modeling fee.

The worst drawback to paying for photos is that they must be negotiated before you take them. This makes it hard to get lively shots as people tend to stiffen up for the camera. But if you shoot first, even with the intention of paying later, there is likely to be an unpleasant scene. The subjects will think that you were "poaching" a picture. This is a bad bargaining position. People often ask for ridiculous amounts of money. You shouldn't have to pay very much, but of course it depends on whom you are photographing. Dandified Masai warriors in full-ochered regalia or Herero women in their voluminous Victorian skirts will naturally want a high fee, while young herdboys might settle for a few coins. Be sure to negotiate a complete deal: one fee covers as many pictures as you want. Otherwise, you may take a snap, but wind up in a new negotiation when you try to take a second. The urge to steal candid shots is sometimes irresistible, but be prepared for problems.

Some people will be enthusiastic about your taking their picture in the hope that you will send them a copy. Such portraits are really precious to them: do remember to send the prints that you promise or there will be some very disappointed folks on the other side of the world. A Polaroid camera is nice to take along — it gives everyone instant gratification!

On Safari

Numerous national park regulations govern the behavior of visitors on safaris. Park rules vary from one country to the next, but they have two common threads: the protection of plants and animals, and the safety of visitors. While few tourists argue with safety rules, they sometimes ignore other restrictions. These rules warrant some thought.

Protection of the animals entails more than simply preventing poachers from shooting them. It also means habitat conservation. Toward that end, off-road driving is now forbidden in most African parks. Such "no off-road" regulations are often resented by tourists, for they upset the wilderness "feel" of safari and make it difficult to photograph animals that are far from the track. But repeated cross-country driving can cause serious degradation of fragile grasslands, and even the passage of a single vehicle can leave near-permanent scars on a desert landscape. So, for the long-term health of the parks, off-road prohibitions should be respected.

Animals are also protected from harassment. It is sad that safari tour drivers, overanxious to please their tourists, sometimes behave without regard to animal activities. It is common, for example, for a driver to spot an animal and immediately drive straight to it for photos. This can disrupt animals in the process of stalking prey or in courtship display. Chasing animals is also too common. It's particularly harmful when young animals are involved, for they frequently get separated and made more vulnerable to their enemies. The most contemptible action is the use of vehicles to herd prey animals toward predators in the hope of producing an instant kill. This is not only against park rules, it is also against the whole spirit of safari. We come to see animals behave naturally. If we are lucky enough to witness the drama of a hunt, it is a privilege, not an entertainment. To see a kill, you need patience and luck. To see an animal butchered, you need only visit a slaughterhouse in your home town.

Visitors are not always directly responsible for such bad behavior, but alas, some encourage it with promises of tips. Others are just the passive accessories of overzealous safari personnel. You can prevent serious harassment of wildlife just by exerting your authority. Remember, it's your safari and you are in control. Don't let your driver disturb the animals because he thinks that it will please you! You can also attempt to prevent other parties from indulging in this sort of thing if you see it happening.

Visitors sometimes "poach" on paying their park fees. This is one area where you should not cut corners, for fees are the lifeblood of the parks. It costs money to patrol against poachers and squatters, not to mention to maintain roads and game tracks for the benefit of visitors. Fees are usually two tiered: a lower rate for residents of the country and a higher one for foreign tourists. Even the higher rates are still quite reasonable when you consider what the fee goes to protect and the fact that most parks don't even collect enough to cover their operating costs. Members of group tours ordinarily don't pay directly, as fees are often included in the tour price. But sometimes tour operators try to avoid payment, and this should not be tolerated. Budget travelers, who have to watch every penny, are more prone to fudging on fees. They sometimes gripe about paying the higher prices, especially where they must be paid in dollars. Another moral dilemma!

It is often argued that little or none of the money paid as fees actually goes to park administration, but winds up going to the national treasury where it is squandered or stolen. In some places, there is a lot of truth to the accusation, and in most countries, the parks do not get back anything near what they earn. But increasingly, national park systems are getting to keep more of their earnings. In some cases, they are becoming semiautonomous entities with budgetary independence. Even where park fees go into a general fund and disappear, it is important from the conservationist's point of view that African governments look upon the parks — and the wildlife habitat that preserve — as money-earning enterprises, lest they be put to other uses.

Official regulations have to be tempered with common sense and courtesy. Littering is illegal; moreover, it's ridiculous to come into a pristine natural area and leave trash behind. Safari drivers often leave picnic refuse in the bush. Make sure they take it out or bury it properly. Take care not to interrupt other parties' game-viewing pleasure by talking loudly while observing animals, driving in front of their field of vision, or passing without pause for a look around: you may scare away animals that you can't see or that don't interest you, but that others may be watching.

Many visitors are unfamiliar with toilet procedures in wilderness areas where there are no toilet facilities. When nature calls, you can ask your driver to stop anywhere he can. If you are in a game park, do not wander any great distance from the car; even just behind the car will do in the utmost emergency, although you can usually find a discreet bush. Please bury, burn, or carry out any toilet paper. It is useful to bring a small plastic spade on safari for burying waste.

CHAPTER THREE

The African Realm:
Tips on Watching Wildlife

AFRICA'S WILDLIFE HERITAGE is fittingly celebrated in superlatives. Such familiar wonders as the elephant, rhinoceros, hippo, and giraffe are only the largest of the continent's astonishing assemblage of mammals. With these march a parade of predators, an immense collection of antelopes, a veritable Ark-full of monkeys and mongooses, aardvarks and insectivores, and a host of other animal oddities. A profusion of colorful birds, weird reptiles, and fascinating insects round out the show. As amazing as the variety of species is the spectacle of numbers, for the African plains are the last place on earth where vast herds still roam in primeval abundance.

Africa's wild creatures do not live in isolation: each species represents a strand in the web forming the community of plants and animals in which it has carved its niche. Even the briefest safari will traverse many such ecological communities and habitats. The eye soon discerns that the African wilds are not a singular entity in which animals occur at random, but an ordered realm where every creature has its appropriate place. Some species are extremely adaptive and survive in a wide spectrum of environments. Others are confined to specific niches or habitats. It would take volumes to describe all of Africa's animals, not to mention their relationships and the habitats in which they live.

A small understanding of African ecology will go a long way toward

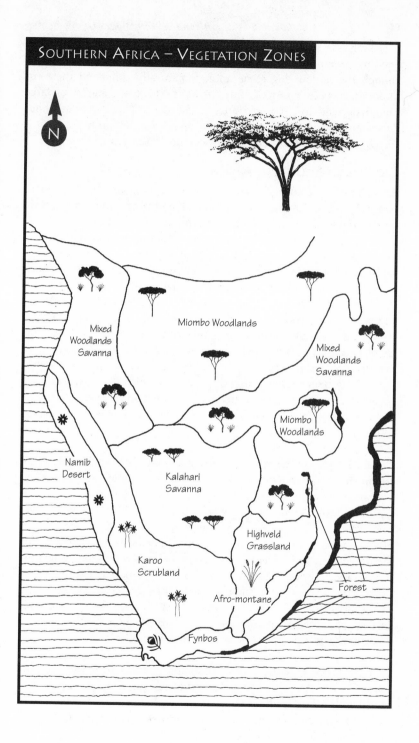

SOUTHERN AFRICA – VEGETATION ZONES

N

Miombo Woodlands

Mixed
Woodlands
Savanna

Mixed
Woodlands
Savanna

Miombo
Woodlands

Namib
Desert

Kalahari
Savanna

Highveld
Grassland

Forest

Karoo
Scrubland

Afro-montane

Fynbos

enriching your safari experience, for the wonder of the animals is heightened by an appreciation and awareness of their total environment. Although the famous big game animals naturally command the most
attention, people who look only for lions, elephants, and other large
mammals tend to get bored after a few days. Those curious about
African wildlife in all its varied forms never have that problem, for it is
impossible to run out of new and fascinating discoveries.

Biomes of Southern Africa

Africa's major ecological zones, or biomes, are defined by their dominant types of vegetation. Climate (rainfall and temperature range) is, of
course, the greatest factor in determining the extent of each biome, although altitude and geology also play important roles. Within each
major vegetation zone, differences in local climate, soil types, and topography account for the growth of specially adapted communities of plants
in particular areas. Such communities, or habitats, are often named for
their characteristic vegetation — for example, knobthorn-marula savanna, mopane woodland, terminalia sandveld, and so on. Marshes,
riverine forests, the various types of woodlands or grasslands, pans
(shallow seasonal lakes), rocky outcrops, and floodplains are examples
of specialized habitats that appear within the larger biomes. Each southern African biome is composed of a mosaic of such habitats, and there
is considerable mixing, especially in transitional areas where one major
vegetation zone melds into another. Ten principal biomes are found in
southern Africa.

FYNBOS: Also known as Cape Macchia, fynbos is a small biome at the
continent's southwestern tip. In this region, a temperate marine climate
—characterized by cold, wet winters—produces a dominant vegetation-
type that looks similar to the scrub found around the shores of the
Mediterranean. Yet the South African fynbos (the word is a corruption
of an Afrikaans word, *fijnbosch*, meaning "fine bush") is celebrated for
the uniqueness and astounding diversity of its plants: proteas, heaths,
restios, and flowering bulbs are only the most remarkable of the many
floral groups found in this biome, which biogeographers call the "Cape
Floral Kingdom." Mountain and coastal habitats give this botanic won-
derland great scenery, but it harbors few large mammals: the rare bontebok antelope is its most celebrated endemic species.

KAROO SHRUBLAND: Karoo shrubland dominates the vast, arid interior of South Africa and extends northward right through west-central
Namibia. With its broiling summers and cold winters, the eastern areas
of the Karoo are mostly characterized by low shrubs and grasslands. The

western parts receive less rain: these semidesert regions are famous for their many succulent plants. Numerous rare and endangered animals live in the Karoo and the interior deserts of Namibia.

NAMIB DESERT: The Namib Desert encompasses the entire coast of Namibia. One of the driest regions in the world, this biome has many unique habitats and fascinating endemic species of plants and small animals (mostly reptiles, insects, and birds).

FOREST: The forest biome is rare in southern Africa and very patchy in its distribution. Native evergreen forests come in two types: coastal forest, which occurs along the littoral of the Indian Ocean, and montane forest, which is reduced to pockets in various eastern mountain ranges with sufficiently high rainfall. Both types of forest harbor small antelopes and specialized birds under a shade-giving canopy of tall evergreen trees.

HIGHVELD GRASSLAND: Highveld grassland is restricted to the high plains of eastern South Africa, where mile-high elevations make for very cold winters. Little of the Highveld remains in a natural state and only remnants of its once abundant wildlife remain. Endemic species include black wildebeest and blesbok.

AFRO-MONTANE VEGETATION: Montane grasslands and mountain fynbos (a scrub composed of proteas and heaths) characterize the zone of Afro-montane vegetation. In southern Africa, this biome dominates the highlands of Lesotho and the Drakensberg Mountains of Natal; it is also dominant on Malawi's Nyika Plateau and occurs in pockets on various other mountain ranges in eastern Zimbabwe and South Africa. Where Afro-montane wilderness is undisturbed, eland thrive, as does a variety of smaller antelopes and upland birds.

KALAHARI SAVANNA: The flat, open expanses of the sandy Kalahari savanna biome are covered with grasslands and scattered trees. Despite the harshness of its arid climate and the absence of surface water, the Kalahari can support large numbers of migratory wild animals. These include springbok, gemsbok, red hartebeest, and eland, and in its wetter northeastern fringes, zebra and wildebeest. Lion, cheetah, leopard, and both brown and spotted hyena are the large predators of this semidesert environment.

MIXED WOODLANDS: Mixed woodlands are characterized by a great variety of thorny acacias and broad-leafed trees. This type of savanna vegetation predominates in northeastern South Africa, including the Lowveld region where Kruger National Park is located, and extends down that country's eastern seaboard into the Eastern Cape Province. In its natural state, this biome supports a full range of African big game.

DRY WOODLANDS: Dry woodlands are another savanna biome. This vegetation-type occurs at lower elevations (up to about 3,300 feet) from Kruger National Park northward into Zimbabwe, Zambia, and Malawi. It also dominates in northern Botswana and the Etosha area of Namibia. Baobab trees are a conspicuous component of the dry woodlands zone, and vast tracts of it are covered with mopane trees. This biome still supports large populations of wild animals and is the favored habitat of elephant.

MIOMBO (MOIST WOODLANDS): Moist woodlands, also known as miombo, are dominant in areas above 3,300 feet in Zimbabwe, Zambia, and Malawi (as well as other countries on the central African plateau). Although these woodlands do receive higher rainfall, which encourages the growth of broad-leafed trees and tall coarse grasses, the "moist" savannas of miombo country, like the other savanna biomes of southern Africa, are subject to the periodic drought of a long dry season. Most of the trees lose their leaves during the dry winter months. The miombo biome takes its name from the deciduous *Brachystegia* (miombo) trees that often dominate its woodlands and sometimes form closed-canopy forests. Just before the onset of the rains, miombo trees sprout new foliage flushed with brilliant hues of purple or red, and the woodlands blaze with color. At other times, when the trees are bare or the woodland grasses stand 10 feet high, extensive travel through miombo can be rather monotonous. Miombo country is also naturally infested with tsetse flies, making it inhospitable to humans and cattle. Huge tracts, therefore, have been left entirely to wildlife. Although few large animals live in the miombo woodlands proper, the shallow valleys (known as *dambos*) that drain the woodlands are filled with grasslands that support more game. Hosting a large but widely dispersed population of elephant, buffalo, big cats, and trophy antelopes, miombo regions are generally more suitable as hunting reserves than national parks.

Savanna: Africa's Prime Wildlife Habitat

Africa's most famous wildlife reserves are almost universally located in the various types of savanna biomes. The savanna owes its extraordinary faunal wealth to its patchwork vegetation. Its blend of grassland, woodland, and bush habitats provides the diversity of niches and abundance of food necessary to support a large and varied population of wild animals. In the classic model, the typical savanna is lightly wooded, with trees spaced widely on open grassy landscapes. In some places, pure grasslands dominate; elsewhere, "bush" country, characterized by denser woods and thickets, is more widespread. Gradations of the three vegetation types are the rule, a condition resulting from a seesaw process of natural succession.

A succession scenario might work something like this: elephants move into an area of savanna woodland that has a generous understory of grass. During the dry season, the pachyderms exhaust the nutritious turf and turn their full attention to the trees. To get at canopy foliage, some trees are pushed over; others die when their bark is peeled off and devoured. After several bruising seasons, the woodland takes on the look of an old battlefield: the grey skeletons of big trees stand among a litter of downed limbs, overturned trunks, and high-rise termite mounds. Seedlings and shrubs, taking advantage of the removal of the old trees, grow rapidly into impenetrable thickets among the wreckage. If fires attack the resurgent bush, these woody plants vanish and open grassland appears in their place. Once shrubs and trees get in a few years of undisturbed growth, however, they become more resistant to incursions by fire. Eventually, trees reach a size that shades out the lower bush, an understory of grass flourishes, and mature woodlands again dominate.

Humans have had a profound influence in shaping the savanna landscape through their use of fire. For generations, African pastoralists have set dry-season fires to encourage a flush of fresh grass to sprout with the first hint of rain. Farmers, too, annually set fires in the bush to clear new land or burn stubble off old fields. Once lit, these fires go untended and rapidly get out of hand. In the dry seasons, whole regions are set ablaze, creating a constant pall that mutes the brilliance of the African sky. Over time, such vast seasonal conflagrations have tended to suppress the regeneration of bush and woodland, and tipped nature's balance toward the spread and maintenance of grassland.

Many African plants have adapted to a regimen of fire. Some savanna trees actually need it to regenerate: their seeds are so hard that the outer layers have to be burnt before they will sprout. Many savanna species have developed fire-resistant bark that enables large trees to withstand repeated "cool" burns (these occur when the grass is fired early in the dry season). Because the grass then retains considerable moisture, it burns incompletely and in patches. Deprived of fuel, a fire moves on before it gets hot enough to ignite and damage the canopies of tall trees. Fires late in the season, when the withered grass is tinder-dry, are much more destructive.

Wild animals also affect the savanna environment. On the one hand, they harm vegetation where they overgraze; on the other, they encourage regeneration by spreading seed and trampling old growth into mulch. Elephants make the most conspicuous modifications to the savanna vegetation. With appetites to match their size, they wreak havoc on woodlands in which they linger, destroying trees and contributing to the spread of grassland. Paradoxically, they wander widely and are constantly distributing the seeds of plants on which they feed. Partially digested seeds are often prepared for germination by passing through the gut of an elephant; digestion strips the protective outer layers, just as fire would. Viable seeds then wind up nicely planted in a fertilizing ball of elephant dung. In general, the feeding strategies of animals contribute to the stability of their habitats because they are keyed to the food and water resources available at any given season. When supplies are low, game migrates or disperses, decreasing the pressure on any particular tract of land. The animals also recycle nutrients rapidly back into the environment: Africa's bushlands are daily fertilized by the droppings of millions of beasts. Although debate rages as to how best to "manage" parks, when wild animals are left with enough territory, they tend to be the best stewards of their land.

Many savanna plants, including most of Africa's acacias, have evolved thorns as a means of discouraging browsing. Although thorns do not afford complete protection against feeding animals, the prevalence of "thornbush" and "thorntrees" is a testament to their utility. While giraffes, elephants, and black rhinos can be seen devouring long acacia thorns without apparent discomfort, the smaller browsing animals have to be more selective. Most large animals favor new growth on which thorns are soft and green; after spines harden into wooden needles, the megafauna tend to leave them alone, preferring to strip foliage (which is less efficient) rather than devour whole limbs, thorns and all.

Acacias are a particularly widespread group of savanna trees. Many species have the flat-topped umbrella shape so characteristic of the most appealing African landscapes. Beside the tall, umbrella-shaped acacias are numerous shrubby varieties, such as the prickly black thorn. In dense stands, these and the spiny seedlings of the larger types form impenetrable thornbush thickets. All acacias are legumes, and their highly nutritious beanlike seedpods are much sought after by animals. Elephants are very fond of them; camps set among acacias routinely attract bulls when the trees are in fruit. Browsing antelopes, rhinos, and baboons also feed avidly on acacia pods, both on the tree and after the pods have dropped to the ground.

Mopane (*Colophospermum mopane*) is one of the most common

trees of southern Africa's dry woodlands zone. These trees dominate huge tracts of countryside in hot, low-lying areas with poorly drained clay soils. Where conditions are right, mopane trees form tall forests, while less favorable areas are covered with a stunted scrub. Mopane leaves have a distinctive butterfly shape; during the heat of the day, they fold up to prevent the loss of moisture. The mopane's green foliage turns to striking fall colors in the dry season, but eventually its leaves drop off. Fresh or dry, mopane leaves and pods are highly nutritious. They are important sources of food for a variety of savanna creatures, which range from the "mopane worm" (a large, colorful caterpillar) to antelopes and elephants. During the rains, many of the large herbivores feed extensively in mopane woodlands, where they find water in the numerous, hard-bottomed clay pans that are characteristic of mopane country. As the rain-filled pans dry up, the animals file out of the interior woodlands to concentrate wherever there are permanent sources of water.

Woodland and bush are habitat for the savanna's "browsing" animals, which eat the foliage of shrubs, trees, and leafy plants. Counted among the browsers are such notables as giraffe and black rhino, and a potpourri of antelopes ranging from the hare-sized dikdik to the spiral-horned kudu and the enormous eland. Most browsers are highly selective feeders that tend to live singly or in small groups rather than in the outsized herds associated with the grass-eaters of the open plains. Trees and bush also provide essential refuge for savanna-dwelling primates, such as vervet monkeys and baboons, as well as a tremendous assortment of woodland birds.

Giraffes (*Giraffa camelopardalis*) primarily inhabit wooded savanna country, although they are often seen crossing nearly treeless plains. Gregarious and ever vigilant, their advantage in height makes it difficult for lions to stalk them without detection. Females join nursery herds after the birth of calves; "creche groups" are sometimes left on their own while the mothers wander off to feed. Bulls may be seen testing their strength against each other in slow motion bouts of "necking," in which contestants stand parallel and intermittently exchange swings of the head. These matches are ordinarily confined to light sparring for place in the dominance hierarchy of local giraffe society. When real fighting does occur, however, true blows are delivered with tremendous force.

The black rhinoceros (*Diceros bicornis*) is a retiring inhabitant of thick savanna bush. Normally a rather solitary animal, a female black rhino is often accompanied by one or two subadults in addition to its calf. The rhino is most active at night, and spends its day napping in the sun or visiting mud wallows. Its eyesight is poor, but its swiveling, funnel-shaped ears are sharp, and its sense of smell is very keen. Tick birds, also called oxpeckers, usually escort rhinos and act as a security alarm to dozing animals; the suspicious birds are quick to fly up noisily when they sense intruders. When frightened, the rhino defends itself aggressively with its front horn. The black rhino has a prehensile upper lip — almost beaklike in appearance — that is used for grasping the leaves and shoots on which it feeds. Its lip and feeding habits distinguish it from the white rhino, for the two species are not colored differently as their names would imply. The white rhino (*Ceratotherium simum*) takes its English name from the Afrikaans word *weit*, which describes its "wide" square jaw, designed for efficiently cropping grass. The white rhino is also much larger, weighing as much as 4.5 tons, as compared to the black rhino's 3,000 pounds. At the turn of the last century, the white rhino was on the brink of extinction. The species was saved when the last handful were given protection in South Africa's Hluhluwe-Umfolozi game reserve. The descendants of these white rhinos have been widely reintroduced to parks and private reserves throughout southern Africa, where they inhabit wooded savannas.

By eating different types of grass, or the same plants at different stages of growth, a whole spectrum of grazing animals is able to share the pasturage of Africa's grassy savannas. Both zebra and wildebeest are very common grazers that feed on identical grasses. Yet wildebeest prefer to eat the moister blades, while zebra readily crop the higher, tougher stems. Tsessebe choose only the tenderest green shoots, and buffalo feed on coarse "rank" grasses — too tough to be chewed by smaller herbivores. Because of the efficiency with which grassland vegetation is used, Africa's grasslands support the continent's greatest game populations; they are the home of Africa's legendary herds. Grazing species such as wildebeest are often found in groups of hundreds, and may concentrate by the thousands when feeding conditions are right.

Some animals take full advantage of the broken mosaic of savanna vegetation by both browsing and grazing. Impala (*Aepyceros melampus*) are one of the commonest antelopes precisely because they exploit the savanna's leafy plants and grasses. Their large, tight-knit herds, which are usually divided into distinct male and female clusters, thrive on the "edges" where grass and bushland meet. Roan and sable antelopes are both inhabitants of open woodlands with tall grass. Roan are primarily grazers, but also browse; sable eat mostly grass but supplement their diet with a higher proportion of leafy foliage than the roan.

Elephants (*Loxodonta africana*), too, do best in mixed bush country. They feed primarily on grass, but also eat immense quantities of leaves, bark, fruits, and pods. Wooded bush also provides elephants with essential cover from their implacable enemy — human hunters. The back-bone of elephant society is the cow-calf family group. Females spend their entire lives within these close-knit sisterhoods, which are composed of a matriarch, her daughters and granddaughters, and their offspring. Such cow-calf herds may number from 10 to 50 animals. Elder females often lead their daughters off to form independent groups, but life-long relationships with the original matriarch and her family are maintained by frequent meetings on a common "home range." Cows are energetic in defense of their young: trumpeting mothers form a daunting circle around their calves, leaving little opportunity for predators to grab a newborn. Ordinarily, baby elephants are vulnerable only if they become sick or get lost. Dry-season food shortages, however, may force cow-calf groups to disperse more widely as they forage, creating situations in which calves are more likely to be taken by enterprising lions.

Bull elephants are gregarious, but are loners at heart and wander as they please. A male gets booted out of his family group at puberty, when the females begin to find his sexual attentions unwelcome. At 13 years of age, he is too big to be bothered by predators, but having been raised in a strong family environment, tends to feel insecure. Newly independent males then seek out the company of others and form loosely organized herds. These associations are constantly breaking up and rearranging themselves according to the whim of individuals; the same bull found wandering alone one day may be accompanied by several colleagues the next, and may have joined completely new chums a week later. When a mature bull encounters a group of cows, he tests their scent to determine whether any are receptive to mating. He may stay with them for several days, but eventually male and females go their separate ways. Over the years, the bulls of a particular region get to know one another quite well; from infancy, they indulge in tests of strength that constantly reestablish their places in the dominance hierarchy. Serious fights between bulls are rare, and usually occur when a stranger, without rank in the local fraternity, emigrates into a new area.

Elephant herds grow larger in the dry season, when the animals concentrate around water. At such times, and when the threat of poaching is constant and strong, elephants may gather in herds numbering in the hundreds. Such large groups normally disperse during the rains.

Predators, the apex of the ecological food pyramid, are necessarily much less numerous than the herbivores upon which they feed: the proportion of hunted to hunters is greater than 100 to 1. Consequently, predators are only really common in those places where prey is abundant.

Africa's abundance and diversity of prey animals supports a magnif-

icent collection of predators. The various carnivores specialize in hunting animals of a weight appropriate to their own. Cheetahs go after
small antelopes, such as springbok and impala, or the young of larger
antelopes, while leopards pursue a somewhat wider range of small- to
medium-sized animals. Lions will take small animals by opportunity.
The average-size impala, however, will barely satisfy the hunger of a single adult male lion, so communal hunts naturally focus on larger animals
such as wildebeest or zebra. Lions are quite capable of attacking prey up
to the size of giraffe and buffalo, and occasionally take young hippos,
rhinos, or even elephants. Hyenas, although conventionally thought of
as scavengers, are formidable hunters in their own right. Working in
groups, they can take animals as large as zebra, and they will attack the
calves of buffalo or rhino. Wild dogs also hunt communally, concentrating on small- to medium-sized antelopes such as impala.

Because of considerable overlap in both habitat and prey, competition
among the meat-eaters is intense. Although we tend to anthropomor-
phize the hunters, describing the lion as noble and the hyena as a skulking coward, these judgments have little to do with the reality of the
animals' lives. Scavenging, territorial fighting, the appropriation of kills,
and intraspecies violence are integral parts of the survival repertoire of
all the hunting species. Violence is a daily fact of their existence. After
all, they must regularly kill animals to survive. It is not easy for the
predators to catch their prey, and every chase holds the possibility of a
debilitating injury — a leg broken from a misstep, a jaw dislocated by a
zebra's kick, a deep wound from an antelope's horn — which may spell
their own ultimate doom. In general, the prey species don't have much
reason to worry about the predators, so long as they are healthy. Nature
has seen to it that the hunters usually succeed in taking mainly the slow
or feeble — the old, the sick, and the very young.

Predators also catch a high proportion of adult male antelopes, which
although healthy, are often put into vulnerable positions because of their
preoccupation with territory, social status, and breeding. Such activities
can leave them alone — and therefore likely to stand out — or pushed to
the edge of a herd, worn out by fighting, or just plain unalert!

Watching Wildlife

The procedures for finding and observing wildlife are best learned
through experience. While advanced methods like tracking are the exclusive province of trained professionals, you can pick up the basics as a
participant on a guided safari and try them out on your own at places
like South Africa's Kruger National Park. Techniques vary according to
habitat and season. A familiarity with the habits of the animals and the

The wooded savannas of southern Africa are prime habitat for the endangered wild dog. Hluhluwe Game Reserve, South Africa. Photo: Allen Bechky.

most effective ways to explore their habitats will add to the enjoyment of your wildlife viewing.

Game Drives

The game drive has come to be the standard mode of wildlife viewing, especially in the African national parks, where both regulations and safety considerations restrict explorations on foot. Even where foot safaris are allowed, game drives generally produce the best opportunities for photography and prolonged wildlife observations. Conditions for vehicular safaris are ideal — cruising savanna game country from the security and comfort of a car, you can encounter a large number and variety of animals simply by chance. In many parks, the animals have lost all fear of vehicles and permit you to drive right up to them. Game drives in such places are always invigorating: you may go from one species to the next — observing zebras here, a giraffe there, a knot of impalas on the right, a trio of elephant bulls dead ahead — as though you were in a great outdoor zoo. But there really is no guarantee what you will see; the animals are free to move around as they please, and may even pass beyond park boundaries. Even in the most prolific game parks, you can get skunked on any particular drive, especially if you *must* see big cats.

The classic safari schedule calls for game drives in the early morning and late afternoon — the hours when animals are most active and photography is at its best. Dawn is a particularly good time for finding predators. Many of the cats hunt at night, and those that have failed to kill are often still on the prowl at first light. In the early morning, successful hunters might be found feeding on their prey, while scavenging hyenas or jackals may be in attendance on abandoned carcasses. Antelopes like to feed during the cool of early morning, then retire to shade to chew their cud. Zebra, buffalo, and elephant also seek shade once the sun reaches full intensity. All resume feeding and movement as afternoon shadows begin to lengthen. For your own comfort, you will do well to pay attention to these daily rhythms of animal life. Aimless driving during the hot midday hours can get tiresome, and you are generally better off conserving your energy for the prime viewing times.

Keep in mind, however, that the "morning and evening" game drive routine can be overdone, and is sometimes employed as much for the convenience of safari operators and lodge managers as anything else. While the cooler parts of the day are undoubtedly optimum for comfort, it is simply not true that there is "nothing to be seen" outside of the standard viewing hours. Much depends on the season and the weather. During southern Africa's cool winter months, few animals will be stirring at the break of dawn, and predators may be on the prowl even at midday. In hot, dry weather, there is a constant traffic of thirsty animals to watering points at which carnivores may lie in ambush. Sometimes you must go out for the entire day to reach some especially worthwhile — but distant — point. On such expeditions, you can take a break while enjoying a bush picnic under a shady tree.

On game drives in savanna parks, pay special attention to areas of minihabitat, such as wetlands and forests. Marshes and swamps often have predators lurking nearby. They are among the best places to view an impressive assortment of herons, ibises, storks, and cranes. Pools and lakes are possible refuges for that most improbable of creatures, the hippopotamus. Rivers also offer the prospect of seeing hippos, as well as crocodiles, and big trees usually flourish along their banks. Where such riparian forests grow particularly lush, they have the feel of tropical jungle. Monkeys, rare birds, and shyer antelopes, such as bushbuck and red duiker, may be glimpsed there by careful observers. Neither riverine forests nor marshes are easily penetrated by vehicles, but resident species often show themselves on game tracks that skirt their edges.

A game drive should not be conducted as a rushed pursuit of animals unseen. In the early stages of a safari, excitement at the prospect of meeting the most famous creatures naturally leads to an emphasis on finding and photographing only the "stars." While there are surely circumstances in which you will want to focus on a particular species, you will do better in general to relax and observe whatever comes up. Obviously, you won't want to spend an entire morning watching a herd of zebra when you are still hoping to locate your first pride of lions. But after you have seen all the celebrities, pay closer attention to the humbler species which, although often easy to find, are usually overlooked. Antelopes are a case in point. Too many people are content merely to catalog each type, get its picture, and go on without taking further notice. Don't make that mistake, for patience and attention to detail will reward you with a deeper appreciation of the unique character of each species, whether it is the tiny dikdik, nervously twitching in response to every sound and smell that drifts its way, or the homely wildebeest, indulging its repertoire of seemingly uncoordinated bucks and kicks. Watch the constant interaction that goes on among the members of herds. Animals groom each other and assert their places in the pecking order; bulls pursue females and fend off rival males; some individuals graze or sleep, while others stand lookout. Always be on the alert for special activity. When you see a zebra rolling on a bald patch of ground, spend a while there watching. The original animal is likely to interrupt its dust bath as soon as you stop to watch, but others may take its place at the same favored spot. Prolonged observation results in the most interesting sightings and best photographs.

Finding the Cats

In heavily visited parks, the tried and true method of finding the big cats is to look for the circle of vehicles that inevitably surrounds them. Finding predators on your own is not so easy, although carnivores are often found on park roads in the very early morning (they like to walk along roads, especially if the fringing bush is thick or wet). Random driving is not terribly efficient; you will do better to zero in on those places where the cats are most likely to be found. Treelines along watercourses are good tracks to follow because cats appreciate shade and take advantage of riverine bush to rest where prey may inadvertently approach. Rocky outcrops and the bases of hills are also promising resting places for big cats. There, too, carnivores find shade among boulders or bushes and enjoy the security of concealment. Outcrops also provide fine vantage points from which to watch for potential prey. In late afternoon, or after rain showers, cats like to sun themselves atop large rocks — a particularly photogenic situation. Most of the time, they are not so obvious. Cats are secretive and can stay well concealed in light bush or high grass, even when not making special efforts to hide themselves. They are easy to miss, so you must search the likely spots slowly and carefully.

No animal is in as much demand for viewing as the lion (*Panthera leo*), for no safari (and, in some quarters, no game drive) is considered a success without a sighting of these big cats. From up close, their huge size and feline grace make an immediate and dramatic impression: adult females weigh more than 250 pounds and full-sized males as much as 440. Yet interest in lions can wane quickly for want of action. Lions sleep a lot, especially during the noontime heat, a habit that leads to persistent accusations of laziness. Such charges are unfounded, for the hours of indolence are punctuated with episodes of explosive violence. A lion's life, like that of other predators, rides an uncertain pendulum swinging between feast and famine. Lions do what they must to survive, no more and no less, and they do it mostly under cover of darkness.

Lions are highly social animals. Ordinarily, a pride might consist of less than a half dozen adults, but in an exceptionally rich habitat, it may have more than 30 members of all ages. At the core of the pride are the adult females who bear the brunt of communal hunting. Males defend the pride's territory against the trespasses of nonmembers and, in so doing, provide a secure environment for raising cubs. While a pride's males seemingly lead the easy life, letting the females kill and appropriating the largest share for themselves, it is not true that males never hunt. At some point, every adolescent male gets ejected from the family by the pride's resident males. The exiles usually form small nomadic bands that must fend for themselves: young males either hunt or they starve. Over the years, the nomads grow in size and toughness until such time as they can successfully take possession of a territory and a group of females, setting themselves up as the lords of a pride. Even afterwards, big males are needed to help females bring down larger prey such as buffalo bulls.

Lions take obvious pleasure in each other's company. They often lie huddled together, bodies touching. When they rouse themselves from midday torpor, they rub sensuously against each other and give warm greetings to pride members returning from other parts of their territory. Cubs are as cute and playful as kittens. They claw and chew as they scramble over the placid adults, and even try to draw the big males into their roughhouse games. A cub can suckle from any lactating lioness, but as its need for meat grows, it must compete for a place at the kill. Among lions, only the strongest get to eat, and starvation is the fate of many cubs — a cruel but efficient way for nature to limit the lion population. Lions breed often, and you may well see mating couples in *flagrante delicto*.

Because stealth and the leopard (*Panthera pardus*) are synonymous, the solitary spotted cat is difficult to find and rates as the number one photographic safari trophy. The leopard's innate need for secrecy is a result of pressure from its larger enemies; even an outsized 175-pound cat

The leopard is the most secretive of the big cats. Londolozi, Sabi Sand Game Reserve, South Africa. Photo: Allen Bechky.

is no match for a pride of lions or a gang of hyenas. The leopard has adopted an arboreal niche in which neither of its foes can compete. It uses its extreme agility and phenomenal strength to carry its prey (for example, a 115-pound reedbuck) high into the sanctuary of a tree. Among the leopard's favorites are acacias and sausage trees, both of which have spreading limbs — ideal for catnaps. Unfortunately for would-be observers, leopards are secretive even at rest: rather than choose a bare branch to lie on, they prefer one hidden in the foliage of a tree's canopy. Typically, the only clue to a leopard's presence is the sudden twitch of a hanging tail. Searching for a leopard is therefore a tedious business involving careful scrutiny of every suitable tree — a survey that is likely to prove fruitless unless you know that a cat is in the neighborhood. Once a kill has been stashed, however, a leopard will stay with it, or return to its larder, until its prey is devoured. Check back repeatedly if you find a carcass hanging. When you do see a leopard, remain absolutely quiet: few become truly accustomed to vehicles, and the sound of a human voice may cause a beautifully relaxed animal to descend in a blur of speed. Once vanished in the grass, a shy leopard is not likely to be seen again.

Where they occur, cheetahs (*Acinonyx jubatus*) are much more easily viewed than leopards because they live in open country and are active during the day. In some reserves, cheetahs readily learn to tolerate vehicles and have even been known to climb atop cars for a vantage point when searching for prey! These sleek, spotted cats can be seen singly or in small groups. Such bands are usually composed of a mother and her full-sized but not yet independent offspring. Male litter mates sometimes stay together when they reach maturity, but females become solitary and bear the sole responsibility for cub rearing. Cheetahs depend on speed rather than stealth to catch their prey. They are remarkably efficient hunters, but lose many of their kills to stronger rivals. The cheetah's spectacular high-speed chases are sometimes witnessed by visitors. Hunts are most likely to take place near dawn or dusk.

Scanning is a useful technique for finding predators that is too seldom employed. It is especially effective in wide, grassy country where great vistas are open to examination with binoculars. Stop periodically to carefully pan the landscape with your lenses, paying special attention to the most likely places. In both morning and late afternoon, this is a good way to discover lions or cheetahs on the move. Cheetahs can often be seen sitting atop termite mounds, which give them a good vantage point for taking a look around. Distant animals that may be in plain view with binoculars would almost surely be missed from a moving car.

Quarry animals often give clues to the whereabouts of predators.

Monkeys and baboons take to trees as soon as they see a lion, uttering sharp, barking alarm calls. Antelopes also have various warning sounds: impalas sneeze, wildebeests snort, reedbucks whistle shrilly. A giraffe that does not look at you when you approach but instead gazes fixedly in another direction is very likely keeping an eye on something more threatening. The presence of vultures is often a telling sign, although not when they are on the wing: circling birds are only soaring on rising thermal currents, searching for food. If you see them coming down, one by one, proceed in their direction for there will likely be a carcass (but not always — vultures also gather to drink and bathe at favorite waterholes on riverbanks). Do not be surprised, however, if no killers are on the scene: most animals that die of natural causes are first discovered by vultures. In the early morning hours, trees festooned with vultures may merely indicate an overnight perch. But at midday, a flock of sitting birds can mean that lions are guarding a kill below. Because the more common types of vultures are ungainly birds that require a good runway to get airborne, they only touch ground after lions have abandoned a carcass. Lions do not tolerate tampering with their food and will kill scavenging birds that get overly impatient.

Hunts and Kills

Almost everyone hopes to see a "kill" during a safari. The chase has elements of beauty as well as drama: both predator and prey have been honed by evolution to play their parts in this ultimate test of survival, and it is fascinating to watch the protagonists perform to their utmost physical capabilities. Yet it is terrible, too, for it is hard to see an animal die, and the final struggle is not pretty. Lions, cheetahs, and leopards ordinarily kill by strangulation, while hyenas and wild dogs literally rip their victims apart. Either way, it is violent, although the end is often oddly passionless: the killer does its part without emotion and, once caught, the victim often accepts its fate with shocked resignation. After the death struggle, you watch the feast, listening to the sound of crunching bones and inhaling the scent of fresh red meat. It can be strong stuff, and some who see it wish their luck hadn't been quite so good. Others feel privileged to have witnessed a key chapter in the natural cycle of life.

Although viewing a kill is primarily a matter of luck, your chances are improved by a long stay in an area inhabited by several resident prides of lions. On a first reconnaissance, you can search for the various prides and assess their readiness to hunt. Often enough, you will find lions stuffed from their last feed. Such cats show no more energy than is necessary to change the position of their bulging bellies or drag themselves to water for a drink. They will not hunt again for several days. Hungry lions *look* much more alert, although activity may consist of nothing more than staring into the distance. When their bones are showing, an absence of prey is often all too obvious. After your initial survey, you can check up periodically on the most likely candidates for a hunt.

A lion hunt is a very slow process. The cats usually start out moving single file, stopping often to lie down and rest; some pride members doze off, while others watch for game. As they get closer to potential prey animals, they gradually spread out into a loose arc. With luck, stealthy flankers can envelope their quarry, putting the pride into an ideal position to launch a successful attack. Lions do not seem to take account of wind direction when they hunt, and it is the wind that frequently defeats their purpose.

When you discover lions in the early stages of hunting, follow along. If no game is near and the cats fall asleep, come back now and then to keep tabs on the situation. When a pride shows signs of movement in the dusk, be sure to return to the vicinity early the next morning. Should they fail to kill during the night, you will have a good chance to see the climax of a hunt. Even when watching the final stalk, however, keep in mind that most hunting attempts end in failure. Time and patience are the keys if the observation of a kill is an important safari goal.

On the other hand, some kills are witnessed merely by luck. Even when watching sleeping lions, it is possible that unwary animals will blunder into their vicinity. The lions' demeanor changes immediately. No longer lazy house cats, they become as taut as bowstrings as they flatten themselves to the ground. If the wind is right and the prey does not sense their presence, the animal may walk right into their midst. It is about as common to see this kind of opportunistic attack as a successful stalk and kill.

CARCASSES: Day and night, death stalks the African herds. Whether victim to predation or disease, each dead animal is a source of food for the various carnivores and carrion-eaters. Carcasses present golden opportunities for wildlife viewing because they bring the gamut of flesh-eating animals together where they can be easily observed. At a kill, you can watch the hunter feed, interact with others of its own species, and respond to different types of animals that arrive with an interest in joining the feast. Lions jealously guard their kills, keeping circling hyenas at bay with snarls and occasional charges. Jackals and small vultures sometimes manage to dart in to grab a stray morsel, but hyenas and larger birds must keep a respectful distance. Cheetahs are on the other end of the spectrum: they are built to run, not to fight, and will yield a kill to any serious challenger. Even a single hyena can appropriate a cheetah's meal.

If an animal has perished from disease, or if lions have abandoned a carcass, the scavengers have their turn.

A crowd of vultures at a carcass provides a fascinating spectacle. Vultures constantly patrol the African sky, scouring the countryside for signs of food. When a bird spies a dead animal, it descends rapidly. Its downward spiral is instantly observed by other airborne vultures that immediately come to investigate, see the carcass, and land in turn. A chain reaction soon brings a steady stream of winged scavengers. Competition becomes heated as dozens of lumbering birds, spreading their wings wide and hissing like angry snakes, bluff and fight for a place on the dead animal. Flocks of white-backed vultures must wait for one of the less common lappet-faced vultures to arrive before they can begin to feed: only this giant has a beak powerful enough to rip open a thick hide. If none of the larger birds turns up, the impatient mob eventually breaks into the carcass through the anus or throat. Vultures are regularly joined at these grisly feasts by tawny eagles, jackals, and marabou storks.

Groups of feeding spotted hyenas (*Crocuta crocuta*) also make interesting viewing. Whether scavenging a carcass or devouring an animal they have brought down themselves, the scene is often one of near frenzy. Hyenas cackle with nervous excitement, anxious to fill up as fast as possible before being displaced by lions or others of their own kind. It is amazing to see the rapidity with which they can dispose of an animal: a small antelope practically disappears within minutes, while a buffalo can be reduced to a skull overnight.

The skulls and animal remains scattered throughout the bush illustrate the role of death in perpetuating life. Nothing is wasted. Leftover bones are gnawed by hyenas and jackals during lean times; horns are slowly eaten away by the larvae of flies.

Night Drives

Although occasionally met in the twilight of dawn or dusk, most of Africa's nocturnal animals are rarely seen by safarists. Such curiosities as aardvarks and porcupines are actually quite common, but during the day, they stay hidden in underground burrows and hollow trees, waiting for the cover of darkness before starting their daily rounds. Where night drives are allowed, these creatures can often be found with the aid of powerful spotlights that pick out the reflection of eyes in the dark. On closer approach, the mysterious orbs materialize into the silhouettes of owls, bush babies, springhares, and civets.

Animals familiar from daytime encounters look different at night, too. Herds of impalas appear as eerie constellations of moving eyes, while hippos prance about skittishly when caught on dry land, and hyenas look positively ghostly. Few safari experiences compare with a night-time sighting of lions at a kill: a circling ring of hyenas and jackals moves furtively just beyond the spotlight's glare, as angry lionesses turn from the carcass to chase the intruders into the darkness. With their eyes glowing ferociously in the beams, lions look immensely scary. Prowling leopards are also more likely to be picked up on night drives than during the day. At night, the leopard can seem a different animal: in parks and private reserves where night drives regularly take place, leopards often learn to ignore vehicles and go about their business undisturbed. It is a great privilege to watch a hunting leopard. If it is successful, it is amazing to see the cat carry its prey into the security of a high tree.

In southern Africa, night drives are featured in some parks and many private game reserves. When they are successful, they are immensely exciting; excessive riding in the dark, however, can get boring (and cold) when there is little game around to be seen. Take warm clothing along on night drives: you may need it.

Waterholes and Blinds

True desert is rare in southern Africa, but vast tracks of savanna annually suffer severely dry conditions during the rainless months that stretch between May and November. Some plants adapt to this periodic drought by dropping their leaves; others store moisture during the rainy season. The baobab tree uses both strategies; its bare limbs and swollen trunk are a familiar sight in many seasonally parched bushlands. Although its vegetation may look lifeless, dry savannas can be extraordinarily rich in wildlife, especially where sources of water remain available. A number of parks are at their best when they serve as dry-season oases in otherwise waterless country.

Finding wildlife in dry habitat is made easier by the scarcity of water: although some antelopes never have to drink, most animals like to slake their thirst daily, and a constant procession of creatures will stream to rivers or waterholes. Observing animals at watering places, whether from viewing blinds or vehicles, is therefore a rewarding game viewing technique. Because lions often take up residence around waterholes, they are risky places for ambush. Prey animals must approach them warily. Giraffes are particularly careful: they will stand a long while, making sure that no cats are lurking about, before attempting to drink. When a giraffe decides that the coast is clear, it must spread its front legs wide to lower its head — a position of utter vulnerability. The giraffe takes only a quick sip and snaps back to attention, then starts the whole process over again. Elephants also take their time: big pachyderms can quaff more than 30 gallons at a session, an amount requiring at least as many trunkloads. After drinking, they throw water or mud onto their heads and backs. A dust bath and a good scratch against a favorite tree or termite mound are the usual finale to this leisurely ritual.

Blinds (also called hides) can be extremely useful in dry country. The best hides allow you to approach unobserved through a tunnel constructed of screening reeds; if the observation platform is located close enough to an active waterhole, the opportunities for game viewing and photography are often fantastic. For good results, however, patience is necessary, and you must remain quiet while you wait for the animals to arrive.

Forests

African forests are a delight to the senses. Moist and cool, perfumed by woodsy fragrance and ringing with bird songs, they seem full of life, and they are. Yet forests are tough places for game viewing because of limited visibility: it's hard to see the animals for the trees. To compound the problem, resident mammals are relatively scarce and tend to be shy or nocturnal. Even the largest mammals are often glimpsed only fleetingly before they vanish into the shadows; when they do stick around, the deep forest twilight makes photography almost impossible. Although avian life is both abundant and interesting (because many extraordinary species are relegated to forest habitat), finding birds in the foliage is difficult and time consuming. None of these conditions makes forests conducive to extensive game drives.

Walking or overnighting in a forest is the best way to appreciate its environment. Birds and monkeys are easier to observe when you are on foot. The sound of their cries or the swaying of branches calls attention to their presence in the treetops — signals that are easily missed from a moving vehicle. Walking also allows you to investigate the many trees, shrubs, and flowers that compete for your attention. If hiking or camping is impractical, you should make a point of pausing in a forest for a rest or picnic. Even such car-side explorations can be revealing.

Aside from riverine tracts, few of southern Africa's closed-canopy evergreen forests still harbor their natural complement of big game animals. Although many such forests would once have been frequented by elephant, black rhino, and buffalo (and a few still are), the mammals most likely to be resident today are leopard, browsing antelopes (notably bushbuck and various types of duikers), bushpig, samango (or blue) monkeys, bush babies, and baboons. With the exception of the monkeys and baboons, most are apt to be active at night. At dawn or dusk, the terrestrial animals are most likely to reveal themselves at the forest's edge or in clearings.

Rivers and Lakes

Large bodies of water are dependable places for finding wildlife. In game country, they are bound to attract thirsty animals to their shores and to provide refuge for specialized aquatic species. Even outside parks, water inevitably signals excellent birdwatching. Soda lakes are often ringed with masses of pink flamingos, while the lusher littorals of freshwater lakes tend to support a greater variety of species. Wherever fish are abundant, pelicans, cormorants, and fish eagles also abound. In shallow waters, these are joined by herons, storks, and smaller waders. Ducks and geese are plentiful, too.

In most African parks, exploration of rivers and lakes usually stops at the water's edge. That's where most of the action is anyway, but it makes a nice change of perspective to get out on the water. River cruises are particularly exciting: as your boat moves upstream, hippos dive and grunt, while crocodiles slip silently from the banks to vanish in the flood. Such an experience is great fun, although such animals are often too scared by engine noise to be closely examined. Where boats can be chartered, however, they offer superior opportunities for birdwatching and can take you to island rookeries and nesting areas, or ply channels through otherwise impassable swamps.

Crocodiles belong to an ancient order of reptiles that has been around in its present form since the time of the dinosaurs. The Nile crocodile (*Crocodylus niloticus*) is widespread in African rivers and lakes. Exceptional specimens can reach a length of 18 feet, and individuals of this species may have grown even bigger before hunting with firearms began. Today, a 14-footer is considered large. Such monsters are dangerous, yet remain afraid of humans. In fact, when you approach basking crocodiles, the largest ones are the first to disappear into the water: only the most wary live to reach great size. Adult crocs have few enemies besides man, but it is a different story when they are young, or even before they are born. Although female crocs guard their nests, whole clutches may be lost to raiding monitor lizards and mongooses. When the eggs hatch, the females carry the young in their mouths down to the water's edge, but the babies are thereafter subject to attack by large birds as well as cannibal crocodiles. Foot-long hatchlings eat insects and frogs, then turn to fish as they grow. When they reach a suitable size and weight, they can attempt to catch large mammals: an unwary animal is grabbed as it drinks, then pulled into the water and drowned. Crocodiles also scavenge on animals that die during river crossings or floods, and a dead hippo is cause for a crocodilian banquet (but mammalian fare is only an occasional boon; ordinarily, crocodiles depend on fish for a living).

Crocs are commonly seen basking on sandbanks in rivers. They are normally extremely wary, and must be stalked in complete silence if they are to be approached for photographs.

The hippo (*Hippopotamus amphibius*) is a source of constant wonder. For one thing, the "river horse" (as the Greeks named it) is much larger than one expects. Resting in a pool with only eyes and ears breaking the surface, it is hard to guess that the average adult hippo weighs about 3,000 pounds; bulls are frightfully large and can weigh over 3 tons. Hippos avoid heat and sun. A pinkish secretion gives their sensitive skin some protection from sunburn, but the animals' main relief is the water in which they spend their day. It's great fun to stand watch over a hippo pool. Although the beasts prefer to stay submerged as much as possible when humans are near, they snort, blow, and keep up a steady stream of amusing action. Hippos are highly gregarious and often pack themselves into compact masses known as pods: one leans on the other, each resting a behemoth head on a neighbor's heavy haunches or sturdy back. When one animal moves, another is displaced, and a dozing herd soon dissolves in a chain reaction of grunts and squabbles. If the hippos' nasal snorts are mirth provoking, nothing tops their toilet habits for laughs: stubby tails are raised with a noisy flapping motion that distributes strawlike excrement into the faces of any rearward companions. Great toothy yawns are also sure crowd-pleasers. Visitors are tempted to pass these exaggerated gestures off as symptoms of drowsiness, but they are really serious threat displays in which bulls advertise their dangerous tusks — up to 3 feet in length — to maximum effect.

The hippo's diet consists primarily of grass. It leaves the water shortly after dark, spreads its dung against a bush or tree, and proceeds on well-marked paths toward grazing areas. Since a hippo eats up to 130 pounds nightly, it may have to travel miles from pool to pasture. Its size is its armor: lions and hyenas rarely attack adult hippos, although calves are at risk.

Few visitors see hippos at night, when they are feeding ashore. On land, and at ease, hippos lumber along on short legs, heads down, cropping grass with their wide, square mouths. They are skittish and, when sensing danger, are quite fast, running with an almost dainty tiptoe gait. In cool weather, hippos are more likely to be ashore during the day, sleeping in tight-packed huddles on sunny sandbanks. If disturbed, however, they are quick to awaken and slip back to the security of water.

Hippos have a profound effect on the aquatic environment and many creatures benefit from their presence. Although crocs occasionally take young hippos, they profit more from hippos in an indirect way: hippos deposit huge amounts of dung into the water, providing a rich source of food for fish. Humans also reap a piscine bounty from lakes that have large hippo populations; sadly, it has been well documented that fish catches decline catastrophically when hippos are eliminated. Although hippos still seem abundant in parks, their numbers have been declining: the total African hippo population is estimated at about 160,000.

Field Guides to Mammals

Ranging from African elephants to elephant shrews, and from aardwolves to zorillas, the variety of African mammals is truly mind-boggling: the antelopes alone total more than 35 species from 11 separate families. Each animal is unique in form and function, and there is simply not enough space here even to mention them all. Although the major species and many others are discussed in the text, the information is far from complete. To fully appreciate Africa's mammalian life, you should carry a field guide along on your trip.

An illustrated field guide is more than an invaluable aide to identification, it is a great reference for information on many aspects of an animal's natural history: the facts of size and weight, habitat and food preferences, reproductive cycles, social behavior, and daily habits are put at your fingertips. *A Field Guide to the Mammals of Africa Including Madagascar*, by Theodor Haltenorth and Helmut Diller (London: Collins, 1980), is quite good and covers the entire continent. Chris and Tilde Stuart's *Field Guide to the Mammals of Southern Africa* (Cape Town: Struik, 1988) is comprehensive for all areas south of the Zambezi. It has informative descriptions and color photos of all species (except marine mammals, for which there are color drawings); even rodents and bats are included in this excellent book. *The Safari Companion: A Guide to Watching African Mammals*, by Richard Estes (Post Mills, Vermont: Chelsea Green, 1993), is no conventional identification guide; this field guide to the behavior of the hoofed mammals, carnivores, and primates is a great resource for keen wildlife observers.

Your pleasure in safari will be increased as the depth of your knowledge about the animals and their habitats deepens. It is highly recommended that you do as much study as possible before you leave home. For further reading, consult the bibliography at the end of this book.

Insects

Most visitors to Africa would just as soon not think about insects, but several types are too important to the continent's overall ecology to pass without notice.

A good number of African parks undoubtedly owe their existence not to an animal that man wanted to preserve, but to one he couldn't get rid of: the tsetse fly. This insect is reviled as the carrier of human sleeping sickness and also transmits the fatal "nagana disease" to cattle. In those areas where tsetses prosper, cattle and people do not; the fly has kept humans out of whole regions of wooded bush country which otherwise would have been settled long ago. Many such tsetse-infested tracts were designated game reserves and later turned into national parks. Because of that, it has been argued that the tsetse has been the greatest conservator of wildlife in Africa. When scientists find the means to eliminate the fly, and they have been doing a good job of that recently, the last wild gamelands will be in serious danger of human encroachment. Try to keep this in mind when tsetses buzz around you in hungry swarms, even if you get a few bites. (In southern Africa, tsetses are now relegated to a few wilderness areas in northern Botswana and Zimbabwe, and to Zambia. Some parks in Zambia are still heavily infested.)

Tsetses are ordinary-sized flies of the genus *Glossina*, recognizable by the peculiar way they fold their wings over their backs: the wings rest one over the other, giving the insect a characteristic cylindrical shape rather than the scissor-winged physique common to other types of flies. Tsetses feed on blood. They rest on the shady underside of bushes or trees and are attracted to passing animals by movement: they consider automobiles to be fair game. Tsetse bites can be subtle or needle sharp, and some people get terribly itchy reactions. Sleeping sickness, however, is rarely contracted in African game parks. (For more information about sleeping sickness, see the Staying Healthy section in chapter 2.)

As you drive through the bush, the imposing spires of termite mounds are sure to catch your eye, for these castles of clay are one of the most striking features of many African landscapes. Termites are voracious primary consumers of vegetation; they harvest immense quantities of grass as well as dead wood. There are many different varieties of termites. Not all of them raise conspicuous mounds, but even where such hillocks are absent, the insects abound. Termites are extremely plentiful in all savanna habitats and play a key role in the lives of many animals.

Termite castles are raised during the rains, when the insects use saliva to fix mud into durable cement; fresh construction can rise inches overnight. The tall towers surround ventilation shafts that reach deep into the earth, providing a cooling system for underground fungus gardens. A variety of small animals live in the tunnels: among the squatters are mongooses, birds, lizards, and snakes. Other animals use termites as a source of food: aardvarks, pangolins, and aardwolves depend on the insects for their survival. "Anthills" that have been torn apart by aardvarks often become the homes of burrowing animals such as warthogs and hyenas. During nuptial swarms, when columns of lace-winged insects spew from the mound like a volcano in eruption, a whole array of animals joins in feasting on them. Baboons, hornbills, eagles, jackals, hyenas — and even humans — relish the fatty abdomens of reproductive termites, the would-be founders of new colonies.

Termite mounds are more commonly seen than the insects themselves. The "white ants" avoid the heat of the sun and mostly venture out at night; during the day, you may find them beneath pieces of downed wood. Where you see fresh work on a mound, you can break off a small piece and the fierce soldier termites will emerge to confront you. But be very cautious about poking into the holes on anthills: they are a favorite refuge for the deadly black mamba snake.

Dung beetles are ecologically important because they rapidly recycle tremendous quantities of fresh excrement back into the earth. These large black "scarabs," which were symbols of rebirth to the ancient Egyptians, are very conspicuous as they roll balls of manure across the plain. Each ball contains a single egg; after burial, a fat grub develops, to emerge in the next rainy season as a "resurrected" beetle. Adult dung beetles have hard shells that make them unpalatable to all but a few large birds (the larvae, however, are eagerly sought by the bat-eared fox; during the lean dry months, this tiny insect-eating canid uses its oversized ears to locate grubs hidden underground).

Although it is not in any sense a comprehensive field guide, *Insects of Southern Africa*, by Erik Holm and Elbie de Meillon (Cape Town: Struik Pocket Guides for Southern Africa, 1993), is a useful and highly portable source of information about the most commonly encountered varieties.

Birds

African birdwatching is arguably the best in the world. Although South America can claim more species, most are hard-to-see creatures of the rainforest. In contrast, excellent visibility in Africa's savanna country makes it easy to appreciate the beauty and diversity of its birdlife. Some 900 species have been recorded in southern Africa (not counting species that only occur in Malawi and Zambia), and it is reasonable for an experienced birder to identify more than 200 types during a typical two-week safari; participants on well-led birding specialty tours can expect to get up to three times that many. But enjoyment of the birds is not restricted to committed listers; birds are so evident a part of the wildlife scene that many people without any previous interest develop a passion for them while on safari.

The brightly colored species are the first to catch the eye. Some of the prettiest are routinely attracted to feeders at camps and lodges: iridescent starlings and golden-yellow weavers are among the regular freeloaders.

On game drives, the sight of a colorful bee-eater or kingfisher perched on a bare branch is a real car-stopper. The lilac-breasted roller, a tame and multihued bird that obligingly poses for the camera, is everyone's favorite. King-sized birds also readily draw attention, whether beautiful, like the elegant crowned crane, or bizarre. The marabou stork falls in the latter category: frocked in sober black and white, its prominent bill, balding pate, and stooped posture give it a distinctly grave demeanor. This conspicuous bird takes its name from an order of Muslim holy men — the *marabout* — found throughout northern Africa.

Africa's birds of prey, ranging in size from the pygmy falcon to the monkey-eating crowned eagle, are another group that piques universal interest. Eagles and vultures are almost constantly patrolling overhead, along with a squadron of miscellaneous hawks, buzzards, harriers, and falcons. Graceful as they are on the wing, these raptors are at their most impressive when perched. No one will fail to be moved when staring into the face of the martial eagle, its fierce eyes burning with all the haughtiness of a medieval warlord.

Among the smaller varieties are many LBJs ("little brown jobs") that would pass unnoticed in your own local city park. But tiny jewel-like species abound, and the assortment of birds is almost endless; an array of shrikes and cuckoos, waxbills and whydahs, hoopoes, hornbills, and honeyguides (to name but a few) seem to pop out of the bush at every turn.

Africa's tropical climate is responsible for this avian wealth, for warm temperatures ensure a year-round food supply of plants and insects. Local abundance varies with the season, however, and some species move around the continent, following the rains in search of the insects, frogs, and fish that multiply in their wake. The exuberance of the rainy season sparks many African birds to breed; mating is serious business, and they put on their most brilliant plumage for the occasion. From October through March, the continent's resident birds are joined by species that migrate to Africa to avoid the Eurasian winter. This migration coincides with southern Africa's summer rainy season, and birdwatching is probably at its best at that time. It is then possible to see massive flocks of the white stork (the one that brings the babies!), now rare in western Europe.

While the average person will be charmed by the birds, the ardent lister will be in heaven. But he or she will face stiff challenges: the sheer variety makes identification a bewildering process, and it is not always easy to catch a good view. Tiny sunbirds won't sit still to be identified, and screening foliage will ensure that the shyer species remain more often heard than seen. LBJs, such as larks and wheatears, blend into their surroundings so well that they are difficult to pick out even 10 feet from a car. Such obstacles will not deter the enthusiast, who will be busy from dawn to dusk pursuing dun-colored larks just as eagerly as the most colorful specimens.

To sort out the birds you will need a field guide. *Newman's Birds of Southern Africa* by Kenneth Newman (revised edition, published in South Africa by Southern Book Publishers, 1995) is the best and easiest to use. The *Sasol Birds of Southern Africa* (in its original form or the recently enlarged version) by Ian Sinclair and Phil Hockey (Cape Town: Struik, 1996) is also excellent. *Roberts' Birds of South Africa* by G. R. McLachlan and R. Liversidge (Cape Town: Voecker Bird Book Fund, reissued 1980) is one of the bibles of African bird lore; it is generally too heavy to tote and is more of a reference book than a field guide. Ken Newman has a separate field guide, *The Birds of Malawi* (South Africa: Southern Book Publishers, 1994), for that country.

Binoculars are *essential* even for casual birdwatching. Spotting scopes are great on lakeshores and mudflats where you can't get close to birds, and for watching birds on nests; they are cumbersome, however, and cannot always be conveniently set up in game parks.

Reptiles

As you might expect, Africa hosts a wide variety of reptilian life. While most species go unnoticed or unobserved, a few deserve mention.

Monitor lizards (or leguaans, as they are widely called in southern Africa) are the continent's largest lizards, growing up to 7 feet in length. The Nile monitor (water leguaan) lives near water and is frequently seen sunning itself in overhanging trees or on the banks of streams. Nile monitors feed on eggs, carrion, fish, and any small animals they can catch, including young crocodiles. Less often seen is the savanna monitor (rock leguaan), a thicker-bodied lizard that can be found far from water. It is a voracious predator and defends itself by lacerating enemies with its serrated tail.

Many types of smaller lizards are routinely encountered. Agamas are conspicuous because of the bold colors sported by males: various species come in bright combinations of red, yellow, orange, and blue. Geckos are often seen hunting moths at night around game lodges and buildings. They have the unusual ability to walk on vertical walls, and can even crawl upside down on the ceiling (do not become alarmed or injure a gecko if you see one in your hotel room: it can do you no harm and may remove a few mosquitoes). Chameleons are more bizarre, although less visible. It is true that they can change their color; equally striking, they can move their eyes, which are set in protruding sockets, in opposite directions. Southern African varieties range from the 14-inch, flap-necked chameleon to various dwarf species, which are as small as 4 inches in length. Chameleons are harmless, although the larger specimens put on fearsome threat displays and can bite if handled. Many Africans regard them as harbingers of evil or bad luck.

Turtlelike terrapins are common around water but rarely stick around for a close-up view. This is not true of the leopard tortoise, a land-dwelling animal that is not noted for speed; it is often encountered crossing the road during game drives, and care must be taken not to run it over. Once seen, the leopard tortoise is easily captured for an examination of its beautifully patterned shell. Leopard tortoises can be handled without fear, but they eject a foul-smelling black liquid, so beware if you pick one up (which you should really do only to remove it from a road). They are preyed on by hyenas, honey badgers, and ground hornbills, but their biggest enemy is fire, which destroys any tortoise that can not find its way underground. Eleven other types of tortoises inhabit southern Africa. Most are endemic species found in the arid regions and fynbos areas of South Africa and Namibia. Several are highly endangered by habitat destruction and reptile collectors.

Although common in most warm habitats, southern Africa's snakes manage to stay well out of sight; on the typical safari, the total number seen ranges from zero to one. But that one can loom large in the imagination. Perhaps because of our fear, it is the dangerous serpents that most grab our fancy: every time we spot a green snake, we would like to believe it is a deadly mamba, ignoring the fact that there are many perfectly harmless varieties of the same color. Contrary to popular opinion, the majority of African snakes are completely innocuous except to the frogs, lizards, and rats on which they feed. Many snakes have no fangs whatsoever.

Africa's poisonous snakes fall into three groups. Colubrid snakes are the most common. With the exceptions of the boomslang ("tree snake") and the vine (or twig) snake, these rear-fanged species are completely harmless to humans. The two mentioned have poisons that are chemically complex, but neither snake is aggressive, and bites are extremely rare.

The most dangerous snakes are the elapids and the vipers. Cobras and mambas belong to the elapid family. These serpents possess short fangs located at the front of the mouth that inject potent neurotoxic venoms. Such poisons attack the nervous system, leading to paralysis of the lungs and heart. A bite can be extremely serious; elapids are responsible for the most cases of sudden death. The "two-step snake" is a myth, however. The effect of any bite varies, and the rapidity or severity of poisoning will depend on many factors, such as the size of the snake, the amount of venom received (none may be injected at all), and the weight of the victim. It takes a massive dose of venom, delivered directly into a vein, to produce immediate death in an adult human. Several types of cobras are capable of spitting their venom up to 10 feet. They aim for the eyes — a tactic designed to protect them from large animals that might otherwise trample on them by accident. The black mamba is the largest and most feared venomous snake in Africa; it reaches a maximum length of 12 feet. By reputation, it is fast and aggressive; it is supposed to be especially protective of the termite mound or rocky outcrop it uses as a refuge. The black mamba hunts on both the ground and in trees, unlike the green mamba, which is almost exclusively arboreal. Note that the black mamba is actually grayish or olive brown in color; solely the inside of its mouth is black. This fact becomes obvious only during the terrifying gaping display that the mamba makes just before it strikes — it's not something you want to see.

Vipers possess hemotoxic venoms that attack tissue and blood. Such poisons are powerful enzymes meant to begin the process of digestion even before prey is swallowed. Most vipers possess wonderfully camouflaged skin that enables them to lie concealed as a means of defense. The puff adder is a common, slow-moving viper. Large specimens are grossly fat. They are active primarily at night, when Africans are prone to step on them in the darkness. The gaboon viper is also a large and beautifully colored snake; its 2-inch-long fangs contain venom with both hemotoxic and neurotoxic agents. It is extremely dangerous, but very rare, and difficult to provoke (in southern Africa, it is mostly restricted to the coastal forests of northern Natal).

Pythons are not poisonous, but fascinate because of their size: they can reach more than 20 feet in length, although such giants are rare. This snake waits in ambush on a game trail, catches its quarry with a firm bite, and quickly coils around the body in an asphyxiating death grip. Prey consists of small- to medium-sized animals, such as monkeys, antelopes, and large rodents. Although a human child could be at risk, an attack on an adult would be accidental: a python simply cannot swallow a full-grown man. But accidents can happen, so it is fortunate that pythons are normally shy and retiring.

Bill Branch's *Field Guide to the Snakes and Other Reptiles of Southern Africa* (Cape Town: Struik, 1988) is the best portable reference book; it has over 500 photos and an informative text. *Snakes of Southern Africa*, by Rod Patterson and Penny Meakin (Cape Town: Struik Pocket Guides, 1986), is a useful little book with beautiful illustrations.

Conservation Notes

While on safari, you will be constantly amazed by the superabundance of animals. Yet the question nags as to how long Africa's wildlife will last. As we enter the 21st century, two storm clouds loom large on the horizon: commercial poaching, the most dramatic and immediate danger, and loss of habitat, the ultimate threat. Both perils are exemplified by the plight of two major species that are already in serious trouble: the elephant and the black rhino.

In many ways, elephants symbolize everything that is wild in Africa. These giants need expansive amounts of space to survive, and even the game reserves are often not big enough to contain them. The African elephant is the largest land animal; a bull can grow to a height of 13 feet and weigh more than 6 tons (12,000 pounds), although most would tip the scales at about 5 tons (10,000 pounds). Females are smaller, but their food requirements are proportionately the same: an elephant eats about 5 percent of its body weight daily. Whereas in the past elephants could migrate at will over vast tracts of countryside, they have been increasingly confined to national parks and game reserves. These parcels have limited carrying capacities and often go through major habitat modifications when their elephant populations get too large. While the conversion of woodland to grassland is good for some species, it has dire consequences for others, including elephants: although elephants depend largely on grass for sustenance, they are basically inhabitants of wooded bush country and require the more varied year-round food sources it provides.

Controversy has raged for years over how to prevent elephants from eating themselves out of house and home. One side advocates "culling" as the solution. In a culling scheme, biologists first determine the number of animals a park can support; its elephants are then counted, the excess number is determined, and teams of expert marksmen go to work. A herd is exterminated in a single deadly fusillade: bulls, cows, and calves are all mercilessly shot down. None are permitted to escape. This brutally efficient technique has several rationales. By removing animals of all ages, the demographic distribution of the elephant population at large is not upset. Annihilation of the entire herd also ensures that no terrified survivors are left to roam the park: elephants have long memories, and traumatized animals could be a hazard to visitors. In addition to keeping the number of elephants within set limits, culling allows parks and national treasuries to reap profits from the sale of ivory, skins, and meat. It has long been employed as a management technique by wildlife authorities in South Africa and Zimbabwe.

In East Africa, park wardens have usually preferred to let nature take its course, trusting to the theory that ecosystems adjust naturally to changes in animal populations. For many years, this laissez-faire policy seemed to work fairly well because there was no shortage of either elephants or other game, but woodlands in some parks were damaged and there were periodic calls for drastic culls. Such appeals invariably sparked acrimonious disputes among wildlife experts. Events made the debate moot: in the 1970s and 1980s, a tidal wave of poaching reduced East Africa's elephant population by more than half. A 1987 survey by researcher Iain Douglas-Hamilton for the United Nations Environment Program (UNEP) put the 15-year — 1973 to 1987 — decrease in elephant populations at 53 percent for Tanzania, 85 percent for Kenya, and 89 percent for Uganda. The situation was equally bad in Zambia and most parts of western and central Africa. It was considered less grave in southern Africa, where Botswana and Zimbabwe still had exceptionally large numbers of elephants. South Africa's herds were undisturbed by poachers, but their total population was relatively small and almost entirely concentrated in Kruger National Park, which was considered to be at its full capacity. The elephants of Malawi, Namibia, Angola, and Mozambique were very hard hit, but their governments refused to admit it. All the southern nations were making money exporting ivory by both legal and illegal means, for there was plenty of collusion between government officials and shady business syndicates to launder poached ivory and market it legally. The inability to control the trade (or to distinguish between legally obtained and poached tusks) led to calls by wildlife conservation groups for an end to all international commerce in ivory. Demands for a moratorium on the legal ivory trade were staunchly resisted by the southern countries, led by South Africa and Zimbabwe. But public opinion came down on the side of a ban: in 1989, a worldwide embargo on the cross-border sale of ivory was approved at a meeting of CITES (the Convention on the International Trade in Endangered Species).

The CITES ban seems to have given elephants a breather: since it was imposed, poaching in most parts of Africa has declined markedly and elephant populations (thought to have reached a low point of between 600,00 and 750,00 continent-wide) have again begun to rise. That is good news, but it has only reignited the debate about culling. The southern African countries still insist that a legal and controlled ivory trade is essential to support their efforts to conserve elephants and wildlife generally. They will attempt to get CITES to repeal the ivory ban at its 1997 meeting. Although they may fail to get their way at that time, it is likely that legal international trade will someday be resumed.

Meanwhile, some conservationists are trying to find nonlethal means to control elephant populations in the national parks. Researchers are investigating chemical methods of birth control that could be used as an alternative to culling. Translocation is another possible option: in the last few years, techniques for tranquilizing and transporting elephants have improved to the point where entire family groups can now be moved instead of killed. Such translocations have permitted surplus elephants to be moved from overpopulated parks and reintroduced to places from which they have long been absent; many parks and private game reserves in South Africa have been the beneficiaries. But translocations are expensive and the number of areas suitable for the reintroduction of elephants is limited. Neither birth control nor translocation provide the hard cash that results from the sale of ivory or the licensing of trophy hunting. The debate between the proponents of the "sustained utilization" of wildlife and those who are morally opposed to the killing of elephants will surely go on.

The black rhinoceros has undergone a much more catastrophic decline than the elephant. Only 20 years ago, this prehistoric-looking beast was a common animal in almost every African game park. But its venerable line may soon be coming to an end: in most places, poachers have completely exterminated the rhino, and in Africa as a whole, its numbers have declined overall by more than 90 percent. In 1994, the total number of black rhinos in the wild was estimated at a mere 2,550.

Since ancient times, the horns and other parts of the rhino's body have been sought-after ingredients in oriental medicines. Rhino horn is made of compacted hairlike tissue, similar to our fingernails. Although its most publicized use is supposedly aphrodisiacal, powdered horn is considered efficacious for any number of disorders; it is mainly used to reduce fevers. Whatever its application, it is still worth its weight in gold throughout Asia. Horns are even more in demand in Yemen, where they are carved into handles for *jambia*, the dagger worn by every adult male. A rhino horn handle is a highly prized status symbol. Thousands have been sold, and the tiny Arabian nation of Yemen is the world's principal consumer of rhinos.

While the scale of commercial poaching can clearly reach appalling heights, it is aimed primarily at the few species for which there are lucrative markets. For less persecuted animals, the critical issue for survival is the preservation of habitat. Although large territories have already been set aside for parks and reserves, wildlife habitat must inevitably shrink as Africa's human population continues to grow. Even before the last surge in poaching activity, it had been estimated that elephants were declining at roughly 3 percent every year, which is about the same rate as that of human increase on the continent. Already the parks are becoming islands in a sea of human habitation. Very soon, Africa's larger animals may be banished from all land that has not been specifically set aside for them. Few parks encompass entire natural ecosystems that meet the year-round requirements of their fauna. In most parks, wildlife populations change as animals migrate to and from surrounding countryside in accordance with seasonal availability of food and water. As the process of "islandization" advances, the carrying capacity of the parks will almost certainly stabilize at lower levels.

Islandization also spells genetic trouble; as animal populations are confined, decreases in local gene pools will lead to a weakening of stocks, especially of rarer species such as rhinos. Their reproduction will require scientific management to protect genetic diversity. Such programs are not only expensive, they also negate the essence of wilderness and wildlife. Distasteful as that may be, in the not-too-distant future, many African parks may be managed like drive-through zoos. Others may simply vanish as the tide of humanity washes away the boundaries of reserves that do not produce huge tourist revenues.

Proponents of sustained utilization maintain that the only way wildlife can survive in the long run is to pay its way: it must be treated as a renewable natural resource to be managed for maximum economic gain. Although some conservationists find this idea distasteful (and it is anathema to animal rights advocates), sustained utilization and the intensive management of wildlife seem to be the wave of the future.

Many African countries are game rich but cash poor. Their governments are anxious to use their wildlife resources to greater economic advantage than that which can be wrung solely from conventional tourism. This is a legitimate end. With proper management, big game trophy hunting, the export of skins and ivory, and the harvesting of meat can all be undertaken on the basis of sustained yields that do not damage healthy populations of wild animals. Such activities undeniably have nasty effects on individual animals, but they can be beneficial to wildlife as a whole: if land can be put to better economic use by leaving it wild than by opening it up to human settlement, more tracts of wilderness are likely to be left intact. Instead of pushing all of Africa's animals into the confines of island-like parks, much vaster territories can be left as undisturbed habitat that will support larger and healthier wildlife populations.

For many of us, the slaughter of wild animals is an unqualified evil and a very emotional issue. Even among conservationists with differing views on sustained utilization, there is general agreement that poaching is a wasteful use of a valuable natural resource. Yet if Africans poach to make a living, that should be no surprise on a continent in which per capita income is measured in mere hundreds of dollars per year. It is true that only a few top traders get rich off the bloody poaching industry, while most of those doing the actual shooting see little of the profit — but their rewards are still relatively good by African standards. At the same time, rural Africans usually see no other cash benefits from having wild animals as neighbors: in the bush, farmers view wildlife more as a nuisance or a source of meat than as an engine for economic gain. Elephants may trample or gobble up an entire field in a single night; lions and other predators are feared as potential dangers to livestock and family; impalas are just plain good to eat. In many African languages, the word for wildlife — *nyama* — is a synonym for meat.

The current strategies of sustained utilization are meant to change attitudes toward wildlife by ensuring that local people and their communities reap tangible economic rewards from conservation. Ecotourism plays an important role in such strategies, for tourism can bring money into a country's economy and create lots of jobs. But until now, most people living on the fringes of national parks have seen little of the money generated by tourists: too often, they have been left out of tourism's process and its profits. This imbalance is now being addressed throughout southern Africa. Various operations, such as Zimbabwe's CAMPFIRE project, seek to involve bush communities in conservation by allowing them to profit from the wildlife that roams their own land. Under these schemes, people are encouraged to tolerate and protect wildlife as an ongoing source of income. Participating communities can earn substantial revenues from leases to tourist camps and trophy hunting concessionaires. Such lodges and hunting outfitters create jobs for local residents as well as outlets for the sale of indigenous arts and crafts. Hunting and controlled culling are also sources of affordable meat.

The jury is out as to whether sustained utilization will succeed in preserving Africa's wildlife. The scientific technology is probably capable of making it work, but there are always thorny questions of political will. In light of continuing human population growth and a ceaseless hunger for land development, maintaining a sustainable environment may not always get priority. Although the economic benefits of tourism can encourage African governments to create parks, reserves that attract few visitors or do not pay their way are potentially in danger of losing their protected status. Some parks have already been annulled by official fiat or lost to de facto encroachment. Technology itself is contributing to the destruction of African wildlife habitat. Through aerial pesticide spraying and the development of effective fly traps, scientists are close to eradicating the tsetse fly in southern Africa — a well-intentioned goal that may have ecological implications far beyond those envisioned by authorities.

Other important wildlife areas, such as the swamps of the Sudd in Sudan, are destined to be dredged or are threatened by dams, as is the lower Zambezi Valley.

Finally, there stands the menace of political instability. As the Ugandan experience has shown, it takes only a few years of anarchy to wreak havoc on a country's wildlife paradises and many, many years for them to recover.

Although the threats are real, predictions regarding "the end of the game" have been rife since the early days of African independence. Yet there are still enough animals around to confound the old-time pessimists. Nor are gloomy trends necessarily irreversible. Research suggests that elephant numbers were probably as low at the end of the last century as they are now, following an earlier period of ruthless ivory hunting. With protection, Africa's elephant population recovered before and may bounce back again if sufficient wild lands remain available. There may even be hope for the black rhino; its cousin, the white rhino, was only saved from extinction by a hair's breadth but is now common in the parks of South Africa. Emergency actions are being taken that will probably ensure the survival of the black rhino in at least a few locales. The emergence of community conservation programs is also a hopeful development. So, too, is the proliferation of private game reserves. All over southern Africa, bush country property owners are converting huge cattle ranches into private wildlife reserves or banding together to form nature "conservancies." Most of these operations are profit-driven businesses designed to cash in on the boom in African tourism; some attract hunters. Although they vary greatly in quality, their net effect has been a tremendous expansion in the acreage devoted to wildlife. In these reserves, game is restocked and managed much as it is in the national parks, and wildlife populations are growing. Big game species such as elephant, rhino, and lion, as well as a host of other animals, are returning to areas from which they vanished many years ago.

In all likelihood, the future of Africa's wildlife reserves will be a mixed bag: some parks will disappear altogether, some will be reduced to the status of wild animal theme parks, and a few will remain large and relatively wild.

Rather than abandon all hope, we must do what we can to aid the cause of African wildlife. A number of organizations fund and manage conservation projects in Africa (a partial list is included in the Appendix of this book) and all of them need financial support. It helps for you to stay informed and spread the word to friends that African wildlife needs help: the slide show that results from your safari could be used to raise a few dollars for your favorite wildlife group. More directly, you can refrain from buying endangered wildlife products and let your government representatives know how you feel about the importation of such products into the United States. (Even today, although we currently do not import ivory, America remains the world's largest importer of live animals, mostly birds, fish, and reptiles for collectors, and wildlife products, such as skins.) Letters to foreign embassies can also be effective; ultimately, boycotts may have to be organized against the tours and products of countries that do not seriously support international efforts to control the wildlife trade.

CHAPTER FOUR

Botswana:
A Desert and a Delta

L ITTLE MORE THAN A DECADE AGO, Botswana was an African backwater, known overseas only to a handful of safari aficionados and big game hunters. Today, the country's name seems to be on everybody's lips, for it has achieved the reputation as the ultimate safari destination.

Botswana's safari attractions are indeed formidable. With such celebrated wilderness havens as the Okavango Delta, Chobe National Park, Moremi Game Reserve, and the Kalahari Desert to its credit, Botswana can hardly qualify as anything but a natural paradise. Its claim to preeminence rests on dual pillars: an abundance of wildlife and an absence of people. Statistics would seem to bear this out. The nation is larger than France but has a mere million and a half human inhabitants, most of whom live in a narrow belt in the southeastern portion of the country. Yet it harbors perhaps as many as 70,000 elephants, the largest remaining population on the continent (the true number of elephants in Botswana is a subject of controversy — estimates range from a high of 80,000 to a low of 30,000). Botswana enjoys a reputation as an untouristed wilderness, where abundant wildlife can be viewed without the necessity of sharing the experience with hordes of other animal watchers.

While Botswana may be relatively new to international tourism, it has been renowned for wildlife ever since the days of the first European

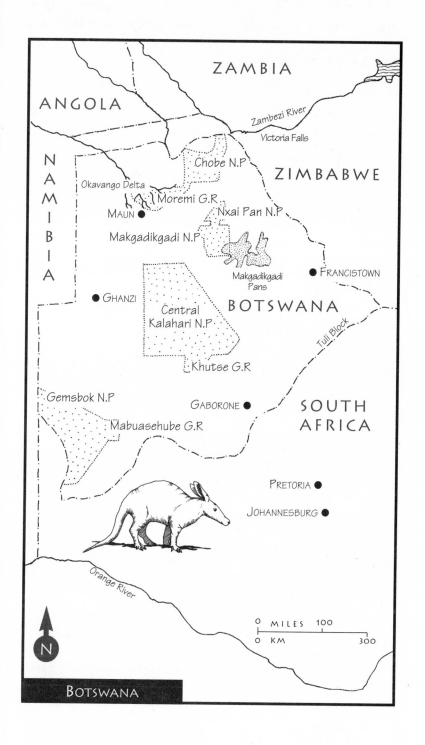

ZAMBIA

ANGOLA

NAMIBIA

Zambezi River

Victoria Falls

Chobe N.P

Okavango Delta

ZIMBABWE

Moremi G.R

MAUN

Nxai Pan N.P

Makgadikgadi N.P

Makgadikgadi
Pans

FRANCISTOWN

GHANZI

Central
Kalahari N.P

BOTSWANA

Tuli Block

Khutse G.R

Gemsbok N.P

GABORONE

SOUTH
AFRICA

Mabuasehube G.R

PRETORIA

JOHANNESBURG

Orange River

MILES   100

KM   300

N

BOTSWANA

explorers. When Livingstone arrived at Lake Ngami in the southern Okavango, local people did not consider ivory to have any special value, and elephants were very common. The explorer heard accounts of "cattle pens made of elephant tusks of enormous size" and found untouched ivory lying among the bones of old elephant carcasses—a sure sign that no hunting was taking place. That changed quickly as hunters and traders swarmed into what was then called Bechuanaland, arming the natives with muskets to assist in their quest for white gold. Other species also suffered in the slaughter that followed, but game continued to hold out in those places remote from the haunts of humankind, especially in the tsetse-plagued woodlands of the north and the thirstlands of the Kalahari. Of course, human activity and habitat encroachment have caused wildlife resources to shrink considerably over the last 150 years. But Botswana has set aside more than 17 percent of its land as protected game areas, and some of its parks offer wildlife viewing to rival that found anywhere on the continent.

Botswana is nearly synonymous with the Kalahari, so it is important to review a little Kalahari geography to understand its central role in the country's ecology. The Kalahari had its origin as a great inland basin, which filled with eolian sands blown in over the ages as the ancient lavas that once covered southern Africa slowly eroded. Kalahari sands now extend from Congo and Angola right down to the Northern Cape Province of South Africa, and across the continent from Namibia to western Zimbabwe. Kalahari sands underlie more than 80 percent of Botswana. This is not to say that the entire country is a desert. The north has wetlands sustained by the Okavango and Chobe rivers and receives more than 20 inches of rain a year, enough to support large tracts of mopane, teak, and acacia woodlands. Rainfall decreases steadily to the south, where it averages less than 10 inches. But statistics do not tell the whole story: over the long dry season between May and October, it almost never rains and any standing surface water quickly evaporates under the combined assault of dry air and fierce sun. Rainfall is also highly erratic, especially in the arid south, where storms can drop a whole year's supply on one area in the space of a few hours but leave a neighboring district without a drop. This seasonal thirstland is the true Kalahari. Although often called a "desert," most of it is a grassland with scattered bush and trees, except in the extreme southwest where bare ground and moving sand dunes appear. But although Botswana is not a desert in the technical sense, water is a scarce and valuable commodity throughout the country—so much so that the Setswana word for rain and the name for the nation's currency are the same: *pula*.

Botswana was not always so dry. Only 35,000 years ago, huge rivers flowed into the heart of the Kalahari (including three great contemporary streams — the Okavango, the Chobe, and the mighty Zambezi), feeding a supersized lake known as Lake Makgadikgadi. That vast inland sea had an hourglass shape. Its western bulb included much of what are today the Okavango Delta, the Mababe Depression, and the floodplains of the Chobe-Linyanti river. The eastern bulb is now the Makgadikgadi Pans. These were connected at a narrow waist by the valley of today's Boteti River. Geologic changes associated with the creation of Africa's Great Rift Valley caused the Chobe and the Zambezi to flow eastward to the Indian Ocean. The Okavango also underwent a metamorphosis, but unlike its sister rivers, its waters were never destined to reach the sea. Because of the Kalahari's flatness, the Okavango's course was altered by minuscule changes in elevation resulting from Rift Valley faulting. The downward slip of the Gomare Fault made the river break into numerous small channels, spreading it into a wide fan shape. Further downstream, an upward movement between the parallel Kunyere and Thamalakane faults dammed the river, forcing it to pond backward. Eventually, sediments carried down by the Okavango formed a vast and shallow inland delta. Only a tiny remnant of water overflowed from the Okavango Delta into the Boteti River. Deprived of its sources, the ancient Lake Makgadikgadi rapidly shrank and ultimately dried up.

Today, only two permanent rivers still flow into Botswana: the Okavango and the Kwando (which ultimately becomes the Chobe). Both have their headwaters in the distant highlands of Angola, then run southward to Botswana. The Chobe forms the country's northern border along Namibia's Caprivi Strip and changes its name several times: it comes down as the Kwando, then meanders through a wide band of marshes as the Linyanti, and finally skirts the edge of the national park that bears its name before joining the great Zambezi. Only the Okavango penetrates deeply into the Kalahari. Shortly after entering Botswana, it broadens into its fan-shaped inland delta, forming an evergreen oasis of wetlands in the midst of dry bush country. It is the great lifeline to the hinterlands of northern Botswana. In exceptional years, its floodwaters reach and fill Lake Ngami. More often, Ngami stays dry while the last of the Delta's waters trickle instead to the southeast, down the Boteti River toward Lake Xau and the burning salt flats of Makgadikgadi.

Most of Botswana is so flat that the sight of a rocky outcrop that would pass unremarked elsewhere is almost a cause for celebration. It is surprising that a country with no mountains or dramatic escarpments — indeed, almost without topographic relief — should nonetheless harbor a wonderful variety of scenic landscapes. Yet anyone who has watched a sunset on the Chobe River, with elephants pouring out of the white dust of the woodlands onto the green of the floodplain, or who has flown over the checkerboard of forested islands, open waters, and reed-covered lagoons that is the heart of the Okavango Delta, could not help but declare Botswana beautiful. Perhaps it is the endless horizons and big skies, or just the pure magic of wilderness, but Botswana has a quality from which few come away unaffected.

Yet no visitors go to Botswana for the scenery (which is more dramatic in neighboring countries). They go to see wildlife, and in this they are not likely to be disappointed.

Most safaris take place in Botswana's northeast, in a belt of wild bushland that nestles against the wetlands of the eastern Okavango Delta and along the meandering course of the Kwando-Linyanti-Chobe river system. This exceedingly rich wildlife region encompasses Chobe National Park and the Moremi Game Reserve — the great reservoirs of Botswana's remaining wildlife — as well as a number of designated Wildlife Management Areas that are reserved for hunting or photographic safari concessions. This northeast region is largely an uninhabited wilderness in which animals can still migrate as the seasons dictate, spreading throughout a vast arc of bush country during the rains, then reconcentrating in the dry season near the waters of the Delta and the Chobe River. This is the realm of Botswana's elephants, where tens of thousands of the great pachyderms still roam at will.

It would be nice to believe that Botswana is one vast wilderness in which African wildlife could roam undisturbed for all time. Certainly a country with as few inhabitants as Botswana would seem to be free of the population pressures that afflict so many African countries. But, of course, that is not the case, for even in so sparsely populated a land, human activity is everywhere evident and human interests are always paramount.

Botswana's population is unusually homogeneous: 95 percent of its people belong to the Tswana tribe (the Batswana), with the remainder being of San (Bushman) origin or from a sprinkling of other groups like the Herero. Such homogeneity helps foster stability, and the country has not suffered any of the tribal conflicts that have divided the energies of so many African nations. That stability has proven to be an important engine for successful development.

For millennia. the sole occupants of Botswana were small bands of San hunters. The cattle-herding Tswana arrived on the dry fringes of the Kalahari between the 13th and 18th centuries, where they settled in widely distributed independent family groups. The hundreds of Tswana clans began to coalesce into larger political structures as a result of the depredations of King Mzilikaze and his Ndebele warriors during the 1830s. Soon thereafter, the arrival of the Afrikaners in the Transvaal put the Tswana under continuous pressure as the Boers sought to expropriate their lands. In 1885, the British acted to end the constant land wars in Bechuanaland by declaring a protectorate over the northern part ruled by the Tswana Chief Khama III, while making everything south of the Molopo River a Crown colony. The northern Bechuanaland Protectorate ultimately became Botswana. The Crown colony was absorbed into South Africa; today, its Tswana people are the dominant group in South Africa's North-West Province.

Bechuanaland was not viewed as one of the more promising parts of the empire, and the British did little more than keep the peace during their tenure. In 1958, they began to prepare the protectorate for independence by establishing a legislative council. Botswana became fully independent in 1966, with Seretse Khama, a direct descendant of the old chief, its elected prime minister. Sir Seretse Khama (he was knighted after independence) became the first president and set the course for Botswana's ship of state, adhering to a constitution that is a model for African democracy. The president is chosen directly in multiparty elections, as are the members of the National Assembly from which government ministers are drawn. A House of Chiefs, consisting of the traditional headmen of the eight largest tribes, consults on matters involving customary tribal affairs. On the village level, issues affecting local communities are hotly debated and resolved at public forums known as *kgotla*. The rights of individuals and opposition parties are constitutionally guaranteed, and — unusual in Africa — have been respected.

Seretse Khama steered the country toward peaceful development. He stayed out of the military conflicts in neighboring Rhodesia and Namibia, even while lending diplomatic support to the black insurgent movements there. It required real political finesse to voice outspoken opposition to the apartheid regime while maintaining some semblance of autonomy from South Africa, the economic giant on which Botswana had to depend as chief trading partner and sole route to the sea. Perhaps Botswana would have become a wholly owned subsidiary if its luck had not come through with the discovery of diamonds a year after independence. A partnership with South Africa's huge De Beers company led to the development of mines at Orapa, Letlhakane, and Jwaneng (Jwaneng is now one of the world's richest diamond mines). Together, the mines earn more than 60 percent of the country's foreign trade revenue, adding a billion dollars a year to the national treasury. With diamonds on the soles of her shoes, Botswana has been able to underwrite education and development projects in the face of droughts and a level of unemployment that would otherwise have proved crippling. The current president, Ketumile (formerly Quett) Masire, succeeded upon Khama's death in 1980, and was re-elected on his own in 1984. Masire has continued Khama's progressive policies.

In Botswana, as in so much of Africa, cattle is king. Among the Tswana, the possession of a large herd is a traditional sign of wealth, conferring a status that cannot be matched in any other way. Hence, even professionals who attain Western living standards like to retain a certain amount of wealth on the hoof, while the most humble citizens aspire to own as many cows as possible, no matter how scrawny. The consequence is that the population of cattle hovers between 2 and 3 million, or up to three animals for every human being in the country. Although large private ranches are found in the heavily populated southeast and in the Ghanzi district in the Kalahari, most of Botswana's cattle are pastured on communal land — a free range for which no one has direct responsibility to guard against overgrazing. Overstocking has caused severe degradation of Botswana's dry rangelands, resulting in catastrophic die-offs of both wild animals and cattle during inevitable periods of drought. Not that cattle do not have real value for the economy: since independence, the country has profited from a deal with the European Community, which buys beef at very favorable prices, making Botswana's meat exports the second largest earner of foreign exchange.

The beef must be free of foot-and-mouth disease to meet European import standards. Because foot-and-mouth outbreaks are regular occurrences in Africa among both domestic stock and wild animals, Botswana constructed and continues to extend a system of veterinary cordon fences. Their purpose is to quickly control foot-and-mouth outbreaks by quarantining diseased areas, and to keep export cattle separated from populations of wild animals that might harbor the disease.

The cordon fences have been immensely controversial because they have contributed significantly to the destruction of the huge migratory herds of game that used to live in the central Kalahari, particularly of wildebeest. Wildebeest are dependent on drinking water and must leave the central Kalahari at the onset of the dry season. When the infamous Kuke Fence was built in 1958, it severed dry-season migration routes from the Kalahari to water sources in the Okavango and the Boteti River, which spills out of the Delta to run along the edge of the Makgadikgadi Game Reserve. In the 1960s, severe drought caused hundreds of thousands of wildebeest and hartebeest to die from starvation and thirst. In the next decade, rainfall was better, and improved grazing led to a revival of the wild herds. But drought struck again. In 1983 alone, an estimated 50,000 wildebeest died along the Kuke Fence and in the neighborhood of Lake Xau, to which the thirsty animals were shunted. This tragedy was reported by wildlife researchers Mark and Delia Owens, whose popular book, *Cry of the Kalahari*, caused a tremendous hullabaloo in the international conservation community. An angered government responded by expelling the Owens from Botswana and threatening to remove the remaining Bushmen from the Central Kalahari Game Reserve, blaming the decline in desert wildlife on their hunting activities. Scapegoating the Bushmen had the effect, wittingly or not, of pushing a wedge between two international constituencies — nature conservation groups and the human-rights lobby. Squabbles about human needs versus those of wild animals obscured debate and took some of the wind out of the conservationists' sails, for the media made the wildlife groups look as though they were working against the interests of a small and powerless group of indigenous people.

While there is no doubt that the fences have contributed to the decline of Kalahari wildlife, they are not the sole or even the root cause. Critics of the Owens point out that massive crashes of the wildlife population are a natural part of a cycle of boom and bust in a region notorious for irregular rainfall and periodic drought. Others say the real culprit is the increase of cattle in the region: competition for grazing and degradation of the range would have caused a decrease in game populations regardless of fencing. The drilling of boreholes opened up the "desert" to cattle ranching, while human settlements blocked migrating animals from getting to water, setting the stage for the decline of wildlife even before the advent of large-scale fencing. Whatever the degree of the fences' culpability, no one can argue that the Kalahari's wildlife has not suffered: in the last decades, zebra and buffalo have disappeared from the central Kalahari, and wildebeest may well follow suit.

Despite the charges of catastrophic effects on the migratory animals of the Kalahari, Botswana's authorities do not consider the fences controversial: they defend them as a necessary tool for the control of foot-and-mouth disease, and the question of taking them down or modifying them to allow for wildlife migration routes is a dead issue. Conservation groups have been successful, however, in getting the government to take migratory routes into consideration in planning any new fences.

The veterinary fences have had one important positive effect on wildlife conservation: the Buffalo Fence, which cordons off the southern Okavango Delta from the surrounding countryside, keeps cattle and people *out*. One has only to look at the difference between the quality of the rangeland on the wilderness side of the fence, where lush greenery prevails, and the parched and dusty ground on the side used by cattle, to appreciate the dire effects of overgrazing. One can also feel the longing with which local people must look at the greener pastures on the other side of the fence.

That hunger for better pasturage can only grow with the imminent eradication of the tsetse fly. The tsetse, carrier of the *nagana* disease that is so fatal to cattle, has been a far more formidable barrier to encroachment on the wildlands of the Delta than any fence could ever be. But a long-term campaign of aerial spraying has taken its toll on the fly, which is nearing extinction in the Okavango Delta. The spraying has been another source of environmental controversy. Not only does it open up the Delta wetlands to the possibility of further encroachment by cattle, it has also been accused of incidentally killing insects and fish, with baneful effects all along the food chain. Once again, government technicians and scientists have come forward to vigorously defend their program. They insist that the chemicals used against the tsetse (a combination of endosulphan and deltamethrine) break down quickly in the environment and cause minimal impact on nontargeted organisms, especially when applied in cool weather. Spraying therefore takes place at night during Botswana's winter months — the height of the tour season (as of 1996, aerial spraying has been suspended, at least temporarily, in favor of a new and less environmentally harmful campaign that uses fly traps to contain the tsetes). Spraying advocates also insist that the program is designed to prevent tsetses from reinfesting cattle-raising areas outside the Buffalo Fence, not to foster expansion into cattle-free zones. Skeptical conservationists remain unconvinced that the final demise of the tsetse will not usher in strong pressures to open up the Delta. In fact, although the normal impulse is to swat these persistent biting flies unto death, some local safari people practice "catch and release" to keep some tsetses around.

The Okavango may one day face the threat of the loss of its very lifeblood — water. A serious proposal was made to dredge the Boro River near Maun to create a reservoir that would provide a water supply for that town as well as serve the demands of the water-hungry Orapa diamond mine. That plan was rejected after scrutiny by the Botswana government and vocal opposition by local people. But water is a scarce resource in the Kalahari region, and there is no certainty that new proposals to utilize the Delta's waters will not surface. The most serious threats could well arise upstream, should Namibia or Angola ever expand development projects that take water from the Okavango before it even reaches the Delta. Namibia already pumps water from the river as it passes through the Caprivi Strip, and its government is pushing hard to significantly increase its off-take.

Fortunately, Botswana's government seems disinclined to allow further encroachment on the Okavango Delta at this time. In fact, the boundaries of the Moremi Game Reserve have recently been expanded in the permanent swamps of the upper Delta to include the extensive papyrus marshes found there, a habitat which was formerly unprotected.

Botswana officially takes a very progressive view on the value of wildlife. The National Conservation Strategy recognizes wildlife's importance as a renewable natural resource and calls for its utilization to bring the maximum benefit to the nation. The plan recognizes that tourism brings money into the country and provides jobs to rural folk. But tourism is only one aspect. Wild animals are a traditional source of food in Botswana, and hunting by local residents is still widely practiced. The Wildlife Department establishes charges and quotas for the number of permits issued annually, as well as for the types and numbers of animals that can be taken. Although citizen hunting provides both income to the economy and meat to the local table, big game trophy hunting by overseas visitors is much more lucrative to the national treasury. A decade ago, it was bringing in the equivalent of 3 million dollars a year in foreign exchange. Because large blocks of land are granted as concessions to professional hunting companies that cater to an exclusive clientele, a mere 5 percent of their quota is killed, yielding a startlingly high revenue per animal bagged. Botswana is celebrated in the international hunting community for the variety of trophies available and the exclusivity of its hunting concessions. Despite its large elephant population and an abundance of foreign hunters willing to pay dearly for the privilege of shooting an elephant, Botswana did not allow elephant hunting from 1983 until 1996, when 27 licenses were issued. The annual number of elephant licenses is expected to increase significantly.

Hunting provides income and meat to Botswana, but it is not without its problems. Citizen licenses are cheap and can be transferred from the original licensee to others, and this gives rise to large-scale commercial meat-hunting operations. Abuses certainly exist: many kills are not reported as required, and violations of hunting rules by both citizen hunters and professional safari outfitters seem to be routine. Overhunting has contributed significantly to an alarming decrease in the wildlife population in some areas. The Wildlife Department acknowledges the problem and is computerizing its operations, a development that should improve the efficiency of its monitoring. It is also converting some concession areas from hunting to photographic use and tightening enforcement of hunting regulations.

Although Botswana's government is often lauded for its environmental sensitivity, decisions on the use of wildlands are always subject to

conflicting pressures. Political considerations can intrude and take precedence over scientific advice. One example is the government's decision to
move ahead with a farming project on the northern Mpandamatenga
Plains to the east of Chobe National Park, an important wildlife migration area. Similar developments in the region have been declared abject
failures by the government's own agricultural consultants, yet authorities
insist on pushing ahead with the scheme. Such actions may indicate that
Botswana's government gets more credit for its conservation policies
than it deserves. Perhaps giving lip service to environmental goals while
pursuing destructive projects is becoming as familiar a public relations
tactic in Africa as it is in the sophisticated Western democracies.

Botswana is investigating the sustainable commercial harvest of indigenous wild plants. Thusano Lefatsheng, a rural development organization, already successfully markets the devil's claw (also called grapple
or *Harpagophytum procumbens*), a reputedly medicinal tuber that
grows in the Kalahari, and is working on the domestication of nutritious
morama beans and the delectable fruit of the marula tree. One of the
group's chief aims is the preservation of indigenous trees, so they stress
the need to harvest without overexploitation. Kalahari truffles are another possible sustainable source of income from the wild.

Tourism remains an important element in Botswana's development
plan. Within the last decade, the industry has grown into the nation's
third largest earner of hard currency, after mining and cattle, and is recognized as a key source of employment in the northern Ngamiland and
Chobe districts. Still, the number of jobs provided to local people is estimated at little more than 1,000. Although this is a windfall for Maun
and a few other northern villages, many citizens question the value of
tourism in their own lives. Perhaps because of their legacy of relations
with South Africa, people are much more reserved than friendly toward
foreigners. Tourists find it difficult to break through to local people, and
there is usually little or no social interaction.

Travel to Botswana slowly increased throughout the 1980s, as word
began to escape that one of Africa's great wildlife paradises was nearly
empty of visitors. This coincided with the great boom in East African
tourism that followed the release of the Hollywood epic, *Out of Africa*.
As East Africa's parks filled up, travel writers and media gurus began to
look for a new safari destination. Abundant wildlife was no longer
enough; it had to be viewed in privacy, without the company of less exclusive onlookers, to fulfill the promise of a true African experience. An
increasing volume of nature documentaries on television and the best-
selling book *Cry of the Kalahari* began to make Botswana a more familiar name. When *National Geographic* devoted an issue to Botswana

at the end of 1990, the floodgates were thrown wide open and the country was propelled to its premier status as a safari destination. But being at the top of everyone's travel list has its price. The rising tide of visitors and safari companies, while tiny in 1980, has multiplied manyfold today: Botswana's old image as a pristine wilderness where one could enjoy game viewing in total privacy (if ever true!) is now largely a thing of the past, at least in the public areas of its national parks (privacy is still possible in private concession areas).

Botswana's official policy is to encourage high-cost, low-volume tourism rather than cut-rate mass visitation. This policy is underpinned by the reasonable assumption that more affluent visitors are willing to pay higher prices to enjoy the privacy of an uncrowded wilderness environment. It is also designed to provide maximum financial gain to the country while minimizing the extent of environmental degradation that inevitably occurs when tourist numbers grow too high. Toward that end, Botswana instituted park fees that are considerably higher than those of any other country in southern Africa; at about US$15 per day, they are more in line with those of Kenya and Tanzania. The fees were adopted with the idea of keeping the parks attractive to more affluent visitors while discouraging low-budget tours and self-drive tourists from South Africa who were coming into the country in great numbers.

The boom in travel has brought strains on the policy of high-cost, low-volume tourism. The high park fees have increased government revenues, but no money seems to go back to the parks. The Wildlife Department remains badly underfunded, public campsites are in a terrible state of disrepair, and motivation among park rangers seems totally lacking. The official policy has been to encourage tourists to stay in high-cost accommodations rather than go camping, so deluxe safari camps and lodges have mushroomed throughout the northern game region. But the number of visitors on lower cost camping tours has also steadily increased, and facilities for them are greatly overstressed. So, too, is the capacity of the parks to provide the "wilderness experience" on which so much of Botswana's appeal is based. Today, it is really only in private concession areas where you can expect to have prime game viewing in privacy. Elsewhere, and particularly in the most wildlife-rich parts of Chobe National Park and the Moremi Game Reserve, you will have to share the bush with others. The opening of a large hotel and an international airport at Kasane can only increase congestion in Chobe National Park, which is already crowded: every day during the busy dry season, hundreds of visitors in dozens of vehicles prowl the game tracks along the Chobe River, while a growing fleet of boats cruises the water. (Plans to limit the number of visitors in high-use areas like Chobe are in the works, but things take a long time to happen in Botswana.) Although game viewing is not affected one whit, this is exactly the same type of high-volume tourism that is so decried in East Africa. Botswana must take care not to kill its golden goose.

Safari Facts

ENTRY: No visas or vaccinations are required for US citizens.

CURRENCY: The currency is the Botswana pula (1997 rate: P3.60 = US$1). If you are participating on a safari tour, you really need not even to change money as you will have few opportunities to spend it, and US dollars are widely accepted throughout the northern game country.

LANGUAGE: English is the official language and is widely spoken by those associated with tourism. Setswana is the most commonly spoken local language.

AIR TRAVEL: Most visitors fly into Maun directly from Victoria Falls, Zimbabwe, or come from Johannesburg via Gaborone. Air Botswana is the principal carrier to Maun, and is the only scheduled domestic airline. Air Namibia connects Maun with Windhoek. The new international airport at Kasane hopes to attract large international carriers, but so far is served only by Air Botswana and charter aircraft.

AIRPORT DEPARTURE TAXES: A tax of P25 (international) and P10 (domestic) is imposed on flights originating in Botswana. The international tax is usually included in your international ticket; domestic air taxes (which apply to charter flights as well as scheduled departures) are often included in the cost of tours booked overseas. Check to make sure you do not pay twice.

LAND TRANSPORTATION: Regular rail service links Gaborone with Johannesburg and with Bulawayo, Zimbabwe. Erratic and slow bus service exists between the towns of eastern Botswana. Avis and Holiday Car Hire have offices in Maun, Kasane, and Gaborone. Car rentals are necessarily quite expensive, especially considering the distances involved in touring the parks.

TOURS: Virtually everyone on tour to Botswana comes to see the game parks of the north. Many take flying safaris of as little as one week's duration, which is just enough to visit three safari camps and have a taste of the principal game areas. But wing safaris of any length can easily be arranged. The better quality overland camping expeditions also include some flights, usually into the Okavango Delta. Overland safaris are generally from 12 to 20 days long. Most tours run between Maun and Victoria Falls, Zimbabwe, the two gateways to Botswana's safari country. Very few tourists visit Gaborone, the capital, except as an airline transfer point. Most safari companies are based in Maun, with the majority of their bookings coming from their offices in Johannesburg or Victoria Falls, or from overseas tour operators. Few have offices in Gaborone; regular travel agencies there will make bookings with safari outfitters.

SHOPPING: Baskets are by far the country's most celebrated craft product. Although they have many utilitarian purposes for rural people, those baskets with the most beautiful colored patterns are naturally made for sale to tourists. The best are woven from *Hyphaene* palm by the Tswana and Mbukushu peoples of Ngamiland. If you are on a tour, opportunities to buy them may be limited to lodge shops or the airport at Maun.

PARK FEES: Although it is a bite for budget travelers, Botswana tries to maximize its revenue from tourism, so their park fees are the highest in southern Africa. Daily entry fees are P50 per person; camping fees are an additional P20. Rates are reduced to P30 for daily entry and P10 for camping for participants on safaris operated by licensed Botswana tour companies.

GABORONE: Botswana's capital is a small modern town without much character. Few tourists spend any time there. It is served by a number of African airlines connecting it with the other capital cities of the region, as well as by British Airways with flights to London. If you plan to spend time in Gaborone, its principal hotels are the *Gaborone Sun*, the *Sheraton*, the *Cresta President*, *Cresta Lodge*, and *Cresta Gaborone*. All are heavily used by business people, so book ahead. The National Museum and Art Gallery contains natural history and ethnological displays.

MAUN: Located at the southern end of the Okavango Delta, Maun is the safari capital of Botswana. It is more an extended village than a town, with dusty sand tracks weaving between simple modern houses and traditional Tswana family compounds. Maun has the notorious reputation of a frontier town, and it has long been the hangout for a collection of professional hunters, adventurers, and safari guides. Indeed, quite a bit of partying (or drinking, at any rate) goes on at the handful of watering holes and lodges where the safari crowd gathers. Aside from getting organized for a safari, there is little else to do. Maun's airport is one of the busiest in Africa, with a constant stream of light aircraft coming and going into the bush. You are very likely to fly to Maun on either end of your safari, but may not be scheduled to spend any more time than it takes to connect to an ongoing flight. If you do have time to kill, there is an excellent shop across the street from the airport check-in hall. To grab a bite, Le Bistro restaurant is about a 10-minute walk from the airport. The only hotel in town is *Riley's Hotel*. It has a pleasant garden and features Harry's Bar, a favorite local meeting place. Several lodges are clustered about 6 miles northeast of town, strung out along the Thamalakane River. *Island Safari Lodge* is favored by overland truck safaris and backpackers, and has a lively social scene. The nearby *Crocodile Camp* is nice and has the best food of all the local lodges. Both of those lodges offer accommodation in chalets, as well as sites for campers. *Audi Camp*, which has tents and campsites, is in the same area. The self-catering *Sitatunga Cam*p is also on the banks of the Thamalakane, but about 8 miles south of town on the road to Lake Ngami. Hippos and crocodiles live in the Thamalakane River, and a stay along the river is pleasant. But be wary of water sports: aside from the crocs, bilharzia definitely occurs around Maun. All the lodges rent boats and *mekoros* (dugout canoes) and arrange safaris into the Delta and the parks. If you are booking a safari locally, it is easier to park yourself at one of the lodges to make inquiries and call around rather than trying to find safari outfitters' compounds.

The Okavango Delta

The Okavango Delta is perhaps Botswana's greatest natural treasure. Here, one of Africa's great rivers fans out to lose itself in the sands of the Kalahari. It is a place of haunting beauty, a world where water and land are so intermarried that it is hard to tell where one leaves off and the other begins. Even more remarkable is that this vast wetland is plunked down in the middle of a near-desert, an oasis whose waters bring myriad life forms to a thirstland where they otherwise could not exist — fish, frogs, crocodiles, and hippos thrive in the heart of the Kalahari. Nor would the nonaquatic species of Botswana's dry hinterlands survive in such abundance without the life-giving floodwaters that arrive in the midst of southern Africa's annual season of drought.

The Okavango River undergoes marked changes in character on its journey to oblivion. The river has its sources in the tropical highlands of central Angola, then flows southward through Namibia's Caprivi Strip. Just where it enters Botswana, the Okavango begins to lose its way on the flat sands of the Kalahari. For 60 miles, its channel is contained between parallel geologic faults. In this long "panhandle," the river meanders over a relatively narrow floodplain, forming hairpin bends as it loops its way through extensive papyrus swamps. Where it spills over the Gomare Fault, the Okavango loses all semblance of a normal river. It breaks into several main channels and a web of smaller waterways and washes over the intervening flatlands, fanning out into a great arc of permanent swamps and seasonally flooded plains. This great Okavango Delta fills with the arrival of the annual flood from Angola, which spreads a shallow veil of water over some 6,000 square miles of countryside. The flood advances so slowly that 95 percent of its water is sucked up by plants or evaporates under the African sun before it reaches the Delta's southern terminus, some 100 miles to the south. There, the last of the Okavango's waters are abruptly impounded by the Thamalakane Fault. Funneled down the small Thamalakane River, they flow past Maun before turning eastward down the bed of the intermittent Boteti River and vanishing into the Kalahari.

The Okavango is a dynamic yet mutable river system. Once it spreads over the flat Kalahari countryside to form its great inland Delta, it is no longer recognizable as the single river it is. Its floodwaters advance on a broad front, moving at a snail's pace of only a half mile a day. Reedbeds and floating mats of papyrus carpet the water's surface. As the slow-moving water flows almost imperceptibly through a sea of reeds and grass, the vegetation filters it, forcing it to drop any heavy silt particles and turning it crystal clear. The flood pulses more quickly through a maze of narrow channels that can broaden into open-water lagoons or just as easily lose themselves in swampy backwaters. The fast-flowing rivulets are kept open by the passage of hippos or *mokoro* (dugout canoe) traffic. But any obstacle — a fallen tree, a raft of floating papyrus, or an abandoned *mokoro* — can block a channel, forcing its water to find another way. New islands appear and grow, channels and lagoons are plugged, then slowly transform into swamp or grassland. In this unstable system, every part is subject to change but remains integral to the whole. For the Delta is a mosaic of wetland environments, interrelated and dependent on the vagaries of the annual floods that come from the north.

The floods are supposed to arrive in the Panhandle in January or February, then slowly filter down to the southernmost Delta to reach Maun by June or July. But they can come early or late, or not at all. Rainfall during the Delta's November to March rainy season also influences the distribution of water, for showers can fill the floodplains long before the arrival of the Angola floods. But most of the rainwater would evaporate soon after the onset of the dry season in May, so the Okavango floods

A mokoro (dugout canoe) safari in the Okavango Delta, Botswana. Photo: Allen Bechky.

bring refreshment to the floodplains of the southern Delta just when they are most needed.

As the river winds through the Panhandle, its channel constantly loops back on itself. At the bends, the floods drop their loads of silt and create sandbars. Crocodiles need such sandy places in which to excavate their nests, and the Panhandle provides many more suitable sites than the lower Delta. As the Okavango's chief breeding grounds, the upper river is well known for both the number and size of its crocodiles. The breeding season occurs between September and February, which coincides with the hot months when the sandbank nesting sites are exposed. The young crocs hatch just before the arrival of the floods. The floodwaters then replenish the nutrients of backwater swamps, in which insects, frogs, and small species of fish quickly start to multiply, providing plenty of food for young crocs. In the dry season, the local villagers bring herds of cattle and goats onto the Panhandle's floodplain to graze and drink. The larger crocs then get the opportunity to grab the occasional cow or goat from the banks of the main river. Big runs of barbel (catfish) and tiger fish that migrate into the upper river to breed between September and November also provide an abundant food source for the Panhandle's crocodiles.

The perennial swamps of the Panhandle and the northern Delta are the realm of the papyrus. These tall sedges grow in dense floating mats held together by a submerged matrix of rhizomes and roots. Although they look luxuriantly green and inviting, few animals live in the papyrus swamps. The plant's stems are tough and low in nutrients, so they are not good eating, and their closely packed mats are at once impenetrable and unstable. Most animals cannot walk on them, for they would sink right through. The notable exception is the sitatunga (*Tragelaphus spekei*). This swamp-dwelling antelope has long, splayed hooves that enable it to walk on floating vegetation — not a bad trick for an animal that can attain 250-plus pounds — and it has the strength to thrust its way through the papyrus thickets. Sitatunga eat papyrus; they prefer fresh new shoots, but also like the feathery umbel that crowns the long stem. They also feed on other reeds and grasses. Sitatunga are related to kudus. Like kudus, they are attractive antelopes, and the males have impressive spiraling horns. They are a much sought-after hunting trophy, but make an even finer prize for the photographer because it is so difficult to catch an unobstructed view of them in the sheltering papyrus. When threatened, sitatunga attempt to quietly sneak off through the reeds, but to escape danger will readily take to the water, where they remain submerged with only their nostrils protruding.

Papyrus swamps are a marginal habitat even for smaller animals.

A small crocodile in a Delta lagoon. Okavango Delta, Botswana. Photo: Allen Bechky.

Weaver birds make their nests high in the papyrus, and swamp warblers call from within, but few animals use the papyrus for anything more than shelter. The water beneath the root mats is dark, acidified by decaying vegetation, and low in oxygen. Freshwater shrimp and other small detritus-eating creatures have adapted to this harsh environment, but the chain of life remains relatively sparse. Conditions improve and animal life increases in both abundance and variety on the swamp's edges, where the papyrus mixes with reeds and gives way to open water.

Unlike papyrus, reeds take root on the bottom and become increasingly dominant in the shallow waters of the Delta swamps below the Panhandle. Although dense beds of tall *Phragmites* reeds tend to line deep channels, widely spaced reeds and sedges provide a more open and hospitable environment for fish, birds, and other aquatic animals. Sedges thrive on the inundated floodplains, forming lush watermeadows that attract herds of red lechwe and a multitude of birds. Among them is the wattled crane that shares the lechwe's predilection for feeding in shallow water. This elegant gray and white bird, with its distinctive drooping facial wattles, is the largest of the African cranes and is probably viewed in the Delta more often than anywhere else. Grasses also flourish on the floodplains. As the waters ebb, the grasslands provide rich pasturage to a succession of animals, large and small. Grazers as diverse as spur-winged goose, warthog, tsessebe, hippo, buffalo, and elephant all feed on the grasses of the seasonal floodplains.

In the swamps, narrow, fast-running channels cut through the thick beds of papyrus and reeds to suddenly open into wide lagoons. These Delta lagoons, locally called *lediba*, are often startlingly beautiful. Their quiet waters are crystal clear, reflecting the flowering water lilies that cover their surface. The widely spaced stems of reeds and bulrushes grow out of the water, and these, too, are mirrored in the placid lagoon. Animal life becomes more abundant and visible in the lagoons. Darters and reed cormorants dive in search of cichlids and small catfish. Diminutive pygmy geese appear in pairs, poking at the submerged bulbs of water lilies, while rafts of yellow-billed ducks glide over the glassy surface. Waterfowl become very evident, and herons abound. The Goliath heron is conspicuous at the water's edge, poised to spear its prey. The smaller purple heron is fairly common, but the rare slaty egret is easily overlooked. The little black egret stands in shallow water with its wings raised umbrella-like above its head, shading the surface for a clearer strike. Perhaps the most entertaining bird is the African jacana (also called the "lily-trotter"), which performs a ballet, nimbly walking on the floating pads of water lilies in search of tiny insect larvae. Hippos spend their days in the lagoons, which are also the preferred hunting grounds for the fiercely predatory tiger fish. Although those animals are hard to see, the wider vistas the lagoons provide make it easier to catch views of lechwe, sitatunga, or buffalo feeding in fringing watermeadows. Both the spotted-necked otter and the larger Cape clawless otter are common in the Delta, where small families of either variety can often be seen swimming and diving in the lagoons, hunting for fish, crabs, and frogs, or just having a good time.

The Delta is studded with islands of every shape and variety. Some are mere islets surrounding a termite mound. Others are crowded with a jungle of feathery wild date (*Phoenix*) palms or a lush hummock of riverine forest. The largest are chunks of Kalahari sand hosting the vegetation of the dry woodlands that surround the Delta. Islands are an important element of the Delta's ecological wealth, for they multiply the niches available to species of both the wetland and dryland communities.

Long, S-shaped islands are typical of the upper part of the Delta, where the river's many channels still carry a lot of silt. Such snaking islands are built by the fascinating process of levee formation: as a river slows down, it drops sand along the bottom and creates levees of decaying vegetation along its banks. Eventually, the river is actually raised above the level of the surrounding floodplain, a situation that comes to an abrupt end when a levee is punctured by an earth tremor or the passage of a hippo. The river then finds a new channel, leaving a winding stretch of infertile sand between the richer soils of its abandoned levees. In time, dense forest occupies the levees and grasses colonize the sandy interior.

Other islands owe their origin to termites. Such islands begin as termite mounds, which the insects raise above the surrounding floodplain over a season or two of drought. When the slow-moving floodwaters arrive, they meet the new obstacle and flow around it, dropping particles of sand against the edge of the island-mound. As silt accumulates and the insects continue to excavate earth from below, the island grows.

Delta islands are usually fringed with dense riverine forest, for they afford a perfect habitat for water-dependent trees that could neither grow on the seasonal floodplains nor on the parched sands of the Kalahari hinterlands. Waterberry trees and wild date palms grow at the water's edge. Behind them are tall stands of sycamore figs, ebony, sausage, marula, and rain trees, knobthorn acacias, and wild mangosteens. Such forests are a treasure trove of bird and animal life, providing food and shelter unavailable in the surrounding marshes. Fruit bats roost in the tall forest trees and feed on the nectar of sausage tree flowers or ripe figs, while nocturnal, rusty-spotted genets prowl in search of tree rats. Bird song fills the forest glades as paradise flycatchers, wood hoopoes, black-eyed bulbuls, puff-backed shrikes, orioles, and black-collared barbets flit from tree to tree, and terrestrial bulbuls, white-rumped babblers, and swamp boubous forage on the forest floor. The trees provide daytime roosting sites for the unusual Pel's fishing owl. This giant but reclusive bird usually spends the day hidden in the thick foliage of a wild mangosteen (*Garcinia livingstonei*). At night, it hunts by dropping from an overhanging branch to pluck unsuspecting fish from the river. Its weird piercing cries are one of the most haunting sounds of the Delta night.

Seasonally flooded grasslands often abut a termite island, and sometimes fill its interior, giving it a curious doughnut shape when seen from the air. In the dry season, such grasslands are dusted with white crystals of trona (sodium bicarbonate), the salty residue of evaporated groundwater. The island grasslands offer forage and dry resting places to lechwe and other large mammals. In many places, island grasslands host groves of tall *Hyphaene* palms, which grow well on saltier soils. The fruits of these graceful fan palms are much enjoyed by baboons and elephants, who shake the thick boles of the trees to bring them raining down. Elephants are important agents in spreading *Hyphaene* palms; they carry the hard seeds in their bellies, then deposit them elsewhere in a fertilizing ball of dung.

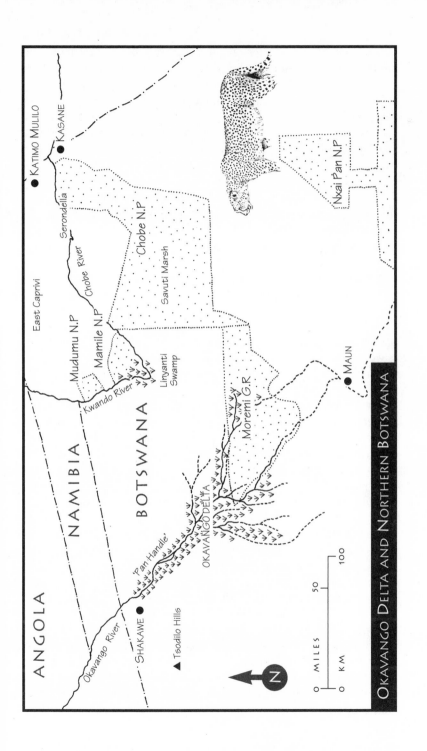

ANGOLA

NAMIBIA

BOTSWANA

East Caprivi

KATIMO MULILO

KASANE

Serondella

Chobe River

Mudumu N.P

Mamile N.P

Chobe N.P

Savuti Marsh

Kwando River

Linyanti Swamp

Nxai Pan N.P

MAUN

Moremi G.R

Okavango River

'Pan Handle'

OKAVANGO DELTA

SHAKAWE

▲ Tsodilo Hills

N

MILES 0   50   100

KM 0

OKAVANGO DELTA AND NORTHERN BOTSWANA

Sand islands become increasingly common in the floodplains of the southern Delta. Surrounded by seasonally inundated grassland, these outposts of Kalahari sand are not subject to flooding and host the vegetation of northern Botswana's rainfall-dependent woodlands. Beyond the fringe of riverine forest and tree islands that marks the highest reaches of the floodplains lie the mopane forests, acacia woodlands, grasslands, and pans of the dry savannas. Where the fingers of Delta rivers advance to their furthest extent, they intersperse with "tongues" of sandveld. These extensions of Kalahari sand reach far out onto the floodplains and support the same vegetation as the sand islands. The largest and best known of the sand islands is Chief's Island, in the Moremi Game Reserve.

Where the grasslands of the floodplains and the woodlands of the dry savannas meet, the greatest number and variety of large mammals are found. Most of the migratory grazing animals, such as zebra, wildebeest, and buffalo, prefer the grasses of the dry savanna. These grasses do not look as lush as those of the floodplains but they are sweeter and are made more nutritious by nitrogen put into the soil by the leguminous acacia trees that are common on the sandveld. The acacias themselves, as well as the mopane, combretum, and terminalias of the savanna, provide highly sought-after fodder for browsing animals such as elephant, giraffe, kudu, and impala.

The larger mammals of the Delta ecosystem move according to the availability of vegetation and water. Each species has its own requirements, but many different types can use the same range by feeding on different plants or even on the same plants in different stages of growth. As the waters advance and recede, a regular succession of herbivores takes place on the Delta floodplains.

Red lechwes thrive year-round on the Delta's watermeadows. They closely follow the rise and fall of the floods, feeding on the lush sedges and grasses that grow in shallow water or at its edge. As the dry season progresses, they follow the waterline and are replaced by reedbuck in drier areas with high grass. Tsessebe and impala also stay in the vicinity of the floodplains throughout the year. The tsessebe search out the tenderest green shoots of medium-length grass, while the impala wander back and forth between the floodplain grasslands and the wooded savanna of the dryland, taking advantage of both habitats to feed on a wide variety of grasses, leaves, fruits, and pods. Zebra and wildebeest start to arrive on the floodplains as the nutritious grasses of the neighboring savannas start to disappear. Big herds of buffalo pour onto the floodplains when the pans of the woodlands dry up and the high-rank grasses they prefer have been exhausted. Although some elephants may be found in the Delta at any time of year, they crowd into the swamps and floodplains in much greater numbers as the dry season advances. In times of drought, herds of elephants may remain in the Delta throughout the year.

Access and Accommodation

In the old days, the only way to get into the heart of the Delta was to travel by boat. But today most visitors arrive by air, flying in to one of the many small strips that serve the various lodges and safari camps. With the proliferation of such camps over the last decade, access to the Delta's interior has become quite easy and there is a wide choice of accommodation. During the tourist season, light aircraft are busy ferrying visitors from one camp to another throughout the day. This is by far the fastest way to penetrate the wetlands, and at the same time it offers the bonus of seeing the Delta from the air.

It's still possible to enter the Delta by boat. You can easily hire a *mokoro* (dugout canoe) and boatman at any of the lodges around Maun and (depending on the state of the flood) set off for the interior of the great marshlands. But it takes several days to get into the cattle-free game area beyond the Buffalo Fence, for it's about 30 miles to the southern end of Chief's Island and the boundary of the Moremi Game Reserve. So even budget tours usually begin with a vehicular or motorboat transfer up to the Buffalo Fence, cutting out about a third of the distance. Powerboats can also be hired in Maun, and a few safari outfitters offer extended trans-Delta tours by boat. Keep in mind that the southern end of the Delta is entirely *seasonal* swamp, so the amount of water will depend on the time of year you visit, local rains, and the progress of the annual floods — it is far more worthwhile to fly in and start your boating safari further up.

Small safari camps abound in the Delta. These fall in two broad categories, although some combine the elements of both: "water" camps feature explorations by boat on rivers, lagoons, and permanent swamps, while "land" camps offer game drives on the seasonal floodplains and in the adjoining savanna woodlands. With few exceptions, Delta camps are small and exclusive, with accommodation in either luxury safari tents or in comfortable cabins. Most of the land camps and a good number of water camps are located on the periphery of the Moremi Game Reserve, and will be described in the Moremi section of this chapter. In this section, we'll discuss only the camps in the Panhandle and northernmost Delta.

Shakawe Fishing Camp, *Xaro Lodge*, *Fish Eagle Lodge* (Drotsky's Cabins), and *Nxamaseri Camp* are located in the upper Panhandle, along the main Okavango River. Xaro is probably the most luxurious camp: it offers luxury safari tents and has a swimming pool. Nxamaseri accommodates its guests in chalets and specializes in fly fishing. Shakawe has a swimming pool; a campsite for overland travelers adjoins the main tented camp. *Guma Lagoon* and *Makwena* camps are further downstream, where the river begins to fan out to form the Delta. All these Panhandle camps are best known for their fishing and birding. Fishing in the Panhandle is always good but is exceptional during the September to December barbel run. Birding, too, is always good; it is particularly rewarding from September through March, when migrants from Europe and central Africa join the area's resident species. Hippos, huge crocodiles, and sitatunga are the large wild animals to be seen along the main river and in the extensive papyrus swamps of the area. The camps of the upper Panhandle also serve as convenient bases for excursions by road to the Tsodilo Hills. Although the hills are only about 20 miles distant, thick sands and a bumpy track make it a very laborious journey.

A mixture of tribal peoples gives the Panhandle region some cultural interest: along the main river, you may see some Herero stockmen bringing their cattle down to drink, while the more numerous Mbukushu and Yei fishermen ply past in their *mekoros*. They catch fish both in traps and by line. San also inhabit the Panhandle region, and are usually to be found at the site of their forebears' famous rock paintings in the Tsodilo Hills. (For more information on the San, see the Tsodilo Hills section of this chapter.)

Touring the Delta

For the avid naturalist, it makes little difference when to visit the Delta: there is always much to see and learn, no matter what the time of year. But local conditions vary according to the ebb and flow of the annual floods and the change of seasons — and these factors can make a big difference in the experience, especially if you are primarily interested in seeing big game.

The "best" time to visit the Delta is considered to be between July and September, when the weather is cool and the Okavango floods have come down to their fullest. As the dry season progresses, increasing numbers of animals emerge from the bushlands of the northern Kalahari to crowd the Okavango floodplains, particularly those of the eastern Delta around the Moremi Game Reserve. Game viewing is then at its peak. The weather is at its most pleasant in April, May, and June; July and August are cold! It warms up considerably in September, and is very hot by October.

Animal watching deteriorates with the onset of the rainy season. Between November and April, the woodlands of the northern Kalahari are flushed with green foliage and its waterholes are full, so most of the large herbivores move away from the environs of the Delta. Over those months, however, local rains replenish marshes and floodplains that have been drying out since the crest of the Okavango floods. The weather is hot and water is everywhere — conditions that are ideal for the growth of plants and the reproduction of insects, fish, and birds. The Delta is therefore lush and bursting with the smaller forms of animal life, but less satisfactory from the point of view of big game viewing or human comfort. Although some camps close during this period, most remain open year-round.

Because the Delta changes character so much between its upper, perennially flooded swamps and the lower, more game-rich floodplains, it's best to plan on visiting at least two different locales, using one water camp and one land camp. This is particularly so if you will be going during the dry season, when you have a good expectation of seeing plenty of game at the land camp. During the rainy season, you may want to cut down your time in the Delta by eliminating a land camp, as getting around for game drives will be sloshy and game will be widely dispersed. You can use the extra days to visit the Kalahari, which is then at its peak of game activity.

Flying low over the Okavango is really a treat: you get a spectacular, bird's-eye view of the wide, flooded plains with their infinitely varied islands, lagoons, and interconnecting waterways. There really is no better way to fully appreciate the extent and complexity of the Delta environment. You will also be able to do a bit of game spotting from the air — picking out herds of red lechwe against the brilliant green of the floodplain, or glimpsing a group of elephant resting under a grove of *Hyphaene* palms on a Delta island.

Once in the Okavango, you'll have several modes to explore the swamps: by *mokoro*, aboard a powerboat, or on foot. The *mokoro* is the prime means of river travel for the Mbukushu people who inhabit the Panhandle; they learned the skills of making and maneuvering *mekoros* from the Yei, who live in the lower Panhandle and in the Delta proper. A *mokoro* may not look like much but it is a real piece of work. Hewn from the trunk of a single tree (ebony and sausage trees are considered the best), these peculiar dugouts are ideal for negotiating the Delta's maze of water and reeds. On river channels or deep lagoons, the boatman uses a paddle. More often, he stands in the back, using a long pole to thrust the *mokoro* forward through flooded grasslands and narrow waterways. A *mokoro* can get through places too shallow, clogged with vegetation, or narrow for any other type of boat, so it is a real boon for exploration. It allows you to glide over a flooded, reed-choked plain to get close to lechwe, or to turn up a tapering hippo path to make a landing on a wilderness island. It is also quiet. Save for the chatter of your companions or polers, you can travel in silence, taking in the sounds of the Delta: the gurgling rush of water through a quick-running channel, the trilling of a swamp warbler hidden in the enveloping papyrus around you, the call of a coppery-tailed coucal bubbling across a lagoon. The slow pace of the *mokoro* has a calming effect that meshes well with the mood of the Delta. Purple herons glide across the sky, and pairs of pygmy geese paddle away into the reeds. You just sit back and relax while the boatman does all the work.

And it is work, too, especially when an already narrow channel wriggles in wasp-waist turns, and the boatman must pole the boat backward, then thrust forward again to break through to open water. Moving again with the stream, you push against the banks of papyrus mats, looking in to see the ferns and tiny plants that grow on the floating mass. It looks solid enough, but if you were to step on it, you could fall straight through. The *mokoro* rides so low in the water that the papyrus around you often forms a high wall, the flowering umbels towering above your own head. In the narrows, you must pay attention. There, you have to carefully lift the sedges out of the way and pass them to the rear, or risk a slap in the head from a slimy, wet umbel.

In the swamps, animal viewing is largely confined to sightings of red lechwe, which are commonly seen feeding on flooded grasslands. Living in the open, they like to keep a pretty good distance and are difficult to approach closely. Sitatunga like to stay well hidden in papyrus or reedbeds, although they can be seen on the edges in the twilight hours. They are probably best viewed when they feed in beds of recently burnt papyrus, to which they are attracted by a proliferation of new green shoots. Papyrus burns well, and large tracts of the Delta's papyrus and grasslands go up in the flames of bush fires during the dry season. The papyrus regenerates quickly from its root mat, however, and the reedbeds bounce back with the arrival of the next rains or floods. A new burn opens up densely overgrown areas, presenting excellent feeding opportunities for various animals and birds. Sitatunga are attracted to the fresh green shoots that pop up on burnt-over papyrus mats, and flocks of open-billed storks are quick to arrive after a fire, for the destruction of the high stems allows them better access to the root mats where the snails and freshwater mussels on which they feed abound.

When you are inside a reedbed or papyrus swamp, visibility from a *mokoro* is often confined to your immediate surroundings. The sudden sound of splashing water will alert you to the presence of large animals, which you might not be able to see. The *mokoro* boatmen are well versed at identifying the sounds: a quick splash followed by an abrupt silence indicates a sitatunga, which will hide in the reeds or quietly sink into the water; more prolonged riffling is made by lechwe as they continue to run through the shallows. A buffalo makes a lot of noise as it retreats through water. Hippos pose a danger to *mekoros*. The boatmen are mindful of this and avoid their daytime haunts in the lagoons, although you will often find yourself using paths and channels cleared by hippos on their nightly forays from their resting places to feeding grounds. If you are lucky, you might come upon elephants while on a *mokoro*. It's very exciting to watch them bathing in deep water, rolling over or bobbing up and down with only their heads and trunks protruding. In the dry season, they wade into *Phragmites* reedbeds to dine on the roots.

Delta water is given a dark color by decaying vegetation, but it is marvelously clear. In fast channels, you can see the sandy bottom where the current keeps it free of plants, and you will have the opportunity to investigate the root mass at the base of papyrus mats and reedbeds. Plants and animals can be seen beneath the water, too: the coiled stems of water lilies, the delicate, pink air sacs of carnivorous bladderworts, and the small fish that dart to shelter in the reeds at the channel's edge. In addition to the beautiful water lilies, you are sure to notice the floating clusters of delicate, white ottelia flowers.

But *mokoro* travel is not for everyone. The boats ride low in the water and, although not as tipsy as they first seem when you totter aboard, you can't fail to notice how little freeboard separates you from the Delta's waters. *Mekoros* tend to leak a bit, too, which can cause concern for camera gear stored on the floor of the boat. A traditional *mokoro* has no seats; a tuft of swamp grass is the only padding available. On deluxe *mokoro* safaris, the boat should be equipped with a padded seat and backrest — which makes all the difference on even a one-hour journey and will be a lifesaver on an extended trip. No *mokoro* offers any shade, however, and it can get hot if you are out in the midday sun (although you could tote along an umbrella). Some people find a long *mokoro* trip claustrophobic, uncomfortable, and even a tad boring.

Delta camps usually keep *mekoros* available to their guests, but larger boats are more the rule for group excursions. Powerboats have the obvious advantage of speed, allowing you to reach a particular lagoon or island without exhausting yourself on the journey. Rushing around should be discouraged, however, as wakes cause destruction to vegetation and nesting animals (particularly to birds that nest on sandbars, like the endangered African skimmer). Engines are also noisy, but you'll have plenty of opportunity to switch off and bask in the quiet of the Delta. The most luxurious boats are flat-bottomed vessels, large enough to provide all the amenities — chairs, cool drinks, shade, and an upper observation deck. You can wander around on board while enjoying expansive views over the reedbeds — something you can't do on a *mokoro*.

At Delta camps, sunset cruises are almost obligatory. And why not? There are few things as pleasant as having sundowners while watching the play of light on sky and water. Another regular event is the fish eagle show. Every big lagoon has its resident pair of these magnificent, white-headed birds of prey, which look similar to the American bald eagle. African fish eagles are commonly seen conspicuously perched atop high trees, and their piercing, territorial cries are often heard ringing out over their domain. The eagles quickly learn when to turn up for a handout. Your guide's whistle and raised hand gets their attention, and a fish tossed onto the water brings them winging in on queue for a spectacular aerial pickup. It's a great photo opportunity, but you must be ready if you want the shot: auto-focus and motor drive help a lot, and fast film is recommended, as the show is usually staged in low evening light.

Birds are by far the most commonly seen animals in the Delta's permanent swamps, so birdwatching is the major game viewing attraction at water camps. The Okavango's juxtaposition of marshes, open water, grassland, and forest ensures a tremendous variety of avian life, large and small. It is the large birds that are most easily seen and appreciated, especially those that inhabit the more open habitats. Around lagoons and rivers, you can expect to see reed cormorants and darters conspicuously perched atop snags while drying their wings, or diving in pursuit of fish. Herons and egrets come in a wealth of sizes and colors, and they are often easily seen along the edges of swamps and lagoons. Ducks and geese are also well represented, with the big spur-winged geese being perhaps the easiest to spot. The smaller species are also abundant, although much more difficult to get a bead on. Everyone takes notice of the black and white pied kingfishers that hover over the water before diving for a fish, or that tiny avian gem, the malachite kingfisher, whose blue and red colors draw the eye whenever it perches on a slender reed.

Delta camps are usually tucked into pockets of riverine forest on the edge of water, and it's a great pleasure merely to soak up nature while relaxing in camp. These shady groves are cool and beautiful and filled with life. At dawn, you'll first be awakened by the fluid notes of the Heuglin's robin, which will soon be joined in a first-rate chorus as the other forest birds chime in. Avian activity tends to carry on right through the morning in the shady forest glades, and again peaks in the late afternoon. The smaller forest birds can be difficult to see, but it's worth keeping your binoculars handy at all times.

At night, bird song is replaced by the piping of reed frogs (which reaches amazing heights in the rainy breeding season), the weird cry of the fishing owl, the repetitive electric-sounding tink of fruit bats, and the deep grunts of hippos. There are also periods of profound silence.

Camping safaris feature all the natural bounty of the Delta, plus a chance for an isolated wilderness experience. Delta camping expeditions do not usually offer the amenities of the permanent camps, although the better safari operators establish seasonal bush camps complete with dining areas, showers, and toilets. Budget groups keep it more simple, traveling by *mokoro* and setting up light camps on suitable islands.

The smaller Delta islands must be explored on foot. Although dangerous animals such as lion, elephant, or buffalo can appear anywhere, their density is low enough that most tour operators do not ordinarily send along someone with a protective firearm: they depend on the bushcraft of guides or boatmen to keep their clients out of harm's way. But extra care must be taken when walking around. On the islands, you'll have the welcome opportunity to get some exercise on walks through grassland and forest habitats. You might get to stalk lechwe or sitatunga or find their distinctive droppings and tracks. Finding Pel's fishing owl involves landing on islands, then padding through forest groves to check their preferred roosting trees. They are wary birds: sometimes you see 'em, sometimes you don't.

Although hippos and crocs live in the Delta, neither species is seen as much as you might expect. Hippos and *mekoros* do not mix, so they are more likely to be seen and approached aboard motorized boats in the bigger lagoons. Crocodiles were overhunted in the Okavango earlier in the century, and it is questionable whether the population has recovered to its carrying capacity, which may be limited by the lack of suitable nesting sites. They are there, however, and you may see crocs sunning themselves at the water's edge. Also watch for the telltale bow wave and bubbles that mark a crocodile's underwater passage across a lagoon.

The Delta's clear waters are inviting, and many visitors get to enjoy a refreshing dip. Because of potential crocodiles, every swim should be approached with caution. Your guides will know the places that are reputed to be crocodile-free, and by tradition, the guides are the first ones in. But people, both locals and tourists, have been taken by crocs in the Delta, so exercise extreme care around water.

Local guides and tour operators insist that the waters of the inner Delta are perfectly safe to drink right out of the rivers and lagoons and are absolutely bilharzia-free. This may be so — and fast-flowing channels in the central area should be free of the parasite — but the US Centers for Disease Control have recorded cases of tourists coming down with bilharzia after safaris in the Delta.

Moremi Game Reserve

The Moremi is one of Africa's great wildlife reserves, giving protection to some 1,200 square miles of the eastern Okavango Delta and fringing dry-country savanna. It encompasses much of the best game country in Botswana, including the richest parts of the seasonal Delta floodplains. Here, the watermeadows and grasslands of the floodplain meet the mopane forests and acacia savannas of the hinterland. With its mix of wetlands and woodlands, Moremi is a park of exceptional beauty. It is in the Moremi reserve (and in the safari concessions of neighboring Wildlife Management Areas) that most of the game viewing in the Delta takes place.

Because it extends from the permanent swamps of the central Okavango Delta right through the floodplains to the wooded country of the northern Kalahari, the Moremi Game Reserve includes all of the habitats of the Delta ecosystem. The Moremi's size and diversity allow it to hold a great variety of wildlife throughout the year. Floodplain animals, such as lechwe, reedbuck, and tsessebe, have plenty of room to move within the reserve, seeking the choicest grazing conditions. The same is true for impala and waterbuck — animals that thrive where grassland and woodland meet. There is also enough dryland habitat to hold at least some of the more wide-ranging migratory species year-round. Small groups of buffalo, elephant, zebra, or wildebeest can be encountered even during the height of the green rainy season. These migrants do disperse widely in the rains, but come crowding back into the reserve when the Kalahari bush country begins to dry out. From May onward, the animal population grows steadily from month to month, with the reserve fairly bursting with game by the time the Okavango floods arrive in the eastern Moremi in July. Although predator populations vary in accordance with the migrations of the herbivores, the year-round presence of prey of all sizes ensures that the Moremi has plenty of resident carnivores. Sightings of lion, cheetah, hyena, and leopard are always a possibility, and Moremi is a particularly good area for wild dogs.

The Moremi was originally put aside as a wildlife reserve in 1962 at the request of local people. It has recently been extended to absorb the Jao and Xo flats, areas of permanently flooded marshland to the west of Chief's Island that were previously concession areas. Such concessions just about surround Moremi, and game wanders freely between them and the unfenced reserve. Although many of these large tracts are open to trophy hunting, the concessionaires often choose not to hunt in areas immediately adjoining the reserve, preferring to use them to establish lodges and camps that cater to photographic safaris.

In essence, the Moremi Game Reserve is divided into three parts: an eastern section (the most accessible to the public), a western sector centered on Chief's Island, and an area of permanent swamps to the northwest of Chief's Island.

The eastern Moremi is composed of a large block of wooded savanna country that fronts the easternmost reaches of the Okavango floodplains. Bounded to the north by the meandering Khwai River and to the south by a band of reedy marshes on the Mogogelo floodplain, this tract is a wide peninsula or "tongue" of dry land that juts into the Delta. At its tapered western tip, near the Xakanaxa Lagoon, the land meets the perennial swamps of the Okavango. With so much wetland at its periphery, the Moremi Peninsula is rich game country, and serves as a conduit for animals migrating back and forth between the Delta and the vast, dry hinterlands to the east. It is also the only section of the Moremi Game Reserve that visitors can reach by road. As such, it is the busiest part of the reserve.

The vegetation of the eastern Moremi is dominated by mopane forest and scrub, although there is a sprinkling of wooded acacia savanna. The usual mix of riverine forest and floodplain grassland prevails all around the edges of the Moremi Peninsula. Its groves of tall mopane trees are particularly beautiful in May and June, when their butterfly-shaped leaves change to golden fall colors. Even after they have dried and fallen, the mopane leaves remain highly nutritious and are much sought after by all the browsing animals, especially kudu, giraffe, common duiker, and elephant. Visibility can be a problem in mopane, especially in dense, leafy scrub. Game viewing is therefore best at the verges of the mopane woodlands, especially along the narrow strips of floodplain that follow the reserve's boundary rivers. Pools in these shallow, reed-choked streams attract hordes of thirsty animals during the dry season. Big herds of buffalo and elephant typically come down to drink every afternoon, and the streams are superb areas for viewing both roan and sable antelope.

Although lagoons are found throughout the Delta, a cluster of large *lediba* (lagoons) among the permanent swamps of the northeastern Moremi are particularly notable for their size and beauty. They are also renowned for massive breeding colonies of colorful waterbirds. The birds are attracted to islets of *gomoti* or water figs (*Ficus verruculosa*), which form dense thickets in shallow water. These tangled fig-tree islands provide multilevel nesting sites for some two dozen species of ibis, storks, and herons. Smaller birds, such as purple herons and sacred ibis, nest within the protective thickets, while the big yellow-billed and marabou storks raise their broods atop the canopy. Nesting and breeding activities start in July and continue through hatching in November, so the colonies are active throughout the height of the tour season. The colonies on the Gedikwe Lagoon are perhaps the largest and most famous. Xakanaxa is the most accessible of the big lagoons, as its shore touches the western tip of the Moremi's dryland peninsula.

Chief's Island is the central feature of Moremi's western section. Ringed by the grasslands and marshes of the floodplains, the island is a huge enclave of dryland habitat in the heart of the Delta. Like the Moremi Peninsula, its interior is dominated by mopane, with a leavening of grassy acacia savanna thrown in. The fauna of both woodland and floodplain habitats is abundant, and many safari camps have been established to take advantage of the excellent game viewing. With the recent extension of the Moremi to include the Jao concession area, a large chunk of permanent marshes and game-rich floodplain to the west of Chief's Island has been added to the reserve.

Beyond the Moremi reserve's western boundary, big concession areas extend throughout the floodplains of the western Delta and a prominent peninsula of fringing dryland habitat called the Sandveldt Tongue. These concessions are used primarily for hunting, but some parts are used for photographic safaris.

Access and Accommodation

Only the eastern section of the Moremi can be reached by road. It's only a 60-mile drive from Maun to the reserve's South Gate and about an equal distance from North Gate to Savuti in Chobe National Park. But the roads are difficult, sand-filled tracks, so distance is no guide to how long it will take; when conditions are dry, figure on three hours from Maun to South Gate, or five between North Gate and Savuti. Wet or dry, four-wheel-drive is mandatory.

Public campsites are situated at each of the two park gates, with another two inside the reserve. Only the *South Gate* and *North Gate* campsites provide tapped water or toilet and washing facilities, and these are poorly maintained. *Third Bridge* campsite is located at the tip of the Moremi Peninsula. Although without facilities, it is a famous swimming spot and therefore very popular (beware: tourists have been attacked by crocs here). The nearby *Xakanaxa* campsite is on the lagoon, and boat trips can be arranged at neighboring lodges. The campsites are all in excellent game viewing areas. In the busy season, they are often crowded with both private travelers and commercial overland safari groups.

The Moremi area abounds with small private safari camps that generally accommodate between 16 and 24 guests. Most of these camps are reached by light aircraft and offer a high standard of service and accommodation that usually includes en suite bathrooms. Activities depend on whether they are land or water camps, and whether or not they are located inside the Moremi Game Reserve. Those outside Moremi do not usually include park entry fees in their rates (those fees are paid locally), but most offer nighttime game drives in their concession areas.

Many safari camps are located in the eastern Moremi. Three camps are strung out along the Khwai River, just outside the reserve boundary at North Gate: *Khwai River Lodge* (24 beds) and *Tsaro Elephant Lodge* (16 beds) both have thatched cabin accommodation, while *Machaba Camp* (14 beds) is tented. Game viewing in this area is superb. Both Khwai River and Machaba feature night drives; Tsaro doesn't, but offers walking safaris. Just outside South Gate, *San-Ta-Wani Lodge* (16 beds) offers tented accommodation, nighttime game drives, and excursions by canoe or motorboat when water levels permit.

A variety of camps and activities are available around the Xakanaxa Lagoon. *Xakanaxa Camp* is a 20-bed tented facility that offers game drives and boating. *Camp Okuti* (20 beds) has the same activities but accommodation is in rustic reed chalets. *Camp Moremi* (20 beds) is tented, with safaris by vehicle or boat. All these camps are within the park, so none offer night drives.

A group of luxurious water camps is clustered among lovely big lagoons just beyond the eastern Moremi's northern boundary. *Camp Okavango* (22 beds) and *Shinde Island Camp* (14 beds) are tented, while 16-bed *Xugana Island Lodge* has reed chalets. All feature boating, fishing, and birding activities, including excursions to the Gedikwe Lagoon. The tented *Kwara Camp* (10 beds) is in the same vicinity, but is primarily a land camp: it highlights night drives and *mokoro* trips as well as daytime game drives.

Another group of safari camps is found on islands off the southwestern end of Chief's Island. They all feature excursions on the water, with dryland game viewing confined to walking. *Xaxaba Camp* (24 beds) and *Delta Camp* (16 beds) are the most up-market lodges: each accommodates its guests in thatched reed chalets. Xaxaba makes use of powerboats and *mekoros*, while Delta offers only *mekoros* and walking; Xaxaba has a swimming pool. Powerboat, *mokoro*, and walking excursions are offered at the more budget *Gunn's (Ntswi) Camp*, where guests stay in chalets that each take up to four occupants; Gunn's also has a campsite for self-catering visitors. *Oddball's* is the most popular destination for budget campers. This campsite has a restaurant and shower block and rents out *mekoros* (with boatmen-guides) and camping equipment. As an alternative to tenting, guests at Oddball's can stay in a rustic reed chalet or a tree house.

Xigera Camp is in a private concession within the Moremi reserve. The 16-bed camp is located in an isolated area to the west of Chief's Island. The concession has permanent waterways and large islands that hold game year-round. As both a land and water camp, Xigera offers boats and *mekoros*, as well as walks and game drives. It is an excellent place for finding sitatunga.

Mombo Camp is located in exceedingly rich game country just off the north end of Chief's Island. As the only lodge in this remote part of the Moremi reserve, it offers exclusive uncrowded game viewing and is famous for its abundant wildlife. The 20-bed lodge uses luxury safari tents. Mombo's sister camp, *Jedibe Island Camp*, is located just outside the new Moremi boundary, deep in the permanent swamps of the upper Delta. A 16-bed tented camp, Jedibe offers explorations on powerboats (or a houseboat) and *mekoros*, as well as walks on nearby islands.

Duba Plains Camp (10 beds) and *Vumbura Camp* (16 beds) are tented lodges on the northern edge of the Moremi reserve. Both feature game drives (by day or night) on the area's extensive floodplains (which are reputed to host huge herds of buffalo seasonally), as well as walking safaris. Vumbura is also a good site for *mokoro* excursions; *mekoros* can be used at Duba Plains if water levels permit.

Chitabe Camp is located in a concession that juts into the southern boundary of the Moremi reserve, just to the southeast of Chief's Island. Although the Chitabe area has plenty of lagoons and waterways, game drives (including night drives) are the featured activity at this 16-bed tented camp.

A couple of safari camps stand out in the concession areas to the west of the Moremi Game Reserve. *Pom Pom* is a 14-bed tented camp on the remote floodplains between Chief's Island and the Sandveldt Tongue. Primarily a water camp, it also offers game viewing from vehicles. Further west is *Abu's Camp*, which is renowned for its elephant-back safaris. Its adult riding elephants (which include the bull, Abu) were originally orphaned cull-survivors that had been shipped to the US and eventually reexported to Africa. They now carry visitors on game walks through the Delta wilds, accompanied by a half-dozen elephant toddlers that make up a nice little herd. The elephants are piloted by trained African *mahouts*, while guests ride on specially designed saddles, or walk alongside. These five-night safaris are very expensive. Although game viewing can probably be surpassed elsewhere, spending time in such close association with elephants is a wonderful educational and emotional experience, so you may find it worth the money.

Another camp in the southwestern Delta, *Horseback Safari Camp (Macateer's Camp)*, is the base for riding safaris. Riders are led by an experienced guide and use excellent mounts; riders stay at the 8-bed tented camp (where they can also do game drives) but have the option to go further afield and spend an overnight in mobile camps or tree houses. On the same concession, the 14-bed *Xudum Camp* offers walks and game drives, as well as *mekoros* when water levels permit.

Touring the Reserve

If you are flying in, a two-camp visit in the Moremi region will make an excellent plan for a Delta safari. Dividing your stay between land and water camps will ensure a varied and satisfactory visit. The water and land experiences will nicely complement each other and allow you to sample a variety of habitats. There is no need to worry about covering the entire reserve: your guides will concentrate on showing you what is in the area around your camps, which is usually plenty.

Overland safari participants will be confined to the Moremi's eastern sector. Even there, it would be best if you can use two different campsites to fully appreciate what the reserve has to offer. The real problem on an overland safari is to get a proper water experience in the Delta marshes. This can be accomplished by flying from Maun to one of the water camps before setting off for the Moremi, or, at a minimum, by hiring a boat from one of the lodges in the Xakanaxa area. The lodges naturally tend to cater to their guests first, so there is always the risk that neither powerboats nor *mekoros* will be available when you want them. Even assuming that you can't hire a boat, you should have an excellent safari in the eastern sector. Game viewing is generally very good, with all dryland and floodplain habitats well represented. The floodplains around the North and South gate campsites are similar in vegetation and fauna, although local game viewing conditions may be better at one or the other at any particular time. A stay at either the Xakanaxa or Third Bridge campsites is also recommended because a good network of roads will let you explore the tip of the Moremi Peninsula and Mboma Island, its furthermost extension into the Delta wetlands.

Chobe National Park

Chobe National Park is one of the great wildlife sanctuaries of southern Africa. The park itself gives absolute protection to some 4,600 square miles of bush country, but to this must be added thousands of miles of wildlife habitat in surrounding hunting blocks and forest reserves. Drawing game from as far away as the Linyanti Swamps, Nxai Pans National Park, and even from Zimbabwe and Namibia's Caprivi Strip, Chobe is a key stronghold for the wildlife of the entire northeastern Kalahari region. It is a legendary elephant refuge, for a great portion of Botswana's 60,000-plus elephant population lives in the park at least part of the year. The massive herds regularly seen during the dry season along the Chobe River are almost an icon of current safari lore.

Chobe is flat country, where sandy tracks lead off through a featureless landscape almost devoid of hills or prominent landmarks. Although its interior bushlands are not wonderfully scenic, the park is botanically interesting, with a good diversity of plant communities providing natural beauty and niches for a wide variety of animals. The region is underlain by Kalahari sands. Where these are shallow and mixed with clay, mopane forest and scrub thrive. Belts of deeper sand support mixed woodlands of Rhodesian teak (also called Zambezi teak) and other dry-deciduous trees. Elsewhere, the sandveld is dominated by grassy acacia savannas. As in the Moremi, Chobe's wildlife disperses widely in the rainy months, when the many small, clay-bottomed pans that dot the countryside hold water. But as the dry season progresses, these waterholes evaporate and game concentrates near permanent water, especially along the Chobe River on the park's northern boundary.

The park is huge, but there are really only two principal game viewing sectors: the Serondella area fronting the Chobe River and the environs of the Savuti Marsh. The Tshinga/Nogatsaa and Linyanti areas have potential to become major venues for game viewing, but they are not currently much used.

The stretch along the Chobe River is the most beautiful part of the park and a legendary place for animal viewing. Here the woodlands come to an abrupt end, dropping off a 50-foot bluff to the grassy floodplain of the Chobe. The view from the high riverbank is terrific; spread before you is the placid river looping over a grassy floodplain speckled with game and flocks of birds, the expansive reedbeds of the Namibian shore stretching far into the distance. A riverine forest crowds the bluff with beautiful shade trees, providing shelter for vervet monkeys, baboons, and mixed parties of birds. This narrow sliver of riverine forest is also the habitat of the boldly marked Chobe bushbuck. With its elegant pattern of stripes and spots, this antelope is arguably the most beautiful subspecies of bushbuck. Because it is restricted to the riparian forest and mixed woodlands near the river, there has been concern that the Chobe bushbuck may be declining in numbers as elephants take their toll on its dwindling forest habitat. The latest research seems to indicate, however, that the antelope's population is holding its own.

Elephant damage is very apparent in the woodlands that extend back from the riverbank. For a mile or more, the ground is littered with the bleached white skeletons of big trees, and most of those left standing show the scars of stripped bark and missing limbs. This is the toll exacted by the huge concentrations of elephants that come lumbering down to the river every evening during the height of the dry season. It is an unforgettable sight, with elephants in columns of hundreds pulsing out of the torn and dusty woodlands to line up and drink at the river's edge. The wreckage of the woodlands is usually offered as an argument for culling the Chobe herds — a controversial step that has not been taken up to this point. But the riverfront woodlands, although damaged, are far from lifeless. Kudu are common in thickets of combretum and woolly caper bush, while herds of impala and small groups of zebra graze the many grassy openings, and there are plenty of giraffe about. Further back from the river, the woods are in better shape. There is elephant damage here, too, but it is not so apparent: you might not notice it, but experts would note an absence of full-sized trees or seedlings of various species and pronounce the woods overbrowsed. The carnage is only clearly evident close to the river, where all the elephants must make their way daily. And even at the riverbank, the onset of the rainy season turns the Chobe sector into a lush green paradise in which visibility is obscured by luxuriant vegetation.

Before Chobe was proclaimed a park in 1968, the interior woodlands were already suffering from logging as the dominant Rhodesian teak trees were cut for their valuable timber. Resident animals are less plentiful in teak forest, but all types of game pass through on their way from the interior bushlands to the river. Roan and sable antelope are often found resting or feeding in grassy patches in the dappled shade of the teak forest.

Since so much of Chobe is seasonally dry bushland, the riverine flats are an important habitat for certain animals that will be found nowhere else in the park. The most notable is the puku, a grassland antelope that is common in Zambia but not found elsewhere in Botswana. Puku, reedbuck, and lechwe are present in small numbers on the Chobe flats, but tend to keep to the moister areas and are usually seen only at a distance. As the river recedes in the dry season, the edges of the floodplain dry out, with the normal succession of grazing animals taking place. Huge herds of buffalo can then be seen on the grasslands, looking very black against the greens and beiges of the plain. Another conspicuously dark animal often seen on the floodplain is the sable antelope, which comes down in small, fleet-footed herds that are quick to take flight.

Game viewing is excellent in the Chobe River area. The woodlands usually produce good close-up viewing of kudu, impala, vervet monkey, baboon, giraffe, roan antelope, and small game such as banded mongoose. Aside from species like the puku or lechwe that are confined to the river flats, many of the woodland animals can also be seen there as they go to water or wallow. Viewing on the floodplain is exceptional because the country is so wide open. Extensive grasslands on the floodplain are the places to look for cheetah. Certain pools are favored by hippos, and the environs of pools are always the place to stay alert for the Cape clawless otter or the Nile monitor, Africa's huge aquatic lizard. The floodplains are always extraordinarily rich in birdlife. Flocks of pelicans, yellow-billed storks, open-billed storks, and white-faced ducks are often present, sometimes mixed in huge congregations with other waterbirds and waders.

Lions and other predators are ever-present in the Serondella area, but hiding places abound in bushy thickets and high grass, and there are many pools and gullies along the river front from which they can drink. For many years, the big cats were more often heard than seen along the Chobe River, but sightings have noticeably improved lately, as they have become less shy. Even so, the Savuti sector is more reliable for lion sightings because it has several resident prides and the number of waterholes there is very limited.

The Savuti area has a very distinctive character. Deep within the sandy western interior of the park, the Savuti Marsh lies midway between the floodplains of the Chobe River and the easternmost wetlands of the Moremi Game Reserve. Savuti is in the Mababe Depression, an exceptionally flat geologic region that was formerly filled by an arm of the old Lake Makgadikgadi. The western edge of the Mababe Depression is marked by the long Magwikwe Sand Ridge (which runs from the Goha Hills southward to within a few miles of the Moremi Game Reserve's Khwai River). The sand ridge is composed of fossilized dunes that once marked the shore of the giant lake. Today, the Mababe Depression is a vast bowl of arid grassland spiked with the twigs of woody combretum bush and scrub mopane.

The Savuti Channel is a most unusual waterway. It starts at the Zibalianja Lagoon in the elbow of the Linyanti Swamps, then meanders eastward over 40 miles of Kalahari sand country to penetrate the Magwikwe Sand Ridge near the rocky outcrops of the Gubatsaa Hills and enter the Savuti Marsh. When it is flowing, the channel's waters are a magnet to game animals, as are the rich grasslands of the Savuti Marsh which it feeds. The odd thing about the Savuti Channel is not that it does not always flow, but that the river's appearance or disappearance has nothing to do with the normal cycle of drought and flood to which both the Okavango and Linyanti river systems are prone. This very flat country is still geologically active, and the slightest underground movements turn the Savuti Channel on and off at irregular intervals. When the Savuti is flowing, the channel's banks become choked with every sort of animal. Hippos and crocodiles then thrive in its water, while dry-season concentrations of elephant and buffalo rival anything to be found in Africa. The Savuti Marsh receives the channel's waters, which keep its grasslands refreshed and verdant long into the dry season, thus allowing it to hold herds of thousands of zebra, tsessebe, and other grazing animals.

In the 1970s, Savuti was one of the most prolific wildlife paradises on the continent. Then, in 1982, the channel abruptly stopped flowing and began to dry out. The disappearance of the river caused incredible suffering to the animals that depended on it. Migrants such as zebra and buffalo quickly moved away to other sources of water, but some animals hung on to their habitual territories in the vain expectation that the river would return. As the water in the channel evaporated, hippos, crocodiles, and catfish crowded into the last pools, which became little more than soupy mud holes fouled with the dung of hippos and elephants. Eventually, the last of the hippos and crocs either took their chances on the thirsty, 40-mile desert trek to the Linyanti Swamps, or perished. A trio of crocodiles opted to outlast the drought by going to ground in caves in the nearby Gubatsaa Hills — a fatal choice, as it turned out. In the bed of the channel, bull elephants dug deep into the sand, excavating at seeps where water lay beneath the ground. The seeps became deep craters into which each thirsty elephant would descend to ponderously sip trunkfulls of precious water.

Terrible drought persisted throughout the 1980s. But even with the arrival of ample rains, still the Savuti does not flow. In the dry season, elephant matriarchs now take their families to the wetlands of the Chobe-Linyanti or to the Delta, but bulls continue to hang around Savuti, where park authorities have sunk a borehole to pump water to the surface. That waterhole has become a famous elephant-watching point. Every afternoon, a parade of bull elephants marches to the pan to drink in its shallow pool, monopolizing it almost to the exclusion of the thirsty impala and giraffe that must wait for an opportune moment to slip in a drink. The viewing is close-up, almost intimate, and many a great elephant photo has been taken there.

Although the huge, dry-season concentrations have vanished with the river, Savuti is still an excellent game viewing area. In the rainy season, thousands of zebras migrate into the Savuti Marsh, along with herds of wildebeest and buffalo. As the dry season commences, most of these animals move toward the wetlands of the Delta or Linyanti, but tsessebe move into the marsh. They are joined by thousands of impala and innumerable sounders of warthogs, ensuring a plentiful food supply to the resident predators. Several large clans of spotted hyena live on the marsh, as do territorial prides of lions. In the woodlands that surround the marsh, giraffe browse on giant camel-thorn acacias, while kudu are common in denser thickets. The marsh and its fringes are also a good place to spot interesting small animals and birds. Prominent among these is the yellow mongoose (*Cynictis penicillata*). Although usually seen reconnoitering alone, up to 20 of these little mongooses can be found living together in burrows excavated in the sand. Bat-eared foxes and black-backed jackals also forage on the marsh. Kori bustards, secretary birds, and ostriches are conspicuous on the open grassland, while the smaller red-crested korhaan is often at its fringes. Male korhaans advertise themselves with a strange series of clicks and whistles and perform a spectacular breeding display that is hard to miss: the cock flies straight up, then suddenly drops back to the ground as if shot out of the air. In February and March, great numbers of beautiful carmine bee-eaters move into the Savuti area. Groups of them can then be seen sitting on the backs of kori bustards: they use the big birds as mobile perches from which to swoop down and catch any insects disturbed as the bustards stalk through high grass.

A forest of dead camel-thorn acacias forms a ghostly landscape around the edges of the Savuti Marsh. The tall snags are the skeletons of trees drowned at a time when the Savuti Channel flowed and turned the marsh into more of a wetland. Camel-thorn snags also stand prominently in the bed of the Savuti Channel. These stately skeletal trees are testimony to the instability of the channel: it takes decades for camel thorns to grow to full size, and they cannot tolerate flooded ground. If the channel remains dry, camel thorns will once again invade its sandy bed and recolonize the marsh, only to be drowned when the river once again reappears.

The rocky nubs of the Gubatsaa Hills rise up close to the Savuti Channel, just a few miles from the point where the riverbed enters the marsh. A tiny gallery of Bushman paintings is found on the solitary Small Quango Hill that overlooks the channel. Near the excellent San portraits of eland, sable, and elephant, some modern "artist" has seen fit to add an engraving of an ostrich. But that has not spoiled the magic of the site. From the flank of the hill, you look down over the Savuti Channel and the wide, game-filled country beyond, and can well imagine what an ideal spot this was for a band of hunters. Several more Bushmen paintings are found on a couple of rock faces a little bit to the north of the main gallery.

The remote Nogatsaa area is much less visited than the Chobe River or Savuti sectors. In this wooded bush country, some 40 miles south of the Chobe River, game gathers around various pans that hold water during the early part of the dry season. Water is supposed to be pumped to the surface at both the Nogatsaa and Tshinga pans, and these are then good places to see game, particularly roan and sable antelope. Pumping has been very intermittent, however, and the Nogatsaa waterhole was actually abandoned several years ago. Park authorities plan to install new pumps at both locations (and may well repair the old Ngwezumba dam, which was destroyed by a flash flood and never rebuilt). The Nogatsaa area was once the place to find Chobe's white rhinos, but the last of these have been captured and moved to a fenced sanctuary for their own protection. Oribi may be seen on black-cotton grasslands near Nogatsaa.

A narrow sliver of parkland extends right up to the Linyanti Swamps on Chobe's northwestern boundary, but very few visitors go there as it is a long journey and animal viewing is better elsewhere. The Linyanti area (most of which is outside the park) is actually excellent game country, although it has suffered from many years of overhunting: its safari concessions were poorly managed, and citizen hunters seriously overexploited its buffalo, zebra, and antelope, thus depleting Chobe park's populations of those migratory species. The surviving animals around Linyanti therefore became very wary and difficult to observe or photograph. Recent reforms aimed at getting citizen hunting under control should result in a reversal of the downward trend in the Linyanti area concession. In the meantime, new conservation-minded operators have taken over the leases in the Linyanti safari areas. They have already revitalized wildlife conservation efforts in the region and have established a number of new and exclusive private camps for photographic safaris. Linyanti is set to become a major game viewing area.

Access and Accommodation

Because of its proximity to the major regional gateway at Victoria Falls, Zimbabwe, the Chobe River sector is the most crowded game viewing area in Botswana. Only 50 miles of good road separate Victoria Falls from the park, but the journey takes a couple of hours because of formalities at the Kazungula border posts. You might also be delayed by elephants on the way! Once in Botswana, it's just a stone's throw to the village of Kasane and the park gate. Kasane also has a new international airport, so there are a limited but growing number of flights coming in directly from Gaborone, Maun, and abroad.

A number of lodges have been built to absorb all the guests. *Chobe Game Lodge* is the only one within the park. This prestigious 47-room luxury hotel overlooks the river flats and is in the middle of a prime game viewing area. Equally comfortable and also on the river, but just outside the park, is the new 220-bed *Cresta Mowana Lodge*. This big hotel complex offers horseback riding and mountain biking in addition to the normal game drives and river cruises. *Chobe Chilwero* is a much more exclusive camp that accommodates a maximum of 16 guests in nice thatched chalets. Located high on a hill above Kasane with magnificent vistas over the Chobe floodplain, it has the best atmosphere of any lodge in the area. *Chobe Safari Lodge*, on the riverfront in the middle of Kasane village, and *Kubu Lodge* (a few miles down river toward the Kazungula border post) offer much cheaper accommodations. Chobe Safari Lodge has some air-conditioned rooms with private baths; its rondavels have neither. Kubu has chalets as well as a campsite. All these lodges offer game drives into the park, as well as boat trips on the river.

For many years, the campsites in the Chobe River sector of the park were all located at Serondella, which is close to Chobe Game Lodge and Kasane. The sites along the river were beautiful but they had too little shade (thanks to elephants thinning the riverine woods) and were crammed in close together. They were also notorious for camp-raiding baboons and monkeys. To alleviate crowding on game tracks near Kasane, the Chobe sector campsites are being moved further west. Safari operators will be able to use private campsites along the river (which are much nicer than those allotted to them at Serondella), while the public campsite will be closer to the Ngoma Gate that marks the western boundary of the Chobe River sector.

There are two permanent safari camps and a public campsite at Savuti. All are located along the now-dry bed of the Savuti Channel. *Lloyd's Camp* features a hide at its own waterhole, which is very active at night. The rustic 14-bed tented camp is owned by Lloyd Wilmot, who is famous for taking selected clients very close to animals on foot. *Savuti South* is a luxurious 16-bed tented camp. Situated near the game scout camp, the public *Savuti Campsite* is overused and its neglected sanitary facilities are in very poor shape — a situation made worse by the local elephants' predilection for tearing up the plumbing to get water. It's not the most comfortable or private site, but this is compensated for by the frequent excitement of game in camp. Animals wander freely through the campsite, so extreme care must be taken when walking around camp at night.

Public campsites are also situated at *Nogatsaa* and *Tshinga*. The Nogatsaa site once had showers and toilets and featured a hide at a nearby waterhole, but the entire complex is now broken down and abandoned. The Tshinga site has no facilities; it has good game viewing and makes an interesting wilderness camp (albeit without shade) when the pump for its waterhole is working. Like the Savuti Campsite, these sites are supposed to be completely rebuilt in the future. Another designated campsite (without facilities) within the park is found near the Linyanti River.

A number of excellent safari camps are located in the Linyanti area to the west of Chobe park. Several small tented camps are found within the Selinda Reserve, a 527-square-mile private concession along the Selinda Spillway, the impermanent watercourse that connects the Okavango Delta with the Linyanti Swamps (it carries overflow water all the way to the Linyanti only during big flood years). The 12-bed *Selinda Camp* is situated on the eastern end of the spillway, while the nearby *Zibalianja Camp* accommodates six guests. Both camps offer boat cruises on the Zibalianja Lagoon, as well as day and night game drives and walking safaris. On the west end of the reserve, *Motswiri Camp* (6 beds) is set on the Selinda Spillway. It offers the same activities, except that it has canoeing (water levels permitting) instead of boating. Multiday walking and canoeing safaris using mobile camps are also done on the Selinda Reserve, as are special "monitoring safaris." These unusual safaris take place during the full moon, when guests can participate in a 24-hour game count.

Three more tented camps are found on a 488-square-mile private concession called the Linyanti Reserve which encompasses the country between the upper Savuti Channel and the Linyanti River. The luxurious *Kings Pool Camp* (20 beds) overlooks the Kings Pool Lagoon, an oxbow lake cut off from the nearby Linyanti River. The camp has a swimming pool, as well as game observation platforms and a double-decker boat used for cruising on the Linyanti. Other activities offered include day and night game drives and walks. The same activities (minus boat cruises) take place at the smaller *Savuti Camp* (8 beds), which is set on the banks of the Savuti Channel. Although the channel is not flowing these days, a pumped waterhole ensures good game viewing right in camp. Another tented camp, *DumaTau*, is near the source of the Savuti Channel. The camp (which has 16 beds and a swimming pool) is sited on a lagoon at the edge of the Linyanti Swamps. The waterways are explored by boat, while game is observed from open vehicles (by day and night), from hides, and on foot.

James Camp is located on the Kwando River. This tented camp offers boat explorations in the Linyanti Swamps, as well as game drives, night drives, and walks.

Touring the Park

During the rainy months (November through March), Chobe's bush-lands are very green and game is widely dispersed. Animals can then be encountered anywhere in the park, although often in small groups. The Chobe River area is still a good bet for viewing a variety of animals and birds: resident specialties like Chobe bushbuck will be around, but you cannot expect to see the spectacle of huge elephant herds at the river. Both the Serondella and Savuti areas have the advantage of open grass-lands in their vicinities, so there are always animals to be seen. Savuti ac-tually offers excellent game viewing in the first months of the year, when the big zebra herds pulse through. At both locales, general game viewing gets easier as the dry season progresses and animals are drawn to either the Chobe River or Savuti's waterhole. The Nogatsaa-Tshinga area is at its best from June to August, as long as the larger pans in the woodlands still hold water; game viewing is excellent right through September and October if the pumps are working at the man-made waterholes. The main attraction of this area, however, is that it there are so few visitors.

Cruises on the Chobe River are very popular and make a nice break from game drives. Boats of all sizes are available for charter at the vari-ous Chobe area lodges, or you can book onto their scheduled cruises. Although these have the potential to degenerate into booze cruises (something which commonly occurs on the evening "sundowner cruises"), game viewing from a boat can be exceptional here: certainly the unobstructed frontal view of the arrival and lineup of elephant herds on the riverbank is tremendously impressive. You may also get your best sightings of Chobe bushbuck: these animals often hug the forested slope of the riverbank, where they are not visible from vehicles on the game tracks above. You'll also get a close-up look at the floodplains on the Namibian side of the river. Aside from the odd reedbuck, you are more likely to see herds of cattle than game over there, for these plains are oc-cupied by humans. The fishermen who work and bathe along the river understandably do not like to be gawked at or, especially, photographed, but they respond positively to a friendly wave.

Because of the ease of access and accommodation, the Chobe River sector is the most congested game viewing spot in Botswana. The Savuti sector is much less crowded, although its campsite may overflow and every vehicle in the area will turn up in the late afternoon for sunset at the waterhole. Here, bull elephants slap mud on their flanks and nurse their drinks, while flocks of doves and guinea fowl flutter at the edge of the pool and herds of impala wait patiently for a turn at the water. Often enough, Savuti's resident lions also turn up. The show is so good, you can't begrudge sharing it with a few other vehicles.

Kalahari Ecology

To the south of the Okavango Delta are the vast sandy bushlands that are commonly called the Kalahari desert. The heart of the Kalahari is a vast, flat savanna of sun-bleached grassland sprinkled with acacia trees and bush. The dry, sandy beds of "fossil rivers" indicate that great volumes of water once flowed there. But today, an absence of year-round surface water is characteristic of the entire region. The deep sands that underlie the Kalahari quickly suck up any rain that falls. Small, clay-bottomed pans pepper the Kalahari bushlands. These do hold water after summer storms, but dry up quickly with the arrival of the long rainless season. For most of the year, the Kalahari remains a place of relentless thirst.

A unique community of flora and fauna, quite different from that of the wetter African savannas, inhabits the arid sandveld of the central and southern Kalahari. As in other desert regions of the world, plants and animals have made fascinating adaptations to an environment in which surface water is rarely available.

Three basic habitats predominate in the Kalahari ecosystem: flat, sandy tracts of grassland and thorny bush, "fossilized" sand dunes, and depressions where water collects (such as pans or the beds of fossil rivers). Because of the relative flatness of the countryside, the best way to appreciate the mosaic of Kalahari landforms and habitats is to see it from the air.

Vast stretches of grassy bushland dominate the sandy flats of the Kalahari plateau. Grasses spring up quickly on this sandveld after heavy rain. For a brief time, the desert is carpeted with green and brightened with flowers. Later, the tall annual grasses wither under the dry winter sun or are killed by frost, but remain standing in sun-bleached clumps among the sand. Even dry, the grass has some nutrient value, and an amazing amount of seed is left lying in the sand, ready to sprout with the next season's rains. Various acacias, growing as full-sized, umbrella-shaped trees or in stubby thickets mixed with other thorny shrubs, dot the grasslands.

In several parts of the Kalahari, prevailing winds have created huge tracts of parallel sand dunes. Over time, the sands of these dunefields have been held in place by vegetation and are now stationary (geologists call them "fossilized" dunes). Water usually lies deep beneath the fossilized dunes, which are crowned with woodlands composed of such trees as leadwood, silver terminalia, and the lovely camel-thorn acacia. The trees push their roots deep into the sand to get at the moisture below.

Pans, large and small, are scattered throughout the Kalahari. Each windswept pan typically has a wooded dune on its leeward side, where windblown sand from its surface has collected and stabilized. The banks of the Kalahari's fossil rivers are also lined with dune woodlands. Here, graceful camel-thorn trees conspicuously mark the winding courses of the shallow valleys. The beds of the extinct rivers are filled with sand and clay, but water often flows underground and, as on the pans, shallow pools may appear briefly on the surface after a heavy rain. Also like the pans, the fertile valley bottoms support short, sweet grasses that grow in profusion during the wet season. These are highly nutritious while green, but quickly disappear once the ground dries up. Afterward, the pans and river bottoms attract animals only to salt licks, where they can eat mineral-rich soil.

The large mammals of the Kalahari have the opposite migration pattern of those in the bushlands to the north. Instead of dispersing during the rains and concentrating near water in the dry season, they collect in large groups during the wet months, the only time of year that surface water is available and there is ample grazing to sustain big herds. Thunderstorms, which are visible from great distances, can cause springbok, gemsbok, red hartebeest, and eland to assemble within days, sometimes by the thousands. Game concentrates and remains in the vicinity of pans and fossil river valleys as long as water and sweet grass remain. There are daily rhythms of game movement, too. Springbok and gemsbok spend the heat of the day in the shade of neighboring dune woodlands, then move onto the open pans or valleys to feed during the cool of the evening and night.

With the arrival of cool weather at the onset of the dry season, the last of the water and short grasses disappear and the game starts to disperse into the surrounding bush. All the desert antelopes can survive without drinking water, but they must break into small groups and wander very widely to find sustenance during the lean, dry months. Flexible feeding strategies are necessary. Eland switch from eating grass to a diet of leafy browse picked from shrubs and trees. The springbok, gemsbok, and hartebeest eat the dry desert grasses, and browse as well. Evergreen bushes and trees, such as the highly nutritious shepherd's tree (*Boscia albitrunca*), become important sources of food. By feeding at night, the herbivores take in extra moisture from dew along with the water content of the plants they eat. The gemsbok and the hartebeest are particularly adept at finding and digging up moisture-rich roots from beneath the sand. Notable among these are the tubers of morama beans and grapple plants. Other vegetable reservoirs are found above ground. Most prized of all are water-filled tsama melons. These and succulent wild cucumbers are key sources of water to the animals of the arid thirstlands.

The predators of the Kalahari follow the same seasonal pattern of movement as their prey. During the wet season, they can set up territories near pans or sections of the fossil river valleys where there is an abundance of game. Prides of lion can then hunt gemsbok and other large antelope, while cheetah rely primarily on springbok. In the dry season, Kalahari lion prides — which are never large — are often forced to disband completely, with members wandering in pairs or even on their own. The big cats then find themselves hunting whatever they can catch: they are just as likely to take small animals such as steenbok, porcupines, or bat-eared foxes as to dine on the large antelope that are their favored prey. Cheetah, and especially leopard, have an advantage in pursuing small animals, but they, too, must work harder to support themselves during the dry season. Throughout the rainless months, the desert predators get all the liquid they need from the animals they eat, although brown hyenas will also readily gorge on tsama melons or ostrich eggs.

The brown hyena (*Hyaena brunnea*) is an interesting carnivore that is a specialty of the Kalahari and neighboring dry regions of southern Africa. This small, shaggy hyena is a consummate forager: it scavenges carcasses and occasionally kills mammals, but a large part of its diet consists of insects, fruits, and vegetables. Brown hyenas forage alone, and for a long time it was believed that they led solitary lives. It turns out that they are highly social animals, living in structured clans much like their better-known relative, the spotted hyena. In the harsh Kalahari environment, the brown hyena has actually taken community living to its ultimate: cubs of various ages are raised in a communal nursery den in which they are fed by all clan members. If a nursing mother falls victim to an accident or a lion, her orphaned cubs still have a good chance of survival. Brown hyenas are highly nocturnal, but they may be seen during the day resting under shady trees.

Prodigious quantities of grass and sand assure a wealth of food and shelter for a great variety of small animals. Harvester termites are incredibly abundant in the Kalahari grasslands. They do not raise mounds, but the holes that lead into their underground nests are everywhere. These insects play a key role in Kalahari ecology: they consume vast amounts of grass and are in turn an essential part of the food pyramid. They are a source of liquid as well as nutrients for a host of animals ranging from predatory insects to lizards and birds and on to a variety of mammals. Foraging for termites in the Kalahari sand, the aardvark excavates good-sized holes throughout the bush. These holes are then used as burrows by any number of other species. Aardwolves also specialize in eating termites, and the insects form an important part of the diet of bat-eared foxes.

The long Kalahari grasses are annual plants that produce a huge volume of seed. Many species of rodents and birds, such as gerbils and sandgrouse, depend on grass seed. These abundant seed-eaters are then consumed by predators higher up the food chain. The small predators of the Kalahari include the black-backed jackal, Cape fox, and black-footed cat. The black-footed cat (also called the small-spotted cat, or *Felis nigripes*) is a tiny but fierce hunter that is a terror to rats, lizards, birds, and large insects alike. Like the Cape fox, it is nocturnal, but is much more rarely seen. The Cape fox (*Vulpes chama*) is a solitary hunter that readily eats wild fruits as well as every sort of small animal. It sometimes becomes tame enough to enter safari camps to scavenge around. Black-backed jackals forage in pairs or small family parties. Their cries are often heard at night.

One of the most endearing animals of the Kalahari is the suricate or meerkat (*Suricata suricata*). These highly social little mongooses live in communal nests burrowed in the sand. While the group is out foraging for insects and scorpions, one always keeps sentry duty, standing or sitting upright while it scans the sky for birds of prey. Suricates often share their burrows with ground squirrels, and sometimes with yellow mongooses as well, forming integrated animal apartment houses.

The ultimate Kalahari apartment dweller is the social weaver. These common seed-and-termite-eating birds construct huge nests of woven straw that can measure 30 feet across. Such an edifice will house hundreds of weavers, each couple with its own nesting hole (they also often harbor a pair of pygmy falcons, the smallest of Africa's birds of prey). The giant nests are built on large trees, such as the camel thorn. On occasion, the weight of the nest will break a supporting limb, bringing the whole complex crashing to the ground.

Many other fascinating animals are tiny inhabitants of the Kalahari's ubiquitous sand. There are legless skinks that swim under the sand, and lizards that swiftly skim over its surface. The weird burrowing frog is only active after rain; it may spend several years in estivation beneath the sand awaiting the next storm. Although many of these small animals may not be seen or identified, you are likely to hear one: the territorial call of the barking gecko is a typical sound of the summer night.

The Kalahari is filled with life, but its secrets are not easily revealed. For those interested only in easy viewing of the large animals, it's better to go elsewhere. But if you can take the heat, by all means visit the Kalahari kitchen!

Touring the Kalahari

Although Botswana is closely identified with the Kalahari, few overseas visitors actually venture into "the desert." Compared to the territory to the north, game viewing is tough and conditions for travel are uncomfortable. But the Kalahari has its own attractions. Chief among them are the Makgadikgadi Pans Game Reserve and the neighboring salt flats of the Makgadikgadi Pans, the Nxai Pan National Park, the Central Kalahari Game Reserve, and the Tsodilo Hills. Each of these places has its own special ecological, geographical, or cultural interest.

Makgadikgadi Pans Game Reserve and Nxai Pan National Park

The salt-encrusted lakebeds of the massive Ntwetwe and Sua pans are collectively known as the Makgadikgadi Pans. Together, these dry lakes form the largest salt flats in the world — over 4,000 square miles in extent. After heavy rains (usually in January and February), large parts of the pans may be covered with vast sheets of inches-deep water. But most of the time, they are bone dry, a wasteland of salt-laden clay, cracked and glistening under the African sun. These ephemeral lakes are all that remain of the huge inland sea — the ancient Lake Makgadikgadi — that once inundated so much of northern Botswana. In modern times, only two seasonal streams fed the pans: the Boteti and the Nata rivers. In exceptional years, the Boteti conveyed some of the overflow of the Okavango as far as Ntwetwe Pan, but those waters are now captured by the Mopipi Dam for use by the nearby Orapa diamond mine. In the northeast, the Nata River still carries a rainy-season spate from Zimbabwe's Matabeleland into Sua Pan.

When the rains are good, some arms of the pans are transformed into shallow lakes that attract masses of flamingos and other wading birds. This occurs most reliably in the Nata Delta, where the river enters the north end of Sua Pan. The flamingos come to feed on the algae and tiny brine shrimp that proliferate in the soda-saturated waters. In good years, the water lasts long enough for the flamingos to breed and raise their young. Their principal breeding grounds are protected within the new Nata Sanctuary, which was created after concern was raised by the development of soda ash mining on nearby Sua Spit. When the Nata floods come down, they flush fish into the pools, and these in turn attract huge flocks of pelicans and other fish-eating birds, adding additional color to the spectacle of the flamingos.

Except for the migrant birds, the Makgadikgadi Pans themselves are not hospitable to wildlife, for nothing grows on their salty surfaces. But grasslands thrive on their fringes, and key wildlife habitat in the region has been protected in the Makgadikgadi Pans Game Reserve and Nxai Pan National Park. Wildlife here includes good herds of zebra and wildebeest, as well as the less water-dependent but equally mobile species that are typical denizens of the Kalahari: gemsbok, eland, red hartebeest, and springbok. The full range of Kalahari predators is also represented. All these animals must necessarily move around a lot in search of food and water. Veterinary cordon fences have cut off the old migration routes to the central Kalahari and the Okavango Delta, but game moves freely between the two sanctuaries and the wild bushlands further north. In the shrinking world of the Kalahari, these unfenced refuges are crucial to the survival of a significant population of game.

The Makgadikgadi Game Reserve is 1,618 square miles in area. It includes a small slice of Ntwetwe Pan, then stretches westward across flat plains to the Boteti River. Most of the reserve is a vast open grassland, with acacia savanna becoming more dominant toward the Boteti and a belt of *Hyphaene* palms conspicuous in the north. In the dry season, thousands of zebra and wildebeest concentrate near the Boteti, where pools persist in the intermittent river. With the rains, they move northward to Nxai Pan and beyond. The desert antelope wander widely during the dry season, when individuals or groups can pop up anywhere. During the rains, the antelope collect in larger herds wherever feeding conditions are most favorable, which is often at Nxai Pan.

The northern boundary of Makgadikgadi reserve coincides with the main highway connecting Maun with Francistown. Game migrates across that highway through a 15-mile-wide corridor of open rangeland that formerly separated the Makgadikgadi reserve from Nxai Pan National Park. That corridor has now been incorporated into the park, officially joining the two game sanctuaries and giving protection to the famous Baines's Baobabs at Kudiakam Pan. This grove (also known as the Seven Sisters) was immortalized in the 1860s when it was painted by explorer-artist Thomas Baines.

Vegetation in the 1,000-square-mile Nxai Pan National Park is dominated by acacia woodlands and thickets, with grasslands covering the fossil lakebeds of its pans. Huge baobab trees are also a conspicuous feature of the landscape. In addition to the migrating animals that wander in from the Makgadikgadi plains, woodlands game such as impala and kudu are present, and elephants come in from the north during the rainy season. Giraffe are abundant in the park, and are often seen feeding in groves of acacias on the many "tree islands" that dot the grassy expanses of the Nxai and Kgama-Kgama pans. It's also a great area for ostrich.

Access and Accommodation

The Makgadikgadi Pans are located midway between Maun and Francistown, which are connected by one of Botswana's main roads. The eastern Sua Pan is most easily reached from the town of Nata. The turn-offs into Makgadikgadi Pans Game Reserve and Nxai Pan National Park are 85 miles from Maun. The drive to this spot was formerly a notoriously dusty journey, but the Maun-Nata road is now paved. Charter planes fly into the strip at Tsoi in the Makgadikgadi reserve.

Camping is the only option if you want to be inside the game parks. There are two campsites in the Makgadikgadi reserve: *Njuca Hills* campsite is located in the Njuca Hills in the eastern part of the reserve (it has no water); *Xhumaga* campsite is near the game scout camp of the same name on the reserve's western boundary. The country to the west of the reserve is a hunting concession area in which licensed safari companies are allowed to set up private camps along the Boteti River. There are two small public campsites with basic facilities in *Nxai Pan*. Although it used to be a popular site, camping is no longer allowed at Baines's Baobabs. Low-cost accommodation can be found at *Gweta Rest Camp* in Gweta village, which is on the main road, about 40 miles east of the turn-offs to the parks' entrance gates.

Jack's Camp is a very unusual tented safari camp. Located on a private concession that adjoins the eastern boundary of the Makgadikgadi reserve, the camp is set near the edge of the seemingly limitless salt pans. Although the wet season is better for seeing the region's migratory herds and masses of waterbirds, game viewing activities are centered year-round on finding the resident creatures of the desert. Night drives and walks in the company of Bushmen trackers are regular features. During the dry months, the pans are explored aboard four-wheel-drive "quad bikes," odd little vehicles that can get to places that ordinary vehicles cannot (guests can have the fun of driving the quads themselves).

Nata Lodge is a good base from which to visit the flamingo breeding grounds in the Nata Sanctuary on Sua Pan. You can stay in chalets or safari tents, or camp; the lodge organizes safaris to the sanctuary and remote parts of Sua Pan. The isolated Kubu Island on southern Sua Pan is a favorite wilderness campsite.

Touring the Makgadikgadi Region

Aside from travelers coming up by road from South Africa, relatively few overseas tourists visit the Makgadikgadi area. Getting there requires a lot of extra travel, which is tiresome and time consuming by land or expensive by air charter. General game viewing is also far less dependable than in the parks to the north, especially during the dry season. Although some estimates put the number of zebra and wildebeest in the Makgadikgadi–Nxai Pan area as high as 100,000, their population fluctuates markedly and the animals are highly mobile, so the chances of seeing them in huge masses are pretty slim. During the dry months, the neighborhood of the Boteti River is the most likely place to catch big herds, but even then, it's a matter of luck. The Makgadikgadi–Nxai Pan region is, however, the most accessible part of Botswana in which to see the wildlife of the Kalahari.

Although the weather can be wet and brutally hot, the best overall time to visit the Makgadikgadi region is between December and early May. In the period after the onset of the rains (whenever they actually do start to fall in this erratic area), the herds of zebra and wildebeest huddled along the Boteti spread out over the open grasslands of the Makgadikgadi reserve and Nxai Pan. Game viewing then reaches its peak at Nxai Pan. In addition to the knots of migrants filtering through from the Makgadikgadi plains, the typical species of the Kalahari antelope are at their most visible because an abundance of food draws springbok, gemsbok, red hartebeest, and eland to collect into herds. Game also arrives from the north, with zebra and elephants coming in from their exhausted dry-season ranges to take advantage of plentiful fresh greenery while the numerous small depressions on the pans hold water.

The landscapes around the great Makgadikgadi Pans are also at their loveliest at this time of year, when the green of the wide grasslands sweeps right down to the azure pools and white flats of the salt pans. If conditions are right, whole bays are tinged pink by masses of flamingos mirrored in their shallow waters. The skies, too, are at their most dramatic. A placid blue vault flecked with cottony clouds can swiftly turn to threatening black as towering cumulus thunderheads bump together to herald a storm, with jagged lightning bolts lashing the ground.

The weather is obviously the wild card: summer storms bring beauty and life, but they also bring some measure of discomfort. In the Kalahari, summer temperatures can soar above 100° F, and several inches of rain can fall in a single shower. Heat stress is inevitable, and no tent is guaranteed not to leak in a torrential deluge. To get the best of the Kalahari, you'll have to pay the price, so consider your level of tolerance for discomfort before you make your plans. The hottest and wettest months are December through February, with rainfall slackening off in March and April. Temperatures moderate considerably in May, but by then game may already be dispersing more widely.

Wet weather makes driving conditions bad. Beneath the seemingly hard-packed surface of the pans lurks gooey mud that can mire even the best four-wheel-drive vehicles. Experienced drivers stick to the edges of the pans or follow in the tracks of cars that have recently passed. If you are exploring without a guide, you must take care not to become lost among the many grassy islands and bays on the edge of the pans: use a GPS (Global Positioning System) or compakjss and map, and keep track of your route and any prominent landmarks.

Central Kalahari Game Reserve

The 20,000-square-mile Central Kalahari Game Reserve is one of the largest protected wildlife areas in Africa. Although its size makes it beckon beguilingly on the map, this is not a place for anyone but the most ardent wilderness enthusiast. Game densities are very low throughout its flat, sandy expanses of acacia bush and grassland, except during the summer rainy season when animals concentrate along its fossil rivers. These shallow valleys once carried vast quantities of water to Lake Makgadikgadi, but like that lake, the rivers have vanished. Short grass now flourishes in their sandy beds in the wake of rain, attracting herds of springbok and gemsbok, while the surrounding tree-crowned dune country harbors red hartebeest and eland. Acacia groves grow on "tree islands" in the riverbeds, and these provide shade and solitude for lion, cheetah, and brown hyena. Deception Valley is the best known of the fossil rivers, for it was there that Mark and Delia Owens camped when they did the research that led to their best-selling book, *Cry of the Kalahari.*

The Central Kalahari was originally declared a reserve in 1961 partly to ensure that the San would have game to hunt and land on which to pursue their traditional way of life. Following the international uproar caused by the Owenses' book, the government of Botswana decided to remove the 1,000 Bushmen living at the Xade settlement near the reserve's western boundary. Although these people graze cattle and plant small plots in the vicinity of the Xade borehole, conservationists do not believe that their hunting activities have had any serious effect on the wildlife population. They attribute the decline of game in the Central Kalahari to fencing and cattle ranching outside the reserve. Nonetheless, the government is committed to resettling the Xade community elsewhere. It remains to be seen if they will then bar the San Bushmen from hunting within the reserve.

The Wildlife Department also plans to establish additional boreholes to encourage a resurgence in the number of wildebeest and hartebeest, two species that have declined markedly in the Central Kalahari in the last few decades.

Access and Accommodation

For many years, access to the reserve was strictly limited, but increasing numbers of safari operators, and even individuals, now receive permits to visit. No accommodation exists, although there are a couple of primitive designated campsites. Most visitors fly or drive to Deception Valley. Road access to Deception is via the village of Rakops, on the Boteti River to the southwest of the Makgadikgadi Pans.

Touring the Reserve

The window of time for visiting is pretty much limited to between February and early May, when temperatures are reasonable and game is likely to be plentiful around the fossil river valleys.

It has to be emphasized that this is an extremely fragile environment that visitors must treat with kid gloves. Vehicle tracks are already scarring the riverbed of Deception Valley, and many of the tree islands used as campsites have been trashed. It's important for campers to be very sparing of firewood, to burn all toilet paper, and to remove all refuse from the reserve.

It's even more important for visitors to be sensitive to the needs of the wildlife. The animals here already live in a very harsh natural environment. Any additional stress can threaten the survival chances of any individual animal. When animals need rest or shelter from the sun, they should not be forced to expend extra energy fleeing from approaching vehicles. Do your game watching from a distance rather than pressing close for the perfect photo.

The network of game tracks in the reserve is not very extensive. In the north, tracks do run up Deception Valley and through intervening sandveld country to such landmarks as Sunday Pan and Piper Pans, or another fossil river called the Passarge.

Other Kalahari Reserves

Khutse Game Reserve is on the southern boundary of the Central Kalahari reserve. Its sparsely vegetated grasslands and small pans harbor the same assortment of wildlife as the larger reserve. There are several public campsites, all without facilities. It is not much visited by overseas visitors, but is a convenient place to do a Kalahari safari if you are spending some time in Gaborone.

Gemsbok National Park is in the beautiful red-dune country of the southwestern Kalahari, but is closed to public access. You can visit the small Mabuasehube Game Reserve, on its eastern edge, if you are a self-sufficient camper. But the game and scenery of this region are much more easily appreciated in South Africa's Kalahari-Gemsbok National Park, which bounds Botswana's Gemsbok park along the unfenced Nossob River.

The Tsodilo Hills
and Other Attractions of Western Botswana

A tiny group of rocky outcrops to the west of the Okavango River Panhandle is the site of one of Africa's most extraordinary collections of Bushman art. The Tsodilo Hills contain over 2,750 individual paintings, spread out among more than 200 different sites. Most of the paintings are images of animals. Eland — an animal of particular spiritual significance to the Bushmen, as well as a prized food source — are common images, as are giraffe, zebra, gemsbok, and other antelope. There are excellent paintings of rhinos — animals that have now disappeared from the Tsodilo area. Scenes of people and cattle and geometric designs round out the collection. Many of the paintings are accompanied by hand prints, which may or may not represent the artists' signatures. Although no date for the oldest paintings has been determined, it is believed that the cattle paintings go back to no earlier than A.D. 700 to 900. The most recent pictures are estimated to be only 100 years old.

The Tsodilo Hills are considered sacred by the Kung Bushmen of the northwestern Kalahari. The Kung believe that their god, Gaoxa, made the hills and various animals while he lived there, and they attribute the paintings to his work. Various stories in which a Bushman and his family were turned to stone describe the creation of the hills. The Mbukushu pastoralists who live in the Okavango Panhandle region also connect their creation story with Tsodilo, believing that their god lowered their ancestors and their cattle from the sky to the summits of the Tsodilo Hills. The Mbukushu have a village near the landmark called the Male Hill. A San village is also located nearby, and this is a fairly reliable place for tourists to meet Kalahari Bushmen (on occasion, there are no San in residence). When they are around the village, Bushmen can be hired as guides. They also demonstrate tool-making and usually have handicrafts ready for sale.

The isolated Tsodilo Hills arise from a vast countryside of rolling fossilized dunes. They are very conspicuous landmarks whether approached by air or by road. There are three principal hills. The southernmost, called the Male Hill, is the highest. The Female Hill is an irregular cluster in the center of the group, and the Child's Hill is the smallest. A tiny isolated outcrop on the north end of the range is unnamed. The majority of the best paintings are on the rock faces and ledges of the Female Hill.

Most visitors to Tsodilo fly in from safari camps in the Okavango Delta for a visit of a few hours. A good number of paintings can be viewed in that time; although you must walk to see them, it's less than a mile from the airstrip to the Female Hill. Several excellent galleries are located along its western base. Many other panels require scrambling up higher, or walking around into the valleys on the east side. Obviously, there is a lot to see, and much will be missed on a short foray. The only alternative to a quick visit is to camp, as there are no accommodations or facilities at Tsodilo. Water is not always available, so make sure you bring your own. The hills are a long drive from Maun; it is a much shorter (but very rough) jaunt if you are based at one of the Panhandle safari camps.

If you are making the long overland trip from Maun to Tsodilo, you will pass by Lake Ngami. Ngami was discovered by Livingstone on his first trans-Kalahari expedition. At that time, the country around the lake was a green oasis, for Ngami was the southern terminus of the Thaoge River that supplied the waters of the western Okavango Delta. The Thaoge has since dried up and, although the lake occasionally receives some of the overflow from the Delta flood via the Thamalakane River, today Ngami is usually just a dry and dusty lakebed surrounded by overgrazed cattle country. In years of exceptional rain or floods, Ngami can fill with a shallow sheet of water that attracts masses of birds.

Drotsky's Cave (also called Gcwihaba Caverns) is another attraction if you are exploring western Botswana overland. These remote limestone grottos, with their typical pillars and dripping stalactites, are of particular interest to spelunkers.

Few visitors venture to the Ghanzi district between the Central Kalahari Game Reserve and Namibia. Although primarily cattle country, the private farms of the region are large and some of them still harbor the fauna and flora of the western Kalahari. The tented *Kanana Safari Camp* is located on a 100-square-mile private reserve to the west of the town of Ghanzi. Kanana offers game drives, but its key activities center on interpretive walks in the company of Bushmen. Excursions can also be made to a little San community located along the nearby Groot Laagte fossil river. The camp can be reached by air charter.

The Bushmen

The Bushmen, or San, are one of the most romanticized groups of people in all Africa. They have been a source of worldwide fascination ever since Laurens van der Post chronicled his 1957 journey in search of them in the film and book, *The Lost World of the Kalahari*. The popular renown of these hardy hunter-gatherers received another boost in the 1980s with the release of the international hit movie, *The Gods Must Be Crazy*. Unfortunately, the reality of the Bushmen's contemporary existence is far less ideal than portrayed in that film.

For millennia, the San, and related indigenous groups, wandered throughout the savannas of southern Africa. Pressed by better armed and organized immigrant peoples, both white and black, the Bushmen were almost completely absorbed or exterminated over the last 300 years. By the beginning of the 20th century, it was only in the wilds of the Kalahari that the San could still practice their traditional hunter-gatherer way of life.

By all accounts it was a good, if hard, lifestyle. By necessity, they lived in small bands so as not to exhaust the limited resources of any particular area. Bushman groups had much the same seasonal dispersal patterns as the wild animals of the Kalahari: in the abundance of the rainy season, when game is concentrated and a bountiful harvest of plants is readily available, they could assemble into larger parties of up to 120 people. In the dry months, they had to split up to forage more widely, even to the point where a man would wander with only his wife and children. While the men were master hunters, exceedingly skilled in the arts of tracking and stalking, and unfailingly deadly with their poison-tipped arrows, it was the women who did the bulk of the gathering, which was by far the more important and reliable method of obtaining food. For although meat was always the favorite meal, plants made up 80 percent of the Bushman's sustenance. Several hundred varieties were harvested from the bush, providing a nutritious and well-balanced diet. Gathering required little time in the rainy season. But the women had to walk much further afield during the dry months: several times a week they would set out to forage for 8 or 10 hours before returning to camp laden with up to 30 pounds of roots and vegetables, usually carrying a young child as well. Setting up grass shelters and moving as the supply of food dictated, a group of San had no need for any material possessions other than those that could be comfortably carried. Everything had utility — the bow, the digging stick, the ostrich egg used as a water container. Animal-skin cloaks doubled as garments and tote bags. Ostrich eggshell beads were used as jewelry — the one concession, along with ritual scarification, to personal adornment.

Although life in the waterless Kalahari would seem impossibly hard, the Bushmen mastered their habitat to an almost unfathomable degree. Even more than the animals of the desert, they depended on underground roots and tubers to provide water in the dry season and developed uncanny skills for spotting the telltale signs that would indicate the presence of moisture-bearing plants hidden in the sand. Other plants indicated where the sands themselves cached water. There they dug miniature sip-wells at which they could draw water from the ground through a straw. Anthropologists generally declare hunter-gatherers to be among the most cheerful of peoples, and the Bushmen were no exception. Within their bands, they practiced a high degree of cooperation: the sharing of tools and food reinforced a social system based on mutual obligation that had real survival value. If one man had no luck in the hunt, he and his family could nonetheless partake in a share of the meat; in turn, he would share when he made a successful kill. Bushmen had no concept of property ownership as we know it. Even disease was looked upon as a communal ill to be cured by trance-dances in which a group member would take the victim's sickness into his own body to exorcise it. Our competitive spirit was also notably absent, even among children's games. It was a remarkably egalitarian society: there were no chiefs, and women had a high degree of social status befitting their importance as providers. The San also had a rich spiritual life, which was reflected in their myths and stories. With charming wit, these stories expressed insight into both human nature and the Bushman's relationship with the animals that shared their world. It's no wonder that "the gentle people" have come to be so highly admired in modern Western culture.

Of course, the Bushmen were capable of the darker aspects of human behavior, too: in the centuries of cattle raids and warfare that eventually saw them exterminated from most of southern Africa, they were fierce warriors, and their poison arrows were greatly feared by white and black adversaries alike.

Today, only a handful of Bushmen still follow the old life as hunter-gatherers, although many others go back to the bush temporarily when wet weather makes conditions less harsh. Little habitat remains where they can still make a living. As cattle have expanded in the Kalahari, they have monopolized water sources and overgrazed the bush, reducing the quantity of game and plants on which the hunter-gatherers depend. In the last few decades, most of the Bushmen have been forced to abandon the traditional way of life. Many have gravitated to cattle ranches, where they work as cowherds receiving little more than food and a place to stay. Others have wound up squatting in small towns or living in government settlements, often in appalling conditions of dependency. Bushmen in towns and farms have changed to a diet of corn meal, which is not as balanced as the varied food of the bush, and malnutrition is a real problem. So is alcoholism. And living in close quarters has produced an epidemic of deadly tuberculosis, as well as venereal disease. Like indigenous peoples in so many parts of the world, the Bushmen have traded a life of self-reliance for a role as the castoffs of modern society. Almost everywhere, they are the objects of ridicule and discrimination.

An estimated 55,000 Bushmen remain today, with about 60 percent in Botswana, 36 percent in Namibia, and most of the rest in South Africa's Northern Cape Province. Although the governments of these countries all profess good intentions for the Bushmen's welfare, with such small numbers their problems can hardly claim political priority.

In Botswana, the government is trying to push the last Bushmen out of the Central Kalahari Game Reserve, the only land in the country that they can call their own. In Namibia, the San's woes are compounded by the legacy of the independence war with South Africa: the South African army recruited Bushmen, many of whom were already refugees from Angola, as trackers and soldiers in the fight against the SWAPO guerrillas, a role that has left them in an awkward position in the newly independent nation. In both countries, the authorities seem intent on getting the Bushmen to completely abandon the old way of life and integrate into modern society. The population of Bushmen seems to be increasing, many of their kids are going to school, and hopefully a good and meaningful future lies ahead. But there are still the problems of discrimination and poverty, and the adjustment from a hunter-gatherer existence to the modern work-a-day world is not an easy one.

Various schemes have been advanced for preserving some elements of the traditional life. In South Africa, several San families have been persuaded to move from the Northern Cape to a private game reserve in the Cedarberg Mountains, a wilderness area near Cape Town from which Bushmen long ago disappeared; the transplanted San are now the reserve's prime tourist attraction. Bushmen are also employed as trackers on several private game reserves in Botswana and Namibia. Such employment may turn out to be beneficial if the people are treated with respect, are decently paid, and get medical care, education, and the choice to determine their own future. At Tsumkwe, in Namibia's Bushmanland district, a community trust is involved with developing its own brand of culturally sensitive tourism. Aside from tourism, Bushmen could use their traditional skills working as rangers in national parks and game reserves, or as technicians in projects for the sustainable harvesting of wild plants. Some indigenous-rights advocacy groups are seeking to secure adequate land to ensure that Bushman bands can sustain the old ways if they choose to do so: in South Africa, for example, lawyers are representing a Bushman community's claims to hunting rights within Kalahari-Gemsbok National Park.

Tourists are often quite keen to meet Bushmen, expecting to find the cheerful innocents depicted in *The Gods Must Be Crazy*. Although such people exist only in the imagination, a few bands of Bushmen actually do live as hunter-gatherers in remote parts of the western and central Kalahari. But the country is vast and there are very few such groups. And, of course, in those places where Bushmen can always be found, they most certainly will be the more sedentary type, who are often much less picturesque than imagined and may be suffering all the corruptions of towns or tourism. Too often, Bushman visits do not live up to expectations.

If the Bushman's ancient way of life has nearly disappeared, its legacy lives on in the rock paintings that abound all over southern Africa. The oldest are estimated to date back some 26,000 years; all painting seems to have stopped about 100 years ago. Many of these artworks are executed with an extraordinary finesse that captures the essence of their subjects in subtle color and graceful line. While the beauty and interest of these works can be appreciated by anyone who cares to visit the better preserved rock galleries, it takes expert study to correctly interpret them. Many have religious or mythological significance. Others depict actual rituals or incidents, such as hunting. A lot of the later paintings, particularly those in South Africa, reveal the Bushman's view of the invasions that overtook them: in various localities, paintings show masted ships, Dutch settlers, red-coated British soldiers, and Bantu raiders and cattle, as well as battle scenes. Most common are pictures of animals and, of course, the Bushmen themselves. Animal paintings often include species that have vanished from the region where the gallery is found. The paintings are always poignant reminders of history and change. In the midst of our contemporary wilderness, you can feel the absence of a people and a vanished way of life.

The Reserves of the Tuli Block and Eastern Botswana

Wild game still flourishes on private land in the Tuli Block, a belt of territory that fronts the Limpopo River, which divides Botswana from South Africa. Although seasonally dry, this area is not part of the Kalahari; its vegetation and wildlife are characteristic of the mixed woodlands biome. The northern portion of the Tuli Block supports a good relict population of elephant, the last of the mighty herds that once roamed along the Limpopo River. Visionary conservationists are proposing to one day link the private reserves of the Tuli area with neighboring gamelands in South Africa and Zimbabwe to form a transborder sanctuary (possibly to be called Dongola International Park).

Currently, the largest and best known of the Tuli Block reserves is the 142-square-mile Mashatu Game Reserve. It occupies the easternmost corner of Botswana, which is squeezed between the Limpopo and Shashe rivers that form the frontiers with Zimbabwe and South Africa. Mashatu is home to some 700 elephants and there is a good range of other game, such as kudu and impala, although large predators are pretty uncommon. (With some fanfare, semitame lions raised by George Adamson of *Born Free* fame were brought in from Kenya to augment the local population, but most of them wound up being shot.) Woodlands and bushy grasslands characterize the reserve. The Limpopo and Shashe rivers are both wide sand rivers that flow only after heavy rains. Luxury safari accommodation and game viewing activities (including night drives and walks) are provided at *Mashatu Main Camp* and its satellite *Tent Camp*. Most guests arrive by air from Johannesburg. The Tuli Block's other tourist-class facility is the *Tuli Safari Lodge*. Less exclusive and pricey than Mashatu, it is popular with South Africans.

The Khama Rhino Sanctuary has recently been established near the town of Serowe, about midway between Gaborone and Francistown. It is the sole refuge for the country's beleaguered white rhinos. The small fenced reserve is in a farming district and is of little interest unless you happen to be in the area.

CHAPTER FIVE

Zimbabwe:
A Heritage in Stone

EVER SINCE ATTAINING its hard-won independence, Zimbabwe has been a bright and shining star in the constellation of African nations. The international goodwill that accompanied the birth of black-run Zimbabwe from the ruins of old Rhodesia has showed considerable staying power. Today, Zimbabwe is one of the great travel destinations of Africa.

To Zimbabwe's many wildlife attractions are wedded the allure of scenic splendor. The misty veil of the incomparable Victoria Falls, the eerie ghost forests along the shores of Lake Kariba, and the wooded valley of the great Zambezi River are all superb backdrops for wildlife viewing. And Zimbabwe's parks ensure that plenty of African fauna is there to be seen. But game can be viewed in greater numbers in neighboring Botswana, and Zambia shares all of the great scenery along the Zambezi. So what gives Zimbabwe its special gloss?

Like Kenya, Zimbabwe enjoys a certain patina of historic — and indeed colonial — romance. Although virtually every visitor today identifies with the justice of the Africans' fight for freedom and self-determination, if you remove the story of the colonial whites, the aura of contemporary Zimbabwe would be considerably dimmed. It is not that anyone admires the colonial mentality of Cecil Rhodes and his cohorts. But *everyone* has heard of Rhodes. The exploits of Rhodes and his min-

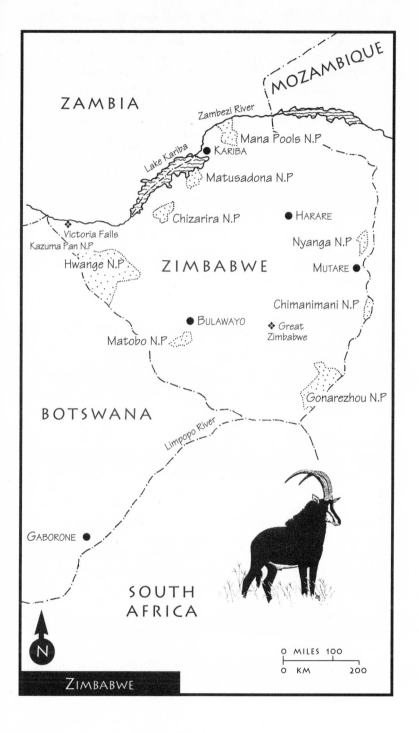

ZAMBIA

MOZAMBIQUE

Zambezi River

Lake Kariba

Mana Pools N.P

● KARIBA

Matusadona N.P

Chizarira N.P

● HARARE

Victoria Falls

Kazuma Pan N.P

Nyanga N.P

Hwange N.P

ZIMBABWE

MUTARE ●

Chimanimani N.P

● BULAWAYO

❖ Great
Zimbabwe

Matobo N.P

BOTSWANA

Gonarezhou N.P

Limpopo River

GABORONE ●

SOUTH
AFRICA

N

O MILES 100

O KM 200

ZIMBABWE

ions in attempting to carve out an empire in "untamed" Africa have left a certain cast on the literature of the continent that has lingered from the novels of Rider Haggard to those of Wilbur Smith. Sensibilities have changed, of course: everyone acknowledges that the conquest of the Ndebele and Shona peoples was accomplished with tremendous effrontery and great violence. That the Africans' land was stolen and the people relegated to second-class status in their own country is inarguable. Yet the story of the birth of the nation, its bloody metamorphosis from white Rhodesia to black-ruled Zimbabwe, has an indelibly romantic element, at least when viewed from afar.

There is both tragedy and drama in the struggle between Europeans and Africans for the land that became Zimbabwe. The Africans were wronged from the beginning. They suffered mightily and ultimately triumphed. Few white settlers could see the justice of the Africans' cause. By their own lights, white settlers worked hard to build their farms and transplant English country life to the African veld. Although the settlers lived comfortably, they did not view themselves as rich, ignoring that their circumstances equated to a very good, if not unattainable, lifestyle in their mother country. The settlers thought they treated their African workers decently, but did not take much interest in improving the lot of those pushed into the native reserves. Most whites, a mere 2 percent of the country's population, were morally blind to the unfairness of their racially based state. Inevitably, the settlers' ante-bellum world was swept away in the cataclysm of the liberation war. Such history is the stuff of epic novels, and no doubt there will some day be a Zimbabwean version of *Gone with the Wind*. In the meantime, you can meet some of the people who lived through the era of struggle on your travels in Zimbabwe.

Of course, the story of Zimbabwe goes back a long way before the arrival of Cecil Rhodes and the white pioneers. It begins with the San bands that left a rich legacy of rock paintings on outcrops all over the country. Those hunter-gatherers were overwhelmed by the arrival of agricultural Bantu peoples, one group of which built the medieval town that we know as Great Zimbabwe. The stone ruins of Great Zimbabwe were at first considered a place of mystery because European discoverers refused to attribute its creation to Africans. We now know that the town was built by forebears of contemporary Zimbabwe's dominant Shona people. Great Zimbabwe's monuments are considered a proud symbol of a glorious African past. The town was actually the seat of a Shona kingdom that flourished between the 13th and 15th centuries. Its wealth was based on cattle and trade, with gold and ivory passing from the hinterlands of contemporary Zimbabwe to the Swahili-Arab enclaves on the Indian Ocean coast. Great Zimbabwe was superseded by other Shona dynasties — the Mutapa, Torwa, Changamire, and later Rozwi kingdoms. These groups also left stone ruins, but the remains of their towns — such as the Khami ruins near the city of Bulawayo — do not possess the mystery of the massive enclosures and towers of Great Zimbabwe, and it is that older town that captures the imagination.

The intertribal *mfecane* disturbances in southern Africa reached Zimbabwe in the 1830s when Nguni raiders arrived and destroyed the Shona dynasty's Rozwi kingdom. The most important of the invaders were the Ndebele,* led by their formidable king, Mzilikazi. He established himself near the rocky Matobo Hills and proceeded to incorporate many of the peoples of western Zimbabwe into a powerful Ndebele kingdom. The Ndebele looked upon the more numerous Shona people of the central plateau as their vassals, while the Shona resented and feared the depredations of the warlike newcomers. These are the roots of an ethnic rivalry that simmers to the present day. Two years after Mzilikazi's death in 1868, his son Lobengula ascended the throne and founded his capital at Bulawayo. The new king was confident of his power, but had to deal with an increasing flow of European visitors. Such visitors had already become commonplace during the 1860s: the old king had allowed Livingstone's father-in-law, Robert Moffat, to establish a mission, and several Europeans attended Lobengula's coronation ceremonies. Lobengula welcomed and assisted white guests, among whom was Frederick Courtney Selous, the hunter-explorer. It was the king's fate to be betrayed by those he befriended.

By the late 1880s, Cecil Rhodes had cast his eye on the territories of the Matabele and the Shona as part of his grand design of empire. Reports of gold had filtered back from the explorer Selous and various prospectors, and Rhodes was keen on leapfrogging any expansion by the Boer republic in the Transvaal, where the rush to Johannesburg's gold reef was already in full swing. Rhodes set about obtaining a concession from Lobengula that granted him permission to mine and colonize in Matabeleland. Robert Moffat's son, John, was instrumental in obtaining the illiterate king's mark on the document: Lobengula relied on the missionary's son to translate, but Moffat deliberately deceived him. Too late, the king tried to repudiate the agreement. In 1890, Rhodes sent the Pioneer Column consisting of 200 soldiers and 500 heavily armed colonists northward to claim Matabeleland and Mashonaland for his

*These people were formerly known as the Matabele, a name that appears in numerous historical sources and is still used to describe western Zimbabwe (Matabeleland), where they are the dominate tribe. Ndebele has come to be the preferred modern usage.

new British South Africa Company (BSAC). Guided by Selous, the column established a series of forts as they occupied the country. Fighting broke out in 1893, whereupon Lobengula fled from Bulawayo, to die of smallpox a year later. Colonization, forced labor, and the destruction of their cattle herds in the devastating Africa-wide rinderpest outbreak led to revolts by both the Shona and Ndebele in 1896. This rebellion is now known as the first *Chimurenga* (liberation war). Fort Salisbury and the European community at Bulawayo were besieged. Reinforcements broke the Shona resistance at Salisbury, and the Shona leaders were hanged the following year. The Ndebele army proved tougher: its *impi* (warriors) and *induna* (chiefs) took refuge in the rugged Matobo Hills, from which they fought the British to a standstill. Finally, an *indaba* (meeting) was arranged. Rhodes attended personally to conclude the peace. The Ndebele won back some of their land and autonomy. When Rhodes visited the grave of Mzilikazi, he was so taken with the beauty of the granite Matobo Hills that he decided that he, too, would be buried there when his time came.

The fledgling colony was named Southern Rhodesia in 1899 to distinguish it from the northern region that would eventually become Zambia. Southern Rhodesia was run by the BSAC until 1923, when it was declared a colony of the British Crown. The colony had a measure of self-rule, but the rights to vote or hold seats in the legislature were essentially restricted to whites. In the 1930s, racist legislation barred Africans from owning land in white areas or working in most skilled trades and professions. A big wave of fresh colonists arrived from England at the end of the Second World War. African resentment and political resistance grew steadily. In 1953, the British combined Southern Rhodesia with Northern Rhodesia and Nyasaland (later Malawi) in a free-trade block called the Federation of Rhodesia and Nyasaland. Attempts to moderate the apartheid-like practices of Southern Rhodesia got nowhere with its white settlers, while African opposition to the Federation was equally vehement in the other colonies. By 1963, the Federation collapsed, with Zambia and Malawi attaining black-ruled independence the following year. That development fueled the determination of the settlers in Southern Rhodesia to obtain their own white-ruled independent state. After negotiations with Britain broke down in 1965, the Rhodesian government of Ian Smith issued its Unilateral Declaration of Independence (UDI).

Britain and the United Nations declared Rhodesian independence illegal and imposed economic sanctions, but it took years before they had any effect. Meanwhile, black nationalists inside the country prepared to go to war. The two principal parties were the Ndebele-backed Zimbabwe African Peoples Union (ZAPU), led by Joshua Nkomo, and the rival Zimbabwe African National Union (ZANU), led by Robert Mugabe, which had primarily Shona support. Armed resistance in the second *Chimurenga* (liberation war) began in 1966, but did not really pick up steam until 1972. After that, it was all-out guerrilla war. The ZAPU forces were based in Zambia, so raid and counterattack raged all along the Zambezi River. ZANU's guerrillas fought primarily from bases in Mozambique. The two groups later combined under the banner of the Patriotic Front. By 1979, Smith's white Rhodesia was exhausted. With superior firepower and training, its army had won most of the battles, but it could not end the widening war. Meanwhile, a good percentage of the white settlers had voted with their feet; fed up with violence and economic hardship, they had left the country by the thousands. Smith's last-ditch machinations failed to get an African government to his liking into place. In the end, he agreed to a constitutional settlement that included universal suffrage but reserved 20 seats for whites in a 100-member parliament. In 1980, British-supervised elections saw an overwhelming victory for ZANU. On April 16, 1980, Zimbabwe officially gained its independence with ZANU leader Robert Mugabe as prime minister.

All over the world, people rejoiced at the realization of Zimbabwe's freedom. Although Mugabe and ZANU were avowedly Marxist, the Western media was so euphoric about black rule that the new nation quickly became the darling of the Western press. Their indulgence glossed over serious abuses that arose as Mugabe sought to strengthen his power. Although the rival Nkomo was initially given an important cabinet post, other ZAPU leaders were soon arrested. By 1981, serious fighting erupted in Bulawayo between ZAPU veterans and ZANU-supporting government soldiers. Over the next years a reign of terror was put into effect in Matabeleland, where the army's elite North Korean–trained troops rampaged in an effort to quell Ndebele opposition to the Shona-led government. Mugabe pushed for a one-party state. Nkomo was briefly detained, then fled the country. When he returned, he agreed to a merger of the two parties, whereupon resistance and repression in Matabeleland came to an end. Yet even today, tribal rivalries linger: complaints are heard in Matabeleland that the region does not receive its fair share of development projects or government funds.

It is still too soon to tell whether Zimbabwe's progress over the last decade and a half is entirely a success story. Although Mugabe's party has a near-unanimous majority in Parliament, he has never succeeded in making the country an official one-party state. With the winds of democratization blowing, it is possible that he will face real opposition in the next presidential election. That could mean change, for the country's economy has not thrived and jobs remain very scarce. The government's early flirtation with Marxism succeeded mainly in scaring away foreign investment. Although Marxist rhetoric has been discarded in recent years, the International Monetary Fund and Mugabe still do not see eye to eye on economic reform, so major grants have not been forthcoming. Zimbabwe is very much an agricultural country; its large and efficient — but mostly white-owned — farms have been the mainstay of food and export crop production. Despite terrific land hunger among the rural people — and counter to the expectations of the left wing of his own party — Mugabe has not moved very far with his espoused plan to break up the large, white-owned farms and redistribute the land to poor Africans. Western (and white) critics predict such a move will produce economic disaster. Yet it has potent political appeal with the electorate, and the president rolls out the plan whenever needed. It is a useful tonic to criticism of corruption in the top echelons of government. Various scandals have led to charges that high-ranking officials have enriched themselves while the common people languish in poverty. If not kept in check, corruption could threaten both the stability of the Mugabe regime and the long-term development prospects of the country. On the positive side, Mugabe's government has vastly improved health care and education for the black population, political opposition is now tolerated, and the economy continues to grow. Best of all — and perhaps surprisingly, given the history — black Zimbabweans don't seem to harbor any great hard feelings toward whites. People are remarkably friendly. Any visitor will certainly feel completely welcome, and will go home concluding that Zimbabwe is doing fine.

The white citizens of Zimbabwe have fared very well since independence. After a postwar period of tension, those who remained rebuilt their lives. They lost all political power (in 1990, a new constitution took away their guaranteed parliamentary seats), but they retain considerable economic influence. Despite the possibility of eventual expropriation, their farms are prospering. This prosperity has reportedly even drawn back some farmers who had previously fled the country. Many white Zimbabweans have opened safari companies or lodges, and they have come to dominate the rapidly growing and lucrative tourist industry. Although the white citizens tend to grumble quite a bit about the economic hardships and difficulties of living under an African regime, they marry that trait with a can-do optimism born of a provincial certainty that they, as well as their farms, lodges, parks, and *country*, are simply without peer.

White dominance of tourism is weakening as a result of a government push toward "indigenization." Under this policy, any new leases for concessions within national parks or game reserves are awarded only to black applicants; as a result, many new lodges are partnerships between experienced white safari professionals and black entrepreneurs who have been awarded the rights to concessions.

Geographically, Zimbabwe's interior is dominated by a central plateau on which elevations vary between 4,000 and 6,000 feet. In the Eastern Highlands along the border with Mozambique, the Nyanga and Chimanimani mountain ranges rise to exceed 8,000 feet. A string of lesser mountains runs down the spine of the central plateau from the Mvurwi Range in the northeast to the Matobo Hills of the southwest. This is called the Great Dyke, a narrow band of 2-billion-year-old crystalline rock that is the source of Zimbabwe's mineral wealth — gold, gemstones, asbestos, and chrome. The high plateau country, with its open savannas and miombo woodlands (which are locally called *msasa* woodlands in honor of one of Zimbabwe's dominant brachystegia trees), is punctuated with massive granite domes (called *dwalas*) and smaller rock koppies (outcrops).* Many of these blocks of ancient stone have eroded into jumbled boulder piles: Zimbabwe is so proud of its balancing rock formations that they are pictured on the national currency. The best farmland in the country is also found on the central plateau. From its heights, the land falls away through agricultural "midlands" to the wildlife havens of the lower bush country. To the north is the drainage of the Zambezi, southward the Lowveld along the Limpopo and Save rivers. In the west, the land merges into the sands of the Kalahari.

Zimbabwe's great wilderness reserves are located in the lowlands along its borders. In the Lowveld adjoining the southeastern border with Mozambique, between the Save and Limpopo rivers, are Gonarezhou National Park and several private nature conservancies, the last strongholds for game in the southern part of the country. But it's in the north that the largest and most famous of Zimbabwe's national parks are located: Hwange, on the Botswana frontier, Matusadona fronting Lake Kariba, and Mana Pools in the lower Zambezi Valley. The resort town at Victoria Falls is the hub for Zimbabwe's principal safari circuit, as well as the site of the spectacular cataracts that are one of Africa's most celebrated scenic wonders.

Zimbabwe is widely (but possibly mistakenly) acclaimed for its

---

*The English term *koppie* derives from the Afrikaans word *kopje* ("little head"), which is used to describe small rocky hills or outcrops. Oddly, koppie is used more often in southern Africa (although it does appear in various place-names in Zimbabwe), while *kopje* is generally employed in East Africa, where the term is familiar to anyone who has visited the Serengeti Plains.

wildlife conservation efforts, particularly its highly publicized CAMP-
FIRE program, which encourages village involvement in conservation.
Zimbabwe's conservation strategy is guided by the premise that wildlife
is a resource that must be used to provide maximum benefit to local people and the country at large, while conserving animal populations on a
sustainable basis. This is a laudable approach, one with which few modern conservationists would quibble. Debate proceeds as to the means
and details of utilization.

CAMPFIRE (the Communal Areas Management Programme for Indigenous Resources) gives the residents of participating communities in
wildlife areas the ownership of the wild animals that live on their lands.
The resource is then managed by wildlife professionals who oversee the
allocation of leases for photographic safari lodges, the sale of permits to
trophy-hunting safari companies, the culling of game, and the distribution of the meat that results to local people. Profits from revenues produced from trophy hunting, tour operations, and the sale of animal
products are then returned to the community. In some areas, CAMP-
FIRE has been successful in changing rural people's attitude toward
wildlife from one of hostility to one of respect for its value. Whereas villagers may previously have viewed wild animals as dangerous pests — the
destroyers of crops, domestic livestock, and human lives — they are now
willing to tolerate the presence of wildlife because of the money it brings
to them and their communities. The program has been touted as a model
for Africa, and although it is not unique, it is a good prototype for a
brand of conservation that preserves wildlife and expands habitat while
directly benefiting the people who live in close proximity with wild animals — and who ultimately compete with them for the land. When the
system works, both wildlife and human populations come out ahead.

Zimbabwe actually has a long history of intensive wildlife management that reaches back to colonial times. The celebrated Operation
Noah project was launched in 1958 to rescue wildlife threatened with
drowning by the mammoth reservoir created by Kariba Dam. Between
1958 and 1961, the project saved thousands of animals from the rising
waters of Lake Kariba and received plenty of favorable publicity from
the world press. No attention was given to the campaign of tsetse fly
eradication that was in progress at the same time. That program, which
had the full endorsement of contemporary wildlife authorities, was designed to eliminate the tsetse problem by denying the flies their food
source — wild animals. Between 1910 and the 1970s, hundreds of thousands of animals were shot in a futile attempt to control the tsetse. Not
that Zimbabwe (then Rhodesia) was alone in practicing this devastating
policy. But the slaughter in the two Rhodesias (later Zimbabwe and

Zambia) was carefully recorded, and the total number of animals killed was truly staggering.

All conservation efforts were eclipsed during Zimbabwe's long struggle for independence. While the guerrilla war raged, game management ground to a halt. As the wilderness regions on the country's perimeter became battlegrounds, much of the local population was removed and wild animals were able to expand their numbers almost unchecked. At independence, Zimbabwe was left with large game populations in all of its parks and hunting areas. In the 1980s, while most African countries were facing the scourge of poaching and experiencing a precipitous decline in elephant populations, Zimbabwe's game managers were complaining that they had too many elephants. Villagers in elephant-bearing districts were suffering the destruction of their crops, and the forests and wooded bush country of the national parks were taking a severe pounding from thousands of hungry elephants.

Even before independence, Zimbabwe's wildlife authorities embarked on a policy of culling. Censuses were undertaken to determine the number of elephants in various parts of the country, while ecologists conducted studies to decide on the optimum carrying capacity of the reserves. The results indicated huge overpopulations in the bushlands along the Zambezi River and in Hwange National Park, and high quotas were fixed for culls in those areas. Over the next decade, thousands of elephants were shot in official operations. (An estimated 44,000 elephants were culled between 1972 and 1992.)

The cull brought in 2 million dollars a year directly to Zimbabwe's national treasury and provided the raw materials to support hundreds of jobs in a thriving ivory-carving industry. But this sanctioned shooting was occurring during the "ivory wars" that were devastating Africa's overall elephant population, and the cull raised the hackles of many foreign conservationists (as well as animal rights activists). Critics questioned Zimbabwe's census methods and population figures. Because the biggest elephant populations were along the borders with Zambia and Botswana, the question of seasonal or long-term migrations had to be considered, and many observers suspected this was not being adequately addressed. It is certain that the widespread system of drilling boreholes for water in Hwange National Park encouraged elephants from the woodlands of the northeastern Kalahari to remain in the park during the annual dry season. Without the boreholes, most of those animals could have been expected to return to Botswana when Hwange's natural waterholes dried up. The boreholes had been drilled precisely to encourage a year-round game population because Hwange is naturally a near-waterless bushland during the dry season. Pumping water turned it into

Zimbabwe's premier game park, where elephants and other animals could always be found, especially during the dry winter months that co-incide with the international tourist season.

Hwange became famous for its large herds of elephants, with a pop-ulation estimated at higher than 20,000. Undeniably, the constant pres-ence of so many elephants was hurting the park's vegetation, particularly in the vicinity of the man-made waterholes. But questions persisted re-garding the timing of the annual elephant census: if done at the height of the dry season, many of the elephants counted would be temporary im-migrants from Botswana that would return there with the rains. To com-plicate matters, during the mid-1980s, the region was in the grip of persistent drought, and Hwange's pumped waterholes became a lifeline that the elephant herds could not abandon. Were a significant number of Hwange elephants actually from Botswana, held in the park by the pres-ence of artificial water sources? Other issues were raised about the ele-phant population along the Zambezi, where intensive poaching was putting tremendous pressure on elephants on the Zambian side of the river. Was poaching causing large numbers of elephants to move to safer havens across the Zambezi — again inflating Zimbabwe's elephant pop-ulation figures and inviting higher than sustainable quotas for its cull? Zimbabwean conservation authorities pointedly defended any criticism of their census methods or culling program. Their responses only invited skeptical critics to complain that Zimbabwe would not allow indepen-dent scientists from overseas conservation organizations access to their data.

In 1989, the international ban on the ivory trade went into effect over the objections of Zimbabwe and the other ivory-exporting nations of southern Africa. Ever since, Zimbabwe has raged furiously against the embargo and has campaigned ceaselessly to have it reversed. Zimbab-wean conservationists are fond of pointing out how much income the ivory ban has cost the country and how that loss of revenue makes it im-possible to properly fund its game management, park maintenance, and antipoaching efforts. But while it's true that income from culling has been lost, that does not tell the whole story.

Zimbabwe could easily have made up the ivory deficit by increasing its revenue from the booming international tourist trade. Zimbabwe's park fees were kept absurdly low: right through 1996, an overseas tourist in Zimbabwe paid a park fee of about US$2.50, while compara-ble entrance fees for nonresidents in Botswana, Kenya, and Tanzania were running from US$15 to US$20 per day (without any adverse effects on the flow of visitors). Even with its low entry fees, Zimbabwe's parks might have paid for themselves, but the money collected did not go to their administration. The funds went instead to the national treasury, at the same time that the government was steadily cutting down on its budget for parks and wildlife personnel. That chronic underfunding led to a breakdown of efficiency and morale: in 1993, 250 park rangers had to be let go for lack of funds — a layoff that was immediately followed by a massive slaughter of rhinos in Hwange National Park. Despite a "shoot to kill" war on poachers along the Zambezi River, skeptics questioned the seriousness of the government's commitment to wildlife protection: poaching was routinely blamed on Zambians or other foreigners, while any suggestion of involvement by high-level Zimbabwean officials was swept under the rug. Such charges persisted, however, and they have only increased as a result of a bitter political battle for control of Zimbabwe's national parks. In 1996, several top people in the park system were dismissed from their posts, but it seems likely that the charges laid against them were trumped up by their replacements — the winners of the power struggle. Some local conservationists suspect that the foxes now have free reign of the chicken coop.

Even with the hint of scandal in the air, big changes are on the way. In 1997, Zimbabwe's Department of National Parks and Wildlife Management became an autonomous body responsible for its own revenue and budget. Park entry fees have been raised to US$5 per day (and may go up to US$10 or even US$20 per day), and all the money collected will be used to run the system. The resulting influx of cash should ultimately ensure improvements in the way the parks are maintained. The department will also keep any money it earns from hunting and culling, and it is anxious to increase those revenues: Zimbabwe will host the 1997 CITES meeting (the Convention on International Trade in Endangered Species), at which it is expected to push hard for a relaxation of the international ban on the ivory trade.

Although overseas visitors are not likely to begrudge paying higher park fees, they are increasingly irritated by the odd three-tiered pricing system used by many Zimbabwean hotels and safari outfitters. Zimbabwe residents get very low "local" rates; a "regional" rate set in South African rand is higher, but is still reasonable. The dollar-based "international rate" — which applies to tourists from the US and Europe — can run as high as three times the local rate, and twice that of the regional rate. This discrepancy leads to all kinds of fiddles on the part of visitors and tour operators alike and feeds a perception that the overseas tourist is being overcharged, as they sometimes pay two or even three times as much for the same services. While most foreign tourists would readily agree that Zimbabweans deserve a break on prices — or at least that off-season rates could be lower when overseas visitors are scarce, no one likes to feel ripped off. Although lower rates for residents apply in most African countries, in Zimbabwe the price differences are obvious and excessive. This should be remedied before word gets around that the country does not give fair value to visitors.

In addition to its national parks, Zimbabwe has designated vast amounts of wild territory as Safari Areas for use by hunters. Big game hunting is a long-established industry in Zimbabwe and, as everywhere, it is very lucrative. Yet in recent years, many of the best professional guides have turned to leading photographic foot safaris. Because of Zimbabwe's exacting standards for obtaining the coveted professional guide license, Zimbabwe's guides are exceptionally good, and this has earned the country a reputation as one of the best places for walking safaris. Walking safaris have become a popular addition to the safari repertoire in Zimbabwe — and almost a fixture of top-quality safaris and camps.

In recent years, increasing numbers of white farmers have been converting their properties into private game reserves. In some areas, property owners have banded together to have their land certified as "conservancies." These admittedly commercial game reserves have become an integral part of Zimbabwe's conservation effort: the funding and care given to private lands make them good sanctuaries for wild animals that are endangered in inhabited areas, or even in the larger but underprotected national parks. Many of Zimbabwe's remaining rhinos have been translocated to conservancy lands for safekeeping.

Through the mid-1980s, Zimbabwe had Africa's largest population of black rhinos (about 1,500) and the country was considered their last great stronghold. But within the space of a few years, their numbers had dwindled to fewer than 300. (Although this figure is the most widely accepted, the actual population may be somewhat higher, perhaps up to 500; it is difficult to obtain the exact number of black rhinos surviving in Zimbabwe because wildlife researchers do not want to further arouse the attention of poachers.) In the national parks, most of the surviving rhinos have been moved to Intensive Protection Zones (IPZs). These are carefully monitored areas within the parks, where, it is hoped, the rhinos can be safeguarded and bred until such time as the poaching crisis eases. This same strategy has worked well in Kenya, where rhinos now thrive only in well-guarded private reserves and specially protected sanctuaries within selected national parks.

Although Zimbabwe's parks are superb examples of wild Africa, they do not offer the easiest game viewing. In most areas, game concentrations are not dense, and thick bush often hinders visibility. Lions and other predators are far more easily seen in other countries — notably in

Kenya, Tanzania, and Botswana. Furthermore, the near elimination of rhinos has deprived the country of one of its primary wildlife attractions. Yet tourism to Zimbabwe has grown enormously over the last decade, for the country has something to offer visitors of every pocketbook and travel style. The most daring are attracted by the chance to do bush walking in the national parks, or to go on canoe and whitewater rafting safaris on the Zambezi. For the less hardy, luxury lodges and safari camps are scattered throughout the bush. At such camps, game viewing safaris can be undertaken without any compromises in comfort. The most exclusive safari operations offer such perks as drives in open vehicles, nighttime game viewing, and foot safaris in the company of licensed professional guides. Budget travelers also have ample opportunity to explore the bush: some parks are easily reached by public transport and have facilities for low-cost accommodation and tours.

Nor are Zimbabwe's attractions limited solely to wildlife. Zimbabwe boasts spectacular scenery and hiking trails in both the mountains of the Eastern Highlands and the Matobo Hills of the southwest. With its San galleries and association with Cecil Rhodes and the Ndebele kings, the Matobo Hills also entice with cultural and historic interest. And, of course, Zimbabwe possesses the greatest archaeological treasure in sub-Saharan Africa — its heritage in stone — the ruins of Great Zimbabwe.

Safari Facts

ENTRY: No visas are required for US citizens. A yellow fever vaccination is needed if you are coming to Zimbabwe from East Africa.

CURRENCY: The currency is the Zimbabwe dollar (1997 rate: Z$11 = US$1). Any foreign currency you bring in must be declared on arrival as you pass through Customs. Local currency is not convertible outside Zimbabwe, so keep exchanges to a minimum and save receipts. Hotels, airline tickets, and safari services must be paid for in US dollars or other foreign exchange. Traveler's checks and credit cards are widely accepted.

LANGUAGE: English is the official language and is universally spoken. Shona is the dominant native tongue, with Ndebele the vernacular in the western part of the country.

AIR TRAVEL: Harare is the principal international gateway and the hub of domestic operations for Air Zimbabwe and Zimbabwe Express. Daily loop flights connect Harare with Kariba, Victoria Falls, and Hwange National Park. Two smaller domestic airlines (United Air and

Expedition Air) fly scheduled routes to various parts of the country. Victoria Falls can be reached directly from South Africa, Botswana, and Namibia, and there are also international flights between Bulawayo, Zimbabwe, and Johannesburg, South Africa. Zimbabwe imposes airport taxes of Z$10 for domestic flights and US$20 (payable in cash only) for international departures.

TRANSPORTATION: A network of excellent paved highways links the major cities, but many of Zimbabwe's roads are gravel. Local buses go everywhere; they are crowded and operate without regular schedules. Reliable (and more comfortable) express buses between the major cities do have schedules; seats should be prebooked. Sunset Tours (in conjunction with Zimbabwe Sun Hotels) runs a convenient daily bus service for tourists visiting the Eastern Highlands, Great Zimbabwe, and the southeastern Lowveld. A wide selection of rental cars is available (theoretically), but must be booked in advance. Hertz, Avis, and Europcar have offices in the major tourist centers. Note that rental car companies usually restrict driving on unpaved roads and they bar travel to remote areas like Mana Pools. US drivers' licenses are accepted. The capital, Harare, is the hub of the railway net. Trains are slow and go mostly at night, but mainline services include dining cars and sleeper compartments in First Class. First Class on regular trains is basic but adequately comfortable. Special steam trains between the city of Bulawayo and Victoria Falls are operated by Rail Safaris. Drawn by vintage steam locomotives, Ivory Class passengers travel in refurbished First Class cars dating from the 1950s. Emerald Class passengers go aboard Private Saloon 754, a coach built in 1929 that features a teak-paneled lounge with a library, upholstered sofas, and panoramic windows. Four-day tours include a game viewing stopover at Hwange National Park.

TOURS: Harare is the country's major international gateway and transportation hub, although many visitors travel directly to Victoria Falls. The principal safari circuit visits Victoria Falls, Hwange National Park, and the Kariba area, which are all linked by daily flights by Air Zimbabwe and Zimbabwe Express. A secondary more culturally oriented circuit includes the Eastern Highlands, Great Zimbabwe, and the Bulawayo region. A list of safari tour operators appears in the Appendix of this book. The largest Zimbabwe tour operator is United Touring Company (UTC), which has regional offices in all major areas. Wilderness Safaris Zimbabwe and Garth Thompson Safari Consultants are highly reputable booking agents. Advance reservations for national park rest camps should be made to: Department of National Parks and Wildlife, P.O. Box CY140, Causeway, Harare. Tel: (263) (4) 706077 or 706078. Fax: (263) (4) 726089.

SHOPPING: Zimbabwe produces a whole range of handicrafts and souvenirs. Masks and other ethnic artifacts, basketry, and wood or stone carvings are all very popular. Ivory products are widely sold and usually come with legal certification. Although the purchase of culled ivory is encouraged in Zimbabwe, it cannot be legally imported into the US or Europe at this time. Products made from crocodile skin can be imported to the US if accompanied by paperwork certifying that the skins come from farmed animals.

SHONA STONE SCULPTURE: While you might find high-quality stone carvings anywhere in Zimbabwe, most of them are repetitive in their themes and are more or less manufactured for sale as souvenirs. Such works are routinely dismissed as "airport art" by critics and collectors. But more than a generation of talented artists have earned Shona stone sculpture a place in the sun, and it is now a hot item in galleries and museums around the world. Although it's tempting to trace the roots of Shona sculpture back to the soapstone birds and carved monoliths of Great Zimbabwe, the modern form owes its origins to mission schools that started art courses in the middle of this century. The unique school of Shona stone sculpture that emerged has won international recognition in the art world. Granite is used, but the most widely used medium is serpentine. Sculpted and sanded, a piece is then heated in fire to facilitate the absorption of wax that brings out the stone's natural color. Black and green pieces prevail, but serpentine comes in various shades of gray and red as well. Green verdite is a harder and rarer stone that is highly sought after by artists and collectors. The themes of the best Shona art are as individual as the artists, although themes are often drawn from the tribe's rich legacy of folklore and traditional spiritual beliefs.

The Harare area is the best place to buy major works by recognized artists, but you can find nice pieces elsewhere. When it comes to art, there is no better rule than "buy what you like." Top quality is going to cost you, especially if you buy large pieces and want to ship them home. If you intend to ship large pieces, stick to purchases from established galleries, pay with a credit card, get the piece properly insured and crated, and *make sure that your shipping address and contact information is ironclad accurate.* Shipping stone artworks by air is devilishly expensive, but the savings over buying such art at home still makes it worthwhile. Although there are no duties on this type of artwork, you may well have to hire a freight agent to clear the packages when they arrive at US Customs.

Harare

At 4,850 feet in elevation, Harare, Zimbabwe's capital, has a moderate climate that contributes to its reputation as one of Africa's nicest cities. Although the downtown area is pleasant enough, you would have to live in one of its tree-shaded suburban neighborhoods to fully appreciate the city's lifestyle potential. Few visitors stay long, as Harare is used mostly as a gateway to the wilder parts of the country. If you are staying in town, pick up a copy of the monthly booklet, *In Harare*, at the Tourist Information Office on African Unity Square, or at any of the major hotels. It will give you ideas of where to shop or eat. Like all big cities, Harare has its share of crime, so beware of pickpockets and do not wander around at night.

THINGS TO DO AROUND HARARE: There's certainly enough to do around town to keep you occupied for a day or two. These are the chief attractions.

National Gallery of Zimbabwe. This museum houses permanent and visiting collections of African art and has played an important role in winning international acceptance of Shona sculpture. The museum shop sells pieces by some of Zimbabwe's top sculptors.

The Kopje. A hilltop viewpoint over the city, this is the site of Zimbabwe's Eternal Flame of Independence, and it will one day also be the setting for the country's parliament building.

Ewanrigg Botanical Gardens. Twenty-two miles from town, these landscaped gardens are known for their collections of African cycads and aloes, which are at the height of bloom in July.

Heroes' Acre. The national monument to those fallen in the liberation struggle.

Epworth Balancing Rocks. Fanciful natural rock formations including the one pictured on the national currency.

National Botanic Garden. An excellent place to investigate the flora of Zimbabwe laid out according to its various habitats.

Mukuvisi Woodlands. These natural *msasa* woodlands are excellent for walking and birdwatching. Guided walking tours take place Wednesdays and Saturdays.

Larvon Bird Gardens. A private aviary featuring over 400 species.

Tobacco Floors. The world's largest tobacco auction takes place here in the morning, daily between April and October.

Mbare Musika. Harare's biggest local market, with loads of fresh produce and local wares in addition to handicrafts.

McIlwaine Recreational Park. On Lake Chivero, this park is Harare's local outdoor getaway. There's a game park and good birdwatching, as well as water skiing and fishing.

Chinhoyi Caves. Limestone grottos and a beautiful sunken pool are featured at this small national park, 90 miles northwest of town. On the way, you pass through a section of Zimbabwe's mineral-rich Great Dyke mountains.

Galleries. Harare's galleries are the best places to see or buy Shona stone sculpture. Aside from the National Gallery (described in this list), there are numerous private salons. At Chapungu Sculpture Park, guides show you around an extensive sculpture garden, explaining the myths and dreams that inspired various pieces. There is also a mock-up of a 19th century Shona village, and tribal dance exhibitions are performed on weekends. Vhukutiwa Gallery is a smaller suburban garden chock-full of works by artists both known and new. Matombo Gallery and Stone Dynamics are both establishments of long-standing repute that feature well-known artists. Nyati Gallery is the newest sculpture garden. Tengenenge is a famous artists' colony located in the countryside, about an hour and a half drive from Harare. Several of Zimbabwe's most respected sculptors live and work in this traditional little village, which can be visited on day tours.

HARARE HOTELS AND LODGES: As you would expect, there is a wide selection of accommodation in and around Harare. The refurbished *Meikles Hotel* has reclaimed its place as first among Harare hostelries. The *Monomotapa* (Holiday Inn Crown Plaza) and *Sheraton* are in the same luxury class. In the middle-price category, the best is the *Bronte Hotel*. It's quiet and has a nice garden, but is difficult to book and has added a less desirable annex — which is where you might wind up. The *Cresta Jameson* is a good modern business traveler's hotel. Budget travelers can find dormitory accommodation at *Paw Paw Lodge* and *Mundawanga Lodge*.

If you prefer, you can stay in various lodges outside Harare that offer pleasant country atmosphere and activities while still close to town and the airport. The luxurious *Imba Matombo* is 15 minutes from town and makes a good alternative to a city hotel, while visitors keen on Shona art can stay at *Chapungu Sculpture Park*. *Landela Lodge* accommodates its guests in a lovely thatched farmhouse and gives them temporary membership in a local country club, as well as hiking, horseback rides, or game drives on the lodge's nearby farm. Similar activities are available at *Wild Geese Lodge*, a small country hotel that receives rave reviews for its cuisine, scenery, and relaxed ambiance. *Mwanga Lodge* also combines the appeal of the bush with proximity to the city, while *Harare Safari Lodge* is set on the shores of Lake Chivero.

Further afield, *Pamuzinda* is a luxury safari lodge about an hour's drive from town. This private game reserve is stocked with cheetah, black rhino, and elephant. *Imire Game Ranch*, near Marondera (also about an hour from Harare but on the way to the Eastern Highlands), specializes in close-up encounters with hand-raised "big five" animals. Visitors there can ride on trained elephants. The elephants are also used on antipoaching patrols and are being taught to plow fields — an agricultural experiment!

Victoria Falls

Giant waterfalls are universally honored as "wonders of the world." Despite the cliché, the great falls of the Zambezi River do not fail to live up to expectations. Here, the wide river plunges over 300-foot cliffs in a cataclysm of falling water, awesome in its power. The Zambezi has been measured to pour as much as 180 million gallons per minute over the falls! At high-flood stage, a roaring, mile-wide curtain of water makes the ground shake and throws a plume of mist hundreds of feet into the air. Visible for 20 miles around, this pillar of spray earned the cataracts their African name, *Mosi-oa-Tunya*, "the smoke that thunders." But ever since David Livingstone first brought them to the attention of the outside world, the falls have been better known by the name of his queen, Victoria.

Livingstone first saw the falls on November 16, 1855. In his journal, he glowingly noted that "scenes so lovely must have been gazed upon by angels in their flight." His Victorian hyperbole struck a responsive cord, and the falls rapidly became an object of fascination to Africa-bound travelers. The first European visitors were limited to the intrepid explorers and exploiters who followed in Livingstone's footsteps. Among them was Thomas Baines, whose paintings gave the world the first visual images of the mighty cascades with their perpetual mist, shimmering rainbows, and tiara of rainforest. Later, Cecil Rhodes instructed that his

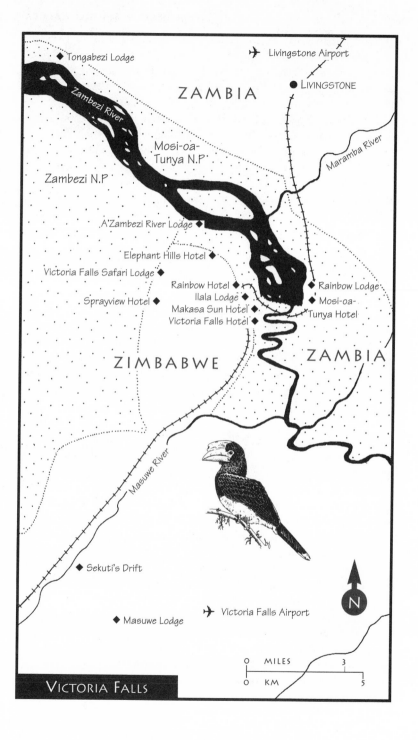

Tongabezi Lodge

✈ Livingstone Airport

ZAMBIA

● LIVINGSTONE

Zambezi River

Mosi-oa-
Tunya N.P.

Maramba River

Zambezi N.P

A'Zambezi River Lodge ◆

Elephant Hills Hotel ◆

Victoria Falls Safari Lodge ◆

Rainbow Hotel ◆
Ilala Lodge ◆
Sprayview Hotel ◆
Makasa Sun Hotel ◆
Victoria Falls Hotel ◆

◆ Rainbow Lodge

◆ Mosi-oa-
Tunya Hotel

ZIMBABWE

ZAMBIA

Masuwe River

◆ Sekuti's Drift

◆ Masuwe Lodge

✈ Victoria Falls Airport

N

O   MILES   3
O   KM   5

VICTORIA FALLS

coveted Cape-to-Cairo railroad should pass within sight of the Falls. By 1904, the railway reached the Zambezi, and the first primitive version of the Victoria Falls Hotel opened for business. From that time, tourists have been visiting the Falls with increasing ease and in growing numbers. Today, it is one of Africa's prime travel destinations.

Although the Falls straddle the border between Zimbabwe and Zambia, the majority of tourists stay on the Zimbabwe side, where the town of Victoria Falls has grown into a busy resort — the principal gateway for safaris in Zimbabwe, Botswana, and Zambia. Victoria Falls, beautiful as ever, are the main draw, but there are plenty of other attractions in the neighborhood. These include game viewing in Zambezi National Park, walking and horseback safaris, canoeing and boat cruises on the wide and gentle upper Zambezi, and whitewater rafting through the gorges below the Falls. The menu of activities has grown steadily with the burgeoning volume of visitors. The planes that carry flight-seeing tourists on the celebrated "Flight of Angels" now compete for airspace with microlight aircraft, helicopters, and float planes (much to the detriment of a peaceful natural environment — the constant drone of airplanes is heard all day). Casinos have been around for some time, but with the arrival of commercial bungee-jumping, risk-takers can now make a safe bet on throwing themselves off the Zambezi Bridge. And after a week or two in the bush, many vacationers are ready for party-time at one of the town's busy nighttime watering holes. These days, there is something for every taste at Victoria Falls.

Access and Accommodation

Victoria Falls has its own international airport. Numerous flights connect it with Johannesburg (South Africa), Windhoek (Namibia), and Maun (Botswana), and it is served daily by Air Zimbabwe and Zimbabwe Express from Harare, Kariba, and Hwange. Vic Falls is also linked by rail to the city of Bulawayo, with service daily on a steam train. The town of Victoria Falls is small but growing, and it increasingly bustles with activity. Its central business district consists of a couple of streets with shops and tourist agencies that intersect at "Wimpy Corner" (in honor of the hamburger joint). It is easy to get around, and bookings for local safari activities can be made at any hotel or tour office. As the major gateway to the safari country of northern Botswana and Zimbabwe, Victoria Falls is a very busy tourist locale.

Accommodation reflects the abundance and variety of its visitors. The *Victoria Falls Hotel* is the oldest and best known in town. Formerly a bastion of colonial atmosphere, the hotel's spacious gardens and its proximity to the Falls still make it a perennial favorite. It has recently gone through extensive renovations and expansion (it now has over 140 rooms). In addition to the normal amenities and a fine dining room, its patio is a popular gathering place for open-air lunches and barbecue dinners. The river views are great at *Elephant Hills Hotel*, a huge new lodge with 276 rooms set high on a hill overlooking the Zambezi, 2 miles above the Falls. (Unfortunately, the hotel's conspicuous location and monstrous size make it visible from miles around, and it does not add to the region's scenic beauty.) It is a prestigious modern resort complete with a golf course, tennis courts, a huge swimming pool complex, conference facilities, and a casino. The well-choreographed "African Spectacular" dance show takes place nightly on its grounds. Cuisine, service, and character at the Elephant Hills Hotel still have a way to go to catch up with its older rival.

The 72-room *Victoria Falls Safari Lodge* is not located on the riverfront, but it overlooks a waterhole where animals come to drink and it has spectacular sunset views over the Zambezi National Park. *Ilala Lodge* is an excellent small hotel on the edge of town but very close to the Falls (a new wing will increase its current capacity of 16 rooms). Its restaurant is highly regarded and the hotel is quiet, except at the public bar and disco, which are popular with the après-rafting crowd. The nearby *Makasa Sun* rounds out the town's selection of tourist-class hotels. This 97-room facility houses the most popular casino in town.

The *Rainbow Hotel* is a cheaper facility that caters mostly to regional vacationers. The *Sprayview Hotel* is the budget choice for the youthful travelers' set; its disco and bar are always busy. The *A'Zambezi River Lodge* is more up-market but has traditionally been priced moderately enough to be popular with budget travelers (it is undergoing extensive renovations, however, so it may soon move into the upper tourist-class category). It has a nice location on the river, but is some 4 miles out of town. Budget travelers can also choose between a campsite in town at the municipal *Victoria Falls Rest Camp* (which is cheap but has security problems) or a quieter one out near the A'Zambezi. If you have a vehicle, you can stay in chalets at the rest camp inside Zambezi National Park.

Several exclusive safari lodges allow you to base yourself in the bush while exploring the Falls region. The Matetsi Private Game Reserve is a huge concession area (195 square miles) that fronts almost 10 miles of river between the Botswana border and the western boundary of Zambezi National Park. Guests stay at either the Matetsi Water Lodge or the Matetsi Safari Camp. The *Matetsi Water Lodge* consists of three separate 12-bed camps strung out along the Zambezi riverbank. Each luxurious little camp has its own dining area and staff. Every chalet is air-conditioned and has its own little swimming pool! The tents at *Mat-*

esti Safari Camp are also superluxurious (each tent is air-conditioned). This 24-bed camp is not on the river, but overlooks a large, grassy *vlei* (a shallow valley) that attracts herds of animals. The various Matetsi camps offer game drives and walks, as well as boating or canoe safaris and excursions to town; the reserve is about 45 minutes by road from Victoria Falls. The 14-bed *Imbalala Camp* is further upriver, just a mile from the Botswana border at Kazungula. This lodge is a favorite with birdwatchers. *Acacia Palm Lodge* is a lovely, owner-run private game re- serve located midway between Victoria Falls and Hwange National Park. It can be used as a base for exploring both areas. The *Elephant Camp* is a tiny (8 beds) thatched lodge on a private reserve some 15 miles from Vic Falls. Its prime attraction is the company of its resident elephant orphans: guests get to ride, bathe, and hang out with a group of appealing and tame young pachyderms.

Masuwe Lodge has a reputation as an exclusive retreat. It is not on the river, but is located in wild bushland only 5 miles from the Falls. Its 10 luxury tents are sited on a rocky ridge overlooking a waterhole where animals drink. Guests are taken on game drives in the nearby Zambezi National Park or ferried to any of the Victoria Falls attractions; the camp's cuisine and ambiance are given top marks. The nearby *Sukuti's Drift Lodge* is a small hotel also noted for its charm and service. *Gorges* is a small lodge perched atop a dramatic precipice. Its 10 chalets over- look the wild rapids of the Zambezi as it flows through the canyons below Victoria Falls.

Tongabezi Lodge is on the Zambian side of the river, but its growing repute earns it mention here. Located upriver, 15 miles above the Falls, its tents and chalets all overlook the broad Zambezi. The most luxurious rooms are marvels of stone and thatch ingenuity that ensure privacy while permitting open-air living. Guests are shuttled to the Falls for ac- tivities, and can take sunrise or sunset river cruises and go canoeing. In the low-water months, Tongabezi establishes a satellite bush camp, *Sind- abezi*, on an island that is just a stone's throw from Zimbabwe's Zam- bezi National Park — and this is the place where elephants may be your neighbors. Tongabezi also sets up *Livingstone Island Camp*, a more basic seasonal camp on Livingstone Island, mere yards above the edge of the Falls. (There are lots of places to stay on the Zambian side of the river; these are discussed in the Victoria Falls and Livingstone section of the Zambia chapter.)

Visiting the Falls

In Zimbabwe, the great cataracts are viewed from Victoria Falls National Park (which requires an entry fee of US$20 per day). A network of trails leads through the rainforest to the riverbank, then along the top of the gorge opposite the waterfalls. Paths are paved to protect vegetation from damage: be sure to remain on them. The park is open daily from sunrise to sunset. It can also be visited on full-moon nights, when you can see mist-bred "moonbows" over the Falls. Views from the Zambian side are also worthwhile, but to cross over, it may be necessary to purchase a one-day visa (US$10 for US citizens; Commonwealth citizens cross free).

The Falls assume a very different character at seasons of high and low water. Water volume peaks in March or April, when the cascades can hardly be seen for all the spray. Walking along slippery paths, you see little more than the curtain of water immediately in front of you. You get soaked, the ground shakes, the sound is deafening. This sense-surround theater is more than a little scary, but the appreciation that it gives you for nature's power is overwhelming.

By July, water levels are dropping and the overall views improve. Rainbows shimmer in the mist as you walk the trail through the rainforest to the Devil's Cataract at the western end of the Falls, where a big stream of water plunges through constantly. From Devil's Cataract, you continue through dripping forest to Main Falls, which also always maintains a heavy flow, then proceed through grassland along the chasm's edge to Danger Point. Here, the 340-foot wall of Rainbow Falls and the Eastern Cataracts are in front of you, and the narrow gorge where the Zambezi recollects to hurl itself downstream through the Boiling Pot is immediately below. As water volume continues to drop, the Falls' curtain of water parts, leaving segments of bare rock exposed between the separate cascades. By October and November, the river is very low with plenty of rock wall showing, and the Eastern Cataracts near the Zambian shore are left nearly dry. But even then, the view from the Zambian side is spectacular from the narrow promontory known as the Knife's Edge: there you look across to Danger Point and get a view up the length of the chasm and the whole line of the Falls. The Zambian view is at its best, however, during the first six months of the year, when water is pouring full force over the Falls. The walk across the Knife's Edge Bridge is then an especially memorable (and wet) experience.

Spray from the Falls nurtures the famous "rainforest" that grows on the opposite side of the gorge. Drenched by constant showers when the river is in flood and moistened by a veil of mist throughout the dry season, this lush, riverine forest adds a special magic to Victoria's environs. Its luxuriant vegetation makes a stark contrast to the seasonally thirsty woodlands that dominate the region. In the rainforest, big evergreen trees of ebony and Natal mahogany form a shady canopy, and the thick, downward-flowing roots of huge strangler figs are very conspicuous. Curlicued woody lianas and feathery wild date palms give the forest a jungle look, but it remains cool in the shade of the forest floor. The shadows are brightened by red fireball lilies, yellow hibiscus flowers, white *Calanthe* ground orchids, and showy flame lilies. Butterflies flutter through the glades, and parties of small birds flit and twitter in the undergrowth. If you are lucky, you can get a look at the pretty Heuglin's robin, although you are more likely just to hear its melodious song. Green pigeons attend fruiting fig trees, and a flash of crimson wings betrays the presence of the crested Livingstone's lourie. Larger animals live in the rainforest, too. It's an excellent place to try for photos of bushbuck, some of which have become amazingly tame. Waterbuck and warthog are also often seen in the park, while overtame baboons have become pests in the parking area at the entry gate.

The Gorges

Below Victoria Falls, the Zambezi River swirls through a series of spectacular gorges that zigzag between vertical walls of volcanic rock. These gorges were carved by the river as it retreated from each of seven successive massive cataracts — the predecessors of the current chasm of the Falls. The river always finds a weak point on which to concentrate the full power of its erosive force. Already, the Zambezi has cut a channel at Devil's Cataract 30 feet deeper than anywhere else on the lip of the Falls, and a heavy flow of water passes through that channel year-round. The river will continue to cut deeper at Devil's Cataract, attracting ever more water until its entire volume is carried through that one cleft. Then the Zambezi will carve a new gorge backward along a fracture of softer rock. Eventually that future gorge will become the line of a new Victoria Falls.

The zigzag canyons are the entrance to the 60-mile-long Batoka Gorge. In the first gorge, sheer walls of red and black basalt tower above the churning whitewater river. Where plants can find a foothold, pale-trunked paperbark trees and rock-splitting figs cling to the cliffs. Further downstream, the gorge deepens but its walls are less steep and more wooded. The river, too, softens in character, with longer stretches of glassy deep water between its wild rapids. Scenery is majestic down the whole length of the gorge. The only means of exploration is by raft, a trip that is universally acclaimed as one of the world's finest whitewater adventures. (For more information, see the Whitewater Rafting section of this chapter.)

River Cruises

Above Victoria Falls, the Zambezi is a wide and beautiful river. The Zimbabwe shore of the river is in Zambezi National Park. Both game and scenery can be enjoyed on leisurely shipboard excursions. Cruises on boats holding 65 to 100 passengers depart daily from the jetty near the A'Zambezi Hotel. There are dawn "champagne" cruises (6:15 A.M.), lunch cruises (12:45 P.M.), and "sundowner" cruises (5:00 P.M.). The sunset "booze cruises" are the most popular. Many companies run sunset cruises on smaller crafts that take only 5 or 10 passengers, and these generally have a higher standard of service and are much better for observing wildlife. Such small boats can be chartered for private parties or for more serious game and birdwatching trips. Cruises are also operated from the Zambian side of the river.

Sunset cruises are indeed pleasant, no matter what style you choose. The big placid river is dotted with islands large and small. Some are palm covered, others mere grassy sandbanks or reefs of exposed rock. Big game viewing is usually pretty limited, but elephants sometimes wander out to browse on island vegetation and hippos can be seen bobbing warily at their favored resting places. The piped whistles of water dikkops carry far over the water as Goliath herons hunt in the reedbeds of the shore and African skimmers dip and glide above the glassy river. The sunset views are always suitably enchanting.

Whitewater Canoeing

The upper section of the Zambezi can also be explored by canoe. The boats used are actually two-person kayaks with covered decks, rather than the open-topped canoes employed on the Zambezi below Kariba Dam. Here in the upper section, the river can flow fast through small rapids, then meander through channels among the myriad islands. Although there are no serious rapids (they are rated up to Class III, depending on the water level), there are riffles and waves big enough to tip a kayak, so you must be psychologically prepared to swim. Testy hippos in narrow channels are another potential hazard. No previous canoeing experience is necessary, but you should be physically fit. Shearwater Adventures, Safari Par Excellence, Frontiers, and Kandahar Safaris operate one- and two-day trips on the Zimbabwe side between April 1 and November 30. Three-day trips from Kazungula, near the Botswana border, run only until the end of June (water levels permitting). Overnights are spent camping in Zambezi National Park, where all types of big game animals can be encountered. Similar canoe safaris are operated on the

Zambian side of the river by Makora Quest, Chundukwa Adventures, and Tongabezi Lodge.

Zambezi National Park

This 209-square-mile park encompasses about half the riverfront between the township of Victoria Falls and the Botswana border. A thin veneer of riverine forest hugs the Zambezi shore, behind which is a mix of Rhodesian teak woodland and mopane scrub. The country holds the wildlife typical of these dry deciduous communities. Although game densities are not high, explorations here can yield sightings of giraffe, kudu, and eland, as well as buffalo, lion, or elephant. It's a very good area for sable antelope. The park is well worth a visit if you are particularly keen and have extra time at Vic Falls. One-day and half-day game drives are easily booked on short notice at any tour office in town.

Because it has relatively few roads, the Zambezi park is a good place to sample alternative forms of game viewing: foot, canoe, and horseback safaris take place here. Experienced riders can participate on Zambezi Horse Trails ranging from half-day rides to multiday trips. These can be booked through Shearwater Adventures. Several companies run professionally escorted foot safaris in the park on a regularly scheduled basis. Shorter walks take place daily, and longer camping expeditions are available.

Walking safaris can also be done in Kazuma Pan National Park. Located on the Botswana border some 50 miles southwest of Vic Falls, the pan is an island of savanna grassland surrounded by teak forests. Roan antelope, oribi, and cheetah are the faunal specialties. There are no facilities in the 122-square-mile park, and the number of camping parties allowed in at one time is strictly controlled.

Flight-Seeing

The bird's-eye view of the Falls and its surroundings is spectacular, so sightseeing flights are a popular activity. The best known is the Flight of Angels, 15- or 30-minute excursions in a twin-engine aircraft. Be prepared for steep banks and dives as you circle for repeated photo runs over the Falls and gorges, then turn upstream for a bit of aerial game viewing. Flights take off every 15 minutes, but demand is heavy during high season, so it's wise to book in advance. If you *really* want to fly, you now have the option of going aloft in a microlight aircraft: it's just you and the pilot out in the wind with fabulous unobstructed views. These flights with Batoka Sky take off from a strip on the Zambian side. Sky diving is another option with either African Extreme (in Zambia) or Zambezi Vultures. Helicopter tours of the gorges are also available.

Masked Makishi dancers are a highlight of tribal dance performances at Victoria Falls. Photo: Allen Bechky.

These are noisy intrusions if you are on a river trip, but if you would rather brave the hazards of flying between cliffs than rafting rapids, you can book with Southern Cross Aviation.

Other Activities at Victoria Falls

As a major tourist gateway, Victoria Falls has developed some good shopping and culturally oriented diversions. These are admirably combined at the Falls Crafts Village, where the traditional architecture, artifacts, and lifestyles of six of Zimbabwe's principal ethnic groups are authentically displayed in an open-air museum. It's a bit touristy — the resident witch doctors will throw the bones to tell your fortune — but it is nonetheless interesting. At 7:00 P.M. nightly, the village puts on a display of traditional native dancing. The show is somewhat less polished than the similar "African Spectacular" (nightly at the Elephant Hills Hotel), and *is* touristy, as is the other show, but it would be a shame to miss one or the other. The Makishi dancers, with their elaborate full-body masks and stilt dances, are particularly appealing. You can buy the elaborate Makishi masks and other artworks at the Falls Crafts Village or one of the neighboring curio shops and stalls. Stone carvers are busily at work here, and their statues are offered by shops, hotels, and street vendors. If you brought along a set of steel chisels for stonework, you could probably get a great trade deal. For the best pieces of Shona sculpture, though, you will probably do better in Harare.

The Zambezi Nature Sanctuary is also worth visiting. Formerly known as the Spencer Creek Crocodile Ranch, crocs are still raised here on a sustainable basis for leather and meat: eggs are collected in the wild, but more reptiles are later put back into the river than would otherwise make it on their own to a survivable size. It's a great place to get close views and photos of crocs of all ages, and to learn about their life cycle and aquatic ecosystem. There is also an environmental education center and a compound with some unusual orphaned animals (like caracal and serval cat). You can sample the croc farm's product at any of the local hotel restaurants.

There is a nice path to walk along the Zambezi, but it is not without risk. A path starts at the Livingstone statue and continues westward to the A'Zambezi Hotel. This area isn't within the national parks (so a professional guide is not required), but there are plenty of animals about, as evidenced by copious elephant and buffalo dung. Although it appears to be safe during daylight hours, people have been attacked by animals along here. If you are tempted, don't try this walk in the twilight, and remain alert at all times.

You won't need any reminders to stay alert if you do the bungee-jump off the Zambezi Bridge: the activity pretty much guarantees the ultimate adrenaline rush. Jumps are organized daily by African Extreme.

Crossing over to the Zambia side is interesting if you want a different perspective on Victoria Falls or simply to check out life in another African country. (For more information, see the Victoria Falls and Livingstone section of the Zambia chapter.)

Whitewater Rafting

In the zigzag gorges below Victoria Falls, the Zambezi plunges through a series of rapids that have made it a Mecca for whitewater rafters. Few would dispute that the river provides the best one-day rafting trip on the planet. Class IV and V rapids (the highest runnable ratings) with huge standing waves and awesome holes provide unparalleled whitewater action for those who dare challenge the "big Z." Many take the dare by joining a professionally operated rafting trip.

The best rafting takes place at low water, when the rapids are more technical and placid pools separate the whitewater drops. The river's flow varies annually, but the rafting season usually gets into high gear by the beginning of August. It is then possible to start at the Boiling Pot, right at the foot of the Falls, which is surely the most spectacular put-in spot imaginable. This is a point in favor of going with one of the Zambian rafting companies, as the only footpath to the pool below the Falls is on their side of the river (Zimbabwean companies must put in a few miles downstream). In any case, low-water runs are long: from August to December the Zambians run Rapid #1 through Rapid #23; the Zimbabwean rafters do almost 14 miles between Rapid #4 and Rapid #24. By January, the river is high and the run is shortened by half, with both Zambian and Zimbabwean rafting companies starting their runs at Rapid #11. High-water runs take place between January and July. Raft trips may not operate from February through May, when water volume may be too high for safe rafting. During high-water runs, the river flows very swiftly, but rocks are drowned and most of the rapids are reduced to a series of standing waves with ratings of Class III and IV.

Most rafters go aboard oar boats — 16-foot inflatable rafts rowed by a single professional oarsperson. Participants should sit in the back if they are content to merely hold on (but you must hold tight, for the aft side of the raft tends to buck in waves, often bouncing out the unprepared). In the front, rafters have to be more active: going into big drops (or "holes"), you are ordered to pile onto the bow in a scrum that adds the extra weight and momentum needed to shoot the raft over the lip of the standing wave on the far side of the hole. Failure to get over a wave can result in a flip, or some tense but exhilarating moments of "surfing."

Rafters are also expected to respond to commands to "highside," with everyone throwing their weight to the side of the raft that faces the waves as it buffets its way through churning rapids. Experienced rafters can opt to go on a paddle boat. Everyone works as crew, paddling under the command of a professional whitewater guide. Paddle boats are more challenging, but the chances that you'll wind up swimming rapids are much greater.

For some, flipping is the highlight of a trip, and it does make good video "carnage" at the end of the day. But swimming a Zambezi rapid can be a very scary experience, one akin to being in a huge washing machine. All you can do is hold your breath as you tumble through the waves feeling as helpless as a leaf in a flood. Fortunately, the Zambezi is a very forgiving river: the sheer volume of water creates a cushion against rocks that protects swimmers from collision, and the holes within rapids are not "keeper" whirlpools that recycle endlessly. So swimmers inevitably pop out in a calm pool at the end of the rapid. Thousands of people now run the river annually, and there have been less than a handful of fatalities since rafting began in 1981. Excellent quality high-flotation life vests are mandatory, helmets are now issued as standard equipment, and there is always a thorough safety briefing at the beginning of each trip. Nonetheless, rafting the Zambezi is not to be undertaken lightly. Although few have died, every year people get injured while being thrown around rafts in pounding rapids. Most suffer only minor cuts or bruises, but bones are sometimes broken. Flips are inherently dangerous and rafting professionals should try to avoid them. Unfortunately, a cowboy mentality prevails among most Zambezi boatmen, many of whom are put onto the river with insufficient professional rafting experience. Although all the rafting companies have safety and risk-management plans, they do little to encourage their boatmen to use the most conservative "lines" (routes through rapids). A casual attitude about risk-taking and boat-flipping is pretty much the norm, so it's lucky that the river is so indulgent.

A number of companies offer daily raft trips. Shearwater, Safari Par Excellence, and Frontiers operate from the Zimbabwe side; Sobek Expeditions, Safari Par Excellence, Raft Quest, and Valley Ventures are licensed to operate in Zambia. All have offices or representatives in Victoria Falls and it is easy to sign up on short notice. Prices are fixed by agreement among the various companies, with the Zambian outfitters allowed to offer a slightly lower price to offset the cost of a Zambian visa (US$10). Each rafting outfitter assembles clients at a convenient location for early morning transport to the put-in; the Zambian companies organize a quick, hassle-free border crossing.

Children under 16 are barred from participation in whitewater rafting. Although there is no upper age limit, everyone should be aware of the pounding one takes on a raft and of the necessity for climbing out of the gorge at the end of the day. It's a stiff hike of almost 700 feet up paths steep enough to be fitted in places with makeshift wooden ladders. Hot afternoon temperatures add to the difficulty of the exit hike. There is also a rocky portage around the fearsome Rapid #9, which is an unrunnable Class VI. It's not mandatory that you carry your raft, but most participants try to help.

In general, hot weather is a good thing when rafting the Zambezi. Water temperature is not bad, but every time you go through a rapid you get soaking wet. Over the course of a day, you can become quite cold, especially in the late afternoon when winds come up and the walls of the gorge block the sun. Although daytime temperatures are pleasant, staying warm is a real concern during the winter months of June through August. At that time, polypropylene (synthetic) clothing, a windproof jacket, and rafting booties would be good to have along. During the warmer months, most people wear bathing suits, although shorts and a short-sleeved shirt do better to minimize contact of wet clothing and skin during the calm stretches between rapids. Bare skin dries and warms quickly in the sun. Unfortunately, it burns easily, too, so be sure to bring along a top-quality waterproof sunscreen. You may want to bring long pants and a long-sleeved shirt to store in the boat's communal dry bag, along with any valuables you take (you need a passport if you are going over the border to raft with a Zambian company). You need shoes for the access hikes and portages, and it's a good idea to wear footwear in the raft: amphibious Teva-type sandals are best, but running shoes will do as long as they will not fall apart when wet. Hats and sunglasses must be secured with snug bands *and* tied to your life vest — otherwise they will surely be lost in the rapids. String is usually supplied for participants, but you might want to bring your own 2-foot length, just in case.

Lunch is provided on one-day trips, and cool drinks appear at that time. Drinking water is brought on the rafts, but you may want to have your own water bottle along for convenience. Make sure it is stored securely or tied down.

Each boat is equipped with a dry bag for storing extra clothing and possessions. Ammo cans are also on hand for stowing cameras. These cans take a daily pounding and are not guaranteed to stay waterproof. If you are depending on your camera gear for more safaris, better weigh the risk of bringing it on the river. Unless you have waterproof equipment, you will not have much access to your camera anyway. Of course, good shots can be had at the put-in and take-out, at lunch, and possibly on some of the long drifts through flat water.

The rafting companies all have their one-day trips videotaped. The videos are swiftly edited and ready for sale at the end of the day. Viewing the day's video highlights at a local pub is the traditional way to wrap up the rafting experience.

Although the waves and rapids get all the attention, the river's flat-water sections have their charm, too. The scenery is gorgeous and primeval, with constant vistas of the deep green river hemmed in by skyward-thrusting canyon walls. Baboons and klipspringers are sometimes seen along the way. Birds are not abundant, although a selection of waders, raptors, and swifts is always present. There is also a good chance to see such rarities as the European black stork and Taita falcon, both of which nest in the gorges — but you'll need binoculars handy for a satisfying view. Crocodiles are sometimes seen in the flat-water pools between rapids. They are usually quite small, and have so far not been a problem for rafts or accidental swimmers collected at the bottom of rapids. But intentional swimming in flat water is not allowed, no matter how hot the day. Although the prospect of crocodiles looms large in the mind before starting a trip, all thoughts of them are quickly banished by the more immediate menace of the rapids.

Longer trips on the Zambezi also take place during low-water season. Shearwater operates two-, three-, and five-day trips. Safari Par Excellence does three- and five-day trips camping on the Zimbabwe side, as well as a two-day Zambia trip that overnights at *Camp Mukuni*, a seasonal full-service safari camp the company puts up in the gorge. The American company Mountain Travel–Sobek pioneered Zambezi rafting and they recreate their original 1981 Zambezi Expedition with a seven-day camping trip that starts at the foot of Victoria Falls and travels the full length of the Batoka Gorge. On this expedition, intervals of flat water grow longer the further down you go. But each day brings more great rapids, some larger than any encountered before. Several portages are necessary, and these are tough jobs when you are carrying expeditionary gear. The hardest is the carry around the torrent of Moemba Falls. Further down, boats must be lined through the Deep Throat rapids. In the last stages of the expedition, the gorge widens and wildlife becomes more abundant, with lots of hippos and large crocodiles to be negotiated. For dedicated river runners, a complete Zambezi expedition is a supreme achievement.

Zambezi rafting could be an endangered species. Zimbabwe is hungry for electric power, and its government is pushing hard to put in a dam on the Batoka Gorge. The dam site has already been selected and preliminary work begun, but the project has been stalled for lack of foreign financial support. If the dam is eventually built, it will create a lake that will drown all the rapids and eliminate even one-day whitewater runs. This is a hot local issue, pitting environmentalists and rafting companies against the government. An alternative source of power already exists in Mozambique's mammoth Cahora Bassa Dam, which has been rendered defunct by years of civil strife. With the Mozambique war over, Cahora Bassa's turbines could be replaced at far less cost than building a new dam, and they would provide abundant electricity to the entire region. But the voices for new development are powerful, and the Zimbabwe government seems indifferent to the loss of the considerable revenues now generated by rafting. Dam advocates are not impressed with such economic reasoning: surely, they counter, tourists would still flock to Victoria Falls, even if there were no whitewater rafting. Perhaps the strongest arguments against a Batoka Dam are really more intangible. What is a wild river worth, after all?

Hwange National Park

Hwange is at once the largest, most famous, and most visited of Zimbabwe's wildlife sanctuaries. Covering over 5,700 square miles of bushland along the Botswana border, Hwange is ecologically an extension of the eastern Kalahari. Here, many of the desert species reach the limit of their range. Mixed with the resident fauna of central Africa's dry woodlands, the desert species add to the park's biological diversity. Consequently, Hwange is reputed to harbor a greater variety of mammals than any other park in Africa. While that may be so, extravagant claims are made that Hwange also hosts the largest numbers. Such exaggerations are hardly necessary, for Hwange is certainly well endowed with wildlife. It has a huge population of elephant and buffalo — somewhere around 15,000 of each — and ample numbers of impala, giraffe, kudu, zebra, wildebeest, lion, and so on down a list that includes rarer species that sometimes wander in from the desert. Hwange has game enough to satisfy anybody, but its animals are *not* usually seen in vast numbers.

Kalahari sands underlie most of the park. On Hwange's northernmost edge, the sand is shallow and basalt outcrops protrude from the underlying bedrock. The hills of the north country are cut by seasonal streams that drain toward the Zambezi. The bush here is dominated by tracts of mopane and terminalia woodlands. It's good country for a variety of game, and is particularly renowned for lion and leopard. A large tract in the Sinamatella area is an Intensive Protection Zone (IPZ) that harbors a good population of black rhino.

Further south, Hwange's landscape assumes the characteristic flattened profile of the Kalahari. Yet it is not quite as flat as it seems: from the air, a pattern of fossilized sand dunes can be discerned in the vegetation below. Woodlands grow thickly on the worn ancient dune crests, which are separated by grasslands in the shallow intervening valleys (locally known as *vleis*). The dune woodlands are primarily forests of Rhodesian teak (*Baikiaea plurijuga*), although they are mixed with a variety of other deciduous trees. Much of Hwange is heavily wooded, but the dense bush is broken by numerous grassy pans. It is in the open grasslands that ring the pans' waterholes that most of the best game viewing takes place. In the southeast, there are also wide grassy plains dotted with big camel-thorn acacias and ilala palms — savannas typical of the eastern Kalahari. These are the places to spot gemsbok and ostrich, or the occasional red hartebeest. But the mix of open grasslands with denser bush makes the southern sector hospitable to a wide variety of game. Its plains and pans are excellent places for viewing sable and roan antelope, as well as small herds of zebra and wildebeest. Giraffe are very common, too, especially where camel-thorn acacias are abundant. Impala are the most numerous of the antelopes, and large groups can be found anywhere in the park. So, too, can elephants and lions.

Hwange National Park undoubtedly has more animals living in it now than at any previous time. It was reputed to have teemed with game when it was a royal hunting ground during the era of Lobengula, the Ndebele king, but most of its animals were wiped out by the ravages of the 1890s' pan-African rinderpest epidemic and indiscriminate shooting. Enough predators and tsetses remained to keep the area inhospitable to cattle, however, and it was declared a game reserve in 1928. In 1949, Hwange was joined with the neighboring Robins Game Sanctuary and achieved national park status. The wardens then set about developing a system of roads and permanent waterholes. Until then, most of Hwange's animals were necessarily migratory, for the park had few natural sources of permanent water. All its rivers and waterholes went dry during its long winter season, when water-dependent species — such as elephant and buffalo — had to migrate to places as distant as the Zambezi River and the Okavango Delta. To keep game in the park, boreholes were drilled on many of the pans, where water was pumped to the surface throughout the rainless months.

The artificial dry-season waterholes proved enormously successful. Hwange's game population soared and the park became a celebrated, year-round wildlife haven. Of course, such human interference in the natural rhythm of the ecosystem resulted in later problems. With water available, game became less migratory, and an increasing animal population put the park's vegetation under year-round pressure. By 1980, elephants were estimated to number over 21,000 animals. Culling has since reduced their population to about 15,000, and Zimbabwe's game managers may well decide to further cut their numbers: South Africa's Kruger National Park is about 40 percent larger than Hwange, yet its elephant population is held below 8,000, which is judged to be its carrying capacity. Hwange's optimal elephant population is difficult to gauge, as its herds still wander widely and many elephants spend a good part of the year in Botswana. Its elephants are an inextricable part of a greater migratory population that really can't be scientifically controlled without regional management.

The importance of elephants as a primary tourist attraction has not been lost on Hwange's tour operators. One outfit has succeeded in getting a particular breeding herd permanently exempted from any threat of a cull. Designated the "Presidential Elephant Herd," these magnificent animals have their home range near Hwange's Main Camp, on the neighboring Hwange Wildlife Estate where a number of private lodges are located. The herd is large — about 120 animals — and includes lots of big tuskers, huge bulls, and great matriarchs. The animals are very relaxed around vehicles and are seen up close by lots of tourists. Giving these elephants special protected status may fly in the face of a scientific rationale for culling, for they do as much damage to vegetation as any others. But perhaps it makes a virtue of necessity — as a cull would raise a huge outcry. Certainly, it makes good commercial sense.

Although Hwange National Park is sure to continue to be in the eye of the culling controversy, it remains a great place to see elephants. That is no longer true for rhinos. Over several decades, healthy populations of both black and white rhinos were built up from animals translocated from South Africa and the Zambezi Valley. The Sinamatella-Robins area was noted for black rhino sightings, while the grassy pans and *vleis* (shallow valleys) around Main Camp were excellent places to observe the larger whites. But poachers virtually wiped out the white rhino population in a devastating blitz in 1993. Black rhinos are thriving in the Sinamatella IPZ, but they are generally seen only when tracked down on foot.

Access and Accommodation

Hwange is easily reached by air or road. Main Camp is only 123 miles from Victoria Falls. Public buses operating between Vic Falls and Bulawayo stop at Hwange Safari Lodge, which is just outside the park and 7 miles from Main Camp. Air Zimbabwe operates daily flights to Hwange National Park's airport, which is only 2 miles from the Hwange Safari Lodge. A United Touring Company bus meets all scheduled flights, taking visitors to either the Safari Lodge or Main Camp for a modest fee. The Victoria Falls–Bulawayo rail line forms the park's eastern boundary, and it's possible to arrive by train: you get off at Dete station, but must arrange transport to cover the 12 miles to Main Camp or the Safari Lodge.

Hwange is a favorite park with budget travelers. It is easily reached by public transport, and offers both affordable accommodation and safari activities. Most budget travelers stay at *Main Camp*. Fees for camping or renting one- or two-bedroom cabins (with twin beds) are very reasonable. Demand for the cabins is accordingly high, and you should reserve them in advance with the National Parks Central Booking Office. Failing that, you can write to the Warden, Main Camp, Private Bag DT 5776, Dete, or call his office at Dete 371 or 372. Visitors bring their own food (which can be supplemented from the camp shop) or eat meals at the camp restaurant. At Main Camp, visitors can book onto game drives with United Touring or Touch the Wild Safaris, which both have desks at Hwange Safari Lodge. Morning and evening, park rangers lead walks to a nearby pan — this is an excellent opportunity to do a foot safari at very low cost. During the full moon, Main Camp rangers also lead convoys of private vehicles on night drives.

If you have your own vehicle, you can base yourself at Main Camp or stay at any of the smaller facilities in the northern sector of the park. *Sinamatella Camp* is beautifully sited atop a rocky, 160-foot-high ridge with magnificent views over the surrounding bush country. You can camp or stay in one- or two-bedroom cabins, cooking for yourself or eating at the camp restaurant. Ranger-led day walks can be arranged at Sinamatella; overnight walking safaris also kick off from there but must be prearranged through the National Parks Central Booking Office. The small *Robins* and *Nantwich* camps are located in the park's northwestern corner. Both offer cabin accommodation; neither has a restaurant. Camping is permitted only at Robins, which also has rangers available to lead walks. Both camps are closed from December to March. Several national park cabin-camps are reserved for the exclusive use of small parties. These include *Deka Camp* (west of Nantwich and reachable only by four-wheel-drive vehicle), *Bambusi Camp* (near Sinamatella), and *Lukosi* (outside the park in the Deka Safari Area). With the warden's permission, fenced picnic areas within the park can be chartered as exclusive campsites by small groups. Mandavu, Detema, and Shumba picnic sites are in the Sinamatella area, where it may also be possible to get permission to spend the night viewing game from the hide on Masuma Dam. In the southern sector, sites are available at Jambile Pan, Kennedy Pan 1, and the Ngweshla picnic site.

The majority of Hwange visitors arrive by air and stay at the Hwange

Safari Lodge or one of the more exclusive private camps. A whole constellation of such safari camps has sprung up around Hwange. Most are on private land along the park's eastern boundary. They are generally expensive, but offer the advantages of open vehicles, walking safaris, and night drives on their properties, as well as superior catering and charm. Some of them feature resident professional guides of the top category.

Hwange Safari Lodge offers the park's only hotel-type accommodation. Moderately priced and located close to Main Camp, it's a good base for safaris into the park and is used as such by minibus tour operators. The waterhole in front of its verandah is much visited by game. It is a fine place to view sable antelope.

An archipelago of excellent small safari camps is run by Touch the Wild on the big Hwange Wildlife Estate that adjoins the Main Camp area. These camps are well located for ease of access to both the airport and the park; they also feature excellent game viewing (of the Presidential Elephant Herd) and night drives. The tiny *Kanondo Camp* accommodates guests in thatched-roofed tree houses. The camp overlooks a busy waterhole that is visited regularly by the Presidential Herd. *Sable Valley Lodge* and *Sikumi Tree Lodge* are sited in the Dete Vlei, a valley that boasts a high population of sable antelope. Guests at Sable Valley stay in thatched chalets, then mount a platform above the dining area to keep watch on the camp's waterhole. Sikumi Tree Lodge is several miles further up the Dete Vlei. As the lodge's name implies, guests sleep in tree houses. It has a swimming pool and is one of the few lodges in the area to accept children. Special arrangements can be made to accommodate the physically disabled. *Katshana Camp*, which consists of six stylish tree houses, and *Makalolo Tented Camp*, are the newest Touch the Wild lodges in the area.

Ivory Lodge features quaint, luxurious tree houses and a swimming pool. It is located on its own 6,000-acre reserve, but is almost 20 miles from the park gate. Ivory's guides and catering are reputed to be excellent, and it is more moderately priced than others in its class. *Detema Lodge* is another moderately priced camp. It is located on the park boundary to the north of Main Camp. Detema offers night drives and walks on its own property, and has direct access rights to enter Hwange National Park.

Although it's located right on the park boundary, *Chokamella Lodge* is an hour and a half drive from the airport or Main Camp. It follows a long and not-very-scenic road along the railway line through the village of Dete. But the lodge itself is close to the Sinamatella entrance, so guests can do game drives in that uncrowded sector of the park and are well situated for rhino tracking in the Sinamatella IPZ. Chokamella vehicles have access to enter the park directly from the lodge property.

Chokamella's thatched cottages and swimming pool overlook a seasonal river. Open vehicles, night drives, and walks with a professional guide are all featured.

Jijima Camp is also over an hour's drive from the airport, but this time to the southeast. This lodge's open vehicles have access over the railway line, so it is well situated for game drives in the productive Kennedy-Ngweshla pans area. Jijima's resident professional guides also take guests on walks and night drives on the lodge's extensive property.

The Hide is a superb lodge sited just outside the park, with very good access to the Kennedy Pans area. It's a small luxury tented camp at which game drives are aboard open-backed vehicles. Walks and night drives are not offered at the Hide, but the camp overlooks an active waterhole that is floodlit for excellent nighttime viewing.

A couple of private safari camps are actually located inside the southern sector of the park. They are a long way from the airport, so road transfers to and from camp take several hours — but there is game viewing the whole way.

The operators of *Makalolo Plains* and *Linkwasha* camps have concessions within a vast restricted wilderness area that covers the entire southern quarter of Hwange National Park. Game is prolific and varied on the pans and *vleis* of these palm-dotted Kalahari grasslands. Both camps feature professional guides, open vehicles, game walks, and night drives. But their principal virtue is their exclusivity. Makalolo Plains is a 16-bed luxury tented camp run by Wilderness Safaris Zimbabwe (a separate 8-bed bush camp is also on the concession). Guests avoid the long drive down by flying from the main Hwange National Park airport to a small nearby strip. Neither Makalolo Plains nor Linkwasha are open during the December–March rainy season. Two other concessions have recently been allocated within the park, so a couple of new safari camps will soon be opening.

Touring the Park

With its superb game viewing, Hwange attracts more visitors than any other park in the country. Such popularity has its price, and Hwange sometimes suffers from congestion. This is particularly true around Main Camp. Patrolled by self-drive visitors from Main Camp and tourist vehicles from the various lodges beyond the gate, circuits near Main Camp can get quite busy. Or at least they seem that way to anyone coming from one of the more remote wilderness parks. Game tracks in the northern sector of the park are less crowded because Sinamatella and Robins camps are smaller than Main Camp, and there are no tourist lodges in the area. It's over 70 miles from Main Camp to Sinamatella, and a further 35 miles to Robins. Keep in mind that there are plenty of animals to delay you, so you should leave Main Camp by 2:00 P.M. to make Sinamatella before dark. It's better to take the whole day to give yourself time enough to watch game at some of the waterholes.

During its summer rainy season, Hwange is a favorite destination for vacationing Zimbabweans and South Africans. The park is then dense with greenery and the animals are much dispersed, so game viewing is harder. But many of the animals drop their young at this season and the birdlife is at its most prolific. Overseas tourists arrive during the cooler winter months, when the trees are bare and animals concentrated around the pump-fed waterholes. The vegetation is then more drab, but the predominant gray of the leafless woodlands is periodically brightened by groves of camel-thorn acacias (*Acacia erioloba*) mixed with Kalahari apple leaf (*Lonchocarpus nelsii*). These trees burst into bloom at the height of the dry season, the yellow acacia blossoms glowing against the massed mauve flowers of the apple leaf.

Game observation is far easier in the dry season, when the best viewing is done simply by watching over the various waterholes. In due course, almost every type of animal will come down to drink. Wary giraffe drink splay-legged, while herds of impala and kudu come and go, and knots of zebra and gnu await their turn. Meanwhile flocks of doves flutter down to the water's edge, and the pool's resident crocodiles cruise back and forth looking for their chance. But the main event at any pan is the arrival of the elephants. This usually takes place at the end of the day, when herds emerge from the surrounding woodlands and surge down to the water en masse. A big herd will transform a waterhole into a squirming bundle of elephants drinking, rolling, bathing, and playing in the mud. It is an unforgettable sight — one for which Hwange's pans are well known.

Viewing platforms or hides have been set up at some of the larger pans, and the viewing from them is often spectacular. The most famous of the platforms is on Nyamandhlovu Pan, which is close to Main Camp. The wooden structure stands 20 feet above the pan, offering an unobstructed view of the waterhole. Some of the action takes place inside the platform-blind, where exceedingly tame yellow-billed hornbills vie for crumbs from onlookers' lunches. In the Main Camp area, another platform is located at Guvalala Pan, further along the road toward Sinamatella. A few miles beyond Guvalala, you can take a loop road back to Main Camp, stopping to check out the many pans on the way.

A less-used track out of Main Camp is the southward loop to Ngweshla Pan. This sandy country is heavily wooded, and in the bushy stretches you may not see much save the occasional kudu or duiker, but there are many waterholes to check out on the way to the Ngweshla picnic site. Waterholes on the Dopi, Jambile, Ngweshla, and Kennedy pans are often visited by big herds of elephants in the late afternoon.

In the Sinamatella and Robins camp area, hides are placed overlooking dams on the seasonal rivers. The larger reservoirs hold hippos and crocs and serve as the usual magnets for every type of game. Professional guides are allowed to take their clients into the Sinamatella IPZ to track Hwange's precious black rhinos on foot.

Over 400 bird species have been recorded at Hwange National Park. Although none are endemic, several are more likely to be seen here than elsewhere in Zimbabwe. Most startling is the crimson-breasted shrike, a bird of thorny thickets. Although its scarlet color is a knockout, its presence is more often given away by a pair's distinctive duet. Also watch for pairs of Bradfield's hornbills in teak forests, and boldly spotted Burchell's sandgrouse when they come to water.

Chizarira National Park

Perched atop a remote Zambezi escarpment, Chizarira is a wilderness refuge more appreciated for scenery than abundant wildlife. Although it does harbor an excellent variety of animals and habitats, game populations are relatively low and the park's isolation from the main tour circuit has left it quite undeveloped. With few roads, it is more suited to game viewing on foot than by vehicle. This makes "Chiz" a favorite with local professional guides, and a magnet for all who enjoy bush walking.

Chizarira ("the barrier") is the Batonka name for a rugged range of hills that rises almost 2,000 feet above the Zambezi Valley. The escarpment's highest point is the summit of Tundazi, a 4,705-foot mountain that is supposed to be haunted by a serpent spirit. The steep wooded hillsides of the Chizarira Escarpment are peppered with small rock piles and isolated towers of weathered stone. Vertical-walled gorges draped with fractured blocks of red and black basalt provide the most dramatic scenery.

Atop the escarpment, the country flattens into a broad plateau. The vegetation is dominated by stunted miombo woodland broken by shallow grassy *vleis*. Perennial springs give birth to several small rivers that cut narrow valleys across the plateau. These gorges are oases of riverine forest and havens for a variety of wildlife.

Chizarira is "big five" country. Elephants and buffalo are the most common large animals, with lion and leopard both well represented. Until quite recently, the park was Zimbabwe's premier haven for black rhino. In 1989, their population was 300; by 1993, it was down to 20. All the survivors were dehorned to make them less a target for poachers, but even that did not save them and it is unlikely that any remain. Impala and waterbuck are the most abundant antelopes, although sable, eland, kudu, and tsessebe are also present.

Chiz is a noted birding hot-spot, with 370 species recorded. Birding hits its peak during the rainy summer season, when migrant specialties such as African broadbill, Livingstone's flycatcher, and Angola pitta may be seen.

Access and Accommodation

Chizarira is a hard day's drive from anywhere. The road is mostly paved from Vic Falls (194 miles) or Hwange (119 miles), but eventually turns into the rough gravel road that passes the park's north entrance before continuing on to Matusadona (110 miles). Chizarira can be reached by charter aircraft. Few safari companies include Chiz on regular itineraries. Those that do usually also feature a licensed guide who can lead walks in the park.

Chizarira Lodge is the only safari camp in the region. Its stone-and-thatch cabins are perched over one of the escarpment's spectacular gorges, and each one has a fabulous view. A waterhole at the foot of the cliff below the lodge is visited by elephants, while baboons are usually seen or heard barking on the opposite side of the gorge. Beyond, huge baobabs and scattered Batonka villages stand out in a vista of woodlands that stretches to the horizon. The lodge is on Batonka communal land, and part of its profits go to the local people. Resident professional guides take guests up to the park for game drives or walks. *Jedson's Camp*, a charming little luxury camp, also features guided boat safaris. It has a hilltop location along the park's isolated southern boundary.

There are several designated campsites inside the park. Two are located close to the escarpment and park headquarters: *Kaswiswi Camp* is on the Lwizilukulu River and *Mbola Camp* is on the Mucheni River. Both rivers are permanent streams and excellent areas for game tracking. *Busi Camp* is located on the remote Busi River in the low country on the south side of the park.

Touring the Park

No one should miss sundowners from the overlook at Mucheni Gorge. Aside from spectacular sunset views of red-rock cliffs and a wilderness landscape that stretches as far as the eye can see, this is a great place for birds of prey. Black eagles quarter the cliffs in search of hyrax, and both the rare Taita falcon and weird bat-hawk are often seen hunting here in the evening.

The park entry road climbs through a gorge filled with evergreen forest. This is a good place for crested guinea fowl and, in summer, Angola pitta, a rare and beautiful bird of the forest floor.

The rocky escarpment woodlands are an excellent place to spot small game like klipspringer and Sharpe's grysbok (*Raphicerus sharpei*), a small steenboklike antelope with a grizzled coat, as well as hyrax and tree squirrels. The bare escarpment woodlands seem austere throughout the dry season, but flush with color when new leaves start to appear in October. The graceful mountain acacias (*Brachystegia glaucescens*) are then especially pretty.

More big game is usually seen atop the plateau. The trees here are broken and dwarfed by elephants. This damage has led to calls for culling, although elephants do not presently seem to be too thick on the ground at Chiz. Grassy *vleis* are usually grazed by herds of impala, waterbuck, and warthog. Animals are particularly drawn to such grasslands after a burn.

The most productive game walks at Chiz are usually patrols along the river valleys. Wide-ranging animals are attracted by the water and greenery, and aside from the increased likelihood of bumping into elephant or buffalo while walking, there are many species to be seen that are confined to the vicinity of forests or riversides. Crocs inhabit some of the larger river pools, and, with luck, otters can be seen foraging along the streams. The sycamore figs and ebony trees of riverine groves attract forest birds such as purple-crested louries and trumpeter hornbills, while a good variety of kingfishers, from the giant to the malachite, can be seen along the rivers.

In the park's remote south, the Chizarira hills drop down to savanna country in the drainage of the Busi River. For much of the year, the Busi is dry, but there can be plenty of game around. Elephants dig for water in the sand river and are attracted to shady groves of *Acacia albida* trees along its banks.

Lake Kariba and Matusadona National Park

When the Kariba Dam was completed in 1958, the waters of the Zambezi were held captive by a great wall of concrete and steel. The local Batonga people who lived along the river were sure that the dam would fail, for Nyaminyami — their serpent-shaped god who personified the indomitable power of the river — would not tolerate such interference. And indeed, Nyaminyami did his best to destroy the offending barrier. Twice — in 1957 and again in 1958 — cataclysmic floodwaters nearly swept away the dam wall. But modern engineering prevailed over the old snake-spirit, and by 1963, a 160-mile stretch of the Zambezi River had been converted into the colossal Lake Kariba we see today.

Nyaminyami's defeat was a disaster for the Batonga, 50,000 of whom where forced out of their homes in the river valley. Primarily a fishing people, they were moved onto higher ground where they were encouraged to take up farming. To this day, most eke out a subsistence living from the seasonally bone-dry bushveld, tending goats and harvesting whatever maize, sorghum, and millet the summer rains will sustain. Some have recolonized the lakeshore, their villages revitalized by a thriving fishery industry. But overall, the Batonga have seen little benefit from the construction of one of Africa's largest hydroelectric projects. Their corner of Zimbabwe remains off the electrical grid, a wilderness where sundown heralds the starry darkness of a primeval African night.

Thousands of wild animals were also removed from the path of Kariba's rising waters in 1958, saved in the celebrated Operation Noah. In some ways, the game fared better than the Batonga, for the rescued animals were naturally well adapted to live in the seasonally dry woodlands beneath the Zambezi escarpments. And with time, the new lakeshore evolved into a prime wildlife habitat as the rise and fall of Kariba's water level converted the fringing bush country into rich grazing lands.

The dam had monumental effects on every aspect of the region's environment and economy, some intended and some unforeseen. As the Zambezi lost its banks, floodwaters crept up the valleys of tributary streams and inundated woody savannas, creating a lake of 2,000 square miles. The artificial lake was almost an ecological vacuum. Vast quantities of vegetation were drowned and their nutrients released, while aquatic species found empty habitats to colonize. A whole new ecosystem came into being, one subject to wild fluctuations before it found its own equilibrium. Nothing illustrates the process better than the history of the "Kariba weed" (*Salvinia molesta*). This small aquatic fern is native to South America, but successfully hitchhiked over to Africa. Washed downstream by the Zambezi, *Salvinia* found Lake Kariba especially to its liking, as its nutrient-rich waters were almost absent of competing aquatic plants. It proliferated like wildfire: within a few years of its first appearance, the weed covered almost a quarter of the lake's surface. Thick beds of *Salvinia* cut off light to the water below and lowered oxygen levels, causing scientists to worry that it would eventually choke Kariba to death. But after its initial burst of fecundity — and for unknown reasons — the weed went into retreat. Today it covers only 1 percent of the lake's surface and has become a respectable member of the ecological community — even winning kudos as a highly mobile hiding place for hatchling fish.

Kariba's planners hoped to exploit the new lake habitat by developing commercial fisheries. The introduction of kapenta, a freshwater sardine native to Lake Tanganyika, proved a spectacular success. Kapenta thrived, and today huge shoals of these 3-inch fish inhabit the lake. They are harvested by a fleet of odd-looking fishing boats. These floating platforms use lights to attract the kapenta to their nets, then haul them in by the ton. The catch is dipped in brine and sun-dried, producing salted sardines that keep without refrigeration. Easily brought to market and stored, they are an inexpensive source of protein for the African diet.

In anticipation of the fishing industry to come, vast tracts of woodlands were bulldozed and burned in an attempt to clear the bottom of the future lake of potential entanglements for fishing nets. Even vaster tracts went uncleared, and whole forests of standing trees were eventually drowned in the lake. Indeed, ghostly forests — the gray snags of dead trees protruding from the water — are emblematic of the Kariba landscape. Underwater, the iron-hard trunks are nearly impervious to decay and may well be on their way toward petrification. Wood-boring beetles weaken the exposed portions of the trees, increasing their vulnerability to waves and storms. Limb by limb, the ghost forests are slowly thinning, but it will take a long time for them to disappear. Meanwhile, the skeleton trees add to the lake's biological diversity by providing niches for life above water and below. Cormorants and fish eagles nest or perch atop the snags, while the submerged trunks anchor aquatic vegetation that provides food and shelter to a community of fish.

Kapenta are not the only fish in Lake Kariba with economic importance. The larger and tastier tilapia (or bream) are also harvested commercially. Delicious tilapia and feisty tiger fish lure droves of sportfishing enthusiasts, and a flotilla of charter boats is there to serve them. Kariba annually hosts a tiger fishing contest which alone attracts hundreds of contestants. The sportfishing industry would itself be a bulwark of local tourism even without the region's safari attractions.

Although tour brochures often portray Kariba as an untouched Eden — an odd characterization for an artificial lake — there have been some problems with environmental pollution. DDT residues and mercury have been detected in Kariba fish: both pose threats to animals further up the food chain and are the inevitable suspects whenever there is a decline in the population of fish eagles. Kariba elephants suffer a peculiar malady not seen elsewhere and widely thought to be caused by a chemical pollutant. Flaccid-trunk (also called floppy-trunk) syndrome may sound like a joke, but losing the use of its nose means starvation to an elephant, and a small number of unfortunate elephants with this deadly condition have been observed in recent years. The cause is still unknown.

Virtually the entire length of Kariba's Zimbabwe shore is excellent game country. In some places, wild animals share the habitat with a smattering of Batonga farms and fishing villages. It is in these communal areas that Zimbabwe's CAMPFIRE project is trying to provide income to local people through managed wildlife utilization. Licensed hunting safaris take place there, as they do in the Charara and Chete Safari Areas, two vast, designated game reserves fronting the lake. But for game viewing, most visitors head to the environs of the Matusadona National Park.

Matusadona National Park occupies a lakefront wilderness between the estuary of the Ume River and the fjordlike Sanyati Gorge. With an area of 550 square miles, Matusadona is not large as African parks go, but its ambiance is genuinely unique. Its lakeshore is scalloped with flooded fingerlike inlets, each bay liberally sprinkled with the snags of drowned trees. This is the watery domain of hippos, crocodiles, and myriad waterbirds. The grasslands of the foreshore teem with game attracted to the flush of green torpedo grass (*Panicum repens*) that perennially hugs the waterline. Scattered herds of waterbuck and the odd buffalo or elephant bull are always to be seen near shore, and it's not unusual to spot zebra, impala, or even bushbuck in the open as well. Huge buffalo herds sometimes spread over the grasslands, and parties of elephant often forage on the grass or lumber down to the water's edge. The extent of the shoreline grasslands varies with the rise and fall of the lake level. Over most of the last decade, the lake dropped steadily, transforming flooded bays into grassland and reconnecting large islands to the mainland. With good rains, that process will reverse. Fingers of water will again move up old channels, and the grasslands will shrink.

Every place the ground rises above the old high-water line, grassland abruptly gives way to wooded bush country. Herds of impala straddle the treeline, advancing onto the grass and retreating to the woods in a daily mini-migration. Kudu and bushbuck also appear at the bushland's edge. The higher ground is dominated by mopane woodland and thickets of tangled jesse bush. Jesse is a particularly dense vegetation composed primarily of scrubby combretum trees (*Combretum celastroides*). Whether in leaf or bare, its twiggy branches make it nearly impenetrable — except to a rhino. Indeed, the jesse makes an excellent hiding place for black rhino — but only a handful of wary specimens remain. Some 20-odd rhinos live in Matusadona National Park's Intensive Protection Zone (IPZ), and they form the only viable population left in the entire Zambezi region. Fat baobabs and other big trees are scattered among the jesse and grassier mopane woods that gradually merge into the miombo woodlands found at higher elevations. This mixed woodland vegetation rises into and over the broken hills of the Matusadona Mountains that form the interior spine of the park.

Matusadona's interior bushlands are the natural habitat of the tsetse fly. Once common in the Kariba region, the fly has nearly been wiped out by a combination of aerial spaying and the use of fly traps. Fly traps are odd devices that consist of rectangles of black cloth impregnated with chemicals that sterilize the flies. The cloth is mounted on poles that swivel with the wind, and a bottle of pungent acetate is set nearby. The black color, movement, and urinelike smell attract the tsetses, who mistake the cloth for a buffalo. Such traps are found throughout the higher portions of the park and the bush country beyond, and are apparently quite effective.

Access and Accommodation

The town of Kariba is the jumping-off point for Matusadona National Park. A paved highway connects Kariba to Harare, but a four-wheel-drive vehicle is needed to reach the park. The sole access to park headquarters at Tashinga is a rough dirt track over hilly terrain, and it is closed during the rainy season. Two ferryboats, the *Sea Lion* and the *Sea Horse,* ply the lake. It's a 22-hour journey between Kariba town and Mlibizi, on the lake's west end. Air Zimbabwe flies daily to Kariba: most overseas visitors arrive by air and immediately transfer by light aircraft or boat to safari lodges around the lake.

Kariba town was originally built to house dam construction workers, but is now the hub of a major resort region. Although the meandering township cannot be described as bustling — elephants and other game animals still wander through its wooded sections — it is a growing center for a variety of commercial activities connected with power generation at the dam, the kapenta fishery, marinas, and safaris. Zimbabweans come to Kariba to fish or go on safari, and like to party. Overseas tourists usually proceed from the Kariba airport directly to one of the safari lodges in the bush. Some tourists have time for a view of the dam from the overlook (where intricately carved walking sticks in the shape of Nyaminyami are sold) and may visit the dam wall before moving off to their hotel. If you have to spend the night in town, the most modern and comfortable hotel is the *Caribbea Bay.* Right on the lake, it is a lively (and sometimes noisy) place with a casino, marina, and Mexican restaurant. Rooms at the *Lake View Inn* have a somewhat frayed colonial charm (baths only), but the hotel offers excellent views and a good restaurant. The *Cutty Sark* and *Kariba Breezes* are the other tourist-class hotels. Several self-catering motels and campsites are also available around town.

A fair number of safari camps are located on the outskirts of Matusadona National Park, and more are coming on line every year. They vary in size and style, but nearly all feature game viewing by boat, vehicle, and foot. Accessible by boat or plane, Matusadona lodges remain open all year, but game drives are often impossible or severely restricted during the rains.

Two long-established camps are sited on Fothergill and Spurwing islands located off the park's eastern shore, although the low water levels of recent years have seen them reconnected with the mainland (and therefore attached to the national park). *Fothergill Safari Lodge* is a well-known, moderately priced camp that accommodates up to 28 guests in thatched lodges. Animal viewing is always top-notch, as the camp is located on Fothergill Island just opposite the section of the Matusadona foreshore that hosts the largest game concentrations in the park. A full range of safari activities is available at Fothergill. *Spurwing Island* is a larger camp (but similar in price) that is popular with white Zimbabweans. Guests are accommodated in tents (without private bath) or in cabins. In addition to game viewing by vehicle, boat, and foot, it offers tiger fishing trips in the lake's scenic Sanyati Gorge.

The exclusive *Sanyati Lodge* is perched on a mainland cliff near the mouth of the Sanyati Gorge. Luxury service includes personal attention, excellent boats, and the best dining in Zimbabwe. It's a bit of a climb up to the lodge — not for the unfit! *Gache Gache Lodge* is located on communal land 10 miles east of Sanyati Gorge and the Matusadona boundary, so activities do not take place inside the park. But the lodge does feature game viewing in canoes and on foot, as well as night drives.

More lodges are found near Matusadona's western boundary, along the wide flooded valley of the Ume River. This area is a long way from Kariba, so guests fly in on light aircraft, then transfer to camp by vehicle or boat. *Bumi Hills* is Lake Kariba's original luxury game viewing resort. Its 20 chalets are set on a hill overlooking the lake. Although recently remodeled, it is upstaged in atmosphere by its elegant new sister camp, *Katete Lodge*. Katete's 16 luxury chalets are decorated to recall the ambiance of safaris in the early 1900s. *Kipling's* is another posh new safari lodge in the Umi area. Its 10 chalets overlook the mouth of the river, with Matusadona park on the other side.

Bumi Hills has a satellite camp, *Water Wilderness*, which is across the Ume River mouth and inside the park. Guests sleep aboard moored houseboats at this exclusive 8-bed floating safari camp, then explore by boat, foot, or canoe. The new *Matusadona Water Camp* has much the same setup and activities. It, too, is a delightful 8-bed camp buoyed in the Ume River estuary, just off the Matusadona shore. Guests commute by canoe or motor launch from floating rooms to a "mother ship" that houses the lounge and dining area. *Musango Camp* is a great 12-bed luxury tented lodge on an "island" off the estuary's western shore. It offers walking and boating safaris (including night cruises) as well as canoe trips among the snag forests of the Ume River. Water Wilderness, Matusadona Water Camp, and Musango are all known for the excellence of their resident professional guides, and these camps have the best access to Matusadona's IPZ, so they are particularly good for visitors keen on rhino tracking. Further up the Ume estuary, *Tiger Bay* is a 36-bed fishing lodge popular with Zimbabweans on holiday. Its resident guides also conduct game viewing excursions into the park by foot, boat, and vehicle.

Well inland and high above the flooded Ume inlet, *Hogwe Safari Camp* is tucked away in the rugged hills of the Zambezi Escarpment. The tiny 6-bed camp is run by John Stevens, one of Zimbabwe's most reputable guides. Bush walking is very much the routine at Hogwe, although interaction with the Batonka villagers who are partners in this safari camp, a CAMPFIRE project, can add another dimension to the experience. Many visitors combine Hogwe with a three-day walking safari in Matusadona National Park. Foot safaris in the park's interior Matusadona Mountains are also the prime activity at the *Matusadona Tented Safari Camp*, which is a 10-bed sister camp of Fothergill Safari Lodge.

At Matusadona, a chartered boat safari is an alternative to a lodge stay. Boats fall into two basic categories: houseboats and cruisers (although some sailboats are also available). Houseboats are more barge-like with accommodation above deck in cabins or open dormitories. Cruisers are yachts with cabins below deck. They are faster and generally more luxurious, and may feature such amenities as air-conditioning — although in the hot season, you may well prefer to sleep on deck. The level of luxury varies with each boat, so be specific about what you want at the time you arrange a charter. All boats come with some kind of tender craft for fishing or game viewing excursions. Game viewing and "camping" on the lake are very pleasant, but to get the most out of a Matusadona National Park visit, you must make sure that you are accompanied by a professional guide licensed to take you on walks in the park.

Several national park campsites and chalets are located inside the park. *Ume*, *Mbalabala*, and *Muuyu* are chalets for self-catering private groups. Public campsites are located at *Tashinga*, *Sanyati*, and *Changachirere*. Tashinga is the largest, but it has excellent hot-shower facilities and is very pleasantly situated on the lakefront among large shade trees. Changachirere is small and suitable for only one party at a time; it is located in the game-rich area opposite Fothergill Island. *Nyanyana* campsite is on the lakefront in the Charara Safari Area, close to Kariba town. Advance reservations for all must be made with the National Parks Central Booking Office.

Fishing and safari camps are beginning to pop up along the western reaches of Lake Kariba. One is the *Senkwe River Lodge*, which is located along the remote shore (about 60 miles west of Matusadona National Park) beneath the Chizarira Escarpment. Game is less abundant (or tame) in the Senkwe area than it is around Matusadona, but there is very little tourist activity, so the camp promises an undisturbed wilderness experience on the shores of the lake.

Touring the Park

Although wildlife viewing at Matusadona National Park is good, it is the lakeside setting that gives the park a charm all its own. Its flaming sunsets are legendary: the spooky flooded forests of the lakeshore are bathed in every hue of purple and orange.

Boat cruises are the most relaxing safaris and are the best way to explore the lakeshore's many flooded inlets. Smaller tender craft and canoes can maneuver through the snags to get close to animals at the shore. But even from a larger boat, you can see wonderful things: watching elephant bulls playfully sparring in the water is a particular treat. If you are doing a multiday cruise or are based aboard a houseboat, you'll have the full water experience: days are passed game viewing, fishing, or soaking up the sun. Swimming looks tempting, but can only be done far from shore in very deep water — where crocodiles *rarely* venture. Moored in a Matusadona bay, you'll be able to sleep on deck under the stars, listening to the sounds of the night: the splash of a fishing crocodile, the honking of a restless Egyptian goose, the bellowing of a disgruntled hippopotamus.

For the most varied game viewing, you'll have to take to vehicles. In most of Matusadona National Park, roads are few and the habitat bushy, so game drives are most productive on the open grasslands of the foreshore and along the fringe of the bush country beyond. Predators are fairly abundant, with lions being the most often seen of the big cats. The cheetah population has been augmented with translocated animals. They are breeding well and are now seen regularly around Fothergill Island. Side-striped jackal are commonly observed trotting on their rounds in the early morning or evening. Game drives may be impossible or severely restricted during the rains.

The lack of roads makes Matusadona's bush country ideal for walking safaris, and many of the lodges keep resident guides on hand to lead such excursions. Hiking cross-country, you follow game trails through patches of mopane and jesse, then emerge onto hidden valleys. Where the lake has retreated, such valleys are mini-extensions of the shoreline, grassy and dotted with skeleton trees. Waterholes and meandering streams attract game into the open valley bottoms, where opportunities for game viewing afoot are good. While exploring smaller creekbeds, you are likely to scare up reedbuck, which bound away to a safe distance whistling their distinctive alarm call. With luck, you will spot elephants and, if the wind is right, maneuver to a position from which you can safely watch them while they remain unaware of your presence. Walkers led by professional guides have a fairly good chance of successfully tracking down a rhino in the park's Intensive Protection Zone.

Most visitors to Matusadona National Park try a couple of hours of foot safari, just for the feel of it. If wilderness bush walking is really up your alley, you can do a multiday backpacking safari that will take you way back into the hills of the Matusadona Mountains. Although rugged, such an adventure will not be cheap, because you will need the services of a fully licensed guide.

Zambezi Canoe Safaris

Below the imprisoning wall of Kariba Dam, the Zambezi is reincarnated a free river. It pushes swiftly through the narrows of Kariba Gorge, then broadens on the floodplains of the Zambezi Valley, where it attains a width of almost 3 miles in some places. The Zambezi is already a majestic stream even before it is swollen by the entry of Zambia's big Kafue River. Wide and strong, it rolls past Mana Pools, then constricts in Mupata Gorge before its junction with its second great tributary, the Luangwa, and its next impoundment in the huge man-made lake of Cahora Bassa.

This 160-mile-long stretch of the middle Zambezi is one of Africa's great wildernesses, a vast zone of remote tsetse-plagued bush that has been left a haven to wildlife. From Kariba to Kanyemba, at the Mozambique border, the Zimbabwe side of the river is virtually uninhabited. With the exception of the portion within Mana Pools National Park, the entire south bank consists of designated safari areas — the domain of professional hunters. Most of the Zambian shore is similarly protected in hunting blocks or Lower Zambezi National Park. The river is the sole highway through these wilds. It is no surprise that Zambezi canoe safaris have become one of Africa's most popular wilderness adventures.

Canoeing expeditions come in various guises. All outfitters use 18-foot, Canadian-style fiberglass canoes. The canoes are remarkably stable and are easy enough to maneuver, once you get the hang of it. It's nor-

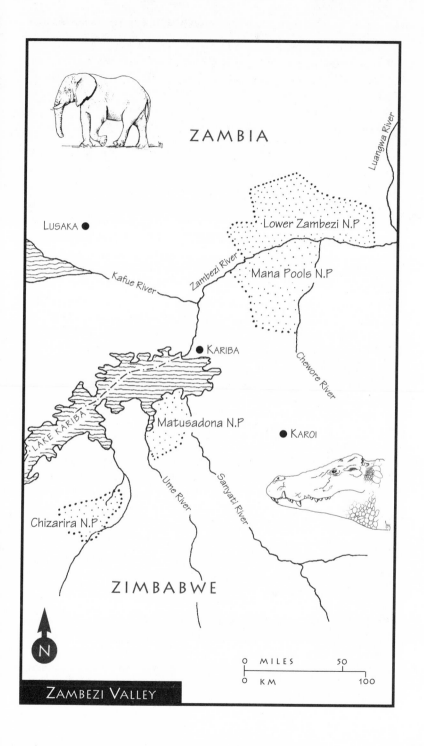

ZAMBIA

Luangwa River

Lusaka ●

Kafue River

Zambezi River

Lower Zambezi N.P

Mana Pools N.P

● KARIBA

Chewore River

LAKE KARIBA

Matusadona N.P

● KAROI

Chizarira N.P

Ume River

Sanyati River

ZIMBABWE

N

O   MILES   50

O   KM   100

ZAMBEZI VALLEY

mally two paddlers per canoe, but some companies may put a third person in the middle when camping gear is not being carried. Groups consist of seven or eight canoeists under the supervision of a single professional guide. Even novices are welcome, although participants should be reasonably fit. Children under 15 are banned from most scheduled trips, but are accepted for chartered expeditions.

Canoeing is not ordinarily strenuous, but it can be hard work when head winds whip up the Zambezi, which happens fairly regularly in the afternoon. Such winds kick up choppy waves that, while not threatening, get you pretty wet and make headway difficult.

Trips always start with a brief lesson in boat handling and safety. Basic concepts of paddling and steering are simple, although maneuvering requires some coordination by the crew — something that can lead to tension.

The basic safety rule is to follow the guide's example and instructions. Guides often know where aggressive territorial hippos hang out and can judge where and when it is safe to pass. They can also read the water for submerged rocks or trees that could capsize a boat. You simply try to keep to the line of the guide's canoe. Life vests are given out, but they are pretty much abandoned by participants after the passage of Kariba Gorge.

Hippos are very abundant in the Zambezi, and your canoe will have to run past many herds on any trip. Crocodiles, too, are very common. Both are very dangerous (for more information, see River Trips in the Living in the Bush section of chapter 2). Swimming in the river is taboo, although the cool water looks very tempting during the afternoon heat. In fact, some people do take quick soaks in clear sand-bottomed shallows — but it is not without risk. So far, croc attacks on tourists have been almost nonexistent, but boats get capsized by hippos every year. This is not surprising, considering that over a thousand canoes now go down the river annually. A few years ago, complaints about the danger posed by the numerous hippos appeared in the press, along with calls for a cull. It's conceivable that authorities will one day decide that hippos have overpopulated the river — a hard assertion to prove, but a surefire justification for culling. So far, the water horses have been left alone and canoeists just have to take their chances.

The sun is, as usual, the most underrated hazard. You'll spend long hours on the river and should be prepared to either cover up or dose yourself well with a good waterproof sunscreen. Local conventional wisdom holds that you can drink directly from the Zambezi River without ill effect, and that the river is bilharzia-free, except around human habitations or in sluggish backwaters.

Most canoe safaris are participatory. Everyone is expected to help pitch camp, load canoes, and assist the guide with cooking chores. Bedding is provided and tents are brought along for emergencies, but generally you set your mattress on the sand, rig up a mosquito net supported by your paddle, and sleep under the stars. Camps are made on islands to discourage roaming lions and hyenas.

On a typical day, you rise early, pack up, and start right after morning coffee and biscuits. After paddling for a couple of hours, there is a midmorning stop for a cooked breakfast. Another paddling session is followed by a long lunch break and siesta. In addition to the stops ashore, there are occasional midriver breaks. Canoes are then lashed together for a lazy Tom Sawyer drift while you sip cool drinks. A final canoeing session in the cooler late afternoon ends in time to pull onto an island and establish camp before dark.

Several companies operate luxury canoe safaris on which there are more comfortable camps. The daily routine is much the same and there is often the addition of a foot safari.

Canoe safaris are really more wilderness adventures than game viewing trips. There is no doubt you will see animals, but aside from myriad hippos and crocodiles, and ever-present aquatic birdlife, any wildlife sightings while paddling should be considered a bonus. The best wildlife viewing trips are those in the Mana Pools/Lower Zambezi Park sector of the river. These combine paddling with foot safaris or game drives ashore, and are accompanied by a fully licensed guide. (Unless otherwise advertised, the majority of canoe trips are led by river guides who are licensed only for canoeing and cannot conduct game walks away from the riverbank.)

Zambezi canoe safaris vary in length and style. Most are variations or combinations of three basic itineraries: from Kariba to Chirundu (two nights) or to Mana Pools (four to six nights), within Mana Pools itself (three or four nights), or from Mana Pools down river to Kanyemba (four to five nights). The complete river journey from Kariba to Kanyemba takes nine nights.

Kariba town is the gateway to the middle Zambezi and the logistical center for a lot of canoeing activity. Many trips start just downstream from the dam wall. Trips on the lower river, within Mana Pools or beyond, usually begin and end at Kariba with road or chartered air transfers.

Kariba Dam is the kickoff point for the first leg of canoeing on the Zambezi, the stretch from Kariba to Chirundu. This journey starts with the run through Kariba Gorge. The river moves pretty fast here. There are some riffles and rocky shoals, but absolutely no whitewater. In this section, you encounter the first hippo pools and see crocodiles on stone ledges. Because the river here is hemmed in by the steep wooded walls of the gorge, there are few other large animals, although you might spot baboons or the odd bushbuck at riverside. Below the gorge, the country and the river widen, and there are lots more hippos. It's a leisurely two-night, three-day trip to Chirundu, where a bridge links Zimbabwe and Zambia. Although all types of animals inhabit the Zimbabwe side of the river (the Urungwe Safari Area), big game sightings are pretty sporadic. The Zambian shore is lightly populated, and you may well see fisherfolk or villagers going about their business at riverside.

Game viewing improves dramatically as you near Mana Pools. Here, the Zambian bank is protected in Lower Zambezi National Park, and game is more abundant on both sides of the river. Elephant and buffalo are often encountered feeding in riverine grasslands and reedbeds. Canoe safaris sometimes come upon elephants standing knee-deep in the river. With caution, bulls can be approached without alarming or threatening them. Waterbuck, impala, and baboons or vervet monkeys are regularly spotted on the banks. Sometimes even lions can be seen from the river. Explorations in smaller side channels yield the best sightings of animals and birds. They also produce more risky adrenaline-producing encounters.

In Zimbabwe, Natureways (Garth Thompson Safaris) offers four-night luxury canoe safaris in Mana Pools. These include the services of a fully licensed canoe and walking guide and camps supported by vehicles and camp staff. Shearwater runs vehicle-supported trips through the park starting from Ruckomechi Camp.

Zambian outfitters run similar game-oriented trips in Lower Zambezi National Park. These usually start with a motorboat ride from the Kafue River down the Zambezi to the park boundary. Safari Par Excellence has established a string of luxury safari camps to accommodate its canoe expeditions. They include game drives and night drives. Shearwater also has permanent canoeing camps in Zambia for its trips on that side of the river. Several of the Zambian lodges along the Lower Zambezi run canoe safaris, too. Walks in Lower Zambezi National Park are accompanied by armed national park scouts as well as the canoeing guide.

Many African canoe aficionados consider the remote sector from Mana Pools to Kanyemba to be the most exciting part of the Zambezi. Although big game sightings may decrease somewhat below Mana Pools, so, too, do the number of canoeing groups, and the sense of wilderness is sublime. The highlight is the passage through the Mupata Gorge, where the Zambezi glides between cliffs up to 500 feet high. This journey is usually done in five nights, which allows lots of time for leisure or tiger fishing.

Mana Pools National Park

Many consider Mana Pools the crown jewel of Zimbabwe's park system. At 858 square miles in extent, it is only Zimbabwe's third largest park, but it is the heart of a much vaster wilderness and encompasses the richest wildlife habitat in the Zambezi Valley.

The riverfront scenery at Mana is exceptionally grand. Here the Zambezi is backdropped by the hills of an escarpment rising up just beyond the Zambian shore. In the broad riverbed, the Zambezi's main channel flows wide and steady, while smaller waterways wind through grassy flats and low-lying islands. A high bank marks an abrupt transition from riverbed to floodplain. Atop this alluvial terrace, big riverine trees flourish. These include such beautiful species as Natal mahogany, sausage tree, and the wide-crowned Zambezi fig. But it is the lovely groves of winterthorn acacias that especially catch the eye, and these trees are almost the trademark of Mana Pools. Scattered on grassy lawns kept cropped by thousands of animals, the tall graceful acacias look as though planted in an English garden. The unique, parklike landscape of the floodplain is so beautiful and game rich that it has earned Mana Pools designation as a UNESCO World Heritage Site.

Mana takes its name from a series of rain-fed lakes on the floodplain. The pools are the gift of the Zambezi, old channels that were carved and abandoned by the meanderings of the great river. In the past, the cut-off channels were periodically refilled when the Zambezi jumped its banks. Since the establishment of Kariba Dam, such floods no longer occur, but the pools still fill during the rains. They retain water well into the dry months, long after all the seasonal waterholes and ephemeral rivers that snake down from the escarpment have disappeared into the sand. The wild animals of the interior bush country then move down to the Zambezi floodplain, where they find water and ample sustenance from vegetation nurtured by rich alluvial soils.

As the dry season progresses, the animals emerge from the escarpment woodlands in ever greater numbers. Early on, there is plenty of green grass on the floodplain. By the end of August most of the palatable grass has been eaten, leaving the ground largely bare save for scattered straw and myriad animal tracks. With food supplies dwindling, buffalo and elephant wade into the Zambezi to graze on island grasslands, and browsing pressure on woody vegetation increases. Mass starvation would threaten without the timely arrival of a bountiful crop.

Mana's big winterthorn acacias are not only beautiful, they are also critically important to the ecology of the park. Each big *Acacia albida* tree produces hundreds of pounds of seedpods a year. The curled, red-brown pods look like dried apple slices (hence another name for the tree: apple-ring acacia). Huge masses of them hang from the branches, providing a nutritious food source for wildlife at the height of the dry season, when little grass is available. The pods are eagerly sought by most herbivores, including buffalo. The abundance of these acacias on the Mana floodplains is an important factor in the park's ability to support a high density of game. Paradoxically, the presence of so many big trees is probably the result of a very low elephant population at the beginning of the century, after unregulated hunting had nearly wiped out the big pachyderms of the Zambezi Valley. Without heavy browsing, the acacias reached full size before elephants reestablished their numbers. Unfortunately, the current abundance of elephants and other browsing animals prevents the trees from regenerating because new seedlings are quickly gobbled up or destroyed. This is a potential long-term threat to the Mana Pools environment.

Impalas are by far the most common antelopes at Mana. In fact, they are periodically culled. Throngs of them are joined on the floodplain by smaller groups of waterbuck, warthog, and zebra. Kudu, eland, and bushbuck are also regulars, and sable antelope are very rare visitors. Baboons seem to be everywhere. Like the impala, baboons readily find forage in the chaff of picked-over grass, and even more easily harvest the fruits of the floodplain trees. Unlike impala, they do not have to wait for figs or acacia pods to fall. Nor do elephants. One of the great sights at Mana is to watch elephants go after acacia pods when the big trees are in full fruit. A full-size bull usually bumps or shakes a tree to make the pods fall. Failing that, he stands up on his hind legs, lifting his trunk high to reach pods from overhead branches.

Three familiar animals are not seen at Mana. The park was a famous stronghold for black rhino, but they were exterminated in the lost war against poachers. More mysteriously, both giraffe and wildebeest are absent from the Zambezi Valley.

At Mana Pools National Park, visitors are allowed to explore on foot unescorted. This unusual feature is a holdover from colonial times. When the park was first established, it was extremely remote and visitors were few. Those who did turn up were mostly white Rhodesians with ample bush experience. It was deemed important that there be at least one park where such people could enjoy the African wilderness without the restrictive rules applied elsewhere. This freedom to roam is still a big part of the Mana mystique.

Access and Accommodation

Mana is open only during the dry season from May 1 to October 31.
Weather permitting, the two safari lodges on its boundaries operate from
April through November.

Mana is hard to get to. The lodges arrange scheduled air transfers
from Kariba, but these flights do not operate daily. Many visitors arrive
on charter flights, which are easily arranged. Mana is a long day's drive
(238 miles) from Harare. Although not far from Kariba town (103
miles), it still takes at least three hours. All visitors must stop at the national park office at Marongora to show or book permits for entry and
accommodation. There is no public transportation and only those with
vehicles are allowed in, so it's difficult for budget travelers to visit the
park.

Keen naturalists will find the last part of the ride to Mana Pools National Park interesting. The Marongora office compound is pleasantly
located in the wooded hills atop the Zambezi Escarpment. It's worth
wandering around the compound, as several fine examples of difficult-
to-identify brachystegia trees are labeled and unusual miombo-country
birds can be seen. Just beyond Marongora, you reach the edge of the escarpment. In the dry season, merely looking into the sere country below
will make you thirsty. By the time you reach the foot of the escarpment,
the vegetation has changed, with the miombo woodlands of the plateau
replaced by the baobabs, mopane, and jesse bush of the low-lying floor
of the Zambezi Valley. You turn onto a gravel road that continues another 45 miles to park headquarters at Nyamepi. It's wild bush country
all the way. The woods are filled with flocks of red-billed hornbills,
wood doves, and white helmet-shrikes, but aside from the occasional
kudu, you see little game until you emerge onto the Zambezi floodplain.

Nyamepi is the park's public campsite. It's a busy place and can feel
overcrowded, but like all Mana campsites, it is well shaded by big riverine trees, has wonderful river views, and is often visited by wild animals.
Fully equipped cabins can be booked at Nyamepi, or at the exclusive
Vundu Camp. There are also a number of exclusive campsites that are
usually reserved by safari tour operators. The most up-market professional guides operate walking and canoe safaris in the roadless Wilderness Area that comprises the eastern third of the Mana Pools National
Park.

Ruckomechi Camp is located just over the park's western boundary,
in the Urungwe Safari Area. Daily transfers from Kariba town are
arranged by road and motorboat. Guests also arrive by canoe, as

Rukomechi is owned by Shearwater and is the terminus for one of their most popular canoe trips. Ruckomechi offers foot and canoe safaris, as well as game drives into the park. It has accommodation for up to 20 guests in thatched chalets.

Chikwenya Camp also has thatched cabins. This excellent 16-bed lodge is sited on the eastern end of the park, in the remote Sapi Safari Area. Walking safaris are the specialty at Chikwenya, although guests can also view game on drives, or from boats and hides.

Touring the Park

Mana has relatively few roads for game drives, although there are ample tracks to explore on the central floodplain around the principal pools. Roads do not skirt the riverbank, and all the tracks that turn down to the Zambezi lead to campsites or lodges.

Of course, the park can be explored on foot. Mana is ideal for bush walking because of the open nature of the floodplain environment. Big game animals are plentiful but visibility is quite good, so it's reasonably safe to walk around (for short distances) as long as you stay in the open and remain alert. That said, it is also easy for the unwary or inexperienced to get in trouble. Gullies or patches of long grass can harbor unseen lions. More seriously, there are plenty of elephants around — and the females are notoriously unpredictable when they sense a threat to their offspring. Even relaxed female elephants in full view are potential trouble. Wind direction can change, alerting them to your presence and altering their mood, while other animals may have inadvertently cut off your safe path of escape. Every year, incidents occur in which visitors get nailed, sometimes with fatal results. That such misadventures are relatively rare is no consolation if it happens to you. It is far safer to walk in the company of an experienced guide. Park rangers are available at Nyamepi to act as escorts. Although they are not required, you may find their eyes and innate caution a tonic for trouble. But even those walking with professional guides sometimes get attacked. There are no guarantees, and any walking is done at your own risk. If you must go on your own, exercise extreme caution in exploring on foot. Stay out of the jesse bush!

The Zambezi Valley is low country, and Mana is very hot from August onwards. Be sure to carry water on your foot safaris.

Canoe safaris are rewarding at Mana Pools National Park, for it is the most game-rich section of the Zambezi. Several of Zimbabwe's top guides offer canoe safaris in the park that combine paddling with foot safaris. Canoes can be rented at the Nyamepi ranger office, but be forewarned that to return the boat, you may have to paddle upriver for half your trip, which is tough work.

The impact of animals on vegetation is easily observed at Mana. On acacias the browse line is consistently at the maximum height elephants can reach. The dense evergreen crowns of Natal mahoganies (*Trichilia emetica*) also have conspicuously flat undersides, but these are kept neatly trimmed by the pruning of kudus and eland. As a consequence, the trees provide terrific shady resting places for animals and humans alike. They are also wonderfully fragrant when in flower.

While impalas, baboons, and elephants may be in constant view on the floodplain, shyer animals tend to spend much of the day in the interior woodlands, hiding in dense thickets of jesse bush or feeding on the dry leaves and bleached grasses of the mopane. Animals like the nyala are most likely seen when they come to water. The nyala lives in the jesse, and it is a prize sighting at Mana. Although very abundant in South Africa, this beautiful striped antelope is rare in Zimbabwe. Late morning is a good time to watch a steady stream of the more common animals — buffalo and kudu, as well as zebra, impala, and baboons — moving down to water. Lions and other predators usually slip down to drink after eating. Keeping watch from a strategic site at one of the pools is a proven game viewing strategy at Mana. Anything can be seen and probably will, if you are given enough game viewing time.

The most famous pool, Long Pool, is the largest. This old river channel often holds water right through the year. Large figs and other riverine trees grow around its edges, where there are many attractive spots for game viewing. The Long Pool area is perennially rife with animals and birds. Crocs inhabit its waters: with luck you can see monsters basking on the banks, but they are wary and will slip into the pool if disturbed. Even then, bony heads, torpedo shapes, and serrated tails of all sizes will poke above the surface everywhere. There may be some real action if there is a hippo carcass in the water, as thrashing crocs twist their bodies to tear off meat. Hippos lay up in the pool, although they may be obscured by the water hyacinths that often crowd the surface of Mana waterholes. Birdlife is always evident. Jacanas, sandpipers, pied kingfishers, and spur-winged geese are usually present, as well as the usual selection of herons and storks.

Lions are the most commonly seen predators at Mana, and it would be an unusual night if you didn't hear the big cats calling. The roars of Mana lions are often answered by prides on the Zambian side of the river. In times of drought, Mana lions have been observed eating a lot of young elephants. It's not certain if the lions are actually preying on elephant calves or whether they are merely scavenging on carcasses. But when food is short, elephant breeding herds tend to split up, with each cow foraging separately. Without the protection of numbers, calves are more vulnerable to harrying attacks, especially if they are already weakened by hunger.

Spotted hyenas and black-backed jackals are often seen. Mana's broken woodlands and abundant impala also make it an excellent habitat for wild dogs, and they are found fairly regularly. Leopard are much more abundant, but usually stay hidden. Cheetah are rare.

The close of the day is always a delight at Mana, where sunsets over the Zambezi are legendary. In the late afternoon, buffalo and elephant are always feeding on the grassy islands, and the mountains of the Zambian escarpment form a nice background. The silhouette of an elephant caught crossing the purple river in front of a fireball sun is the defining photo image at Mana Pools. It can be collected almost any evening.

The Eastern Highlands

From Harare, a narrow sliver of high country at altitudes between 5,000 and 6,000 feet extends eastward all the way to the Mozambique frontier. These uplands, known as the Eastern Highlands, rise to their apogee in the 8,000-foot peaks of the Nyanga Mountains, the northern end of a spectacularly broken string of peaks and deep-cut valleys that runs for 190 miles along the border. The Eastern Highlands are in Manicaland, Zimbabwe's easternmost province, named for its Shona-speaking Manyika people

The Eastern Highlands possess the most stunning scenery in the country. Rhodesia's colonial settlers loved the place for its greenery and cool climate, so reminiscent of their home islands. They set out to duplicate the British countryside. They built English-style country hotels, laid out formal gardens and golf courses, stocked mountain streams with trout, and made the region their vacation land. Still popular with Zimbabwe residents, the Eastern Highlands now also attract international travelers looking for an alternative to game country safaris. Although there is interesting fauna about (for birders, the region is one of the most fascinating parts of the country), the Eastern Highlands are mostly celebrated for their mountain scenery and colonial-era ambiance.

The Eastern Highlands are divided into three principal areas of interest: the Vumba Mountains, the Nyanga region, and the Chimanimani Mountains. Each has a distinctive character and appeal. The highest mountains are found in the Nyanga, an upland plateau that is also the most developed as a European-style resort. The Vumba Mountains, with their lush forests, have a more African feel, although there, too, are found excellent resort hotels. The Chimanimani are rugged and roadless, the realm of backpackers and mountain walkers.

The town of Mutare is the capital of Manicaland Province and the gateway to the Eastern Highlands. It's 163 miles from Harare, only a three-hour drive on an excellent paved road. The highway passes through Marondera, a small town, but still Zimbabwe's third largest, and a major agricultural center. The drive to Mutare is particularly pleasant in September, when Zimbabwe's *msasa* trees shoot out new foliage in glorious hues of red and pink. Mutare can also be reached by public bus or overnight train. From Mutare there is public transport into the Nyanga and Vumba, but a car is clearly the preferred way to get around. Mutare is also the main rail and road link to Mozambique, and it is the portal to the 185-mile Beira Corridor that connects Zimbabwe with its closest seaport. Now that peace has been restored to Mozambique, Mutare will no doubt see quite a bit of traffic going to the coast.

Mutare has a gem of a setting. It is only 3,674 feet high, yet is surrounded by mountains, with the Vumba rising only 6 miles to the south. The *Manica Hotel* is the best in town, but if you have a vehicle you will probably move on to more charming lodgings in the nearby mountains (the *Inn on the Vumba* is only 5 miles from Mutare). If you do spend time in town, you'll want to see the Mutare Museum. It has ethnological and archaeological collections, as well as displays on the fauna, flora, and geology of Manicaland. There is also a collection of old vehicles and a large aviary on the grounds. The Aloe Garden and Park specializes in those African succulents, which bloom from May until August. Cecil Kop Nature Reserve is very zoolike. You might prefer a nature hike on Murahwa's Hill, where there is a natural stone gong. La Rochelle is a colonial estate with once-carefully landscaped gardens. It is just north of town, near the gold mining village of Penhalonga.

The Vumba Mountains

Although not particularly high (their highest peak, Castle Beacon, is only 6,270 feet), the Vumba are stunningly beautiful. Vumba literally means "mist," and in these Mountains of Mist, blue-gray granite domes suddenly appear to hover above luxuriant, forest-covered hills, only to vanish again in banks of swirling cloud. The year-round mists and an annual rainfall of over 60 inches nurture a riot of vegetation. Msasa trees carpet the lower slopes. These are replaced with evergreens like mahogany and cedar in the higher montane forest, with montane grassland and scrub crowning some of the highest promontories.

The best places to take in the nature of the Vumba Mountains are the Bunga Forest Botanical Reserve and the Vumba Botanical Gardens.

Both are accessible by an excellent road that cuts through the heart of the Vumba, passing beneath the peaks of Cloudlands, Lion Rock, and Castle Beacon. The Bunga reserve has steep walking trails through dense native forest. The more celebrated Vumba Botanical Gardens is much easier to explore. On its manicured trails, exotic flowers from around the world flourish within a verdant setting of natural African vegetation. As a bonus, when the weather clears, there are great vistas down to the plains of Mozambique. In addition to 75 acres of tended garden, another 420 acres of indigenous forest are protected in the adjoining Vumba Botanical Reserve. The wild portions of both the Vumba and Bunga reserves are inhabited by shy forest animals such as samango monkey, bushpig, tree civet, and blue duiker. Birds are everywhere in these forests. Some fine specialties include orange thrush, bronze sunbird, Swynnerton's robin, and black-fronted bush shrike. The Chirinda apalis, Robert's prinia, and red-faced crimsonwing are virtually endemic to this part of Zimbabwe.

A variety of accommodation is available in the Vumba. The *Leopard Rock Hotel* is the most prestigious resort. Princess Elizabeth (not yet Queen of England) and her mom stayed there in 1953: such royal names in the guest book ensure a hotel's renown. The hotel's chateaulike building was badly damaged in Zimbabwe's independence war, but has recently been renovated. Set beneath a granite dome just south of the Vumba Botanical Gardens, with a championship golf course, the Leopard Rock really is elegant, although service is not yet world-class. The *White Horse Inn*, *Impala Arms*, and *Eden Lodge* are English-style country hotels in the mountains, and there are a number of guest houses as well. A trailer park and campsite is located in the Vumba Botanical Gardens.

A scenic loop road encircles the Vumba Mountains. Crossing the range, it passes through changing landscapes varying from the evergreen Vumba forests to coffee and eucalyptus plantations in the high Essex Valley, then to the banana groves and tobacco farms of the tropical Burma Valley. On this circuit, you not only look down into Mozambique, but get westward views to the Save River in Zimbabwe's Lowveld.

Nyanga National Park

The Nyanga high country offers a strange hybrid of civilized charm and primitive montane grandeur. Its rain-swept peaks and misty moorlands are the breeding grounds of rivers that plunge in spectacular waterfalls from green plateaus into deep gorges. The entire Nyanga is littered with mysterious stone structures, the remains of a vanished culture. Yet spread among the granite domes, rushing waterfalls, and ruined stone forts are trout-filled dams, golf courses, tidy farms, and colonial-style hotels.

The centerpiece of the region is Nyanga National Park. Inspired by its scenery, Cecil Rhodes established an estate there that was willed to the country upon his death and later became the nucleus of the park. The Rhodes estate is located in the park's central area near Nyanga Dam. Today, his farmhouse is part of a hotel and the stables have been converted into a museum. A lot of the Nyanga region was cleared, its native forests replaced with farms, orchards, and pine plantations. But patches of evergreen forest remain, especially in the southern Mtarazi section of the park, and there are plenty of natural montane grasslands and heath-covered moors beneath the granite mountains. Inyangani (8,507 feet) is the biggest peak, and the highest point in Zimbabwe. It is not particularly imposing when viewed from the park, but a marked path leads over moorlands to its broad summit where walkers may be treated to impressive views of the Honde Valley 3,000 feet below (*if* weather permits). Weather is problematic in these storm-prone mountains, and hikers should be well prepared with warm clothing and wet-weather gear. Visitors have vanished in the past, and local legend has it that the mountain is possessed of spirits unkind to trespassers.

You need not climb the heights of Inyangani for great scenery, as many of Nyanga's attractions are easily reached by car. World's View lookout point offers a westward vista over Zimbabwe's Highveld, while the Honde Valley lookout perches some 5,000 feet above the plains of Mozambique. Just nearby, Mtarazi Falls tumbles over the edge of the escarpment for a drop of 2,500 feet, the longest in Zimbabwe. The cascades of the larger Pungwe River are not as high, but they make a strong impression as they jump a 797-foot precipice into the mouth of a 6-mile-long gorge. The small but beautiful Nyangombe Falls can also be reached by road.

Nyanga's ruins are spread all over the park and beyond — their sheer extent is astonishing. Stone-walled forts and pit structures abound throughout the region, and there are literally hundreds of miles of rock terraces. These stoneworks date from at least the 15th century, but some may be up to 1,000 years old. Their original purposes are a somewhat controversial subject. The sunken pit structures are 6 to 9 feet deep and 10 feet across. Each is lined with stone and entered by an underground tunnel. In colonial days, they were thought to be "slave pits," but they were more likely used as pens for livestock. Nothing could get in or out of such an enclosure without alerting the owners, who slept in a hut above the tunnel entrance. A reconstructed pit structure is located near

Nyanga Dam. Also a subject of controversy are walled "forts" that are found everywhere atop high ground. Although they have the character of defensive works, some researchers claim they were merely lookout posts. The best known sites in the park are Nyangwe Fort and the Chawomera Ruins, where there are forts, pits, and terraces. The region's most extensive ruins are the Ziwa and Nyahokwe sites in the low country to the northwest of the Nyanga plateau. Now overgrown with euphorbia bush, their terraces, walls, and grinding stones are clearly the remains of agricultural communities.

Nyanga National Park is only an hour's drive north of Mutare, although there is a shortcut to Juliasdale village if you are coming directly from Harare. Accommodation in the park is available at national park self-service chalets at the historic *Rhodes Nyanga Hotel*, which incorporates the buildings of the original Rhodes estate and has plenty of colonial atmosphere (the old stone farmhouse is now the hotel dining room). The posh *Troutbeck Inn* also has colonial charm and is the best resort in the region. It features golf, tennis, and all the recreational amenities. It is north of the park, close to the artificial Connemara Lakes and the famous World's View vista point. The charming *Pine Tree Inn*, as well as the *Brondesbury Park Hotel* and the *Montclair Casino Hotel*, is located near Juliasdale, a pretty region of fruit farms, msasa woods, and pine plantations just south of the park entrance. The basic *Nyanga Holiday Hotel* is outside the pretty English-style village of Nyanga, on the north edge of the park. An outfit called Far and Wild runs a rustic log cabin camp near the Honde Valley Viewpoint. It is their base for guided hikes and mountain bike adventures, as well as Class IV whitewater rafting trips on the Pungwe River (which unfortunately is slated to be flooded by a dam).

From a base in the highlands, you can visit some interesting areas around the Nyanga. A steep, switchbacked road leads down into the hot, dry Honde Valley, where the Stonehenge-like boulders called the *Masimiki* ("rocks that stand upright") form a natural monument. Beyond the Pungwe River, the road climbs into lovely, green, coffee-and-tea plantation country at the base of Inyangani Mountain. The verdant Aberfoyle Plantation is set in a wonderful location beneath its towering escarpment, and you can spend the night at the *Aberfoyle Country Club*. To the northwest of the Nyanga Mountains, the Ziwa and Nyahokwe ruins can be visited on a gravel track accessible through Nyanga village.

Chimanimani National Park

The gleaming white peaks of the Chimanimani Mountains are the wildest and most rugged of Zimbabwe's high ranges. Unlike the dark granitic domes to the north, the Chimanimani are composed of quartzite, and their bare crags reflect brilliantly white when exposed to the African sun. They are arranged in three parallel ridges, of which the easternmost, running right along the Mozambique border, reaches heights of almost 8,000 feet. No road penetrates beyond the first valley, and that is just a rough track to the ranger base camp in the north end of Chimanimani National Park. Without any access or lodge accommodation, the Chimanimani remain a true mountain wilderness that can only be explored by avid hikers.

The park is reached through the village of Chimanimani, about 90 miles south of Mutare. You can spend the night in the basic but comfortable *Chimanimani Hotel,* or continue up a 12-mile track that winds up to the park base camp at Mutekeswane, where there are campsites and hot showers. Before you go up, it's a good idea to check in at the Outward Bound School just outside the park to pick up maps and information, particularly about water sources during the hot dry months of September and October.

From base camp, it's about a three-hour walk over a 1,600-foot ridge to a communal mountain hut overlooking the Upper Bundi Valley that drains Chimanimani's central cluster of four high peaks. Binga (also called Kweza) is the highest at 7,992 feet, although the other three are nearly as big. This area is very beautiful and there are many places to explore, so it is worth a one or two night stopover. There are a number of caves that make nice private campsites. You can make a circular tour by descending through the Hadrang Valley that leads directly to the Outward Bound School and the nearby Tessa's Pool, a favorite swimming hole. You can also do a longer trek by following the Bundi River southward to the Southern Lakes and returning to base camp on the Banana Grove Track. It's possible to trek even further south, but the main path crosses into Mozambique, which you should avoid doing.

Chimanimani's mountain passes were supposedly once used as trade routes between the old kingdoms of Zimbabwe and the coast. More recently, they have been used by refugees fleeing the war in Mozambique. They chose a hard route, for although the peaks are enticing in the sunshine, they are frequently veiled in cold mists or violent lightning storms. One prominent path above the Upper Bundi Valley is called Skeleton Pass, for obvious reasons. Although hikers would presumably be better equipped than thinly clad people from the coastal plain, they should definitely take heed of the weather in these mountains.

The Chimanimani Mountains have interesting fauna and flora. Beneath their austere peaks, mineral-rich sandy soils support a rich variety of vegetation. Montane grasslands and fynboslike scrub — the habitat of proteas, heathers, and everlasting flowers—dominate upland valleys and ridges. Lower down, dry montane forests of cedar and yellowwood nestle in protected valleys. Large mammals do better in the Chimanimani wilderness than in other parts of the Eastern Highlands. Although not abundant, eland are often seen, and sable antelope, bushbuck, and klipspringer are also present. Blue duiker and samango monkeys are restricted to forest, but troops of baboons can be found anywhere. So, too, can leopards, which although rarely seen, are known to inhabit the park. Aside from the bokmakierie shrike, which is not found elsewhere in Zimbabwe, most of the birds in the high parts of the Chimanimani can be seen elsewhere.

Just at the southern end of the range, however, are a couple of birding hot-spots. These are the Rusitu and Haroni Forest Botanical Reserves, pockets of lowland forest right on the Mozambique border. Over 250 species have been seen here, including such beauties as the Vanga flycatcher, fire-crowned bishop, and chestnut-fronted helmet shrike. Unfortunately, the reserves are suffering from tree cutting, and they are difficult to get to. It's easier to visit the Chirinda Forest Botanical Reserve, which is located near Mt. Selinda, the southernmost peak of the Eastern Highlands chain. This refuge protects a tropical forest of large evergreen trees. Among them is Zimbabwe's "big tree," a 216-foot red mahogany (*Khaya nyasica*). The forest also harbors tree civets, sun squirrels, black-fronted bush shrikes, and myriad butterflies. The *Kiledo Lodge* (near Chipenge town) makes a cozy base for visiting these forest reserves.

Gonarezhou National Park

Among Zimbabwean conservationists, Gonarezhou enjoys a long-standing reputation as one of the most interesting wilderness havens in the country. Covering 1,930 square miles of Lowveld bush, it is Zimbabwe's second largest park and its least visited. As such, it has always been appreciated as much for its wilderness atmosphere as its fauna. Abutting the lowlands of Mozambique, the park is the habitat of unusual species such as Lichtenstein's hartebeest, nyala, and suni antelope—animals absent or rare elsewhere in Zimbabwe. The name Gonarezhou means "place of the elephants." Its wooded bushlands were the traditional territory of the nation's biggest tuskers, where huge bulls carried ivory in excess of 100 pounds on each side.

Unfortunately, Gonarezhou National Park has a troubled history. The Lowveld country between the Limpopo and Save rivers is indeed great wildlife habitat. But at the turn of the century, it attracted poachers who just about wiped out its elephant herds. Later, tsetse control shooting destroyed thousands of buffalo and other herbivores. Threatened by the advance of large-scale farming, Gonarezhou was finally set aside as a game reserve in 1968, and given national park status in 1973. By then its wildlife populations had rebounded, but visitors were kept out, first by the independence war, and afterwards by the threat of guerrillas and bandits spilling over from Mozambique.

The rains fail periodically in the eastern Lowveld, and drought hit hard between 1991 and 1992, causing immense suffering. Forced to stay near a handful of remaining waterholes, the wild animals gobbled up every bit of greenery before starting to die en masse. Park authorities waited too long to act. By the time they began to implement a rescue plan, bleached bones and desiccated carcasses lay scattered throughout the bush. Almost all the park's hippos had already died, although several hundred were being kept alive by supplementary feeding on nearby farms. Park wardens and local conservationists embarked on an emergency program that called for the repair of broken boreholes, along with the culling of some animals and translocation of others to nearby private nature conservancies. Priority was given to saving the rare hartebeest, as well as sable and roan antelope, and waterbuck. A couple of hundred buffalo were also captured and penned on private farms. Several thousand impala were shot.

Elephants were the biggest problem. Numbering some 2,000 more than Gonarezhou National Park's estimated carrying capacity of 6,500, they devastated huge swaths of vegetation. The park's ancient baobabs were particularly hard hit — they were literally ripped apart by starving pachyderms. Culling crews set to disposing of excess elephants, while translocation teams attempted to capture calves. In the process, they discovered techniques to capture and move adult elephants. For the first time, entire family groups were successfully translocated. Over 1,100 elephants were moved out of the park, with some 200 taken to reserves in South Africa. Those translocations had effects far beyond Gonarezhou's boundaries, for they have opened up new possibilities and controversies concerning the conservation of the African elephant.

When the rains returned, Gonarezhou's vegetation and wildlife began to recover as they had in the past. With good management and peace in Mozambique, the park will eventually regain its proper place as a major refuge. Already, it is attracting more interest and development. The wildlife rescue effort prompted by the drought resulted in the creation of several neighboring private game reserves and conservancies. Some of the elephant and buffalo translocated from the park remain in the private reserves, which have also established small breeding herds of black rhino.

Access and Accommodation

Gonarezhou is a dry-season park open from May 1 to October 31. Four-wheel-drive vehicles are needed in the park.

Travelers from the Eastern Highlands come by road via the Save River Valley, where the broad, sandy river moves through hot country well sprinkled with massive baobabs. It's 156 miles from Chimanimani to Chiredzi (or 126 miles from Masvingo, near Great Zimbabwe), then a further 36 miles to the park. United Air (booked through Air Zimbabwe) and Expedition Air have scheduled flights to Buffalo Range, and arrangements can be made to have flights extended to some of the private reserves (or charters can be booked from Buffalo Range).

Chipinda Pools and *Chigulu* rest camps offer shaded platform campsites with communal washing facilities. Many lovely private sites (without facilities) are spread along the Runde River. The *Fishans* campsite has great views of the Chilojo Cliffs.

In the southern Mabaluata section, the *Swimuwini Rest Camp* is set on a baobab-studded bluff overlooking the sandy Buffalo Bend of the Nuanetsi River. Long closed because of the independence war and security problems in neighboring Mozambique, its chalets and campsites will no doubt be popular when the camp is again up and running.

Several nice lodges are located outside the park. *Nduna Safari Lodge* is on the neighboring 175-square-mile Lonestar Reserve, which is owned by the Malilangwe Conservation Trust. Built into a rocky cliff overlooking a lake, this 12-bed lodge offers canoeing and an abundance of Bushman rock paintings, as well as game viewing. In addition to the typical Lowveld species, white rhinos are found at Lonestar, and day trips are run into Gonarezhou. The beautiful 16-bed *Mahenye Lodge* is set on an island in the middle of the Save River, which marks the park's northern boundary. Guests cross the river for game drives in the park; canoeing (during the rainy season) and visits to a nearby Shangaan village are also featured. Mahenye is a CAMPFIRE project on communal land, so the local community is involved. That is also the case at the nearby *Chilo Gorge Camp*, which is also built on an island on the edge of the park and offers 14 thatched chalets.

Further north (and too far for game drives in Gonarezhou) is the Save Valley Conservancy. This huge private reserve covers 1,273 square miles of country on the west bank of the Save River. Like the other private reserves in the region, it supports a full range of Lowveld wildlife in low but rapidly growing densities. It harbors both black and white rhino. The 18-bed *Senuko Safari Lodge* (opened in 1996) is the principal safari camp in the conservancy, but with 21 separate landowners, more lodges are sure to open.

For a different Lowveld experience, Biza Saddle Safaris run two- to five-day horseback trips on the 328-square-mile Chiredzi River Conservancy, about 30 miles north of Gonarezhou. Rides and foot safaris take place along the Chiredzi River, with overnights at comfortable bush camps. Black rhino and elephant may be seen on the rides.

Touring the Park

Because of its size and lack of development, Gonarezhou National Park is mostly the territory of self-sufficient camping safaris. Game viewing is not easy, as animals are not currently abundant and they are skittish around vehicles.

Much of Gonarezhou is trackless wilderness covered with mixed woodlands and mopane, with patches of riparian forest along the principal rivers. The park is split into two distinct sectors. In the north, the Chipinda Pools area offers dramatic scenery along the Runde River. After exiting a series of hippo and croc pools near park headquarters, the Runde cuts through a range of hills as it tumbles down the Chivilila rapids. The river spreads out on the flats beyond, forming a wide, sandy bed beneath the celebrated Chilojo Cliffs, the flat-topped, ocher-colored cliffs that are Gonarezhou's most striking scenic feature. The Runde follows the base of the bluffs for 20 miles before making its junction with the larger Save River at the seasonally flooded Tambahata Pan, just before the Save crosses into Mozambique.

The Nuanetsi River runs along the southwestern boundary of the park. It is the principal game viewing area in the Mabalauta sector. Nyala antelope live in the river's fringing forest, and there are crocs in its pools. Only 15 miles separate the Nuanetsi from the Limpopo River and South Africa's Kruger National Park. Elephants have no respect for human borders and used to move almost at will between the two sanctuaries. The Nuanetsi was the favored area for Gonarezhou's famous tuskers, but it's doubtful if any big boys are still hanging around. Perhaps they are and there has simply been no one to report their presence, for this section of the park has been closed for years.

Great Zimbabwe

The ancestors of Zimbabwe's Shona people left a heritage of stone architecture unique in sub-Saharan Africa. The sites of more than 150 such *mazimbabwe* ("houses of stone") are spread over the country's central plateau. The largest and most magnificent are the ruins of Great Zimbabwe.

Great Zimbabwe flourished between A.D. 1200 and 1550, when it was the seat of temporal and religious authority for an early Shona kingdom. Located in a fertile, well-watered valley at the southern edge of the central plateau, the kingdom's prosperity was based originally on cattle and iron smelting. Later, its strategic location allowed its rulers to control a trade route between the Zimbabwe plateau and the Swahili towns of the coast via the valley of the Save River. Gold, which had little value in the interior, was exported to the coast in exchange for cloth, pottery, and other wares from as far away as Persia and China. The increasing wealth of the city's elites allowed them to indulge in the construction of massive stone edifices.

Nearby granite hills provided a ready source of building material. Exfoliated granite rocks were easily split into handy bricklike shapes. These formed the blocks for the unmortared stone walls that are such a prominent feature of Great Zimbabwe's architecture. The other building material was *daga*, a cementlike mixture of gravel and clay that was hardened by fire. *Daga* was used to construct floor platforms and molded into the walls of huts, which were later roofed with thatch. None of the stone enclosures at Great Zimbabwe were roofed. Typically, groups of *daga* huts were built and then surrounded by stone walls to make discreet enclosures. The red or yellow remains of *daga* buildings can be seen all over the ruins site, but the huts themselves have vanished, leaving only the more durable stone walls.

The Great Zimbabwe ruins are divided into three sections: the Hill Complex, the Great Enclosure, and the Valley Complex. The oldest is the Hill Complex, on a 300-foot-high, boulder-strewn cliff that dominates the north side of the valley. Construction on the Hill Complex followed the granite outcrops' natural contours, with large and irregular boulders left in place and incorporated into enclosures by connecting stone walls. The Western Enclosure is thought to have been the original royal quarters, while the Eastern Enclosure was probably the city's ceremonial center and the site of a shrine sacred to the Shona god Mwari. Most of Great Zimbabwe's renowned stone birds were found in this enclosure, as were numerous monoliths — upright granite slabs that were characteristic ornamental or symbolic objects at Great Zimbabwe. A nearby cave may have been used as an oracle, as sounds resonating from within could be heard far down the valley. Another enclosure was apparently used as a gold foundry. Narrow, winding passages squeezed between natural boulders and stone walls connect the various enclosures of the Hill Complex with each other, and to the ruins in the valley below.

The Great Enclosure is the most striking edifice at the ruins, and by far the largest. Known as Imba Huru, "the house of the Great Woman," it is usually described as the residence of the queen mother and the royal wives. The Great Enclosure is a huge elliptical structure. As wide as a football field, it is surrounded by a massive Outer Wall up to 32 feet high and 17 feet thick, and more than 820 feet in circumference. This incredible wall was put up around a group of older structures that were already enclosed by a high wall on their eastern side. When the Outer Wall was built, construction began on the Great Enclosure's northwest end, and originally the Outer Wall may have been intended to merely join the original eastern wall. But the builders continued right around with the new Outer Wall, leaving a narrow parallel passage between the two walls. As construction of the Outer Wall proceeded, the quality of work got better. The wall reaches its greatest magnificence in the vicinity of the Conical Tower, where its mortarless stones are meticulously laid and an intricate chevron pattern graces its top rim.

The celebrated Conical Tower was put up on the southeast side of the Great Enclosure, between the old and new Outer Wall. This odd structure is 18 feet in diameter and over 30 feet high. It may be a representation of a grain bin, and therefore a symbol of power, as grain was given the king in tribute — or it may have had phallic significance. The tower is solid and obviously had purely ritual or religious importance.

Other structures are found throughout the Valley Complex. Although far less imposing than those on the Hill Complex or in the Great Enclosure, these less-exalted sites have yielded important archaeological discoveries, including the famous stone bird that has become the national symbol of Zimbabwe. Buildings in the Valley Complex include the stone walls of houses for nobles and the *daga* (cementlike) remains of commoners' houses.

By some estimates, Great Zimbabwe's population reached a height of 10,000 to 20,000 people, although more conservative researchers have put the number at only a tenth of that total. Some theories maintain that the city was abandoned suddenly because of ecological collapse brought on by the demands of its large population of humans and cattle, but it's equally possible that the opening of new trade routes through the Zambezi Valley led to a shift in the geographic power base of Shona society. Whatever the true reason, by about 1550, Great Zimbabwe had lost its place as a political and trade center, and no new construction took place after that time. It seems to have maintained some status as a religious shrine well into the last century.

For many years, Great Zimbabwe was cloaked in an aura of pseudo-mystery regarding its origins. From the time of its discovery, white Rhodesians embraced far-fetched theories about the ruins, preferring to attribute the monuments to ancient Phoenicians or the Queen of Sheba — to anyone, really — rather than accept that they were the work of native Africans. Such racially based theories circulated throughout the colonial era and well beyond, despite the solid scientific work of archaeologists that testified to their unique African provenance. Today, in overreaction, some feel obliged to ascribe a level of sophistication to the culture of Great Zimbabwe that did not exist, comparing its technical achievements favorably with those of contemporary Europe. Such hyped-up claims are unwarranted and unnecessary, for Great Zimbabwe stands on its own merits — a glorious manifestation of the creative genius of Iron-Age Zimbabwe. For that reason, the ruins have been designated a UNESCO World Heritage Site.

Access and Accommodation

Great Zimbabwe is easily reached by road. The ruins are 17 miles from the town of Masvingo, which is connected to Harare by 181 miles of excellent road. Masvingo is 185 miles from Mutare. The Zimbabwe Sun hotel chain runs daily buses from Harare and Mutare to its Great Zimbabwe Hotel; these are very convenient. The luxury Blue Arrow bus service connects Masvingo with Harare and Bulawayo. Several domestic airlines also have scheduled flights to Masvingo.

The luxury lodge called *The Lodge of the Ancient City* has an imaginative design. Slabs of stone were liberally used in its construction to create an atmosphere that recalls the architecture of the old Shona kingdom. The older *Great Zimbabwe Hotel* is comfortable and has a wonderful location just a stone's throw from the ruins. There is also a campsite near the park gate. Cheaper hotel accommodation is available in Masvingo, where local bus tours can be booked to the ruins.

Several small lodges and campsites are located a few miles from the ruins on the south shore of Lake Mutirikwe (formerly Lake Kyle). Lake Mutirikwe Recreational Park is mostly of interest to Zimbabwean vacationers. It offers fishing and a north-shore game park, where you can view white rhinos from horseback.

Touring the Ruins

Great Zimbabwe's setting, in a beautiful wooded valley flanked by granite koppies, heightens the atmosphere of mystery surrounding the unique stone monuments of a vanished civilization. An overnight stay at the ruins is recommended to give yourself enough time to absorb a sense of place and take a good look around with both morning and afternoon visits. Those are by far the best times to tour the ruins, for both ambiance and photography. Use the hours of golden sunlight to explore and enjoy the monuments, and the less choice times to check out the museum, where seven of Great Zimbabwe's celebrated stone birds are on display. These have become national emblems, appearing on the country's currency, flag, and coat-of-arms. The museum also contains informative exhibits and other artifacts.

The ruins are open daily from 8:00 A.M. to 5:00 P.M. There is an entry fee, and guides are available for hire on the site.

Bushman rock painting at Nsvatuke Cave, Matobo National Park, Zimbabwe. Photo: Allen Bechky.

The Great Zimbabwe ruins suffered badly from the ravages of early treasure hunters and disastrous archaeological excavations. Concentrating on the stone monuments and preoccupied with the search for evidence of a non-African origin, amateur investigators dug through layers of *daga*, destroying much of the ruins' archaeological potential. They threw away innumerable artifacts that would have yielded a much deeper understanding of the material culture of Great Zimbabwe's society. The worst damage was done by the first official curator of the site, whose extensive but inept excavations between 1902 and 1904 did irreparable harm. Further damage and flawed reconstruction by the authorities continued until 1936. But don't let this archaeological tragedy spoil your visit — the fascinating ambiance of Great Zimbabwe has come through intact.

Matobo Hills National Park and the Bulawayo Area

Few places in Africa combine so much history and natural beauty as the Matobo Hills. Their hard primeval granites have battled the forces of wind and water for 2 billion years. The result is a veritable forest of jumbled rock piles and massive granite domes crowned by castle rocks and balancing boulders. It is a geography for mystics, a place that has inspired humans since the dawn of history. The Bushmen left painted gal-

leries in caves and clefts all over the Matobo Hills. Then came Shona
peoples who worshipped at oracle caves sacred to their god Mwari.
When the wandering Ndebele king, Mzilikazi, settled near the hills, he
named them *matobo* ("the bald ones") because the round boulders atop
their summits reminded him of the shiny pates of tribal elders. The Ndebele proceeded to adopt the Shona's sacred sites as their own. Cecil
Rhodes was so struck by the majesty of the Matobo landscape that he
arranged to be entombed there. Even today, Ndebele ceremonies continue to take place in these hills, while New Age devotees consider the
Matobo Hills one of the planet's potent "power points."

The Matobo Hills and their surrounds have been the setting of major
events in Zimbabwe history. By the end of the Bushmen's tenure, the earliest Shona culture was evolving in the area, as evidenced by archaeological remains from the Leopard Kopje site (at the Khami ruins near
Bulawayo). More advanced Shona cultures later built the stone terraces
of the Khami ruins, as well as those of the more distant Nalatale ruins.
Then came the Ndebele. Following Mzilikazi's death, his son Lobengula
established his royal capital at Gubulawayo, alternatively translated as
"the place of slaughter" and "the place of the persecuted man." Either
way, the name unintentionally proved prophetic, for the mercenaries of
Rhodes's British South Africa Company later chased Lobengula from his
compound, and Bulawayo became the focus of bloody fighting during the
first *Chimurenga*. During that 1896 liberation war, the Ndebele army
found the Matobo Hills an impregnable stronghold. Rhodes himself had
to come to the Matobos to attend the series of open-air *indabas* ("meetings") with the Ndebele *indunas* ("chiefs") that concluded the peace.

As if splendid scenery and historic sites are not enough, the Matobo
Hills are also a great place to investigate African flora and fauna. The
heart of the wilderness is protected in Matobo Hills National Park. Its
granite rock outcrops (koppies) provide ideal nesting places for birds of
prey, and the park hosts a superlative variety of raptors. It is particularly
famous for its black eagles, which are sustained by an abundance of rock
hyrax. With its multitude of koppies, there can't be better habitat for
klipspringers, and they are very common. Baboons also use the rock outcrops, finding night roosts on steep cliffs. Although the highest concentration of large mammals is kept in a fenced game park, animals can be
found throughout the Matobo area. Its valleys, grassy flats, and wooded
groves harbor impala, reedbuck, steenbok, bushbuck, and sable antelopes. White rhinos are a local specialty, and can even be found beyond
the confines of the game park. Careful observers will find ample signs of
leopards, although the cats themselves are rarely seen.

Botanically, the park is extremely interesting. Paperbark commiphoras and rock-splitting fig trees cling to cliff faces, and brilliantly colored lichens cover granite boulders with a Jackson Pollack palette of reds, greens, and yellows. The wooded valleys that fill the narrow gaps between boulder-strewn ridges contain a fantastic variety of trees. An array of terminalias, combretums, albezias, brachystegias, and others — including kudu berry (notable for its exceptionally long Latin name, *Pseudolachnostylis maprouneifolia*) — compete for attention by displaying brilliant foliage and unusual seedpods.

Access and Accommodation

Matobo Hills National Park is only a half hour's drive from the city of Bulawayo. That city can easily be reached by road or rail from either Victoria Falls (273 miles) or Harare (273 miles), and there are regular Air Zimbabwe flights connecting them as well. It's 174 miles of paved road to Masvingo.

Self-service national park chalets with kitchens are located at *Maleme Rest Camp*, which is set on a koppie above the nearby Maleme Dam. There are campsites at Maleme as well as several other places around the park.

Two luxury lodges are located in the hills just outside the park. *Matobo Hills Lodge* is a 40-bed facility featuring an open-air dining area and a beautiful natural-rock swimming pool. The lodge offers special historical and ethnic tours in addition to game drives, walks, and horseback riding. The attractive *Amalinda Camp* is cleverly built into a koppie; its dining area is a natural rock shelter, and one of the guest rooms has a genuine Bushman painting on the wall. Amalinda guests enjoy the normal Matobo activities, plus elephants: a trio of tame adolescents live on the property and are available for riding. The *Big Cave Camp* is also set among massive boulders on a Matobo koppie. The 8-bed camp is on its own 2,000-acre wilderness reserve that abuts the park.

Plenty of accommodation is available in Bulawayo. Tops for charm is *Nesbitt Castle*, an authentically wrought stone castle with crenulated walls, griffin statues, and opulent decor. *Induna Lodge* is a small hotel in the suburbs, noted for personalized service that includes private tours to any of the sites in the Matobo-Bulawayo area. The *Bulawayo Sun* and *Cresta Churchill* hotels are oriented more toward business travelers than tourists. Midrange hotels include *Grey's Inn* and the *Selborne*. On the budget end, there is a *Youth Hostel*, a *Y.W.C.A.*, and any number of cheap hotels.

If you are staying in town, you can catch various daily excursions with United Touring Company. For a more personalized visit to the Matobo Hills, go with Black Rhino Safaris.

Several lodges and game ranches are located in the region. *Malalangwe Lodge* is a huge ranch in grassy koppie country to the west of Bulawayo, with game as well as Bushman and Shona caves on the property. *N'tabazinduna Lodge* is a tiny bush camp atop "the hill of the chiefs." *Jabulani* is an 8-bed lodge on a working farm about an hour and a half east of Bulawayo. It makes an excellent base for visiting the Nalatale ruins, only 9 miles distant.

The Bubiana Conservancy (with accommodations at *Nyala Lodge*) and *Sondelani* (with its own lodge) are private game reserves more than 100 miles from Bulawayo, in the low country to the south of the Matobo Hills. Black rhinos are bred in the Bubiana Conservancy, while Sondelani has a resident elephant herd.

Touring the Park

Most of Matobo's famous attractions can be visited on a one-day road tour, although one could profitably spend a lot more time in this park. Tours usually take in a couple of the more prominent Bushman caves, and may include a visit to the game park.

No one fails to stop at World's View (or more properly "view of the world" as Rhodes called it), the vista point on the summit of Malindidzimu ("the place of spirits") mountain. The wide vista from atop its broad granite dome is indeed stupendous, and it's easy to see how Rhodes could identify with the grandeur of the Matobo country. He chose his final resting place among a cluster of huge, wind-polished boulders that form a noble natural monument for his grave, which is marked with a simple brass plaque. After his death in 1902, his body was conveyed from Cape Town to Bulawayo by train, then drawn on a caisson to Malindidzimu. Thousands of Matabele warriors attended the funeral to give their conqueror a singular farewell, shouting "*Bayete*," a salute reserved for kings. Now it is quiet but for the wind. Bright, red-and-blue flat lizards (*Platysaurus intermedius*) are always conspicuous at the grave site. Less obvious, but worth looking for, are rock elephant shrews. These long-nosed little mammals scuttle out from beneath the boulders, then just as suddenly disappear.

Two other simple graves share the Malindidzimu site. Notably, one belongs to Sir Leander Starr Jameson, Rhodes's loyal lieutenant and leader of the notorious Jameson Raid that helped precipitate the Boer War. There is also one large heroic-style monument on the hill. It commemorates Major Allan Wilson and the 33 members of the Shangani Patrol (the Rhodesian version of Custer's Last Stand), who were wiped out while pursuing the fleeing Lobengula.

Bushman rock paintings are found all over Matobo Hills National

Park. Several of the best known galleries are easily reached by road. The paintings at Nsvatuke Cave are particularly beautiful, with superb color and lifelike perspective. In one painting, a kudu, tail raised in alarm, runs in full flight. In another, a magnificent giraffe gallops behind a cruder zebra. Here and there among the animals are human figures. Some have careful dimension; others are little more than stick figures. Faded by time and, sadly, abused by visitors, the gallery is nonetheless affecting. The paintings at the massive Pomongwe Cave were spoiled by a well-meaning but foolhardy scheme to protect them: an application of varnish stained them with ugly brown splotches. Artifacts excavated at Pomongwe indicate the cave was a human occupation site as far back as 35,000 years ago. The paintings at the White Rhino Shelter have lifelike line drawings of animals, rather than polychrome paintings. The gallery at Silozwane Cave is celebrated for its many excellent paintings, including those of fish and a winged termite. Off the beaten track and seldom visited, Silozwane is located on communal land beyond the southern boundary of the park, and the cave is rumored to still be used for Ndebele rainmaking ceremonies. Inanke Cave is reputed to have the most extensive and beautiful gallery, but a stiff hike is required to get there. For the steep climb to the top of Inanke dome, allow for a round-trip hike of six hours from the Toghwana Dam campsite.

Although park authorities have not gotten around to banning the practice, you should not use flash when photographing Bushman paintings. The light breaks down their ancient pigments. Although an individual shot will not do much damage, the harmful effects compound when multiplied by those taken by hundreds of visitors.

Matobo's Whovi Game Park requires a separate entry fee. It has a wide selection of antelope and other plains game such as giraffe and zebra, as well as a good number of white rhino.

Walking is allowed anywhere in Matobo except in the game park, and the country is a rambler's dream. Short trails to popular sites are well marked, but elsewhere you must take care not to get lost. Carry plenty of water while hiking. Many leopards inhabit the park, but you needn't worry about them. You do have to be alert for snakes: the koppie-studded Matobo terrain is ideal habitat for black mambas and they are supposed to be fairly abundant.

Touring Bulawayo and Nearby Attractions

Bulawayo is Zimbabwe's second largest city. It is a pleasant town with wide, jacaranda-lined streets and two large city parks. The Museum of Natural History, located in Centenary Park, is one of Africa's finest. It houses extensive collections of birds and animals, as well as displays of minerals, ethnic and archaeological artifacts, and items from the colonial era. Other places of interest include the Railways Museum, with its collection of steam engines and antique rolling stock, and the Mzilikazi Arts and Crafts Center, where pottery, sculpture, and paintings are made. Old Bulawayo is a reconstruction of Lobengula's royal kraal. Outside town, the buildings of the Cyrene Mission are noted for the colorful African motifs of their murals. The Chipangali Wildlife Orphanage is a refuge for injured animals and a breeding center for rare species, including an especially fine collection of duikers.

The archaeological site at Khami ruins is 14 miles west of Bulawayo. Khami was the capital of the Shona's Torwa dynasty, one of the successor states to Great Zimbabwe. It flourished from 1450 to 1650. Like Great Zimbabwe, it was mostly a *daga* settlement, but its square, multiroomed huts have disappeared, leaving a series of terraces decorated with stone walls. A maze of passages leads up through the terraces to the top, where the king's palace stood. The site overlooks a pool in the Khami River. On the other side, Leopard Kopje was the site of a seminal Shona culture that produced fine pottery and metalwork about 1,000 years ago.

The Nalatale ruins, about 75 miles east of Bulawayo, are the masterwork of Shona decorative stone masonry. The great wall at Nalatale incorporates multiple design motifs, including various chevron and herringbone patterns. It was built by the Rozwi dynasty that was also responsible for the nearby Dhlo Dhlo ruins.

CHAPTER SIX

Zambia:
Paradise Lost and Found

ZAMBIA LIES AT THE HEART of south-central Africa. A country the size of the Dakotas, Iowa, and Minnesota combined, a huge proportion of its territory remains committed to the wild. Its 19 national parks and 31 game management areas are scattered from the shores of the Great Rift Valley's Lake Tanganyika to the fringes of the Kalahari. The landscape is dominated by a gently undulating plateau at elevations above 4,000 feet. Zambia's latitude gives it a climate more tropical than that of its southern neighbors, and some of its habitats and species show more affinities to those of central Africa than to those further south. Rainfall averaging between 30 and 40 inches a year ensures that its wildlands are well watered. Three great rivers traverse the country: the Luangwa, the Kafue, and the Zambezi. These rivers and the wetlands of the Bangweulu Swamps nurture Zambia's most important wildlife reserves.

Zambia's premier safari attraction is the Luangwa Valley, and South Luangwa National Park is without doubt one of the finest in Africa. Few of the other Zambian parks ever make it to tour itineraries. This is not for lack of interest: other parks in Zambia encompass a wonderful variety of rich habitats and host an abundance of animals, including a number of species absent elsewhere in southern Africa. The country has long been a favorite stalking ground for big game hunters, but has been largely ignored as a safari tour destination. As a consequence, its neglected parks have remained undeveloped and unknown. This situation could change soon: as the parks in neighboring countries fill with visitors, the novelty and wildness of the Zambian sanctuaries make them increasingly attractive. Zambia has great appeal for those who want to experience the real Africa.

Zambia figured very prominently in the career of David Livingstone. When the explorer first wandered through, he marched up the Zambezi, following its course through the western reaches of the country. He later retraced his steps to discover Victoria Falls, then pursued the great Zambezi River to the sea. In 1866, he crossed the Luangwa Valley, moving northward in his errant search for the sources of the Nile. A few years later, after being "lost" and found by Stanley, he succumbed to fever in northern Zambia's Bangweulu Swamps.

In colonial days, Zambia — then Northern Rhodesia — always took a back seat to its southerly sister "colony." (Technically, Northern Rhodesia was officially governed as a "protectorate," not a Crown colony.) Under separate administration, its exploitation and development lagged until the 1920s when big mining operations started in the Copper Belt adjacent to the salient of the Belgian Congo's mineral-rich Katanga Province. Although the mines ultimately became the source of great riches, the profits went primarily to Rhodesian and South African companies. Aside from the creation of thousands of jobs for migrant laborers, little financial benefit accrued to the northern colony. Europeans came to manage the mines, but overall the number of permanent settlers in the north remained quite small. While the white community in the south became essentially self-governing, Northern Rhodesia was administered more closely by the British Crown. This had the unintended effect of sparing native Africans the worst of the racist legislation that became the bedrock of political life in the south. When the British tried to federate the two colonies with Nyasaland (later Malawi), rioting by workers in the Copper Belt and unbudging opposition from African politicians thwarted the attempt. Although the merger might have had long-term economic benefits for the region, the Africans feared — with reason — that the union would be dominated by the white regime in Southern Rhodesia. The Federation of Rhodesia and Nyasaland lasted a mere decade, from 1953 to 1963.

Kenneth Kaunda emerged as the head of the national movement in Northern Rhodesia and became president of the new Republic of Zambia when it attained independence in 1964. Like Julius Nyerere in Tanzania, Kaunda had a vision for building a prosperous future based on his

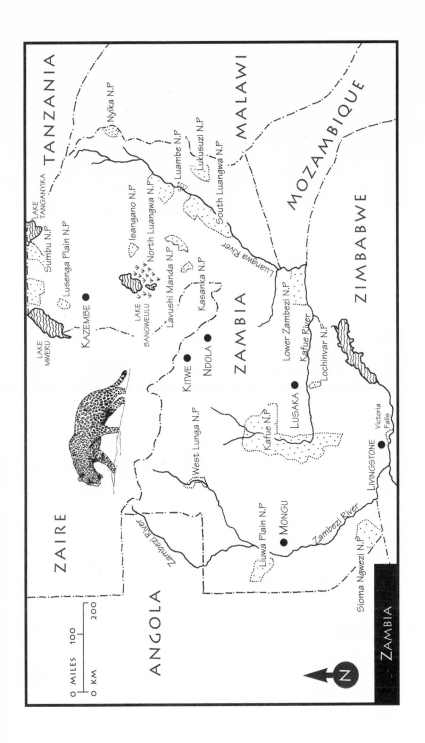

ZAMBIA

own brand of African socialism. The prospects for the new nation looked quite good. The country was more than self-sufficient in food production, and the tremendous reserves of rich ore in its Copper Belt fairly glowed with promise to provide the income that would fuel development nationwide. Instead, things fell apart. Within a few years, the state took control of all aspects of the nation's economy. The mines and other large enterprises were nationalized and run under the aegis of "parastatal" corporations. Zambia was also converted into a one-party state under Kaunda's United National Independence Party (UNIP). The results were disastrous: chronic inefficiency became wedded to a culture of corruption, and Zambia's economy went into perpetual stagnation. Agricultural production plummeted: once the breadbasket of central Africa, Zambia became increasingly dependent on food imports. Admittedly, the economic decline was influenced by external factors, specifically a steady retreat in world prices for copper and the disruptions caused by wars in neighboring countries of southern Africa. Zambia's support for African liberation movements cost the nation dearly, especially as it became increasingly embroiled in the Zimbabwe independence war. As the president of a "front line state," Kaunda played the statesman on the international stage. That role earned him kudos abroad that helped mask the deficiencies of his government at home. It did nothing to reverse the country's dismal economic performance or the misery of its people. By 1991, Zambians had lost the faith. In a historic democratic election, Kaunda was turned out in a landslide victory for the Movement for Multi-Party Democracy (MMD), led by Frederick Chiluba. To his credit, Kaunda accepted the will of the people with good grace and left power peaceably. He later maneuvered tirelessly to get his old job back, but was prevented from running in the 1996 elections by questionable "legal" technicalities.

Chiluba has made some headway in liberalizing the economy. His government has been selling off inefficient, state-owned enterprises, loosening rigid price controls, and encouraging foreign and private investment. Yet one major problem is beyond anyone's control: the foreign exchange surplus that should have emanated from the bounty of the mines has been frittered away by years of corruption and mismanagement, and the downturn in the price of copper makes it unlikely that the mines will be able to spur an economic boom before their reserves of ore begin to peter out in the early years of the next century. Shaking up entrenched bureaucracies and reversing pervasive corruption is proving an even tougher battle than getting the economy rolling, and there is already a certain amount of popular disillusionment with the government's reforms.

Zambia's 8.5 million people are divided among many tribal groups that speak a total of 73 different Bantu dialects. The principal tribes are the Bemba in the northeast, the Chewa in the east, the Tonga in the south, and the Lozi, Lunda, Kaonde, and Luvale in the west. With the exception of the Tonga, whose tenure in Zambia goes back over 900 years, and the Ngoni, a martial tribe that swept up from the south in the 19th century, most of these peoples originally came from areas in what is now Congo. Despite considerable recent migration to Lusaka and the cities of the Copper Belt, most of Zambia's people still live on the land. Within the national identity, traditional culture remains very strong. Tribal kings and local chiefs still wield considerable influence over their people, and the government encourages the celebration of tribal rites and ceremonies. The most famous is the *Kuomboka*, the annual procession of a colorful flotilla carrying the Lozi king and his court from the inundated Barotse Plains to his wet-season capital on high ground above the Zambezi flood zone. Unlike many other places, traditional music and dance still enjoy considerable popularity in Zambia. Dance performances at "cultural villages," which in most countries are put on solely for the enjoyment of foreign tourists, are mainly attended by local people. Zambian radio features traditional music and songs, and anyone who spends time in the countryside will hear the beating of village drums during the night.

In Livingstone's day, Zambia was one of the earth's great wild paradises. The wooded savannas of the vast Zambian plateau were only sparsely populated by human beings. Uncounted herds of wild game thrived on the grassy floodplains bordering the great rivers and marshes, while elephants roamed at will in trackless woodlands, and rivers teemed with hippos and crocodiles. The intervening century and a half has seen a shift in the balance between humans and animals. Zambia's once-teeming wildlife populations have been tragically reduced. The tragedy lies in the waste of a resource that could well serve the people.

The worst damage to Zambia's wildlife occurred within the last two decades, during which numerous superb game areas fell victim to the ravages of unrestricted poaching. The poaching firestorm was a stepchild of the neglect and corruption under which the entire country suffered. There was money to be made and wildlife authorities were not immune to the virus: complicity with poaching activities reached from rank-and-file game scouts up to the highest levels. Park wardens, police, government ministers, judges, and diplomats (both Zambian and foreign) were all involved. Whole parks — remote and unvisited — were simply relinquished to poachers. In some areas, volunteer honorary rangers helped to enforce the game laws; the Save the Rhino Trust fought a valiant but losing battle against rhino poachers in the Luangwa Valley and Lower Zambezi areas, but no doubt prevented overall wildlife losses from being even worse than they might have been.

Nor was it only rhinos and elephants that were relentlessly pursued. The Zambian people readily eat game meat, and commercial poachers devastated whole parks. In many places, wild herds were reduced to scattered groups or even isolated individuals. Even today, subsistence hunting remains rampant, and organized poaching gangs have so reduced game populations that some formerly prime areas are no longer of much interest to wildlife-viewing tourists. Buffalo, hippos, and antelopes of every stripe and size have literally gone to pot.

There is now hope for recovery. A new awareness of the potential for tourism has animated the Chiluba government. It is trying to strengthen and reform Zambia's National Parks and Wildlife Service and is getting the courts to treat poaching offenses seriously. Private investors are revitalizing the tourism sector of the economy, with many new lodges and safari companies opening up in areas that were formerly abandoned to poachers. Most significantly, the concept of community conservation is widely taking hold. Various organizations — both governmental and private — are trying to educate villagers in game areas to the importance of sustainable wildlife conservation and to make sure that the communities themselves receive tangible economic benefits from tourism. ADMADE (Administrative Management Design for game management areas) is a government-backed program that seeks to involve directly in conservation the inhabitants of the game management areas (GMAs) around the national parks. The program aims to win the critical support of local chiefs and get villages to establish units of community game scouts to guard against poaching. Meanwhile, wildlife-generated revenue from tourist lodges and professional hunting safari companies is plowed back into the villages, while the meat derived from hunting safaris is distributed to local people. So far, the concept has enjoyed some success in the Luangwa Valley and is being spread to other parts of the country. Of course, there are problems: projects born of good intentions can still succumb to inefficiency, corruption, or lack of funds. Yet such community-based programs probably represent the last best hope for Zambia's wildlife. If the people who live around the parks and GMAs see wildlife as a sustainable source of meat and income, they may well put a stop to poaching and get behind the conservation banner. The Zambian wilds could once again become a wildlife paradise.

Safari Facts

ENTRY: US citizens need visas (US$20 for multiple entry). Get one in advance if you are arriving by air. Visas can easily be obtained at the Livingstone border post if you are arriving overland from Victoria Falls. They are also available at the Siavonga border post at Kariba Dam, opposite the town of Kariba, Zimbabwe.

CURRENCY: Zambian currency is called the kwacha (1997 rate: K1450 = US$1). Traveler's checks are universally accepted; credit cards are only useful at major lodges, hotels, airlines, and so on.

NATIONAL PARK FEES: US$15 per day at South Luangwa National Park. Other parks vary: all are much lower and some are completely free.

LANGUAGE: English is the official language.

AIR TRAVEL: Lusaka is the principal international gateway city, although many travelers fly into Victoria Falls, Zimbabwe, and cross over the border to Livingstone. Lusaka is served from Europe by British Air and is connected to most capitals in East Africa and southern Africa by the various national airlines as well as the two main Zambian airlines: Zambian Express and Aero Zambia. Zambian Express also flies from Johannesburg, South Africa, directly to Livingstone (at Victoria Falls) then connects to Lusaka and Mfuwe, in the Luangwa Valley. Air Malawi has direct service into Mfuwe from Lilongwe, Malawi. Several small airlines operate scheduled services (using light aircraft) that are useful for safari travel in Zambia. For example, Lunga Air conveniently links Victoria Falls (Livingstone) with South Luangwa, Lower Zambezi, and Kafue national parks. Proflight goes between Lusaka and Livingstone, as well as between Lusaka and the Luangwa Valley. Tropic Air flies between Luangwa and Harare, Zimbabwe. Tongabezi runs air charters from Livingstone to Lower Zambezi National Park.

TRANSPORTATION: Distances are long, so most tourists travel by air. A network of badly paved highways connects the principal towns; once you're off those pot-holed highways, you're on rugged dirt roads. Self-drive car rentals are not readily available for safaris, although Avis and Hertz do provide cars with drivers. Chauffeur-driven cars are also available from Zungulila Zambia and Big 5 Tours, two tour operators in Lusaka. Railroads link Lusaka with Livingstone and with Tanzania. Public buses between towns are crowded and unreliable.

TOURS: Although Zambia is linked to southern Africa's tour circuits, it has a very different character than its southern neighbors. The country's long economic decline put its infrastructure into pretty bad shape. Notorious transportation difficulties coupled with indifferent hotel service and high prices were major obstacles to tourism in the past (the national airline, Zambia Airways, was in such a shambles that it finally had to close down). Zambia's bad reputation is only now being turned around.

New (and more reliable) private airlines are servicing the main visitor destinations, while quality lodge and tour operators are steadily improving safari services. But the overall poverty of the country means that travel in Zambia still has rougher edges than it does further south.

Zambia's primary safari destinations are Victoria Falls and South Luangwa National Park. The Falls need no introduction. South Luangwa teems with wildlife, and many top-notch safari outfitters run lodges and camps there. Game viewing in Luangwa will satisfy the highest expectations, and the park is also famous as a venue for walking safaris in game country. All the other Zambian parks are less accessible and game viewing in them is generally more limited. Several areas are particularly noteworthy: the Bangweulu Swamps and the Kafue Flats are two of southern Africa's great wetlands. Both are inhabited by herds of endemic species of lechwe antelope and are also celebrated bird sanctuaries. The Kafue and North Luangwa parks are excellent game areas that have been hurt by poaching, but they still offer superb opportunities for wilderness safaris.

Zambia is one of Africa's leading adventure destinations. It was the first country to allow walking safaris in its national parks — and these are regular features in most game areas. The country also offers canoeing on the Zambezi above Victoria Falls and below Kariba Dam. Lower Zambezi National Park, opposite Zimbabwe's celebrated Mana Pools, is the finest place to take canoe safaris in big game country. Whitewater rafting on the Zambezi is also a Zambian specialty.

Most visitors confine their Zambia tour to South Luangwa National Park and the town of Livingstone (at Victoria Falls). There are no other regular tour circuits, although a few safari operators run special expeditions that combine South Luangwa with North Luangwa and the Bangweulu Swamps. Visits to lodges in Kafue or canoe safaris in Lower Zambezi National Park are easily arranged. Remote parks such as the Liuwa Plain and the Nyika Plateau require special arrangements. A list of safari operators appears in the Appendix. If you arrive in Lusaka on your own, you can make tour arrangements through Bushwackers or Africa Tour Designers.

SHOPPING. Zambian basketry is extraordinary, and the woven reed mats, pottery, copper crafts, and ethnic artifacts are interesting.

SECURITY: Zambian police and soldiers have been known to be zealous in enforcing regulations against taking pictures of bridges, airports, dams, or government installations. Such rules may be lightening up, but it's best to get permission if in doubt. Street crime is a problem in

Lusaka. Take a taxi anywhere around town, and leave valuables in your hotel safe.

LUSAKA: Zambia's capital is a sad and run-down place. There isn't much of special interest to see or do, so most tourists only visit Lusaka if air schedules force an overnight stopover. If that happens, you are most likely to spend your time relaxing around your hotel. In town, the best-rated hotels (local five-star) are the *Intercontinental* and the *Pamodzi*; neither offers great service or ambiance. The former *Ridgeway Hotel*, a four-star hotel notable for its lively garden restaurant and well-stocked Zintu Handicrafts Shop, has been totally refurbished and is now known as the *Holiday Inn Garden Court*. *Andrews Motel* (which has a pool) and the *Lusaka Hotel* (which doesn't) are cheaper and cater to Zambian businessmen. If you venture downtown, you'll find all the shops, airline offices, and travel agencies on a small section of Cairo Road. A few markets and souvenir stores are scattered around town, and tours can be undertaken to view the government buildings or visit gemstone-grinding factories. The Munda Wanga Botanical Gardens are pretty run down, but you can walk in them safely.

The best place to stay around Lusaka is about a half hour's drive outside town. *Lilayi Lodge* is located on its own private game reserve stocked with 16 species of antelope. It's a good place to get photos of hard-to-shoot animals like roan, sable, eland, and Lichtenstein's hartebeest in a natural miombo setting. You can walk, do game drives, or take horseback rides around the reserve. The lodge is charming and comfortable, and the food is excellent. They also book helicopter excursions along the Kafue and Zambezi rivers. The lovely *Lechwe Lodge* makes another nice out-of-town alternative, although it is considerably further out of Lusaka and not as convenient to the airport. This new private reserve is sited on the banks of the Kafue River and makes a good base for visiting Lochinvar National Park on the Kafue Flats. The lodge offers game viewing and cruising or canoeing on the Kafue River, as well as horseback riding and tours of the lodge's fish farm.

The Luangwa Valley

One branch of Africa's Great Rift Valley cuts a 400-mile-long gash through eastern Zambia. Although tectonic forces created this 3,500-foot-deep cleft, the Luangwa River is now the dominant architect of the valley's landscape. Changing its course with every annual flood, the river nurtures one of Africa's most outstanding wildlife areas.

Fed by innumerable tributaries from the surrounding plateau country, the Luangwa River gains irresistible force during Zambia's rainy season.

The river then swells to a red torrent, colored by the soils carried in its flood. The Luangwa regularly bursts its banks as it pushes its way through the loops and bends that mark its course over the valley floor. In its rush to find the easiest path downstream, the river is continually tearing at its banks, forming new channels or cutting off meandering loops, then damming them with silt. Such cutoff channels, locally known as *luangwa wafwa* ("the dead Luangwa"), are distributed all over the floodplain. Newly discarded channels may still flow during the spate, but their wide, sandy beds are left dry and empty when the floods subside. Older channels, more disconnected from the river, also fill during the rains. The distinctive, crescent-shaped lagoons of oxbow lakes form in the deeper bends of abandoned channels. The deepest lagoons retain water all year, providing permanent refuge to aquatic animals such as hippos and crocodiles, as well as refreshment to thirsty land animals. Shallower cutoff channels dry out completely during the rainless months, but their waters are replaced by luxuriant lawns of grass. Such *dambos* are key grazing grounds when the valley's animals crowd down to the floodplain at the height of the annual drought. Shady riparian forests grow on the old riverbanks that border lagoons and disused channels. These higher areas do not flood and are an important year-round source of food and shelter for a tremendous variety of animals and birds. This flux of microhabitats with vegetation in differing stages of succession enables the Luangwa floodplain to support an astonishing wildlife population.

Although some species remain on the floodplain throughout the year, many animals spread more widely during or immediately after the rains. Most of the valley floor is dominated by seasonally dry woodlands. Mopane trees are very widespread, although there are also extensive tracts of scrubby bush and some open grass plains. Riverine forests and grasslands accompany the courses of the Luangwa's major tributary streams, while miombo woodlands prevail on the foothills and walls of the enclosing escarpments. The western side of the valley is abruptly marked by the steep hills of the Muchinga Escarpment, which rises to a high point of 5,085 feet, towering more than 3,000 feet above the valley floor. Some 60 miles separate it from the less dramatic hills that define the eastern side of the Luangwa Valley. In this vast and varied environment, wildlife has enough room to indulge in any necessary seasonal migrations. Although animals, particularly elephants, used to range into the surrounding plateau country on well-established game trails, the valley is a functionally self-contained ecosystem. This makes it almost unique among southern Africa's wildlife regions. Unlike Kruger,

Hwange, or Etosha, the confines of the Luangwa Valley meet the year-round needs of its resident wildlife, and its parks are unfenced.

Virtually the entire Luangwa Valley is divided into game management areas and national parks. In the GMAs, humans share the land with wildlife, and hunting takes place. The largest and most important of the four parks in the valley is South Luangwa National Park (3,535 square miles). Further up valley is North Luangwa National Park (1,800 square miles). The tiny Luambe National Park (128 square miles) is located between the two major reserves, while the nearby Lukusuzi National Park (1,062 square miles) straddles the eastern side of the valley and the miombo woodlands atop the plateau.

The Luangwa Valley is one of the most prolific wildlife areas in southern Africa. Until the early 1970s, the Luangwa watershed was thought to harbor upwards of 100,000 elephants and over 5,000 black rhinos. Although poaching has trimmed its elephant population by over 80 percent and rhinos have been all but eliminated, the habitat remains intact and all other species associated with the valley are thriving.

Impala and puku are the most common Luangwa antelopes. Large groups are often seen feeding together on the short grasses of the floodplain. The puku (*Kobus vardonii*) looks much like a sturdier version of an impala, but the resemblance is superficial — it is actually a closer relative of the waterbuck. Unlike impala, puku are almost exclusively grazers and are practically restricted to floodplain grasslands. While they avoid inundated ground, they like tender green grass, so they collect where new grass is springing up in the wake of retreating water, or in areas where long, coarse grasses have been cleared away by buffalo. During the mating season, male pukus establish small individual territories on communal breeding grounds. Each male defends his plot against other bulls, but females wander freely from one territory to the next. Although common in Zambia (and found in parts of Tanzania), puku are rare and unlikely to be seen elsewhere in southern Africa.

Two animals are unique to Luangwa, and even within the valley have oddly limited distributions. Cookson's wildebeest is the local subspecies of this widespread antelope. It is more reddish than its kind elsewhere, and is most numerous in the northern part of the valley, especially on the east side of the river. It is rarely seen below South Luangwa's Nsefu sector. Thornicroft's giraffe is another Luangwa endemic. Although the difference between it and other giraffes in southern Africa is slight (adult Thornicroft males develop dark brown patches on the neck that contrast with black patches on the body), the Luangwa giraffes are a distinct population, well isolated from their nearest kin. They are restricted to the

The puku is abundant on the Luangwa floodplains. South Luangwa National Park, Zambia. Photo: Allen Bechky.

south end of the valley and occur almost entirely on the east bank of the river. Their range seems to be extending northward, where it reaches as far as the Nsefu sector of South Luangwa National Park.

Hippos are superabundant in the Luangwa Valley. Their population density is officially estimated at over 48 per kilometer of river; that would yield some 12,000 hippos in South Luangwa National Park alone — but there could well be twice that many. Pods can be seen in every suitable bend of the Luangwa River, as well as in all the larger lagoons. Their weird grunts and bellows are one of the most typical sounds of the Luangwa night. The hippo population bounced back quickly from an anthrax outbreak between 1987 and 1988 that killed about a third of their number. By 1995, their population was again sufficiently high to permit more than 500 to be shot in a sanctioned cull. Many Zambian conservationists support culling hippos because of the overgrazing they do during the dry season. Such culls also supply needed meat and income to the valley's villagers.

Although their population has suffered a drastic decline in the last 20 years, there are still some 15,000 elephants in the Luangwa Valley. Elephant-caused damage to vegetation is very evident in some parts of

Thousands of hippos inhabit the Luangwa River. South Luangwa National Park, Zambia. Photo: Allen Bechky.

South Luangwa National Park. Poaching pressures tend to keep the survivors in the better-protected tourist sectors even during the months when they might normally disperse more widely. Whole tracts of mopane forest near the floodplain have been turned into coppiced scrub and grassland. Such thinning is not entirely negative, for the spread of grasslands has been accompanied by an increase in the number of wildebeest and zebra. Such grazers benefit, but it's not good news for the mopane trees themselves, which don't produce seed unless they get to a sufficient height.

A handful of rhinos still survive in the valley. Their numbers are so low that the Luangwa population may no longer be genetically or numerically viable. Yet with so few rhinos around and so much trackless bushland to hide in, it's hardly worth a poacher's effort to search for them. If community-oriented conservation efforts really take hold and the government gets serious about punishing high-level poachers, it's quite possible that rhinos will start to appear and that the park could someday be a safe haven for them.

Zebra and buffalo are plentiful and wide ranging throughout the Luangwa Valley. The zebra tend to occur in small groups, while buffalo appear in their usual way: in either big breeding herds or small parties of tough old bulls, locally known as *kakuli*. Buffalo are the favorite prey of Luangwa's lions. Baboon, warthog, and waterbuck are also quite common. Bushbuck are shy and singular, but are regular residents of the riverine forests. Kudu and eland inhabit the woodlands, but descend to the floodplain as the dry season progresses. Roan antelope rarely venture down to the floodplain. Both they and Lichtenstein's hartebeest favor the miombo forests of the valley edges, while sable live in the foothills of the Muchinga Escarpment. Sharpe's grysbok is the smallest of the valley's antelopes. A shy inhabitant of woodland and thickets, it is not often seen except on night drives, when it is sometimes encountered near villagers' gardens outside the parks.

Lion and leopard are both very common in Luangwa. With the park's abundance of trees and small game, there is no finer country for leopards and they are seen on most night drives in the park. In the valley, a pack of hyenas will often follow a leopard as it hunts. They appropriate its kill if the cat is not quick enough to get the carcass up a tree. Thus deprived of the fruits of their labor, Luangwa leopards have to work doubly hard — perhaps another reason they are so often seen on the prowl. Cheetahs are very rare, and wild dogs occur sporadically. The only jackal in the valley (and in Zambia) is the side-striped. The most timid member of the jackal clan, it is not often seen. Eight species of mongoose are found in the valley, including the little-known bush-tailed and Meller's varieties.

The Luangwa Valley is tsetse country. The presence of the fly and heavy annual flooding have served as brakes on human colonization, so the 400-mile-long valley is lightly populated. Because of the tsetse, the people who do live there cannot keep domestic livestock. They are small-scale farmers whose staple food crops are maize and sorghum. They also plant sunflowers and cotton as cash crops.

Luangwa's people have to coexist with the valley's abundant wildlife. Man-eating lions and crocodiles are but two of the potential hazards of living in the valley, where defending fields from wild animals is a way of life. Zambia's National Parks and Wildlife Service has always done plenty of "control shooting" to discourage elephants from crop-raiding, even while its scouts try to prevent poaching inside the national parks. Traditionally, Luangwa's human residents have supplemented their diet with game meat, so "poaching" by local people is constant and widespread. Such subsistence hunters use a variety of means. A few carry old rifles, even homemade muzzle loaders, but wire snares are far more widely employed. The commercial poaching gangs that go after elephants are infinitely more lethal and highly organized. They use automatic weapons and have vehicles at their disposal. They are also backed by a sophisticated network of middle men and protectors within the various enforcement and judicial bureaucracies.

A lot of effort has recently gone into wooing the valley's inhabitants away from their natural sympathy to poachers. Several organizations are working to build support for conservation by directing wildlife-generated income back to local communities. In 1988, the Luangwa Integrated Resource Development Project (LIRDP) was given the brief to manage South Luangwa National Park and the neighboring Lupande Game Management Area, while funneling some of the profits from wildlife activities back to local residents. The LIRDP increased revenues by raising park entry fees and leasing concession areas to professional hunters and tourist lodges. The funds were used for such things as improving local transportation services and building village maize-grinding mills. Although there was criticism on specifics, reaction to the program was generally favorable. But while LIRDP got the conservation ball rolling, it inevitably stepped on a lot of toes in the process. The situation was muddled by the national election of 1991. With the change of government, LIRDP's influence declined relative to that of a rival project, ADMADE. ADMADE is a nationwide program that professes the same goals as LIRDP: conservation to benefit local people through sustainable use. ADMADE also strives to use wildlife revenues to fund community projects and has been particularly active in hiring and training village game scouts, who could form an effective, paid cadre in the war against poaching. ADMADE has its own set of international donors, and it is more closely identified with the new Movement for Multi-Party Democracy (MMD) government than LIRDP. To further complicate matters, a private foundation created by researchers Mark and Delia Owens has developed its own community-oriented antipoaching program around North Luangwa National Park. These groups are all well meaning, but there has been inevitable turf fighting among the various organizations, their foreign donors, and competing government bureaucracies. Because it's Zambia, funds for local projects — such as the pay for newly organized groups of village wildlife guards — are often late in coming, or simply disappear. Similarly, quotas for legal hunting licenses are routinely exceeded or ignored. Despite such frustrations, progress has been made. Poaching is down, community benefits and support are becoming more apparent, and tourism is growing. The future looks somewhat brighter for conservation in the Luangwa Valley than it has in many years.

South Luangwa National Park

The most important wildlife sanctuary in Zambia is South Luangwa National Park. Most of its 3,535-square-mile area extends from the Luangwa River's west bank to the crest of the Muchinga Escarpment. Only the remote and little-visited southernmost sector around Luamfwa Lagoon and the small salient of the game-rich Nsefu sector are east of the river. Nsefu and the central area around Mfuwe Lagoon are the primary safari areas.

This huge park is almost entirely wilderness. Game tracks are very few and are virtually all concentrated on the stretch of floodplain between the Mfuwe area and the Nsefu sector. The rest of the park can only be explored on foot. While it is famous for its bush walking safaris, very few visitors mount the major expeditions necessary to explore deep into the interior. Although such adventures are surely rewarding, they are hardly necessary — game viewing on the rich alluvial floodplains of the Luangwa rivals the best found anywhere in Africa.

Access and Accommodation

Although South Luangwa is officially open year-round, the safari season runs from June 1 through October 31. Almost all lodges and safari camps are closed during the intervening rainy months because (except on the few all-weather roads in the Mfuwe area) it is then impossible to get around. Flooding makes most of the park completely inaccessible to vehicles, while over-the-head-high grass makes bush walking dangerous. During the rains, game is widely dispersed throughout the park and neighboring game management areas, although elephants are still plentiful on the floodplain grasslands and birding is exceptional. As the dry season progresses, the animals come down from the higher portions of the valley. They move toward the lagoons and *dambos* of the floodplain and gradually pack into the area around the main river. At the height of the dry season, a parade of impalas, pukus, waterbucks, and baboons always seem to be in view along the Luangwa River, where hippos rest and crocodiles laze on exposed sandbanks. Hippos are crowded into the remaining suitable pools, so fights and aggressive behavior are commonly seen and constantly heard.

The valley floor averages less than 2,000 feet in elevation, so temperatures are always warm. From June through August, the weather is quite pleasant for walking safaris. September and October have optimal game viewing, but it is dry and hot.

Few nonresidents make the long, 425-mile drive from Lusaka to South Luangwa National Park. Almost everyone arrives by plane at Mfuwe airport, which is now well served by a variety of airlines. Mfuwe has immigration facilities to handle international arrivals. Air Malawi flies in directly from Lilongwe, Malawi, and Tropic Air arrives from Harare, Zimbabwe. Zambian Express flies to Mfuwe several times a

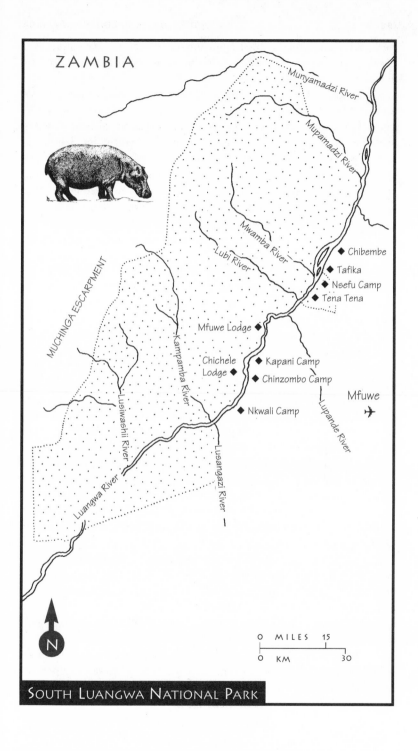

ZAMBIA

Munyamadzi River

Mupamadzi River

MUCHINGA ESCARPMENT

Mwamba River

Lubi River

◆ Chibembe
◆ Tafika
◆ Nsefu Camp
◆ Tena Tena

Mfuwe Lodge ◆

Chichele
Lodge ◆

◆ Kapani Camp
◆ Chinzombo Camp

◆ Nkwali Camp

Mfuwe
✈

Kampamba River

Lusiwashii River

Luangwa River

Lusangazi River

Lupande River

O   MILES   15
O   KM   30

N

SOUTH LUANGWA NATIONAL PARK

week (allowing a direct flight from Johannesburg via Livingstone and Lusaka). Lunga Air and Proflight also have multiple regularly scheduled flights, but use smaller aircraft.

One of the great pleasures of Luangwa is the relative scarcity of visitors. Although each arriving plane may be full, after everyone is collected by the representatives of the various lodges, the airport crowd is well dispersed and not to be seen again until it returns for departure.

Except for the simpler bush camps that are used exclusively for walking safaris, Luangwa's private lodges and camps all have much the same daily routine: morning game drives or walks plus a late afternoon drive that includes a stop for sundowners, then continues into the night using spotlights. The exceptions are a couple of self-catering, self-drive camps used pretty much exclusively by Zambian residents and overland truck expeditions: in the Mfuwe area, a budget camp near the Crocodile Farm is open all year and the Chipata branch of the Wildlife Society of Zambia runs *Wildlife Camp*, which has chalets, a dormitory, and campsites. The former government-run camps in Luangwa have all been closed or leased to private concessionaires.

South Luangwa's central Mfuwe sector is a prime tour area. It's only a half-hour drive on a paved road from the airport to the park gate at the Luangwa Bridge. This makes the lodges around Mfuwe exceptionally convenient, and the sector's all-weather roads allow several of them to stay open even in the wet season. The camps on the east side of the river do most of their game drives in the park, to which they have quick access over the bridge. These camps (Kapani, Chinzombo, and Nsefu, described below) also share a private "pontoon" that can ferry their vehicles across the Luangwa for game drives. For walks, those camps have boats on hand to punt guests across the river, directly into the park. Because of the number of lodges in the area, game tracks around Mfuwe get a lot more use during the busy dry season, but real crowding is rarely a problem: this could change in the future, depending on the extent of further camp development.

Kapani Lodge was owned and overseen by Luangwa's grand old man, Norman Carr, until his death in 1977. He was the legendary former warden who pioneered commercial foot safaris in Luangwa and made them a park specialty. Kapani is probably the most comfortably appointed camp in the valley. Its eight twin-bedded cabins include such niceties as overhead fans and a fridge on the verandah, and the lodge has a swimming pool. The camp overlooks the Chinzombo Lagoon, where wildlife is always in view. Kapani is headquarters for three satellite bush camps, *Luwi* (six beds) and *Nsolo* (eight beds), both on the Lubi (sometimes spelled Luwi) sand river, and *Kakuli* (eight beds), which is near the confluence of the Lubi with the Luangwa River. These seasonal camps are constructed of grass and thatch. They are primarily used for foot safaris (although game drives are also done from them), and Nsolo has an excellent hide over a well-used waterhole, which is spotlighted at night. A fine multiday safari can be made walking down the Lubi from one camp to another. In the past, Kapani has remained open year-round, but now closes from mid-January through February.

Chinzombo is another first-rate lodge. Located in a shady grove right on the banks of the Luangwa, Chinzombo accommodates up to 18 guests in its nine cabins. It has a swimming pool and is open from mid-April until mid-January. Like Kapani, it operates two remote seasonal bush camps (*Kuyenda* and *Chamilandu*) with chalets built of grass and thatch. Kuyenda and Chamilandu have six beds each and are only open in the dry season. Kuyenda offers both walks and game drives, while Chamilandu — set on the west bank of the Luangwa — is primarily a walking camp. Chinzombo Lodge also specializes in organizing old-fashioned camping expeditions on which you walk with a column of porters to explore the further reaches of the park. These are led by long-time Luangwa guide, Phil Berry.

Nkwali is a six-chalet camp in the same area as Kapani and Chinzombo. It offers simpler, but comfortable, accommodation and is open from April to the beginning of January (it is the sister camp of Tena Tena in the Nsefu sector). Nkwali has good access to walks in the nearby Nchindeni Hills that rise to the east of the river. The hills offer great views over the valley and the opportunity for a bath in natural hot springs at their base.

Mfuwe Lodge is inside the park. Situated on the permanent Mfuwe Lagoon, it is in the middle of a superb game viewing area. For many years, Mfuwe was a neglected, government-run facility, but the derelict old camp has been torn down and a new private lodge is in the process of being built on this excellent site. It is the same story with the formerly government-owned *Chichele Lodge*, which has fine views from its perch atop President Hill (so called because the lodge shared the site with the Zambian head-of-state's safari retreat). Chichele, too, is being completely redeveloped by a private licensee. Both of the old lodges were quite big (48 beds and 32 beds, respectively), but they were nearly always empty: if the new camps that replace them are equally large, they will have a major impact on the number of safari vehicles patrolling the Mfuwe sector.

Several other seasonal camps are located to the south of the Mfuwe-

Chinzombo area. *Tundwe Camp* is a rustic lodge on the Luangwa River, just across from the park. It is used for walking safaris in the park and in the nearby Nchindeni Hills, but has limited opportunities for game drives in the vicinity of the camp (although drives can be organized into more distant parts of the park). *Kapamba Camp* is inside the park. It is set on the banks of the Kapamba (also spelled Kampamba) River, close to its junction with the Luangwa. *Luamfwa Lodge* is located on the banks of a floodplain lagoon in the remote southernmost section of the park. Formerly a government-run camp, it has been closed for many years, but is slated to be privatized and rebuilt.

The Nsefu sector is a game-rich wedge of land on the east bank of the Luangwa, some 15 miles north of Mfuwe. A number of seasonal lodges are clustered in or around Nsefu. It takes about an hour to drive the dirt roads from the airport to the Miliyoti Gate that marks the entrance to Nsefu sector. The track passes through a countryside where small villages — with their grass huts, raised wooden granaries, and untidy fields of sunflowers, sorghum, and cotton — are interspersed with wild bush. After passing the entrance gate, it can take anywhere from a half hour to an hour and a half to proceed to the various lodges in or around the Nsefu sector. The long drive to the lodges to the north of the Nsefu sector can be avoided by flying into the Lukuzi airstrip: Tropic Air will extend its regular Harare-Mfuwe flights to Lukuzi if they have passengers, and a local charter company offers daily services (during the safari session) between Mfuwe and Lukuzi.

Two superb camps (Nsefu and Tena Tena) are located inside the Nsefu sector. *Nsefu Camp* is a gem, with six white-washed rondavels overlooking a scenic loop of the Luangwa. An excellent hide over a small waterhole is active during the day. Walks can be arranged at Nsefu but game drives are more typical. At *Tena Tena*, the Nsefu sector's luxury tented camp, daily walks and game drives are conducted, and six fully equipped safari tents are set up beneath grass thatch shelters. Tena Tena, too, has magnificent views from its mahogany grove on the banks of the Luangwa. A two-tiered hide affords superb, close-up opportunities for wildlife photography. Tena Tena is the flagship camp for Robin Pope, one of Zambia's best known guides. Robin Pope Safaris also runs five-day walking safaris (using vehicle-supported mobile camps) along the remote Mupamadzi River on the northern end of the park.

Tafika Camp is located just to the north of the Nsefu sector. This eight-bed bush camp, with its rustic, grass-thatched chalets, has good access to both the Nsefu sector and the main body of the park by means of a nearby "pontoon" ferry across the Luangwa. Tafika offers two unusual activities in addition to the normal walks and game drives: scenic microlight flights and canoe safaris. The highly adventurous canoe trips on the Luangwa take place only during February and March, when the river is in its high-water stage. Tafika also operates *Mwaleshi Camp* in North Luangwa National Park (for more information, see the North Luangwa National Park section of this chapter).

A couple of private safari camps are found on the west side of the Luangwa, opposite the Nsefu sector. *Kaingo* is a nice eight-bed camp that offers both walks and game drives, while *Kakuli* is one of the bush camps owned by Kapani Lodge. Several other sites in the area (including the old *Lion Camp*, which is now a self-catering facility) may be up for lease, so new seasonal tourist-class safari camps may soon appear.

Chibembe Safari Lodge is located 8 miles beyond the northern boundary gate of the Nsefu sector. A stretch of villages and cultivated plots separates it from the park. Chibembe is beautifully sited in riverine forest on a high bank above the main Luangwa channel. The lodge has a swimming pool and was built to accommodate up to 40 guests in wooden chalets (its capacity has declined almost by half, however, because the Luangwa has been eating into its bank, causing a number of chalets to fall into the river). Because of its size, Chibembe has a busier, less personal atmosphere than Luangwa's smaller camps. It is nonetheless a very pleasant place, where animals are constantly in view along the river. Several years ago, Chibembe began to care for orphaned elephant calves. With considerable effort and expense — and heartbreak — the lodge staff has attained a certain expertise in the difficult process of raising nursing calves. Although the original calves didn't survive, Chibembe still attempts to rescue orphans. Baby elephants are a bundle of trouble but great fun to be around, and there may well be one or two in residence when you visit. Chibembe does most of its game drives in the Nsefu sector, but its vehicles also have access to the main body of the park via the nearby "pontoon" ferry.

Chibembe is the base for popular Wilderness Trails walking safaris. Each year, the lodge sets up three very simple bush camps in a roadless concession area on the west side of the Luangwa River inside the park. A maximum of seven clients participate on a three-night foot safari (two camps are used on each safari). Walking with a guide and an armed national park game scout, you explore the lagoons and streams of the game-rich Luangwa floodplain.

Chibembe also runs a remote seasonal camp called the *Mupamadzi River Camp*, which is open from July through October, and is a two and a half hour drive from Chibembe. A three-night stay is recommended to explore its vicinity, which includes the mile-wide floodplains of the permanent Mupamadzi River and the big grassy Chifungwe and Lundu plains. This simple bush camp takes a maximum of six guests, who do all their game viewing on foot.

Touring the Park

Because of the time needed to get there and the quality of its game viewing, a minimum stay of four nights in South Luangwa National Park is recommended. A longer visit using two or more camps in different parts of the park would also be very worthwhile. Most Luangwa safari camps use "open" vehicles — a boon to good game viewing.

With few roads and plenty of wildlife, South Luangwa has a deserved reputation for foot safaris, which have become a park standard. These come in many forms. Most lodges offer brief morning or afternoon walks, and some run multiday treks with nights in seasonal bush camps. All foot safaris share some characteristics. Walking groups are limited to a maximum of six or seven participants. They are always accompanied by an armed national park game scout and the safari operator's guide, or "trail leader." The armed scout is responsible for the group's safety. Scouts vary in their quality and ability to communicate, but generally they know their business: in the off-season, they are very likely doing elephant-control work. Trail leaders provide natural history interpretation. Luangwa safari guides are required to pass qualifying written and oral exams, so the quality of their information and level of professionalism is generally excellent. Walking groups are also accompanied by a tea bearer, who makes a fire and prepares a refreshing brew during a mid-morning break. Most walks are not long-distance marches, but leisurely patrols of likely game areas, with plenty of time taken up in observation of whatever comes along. Walks early in the season (June and July) are usually longer because the weather is so fine. Daytime temperatures soar as the dry season progresses, so late-season walks are short or else they extend into the hot part of the day. The tradeoff is that game viewing is vastly better later in the season, when animals are crowding down to the lagoons and *dambos* of the Luangwa floodplain. Participants need only carry their cameras, binoculars, and perhaps a daypack (bringing a water bottle is a good idea).

Several safari companies organize longer expeditions to remote portions of the park. By their nature, these journeys are more arduous, although porters or vehicles are used to transport mobile camps and all baggage. Several major streams — notably the Kapamba in the south and the Mupamadzi along the remote northern park boundary — usually continue to flow from the Muchinga Escarpment right through the dry season. These clear-water tributaries make interesting routes into the trackless wilderness regions beyond the Luangwa floodplain.

Walking safaris are not necessarily without discomfort, and game drives usually yield closer viewing of big game and better photographs. Yet walks enable you to appreciate the subtleties of the variable Luangwa environment. Crossing the floodplain on foot, you discover the many hidden streambeds that must be negotiated, as well as the variety of *dambos* and lagoons. One *dambo* is covered in short green grass attended by puku. The next is bottomed with gray mud, and is so cratered with the footprints of elephant, buffalo, and hippo that it is difficult to walk on. Another lagoon holds water, its surface covered with Nile cabbage. Hippos watch you warily, with little water cabbages vainly camouflaging the tops of their enormous raised heads. Jacanas tiptoe across the floating vegetation, while a Goliath heron remains poised to strike an unwary frog. You jump at the slap of a 5-foot-long monitor lizard as it hits the water after dropping from an overhanging limb, then hear the whistle of an alarmed puku. What has disturbed it? You walk across burnt grasslands — charred stems scratching and blackening your legs while the hot sun beats down — then discover the blissful, deep shade of a lagoon-side Natal mahogany tree. You may even have some close encounters with elephants or lions. Bush walking is not for everyone, but Luangwa is certainly a good place to experience it.

Night drives are another regular feature at Luangwa safari camps. Leopards are commonly seen, and it's not unusual to follow them on their rounds or even observe a kill. Although drivers will approach most animals fairly closely, they give hippos a wide berth and do not like to put them in the spotlight. These skittish animals are easily confused and may accidentally run into a vehicle. Lions, hyenas, and myriad odd creatures — even crocodiles moving overland — can appear in the spotlight's beam. Perhaps one of the most startling is the pennant-winged nightjar, a nocturnal, insect-eating bird. Breeding males carry 2-foot-long streamers on their wings that are more than twice the length of the body, causing them to flutter, ghostlike, through the night sky.

As you might expect, Luangwa birdlife is abundant and interesting. With its wealth of lagoons and waterways, there are always ample numbers of herons, storks, fish eagles, jacanas, and other waterbirds. Pel's fishing owls inhabit the riverine forests that border lagoons. The Chipera Lagoon in the Nsefu sector is a famous breeding site for yellow-billed storks. Between March and the end of July, more than a thousand pairs nest in ebony trees overlooking the lagoon. Flocks of brilliant-green Lillian's lovebirds are a common sight in wooded areas throughout the year. Bee-eaters nest in holes excavated in high, exposed banks along the Luangwa. Colonies of carmine bee-eaters make a particularly splendid sight when they assemble during the breeding season. Less colorful, but possibly even more spectacular, are incredible masses of red-billed que-leas that gather at dusk on favorite roosting sites. Millions of these small finches cross the sky in continuous undulating lines that look like columns of smoke.

A "fish out" at a dying lagoon is another remarkable and regular event you might witness in Luangwa. As the dry season advances, many lagoons shrink down to murky pools. Shoals of catfish flounder in the thickening mud, which becomes a feasting ground for their enemies. Crocodiles cruise the dwindling lagoons, tearing at the frantic catfish, while flocks of ravenous birds join in the attack. In a matter of days, the dive-bombing fish eagles, squadrons of white pelicans, and relentless companies of yellow-billed storks pluck out the helpless fish and move on to another pool. A few catfish always manage to escape into the mud, digging deep into the ooze where they cocoon to pass the dry months. The survivors burst out with the rains — the progenitors of the next year's abundant catch.

North Luangwa National Park

Wilderness is both the glory and the curse of North Luangwa. Without development of any sort, the park was virtually abandoned to poachers for most of the last 25 years. Nearly all of its elephants were slain, and large poaching gangs were so bold as to set up commercial "bush meat" operations — shooting animals and smoking meat in the park, then transporting it to villages and cities.

North Luangwa's plight has received a lot of attention in recent years as a result of publicity generated by American researchers Mark and Delia Owens. Their attempt to study wildlife there necessarily degener-ated into a struggle against the active and entrenched poaching gangs that used the park as their theater of operations. If their 1992 book, *The Eye of the Elephant*, is to be believed, the scourge of poaching has been sub-stantially reduced. It will take some time, however, for the elephant pop-ulation to recover and for the animals to become habituated to human observers. (In 1996, the Owens had to pull out of the country due to con-troversy surrounding the death of a poacher; at this time, it's not known whether they will be able to resume their efforts in North Luangwa.)

Stretching from the west bank of the Luangwa River up to the top of the Muchinga Escarpment, North Luangwa National Park protects the same habitats and wildlife as South Luangwa. The park has tremendous potential as a major wildlife sanctuary. For the moment, it is still com-pletely undeveloped. It is really only suitable for visitors who wish to do most, or all, of their explorations on foot, and for those who crave a wilderness experience more than easy game viewing.

The heart of the park is the Mwaleshi River. This clear-running permanent river comes down from the Muchinga hills, then widens into a broad stream only inches deep as it passes over the valley floor on the way to its junction with the Luangwa. It is thus a convenient route for traversing the park. You can follow its course from the Luangwa upwards into the hills of the escarpment, where you can explore wooded glades, secret waterfalls, and streamside bamboo groves. Game is not as abundant as it is in the better protected South Luangwa National Park, but there are still large herds of buffalo along the Mwaleshi, and plenty of lions. Elephants are present, too, but very shy — they tend to panic and run at the first hint of human presence. There are many good camping sites in wooded groves along the Mwaleshi. (In one, a hungry lioness, injured and quite desperate, took a well-known hunter out of his tent in a famous man-eating incident.) The shallow Mwaleshi is bilharzia-free and (almost) devoid of crocs in the dry season, so you can splash in its cool waters. Use caution, however, and stay out of any pools in the river, as hidden crocs may still be lurking.

Access and Accommodation

The park is about a five- to seven-hour journey from the various camps in South Luangwa National Park. The road goes through Luambe National Park and passes by several villages, but mostly it is just wild bush in the hunting blocks along the Luangwa.

There are only a couple of seasonal bush camps in North Luangwa. *Mwaleshi Camp* is a six-hour drive from Tafika Camp in South Luangwa. It is open from mid-July to mid-October. A minimum three-night stay is required, and four is optimum. Mwaleshi is a simple bush camp with grass structures, limited to a maximum of six clients (safaris require a *minimum* of four). Game viewing and explorations are conducted on foot. The eight-bed *Buffalo Camp* is another seasonal bush camp located on the Mwaleshi River. It is used as a base in North Luangwa by Shiwa Safaris.

North Luangwa National Park can also be reached from the west via the town of Mpika, from which a rough track descends the Muchinga Escarpment. Shiwa Safaris uses this route to enter the park and access Buffalo Camp. The company starts their safaris from their estate at Shiwa Ngandu — the Bemba chiefs' Lake of the Sacred Crocodile — where they maintain a chalet-style safari camp at the palm-fringed *Kapishya Hot Springs*. Guests can tour (and even stay in) the baronial *Shiwa Ngandu* manor house that overlooks the lake.

Several other safari outfitters also operate mobile camping trips to North Luangwa, usually coming up from the south park. Wild Zambia

Safaris uses the Muchinga track to combine North Luangwa with visits to the Bangweulu Swamps and Kasanka National Park.

The Bangweulu Swamps and Kasanka National Park

The Bangweulu Swamps are one of Zambia's most intriguing wilderness regions. Seventeen rivers glide from surrounding miombo country into a shallow, flat-bottomed bowl to create one of Africa's most extensive wetlands. David Livingstone described the swamps as a "world of water." Here marshes, lily-covered lagoons, papyrus swamps, grassy watermeadows, and meandering streams blend in an atmosphere reminiscent of Botswana's Okavango Delta.

The Bangweulu region has tremendous potential as a wildlife paradise, although its game populations have been much reduced by poaching. Bangweulu's marshes and watermeadows are home to the black lechwe, which is found nowhere else. Its drier floodplains are habitat to tsessebe and reedbuck, while papyrus swamps shelter sitatunga. Its lakes and watercourses are havens for hippos, crocs, and clawless otters. Elephant and buffalo are present if not plentiful, and lion and leopard are definitely around. Birds are abundant and varied, with over 400 species recorded. There is probably no better place to see the shoebill stork, a secretive, whale-headed denizen of central African swamps that just about tops every birder's wish list.

The heart of the Bangweulu Swamps is a game management area, rather than a national park, and villagers are allowed to harvest the swamps' bountiful fish. Three national parks — Lavushi Manda, Isangano, and Kasanka — are located around the fringes of the swamps. Lavushi Manda is a miombo park in the hills on Bangweulu's southeastern edge, and a good part of Isangano is actually within the swampy plains, but both these parks are completely undeveloped and largely unprotected. Only Kasanka National Park is up and functioning as a safe haven for wildlife.

Kasanka is the site of a fascinating experiment in African conservation. In 1986, the management of the neglected and poached-out park was given over to a private trust. With the avowed goal of providing jobs and income to surrounding communities, 30 guardposts were set up, bridges and roads were repaired, and several small safari lodges were built. Since the trust got involved, not an elephant or hippo has been poached, and Kasanka's wildlife population has rebounded. A formal 10-year management contract was signed with the National Parks and Wildlife Service in 1990, and the trust corporation is starting educational, health, and agricultural projects in neighboring villages. Kasanka looks like a community-oriented conservation project that really works.

Kasanka National Park is small (only 167 square miles) but has a very interesting variety of habitats and animals. Although not part of the Bangweulu Swamps, Kasanka is well watered with rivers, lagoons, *dambos*, and floodplains. Puku are the most common antelope. Lechwe are absent, but tracts of papyrus swamp are known for their resident sitatunga. Pockets of *mushitu* (relict forest) are one of Kasanka's most unusual habitats. These groves of closed-canopy swamp forest, in which evergreen trees reach 100 feet, are outliers of the vast tropical jungles of Congo. They harbor the yellow-backed duiker and, during the rains, are the roosting place for a million-strong colony of fruit bats. Blue monkeys (a subspecies of the samango monkey found in South Africa and Zimbabwe) inhabit the *mushitu* as well as the gallery forests found along Kasanka's rivers. Hartebeest and sable live in the miombo woods. Elephant, bushpig, hyena, and leopard are all resident animals, although not always seen. Birdlife is great: the tree-fringed steams are excellent places to spot African finfoot, Pel's fishing owl, and half-collared kingfisher. Ross's lourie, a deep-blue turaco with a red crest and flashing crimson wings, is a spectacular forest resident. The shoebill is sometimes seen in Kasanka.

The Bangweulu wetlands drew David Livingstone, who thought he was nearing the sources of the Nile. Actually, the rivers that feed the Bangweulu marshes are the headwaters of Africa's longest river, the Congo. Livingstone never realized his mistake: he died at Chitambo's village on the edge of the great swamps. A monument marks the place where the explorer's heart was buried. His body, preserved with salt, was carried back to Zanzibar and hence to England, where it was entombed in Westminster Abbey.

Access and Accommodation

Kasanka is about a six-hour drive from Lusaka, most of it on the major Great North Road. It can also be reached by charter aircraft. Kasanka and Bangweulu combine well with overland safaris coming from North Luangwa via the town of Mpika.

At Kasanka, two 10-bed lodges are open all year: *Wasa Lodge* and *Luwombwa Fishing Lodge* both accommodate guests in thatched rondavels. Wasa Lodge is on a lake, while the fishing lodge is located on the Luwombwa River. *Musande Camp* also takes 10 guests, but uses luxury safari tents sited along the Luwombwa. It is open from June to October. The *Kankonta* camping site is also on the Luwombwa. These camps are all run by Kasanka Wildlife Conservation Ltd. The camps offer motorized boats, canoes, guided walks, and game drives.

The Bangweulu Swamps proper begin about 30 miles north of

Kasanka. They are reached by rough roads that may be impassable during the rains. There are two camps in the swamps: *Nsobe Safari Camp* has chalets, but the tented, 10-bed *Shoebill Island Camp* is the prime tourist lodge. It is accessible by charter flight. Activities include walks, game drives, and explorations by boat.

Touring Kasanka and Bangweulu

The Bangweulu Swamps are really a birdwatcher's paradise. The great prize is the shoebill. This odd-looking stork has a big head and a wide, rounded bill that earned it the scientific name *Balaeniceps*, or whale-head. It scoops up frogs, snakes, nestling birds, and other animals from the papyrus swamps and reedbeds that it inhabits. Because it often stands quietly in screening swamp vegetation, it is not always easy to see, but the wetlands of Bangweulu are the place to try. Many visitors are successful. Whether you catch a glimpse of the shoebill or not, you'll see hordes of wetland birds and scattered groups of black lechwe.

Movement in Bangweulu can be restricted by the nature of the swamps. There are a limited number of roads, although waterways can be explored by boat or canoe. You may get a chance to do some walking on boggy mats of floating vegetation and on seasonal floodplains.

Kasanka is easier to get around. Wasa Lake and the Luwombwa River can each be explored by either motor launch or canoe. Angling for tilapia and tiger fish is good. The park roads are in good repair. Walking is the best way to explore the *mushitu* and riverine forests. Kasanka has an excellent tree-hide set up above a papyrus swamp to facilitate viewing of sitatunga.

The Livingstone Memorial is located 28 miles from the main Kasanka entrance gate. Chief Chitambo IV, the great-grandson of the chief who extended hospitality to the fever-wracked explorer, encourages visitors to his village. In addition to viewing a performance of traditional songs and dance, guests are invited into people's homes to sample local fare, and can witness everyday activities such as the preparation of cassava or canoe building. The chief is working with local conservation efforts and plans to open a craft market and library that will feature books about Livingstone.

Kafue National Park

At 8,650 square miles in area, Kafue National Park is one of the largest wildlife sanctuaries in Africa. This immense wilderness of well-watered miombo woodlands and seasonally flooded plains hosts a tremendous variety of species and some unique habitats. Its marshy Busanga Plain — teeming with herds of lechwe and puku, and dimpled with hippo wallows — should alone qualify Kafue as a major safari destination. Yet the park remains virtually unknown and unvisited.

Kafue owes its obscurity to factors both natural and human. The park is dominated by miombo country, a habitat that does not make for easy game viewing. In the miombo, the density of large animals tends to be fairly thin, with small herds or individuals spread out here and there among the woodlands. Trees and high grass impede visibility, while providing ideal habitat for tsetse flies. Such drawbacks make Kafue a hard sell for mass tourism, but they are factors inherent to the habitat. The real problem is that years of government neglect and declining tourism have seen Kafue ravaged by poachers. As in so many parts of Africa, its rhinos are gone, its remnant elephant population hard-pressed. But the poaching menace reaches truly alarming proportions in Kafue, where the slaughter encompasses far more than the usual hunt for tusks and rhino horns. Highly organized gangs have turned the park into the site of a commercial meat-packing industry. Each rainy season, the poachers attack the park. While poorly equipped and unmotivated game scouts are confined to their posts by impassable roads, the poaching gangs are free to set up miles of deadly snare lines to catch antelopes, and to shoot hippos and buffalo at will. The resulting meat is dried on huge wooden racks, then carried by porters to fringing villages, from which it is trucked to market in the hungry cities of Zambia's industrial Copper Belt.

Over the years, Kafue has suffered a devastating downward spiral. As the park was progressively plundered by poachers, its wildlife population declined, rendering game viewing ever more difficult, hence attracting fewer tourists. Eventually all its safari camps fell into decay and the country's leading tour outfitters wrote the park off completely, leaving the poachers even freer from restraint. This vicious cycle of decline has far-reaching implications for conservation throughout Africa. Yet there are glimmers of hope. As Zambia's safari industry revitalizes, tour operators are starting to come back to Kafue. Several new camps have opened, and some outfits are running mobile camping safaris into the park.

Kafue is quite different from Luangwa Valley and makes a good complement as a safari destination. Higher in altitude, it is probably Africa's finest miombo park. Myriad small rivers drain the shallow valleys of its miombo country and eventually flow into the big Kafue River, which winds its way for 140 miles through the park. Most game viewing takes place near the river or on the grassy *dambos* along its seasonally flooded tributaries.

Kafue's most astonishing attraction is its Busanga Plain — an ecosystem much like that of Botswana's better known Okavango Delta. This broad depression in the park's far north is a sump for the many streams that discharge from the surrounding miombo. The plain is inundated during the rainy season, when it is turned into a shallow sea of flooded grass. Only occasional termite-mound islands — often crowned by a single fig tree or a bushy grove of wild date (*Phoenix*) palms — rise above the flood. The watermeadows and pools at the heart of the Busanga Plain stay moist right through the dry season. Waterbirds then concentrate around pothole depressions. Spoonbills, squacco herons, egrets, and wattled or blacksmith plovers can all be seen in great numbers. Most startling are concentrations of large cranes — both wattled and crowned — that stalk the grassy flats. The watermeadows are the habitat of the red lechwe, and these handsome antelope are present in good-sized herds. Puku mix with the lechwe where they can, but do not actually venture onto flooded ground. Bands of wildebeest and zebra — as well as unusually large herds of roan antelope — graze the dryer grasslands. Sable and eland inhabit the wooded fringes of the plain. Where the high grass has been burnt off, it is easy to see pairs of diminutive oribi. The Lufupa River drains the waterlogged plains. At its headwaters, the river is little more than a meander connecting scattered pools. Hippos crowd these mud puddles in the dry season. This makes for terrific hippo watching, but the many skulls and piles of hippo bones scattered on the plain attest to the animal's vulnerability to poachers.

A belt of drier grassland surrounding Busanga's marshy core is inhabited by incalculable billions of termites. The social insects have thrown up tens of thousands of small gray mounds. Individually, these anthills are nothing to write home about by African standards: few attain a height of more than a foot or two. But after fires have burned off the concealing high grass, the mounds seem to cover the entire plain, rising everywhere from a green carpet of new growth. The tallest mounds line both sides of the plain's lonely dirt track. They look like ruined columns strung out along a causeway through some immense ancient city. It is an altogether startling and unique landscape.

Kafue has an excellent variety of wildlife. The park is one of the best for sable and roan antelopes, and the miombo is the realm of the unique Lichtenstein's hartebeest, with its very odd-shaped horns. The grassy *dambos* that punctuate the miombo are home to oribi and reedbuck, while gallery forests provide habitat for the yellow-backed duiker (*Cephalophus sylvicultor*), a rarely seen nocturnal antelope that occurs in no other major park in southern Africa. This largest of all duikers is a denizen of the moist forests of central Africa, but is also found in the *mushitu* of western Zambia. Kafue's waterbuck differ from those found in Luangwa and the rest of southern Africa. Kafue's Defassa waterbuck has a white rump, unlike the common waterbuck, which has a distinctive crescent ring on its behind. Red lechwe, which are absent from Luangwa, abound on the Busanga Plain.

Although the official tourist map notes that "Buffalo, Elephant, and Lion may be seen in all areas of the park," this is no longer true for at least two of these species. Kafue's elephant and buffalo populations have been hard hit by poachers, and both species are rare and skittish, especially in the northern sector of the park. Hippos, too, have suffered, although they are still regularly seen in the Kafue River. Lion and leopard are both quite common and likely to be encountered on night drives. The park is ideal country for wild dogs, and there are plenty of impala and puku for them to pursue.

Access and Accommodation

An excellent, 150-mile paved road connects Kafue's eastern boundary with Lusaka. This highway continues straight through the park, dividing it into northern and southern sectors. The first part of the journey is through populated agricultural districts. At the town of Mumbwa (30 miles from the park), a dirt road shoots off to the safari camps on Kafue's northeastern border. Beyond Mumbwa on the main road, you enter game country and pass through a good stretch of mature miombo forest (sometimes called "cathedral miombo" because of its tall trees) before the landscape opens up in the shallow valley of the Kafue River. The ride to the park takes about three and a half hours, but rough tracks within the reserve can more than double the time necessary to get into some of the more distant camps. Kafue can also be reached overland from Livingstone. It takes most of a day to negotiate the 126 miles of rough road between the Zambezi and Kafue's southernmost sector along the Nanzhila River. Air charters can be arranged.

All the government-run camps in Kafue are pretty decrepit by international safari standards, and some that appear on official maps and literature are actually defunct. *Chunga* (just a few miles south of the tar road) is the principal government rest camp within the park; *Ngoma*, formerly another main camp about 40 miles south of Chunga, is now just a collection of derelict old buildings. The more modern *New Kalala Camp* and *Musungwa Lodge* are much better facilities located in the Ngoma area, but are just beyond the park boundary, near the Itezhi-Tezhi Dam on the Kafue River. All these camps offer accommodation and meals, and are open year-round. They are used chiefly by Zambian residents. Activities at both Musungwa and New Kalala include fishing and game viewing cruises on the river, as well as escorted game drives. *Nanzhila Cam*p, in the park's far south, is supposed to be open from June to November, but it is in a state of advanced decay and may be closed. *Ntemwa Camp*, close to the Busanga Plain, is currently closed. Campers may pitch their own tents at Chunga, New Kalala, and Lufupa camps, and at the Wildlife Conservation Society camp on Lake Itezhi-Tezhi.

A new, privately owned camp, *Puku Pan Safari Camp*, has opened near Chunga in Kafue's southern sector. Puku Pan's seven comfortable thatched chalets face the Kafue River. Guests explore the park in open four-wheel-drive vehicles, by boat, and on foot.

Busanga Trails operates a string of simple, fully catered safari camps in Kafue's northern sector. *Lufupa* is the main camp. It features boat rides and fishing on the Kafue and Lufupa rivers, as well as game viewing on both day and night drives, and expeditions to its satellite camps. *Kafwala Camp* is set in deep woods along a rocky stretch of rapids on the Kafue. *Shumba* is a bush camp on the Busanga Plain. Located on a small island among massive fig trees, it is well positioned for exploring the most game-rich portion of the park. Catering mostly to a local clientele, the level of service at Busanga Trails is not up to the highest safari standards. Game drives are done in open vehicles, but drivers and guides are not well tutored in natural history and concentrate mostly on finding the big cats. That said, the outfit deserves credit for not abandoning the park in its time of distress. Without the presence of its camps, the poachers would have free reign year-round. As it is, the park gets a little relief from June to October or November (depending on the onset of the rains), when the Busanga Trails camps are open.

Several other private camps are scattered around Kafue's northeastern edge. *Lunga Cabins* is a new 12-bed luxury camp on the Lunga River, a major tributary to the Kafue. It features motorized boat excursions and canoeing on the Lunga (including an optional overnight canoe adventure accommodated in a simple bush camp), as well as game drives and walks. The *Busanga Bush Camp* is set up seasonally to accommodate Lunga guests who want to visit the Busanga Plain. It takes about three hours to reach the little satellite camp, which consists of three thatched huts (with en suite bath and toilet) on a fig tree island. Night drives are done at Busanga Bush Camp. Lunga Cabins is open from April through December; the Busanga Bush Camp necessarily has a shorter season (June to October). Lunga operates a reliable scheduled air service that links it to Livingstone, Lusaka, Luangwa Valley, and Lower

Zambezi National Park. For ease of access and level of service, the Lunga camps are the best option for a safari to northern Kafue and, especially, to the Busanga Plain.

Hippo Camp is a new tented lodge run by an experienced Zambian guide. Offering walks, game viewing by vehicle or boat, and night drives, the camp is located on the Kafue River, near the Lunga confluence. *Leopard Lodge* is in the same area, but accommodates guests in chalets. It is open from June through January.

Chundukwa Adventure Trails sets up the six-bed *Nanzhila Tented Camp* as a base for its safaris in Kafue's southernmost wilderness. Vehicular explorations and night drives are offered, but the camp specializes in walking safaris in the company of an expert guide. The Nanzhila area harbors a good range of game that includes roan and sable antelopes as well as all the predators.

Touring the Park

Kafue is a huge park, but you are likely to see only the locality where your camp is situated. A few mobile safari outfitters are doing more extensive expeditions around the park, particularly in the southern area along the Nanzhila River. Elephant and buffalo are reputed to be seen in that region, as well as in the central area between Chunga and Ngoma camps. Those animals are less likely to be encountered in the northern half of the park, although its Busanga Plain undoubtedly offers the most prolific game viewing overall. Aside from Busanga, daytime drives will not produce great quantities of game: you should count more on the quality of sightings than quantity. Night drives are quite good for seeing the predators.

Many of Kafue's safari camps offer river cruises. The Kafue is an old river with a well-developed channel navigable by small boats even in the dry season. Its high banks are covered with dense riparian forest and thickets that overhang the water. These provide convenient perches for kingfishers, cormorants, darters, and fish eagles. The unusual Peter's finfoot is often seen swimming in the river but quickly disappears behind screening vegetation. Baby crocodiles and Nile monitors rest on horizontal branches or floating logs. Big crocs often haul out on the wooded riverbanks, as there are relatively few sandy bars or rock ledges. Kafue hippos are generally wary: little more of them will be seen than their protruding eyes and ears, unless you encounter them on land at night.

The riverine forest is excellent for birding afoot. Half-collared and giant kingfishers, wattle-eyed flycatchers, and Livingstone's louries are some of its residents. Just back from the riverbank, the vegetation includes wide-boled *Hyphaene* palms and a variety of flowering trees. These make birding around safari camps a pleasure, and they are good places to spot swallow-tailed bee-eaters and collared palm thrushes.

Victoria Falls and Livingstone

No visitor to Zambia will miss Victoria Falls. Although the lion's share of tourists flock to the bustling resort town on the more sophisticated Zimbabwe side, there is something to be said for seeing the Falls from the Zambia side. Zambia offers the same range of activities along the Zambezi — rafting, canoeing, river cruising, and fabulous views of the Falls — but as yet, the north bank of the river maintains a much more relaxed, African pace to its tourism. Game viewing options are somewhat more limited, but no one can accuse Zambia of being too touristy.

Access and Accommodation

Visitors coming from Lusaka or Luangwa Valley fly into Livingstone Airport. Zambian Express has service a couple of times a week from Johannesburg and Mfuwe, and there are now increasing numbers of air charters. Many visitors enter or leave Zambia by crossing over the Zambezi Bridge from Victoria Falls, Zimbabwe. Zambian visas are required but can be obtained at the border post (upon payment of fees in US cash). One-day visas are US$10. Longer-term visas are US$20. Multiple-entry visas can be obtained in Livingstone for an additional US$5. (Visa prices are subject to change.)

Zambia has a good variety of accommodation available around the Falls and along the upper Zambezi. The *Musi-o-Tunya* is an Intercontinental hotel located a stone's throw from the Falls. It is modern comfortable rather than elegant (it has a nice swimming pool), but is pleasant and brilliantly situated for walks to the various viewpoints above the cascades. The *Rainbow Lodge* is a run-down but passable government rest camp with a range of chalets. Less than a mile upriver from the Falls, it has fine views of the eternal pillar of mist.

Wasawange Lodge is a new luxury lodge close to Livingstone and the airport. Its six ethnic-style chalets feature color TV and air-conditioning, and the lodge has a sauna and jacuzzi in addition to a pool; it is very comfortable but does not have a bush atmosphere.

The *Victoria Falls Holiday Village* is a campsite located near the confluence of the Maramba River and the Zambezi, about 2 miles above the Falls. It offers hot showers, barbecues, and a snack bar.

Thorntree Tented Safari Camp has a very hospitable ambiance and a great location overlooking the Zambezi. With Mosi-oa-Tunya National Park next door and Zimbabwe's Zambezi National Park across the river,

Thorntree has excellent game viewing, yet it has quick access to the myriad activities around Livingstone and the Falls. The camp is comfortable and offers good value. Its owner is a professional guide who conducts luxury mobile safaris.

The most elegant place to stay on the Zambian side of the Victoria Falls is *Tongabezi Lodge* (for more information, see the Victoria Falls section of the Zimbabwe chapter). This lovely safari camp is 15 miles above the Falls, but guests are taken to the Falls for viewings and catered lunches on Livingstone Island, from which the explorer got his first close-up view of the cascade. Tongabezi opens a seasonal camp on the island and does a variety of canoe safaris and launch cruises on the river. Another luxury camp, the colonial-style *Amanzi*, has opened up near Tongabezi Lodge. With 10 chalets, this camp has such amenities as croquet and a tennis court in addition to offering all the local safari activities. *Chundukwa Camp* is 10 minutes up-river from Tongabezi. This small reed-and-thatch safari camp runs canoe and horseback excursions along the Zambezi, as well as safaris to Kafue National Park. The nearby *Kubu Cabins* is a relaxing and comfortable bush camp with chalet accommodation. All these safari camps are on the riverfront facing Zimbabwe's Zambezi National Park, where elephants and other animals can be seen when they come to water.

The *Zambezi Royal Chundu Lodge* is also on the broad upper river, but it is a long way (34 miles) from the Falls; this fishing and safari camp is only 6 miles from Botswana's Kazungula border post. *Taita Falcon Lodge* is poised above the spectacular gorges below the Falls, and is named for the rare bird that nests on the cliffs. It takes about 45 minutes on rough roads to get to this new lodge, which has a pool and is located on tribal land. Rugged trails offer the opportunity for treks into the gorges.

Touring the Falls and Livingstone

The Falls are within Mosi-oa-Tunya National Park (which has an entry fee of US$3). Paths lead around the edge of the abyss to viewpoints above the Eastern Cataracts, the Boiling Pot, and the various gorges. The walk over the footbridge to the Knife's Edge is particularly rewarding. There is considerably less wildlife right around the Falls area than there is on the Zimbabwe side. On the other hand, the Falls are accessible at night. The view of the lunar rainbow over the Eastern Cataracts is quite spectacular on full-moon nights.

Scenic cruises on the Zambezi operate several times daily on the *Makumbi* riverboat, and there are other "booze cruise" boats as well. Several safari lodges offer canoe excursions on the upper river. Makora

Quest is the leading Zambian canoe operator. It runs multiday white-water canoe expeditions aboard covered-deck kayaks. Raft Quest, Sobek Expeditions Zambia, and Safari Par Excellence operate exciting whitewater rafting in the gorges below the Falls. These Zambian companies have the jump on their Zimbabwean rivals because of their ability to start their trips at the Boiling Pot, right at the foot of the Falls. (For a full description of rafting and canoeing in the area, see the Victoria Falls section of the Zimbabwe chapter.) Batoka Sky's adventurous flight-seeing excursions aboard microlight aircraft are a Zambian exclusive. Batoka Sky has its own airstrip just outside Livingstone.

Although not large, Livingstone is a real African town, not a resort, so explorations there give you an opportunity to encounter genuine African culture. Its ramshackle atmosphere belies its former glory as a colonial administrative center. The original European settlement was at the Old Drift — a ford on the Zambezi a few miles upriver from the Falls. The colonists, plagued by malaria, were forced to move inland to found Livingstone, which became the capital of Northern Rhodesia. Like the town it's in, the Livingstone National Museum has lost its colonial polish and could use a coat of paint. It does house excellent historical, archaeological, and ethnological collections, including an exhibit of David Livingstone artifacts. The Steam Railway Museum is also interesting, although in bad shape: the old locomotives and rolling stock are rusting away.

Elephants and hippos can be found all along the Zambian side of the Zambezi, although they generally lie low until nightfall. Game is pretty abundant in Mosi-oa-Tunya Game Park, which is a pleasant place for bird and animal watching along the Zambezi. This small, fenced reserve has been stocked with white rhino (dehorned for their protection) and giraffe, and there are any number of impala, zebra, baboons, and other small animals. Elephants and hippos find their own way in, but there are no large predators. Perhaps Mosi-oa-Tunya Game Park's most interesting feature is the Old Drift Cemetery — all that remains of the original white colonists' settlement. It is sobering to read the tombstones. Most belong to men in their 20s and 30s who died of the ubiquitous "fever." It makes you realize how much more risky African travel was in the old days.

Maramba Cultural Village is located on the road between Livingstone and the Falls. It was set up to preserve Zambian arts and crafts. Dance performances there are excellent: they have a much more spontaneous feel than those in Zimbabwe largely because they are thronged by local people who obviously enjoy the shows. Dances takes place from 3:00 to 5:00 P.M. on Saturdays and Sundays, which is a good time of day for photography. Admission is about US$1. For a taste of everyday life and demonstrations of traditional skills, visits can be made to the village of Chief Mukuni, an important traditional ruler in the Livingstone region.

Sioma Falls and the Parks of the Western Province

The Victoria Falls–Livingstone area is the base for explorations to little-known destinations in westernmost Zambia. These include Sioma Falls and the nearby Sioma Ngwezi National Park, as well as the vast flood-plains of Barotseland and Liuwa Plains National Park. The dominant feature of this part of Zambia is the mighty Zambezi River.

The remote Sioma Falls are located about 175 miles upriver from Victoria Falls. Sioma Falls (also called Ngonye Falls) do not have the height or power of Victoria, but they are magnificent in their own right. They are at their best during or just after the rains, especially in June and July, when the volume of water is just right for viewing a multitude of little waterfalls and rivulets as they drop over a huge basalt ledge. A nice rustic tented camp is located near the falls: *Maziba Bay River Lodge* accommodates up to 12 guests (and has campsites available, too). Aside from excursions to Sioma Falls, the camp offers kayaking in the Class III rapids below the cascades, tiger fishing, river cruises in a Zodiac, and microlight flights. It also runs game viewing excursions into the nearby Sioma Ngwezi National Park.

Sioma Ngwezi occupies a huge tract of Kalahari woodland along the three-cornered Angola-Namibia border. Game is present, but poaching is still rife, so the animal population is both sparse and shy. Elephants do occur, and giraffes, which are otherwise rare in Zambia, are a park specialty.

One hundred miles to the north of Sioma Falls, the town of Mongu is set on a rise above the Zambezi's Barotse floodplains. The Lozi people of Barotseland maintain one of the strongest of Zambia's traditional monarchies, and the Lozi king (the *Litunga*) and his palaces are near Mongu. The annual *Kuomboka* festival takes place when the Zambezi's floodwaters inundate the plains and the *Litunga* moves his court from his dry-season palace on the flats (at the village of Lealui) to his wet-season residence on higher ground (at Limulunga). The procession of the *Litunga*'s flotilla is one of the most colorful of Zambian tribal ceremonies, but it is difficult to try to attend: the procession usually happens in March or April, but the date varies wildly, and in dry years, the *Kuomboka* does not take place at all.

The heart of the 1,430-square-mile Liuwa Plain National Park is a vast expanse of treeless grasslands that stretch to every horizon. Belts of trees and palm islands extend onto the grass sea, and the plain is surrounded by miombo woodlands. In spite of heavy poaching pressure (from locals as well as hunters from neighboring Angola), Liuwa supports good resident herds of zebra and tsessebe and provides ample sightings of lion, wild dog, and hyena. The park is the site of a mass wildebeest migration, when many thousands of blue wildebeest congregate on the plains at the beginning of the rainy season. This usually takes place in November, which is considered the best month to visit (even though the weather can be very hot). Liuwa is very much a wilderness park, and is very difficult to get to; it is unwise to go with a single vehicle. A handful of Zambian safari companies run trips there, and they usually coincide with the wildebeest migration. A tented camp, the *Royal Barotse Safari Camp*, is due to open in Liuwa. The best access will be by air charter.

Zambezi Canoe Safaris and Lower Zambezi National Park

Zambia lagged behind Zimbabwe in getting Zambezi canoe safaris started, but it is catching up fast. Zambian canoe outfitters now operate trips down the length of the Zambezi Valley, from the foot of Kariba Dam to the Mupata Gorge. By far the favorite venue, however, is the stretch of river fronting Lower Zambezi National Park.

Lower Zambezi National Park occupies 1,598 square miles of prime wilderness in the Zambezi Valley. Here the wooded hills of the Zambezi Escarpment — which reach 3,000 feet above the valley floor — come to within a few miles of the riverbank. This creates a dramatic backdrop to explorations along the Zambezi. The amount of bountiful floodplain habitat in the park is small when compared to that of the less prolific miombo woodlands of the interior hill country. Nonetheless, game viewing on the floodplain is good, especially during the dry season when animals are drawn to the river. The park is located opposite Zimbabwe's Mana Pools, and together these sanctuaries form the most game-rich section of the Zambezi.

Lower Zambezi park was closed all through the years of Zimbabwe's independence war. Later, it was badly hammered by poachers, some of whom were crossing the Zambezi to pot rhinos in Mana Pools. Rhinos were wiped out on both sides of the river, and the elephant population on the Zambian bank was very severely reduced. Poaching has slackened, but the damage will take time to repair. Elephants are wary and much less abundant than in Mana Pools — no one talks of culling on the north bank — and game is generally thinner on the ground. The variety of Lower Zambezi species, however, is quite good, with elephant, buffalo, hippo, crocodile, zebra, impala, kudu, and waterbuck the most commonly observed large animals. Lion and leopard are both abundant.

Although its elephant population is down, the Lower Zambezi environment is in good shape. Heavy poaching has saved its floodplain vegetation from excessive elephant damage. *Acacia albida* seedlings have been able to survive, something that has proved almost impossible across the river. These pod-rich winterthorns, which are so important to many species as a dry-season food resource, are found in a much greater variety of sizes and ages in Lower Zambezi park than in Mana Pools: when the big trees in Mana succumb to old age, elephants will find new groves to exploit on the Zambian bank.

Lower Zambezi National Park is becoming increasingly popular as an alternative to Mana Pools. In the last few years, several small lodges have opened in the park or its vicinity. All cater to canoe safaris, but also offer drives by day and night. All Zambian canoe outfitters are given leases to establish their own private camps, so the number of parties using the park at any one time is pretty carefully controlled. Walking in Lower Zambezi National Park is allowed in the company of armed game scouts.

Access and Accommodation

Kariba, Zimbabwe, is the most often-used gateway to canoe safaris and lodges on the Zambian shore of the lower Zambezi: Kariba has a convenient airport, while Siavonga, the Zambian town on the opposite side of Kariba Dam, is only now scheduled to build a registered airstrip. Some canoe safari groups actually cross the Kariba Dam to rendezvous for the start of their trip in Siavonga; others proceed by road from Kariba to Chirundu (about a two-hour drive), where they cross the bridge to Zambia and continue (by boat or vehicle) to a put-in on the Kafue River, near its confluence with the Zambezi. Visitors to the Zambian safari lodges on the lower Zambezi generally arrive by boat from Chirundu or fly in directly to local airstrips. Good access from Lusaka is also possible by a combination of road and boat via the town of Gwabi, on the mouth of the Kafue River.

Zambia has not developed Lake Kariba's resort potential as much as Zimbabwe. It may not be possible to do so, as Zambia did not establish any national parks on its side of the lake, and game densities there are low. Nonetheless, there are signs of life in the tour industry at Siavonga. The new 60-bed *Manchinchi Bay Lodge* is the rendezvous point for some canoe trip operators. The 80-bed *Zambezi Lodge* (the meeting place for Safari Par Excellence canoe safaris) and 60-bed *Kariba Inns* round out the hotel selection. All have pools and air-conditioning. They cater mostly to fishing enthusiasts and Zambian visitors. The Manch-inchi and Zambezi lodges have water sports facilities. Downriver, near Chirundu, *Gwabi Lodge* is a 12-bed, chalet-style hotel with a swimming pool overlooking the Kafue River. It makes a convenient overnight stop before jumping off on a canoe safari.

Safari Par Excellence and Shearwater are the principal operators of scheduled canoe safaris on the Zambian side of the lower Zambezi. Both run a variety of scheduled tours: Safari Par has one-day trips through Kariba Gorge, as well as three-day trips that run through the gorge to Chirundu, and longer four- and five-day trips that go into Lower Zam-bezi National Park. Most Shearwater canoe safaris start at Chirundu and spend the first night in a traditional Zambian village before contin-uing down to the park for another two to three nights in game country. Both companies have several bush camps within the park to accommo-date guests on their canoe safaris. They also have programs that include stays at one or another of the luxury lodges along the Zambezi, and will set up special safari itineraries by request.

The very comfortable *Royal Zambezi Lodge* is set on the banks of the great river, just above the entry of the Chongwe River that marks the boundary to Lower Zambezi National Park. The lodge accommodates 14 guests in luxury safari tents and offers fishing or launch cruises on the Zambezi, as well as game drives by day and night. Some Shearwater canoe safaris include a stay at Royal Zambezi.

Kayila Lodge is another excellent permanent camp on the edge of the Zambezi. Up to 12 guests stay in luxury safari tents or the camp's tree house. Kayila is a flagship camp for Safari Par Excellence, the canoe sa-fari operator, and the lodge features game drives or walks, fishing, boat-ing, and canoeing.

Within the park, *Chiawa Camp* is a seasonal 14-bed tented lodge with shared bath and toilet facilities. Canoeing, fishing, launch cruises, game drives, and night drives are the daily routine.

Chifungulu is an interesting tented camp operation deep inside the park. Guests fly into the remote Jekki airstrip, then transfer by a 45-minute game drive to camp. Chifungulu is run by the Tongabezi Lodge (of Victoria Falls fame), and its design combines high style with an au-thentic bush atmosphere. There are actually two camps: Sausage Tree and Potato Bush. *Sausage Tree Camp* accommodates up to 12 guests in round, marquee-style tents with reed walls and en suite toilet and bath. The effect is very light and open, and not for the timid, for there is plenty of game around. Activities include excursions by boat or canoe, as well as walks, game drives, and night drives. The smaller sister camp, *Potato*

Bush Camp, is further downstream, and a safari can include both camps, as they are easily linked by canoe.

Touring the Park

Canoeing the Zambian side of the Zambezi River gives you more of an opportunity for cultural experiences, if you want them. Once you are out of Kariba Gorge, small villages and farms occur sporadically until you enter the hunting area bordering the national park. As you travel along the river, you encounter women washing clothing and men fishing, and village visits can be arranged. The chieftainess of Chiawa encourages visitors to her village (the village is used for overnight stays by many Shearwater canoe groups). Such social calls are not choreographed tourist events and give you a chance to meet ordinary people.

Although game is more abundant in Mana Pools, canoeing in Lower Zambezi National Park has some advantages. Most of the big islands are on the Zambian side of the river, so a lot of canoeing takes place in narrow channels rather than on the main stream. The channels harbor lots of birdlife. Canoeing in the smaller channels can also result in close confrontations with large animals: there is even the possibility of short portages around feisty hippos.

For details on canoeing the lower Zambezi as well as the mechanics of canoe safaris, canoe safety issues, and a review of the attractions of the various sections of the Zambezi Valley, see the Zambezi Canoe Safaris section of the Zimbabwe chapter; for additional natural history information that is also relevant to Lower Zambezi National Park, see the Mana Pools National Park section of the Zimbabwe chapter.

Lochinvar National Park

One hundred miles before its junction with the Zambezi, the Kafue River pulses through its own wide floodplain. In the rainy season, the big river jumps its banks, converting the Kafue Flats into a shallow grassy sea. It is ideal habitat for lechwe — the semiaquatic antelope which readily takes to flooded ground. The flats are home to the Kafue lechwe, whose black leg markings distinguish it from the more widespread red variety. The lechwe, which will feed in water up to 3 feet deep, follow the rise and fall of the Kafue floods in an annual mini-migration. At one time, vast herds of these antelope inhabited the Kafue Flats. Farming encroachment and unrestricted hunting in this century greatly reduced their numbers, but an estimated 30,000 lechwe still crowd the floodplain grasslands of Lochinvar National Park.

The 160-square-mile park is also a noted bird sanctuary, with over

428 species recorded. Huge flocks of waterfowl congregate on the Chunga Lagoon, while an array of waders and herons stalk its grassy wetlands. Rarities include Baillon's crake, Denham's bustard, and the wattled crane. In addition to the birds and lechwe, wildebeest, zebra, hippo, and crocodile are Lochinvar residents. Hot springs and a prehistoric archaeological site round out the park's attractions.

A second national park, Blue Lagoon, was created to protect floodplain habitat on the north bank of the Kafue, but it was taken over as a base by the Zambian army some years ago. The park appears on maps, but no one knows how its wildlife has fared or when it will be reopened to the public.

Access and Accommodation

Lochinvar is about a three-hour drive from Lusaka (145 miles). It is accessible year-round. In many ways, the park is at its best during the rainy-season floods (from December through May), when the lechwe are forced onto the upper edge of the flood zone and tremendous concentrations of birds are present, including many European migrants. The lechwe mate in December and January, and there is plenty of interesting courtship activity. It's not always easy to get close to the lechwe because of soggy ground, but viewing them in big numbers is exciting. The concentration of lechwe is so great that the shuffling of their feet creates the sound of a fast flowing rapids, even though they are feeding in standing water.

Lochinvar Lodge is an attractive old Cape Dutch-style brick farmhouse, but it is state-owned and not currently up to a great standard. The Worldwide Fund for Nature (World Wildlife Fund) has a campsite just outside the park gate. Both the Lochinvar Lodge and the camp are used primarily by Zambians. Tourist-class accommodation is available from May to November at Lechwe Lodge (described in the Lusaka section of Safari Facts in this chapter), about two hours away.

Lake Tanganyika and Sumbu National Park

Sumbu National Park is located along the shores of Lake Tanganyika. Most of its 789-square-mile area comprises inaccessible miombo woodlands, so game viewing takes place primarily along the lakeshore. Elephant, hippo, buffalo, puku, and even lion are resident animals, as are hartebeest and both yellow-backed and blue duikers. Because it is remote and its game species can be seen more easily elsewhere, Sumbu is mostly of interest to sports fishing enthusiasts and Zambian residents seeking a getaway vacation at the beach.

Lake Tanganyika is the longest and deepest of Africa's Rift Valley lakes. It reaches a nadir of 4,710 feet. Although those profound depths are almost sterile, its crystal-clear upper waters teem with fish. Among them are monster Nile perch that can weigh over 100 pounds, as well as toothy Goliath tiger fish and giant vundu catfish. These are the trophies that draw Zambian fishermen. Also present are myriad varieties of cichlids. These small and colorful species, the delight of freshwater aquarium hobbyists, can be viewed by divers and snorkelers. Other interesting lake inhabitants include endemic water cobras, which are poisonous but not notably aggressive, and hippos and crocodiles.

The lake and Sumbu are located in the remote northernmost corner of Zambia. They can be reached by road, but Sumbu is so far off the normal tour routes that overseas visitors who are not on a self-drive, transcontinental trip will have no access except by air. Domestic airlines serve Kasaba Bay a couple of times a week, and charter flights can be arranged. *Kasaba Bay Lodge* and *Nkamba Bay Lodge* are both located inside the national park and are therefore better for game activities, while the newer *Ndole Bay Lodge* is situated just over the park boundary. All offer fishing, swimming, and beach activities (Ndole Bay has water skiing), in addition to game drives and guided walks to blinds hidden at waterholes. Nkamba also runs night boat rides to spotlight crocodiles, which are common on Nkamba Bay. The new *Tanganyika Lodge* offers guided diving and snorkeling excursions.

Nyika National Park

At over 7,000 feet in altitude, the high country of the Nyika Plateau stands in marked contrast to any other Zambian environment. Atop the Nyika is a cool montane world of grassy bald hills, where pockets of yellowwood forest are tucked into hidden valleys. It is not big game country, although roan antelope, eland, and reedbuck range its wide grasslands and leopard are not at all uncommon. Rather, these uplands are a good place to explore on foot, savoring distant views, displays of wildflowers, and the cool mysteries of mountain forests.

The Nyika Plateau straddles the border between Zambia and Malawi. The Zambian portion is small, with only 50 square miles protected in Nyika National Park. Access is difficult because it is located some 200 miles north of South Luangwa. There is a simple, eight-bed, self-catering rest house in the park. Robin Pope Safaris schedules several expeditions a year to the Nyika. Otherwise, most overseas visitors approach the plateau from the Malawi side. (For more information, see the Nyika National Park section of the Malawi chapter.)

CHAPTER SEVEN

Malawi:
Land of the Lake

WHERE THE EASTERN ARM of Africa's Great Rift Valley cuts into southern Africa, it forms a deep trough filled by the waters of Lake Malawi. Some 360 miles long and 50 miles wide, the lake is synonymous with the slender little country that fronts its western shore.

For a nation of its size, Malawi possesses a diverse geography. Steep escarpments divide the gently undulating 4,000-foot-high central African plateau from the trough of the Great Rift Valley. Brachystegia woodlands (miombo) are the natural vegetation of the plateau, but most of it has been cleared for the cultivation of maize and tobacco. In contrast, the Rift Valley (where Lake Malawi's surface is 1,555 feet above sea level) is more tropical; it is the place of baobab and mango trees, of sugar and cotton farms, and of thatch-roofed fishing villages strung out along the shores of the inland sea. In Malawi's north, a narrow band of plains hugs the edge of the lake, and immense escarpments rise close to its shore. These climb directly into the bracing highlands of the Nyika and Viphya plateaus, which respectively reach over 8,000 and 6,500 feet. In the south, the lakeshore plains are wider, and they merge into the valley of the Shire River, which spills out of the bottom end of the lake. Floodplains and marshlands border the course of the Shire as it flows southward toward the Zambezi. The Shire Valley, which eventually drops as low as 121 feet above sea level, has a hot and humid cli-

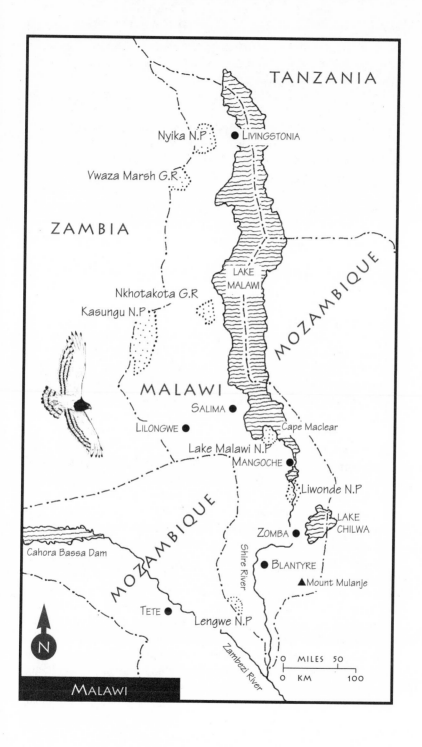

TANZANIA

Nyika N.P ● LIVINGSTONIA

Vwaza Marsh G.R

ZAMBIA

LAKE
MALAWI

MOZAMBIQUE

Nkhotakota G.R
Kasungu N.P

MALAWI

SALIMA ●

LILONGWE ●

Cape Maclear

Lake Malawi N.P
MANGOCHE ●

Liwonde N.P

LAKE
CHILWA

ZOMBA ●

Cahora Bassa Dam

MOZAMBIQUE

● BLANTYRE

▲Mount Mulanje

Shire River

TETE ●

Lengwe N.P

MILES 50

KM 100

Zambezi River

N

MALAWI

mate. Southern Malawi also has its mountains: the Shire Highlands reach almost 7,000 feet atop the Zomba Plateau, and Mount Mulanje, at 9,849 feet, is the highest range in the country.

With its gigantic lake, dramatic escarpments, and imposing mountains, Malawi certainly does not lack for scenery. But with nearly 10 million inhabitants, the Indiana-sized country is densely populated. As a consequence, most of its wildlife has vanished and its parks are small by African standards. Although Malawi tries to market the friendliness of its people as a major tourist attraction (its publicists style it "the warm heart of Africa"), neither its culture nor its scenery succeeds in drawing large numbers of overseas visitors.

Malawi has played second fiddle as a travel destination ever since the days of David Livingstone. The great explorer first visited as a diversion from his failed attempt to take a steamboat up the Zambezi River. Blocked by the rapids of the Cahora Bassa Gorge, Livingstone instead followed the tributary Shire River to its source and in 1859 discovered what he called "Lake Nyasa." His descriptions of the slave trade that flourished there inspired other Scottish missionaries to set off for the lake. In 1875, they launched the steamboat *Ilala* and founded the first of several "Livingstonia" mission stations. By 1891, Nyasaland was formally declared a British protectorate. Always somewhat of a poor sister to the neighboring Rhodesian colonies (to which it was briefly federated), Nyasaland became the independent nation of Malawi in 1964, led by Dr. Hastings Kamuzu Banda.

Banda proved an able but autocratic ruler: he liked his job so much that he assumed the office of "Life President." His policy of cooperation with South Africa earned the disapproval of fellow black African presidents, yet Malawi's economy (which was based on the export of tobacco, cotton, and tea, as well as the remissions of Malawians working in South Africa) remained afloat, even if its people stayed poor. Banda maintained stability by tolerating no opposition. As the Life President aged into his nineties, however, the corruption of his regime became increasingly evident: ignoring the abuses of the clique around him, Banda could well have been described as "the cold heart of Africa." In 1994, he was turned out of office and replaced with a multiparty government.

Malawi has traditionally attracted South Africans to its lakeside resorts; until the end of the apartheid regime, it was one of the few African countries that welcomed South African passport holders. The lake has also long been a popular hangout for the low-budget backpacker and overland-traveler set. Visitors enjoy relaxing at its unpretentious resorts and meeting local villagers, who are almost unfailingly polite, friendly, and poor. Everyone agrees that the lake is a great place to take a vacation from the rigors of bush travel. But as a safari destination, Malawi is simply overshadowed by its competitors in East and southern Africa.

Paradoxically, Malawi has a lot to offer nature-oriented travelers, for it has some lovely, uncrowded parks with highly unusual environments. None is more unusual than Lake Malawi National Park, which was created expressly to protect its exceptionally diverse collection of freshwater fish. Nyika National Park and Mulanje Forest Reserve are outstanding enclaves of Afro-montane habitat, each with its own character and singular communities of fauna and flora. Kasungu National Park is an excellent place to see the wildlife and vegetation typical of miombo woodlands, while Liwonde National Park offers fine game viewing (notably of elephants and sable antelopes, as well as hippos and crocs) in a beautiful setting along the banks of the Shire River. The tropical thickets of Lengwe National Park harbor such rare species as nyala and suni antelope. In addition to the major national parks, a number of other game and forest reserves are scattered around the country. Although big game may not be superabundant in Malawi's parks, it is well represented: all the large mammals (with the exception of the giraffe) are present, as is a wide variety of antelopes and small animals. With over 600 species of birds recorded, Malawi's avifauna is particularly interesting. Birders can pick up a lot of odd species, especially during the rainy season (from December to April), when the country is popular with birding safari groups. Malawi also draws other types of outdoors enthusiasts. Its high mountains are especially attractive to walkers and trekkers, while the lake is a treat for kayakers, divers, and sailors.

Malawi is not a glamorous country, yet that is part of its charm. It is likely to remain an offbeat destination. But those who venture to its wild places will certainly discover much to suit their interests.

Safari Facts

ENTRY: No visas are required for US citizens. A yellow fever vaccination may be necessary if you are coming from an infected area.

CURRENCY: The currency is the Malawi kwacha (1997 rate: MWK15 = US$1). Traveler's checks and hard currencies can be exchanged at banks or authorized hotels. Credit cards are accepted by major vendors.

LANGUAGE: The official languages are English and Chichewa.

AIR TRAVEL: Malawi's Lilongwe International Airport (near the capital, Lilongwe) is served by KLM from Europe and by South African

Airways from Johannesburg. Air Malawi flies internationally to Johannesburg and other regional capitals: it also serves Mfuwe, Zambia, the gateway to the Luangwa Valley, making a safari there an attractive combination with a visit to Malawi. Domestically, Air Malawi flies daily to Blantyre and has scheduled flights once a week to Club Makokola (on the southern shore of Lake Malawi). Sefofane Air Charters (booked through Central African Wilderness Safaris) flies a six-seater plane on scheduled routes to the lake and to the Luangwa Valley.

LAND TRANSPORTATION: Some of Malawi's main roads are paved and well maintained, but elsewhere road conditions are often very poor. Coachline runs a comfortable four-hour bus service twice daily between the cities of Lilongwe and Blantyre; elsewhere, buses are slow and stop often. Avis is the largest car rental agency; it has offices at the international airport, as well as all the major towns and tourist resorts. Other reputable rental companies include Central Rent-A-Car and Car Hire Limited.

PARK RESERVATIONS: Bookings for public rest camps or campsites in national parks and game reserves should be made with the Booking Officer, The Department of National Parks and Wildlife, P.O. Box 30131, Lilongwe 3, Malawi. Tel: (265) 723505. For hut accommodation on Mulanje, contact Chief Forest Officer, P.O. Box 50, Mulanje, Malawi. For Mvuu Camp or Mvuu Lodge, contact Central African Wilderness Safaris. Tel: (265) 781393. Fax: (265) 781397.

DRESS CODE: Under the Banda regime, long-haired men were refused entry to Malawi and women who wore pants or revealing attire (outside of beach resorts) were liable to arrest. This notorious dress code has been scrapped by the new government.

TOURS: The vast majority of visitors confine their explorations to the southern part of the country, where they spend a few days at a lakeshore resort. Tours to the highlands of the Zomba Plateau and Liwonde National Park easily combine with such a lake visit; in the south, distances are not great and main roads are usually adequate. Far fewer overseas visitors venture to Malawi's north, which takes more time and effort.

As the site of the international airport, Lilongwe, Malawi's capital city, is the major gateway to the country. The government buildings are spread out among the parks and gardens of the "new town," while the "old town's" commercial district is very small. Although Lilongwe is pleasant enough for a layover, there is little to tempt a tourist to tarry longer than necessary. The Lilongwe Nature Sanctuary is a nice place to go for a bird walk in relatively wild bush (leopards and hyenas occur there); the more distant Dzalanyama Forest Reserve is a good day trip for keen birders anxious to see species of the miombo woodlands. The large and modern *Capital Hotel* is Lilongwe's best; it is located outside of town in an area with plenty of park land. The older but quite adequate *Lilongwe Hotel* is in the town's commercial center.

Lake Malawi

Lake Malawi is a beautiful and intriguing body of water. The southernmost of Africa's great lakes, it fills one of the deepest clefts of the Rift Valley and is surrounded by escarpment mountains. The scarps are most spectacular in the north, where they plunge directly into the lake and drop to its bottom, which, at a depth of 2,310 feet, is some 755 feet below sea level. Nothing lives in the cold deeps, where there is no light and little oxygen, but the lake's upper waters and shallow areas teem with life. The southern end of the lake is less than 300 feet deep and its waters are particularly rich. An abundance of plankton supports shoals of fish, which in turn provide 70 percent of the protein for Malawi's human population.

Lake Malawi is distinguished by the amazing biodiversity of its fish; it vies with nearby Lake Tanganyika for the greatest number of species found in any freshwater lake on earth. Somewhere between 600 and 1,000 species inhabit its waters (new ones are discovered all the time, so it is impossible to come up with an exact number). Of these, more than 350 are endemic species belonging to a fascinating family known as the cichlids. Cichlids are small, often brilliantly colored fish that have the unusual habit of mouth-brooding. Although the males often build elaborate nests to attract a mate, once the eggs are laid, the female collects them in her mouth. She keeps them in her mouth until they hatch, after which the tiny fry will retreat to its safety whenever danger threatens. Some types of cichlids prefer sandy habitats, others favor rocks.

In Lake Malawi, the rock-dwelling fish, locally known as *mbuna*, are particularly colorful and diverse. Every isolated island or cluster of underwater boulders has evolved its own resident species, and every possible niche has been exploited. Like Darwin's finches in the Galapagos, each of which has a distinctive bill, the *mbuna* have developed different mouthparts to accommodate their eating habits. Most graze on the carpets of algae that cover the underwater rock gardens, others feed on small animals, and a few survive by nibbling on the fins or scales of bigger fish. *Mbuna* are much studied by scientists and are prized by collectors worldwide as aquarium specimens.

Mbuna are great fun for snorkelers and divers to watch, but they are no good to eat. Other species in the lake are key sources of sustenance for Malawi's large human population. Lake Malawi's offshore waters are patrolled by huge schools of edible fish. These are netted by local fishermen working from small boats or traditional dugout canoes, known as *bwato*. Most fishing takes place at night, when fish are attracted to lights. Hauled ashore with the dawn, the smaller species are sun-dried on the large wooden racks visible in any fishing village. Larger fish are smoked over open fires. *Chambo* is one of the most desirable eating fish and the *kampango* catfish is a local delicacy. The *Bathyclarias* catfish, locally called *vundu*, is the largest fish in the lake; these catfish can attain weights of over 100 pounds. Other interesting species are the elephant-snout fish (a deepwater bottom-dweller), and the *mpasa*, or lake salmon, which swims upstream to spawn in the rivers that drop from the Rift Valley escarpments.

Because of its vital importance as a food source, maintaining Lake Malawi's fish population is crucial to human welfare. Overfishing is already a concern, but schemes to introduce nonnative species (like the Lake Tanganyika sardine) could well pose a greater threat. Although such plans are well intentioned (they are meant to boost the production of the fishery), their long-term effects on the ecosystem are unknown and unknowable.

Lake Malawi is home to other creatures besides fish. Hippos and crocodiles are the largest animals, although fish-eating birds such as kingfishers, pelicans, darters, gulls, and terns are much more conspicuous. Hammerkops and fish eagles are common around the shores of the lake, while large colonies of white-breasted cormorants are found on several offshore islands. One local animal oddity (not mentioned in tour brochures) is the lake fly, which exists in vast numbers and forms an important part of the food chain that leads directly to the human dinner table. Although local villagers actually collect and eat lake flies, these tiny insects are far more significant as fish food: their larvae live in the water and are consumed by shoaling fish. When the weather is calm, the adult flies emerge in a nuptial flight, and dark clouds of them can be seen swarming over the lake. They are quite harmless. The same cannot be said of the bilharzia-causing organism that can be found in vegetated shoreline areas: although the waters around beach resorts and the Cape Maclear Peninsula are often claimed to be bilharzia-free, a few cases of the disease have been documented among tourists. In general, however, the risks of contracting bilharzia, or of fatal encounters with hippos or crocodiles, are low in the places in Lake Malawi frequented by tourists.

The lake's southern region is the most often visited. Easily accessible by road from either Lilongwe or Blantyre, this is where Lake Malawi National Park and the principal beach resorts are located. The park is at Cape Maclear; the resorts are spread out along the western lakeshore from Livingstonia Beach (near Salima) to the town of Mangoche, at the south end of the lake. The beach resorts are divided into two types: tourist-class hotels (most are comfortable rather than truly luxurious) and guest houses or campsites that cater to the overlander and back-packer crowd. The beach hotels all have water-sports equipment and offer boating excursions and tours to nearby places of interest. Both tourist-class and budget establishments have fairly laid-back atmospheres: the main activities are swimming, water sports, and sun worshipping, although visits to fishing villages and bargaining with local people for hand-crafted curios are part of the daily routine.

Two important beach hotels are located between Cape Maclear and Mangoche. *Club Makokola* is the largest and most popular beach hotel. Its pleasant lakeside cottages front a manicured sand beach speckled with shady umbrellas; it also has a wing that is set back from the water. Rooms have air-conditioning or fans. It has full water-sports facilities (including a dive shop), as well as a pool and tennis courts. Club Mak, as it is called, is the headquarters for Rift Lake Charters, which runs multiday sailing and camping safaris to the national park at Cape Maclear aboard 26-foot catamarans. Smaller sailboats can be rented for day use: the lake sailing is excellent, but due care must be paid to the onslaught of strong winds that can kick up 5-foot waves. *Nkopola Lodge* is a beach-side hotel very similar to Club Mak and located close by. The *Sunbird*, a large boat that can accommodate 16 to 25 people, takes guests from either of the two hotels on sunset cruises to nearby Boadzulu Island; it is also used for snorkeling and diving trips to Cape Maclear. Club Mak and Nkopola Lodge are both about 215 miles (about a five and a half hour drive) from Lilongwe. From these hotels, it takes little more than an hour to drive up to Lake Malawi National Park. Club Mak has its own airstrip.

The *Livingstonia Beach Hotel* is the classiest of the beach resorts. It is located near the town of Salima and is only about a two-hour drive from Lilongwe. All its rooms are pleasant, but the best are spacious, white-washed rondavels set away from the main lodge. The hotel has a pretty setting on a secluded lagoon with a half-mile of private beach and offers a full range of water sports (except diving). Although it is too far (about a four-hour drive) for day trips to Lake Malawi National Park, the hotel runs boats out to a nearby island where there is good snorkeling. Hippo pools are also in the vicinity, as is an interesting tropical fish farm where *mbuna* are collected and bred for export. The hotel also runs a well-organized campsite (called *The Steps*), which is located within walking distance of the lodge. *The Wheelhouse*, another campsite in the Livingstonia Beach area, is popular with overland truck expeditioners.

Clear waters and rocky coves make Lake Malawi National Park the best place to observe fish and study the underwater ecology of the lake. The park occupies most of the scenic Cape Maclear Peninsula, which juts out into the lake's rich southern waters. Here, steep, tree-covered hills tumble down to beautiful, boulder-strewn bays and sandy beaches. The 34-square-mile Lake Malawi National Park covers the tip of the peninsula and includes a dozen offshore islands. The park was created primarily to protect the many species of *mbuna* found offshore, as well as the spawning grounds of several important, food-producing types of fish. Toward that end, the park boundary extends about 300 feet out from shore and surrounds the various islands. Unlike most national parks, several fishing villages still exist as enclaves within its boundaries. The Lake Malawi Education Center is the park's visitor center, housing two large aquariums stocked with fish native to the lake. It is a vital source of conservation information for local villagers and is very popular with visitors. The Education Center is located at the park's rest camp (the Golden Sands Holiday Camp), which is built on the site of the original Livingstonia Mission: a couple of graves are all that remain of that historic settlement.

Most park visitors want to get underwater for fish-watching. Many species of colorful *mbuna* can easily be observed at Otter Point, the prime mainland snorkeling area. True to its name, the spotted-necked otter can sometimes be found here; the larger Cape clawless otter also occurs, but is rarely seen. The various islands also have excellent diving and snorkeling sites accessible by boat. Mumbo and Boadzulu islands host significant breeding colonies of white-breasted cormorants.

Lake Malawi National Park is reached by 12 miles of narrow track that cuts off from the main lakeshore road (near the little port of Monkey Bay) and winds through the wooded hills of the Cape Maclear Peninsula. Baboons, klipspringers, hyrax, and other small animals may be seen in the woodlands; larger species such as zebra and kudu live there, too, but are very shy. The road ends at the *Golden Sands Holiday Camp*, which shares a wide, sheltered bay and a long stretch of sandy beach with the fishing village of Chembe. Golden Sands is pretty run down: it offers basic self-catering cabins and a campsite. It does have a prime location at the end of the beach, quite near the rocky headlands of Otter Point, and there are always rumors that it will one day be replaced with a tourist-class lodge. For now, the best choice for accommodation in the area is *Chembe Lodge*, a fully catered tented camp designed to ap-

A scenic bay at Cape Maclear, Lake Malawi National Park, Malawi. Photo: Allen Bechky.

peal to the adventurous budget traveler. It has equipment for many different water sports, including an on-site dive school. It also runs a three-
day sailing safari featuring snorkeling and diving, with nights spent
camping on nearby Domwe Island. The celebrated *Mr. Stephen's Rest-
house* is also located on the beach at Chembe. This long-time favorite
backpacker's resort has simple rooms and a basic menu, as well as an
easygoing traveler's ambiance. Mr. Stephen's pick-up truck provides
transport to the main road at the port of Monkey Bay.

   Another option is to explore Cape Maclear (or more remote parts of
Lake Malawi) aboard sea kayaks: Kayak Africa runs six-day expeditions
from a base at Monkey Bay, from which one paddles to thatched camps
on Mumbo and Domwe islands for snorkeling, diving, and fishing.

   Monkey Bay is the home port for the *Ilala II*, a large ship that ferries
people and goods to the various towns along the lakeshore. Although it
has cabins (with shared baths and toilets) and catering for first-class passengers, the *Ilala* is by no means a luxury cruiser; it provides an unusual
and no doubt memorable way to experience the lake and get up to its remote northern reaches. The *Ilala* first crosses over to Makanjila on the
southeastern shore, then stops at Chipoka and Nkhotakota (major ports
of call on the west side of the lake) before looping over to Likoma Island, which is actually an enclave very close to the Mozambique shore.

An unusual feature at Likoma is an English-style cathedral. Finally, the *Ilala* gets up to Nkhata Bay, which was the northernmost point reached by Livingstone on his explorations of the lake. The most spectacular scenery lies beyond, where the *Ilala* glides beneath great escarpments on the way to Chilumba, before turning southward again. A return trip to Monkey Bay takes a full six days, but it's possible to disembark at Nkhata Bay and come back overland (arrangements can be made to have a rental car sent up to meet you there). First-class cabins on the *Ilala* must be prebooked; conditions of travel in second or third class are too rough for most Western travelers.

Road travel is possible along most of Lake Malawi's western shore. The lakeshore road passes through Nkhotakota, which was once an Arab slaving center. As in many of the villages along the southern part of the lake, the call to prayer is often heard issuing from village mosques, for a good portion of the population is Muslim. Another Arab legacy is the presence of sailing boats called dhows, which are most often seen crossing the lake between the Salima area and Makanjila. The *Chintheche Inn* is a beachfront hotel 30 miles south of Nkhata Bay. It is popular with Malawi's expatriate community and makes a good overnight stop if you are traveling the northern lakeshore. The ruins of the second Livingstonia settlement are located nearby at Bandawe.

The lake's north end is renowned for its scenery, especially the portion around the present Livingstonia Mission. That famous Christian community is perched atop an escarpment located between the lakeshore and the heights of the Nyika Plateau. The area offers splendid vistas across the lake to the remote Livingstone Mountains in Tanzania (although views are obscured by atmospheric dust and smoke in September and October, the late dry season). Unlike the two failed Livingstonia missions, this one succeeded because of its healthy, malaria-free site. The community, founded in 1894, is still going strong. Livingstonia is reached from the lakeshore by mounting the 20 hairpin turns of the infamous Gorode Road. At the settlement, there is a stone church (with a stained glass window that shows Livingstone preaching at the lakeshore) and a little museum devoted to the history of the Scots missionaries and their Presbyterian community. Rest-house accommodation is available in the *Old Stone House*, where the museum is located.

Liwonde National Park

Situated alongside the wide Shire River, Liwonde National Park offers fine wildlife viewing in a lovely tropical setting. Its proximity to the southern lakeshore and the Zomba Plateau makes it Malawi's most popular game park.

The Shire River, along with the shallow waters of Lake Malombe from which it flows, forms Liwonde's western boundary, while the walls of the Rift Valley press close to its eastern side. The combination of aquatic and bushland environments gives the 226-square-mile park an excellent variety of vegetation, scenery, and animals. Along its 25 miles of riverfront and lakeshore floodplain are marshes, grasslands, palm savannas, and luxuriant riverine forests that create a year-round paradise for water-loving birds and animals. Hippos, crocodiles, and aquatic birds are always to be found at river and lakeside, while waterbuck and reedbuck are permanent residents of the floodplain grasslands, and bushbuck browse its riparian forests. Impala, kudu, and yellow baboon are all common residents. Further back from the water's edge, mopane woodlands and other types of dry deciduous forest dominate the park's lower elevations, and miombo takes over on its hills. The woodlands are the realm of elephant and sable antelope. All the animals crowd down toward the lakeshore or riverside during the dry winter season, when big game viewing is at its peak. Lions inhabit the park (in fact, Liwonde used to have a reputation as man-eater country), although they are more often heard than seen. Liwonde's bird list tops 400 species; specialties include Lilian's lovebird, collared palm-thrush, Boehm's bee-eater, Livingstone's flycatcher, and Angola pitta. More rarities (like the bar-tailed trogon) occur in the evergreen forests of the neighboring Mangochi Forest Reserve, atop the hills of the eastern escarpment. This reserve is also a rainy-season retreat for some of Liwonde's elephants.

For many years, Liwonde's wildlife populations were dropping as a result of encroachment by growing numbers of humans. In the last decade, the trend has been reversed by a South African–backed effort to strengthen the park and improve its relations with neighboring villagers. An electric fence is going up around the park to keep the villagers out and the animals in, and various projects are providing outlying communities with services such as health clinics and alternative sources of firewood. The results have been positive all around, with local people getting more economic benefits and the animals receiving better protection. Crop raiding by elephants and attacks by lions have been reduced in frequency, and poaching has been controlled to the point where a pair of black rhinos have been reintroduced (albeit to a well-defended, fenced sanctuary within the park).

The Shire River provides the opportunity for relaxed game viewing from boats, so cruises along the river are very popular with visitors. Liwonde's system of game tracks covers a good range of habitats. One route runs from the main entrance (at the park's south end, near the village of Liwonde) upriver to Mvuu, which is the park rest camp. Side tracks cut off to go around Chiunguni Hill (near the south entrance), which displays a fine example of tall miombo forest and offers great views of the Shire Valley. In the north, several tracks wind into the woodlands of the eastern hills. Many tracks in Liwonde are really usable only in the drier months, when visitors concentrate their efforts on the game-thronged riverine and floodplain areas. During the rains, some tracks are impassable and Mvuu may then be reachable only by boat. Park rangers can be hired to escort bush walks in Liwonde.

Mvuu Camp is an experiment in public-private cooperation: the old government camp has been replaced with a new rest camp built and run by a private company. Mvuu's tree-shaded, 24-bed main camp fronts the Shire River and offers accommodation in either tents (with shared facilities) or chalets; a restaurant and bar cater to those who do not wish to cook their own meals. There is also a campsite. A separate camp, the luxurious *Mvuu Lodge*, is situated at a secluded spot overlooking a lovely, forest-fringed lagoon. It accommodates a maximum of eight guests. Activities at Mvuu include escorted game drives, walks, and river cruises aboard a small motorized boat ideal for birding and game observation (all are free for guests at Mvuu Lodge; main camp residents must pay separately for each activity desired).

Kudya Discovery Lodge is set on the west bank of the Shire River, opposite Chiunguni Hill and the southern entrance to the park. This 30-bed hotel can be used as a base for game drives; the hotel also operates three-hour game viewing cruises aboard the *Shire Princess*.

The Shire Highlands, Zomba Plateau, and Mount Mulanje

The Shire Highlands rise to form the eastern wall of the Shire Valley. In contrast to the tropical heat of the river country, these verdant hills have a cool climate. Attracted by the pleasant and healthy environment, the British founded their colonial capital at Zomba, beneath a plateau on the north end of the highlands chain. They established the trading center of Blantyre near its southern terminus. After independence, Malawi's government offices abandoned Zomba for Lilongwe, but Blantyre remains the country's largest city and its commercial hub. Although not itself a tourist attraction, Blantyre's location makes it the gateway to the beautiful tea-growing districts of the southern highlands as well as Mount Mulanje and Lengwe National Park. The prime accommodation in Blantyre is the *Mount Soche Hotel*, which is named for the highest of the three mountains that surround the city. Mount Soche reaches 5,289 feet, while the more accessible Michiru Mountain (4,833 feet) is a nature conservation area with well-marked hiking trails.

With its many old colonial buildings (which now house the University of Malawi), the little town of Zomba has much more charm than Blantyre. Located 43 miles from that city and 100 miles south of Lake Malawi, the town sits at the foot of the lush Zomba Plateau. This high tableland, towering more than 3,300 feet above the surrounding countryside, reaches elevations of up to 6,841 feet. It is one of the most accessible and scenic mountain areas in the country. Separate "up" and "down" roads connect to a 15-mile gravel track (easily negotiable in the dry season) that encircles the rim of the plateau. The uplands are not a wilderness area; the plateau is largely covered with forestry plantations of pine and Mulanje cedar, although there are also tracts of montane grasslands and patches of native evergreen forest. Mountain streams are lined with tree ferns and other lush riverine vegetation, and there are several trout-filled dams and picturesque waterfalls. Mammals are rare, but the bird fauna is quite different from that of the surrounding lowlands. The Zomba Plateau is an attractive place to explore on horse or on foot, but most visitors are content to tour by car and enjoy stunning vistas from the ring road's viewpoints. When the weather is clear, there are great views in every direction, especially westward over the Shire Valley and southward toward the heights of Mulanje, 25 miles distant across the flat expanse of the Phalombe Plain. There is a campsite atop the plateau, but a stay at the *Ku Chawe Inn* is a real treat. This fine hotel, with its gracious architecture and beautiful gardens, is perched on the southern edge of the plateau and commands panoramic views of Zomba town and Mount Mulanje.

Mulanje is a fascinating mountain. The massif rises to almost 9,000 feet in splendid isolation from the plains around it. Its lower flanks are clothed in verdant tea plantations and brachystegia woodlands. The slopes rise smartly above the plains for some 3,000 to 5,000 feet, then level out on a series of plateaus. At elevations of 6,000 to 7,000 feet, these plateaus form the shoulders of the mountain. On the plateaus, rolling montane grasslands are cut by deep ravines and hidden basins that harbor roaring streams and evergreen forests. The scenery is everywhere grand: spectacular waterfalls drop off the edges of the grassy moors, and towering above them are jumbled boulder fields and massive chunks of granitic rock that form the mountain's brooding peaks. Twenty summits on Mount Mulanje reach above 8,000 feet; Sapitwa Peak tops out at 9,849 feet, the highest point in Malawi.

The grandeur of Mulanje's mountain scenery is enhanced by its for-

bidding atmosphere. The weather is moody and the mountain is frequently enveloped in blinding mists. Even in the winter "dry" season,
banks of clouds brewing up over neighboring Mozambique herald the
onset of the *chiperone*, a dense and treacherous fog that enshrouds the
highlands for days on end. Although such inclement weather is inconvenient (and even dangerous) for visitors, the dampness nurtures eerie
forests of Mulanje cedar (*Widdringtonia cupressoides*). Ancient specimens of these impressive trees (some 200 to 300 years old) reach upwards
of 130 feet in height, and their graceful branches are well draped with
beards of lichen and moss. Everyone who goes to Mulanje comments on
the primeval feel of its somber cedar forests. Although reduced in extent
by fires, by cutting (which is now discontinued except for dead trees), and
by the spread of exotic pines, the cedar groves retain a special magic.

Even aside from its cedars, Mulanje has plenty of botanical interest.
Primitive tree ferns and an endemic cycad grow in its streamside forests,
and the mountain supports many types of orchids. Its grasslands are seasonally carpeted in red-hot poker lilies and everlasting daisies, while the
proteas and heaths typical of Afro-alpine vegetation occur at higher elevations (the recent discovery of a restio suggests a link between Mulanje's montane vegetation and that of the fynbos of South Africa's
Cape). The white flowers of the woody-stemmed staghorn lily grace the
rocky crags of Mulanje's peaks. As on the Zomba Plateau, mammals are
relatively rare on Mulanje, but its upland birdlife is interesting: red-
tailed flufftails and swee waxbills inhabit the grasslands, while bar-tailed
trogons and red-faced crimsonwings live in its forests. The augur buzzard and white-necked raven are both common residents of Malawi's
mountains.

Mulanje is best reached from Blantyre via Thyolo, a delightfully green
district covered with tea estates. The lower flanks of Mulanje are also
planted with tea, and secondary roads lead around the mountain to the
various trailheads. No roads penetrate to the Mulanje highlands, however, so the only way to fully appreciate the mountain's mystique is to
walk up. Porters are available for hire at any of several trailheads; these
strongmen normally carry heavy planks, hand-cut in saw pits, down
from Mulanje's forests. Six huts run by the Department of Forestry (each
accommodating from 8 to 20 persons) provide welcome shelter to
trekkers and climbers. Mount Mulanje offers challenging rock climbing;
one route on Chambe Peak is over 5,500 vertical feet long! Climbers and
trekkers must stay alert to the weather: the *chiperone* fog is treacherous,
and hikers can easily become lost in the mists and suffer falls or hypothermia. Although the *chiperone* occurs primarily between mid-April
and the end of September, the best climbing season is considered to be

from April to July. Simple, self-catering accommodation can be found at the foot of the mountain at the *Likhabula Forestry Resthouse*, which can be used as a base camp for day hikes. It is located some 6 miles from the town of Mulanje. Campers can also stay at the nearby *Mulanje Club*.

Lengwe National Park

Located on the western side of the Shire Valley, flush against the Mozambique border, the 346-square-mile Lengwe National Park has a hot, lowland climate. The most important sector of the park is part of the Shire floodplain, where dense thickets and patches of forest provide excellent habitat for nyala antelope and other animals associated with the hot coastal plains of Mozambique and South Africa's Natal. Lengwe is on the northernmost tip of the nyala's range and the park is an excellent place to view those beautiful striped antelope. Suni antelope also inhabit Lengwe's thickets, as do such avian specialties as Venga (black-and-white) flycatcher, barred long-tailed cuckoo (or barred cuckoo), gorgeous bush shrike, and crested guinea fowl. Lengwe is only 48 miles from Blantyre. The park has a tiny self-catering rest camp. The best developed game tracks are in a small eastern portion of the park, where hides that overlook artificial waterholes facilitate dry-season game viewing (the best way to photograph the shy nyala is from a hide). Tracks through the brachystegia and mopane woodlands of Lengwe's western wilderness area yield less game but lead to some odd sandstone formations. Rangers can be hired to accompany walks: buffalo and leopard are present in Lengwe.

Nyika National Park

The remote Nyika Plateau is one of the largest and most interesting montane wildernesses in southern Africa. Great vistas are created by the craggy escarpments that drop away on all sides of this vast upland territory, where climate and terrain seem more akin to the moors of northern Europe than the bushlands of tropical Africa. The chilly atmosphere is the gift of lofty altitudes: most of the Nyika highlands average 7,000 feet above sea level and a few peaks rise above 8,500 feet. The high plateau is crowned with sensuously rolling, grass-covered hills speckled with dark patches of dense forest. Most of it is protected within Malawi's 1,224-square-mile Nyika National Park (another 50 square miles on the western edge of the Nyika Plateau belongs to the Zambian park of the same name).

In addition to its fine scenery, the Nyika Plateau has an unusual array of plants and animals. Although not a place for classic big game viewing, it is a superb locale in which to investigate the nature of Africa's mountain environment.

The lower slopes of the Nyika Plateau are covered in brachystegia woodlands; higher on the precipitous escarpment, the miombo woods are replaced by a montane scrub of proteas and heaths. Grasslands dominate on the rolling hills atop the plateau, where there are also boggy *dambos* (shallow river valleys) and scattered tracts of moist evergreen forest. Nyika's forests are one of its most unusual habitats. Thought to be the remnants of once-vaster woods, their shady confines harbor species typical of East Africa's montane timberlands: in a couple of relict "juniper forests," the tall African juniper (*Juniperus procera*) reaches the southernmost point of its range. Elsewhere in the Nyika forests, African olive trees, yellowwoods (podocarpus), and other buttress-rooted giants create a cool but junglelike atmosphere replete with hanging orchids and other epiphytic plants.

Unlike the mountain forest reserves of southern Malawi (on Mount Mulanje and the Zomba Plateau), the countryside surrounding the Nyika Plateau is not heavily populated. That, and the better protection given a national park, account for the Nyika's relative abundance of game and add to its wilderness character. The faunal community of the high plateau is unusual: eland and klipspringer are expected in such a montane area, but atop the Nyika, those animals are joined by southern reedbuck (not the mountain variety), as well as by zebra and roan antelope. The reedbuck is found year-round on the grassy uplands, while herds of zebra, roan, and eland (sometimes in groups 100-strong) roam the grasslands only during Malawi's warm rainy season (from October to April); in the cold winter months, the herds seek shelter and better grazing in the lower brachystegia woodlands. Elephant, buffalo, lion, and other bush country animals inhabit the lower regions of the park, while the moist montane forests shelter bushbuck, blue (samango) monkey, and bushpig, as well as both blue and red duikers (the gray duiker inhabits the grasslands). Leopard are common and seen fairly often atop the plateau, where they find plenty of small prey year-round in both forest and grassland. Serval cats and side-striped jackals also hunt the high grasslands. Game viewing on the plateau is at its best during the rains, when the weather is warmer and there is an abundance of nutritious grass.

Birding on the Nyika Plateau is at its best early in the rainy season (November and December), when many migrants are present. The plateau grasslands are habitat for two conspicuous large birds: the odd Denham's bustard stalks the open prairies, and the wattled crane, which is rare elsewhere, is commonly seen around the Nyika's upland *dambos*. The smaller redwing francolin is a common grasslands bird. The evergreen forests host many unusual species. These include rare forest robins (like the olive-flanked robin and white-chested alethe), as well as such fruit eaters as Livingstone's turaco (or lourie), bar-tailed trogon, and Cape parrot.

The Nyika Plateau is famous for its wildflowers. It is especially renowned for its orchids, of which there are over 120 terrestrial species. Floral displays peak in the wet season, although many grassland flowers appear again following dry-season fires, and there are always some plants to be found in bloom: everlasting daisies deck the grasslands during the dry months, when the heathers also blossom.

A network of park roads (all unpaved) facilitates game viewing, while paths lead to several places of special interest best explored on foot, such as the Juniper Forest and the Zovo Chipolo Forest. Fingira Rock is a massive outcrop that contains a Stone Age rock shelter site, and Lake Kaulime, the Nyika Plateau's only natural standing body of water, is thought to be inhabited by a snake-spirit that protects the plateau's wild animals. Chisanga Falls is the most spectacular cataract in the park, while the best vistas of Zambia and the western escarpment are seen from the Domwe Viewpoint. Jalawe Rock also offers great views: elephants can be seen below in the Chipome Valley, which separates the main plateau from the rugged and roadless mountains of the Nyika's northern side. That area, and other remote parts of the park, can be explored by trekkers on multiday camping safaris; a game scout must accompany such wilderness walks and porters can be arranged. In most areas of the park, day hikes are permitted (with or without a ranger-guide). Heart of Africa Safaris runs excellent horseback trips on the plateau. These range from morning rides to five-day expeditions staying in special camps.

Although there are no hotels on the Nyika Plateau, self-catering accommodation is available. The main rest camp is *Chelinda*, which is set between a trout-stocked dam and a pine forest (although the trees of this pine forest are not native, these woods are reputed to be a good place for leopard). A major upgrade for Chelinda is supposed to take place in the near future, but for now this small camp has only four chalets (each with two double bedrooms, a bathroom, a kitchen, and a living room with fireplace) and six double rooms in a separate building (with communal bath and kitchen). There is also a campsite. Another rustic four-person cabin is located at the Juniper Forest. Visitors can also stay at a self-catering rest house that sleeps eight on the Zambian side of the park.

Located in the far northern reaches of Malawi (some 315 miles from Lilongwe), Nyika National Park does not appear on many tour itineraries. Although an airstrip at Chelinda allows air charters, most visitors go by road. A trip to Nyika is easily combined with a visit to Livingstonia, which is situated below the plateau's eastern escarpment. Another interesting nearby area is the Vwaza Marsh Game Reserve. Although this 385-square-mile sanctuary supports a good range of large mammals (including elephant, lion, buffalo, hippo, and many types of antelope), it is most noted for its birds, especially the aquatic species that thrive in its wetlands and waterways. A self-catering tented camp is located at Lake Kazuni, a prime area for birds and hippos.

Kasungu National Park

Kasungu is an atypical national park. This 905-square-mile sanctuary is an excellent place to check out the fauna and flora of the miombo — the brachystegia woodlands that were once the dominant natural vegetation of the central African plateau. In Malawi, this type of woodland has been largely cleared or degraded by human activities. Although miombo does not support high densities of large mammals, it is good game country with a wide variety of species, including the most sought-after trophy animals. Consequently, miombo areas are more often used for hunting than for photographic safaris.

At Kasungu National Park, the brachystegia woods cover the higher ground on a slightly rolling landscape, with grass-covered *dambos* filling the shallow intervening river valleys. During the rains, bulk grazers like elephant, buffalo, and zebra are drawn to the grasslands in the park's major river valleys. When the tall grass becomes unpalatable, most of those big animals retreat to the woodlands and smaller *dambos*. After dry-season fires clear off the old herbage, many antelopes are attracted into the open valleys by a flush of new growth. The river valleys and *dambos* are therefore the best areas for game viewing year-round.

Kasungu hosts a very good selection of animals, although most are not easily seen. The park has a population of some 300 to 400 elephants; the signs of their presence are abundant, but they are rarely in view. Buffalo, zebra, and hippo, as well as antelope such as reedbuck, impala, oribi, and waterbuck, are more commonly seen. Trophy antelopes like kudu, sable, and roan are found, and the miombo-dwelling Lichtenstein's hartebeest is a park specialty. Lions are the most frequently encountered of the big predators, although leopards, cheetahs, spotted hyenas, and wild dogs all occur.

Most game viewing in Kasungu takes place in the southern part of the park, along the broad valley of the Lingadzi River and its tributary *dambos*. The remote northern section is only accessible to four-wheel-drive vehicles. Kasungu's seldom-visited western reaches, along the Zambian border, are quite pretty: rounded domes of naked granite rise above a high-canopied miombo forest of tall brachystegia and julbernardia trees. It's a nice area to explore on foot (game scouts can be hired for walks):

there are rock shelters with simple paintings (some probably of recent origin), as well as a couple of iron-smelting kilns dating to about 1930. The remains of fortified villages, mementos of 19th century tribal wars, are also found in the park.

Accommodation at Kasungu is found around Lifupa Dam, which provides dry-season refuge to the park's hippos and affords good bird-watching opportunities. *Lifupa Camp* has 10 reed chalets (with shared toilet facilities) and a campsite. Although primarily a self-catering camp, meals and game drives are provided to guests paying an inclusive rate. The rondavels of the old government-run *Lifupa Lodge* have been de-molished: they are to be replaced with a privately operated 40-bed lux-ury lodge. Kasungu is located 102 miles from Lilongwe.

The Nkhotakota Game Reserve is another interesting miombo area. Located due east of Kasungu, the reserve encompasses 700 square miles of rugged country along the Rift Valley escarpment above Lake Malawi. All the miombo species inhabit the reserve, but there are no game view-ing tracks, so its main attractions are mountain scenery, wilderness walking, and fishing: the Bua River is a major spawning stream for the lake salmon that migrate up from Lake Malawi between April and June. Campsites are located near several ranger stations; to hire game scouts to act as walking guides, arrangements should be made in advance.

CHAPTER EIGHT

Namibia:
Africa's Southwest Desert Country

LIKE ITS GEOGRAPHICAL COUNTERPART in North America, the African southwest is desert country. In fact, Namibia takes its name from the Namib, the great swathe of desert that stretches the length of its 800-mile-long Skeleton Coast. This Namib Desert is one of the driest places on earth.

With its vast empty plains, isolated mountains, and massed dune seas, the Namib forms a cordon of desolation that reaches from Africa's Atlantic beaches up to the base of the continent's 3,000-foot-high western escarpment. Elevations climb still higher, to over 5,000 feet, on the savannas of the central plateau that is Namibia's agricultural heartland. Although naked ground is largely confined to the near-rainless coastal strip of the Namib proper, the entire country has a very dry climate and its landscapes are usually painted in earth tones. Rainfall rises with altitude, but storms are everywhere freakish and seasonal, and most rainy seasons are disappointingly light. Scattered mountain ranges lend grandeur to the scenery along Namibia's western escarpment and punctuate the landscapes of the central plateau as well as those of the country's parched southern steppes. To the east, the country flattens into the vastness of the

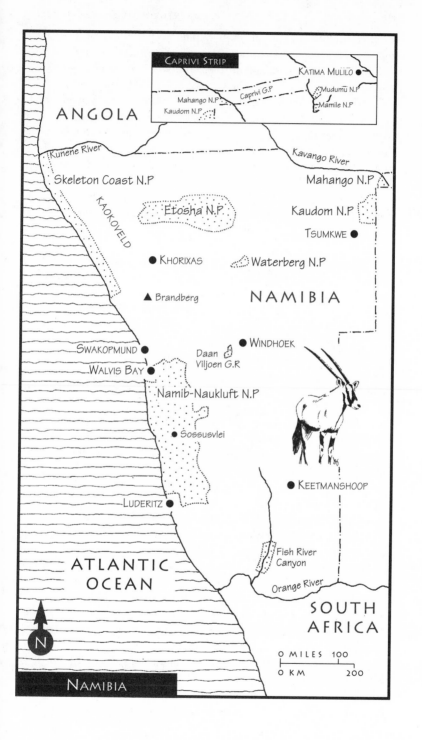

CAPRIVI STRIP

KATIMA MULILO ●

Mudumu N.P

Mahango N.P
Caprivi G.P

Kaudom N.P

Mamile N.P

ANGOLA

Kunene River

Kavango River

Skeleton Coast N.P

Mahango N.P △

KAOKOVELD

Etosha N.P

Kaudom N.P

TSUMKWE ●

● KHORIXAS

Waterberg N.P

▲ Brandberg

NAMIBIA

SWAKOPMUND ●

WINDHOEK ●

Daan
Viljoen G.R

WALVIS BAY ●

Namib-Naukluft N.P

● Sossusvlei

KEETMANSHOOP ●

LUDERITZ ●

ATLANTIC
OCEAN

Fish River
Canyon

Orange River

SOUTH
AFRICA

N

0 MILES 100

0 KM 200

NAMIBIA

Kalahari sandveld, a land of gently undulating red dunes, well vegetated with thornbush and coarse grasses but absent of surface water.

Except at its southern and northern borders, Namibia has no permanent rivers or natural lakes. The Orange River marks the southern frontier with South Africa. On the northern frontier, the Kunene River divides Namibia's wild and remote Kaokoland from Angola. Between these two rivers, no major stream flows year-round, and both the Kunene and the Orange are mere ribbonlike oases of greenery surrounded by desertscapes. Only in the northeast corner of the country, in the odd appendage known as the Caprivi Strip, is there an abundance of water, courtesy of the Okavango, Zambezi, and Kwando rivers that flow from the north. The Kwando changes its name three times during its short passage through the narrow Caprivi. It nurtures the swamps of the Linyanti and Chobe floodplains, forming aquatic habitats similar to those found in neighboring Botswana's Okavango Delta.

Namibia's ethnic mix is fascinating. Of the various culturally distinct groups of black Africans, the Ovambo (also spelled the Owambo) are by far the largest: they account for over half Namibia's total population. The Ovambo home territory is in the far north, where they traditionally lived by farming and fishing. Their land, which is so lush when its numerous *oshana* (seasonal waterways) are refreshed by life-giving rainy-season floods, is otherwise pitifully dry and overexploited. As a consequence, the Ovambo have immigrated to all parts of the country to find work. Other principal groups include the Kavango people of the northeast Okavango River country, the Herero of the central region (whose women are famous for their multilayered Victorian dresses), the Damara and Himba of the northwestern Kaokoveld, and the Nama of the arid south. Whites make up about 10 percent of Namibia's population, and can be divided into three "tribes" — the Germans, the Afrikaners, and the English — each with its own language and traditions.

Namibia's earliest human inhabitants were small bands of Khoisan hunter-gatherers. San Bushmen wandered the country's interior, while Hottentot *strandlopers* ("beach walkers") foraged on the Atlantic coast, and an unknown people left extravagant galleries of engravings and paintings on the rocks of Damaraland. Those folk were likely the ancestors of the modern Damara, who, although racially Negroid, speak a Khoisan language and are thought to have lived in Namibia for at least 3,000 years. Their tenancy long predates the arrival of the Herero pastoralists who emigrated from Angola some 300 years ago. Thereafter, the cattle-herding Herero held sway on the grasslands of northern Namibia until they clashed with the Nama, who were called "Hottentots" by the Cape Dutch. Pastoral Nama clans had long occupied Namibia's parched southern region. In the early 1800s, the Nama were joined by newcomers of mixed Dutch-Hottentot blood who brought new technologies from South Africa. With horses and guns, Nama clans bearing Afrikaner names (such as the Witboois) bore down on the hapless Herero. Stripped of their cattle, some Herero fled back to Angola where they were reduced to near-starvation and became known as *Himba* ("beggars"). The Herero of central Namibia were "saved" by the arrival of white traders, who gave them guns in exchange for cattle and land.

Although 15th century Portuguese mariners were the first Europeans to set foot on the Namibian shore, they left nothing to mark their passage save stone crosses and place names on their maps. It took almost 300 years before Europeans came to stay. The first white presence was that of American and English whalers who established small onshore outposts at Swakopmund and Walvis Bay. By the mid-1800s, a vanguard of hunter-explorers, Boer *voortrekkers*, and German missionaries were penetrating the Namibian interior. The German missions had the unintended effect of sparking colonial interest back in the home country. Although the Cape colony maintained its enclave at Walvis Bay and held title to a string of offshore guano islands, the British were reluctant to undertake the expense of administering a seemingly worthless and war-torn desert region. This gave German businessman Adolf Luderitz the opportunity to establish a trading post at Angra Pequena (now Luderitz Bay) and stake a claim to the coast as far south as the Orange River. In 1884, Luderitz persuaded the German government to declare a protectorate over his domain, which became known as South-West Africa. Shortly thereafter, the European nations signed treaties agreeing to the colonial partition of the continent. The British formally recognized German rights to the Namibian interior as well as the coast, and were even compliant in letting the Reich lay claim to a northern territory stretching all the way to the Zambezi — the finger of land that came to be known as the Caprivi Strip.

Colonization was facilitated by the pan-African rinderpest outbreak that reached South-West Africa in 1897. With their cattle dying en masse, the Herero sold much of their land to German farmers in exchange for food or vaccine for their remaining livestock. Continual warfare between the Herero and the Nama was also exploited by the Germans. Divide and conquer proved a good strategy for the Germans, and separate Herero and Nama revolts were brutally quashed in 1904. The Herero insurrection was particularly nasty: a number of European colonists were killed at its start, and the German General von Trotha subsequently waged a retaliatory war of extermination. After his well-armed forces, the *Schutztruppe*, massacred the Herero gathered at the Waterberg Plateau, the survivors fled eastward into the waterless Omaheke desert, a part of the great Kalahari thirstlands. Von Trotha gave them no quarter: German troops sealed off or poisoned the wells at the desert's edge and summarily executed any Herero who attempted to return. Several thousand refugees made it through the Kalahari to resettle in present-day Botswana, but some 60,000 Herero are thought to have perished of thirst and starvation before the German government relented on its merciless policy. A census in 1911 indicated that three-quarters of the Herero population died as a result of the war or incarceration in forced-labor camps, as did about half (some 10,000) of the Nama.

Although German rule proved short-lived, it had an enduring effect on the country's character. What is now the so-called traditional Herero dress (or at least the typical woman's costume of voluminous patchwork skirts and a boat-shaped cap) is a German legacy: German missionaries induced the Herero to abandon their traditional state of undress in favor of modest Victorian attire, and the fashion has stuck to this day. Colonial farmhouses, churches, *Schutztruppe* forts and memorials, even castles, are still found spread all over Namibia. Indeed, whole towns retain so much German atmosphere they could be in northern Europe. But the mementos of German occupation go beyond mere architecture: cafes, beer gardens, and restaurants are only the most visible manifestations of a prosperous German-speaking community that still strongly identifies with its tribal roots. In Tanzania — the former German East Africa — contemporary society shows barely a trace of Teutonic influence. In contrast, the deep German vein in Namibia, so unexpected in such a remote corner of Africa, is quite startling to visitors — unless they happen to be German: German literature of exploration is replete with stories of South-West Africa, and modern Namibia seems to attract German tourists like a magnet.

During the First World War, the German colony of South-West Africa was quickly gobbled up by South African forces in 1915. It was afterwards administered by South Africa under the mandate of the League of Nations. Although the terms of that mandate prevented outright annexation, the territory was run more or less as a province of South Africa. After the Second World War, there was considerable wrangling with the United Nations over the status of South-West Africa. To keep step with South African racial policy, apartheid was enforced and, by 1966, the various black tribes in South-West Africa were assigned territorial homelands. The United Nations then terminated South Africa's mandate, renamed the territory Namibia, and recognized the South-West African People's Organization (SWAPO) as the "representative" of the Namibian people. Years of diplomatic deadlock passed while SWAPO waged a guerrilla campaign. Aside from the odd act of terrorism, military action was largely confined to the northern border with Angola. Any solution was complicated by Cold War politics: Namibian independence became inextricably tied up with the Angolan civil war that pitted Cuban soldiers against South African troops and Soviet interests against American.

After years of complicated maneuvering, United Nations–sponsored elections led to Namibian independence in 1990. Sam Nujoma, the SWAPO candidate, won the presidency under a democratic, multiparty constitution. Although Nujoma was a Marxist firebrand during the war years, he has so far led the country on a moderate path. The Namibian government has been working harmoniously with the large South African corporations that control the economy.

Namibia's mineral resources are its economic trump card. Diamonds provide the bulk of the country's income: the marine gravels of the southern coast are among the richest sources of gemstones in the world. Elsewhere, mines extract uranium, copper, tin, and other precious metals. Karakul lamb skins are Namibia's most valuable agricultural product. Offshore fish stocks have declined over the years, but the fishing industry remains a valuable fount of foreign exchange. Although mining and fishing provide a certain number of decently paid jobs, the country is struggling to deal with unemployment and undereducation among its African population. This has necessarily left Namibia's whites in a privileged position. The preponderance of productive farms and businesses are European-owned, with Africans working mainly as low-paid laborers. The development of tourism, while not likely to put many blacks into ownership positions, is a good job spinner and is increasingly important to the economy.

Namibia has established a reputation for an advanced outlook on wildlife conservation. The nation's constitution mandates both environmental protection and the sustainable use of natural resources: wildlife and ecosystems are therefore to be cherished and preserved, but they are also to pay their way. A system of parks and nature reserves reflecting the diversity of Namibian habitats is carefully monitored by the Ministry of Environment and Tourism. The system was originally modeled along the lines of the South African national parks, and even today there are many similarities in administrative style. Both wildlife and visitors are intensively managed: game animals are culled or translocated as conservation officials deem necessary, and rules for visitors are strictly enforced. Ecotourism is being heavily promoted as an incentive for conservation on private land as well as in the national parks. Wildlife is also exploited consumptively to produce revenues from sport hunting and to harvest commercially valuable products. These activities, too, are controlled by the Ministry of Environment and Tourism.

Despite Namibia's newfound zeal for wildlife conservation, there is relatively little big game left to save. At one time, the entire country teemed with animals. Place names in the southern region — such as the Oliphants (Elephant) and Lowen (Lion) rivers — testify to the presence of Africa's megafauna at the time of European discovery, and indeed the descriptions of early explorers are filled with tales of excellent big game hunting. But the southern region's elephants and lions were long ago shot to extinction, its wild bushlands fenced and converted into cattle and sheep ranches on which predators were shot on sight (and still are today). Wildlife fared better in the remote north.

From 1907 to 1970, the entire northwestern corner of the country, from the current boundaries of Etosha National Park all the way through the Kaokoveld to the Skeleton Coast, was a protected game reserve. The Himba and Damara people who lived there did little harm to the resident wildlife population, and animals thrived in that harsh semidesert region. When South Africa's "homelands" policy was put into effect in Namibia, the Kaokoveld was cut out of what was then called Etosha Game Park (the rest of the reserve became Etosha National Park). The loss of game reserve status was disastrous for the Kaokoveld's wildlife: a combination of unrelenting drought and unrestricted hunting saw animal populations tumble throughout the 1970s and 1980s. Poaching, for both sport and profit, was carried out by whites as well as indigenous hunters: even high government officials and officers of the South African army were involved in illegal hunting. The SWAPO war took its toll: in addition to recreational hunting by South African troops, thousands of rifles were distributed among local tribesmen. Although meant to be used for defense against terrorists, the guns were instead trained on the fauna of the Kaokoveld — the territory of Namibia's celebrated "desert elephants" and "desert rhinos." The populations of both species crashed to dangerous levels, and it was not only those animals that suffered. The black-faced impala, an animal naturally endemic to the Kaokoveld, was only saved by establishing a small population within Etosha National Park. Giraffes, also once common in the north, were widely pursued by native hunters on horseback. Run to exhaustion, they were easily dispatched with firearms.

Independence seems to have reversed the downward spiral in the fortunes of Namibia's wildlife. A growing realization of the potential for income from tourism has sparked a corresponding enthusiasm for wildlife conservation in both the private and public sectors. Several new national parks have been proclaimed recently, and there has been almost a mania among private landowners to open their own game lodges or combine with neighbors to create huge private game reserves. While these areas will take some years to be restocked to their full carrying capacities, and some of them suffer from a contrived, theme-park atmosphere, the overall effect on Namibia as a game viewing destination is to the good. For although Namibia hosts a fascinating assortment of wildlife, most of its endemic specialties are small creatures peculiar to its desert habitats. While insects, lizards, snakes, rodents, and little brown birds may delight ardent naturalists, they are not the types of animals to satisfy tourists bent on the traditional big game safari; aside from kudu and a few other species of antelopes that thrive on farmlands, large mammals are neither abundant nor easily seen in Namibia.

The country's one haven for world-class big game watching is Etosha National Park. Although fenced and half its original size, Etosha is still a huge sanctuary that harbors abundant herds of antelope and zebra, as well as plenty of lion and elephant, and a number of rare and endangered species.

Namibia possesses several endemic large mammals that are particularly rare or beautiful. The most notable are its desert elephants and desert rhinos, the Hartmann's mountain zebra (a hardy inhabitant of the pro-Namib thirstlands), the unusual black-faced impala, and the tiny Damara dikdik, the smallest of southern Africa's antelopes. With the exception of the desert-dwelling Hartmann's zebra, most Namibian specialties are subspecies — that is, they are varieties of animals found elsewhere. This is true of the Damara dikdik and the black-faced impala. Namibia's desert-adapted black rhinos are also a distinct subspecies (*Diceros bicornis bicornis*). The so-called desert elephants do not fall in this category: although they have made remarkable behavioral adaptations suited to survival in their harsh environment, they are genetically identical to savanna-dwelling African elephants. But such fine distinctions do not mean that Namibia's rarest large animals should not be treasured and preserved: once annihilated, rhinos or elephants reintroduced from other places are unlikely to adapt to life in the Namib, and those species will be forever banished from their desert habitat.

Namibia's black rhino population is not huge, but its 500 animals are significant on a continent where the species hovers on the brink of extinction. Their numbers are deemed high enough that they can be moved to recolonize suitable areas: Namibian rhinos are now being translocated to parks in South Africa to replace those that once roamed widely in dry country habitats. Rhinos are fairly abundant in Etosha, which received an influx of threatened animals translocated from the Kaokoveld during the 1970s. Today, there are very few in Namibia outside Etosha, and those living in the desert number no more than a handful. Strenuous efforts are being undertaken to save the last of the Kaokoveld's hardy desert rhinos. Perhaps the most imaginative scheme was set up by conservationists Garth Owen-Smith and Margaret Jacobsohn. For over a decade, they have tried to involve local communities in the conservation of desert wildlife. They have been hiring community game guards as "auxiliaries" to the regular wildlife authorities and trying to make sure that some of the profits from ecotourism get back into the hands of local people. The project has actually been fairly successful in reducing poaching. Rhino numbers have been holding their own or even increasing slightly in recent years, while elephants are once again expanding their range in Damaraland, the southern portion of the Kaokoveld. Elephants recently appeared in the valley of the Ugab River near the Brandberg Mountain — an area where they have not been seen since the 1950s.

The desert elephants have engendered plenty of debate. When the Kaokoveld was protected within the former Etosha Game Park, the elephants of the region were free to range widely. Since the reduction in the size of the park, fencing discourages most of Etosha's elephants from moving westward. The Kaokoveld's elephants are now divided into three populations: an eastern group which sometimes moves into Etosha, the desert elephants of the Namib, and a transitional group which lives in the scrubby eastern savannas (known as the pro-Namib) between the park and the coastal Namib thirstlands. The true "desert elephants" primarily inhabit the Kaokoveld's river valleys, which run westward down to the Skeleton Coast. Most of the streams in these river valleys flow only after exceptionally heavy rains, but water is always found percolating beneath their sandy beds; here and there, it gets forced upward by rock strata to form life-giving pools. The vegetation in the river valleys is sufficient to sustain elephants, but they must sometimes undertake long treks (of up to 60 miles) to find water. On occasion, the elephants are seen moving over dunes or bare flats as they pass from one river valley to the next. When circumstances require, elephants from the transitional population may move westward to the desert or eastward into Etosha National Park. The transitional population lives in a wetter and better vegetated area, but it is still very arid (it receives only about 6 inches of rain annually). A country of sere red-rock buttes and open plains peppered with stunted bush or wisps of sun-bleached grass, the Kaokoveld easily fits most people's concept of desert — so the elephants of the eastern Kaokoveld are popularly called "desert elephants" even though, technically, they are not.

Namibia has become a major focus of concern for cheetah conservation. With an estimated 2,400 resident cats, it has the highest cheetah population of any African country, harboring about 20 percent of the continent's total. Unfortunately, very few of Namibia's cheetahs live in areas where they are afforded protection: 95 percent of them are found on commercial farmlands. Indeed, they are not thriving in Namibia's parks: Etosha, once a stronghold for cheetahs, has suffered a decline because of heavy competition from lions and hyenas. Cheetahs have done better on the private cattle farms, where the rival predators have been eliminated or severely reduced in number. Of course, Namibian farmers wage war against cheetahs, too: they are regularly trapped and shot on the farms, and it is a bit of a mystery as to how these animals — which are active during the day — have hung on as well as they have, especially in light of a behavioral pattern that has not been observed in cheetah populations elsewhere. For unknown reasons, Namibian cheetahs habitually visit certain "play trees" at which they are easily trapped. Although most ranchers are still openly hostile to the cheetah, international support for the animal may be turning them around. The Namibia-based Cheetah Conservation Fund (run by American researchers Danny Krause and Laurie Marker-Krause) is trying to teach farmers new ways to reduce livestock losses caused by cheetahs. They are promoting the use of Anatolian guard dogs and donkeys, both of which readily chase off cheetahs, as deterrents to livestock predation. They are also working in the public schools to promote cheetah awareness and affection among children — a tactic that gets the message to the farmer in his own home.

Namibian landowners legally own the wild animals that live on their properties. Farmers are delighted to have antelope such as kudu, eland, or oryx around; they can charge visiting trophy hunters high fees or shoot the animals themselves, then dry and sell the meat as *biltong* (jerky). Either way, the farmer makes money from the game animals on his land. As a result, wildlife is often tolerated or even encouraged. This does not necessarily translate into good wildlife management, however, for even on game ranches, predators are often killed on sight. No matter whether the victim was a gemsbok or a cow, a Namibian farmer gets irate when he finds a carcass he suspects was killed by a predator: it could have been money in his pocket.

Hunting has long been a source of wildlife-generated income in Namibia. The country is a favorite destination for South African hunters seeking trophy antelopes and *biltong*. Although its "big game" species are by and large too depleted for it to compete as a major international hunting venue, some hunters are attracted by the lure of exotic trophies unavailable elsewhere. A number of Namibian safari outfitters advertise hunts for cheetah and even white rhino, species that are completely protected in most African countries. Because white rhinos are not currently considered endangered (they breed well and are routinely sold to private game farms) and cheetahs are still viewed as stock-killing vermin, the opportunity to convert them into cold cash is often too tempting to pass up. Although most trophy hunting takes place on private game farms, the practice is strictly regulated by the Ministry of Environment and Tourism, which sets seasons, quotas, and closures on the various species that may be taken.

Namibia's policy of sustained use extends to its marine wildlife resources. The country has expanded its zone of territorial waters in the Atlantic to better control its fish stocks, the basis for an industry important to the export economy. The waters of the Skeleton Coast also support vast numbers of seabirds, of which Cape cormorants and gannets are especially common, and these provide a renewable wildlife product for harvest. Originally, the island nesting colonies of these fish-eating birds were mined for their guano, which is a valuable fertilizer. Later, huge platforms were placed offshore as roosting sites to attract the birds. These platforms achieve a thick white coating of bird droppings and are regularly stripped of their guano for export.

Sealing, too, is a source for foreign exchange. The Cape fur seal (*Artocephalus pusillus pusillus*) is very common along Africa's southwest coast. Its population is estimated between 800,000 and one and a half million, about two-thirds of which live in Namibia. The seals congregate in vast breeding colonies. Most are located around the port town of Luderitz on the southern Skeleton Coast. The largest colony is at Cape Cross, where the population has been estimated as high as 100,000. Culling operations have long taken place at Cape Cross, where there is a factory for processing animals taken in the seasonal kill. In past times, seal pups were harvested for their silky pelts. After animal rights protests led to a collapse of demand for sealskin coats in Europe and the Americas, the primary market shifted to the countries of the Far East, where seal penis is considered an aphrodisiac and retails for over US$1,000 a pound. With dried seal genitals fetching such amazing prices in Asia, the Namibian government has been willing to weather the usual storms of controversy associated with the commercial slaughter of marine mammals. Aside from unresolvable disputes regarding the ethics of culling, there remain hard scientific concerns about population dynamics and sustainability. Although the seal population seemed to grow throughout the 1980s, their numbers suddenly crashed in 1994 due to a decline in their food supply. Even afterwards, Namibia's commercial fishermen still contend that seals take too much of *their* resource, and continue to demand massive culls. Conservationists have rallied to the cause, and the bust in the seal population can only add fuel to the fires of contention surrounding the cull.

With only a million and a half people spread over a territory twice the size of California, Namibia might seem a pristine African wilderness, empty and untouched by humankind. Indeed, some of it is, particularly along the empty beaches of the Atlantic coast and in the adjacent droughtlands of the waterless Namib interior. There, several large and remote tracts are virtually inaccessible: they are cut off to all but a handful of visitors by land grants to private concessionaires and diamond mining companies. Elsewhere, the signs of human presence are almost everywhere, and most of the country seems tame compared to other African wilderness destinations. Even in seemingly empty bushlands, roads are enclosed by ubiquitous fences that inhibit a sense of unbounded wilderness. Crisscrossing tire tracks have the same inhibiting effect in many parts of the desert. Wildlife encounters are also sometimes tainted by human control. In parks and on private lands, game animals are shunted around at will, their numbers and variety shuffled in the name of management. Some private reserves haphazardly introduce nonnative animals without much regard to the natural habitat. Only Etosha has a multitude of the African megafauna on view, and there, heavy regulation and high visitation detract from a wilderness safari atmosphere. All this is not to say that wilderness experiences cannot be enjoyed in Namibia; they can, but you must go the extra mile and bear the additional expense of getting off the beaten track.

Making the most of touring Namibia takes good infusions of time or money. The country has an excellent network of tar highways and well-maintained gravel roads, but distances are vast. Getting around by car means long hours on the road, with days often spent driving at high speed to cover the great stretches of ground between vital destinations. The alternative is to go by air: small planes are readily available for charter (and there are numerous regularly scheduled wing safaris), but the cost is high. The heavy expense of flying reflects both hours logged in the air and the necessity for planes and pilots to overnight in the bush or deadhead back to base.

Caveats and costs notwithstanding, Namibia is a fascinating travel destination. Its attractions are undeniable. Scenic grandeur abounds in the dunes of the Namib and the buttes of its desert mountain ranges, and few places can match the fearsome loneliness of the Skeleton Coast for wilderness character. While Namibia is not the greatest country for classic big game safaris, it does offer that spectacle at Etosha. Moreover, the bizarre flora and fauna of the Namib — each species a miracle of evolutionary adaptation — are the source of endless wonder. The oddities of Namibia's wildlife, the hostile beauty of its geography, the strange environments of the Namib and the Skeleton Coast, and a remarkable cultural mix combine to give Africa's southwest desert country an ambiance all its own.

Safari Facts

ENTRY: No visa or vaccinations are required for US citizens.

CURRENCY: The Namibian dollar is fixed to equal the South African rand (1997 rate: N$4.5 = US$1). The South African rand can also be freely used in Namibia. Major credit cards are accepted in the city of Windhoek and in larger hotels. Smaller game lodges usually accept US dollar traveler's checks. There is an official exchange bureau at the airport, and plenty of banks, hotels, or bureaus in Windhoek at which to exchange for local currency.

AIR TRAVEL: Most overseas visitors fly into Windhoek, which is served by Air Namibia, Lufthansa, South African Airways, and several regional airlines. Air Namibia connects Victoria Falls directly with Etosha and Windhoek (via Katima Mulilo in the Caprivi Strip). Air Namibia also has a pretty good network of flights that link some of the prime areas of tourist interest. Several small companies specialize in flying safaris and charter flights.

LAND TRANSPORTATION: The country is served by an excellent network of well-maintained roads, both paved and gravel. Because Namibia is big and distances between destinations tend to be long (and the roads seem empty), there is a tendency for drivers to speed. This temptation should be resisted: loose gravel on dirt roads makes them slippery, as many self-drive tourists discover to their pain. Wild animals, especially kudu, are another road hazard: slow down and be extremely careful at dawn and dusk, and avoid traveling at night. Legal speed limits are already high (75 mph on tarred roads and 62 mph on gravel), but novices to African roads should take it easier, especially on gravel.

CAR RENTAL: Avis and Budget have offices in Windhoek and Swakopmund. Other major companies include Imperial, Tempest, and Kessler 4x4 Hire. A company called Camping Car Hire rents camping equipment along with its vehicles. Due to wear and tear and the cost of vehicles and spare parts in Namibia, rates are high and insurance is very expensive (and deductibles are large). An international driver's license is officially required.

PARK RESERVATIONS AND FEES: Namibia's parks have a centrally controlled booking system run by the Ministry of Environment and Tourism. Bookings for all accommodations in national park rest camps, as well as for park hiking trails, should be made in advance at the reservations office in Windhoek. Applications should be addressed to: Ministry of Environment and Tourism, Reservations Office, Private Bag 13267, Windhoek. The telephone number is (061) 236975 and the fax is (061) 224900. Making reservations is a tricky process as each rest camp has various types of chalets (typically one- or two-room bungalows with two to four beds), and each is offered at a different price. Applications should include your passport number, address and full communications information, type of accommodation requested, number of adults and children in the party, and the dates of arrival and departure (with alternative dates). The Ministry of Environment and Tourism Reservations Office will send you a conditional reservation form, and after you receive this, you must make immediate payment. Bookings can also be made in person at the office in Windhoek (in the Oude Voopost Building at the corners of Meinert and Moltke streets and Independence Avenue), or at the Tourist Rendezvous on Independence Avenue. Accommodation *might* be available at a rest camp if you just show up, but you cannot count on it. Bookings for the various hiking trails in the park are hard to get and should be made well in advance. Entry fees in Namibia differ at each park (and seem to increase annually), but they are always very low: rates vary from N$20 for Etosha to N$10 for less popular parks like Waterberg. Entry fees do not have to be paid in advance.

SCHOOL HOLIDAYS: Getting bookings for accommodation in park rest camps or hiking trails during Namibian school holiday periods is really tough. Exact dates vary each year, but they occur at Easter, Christmas, and during a spring break around the end of August. Each holiday period lasts about one month.

TOURS: A great number of tour operators run custom-made safaris as well as scheduled departures of fixed itinerary tours. See the list of safari tour operators in the Appendix for more information.

SHOPPING: African artifacts and curios of all sorts are readily available in Windhoek. These run the gamut from Herero dolls to Kavango baskets and Bushman bow-and-quiver sets. Rock hounds will find an unbelievable variety of minerals on sale, gemstones included. Chic clothing of karakul sheepskin (marketed under the name Nakara) is sold at several designer emporiums. Hand-woven karakul carpets are also featured at finer shops. The National Art Gallery of Namibia has a shop in the Alte Feste complex. Other noteworthy stores include the Namibian Crafts Center (a handicrafts supermarket) and the Bushman Art and African Museum. There are plenty of others, as well as street vendors.

MEDICAL EVACUATION: 24-hour emergency evacuation can be arranged with Medical Rescue International (MRI) in Windhoek. The telephone number is (061) 23-0505 at all hours. They offer air rescue insurance. Medicity Windhoek is a modern private hospital in Windhoek.

Windhoek

Squeaky clean and surrounded by scrub-covered mountains, Namibia's capital seems like some small German city plunked down in the midst of the Arizona desert. With an architecture that mixes the old German colonial style with modern towers and malls, Windhoek's cleanliness and compact size make it a pleasant enough place to stop over on either end of a Namibia tour.

Sightseeing in town is limited to a few historical sites. The Railroad Station, the Christuskirche (Evangelical Lutheran Church), Heinitzburg Castle, and the Tintinpalast, which today houses the Namibian parliament, are some of the most prominent architectural relics of the German days. Another complex of colonial buildings, the Alte Feste, houses a collection of independence-movement memorabilia as well as a National Art Gallery–sponsored shop that highlights traditional Namibian handicrafts. Shopping is a prime tourist activity in Windhoek. In addition to the various shops and galleries clustered along Independence Avenue and neighboring downtown streets, a host of street vendors sell all kinds of Namibian crafts. Every other Saturday, vendors gather for the Street Market, which takes place at the Post Street Mall. This colorful postmodern shopping center is graced by the presence of the unusual Meteorite Fountain and the old Kaiserkrone Hotel, which features an outdoor beer-garden. Such German-flavored gustatory retreats are sprinkled liberally around central Windhoek.

Advice regarding events or tourist facilities is available at the Windhoek Information and Publicity office in the Post Street Mall and at the Namibia Tourism office near the Kudu Statue on Independence Avenue. Both offices book national park camps.

Windhoek has two airports. Windhoek International is a very modern airport located 25 miles east of town. An airport bus is supposed to meet every flight; alternatives are expensive because taxis are not always waiting at the airport and tour operators charge a premium rate for airport transfers. Eros Airport is virtually in town (3 miles from the city center). It is a very busy center for light aircraft and is the gateway for the many scheduled air safaris and charter flights that serve the needs of tourists.

The *Kalahari Sands* is Windhoek's principal downtown tourist hotel. This 184-room tower on Independence Avenue is centrally located both for shopping and transport (the taxi and bus stand across the street is the terminal for the bus to Windhoek International Airport). The Kalahari Sands' pride of place has now been eclipsed by the new *Windhoek Hotel and Country Club*, a mammoth, five-star luxury hotel, entertainment, and golf-course complex on the outskirts of town. Other hotels include the affordable downtown *Continental Hotel* and the business-oriented *Hotel Safari*, which is located next to Eros Airport. Windhoek's colonial-era *Heinitzburg Castle* (built in 1884) has recently been converted into a comfortable small hotel. The *Villa Verdi* is a stylishly decorated 12-room hotel a few minutes walk from the city center. Windhoek also has a number of German-style pensions (bed-and-breakfasts): the best is the *Pension Kleines Heim*; the *Hotel-Pension Cela* is recommended for those on a budget.

There are some places of interest outside Windhoek that can be visited or included into more wide-ranging itineraries. To the south, the town of Rehoboth is the center for the Baster people, a distinctive mixed-blood group descended from Cape Dutch whites and Namas who settled the town in 1870. A museum documents Baster culture and history, and the town is known for its hot springs spa. To the north, on the way toward Etosha, is the town of Okahandja, where the great Herero chiefs are buried. Every year on August 26, Herero in brilliant red garb gather by the thousands to celebrate Heroes' Day and honor their ancestors. *Gross-Barmen Hot Springs* is a well-known spa and government rest camp near Okahandja.

The Daan Viljoen Game Park is only 15 miles from Windhoek. It is set in the Khomas Hochland, a pleasant hill country that divides Windhoek from the deserts to the west. The park has a variety of game and some 200 recorded varieties of birds, but no dangerous animals, making it possible to take advantage of its hiking trails. Day visitors must make reservations in advance with one of the official reservations offices in Windhoek and leave by 6:00 P.M. The *Daan Viljoen Rest Camp* has chalets to accommodate overnight visitors; it also has campsites, a restaurant, and a swimming pool.

To travel between Windhoek and the coast, several routes across the Khomas Hochland can be used. Windhoek, on the country's central plateau, is at an altitude of 5,400 feet. The western roads go yet higher, reaching 8,340 feet on the Gamsburg Pass before plunging toward the coastal plains of the Namib.

The Skeleton Coast and the Namib Desert

Southern Africa's wave-tossed Atlantic shore is at once one of the wildest and least hospitable coastlines imaginable. Hidden under a perpetual shroud of dense sea fog, its relentless waves, uncharted reefs, shifting sandbars, and treacherous currents have long made Africa's southwest coast a notoriously dangerous passage for mariners attempting to round the Cape of Good Hope. Old-time sailors had reason enough to fear: if the crew of a foundered ship survived the angry surf, worse terrors awaited ashore. There they found themselves marooned in the Namib Desert, a 100-mile-wide strip of waterless dune and rock stretching hundreds of miles to north and south. Rescue was near impossible; the only salvation was to trek across the pitiless desert. Many ships did go down, leaving their wrecks among the bleached bones littering the beaches of the infamous Skeleton Coast.

Although fearsome and sometimes deadly to humans, Namibia's plankton-rich coastal waters support an exuberant marine ecosystem. At one time, these waters were the wintering grounds for abundant baleen whales from the Antarctic. American whalers were among the first to exploit the southern right whales that teemed along the Skeleton Coast. Relatively few remain, but whale bones are still scattered on the beaches, along with the remains of fur seals and other sea creatures tossed up by the unrelenting waves. Indeed, the coastal waters are still amazingly rich, for the cold, upwelling Benguela Current is packed with nutrients from the ocean depths of the Antarctic. Great shoals of filter-feeding fish, such as pilchards (sardines) and anchovies, feed on plankton, and these in turn support larger pelagic fish, as well as Cape fur seals, seabirds, and humans. Like the whales, commercial fishing stocks have been greatly reduced by overexploitation, but fish are still bountiful enough to draw thousands of South African surf-casters annually. Even their catch has declined in recent years, however, and the government is tightening bag limits.

Birdlife along the Skeleton Coast is abundant and varied. Long lines of Cape cormorants are a common sight streaming over the sea, and the black-and-white Cape gannet is commonly observed diving headlong into the water. The flightless jackass penguin forms colonies on offshore islands, but individuals are sometimes seen on mainland shores. A wide variety of gulls and terns ply the coastal waters, including the Damara tern, which is endemic to Africa's south Atlantic shores. Coastal lagoons, particularly those at Walvis Bay and Sandwich Harbour, are avian paradises. In addition to seabirds, these protected waters attract a vast array of waders, waterfowl, and other aquatic species including flamingos and white pelicans. Flamingos are also common at commercial salt ponds along the central coast.

The Namib Desert is Namibia's most unusual ecosystem. It is essentially the gift of the Benguela Current, for the tropical sun burning down above the cold sea produces a temperature inversion that prevents airborne moisture from falling as rain. As a consequence, the Namib is one of the driest regions on earth: at the coast, rainfall *averages* less than half an inch per year (and rises to a maximum of 4 inches in the interior eastern desert), and any particular locale may go years without *any* rain. This thirstland of rock and dune occupies coastal plains that extend as far as 100 miles inland, up to the foot of the continent's western escarpment.

The Namib's southern portion, roughly from the Orange River up to Swakopmund, is dominated by a vast sea of sand. Over eons, the Orange has washed down eroded soils from the interior mountains of South Africa and Lesotho and dumped them into the Atlantic, where prevailing southwest winds drive them back ashore. The sand piles up to the north of the Orange River mouth, forming wandering barchan dunes that move northward with the wind (barchan is the geological term for windblown, mobile dunes). Between Luderitz and Walvis Bay, a distance of almost 250 miles, massive dunes bury the land under their suffocating weight. This southern dune sea ends abruptly at the Kuiseb River. Its rainy-season floods are strong enough to wash away encroaching sand, and only the river's mouth is drowned beneath high coastal dunes. Although there are two major dunefields on the northern Skeleton Coast (between Torra Bay and the Hoarusib River, and again from Cape Frio to the Kunene River mouth), dunes along the central Namibian coast are limited to patches of the small and highly mobile barchan type.

The Namib changes character radically north of the Kuiseb. From Swakopmund to Torra Bay, dunes are supplanted by the seemingly bare lichen-covered plains typical of the central Namib. Here and there, isolated mountains tower above these barren flats. A series of parallel river valleys cut westward across the desert. Although most of these streams rarely carry surface water, they form linear oases in which springs and underground moisture support richer vegetation. They are vital arteries and refuges for desert wildlife.

A combination of cold water and warm sun gives rise to the fog that is so characteristic of the Namib coast. Dense shoals of low-lying cloud hover over the ocean. Prevailing southwesterly winds push the fog landward nightly, when it moves up to 40 miles inland, passing over the sand dunes and gravel flats of the western Namib. Where dune crests and hills (or even plants and rocks) catch the mist, condensation occurs and drops of moisture form. In a region where no rain may fall for years at a time, these fog-borne drops are precious. A whole community of plants and animals has come to depend on the fog for survival, for it is their only regular source of water. In addition to perpetual drought, the plants and animals of the fog zone have to contend with burning midday temperatures. Further inland, beyond the reach of the fog, temperature variations are even more extreme and there is no daily delivery of nocturnal moisture. Life has to adapt to a regime of fiendish heat and unrelieved drought for at least half the year.

The plants and animals of the Namib have evolved an amazing array of adaptations to their brutal environment. More than anything else, this is what makes the desert so endlessly fascinating to students of nature. The western Namib possesses a variety of habitats, each with its own community of flora and fauna. Beach strand, gravel plains, rocky outcrops, riverbeds, and sand dunes are the major habitats.

On the beach, the main food source for animals is organic litter tossed out by the angry ocean. Primeval creatures like fishmoths and isopods scuttle among tangles of stranded kelp. At night, gerbils emerge from fringing sand dunes to feast on scavenging insects. Cape foxes, jackals, and brown hyenas patrol the beaches in search of the washed up bodies of seabirds and marine animals. In former days, even lions were known to scavenge seal carcasses along the shore.

Sand dunes are one of the most challenging habitats in the Namib ecosystem. Small dunes and interdunal valleys support vegetation, but the heights of massive sand ridges are too inhospitable an environment for plants. Although bare, such sand mountains are far from lifeless. Atop the dunes, wind-borne detritus forms the base of the food pyramid: seeds and dry bits of plant or animal remains are tossed up by winds that blow from the more vegetated parts of the desert. Detritus deposited onto a windward duneslope is exposed as sand tumbles down the slipface below the leeward crest. The relative abundance of food ensures a greater concentration of animals, so slipfaces are the best places to observe the fauna of the dunes. Tenebrionid beetles and other invertebrates forage there for seeds and bits of organic refuse. The insects attract a variety of predators. Each species has developed fascinating strategies for survival in the sand.

Tenebrionid beetles are widespread in southern Africa. The most fa-

miliar are known as tok-tokkies because of the males' odd habit of tap-
ping their abdomens against the ground to produce a sound that attracts
amorous females. In the Namib, tenebrionids have shown a remarkable
degree of speciation, with each variety developing adaptations peculiar
to its niche. The black *Onymacris unguicularis* is celebrated for performing nighttime head stands atop dune crests. This behavior allows
water droplets condensed on its own body to run downward to its
mouth. To trap their water, the flying-saucer-shaped *Lepidochora* beetles
dig narrow trenches on dune slipfaces. Several species of Namib tenebrionids sport bold black-and-white coloration, others have less flashy
designs. By using behavioral adaptations such as "stilting" — standing to
full height atop long legs to catch cooling breezes — some tenebrionids
can remain active in the heat of the day. Others must stay hidden under
insulating sand until nightfall.

Several fascinating lizards inhabit the dunes. The shovel-snouted
lizard (*Aporosaurus anchiete)* is a diurnal predator that swiftly pursues
its insect prey atop the sand. When surface temperatures get too hot, the
lizard performs a "thermal dance," raising its forefeet and tail in the air
to minimize contact with the ground. When threatened, *Aporosaurus*
dives effortlessly under the sand, a move facilitated by its flattened
snout. The ability to "swim" beneath sand obviates the use of tunnels
and is an adaptation employed by many denizens of the dunes. The
desert-plaited lizard (*Angolosaurus skoogi*) shares this talent. Nearly a
foot long, this diurnal resident of scrub-covered dunes can disappear
with astounding rapidity. The *Palmatogecko rangei*, or web-footed
gecko, spends its day in a burrow. This bug-eyed nocturnal lizard has a
rather emaciated and eerily semitransparent body. It hunts insects and
spiders on the nighttime dunes, when it also draws its water from condensed fog. The 10-inch Namaqua chameleon (*Chamaeleo namaquen-
sis*) forages on dunes and rocks, and can even be found along the
seashore. This voracious lizard eats any animal it can swallow, including
insects, other lizards, and even small snakes.

Lizards are not the only hunters on the dunes. In fact, they are themselves preyed on by a number of other dune residents. The sidewinding
adder (*Bitis peringueyi*) is a small (10 to 11 inch) snake with the same
distinctive style of locomotion as the American sidewinder rattlesnake —
a textbook example of convergent evolution! The parallel undulating
lines of the adder's tracks are unmistakable, but the snake itself is hard
to see: it has the habit of burying itself in the sand with only its eyes protruding above the surface. It sometimes waves the tip of its tail above
ground to attract its lizard prey. At night, the adder drinks fog water collected on its own scales. The golden mole (*Eremitalpa granti*) spends the

day underground. At night, it swims upward and emerges to patrol the dune surface. It eats insects and other invertebrates and readily takes the weird *Palmatogecko*. Fearsome white lady spiders are also enemies of the gecko: at 4 inches across, these fast-moving nocturnal arachnids are quite capable of killing small lizards. One type of white lady (*Leucorchestris*) jumps into the air when threatened and performs the maneuvers that have earned its alternative name, "the dancing spider." When escape proves necessary, another white lady (*Carparachne*) rolls itself into a ball and swiftly rolls away down the slipface.

Barren, gravel-covered plains are a conspicuous feature of the central Namib. These seemingly lifeless flats are actually carpeted with a crust of lichens — primitive plants that are symbiotic combinations of algae and fungi. The Namib lichens get their moisture from fog. In the morning, they are colored with soft shades of green or bright orange, but they fade as they dry up with the heat of the day. Although not a place of great beauty or a haunt of large animals, the Namib's lichen fields are one of its most delicate habitats. Off-road travel is especially destructive to the gypsum plains of the central Namib, where the weight of vehicles breaks the lichen crust, killing the plants and leaving tire tracks as permanent scars. The Namib's most colorful lichens — which form bright galleries mixing oranges, black, greens, and whites — tend to occur on rocky outcrops.

The Namib's scattered hills and mountains get more moisture and support a wider variety of plants than the sere coastal plains. Succulent aloes and euphorbias, as well as many other attractive species, thrive on the rocky hillsides. Among them are the tiny *Lithops*, minute gray-green succulents that pass as "living stones" when not graced with a blossom. Locally called "Bushmen's buttocks," these small bilobed plants are much sought after by horticulturists and have become endangered by overcollecting. The cactuslike *Hoodia*, with its cluster of large, petunialike flowers, also grows on rocky ground, as does the conspicuous *kokerboom*, or quiver tree (*Aloe dichotoma*).

The *Welwitschia mirabilis* is the most famous Namib plant. This curious link between the cone-bearing gymnospores (the group to which pine trees belong) and flowering plants is particularly interesting to scientists, but holds an almost equal fascination for laypeople. The welwitschia is a long-lived plant (some large specimens are estimated to be over 1,000 years old) but not pretty: a winding tangle of stringy, ribbonlike leaves seems to sprout from its central woody core, forming an untidy prostrate mass that hugs the desert floor. In reality, the welwitschia has only two leaves. These get shredded by the wind and chewed on by desert animals for their moisture (the tough fibers are spit out). Male and female plants are distinguished by their distinctive cones, which are often inhabited by the brightly colored welwitschia bug. Welwitschia plants grow on the Namib's gravel flats, especially along the shallow beds of dry watercourses. A 10-foot-deep taproot is supplemented by surface roots that can suck moisture from fog-dampened ground. The leaves, too, may be able to absorb fog-borne moisture.

The endemic nara plant (*Acanthosicyos horrida*) is less well known than the welwitschia but it may well be more important to the ecology of the Namib. Nara grows in sandy places, wherever its roots can penetrate to underground water, and it is common in the dry riverbeds that traverse the coastal desert. The leafless plant forms spiny thickets and is unpalatable to game until it produces its melonlike fruit. Nara fruits are a welcome source of food and moisture for animals as diverse as insects, Cape foxes, gerbils, giraffes, gemsboks, and rhinos. The fruits have historically been an important food for hunter-gatherer groups of human beings, and are still harvested annually by the Topnaar Hottentots who live along the Kuiseb River south of Swakopmund.

Although they flow only with the greatest irregularity, the Namib's major rivers are crucial habitat in the ecology of the desert. Even when dry, they remain linear oases in which plants and animals that cannot tolerate the surrounding desert can continue to thrive. Vegetation is much more diverse, as many plants associated with higher rainfall areas are able to survive by making use of subterranean water. Tall trees such as leadwood, camel thorn, and winterthorn acacia are found along the sandy channels, providing shade and sustenance to birds and animals alike. Scrubbier tamarisk trees grow in dense thickets in the riverbeds. Animals, too, make use of the underground water. Gemsbok and Hartmann's mountain zebra dig for water in the sand, a task made easier by the excavations of elephants in the northern river valleys. Where these linear greenbelts snake across the desert landscape, they are the highways for the east-west movements of wild animals and domestic stock. As such, they are essential for the survival of the remaining desert elephants and rhinos of the Namib's wild northern Kaokoveld.

The eastern desert, beyond the fog belt, is known as the pro-Namib. Although total precipitation here is higher, rain still arrives with painful irregularity and then only during the broiling summer months between October and March. Dew replaces fog as a water source for some species, but the long months of annual drought generally require different survival strategies for plants and animals. Succulence or the ability to put down deep roots remain useful adaptations for many plants. For others, the key to survival is the ability to set large amounts of seed that can withstand months or even years of aridity. When the rains do come, seeds quickly germinate and the desert bursts with life. The bare pro-Namib plains are then briefly transformed to fields of grass. Even after their verdant greens have faded to the pale shades of the desert, the grasslands continue to attract the large animals typical of the Namib — springbok, gemsbok, and ostrich. Flash floods periodically pour down from the interior mountains, scouring normally dry gorges and filling the thirsty beds of sand rivers. For a time, the big rivers of the Namib may actually flow, bringing a new lushness to the riverbed oases. As the rivers subside, grasses pop up in the wet sand. It is a time of plenty in the Namib, and many of the large migratory animals can extend their ranges westward into parts of the desert where they cannot exist in drier times.

Marginally higher rainfall makes the pro-Namib the richer part of the desert ecosystem. Migration is the rule for the large animals of the desert — they must move quickly to take advantage of fleeting feeding opportunities. The desert migrants — the gemsbok, springbok, and Hartmann's mountain zebra — are usually found in small bands, although good grazing may bring them briefly together into larger aggregations. All these animals, as well as ostrich, can be found in suitable habitat throughout the Namib and pro-Namib. Elephant, rhino, lion, and giraffe are now restricted to the northern part of the desert.

The black rhino is well suited to life in the pro-Namib, where it finds sufficient browse even in the driest of times. Although the rhino likes to drink and frequently visits springs or waterholes, it can largely meet its liquid requirements by feeding on moisture-rich succulent plants. The Namib rhinos are especially fond of the common *Euphorbia damarana*, a spiny succulent widespread in rocky areas. Poaching has reduced the "desert rhinos" of the northern Namib to a mere handful.

Hartmann's mountain zebra (*Equus zebra hartmannae*) is a resident of Namibia's western escarpment and the pro-Namib. This hardy zebra looks superficially much like the common variety, but is distinguished by a pouchy-looking dewlap on its throat and an odd gridiron pattern on its lower back. Even more than by physical characteristics, this desert animal is differentiated by habitat. It lives in the rocky uplands and gorges of the pro-Namib, where it supplements its grazing with browse from trees and bushes. It must drink, so it is commonly found in the vicinity of springs. When necessary, it uses its powerful hooves to dig for water in the sand of dry riverbeds. After the rains, Hartmann's zebra will venture down onto plains adjacent to its mountain fastnesses to take advantage of the grazing offered by the ephemeral desert grasslands. Although Namibia's population of Hartmann's mountain zebra was probably over 100,000 in the 1950s, it is now estimated at less than 10 percent of that number.

Touring the Namib and Skeleton Coast

Although the Namib and Skeleton Coast span the length of the country, huge chunks of their territory remain closed to the general public. A vast southern portion is taken up by the *Speergebeit* (the "forbidden region"), which consists of official Diamond Areas where mining companies guard concessions that are off-limits to public entry. Admission to this region is highly restricted, although some of the more interesting features around the town of Luderitz can be explored in the company of a licensed tour operator. Similarly, the northernmost half of Skeleton Coast Park, which stretches from the Hoarusib River all the way to the Angola border, has been granted as a concession to a single tour operator. The central area, from Walvis Bay up to Terrace Bay in Skeleton Coast Park, is the most easily accessible and highly visited portion of the coastal desert. Access to this part of the coast and the adjacent inland regions of the Namib, especially those in Namib-Naukluft Park, is centered on the booming tourist town of Swakopmund.

Perhaps the most evocative image of the Skeleton Coast is that of a wrecked ship being smothered by desert sand. Although photos of beached ships are widely displayed, such striking sights are seen by very few: wrecks do not last forever, and those that are still in good shape are all in very remote or inaccessible sites. Three prominent wrecks are located along the dune-fringed coast between Walvis Bay and Conception Bay. They are usually seen only from the air.

Namib-Naukluft Park

Namib-Naukluft Park is one of the largest protected nature reserves in the world. An extraordinary range of desert habitats and landscapes are encompassed within its 9,140 square miles. Most of this vast territory remains trackless and completely inaccessible to the public. Four prime areas are open to exploration: the Namib section showcasing the desert between the Swakop and Kuiseb rivers, the coastal dunes and lagoons at Sandwich Harbour, the interior Naukluft Mountains, and the celebrated dunes at Sossusvlei.

The Namib section contains all the habitats typical of the central desert. The barren gravel flats, rocky mountain outcrops, and dunes of the fog-nurtured coastal desert are all represented, as are the grassier plains and tree-fringed watercourses of the interior pro-Namib. As wide open plains predominate over much of this section of the park, some of its landscapes are notably lonely and bleak — a seemingly empty wilderness of bare rock and stunted plants. But here and there, solitary mountains rise forlornly above the barren flats. These rocky islands lend scale to the vastness of the desert and give an impression of limitless space.

The boundary of the Namib section lies just beyond the coastal dunes outside Swakopmund. Proximity to town allows it to be explored on day trips, making it the most accessible part of the Namib and a very popular venue for desert explorations. Two major roads (one connecting to Windhoek, the other to the Naukluft and Sossusvlei areas) traverse the Namib section of Namib-Naukluft Park, and it has a good network of tracks on which to explore.

The most popular route in the park is the Welwitschia Trail that parallels the course of the Swakop River. This track leads to the riverbed oasis of Goanikontes. The site of an old colonial farm, it is still lush with eucalyptus, casuarina trees, and date palms — all species introduced by the Germans. Further along are the Welwitschia Flats, where large numbers of those weird plants grow in shallow watercourses. The nearby Giant Welwitschia, reputed to be 1,500 years old, is enshrined within its own protective fence. The scenic highlight of the Welwitschia Trail is the area called the Moon Landscape, which offers a panoramic vista of eroded desert badlands.

The Welwitschia Trail can easily be explored on a half-day tour out of Swakopmund. Full-day trips can be extended to many other interesting spots in the Namib section, where a number of designated wilderness campsites invite even longer forays. Mountains such as the Hamilton Range and the Vogelfederberg must be explored on foot to find their hidden flora and fauna. You are more likely to see the larger desert animals such as springbok, ostrich, gemsbok, and even Hartmann's zebra while driving through the grassier plains of the eastern Namib, particularly around the Tinkas Flats and the Ganab campsite. The narrow chasm of the Kuiseb Canyon can be viewed by taking a short detour while traveling the main road from Swakopmund to Sossusvlei. Less often visited is the remote and fascinating campsite at Homeb. Here, the tree-lined course of the Kuiseb River marks the abrupt edge of the great southern dune sea, which rises up immediately on its south bank. Homeb is an excellent place to look for the fauna of both dunes and river oases.

Camping in the Namib ensures adequate time to explore on foot, search for the desert's elusive wildlife, and savor the colors of its scenery at the best times of day. Camping is allowed only at designated sites; permits must be obtained through the Reservations Office in Windhoek or at the office in Swakopmund [Namib-i, Roon and Kaiser Wilhelm Street,

P.O. Box 1236, tel. (40) 2224, fax (40) 5101]. All campsites in the Namib section of the park are basic and small (limited to single parties of up to eight persons); firepits and toilets are provided, but you must bring water and firewood. The campsites at *Bloedkoppie*, a granite outcrop near the Tinkas Flats, and on the Kuiseb River at *Homeb*, are particularly appealing. The *Ganab* campsite is in a good wildlife area.

Sandwich Harbour is one of the prettiest spots on the Namibian coast. Squeezed between the titanic sands of the Namib dune sea and the wild waves of the Atlantic, the placid blue lagoon with its fringe of emerald reeds makes a startling sight. A trip to Sandwich Harbour also affords an opportunity to explore the great dunes of the Namib while doing some excellent birdwatching. Sandwich is completely undeveloped, so there is no accommodation or camping. It makes a fine day trip from Swakopmund, and a stop at Walvis Bay lagoon can be included on the way.

Sandwich Harbour and Walvis Bay provide key wetland habitat for tens of thousands of migratory waterbirds. The Walvis Bay wetlands are a protected bird sanctuary that supports the gamut of Skeleton Coast species. Gannets, cormorants, and terns fish its open waters, while whimbrels and other waders work the tidal mudflats. The Walvis lagoon is a good place to see flamingos, which usually crowd its shallow waters in large numbers.

The more remote lagoon at Sandwich Harbour can only be reached by four-wheel-drive vehicle. The track southward from Walvis Bay traverses the big dunes that choke off the Kuiseb River's mouth from its exit to the sea. Some Kuiseb water is still surmised to pass under the dunes to reach the Sandwich lagoon, as evidenced by the presence of freshwater reeds. At Sandwich Harbour, the great dunes press right down to the shore of the lagoon, which is separated from the Atlantic by a narrow wave-lashed sandspit. The waters of the lagoon are an extremely fertile breeding ground for fish. Sharks and fur seals can be seen feeding in the lagoon, as can all the fish-eating seabirds. Flamingos and other waders stalk its shallower parts, while gemsbok and brown hyenas sometimes visit its shores.

The Naukluft Mountains form a salient on the eastern edge of the Namib-Naukluft Park. Rising to over 6,000 feet in elevation, these marble mountains catch more rain than the desert below. They periodically send flash floods racing down to the dry riverbeds of the Namib. The Naukluft's dolomite-limestone peaks are cut by deep canyons that hold hidden springs and pool-filled grottos. Hartmann's mountain zebra, klipspringer, hyrax, and black eagle are the animals most likely to be seen in this section of the park.

The world of the Naukluft belongs to the hiker, for it can only be properly explored on foot. Two circular walking trails, the 11-mile Waterkloof and the 6-mile Olive, make great day hikes from the *Naukluft* campsite. This camp has hot-water washing facilities and space for four parties of up to eight members each. Really hardy backpackers can undertake the challenging Naukluft Hiking Trail. It can be done as an eight-day, 75-mile expedition or reduced to a four-day, 36-mile trek. Because of high summer temperatures, these longer hikes take place only between March and October. They are limited to 12 participants. Space for both the Naukluft campsite and the Naukluft Hiking Trail is tightly controlled and must be prebooked with one of the reservations offices in Windhoek or Swakopmund. Comfortable catered accommodation in the Naukluft area can be found at *Bullsport Lodge*, which offers fine mountain hiking on its own extensive property. An official trail for four-wheel-drive vehicles has recently opened in the mountain section of the park; access to the Naukluft 4x4 trail is limited and advance bookings must be made.

The southernmost public section of the Namib-Naukluft Park includes Sesriem Canyon and the famous dunes at Sossusvlei.

Sossusvlei is probably the most spectacularly scenic landscape in the country. Giant dunes surround Sossusvlei, a cul-de-sac valley thrust into the heart of the Namib's sand sea. Here, majestic 1,000-foot-high dunes tower into the sky, dwarfing the camel-thorn acacias on the pan below. It is a magic place of stark simplicity, where twisted acacias are silhouetted against the sinuous ripples of mountainous red dunes.

Sossusvlei is the creation of the Tsauchab River, a now-temporary rainy-season stream that finds its headwaters in the Naukluft Mountains. In former times, it cut the narrow gorge at Sesriem as it flowed westward toward the Atlantic. Later, flash floods kept its channel free of sand even after its path to the sea was buried under encroaching dunes. Even now, during exceptionally rainy years, the Tsauchab's floodwaters sometimes inundate Sossusvlei, transforming the dry pan into an inland lake—a most astonishing appendage to the desert dunescape. Ducks and waders then join the gemsbok that are the more typical inhabitants of Sossusvlei. The nearby Dead Vlei, a side valley long ago cut off from the floods, is eerily dotted with the upright skeletons of acacias estimated to be 500 years old.

The Sossusvlei dunes are among the highest in the world. Sculpted by both easterly and westerly winds, they possess striking, multifaced, star-shaped undulations (geologists call such formations star dunes). Their "red" sands result from each grain's covering of iron oxide, a phenomenon absent from the younger dunes of the coast. The intensity of color

Spectacular thousand-foot-high red dunes encircle the pan at Sossusvlei, Namibia. Photo: Allen Bechky.

shifts with the movement of the sun, providing a day-long light show of dancing hues that range from pale apricot to blood orange.

The best time to visit Sossusvlei is early morning. When the sun peeps over the horizon, the red dunes positively glow under its soft light and a distant crown of purple-tinted sea fog is visible in the west. It is a photographer's dream. Unfortunately, the short window of time for optimum light necessitates a dusty race to the head of Sossusvlei. Every visitor wants to be early, so there is a rush of vehicles along the Tsauchab corridor. Once arrived, there is room enough for all to explore or climb to the top of one of the mountainous dunes. Needless to say, climbing the dunes is not easy for everyone; deep sand makes it hard going up, and it rapidly becomes hot once the sun gets into the sky.

Sesriem is a narrow, steep-walled gorge formed by the Tsauchab River. It takes its name from the number of lengths of leather ox-team reins (*riem*) early settlers needed to draw a bucket of water up to the lip of the gorge. Some interesting rock formations are found within the canyon, but it pales in scenic significance with the better known Sossusvlei dunes.

Sesriem is the gateway to Sossusvlei, however, and its campsite at the park entrance is heavily utilized. *Sesriem Campsite* has hot-water washing facilities but it already struggles to serve up to 144 campers, and the camp may well have to be enlarged: already many parties that cannot find official slots at Sesriem merely pitch their tents illegally outside the gate. Advance booking is essential. It's 39 miles from the Sesriem gate to the Sossusvlei car park. The road continues for another 2.5 miles, but this last bit can only be negotiated by four-wheel-drive vehicles. Concerns about the volume of vehicles using the Sesriem-Sossusvlei track (as well as littering and wood gathering by unsupervised campers) may soon lead to new regulations that reduce access to Sossusvlei.

A number of lodges have opened on private land just outside the Sesriem/Sossusvlei area. *Namib Naukluft Lodge* is a 26-bed facility, while the *Sossusvlei Karos Lodge* is a larger complex (90 beds). Both offer modern luxury accommodations, excursions to Sossusvlei, private airstrips, and shuttle services that allow guests road access from Windhoek. The Karos Lodge rents out 4x4 vehicles and conducts escorted game drives on its extensive (172 square miles) property; it is also a convenient base for going aloft on an early morning balloon ride. The balloons are actually run by Namib Sky Adventure Safaris from their base on the neighboring NamibRand Nature Reserve. Their 12-bed tented *Mwisho Camp* is one of several small camps on the huge NamibRand reserve. The 10-bed *Wolwedans Dune Camp* is the flagship lodge. Its tents are built on a boardwalk above the desert floor. Located some 60 miles south of the Sesriem gate, Wolwedans is a rather long round-trip drive from Sossusvlei, but admirably suited for exploring NamibRand. This 470-square-mile conservancy (which is supposed to expand to 585 square miles) lays claim to being the biggest private game reserve in southern Africa. Sharing a 60-mile-long boundary with the Namib-Naukluft Park, its landscapes and wildlife are typical of the pro-Namib. Other accommodations near the Namib-Naukluft's southern sector include *Kulala*, a 24-bed tented camp on a farm near Sesriem, and the 10-bed *Zebra River Lodge*. This charming little lodge is a bit far from Sossuvlei, but its location in the escarpment mountains at the edge of the desert makes it particularly attractive to hikers.

Swakopmund

Founded in 1892, Swakopmund served as the German colony's principal port. In modern times, the old town evolved into Namibia's seaside resort. It appeals to widely different constituencies. Namibians go to beat the heat of their ferocious summers, while South Africans flock there for the fishing. But for overseas visitors, Swakopmund is primarily a gateway to the Skeleton Coast and Namib Desert.

The town still has a very German atmosphere. Fine old colonial buildings have been restored and converted into hotels, galleries, and public buildings. Newer buildings generally go up with harmonious architecture, so the town maintains much the feeling of a north German seafront city. That impression is reinforced by its many German restaurants and cafes.

Swakopmund (or nearby Walvis Bay) is served daily by scheduled Air Namibia flights from Windhoek. Three roads connect it with the capital. The main highway follows the route of the railway line in a northward loop via the towns of Okahandja and Usakos. The others forge more precipitous routes across the western escarpment and through Namib-Naukluft Park. Anyone traveling between that park and the Skeleton Coast or Damaraland will necessarily spend a night or two in Swakopmund.

A wide range of accommodation is available in town. The *Swakopmund Hotel and Entertainment Centre* is the latest and largest: although it incorporates the colonial-era German railway station in its central area, it is theme-park modern. The *Hansa Hotel* dates to 1904. It is tops in sophisticated elegance. The *Strand* and *Schweizerhaus* hotels are modern, boxy, and medium grade. There are many other hotels and comfortable pensions. Campers often stay at the municipal rest camp.

Around town, visitors can walk out on the old breakwater ("the Mole") or visit the lighthouse built in 1903. Swimming and windsurfing are available if you care to brave the cold sea. A brand new aquarium highlights the marine fauna and flora of a typical Skeleton Coast reef. There is also a natural history museum, shopping, and those German pastry shops to keep you entertained. Further afield, there is the coast and Namib-Naukluft Park to explore. Four-wheel-drive vehicles can be rented from Avis, Budget, or Bonanza Car Hire; Charley's Desert Tours and Wilderness Safaris Namibia run one-day escorted tours. Other activities around Swakopmund include horseback or camel rides, dune skiing, and paragliding.

Walvis Bay is only 22 miles south of Swakopmund. Since its incorporation into Namibia in 1994, this town has served as the country's seaport and the base for its fishing industry. It is a popular place with sports fishermen and its lagoon is a wonderful birding spot, where flamingos and legions of shorebirds can be easily observed. Bird Island, one of the huge guano platforms that attract large numbers of seabirds, can be seen offshore on the way to Walvis Bay. Flamingos are also abundant on the man-made commercial salt pools to the north of Swakopmund

The National West Coast Tourist Recreation Area occupies the 120-

mile-long stretch of shore between Swakopmund and the Skeleton Coast Park. This part of the coast is free of dunes and rather bleak but is a favorite with fishermen: they come in droves to cast into the surf. Little knots of them and their ubiquitous pickup trucks can be seen all along the beaches. Aside from the *Jakkalsputz* caravan park at Henties Bay, the campsites designated for them are all named solely according to their distance from Swakopmund: *Mile 4*, *Mile 14*, *Mile 72*, and *Mile 108*.

Fifty miles north of Swakopmund, at Henties Bay, the paved highway turns inland toward Brandberg (the highest mountain in Namibia) and the town of Khorixas in Damaraland. Continuing north toward the Skeleton Coast Park, a salt road parallels the beach all the way to Terrace Bay and beyond. Scenery along this section of coast is rather monotonous: miles and miles of wave-beaten beaches are backed by seemingly endless gypsum plains. For many visitors, the high point of this journey, as well as the turnaround point, is the seal colony at Cape Cross.

The Cape Cross Seal Reserve is one of the largest breeding colonies for the Cape fur seal. During the mating and pupping season, up to 100,000 seals haul out in black masses that cover the reserve's sandy beaches. Many thousands are present at any time of year. To prevent disturbances that could stampede the animals, a wooden fence separates the seals from the viewing area. Black-backed jackals, which prey on young pups and scavenge on seal carcasses, are usually on hand. Seal colonies are very pungent, a fact that upsets some visitors. So, too, does the ugly building for processing seals taken in the annual cull. A replica of the stone cross erected by Portuguese explorer Diogo Cão in 1486 is also located at Cape Cross.

The Brandberg and Spitzkoppe mountains are located in the pro-Namib to the east of the coastal recreation area. Each is an isolated mountain, separated from the other by some 60 miles. Brandberg is a much more massive mountain and, at 8,465 feet, the highest peak in the country. It is famous for the large number of rock paintings found there, especially the so-called White Lady. That image was formerly "controversial" because it was originally purported to depict a Caucasian woman, an interpretation that has since been discredited. The faded painting, which had to be sealed behind iron bars to protect it from vandals, is only one of hundreds on the mountain. Spitzkoppe, too, harbors innumerable rock paintings. The beautiful granite of its soaring peak (5,771 feet) and sheer satellite spires earns it the special affection of rock climbers. A *community-owned campsite* is located at the foot of Spitzkoppe, and the *Brandberg Rest Camp* is located near the village of Uis.

Skeleton Coast Park

The Ugab River marks the southern boundary of the Skeleton Coast Park. From there, the park extends all the way to the Angola border — a distance of some 300 miles. This incredible sweep of lonely coastline and empty desert is one of southern Africa's least visited wildernesses. Of the park's 6,600 square miles, only its southern half is open to the general public, and even there access is severely limited by lack of accommodation.

Although the Skeleton Coast Park's habitats share many affinities with those of the southern and central Namib, there are differences. Gravel plains continue to hug the coast, but ever-moving barchan dunes begin to pop up and eventually swell into large dunefields. These northern dunes do not reach right to the seashore as they do in the south, but form a discontinuous belt of inland sand that pushes all the way from Torra Bay into Angola. The Namib coastal plain is also narrower at its northern end, and the transition from barren desert to greener pro-Namib savanna is more abrupt.

The northern desert is marked by many riverbeds that cut through the park to the sea. Their occasional floods restrict the growth of the northern dunefields, and their waterholes allow large animals to penetrate deep into the desert. The "desert elephants" are regularly found along the courses of the Hoanib and Hoarusib rivers. Giraffe, too, frequent the riverbeds, and lions occasionally follow the rivers down to the coast. The possibility of seeing such big game animals, in addition to the more typical desert fauna, makes Skeleton Coast Park a much more interesting wildlife area than the southern Namib.

For some years, lions were absent from the Skeleton Coast, but several have recently been translocated to the Uniab River between Torra and Terrace bays. The Uniab forms a little delta at its mouth. Here, reed-encircled pools attract groups of grazing springbok and gemsbok, and these may well encourage the lions to stick around. The pools and a trickling waterfall in one of its streambeds make the Uniab a favorite hiking area; walkers there should now be extra alert because of the presence of lions. Park rangers escort a three-day backpack trip along the Ugab River. It is relatively well wooded, and was once a favorite haunt of black rhino.

Terrace Bay Rest Camp has the only catered accommodation in the park. The camp was originally a diamond mine; it was converted to a rest camp after the venture was exposed as a huge scam. Rooms are inclusive of full board. Self-service camping is only permitted at Torra Bay, but that site is only open in December and January. It is a favorite with fishermen. Bookings for accommodation or campsites in the park, or for hikes on the Ugab Trail, must be made in advance with the Reservations Office in Windhoek.

From Torra Bay, a scenic track goes eastward to the park gate at Springbokwasser, then continues toward the town of Khorixas. It is an appealing route into the wilds of Damaraland and the Kaokoveld.

North of the Hoanib River, the Skeleton Coast is a closed wilderness area. One company, Olympia Reisen, has an exclusive concession to operate in this section of the park. They run flying safaris and accommodate guests at a couple of small permanent camps. Their clients get to explore the dramatic canyon of the Hoarusib River, where the rock walls of the gorge seem to hold back mountains of sand, and clients have a chance to encounter desert elephants. They also visit the odd Roaring Dunes (yes, they rumble as you slide down) and the fur seal colony at Cape Frio. It's a wonderful area but, like all wing safaris in Namibia, the price of admission is very high.

The well-respected Skeleton Coast Safaris (the original concessionaire in the northern sector of Skeleton Coast Park) still operates excellent flying safaris in the region, but their camps are now all outside the park. They land at Terrace Bay and explore the coast by Land Rover, then fly on to camps in the remote interior valleys of the Kaokoveld.

Luderitz

Luderitz is a funny little fishing harbor set amidst the vast *Speergebiet*, the forbidden Diamond Area (a diamond-mining concession) of the southern coast. Luderitz was the original German settlement in South-West Africa and the site of a wild diamond boom after gems were discovered there in 1908. Later, mining operations shifted south toward the richer diamond fields closer to the mouth of the Orange River.

With its fine old colonial-era buildings, Luderitz retains its German flavor, a charm enhanced by the unique setting of its rocky bay. There are plenty of places to fish or explore around the shores and inlets of the Luderitz enclave, including the replica of the original Portuguese cross set up on Dias Point in 1488. Dining on crayfish (rock lobster) is a favorite activity. Birding is quite good: in addition to the normal Skeleton Coast seabirds, a colony of penguins can be viewed close to the shore on Halifax Island. For decades, travel into the surrounding Diamond Area was completely off-limits. Now the Kolmanskop Tour Company is authorized to run trips to some of the interesting places in the *Speergebiet*. These include the ghost towns of Pomona and Elizabeth Bay (where there is also a modern diamond mine), the huge seal colony at Atlas Bay, and the striking Bogenfels, a 180-foot rock arch rising from the ocean. Bookings must be made in advance to get security clearance. A permit is required (but not a tour) to visit the ghost town of Kolmanskop, which is very close to Luderitz. Kolmanskop is quite eerie, as its old buildings are being progressively buried under encroaching dunes.

Luderitz is served by Air Namibia. A visit can be included as part of a road tour in the southern part of the country. On such a road tour, "wild horses" can be seen along the way at the Garub waterhole. These feral horses are probably the descendants of animals abandoned by the German *Schutztruppe* during the First World War. Small hotels are the rule in Luderitz; the best is the *Bay View*.

The Kaokoveld: Damaraland and Kaokoland

Northwestern Namibia is one of the most fascinating parts of the country. The "Kaokoveld," as this area is called by conservationists, is a geographic buffer between the harsh deserts of the Skeleton Coast and the gentler savannas of the central plateau. Rugged and mountainous, its desert ranges spawn the flash floods that replenish the pro-Namib's thirsty river valleys and sometimes burst through to the sea. It is the territory of desert elephants and cattle-herding Himba nomads. The Kaokoveld has long been renowned for its spectacular scenery, odd geological formations, unusual wildlife, rock art, and tribal peoples. It is divided into two districts: Damaraland (now officially called Erongo) in the south, and Kaokoland (now Kunene) in the far north.

Damaraland is the more visited region, especially the southern part around the town of Khorixas, a convenient crossroads for travelers moving between the Etosha Pan and the Skeleton Coast. Several sites of geologic interest are clustered close by. The Petrified Forest features 250-million-year-old fossilized logs deposited by some ancient flood. At Burnt Mountain, colorful rocks are cached in a slag-heap of charcoal-hued desolation. Vertical basalt columns make up the Organ Pipes formation. The key attraction around Khorixas, however, is the tremendous gallery of rock engravings at Twyfelfontein. Here, thousands of individual petroglyphs are etched onto rock slabs above the "doubtful spring." These include wonderful renditions of rhinos, giraffes, zebras, antelopes, birds, and elephants. One favorite is a lion that displays a symbolic paw mark at the tip of his oddly L-shaped tail. Animal tracks, human footprints, and geometric designs are also prominent. Engravings of human figures are rare, but they appear in paintings found at the site. Although human presence at Twyfelfontein is estimated to go back 6,000 years, the identity of the artists remains uncertain.

Damaraland no longer teems with wildlife, but the animals seen in the rock engravings are all still around. Riverbeds are the most likely places to encounter desert elephants, and may yet harbor a few black rhino. After years of poaching, animals tend to be shy and are largely nocturnal. Hartmann's zebra, giraffe, steenbok, baboon, and the desert antelopes are the most likely species to be encountered. Birdlife includes such endemics as Herero chat, Damara rockrunner, and Ruppell's korhaan.

A large government rest camp at *Khorixas* offers bungalow accommodation, campsites, a restaurant, and a swimming pool. To the east of Khorixas, the comfortable 48-bed *Vingerklip Lodge* has a nice setting in the Ugab Valley facing the landmark "finger" of rock for which it is named. Close to Twyfelfontein, the *Aba-Huab Camp Site* allows a more bush atmosphere: it features A-frame shelters and hot-water showers. Elephants are sometimes seen in the valley of the Aba-Huab River. They can also be encountered around *Huab Lodge.* Located on the Huab River, it is the area's most up-market safari lodge. In addition to a pool, it has its own natural thermal spring. The *Damaraland Camp* is also in the Huab Valley. This small tented safari camp is a partnership with the local community. It has comfortable facilities and a grand vista toward the imposing mass of Brandberg. It is near Twyfelfontein and offers guided hikes and drives in search of desert elephant.

Further north, *Palmvag Lodge* is situated in an excellent elephant area. Set in a straggling grove of *Hyphaene* (makalani) palms, this seven-bungalow lodge and campsite is adequate rather than luxurious, but it has sole access to a vast concession of desert country in the upper drainage of the Uniab River. This is a prime area for desert rhinos as well as elephants, and Namibia's Save the Rhino Trust (SRT) operates special "Bicornis Safaris" out of Palmvag. Up to 12 participants spend four nights (divided between the lodge and mobile camps) with an SRT patrol, tracking and monitoring desert rhinos. Palmvag is located on the main (and only!) road leading northward to Kaokoland.

Edenteka Mountain Camp is off the main road and is only accessible by four-wheel-drive (they pick up clients at a designated parking spot). *Edenteka* is a 600-square-mile concession and tented camp operated as a wilderness wildlife reserve. Its red-rock, flat-topped buttes and boulder-strewn plains give the landscape the flavor of New Mexico, but its plant and animal life could only be Namibian. Scrub mopane and stunted leadwood grow along its washes, while clumps of *Euphorbia damarana* dominate its wide-open rocky plains. The euphorbia is a favorite food for Edenteka's most sought after residents — black rhinos. These are carefully monitored by local game guards, and have increased in number and security in the last few years. The 20-bed tented camp is comfortable but not luxurious; water is in short supply, so bucket showers (with hot water) are the rule. Walks and game drives are conducted daily. Multiday camping safaris are arranged for those who want to explore more extensively on foot or track desert rhinos.

Strange plants like the bottelboom *(the "bottle tree") are found in the deserts of the Kaokoveld. Edenteka, Namibia. Photo: Allen Bechky.*

The Kaokoveld's far north is one of the last bastions of wilderness in southern Africa. Until recently, Kaokoland — the remote territory between the Hoanib and Kunene rivers — was completely off the map as a Namibian tour destination. Aside from its wilderness mystique, Kaokoland's great attractions are its rugged scenery — particularly that along the ever-flowing Kunene River — and its Himba people.

The Himba are celebrated for their traditional way of life. In their remote and arid homeland — a region devoid of farms and fences — the Himba have been able to remain pastoral nomads, moving their herds of cattle at will through the semidesert.

The Himba are an offshoot of the Herero. Stripped of their cattle and driven into Angola by Nama raiders in the middle of the 19th century, the fortunes of these *ovaHimba* "beggars" were turned around by a charismatic hero-chief named Vita. Allying himself with the Portuguese, Vita led his warriors on a series of victorious campaigns in which they amassed cattle as booty. With their herds restocked, most of the Himba recrossed the Kunene in 1920 and spread out in the land they called *okaoko* (the "left side" or south bank of the river).

The Himba way of life still revolves around cattle. Their prized animals are not merely a source of food: they are the symbols of wealth and status. In everyday life, cattle are relied on for their milk products; slaughter is reserved mostly for ceremonial feasts on such occasions as births, marriages, initiations, and funerals. It is goats and sheep that regularly provide meat for the cooking pot. Even though Himba families keep home kraals, raising stock in semidesert conditions requires great mobility; when necessary, the menfolk still drive their herds long distances to find suitable grazing.

Unlike their Herero kin, the Himba have not given up their traditional mode of dress. A Himba woman's costume has become familiar from the ubiquitous photos of ocher-tinted, bare-breasted women that adorn Namibian tour brochures. A sensible adaptation to hot country, clothing consists of no more than an animal-skin apron or skirt. Naked torsos are heavily adorned with metal-studded belts and coiled leather necklaces, while copper bangles and beaded anklets encircle the limbs. A large white seashell often dangles conspicuously from the neck. A married woman's coiffure is particularly elaborate: the hair, woven with plant fiber and smeared with ocher, hangs in long braids and is topped with a dimpled leather headdress. Ocher-impregnated fat is smeared from head to toe, tinting the women and all their leather gear a dusky orange-brown. Himba men also go bare-chested and wear a leather skirt. Married men wear tight-fitting turbans of ochered leather or cloth, while boys sport punk hairdos with shaven sides and a braided pigtail down the back. Men, however, are increasingly adopting Western clothing.

Other changes are also coming to the Himba. The drilling of wells has encouraged permanent settlements. These and the growing numbers of their cattle have led to degradation of the fragile rangelands of the desert environment. A controversial dam on the Kunene River will displace several thousand Himba from their home kraals, yet many young men favor the dam for the jobs it is supposed to bring. Tourism, too, takes its toll: the combination of camera-happy tourists and cash-poor but photogenic subjects tends to engender bad attitudes all around. Various projects are attempting to moderate the negative cultural effects of tourism while allowing local people to profit from the sale of their handicrafts.

Some of the most awesome landscapes in the Kaokoveld occur in the country just south of the Kunene River. Here mountain ranges crowd almost to the banks of the Kunene. Tucked between their desolate ridges are beautiful sequestered valleys. Perhaps the most spectacular is the Marienfluss, where the bare blocks of desert mountains fall away sheer to the sand-filled valley floor, although some would give the prize for scenic grandeur to the even more remote Hartmann Valley. The Kunene River itself is a magic sight: a green ribbon of running water and fringing forest that cuts through a wasteland of naked rock and sand. The most celebrated spot on the Kunene is Epupa Falls, which has become a synonym for remoteness and beauty. Here the river drops 130 feet in a paradisiacal setting of makalani palms and massive baobabs. Sadly, Epupa's charms are condemned to be drowned by a hydroelectric dam. Upriver, where the Kunene first enters Namibia, is Ruacana Falls. The stretch of river between the two cataracts is a venue for rafting expeditions.

Kaokoland's isolation and lack of amenities make it accessible mostly to self-contained camping expeditions, whether operated as overland safaris or fly-in trips. Several safari companies have established small camps for their clients along the Kunene River. Epupa is the most popular destination, and a number of such campsites have sprung up there: these include *Epupa Camp* and *Omarunga Camp*, which both cater to fly-in clients. Skeleton Coast Flying Safaris keeps its own *Otjaivera Camp* on the Kunene in the remote Hartmann Valley; it also has *Nunib Camp* near Porros on the Hoarusib River and *Kuidas Camp* in the Huab Valley. On Kaokoland's southern boundary, there are two established campsites along the Hoanib River: *Khowarib Camp* is a community-owned conservation project set up with the backing of the Save the Rhino Trust. It has traditional huts and A-frame camping shelters. The nearby *Ongongo Camp* is similar, and offers swimming in a clear pool at the base of a waterfall. At both camps, visitors must bring their own equipment and food. *Fort Sesfontein*, a recreation of an original German outpost, is the only safari lodge in the area.

Etosha National Park

Etosha is one of Africa's legendary wildlife paradises. Immortalized in countless photos and documentary films, the park has become almost a mystical destination. It is the only park in Namibia to offer top-notch big game viewing and is far and away the biggest tourist attraction in the country. Visitors come expecting superb wildlife sightings. Few go home disappointed.

Etosha's unique collection of animals mixes Namibia's characteristic desert species with those of Africa's dry savannas. Herds of wildebeest and zebra join throngs of springbok and oryx on Etosha's open plains. A population of some 1,500 elephant ranges widely throughout the park, while giraffe and kudu are also abundant and widespread. Etosha is home to two of Namibia's most unusual species: the Damara dikdik and the black-faced impala. It is also Africa's foremost refuge for the black rhinoceros, and a few white rhino have recently been introduced. Another specialty, Hartmann's mountain zebra, inhabits the drier western section of the park. Etosha is also a good place to see red hartebeest, a scarce, dry-country antelope. The large number of herbivores supports a good population of predators. Some 300 lions are thought to inhabit the park, and an estimated 20,000 springbok provide ample prey for cheetahs. Both spotted and brown hyenas are found at Etosha, and leopards are quite common.

Etosha's repute rests not only on the variety and abundance of its game but on the relative ease of seeing it. In the dry season, which is the prime time for visiting, game is heavily concentrated along the southern edge of Etosha Pan, and animals are easily observed at waterholes as they come to drink.

At Etosha's heart lies the 2,400-square-mile Etosha Pan, "the great white place," from which the park takes its name. The pan is an ancient lakebed. At one time, the lake was fed by the Kunene, but it shriveled and dried when that river changed to its present course. Etosha Pan is now a vast sea of cracked white clay, a salt desert where nothing grows. Baked by sun and whipped by desert winds, its white surface is a spawning ground for mirages and dust devils. The pan still receives water from seasonal rivers that filter down from the rain-fed *oshana* waterways to the north. In normal rainy seasons, these streams carry enough water to cover some parts of the lakebed, but most of it is left dry. Only in exceptionally rainy years does the pan fill. Then Etosha Pan is again a vast lake, most of which is merely inches deep.

Although the pan itself is a virtual desert, a belt of fertile sweetveld savanna fronts its southern shore. Here, the availability of tasty vegeta-

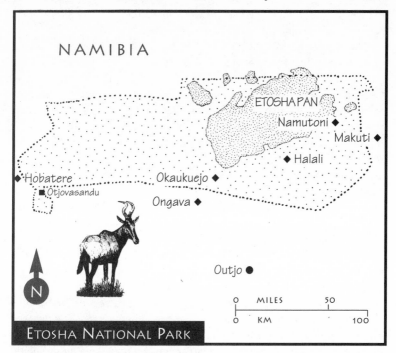

NAMIBIA

ETOSHA PAN

Namutoni ◆

Makuti ◆

◆ Halali

◆ Hobatere

Okaukuejo ◆

■ Otjovasandu

Ongava ◆

Outjo ●

N

```
0        MILES        50
0         KM              100
```

ETOSHA NATIONAL PARK

tion and permanent waterholes attract masses of game during the dry season. A carpet of short grass and dwarf shrubs covers the pan-side plains. The sweet grasses are extremely palatable to grazing animals and attract big herds of springbok, zebra, and wildebeest, while browsers such as giraffe and rhino feed on the low-growing shrubs. A series of natural springs trickle from a layer of white calcite limestone that demarcates the edge of the pan. Deeper onto the plains, woodlands appear and artesian springs shoot water to the surface. These natural "fountains" have been supplemented with man-made waterholes. The water draws a steady stream of elephants and other thirsty animals out of the dry woodlands that dominate the park's hinterlands.

Average annual rainfall in Etosha increases steadily from west (10 inches) to east (17 inches), with corresponding changes in vegetation. Away from the margins of the pan, wooded savannas dominate the eastern half of the park, while shrub and thorn savanna prevails in the west. Much of the park is covered by great tracts of mopane in guises ranging from spindly scrub to open forests. Acacia thornbush is widespread, and a variety of big trees thrive in woodlands along the rainier eastern edge of the park. The mopane and mixed woodlands are key habitat for elephants and other browsers. Elephants feed in them extensively during the wet season, then move back toward the pan to take advantage of the numerous waterholes during the dry months.

The eastern half of the park is the most prolific game area, and the only section open to the general public. It includes the whole of Etosha Pan and extends to smaller satellite pans and plains to the west of Okaukuejo. Aside from a couple of rocky outcrops at Halali, the landscape is almost unrelievedly flat. A break in the topography occurs along the park boundary to the southwest of Okaukuejo, where a long dolomite ridge is known as the Ondundozonananandana hills. This tongue-twisting name means "the place where the calves go but do not return," indicating that it is a good place for leopards. It may be, but no roads go there, so it cannot be explored.

The little-visited western half of Etosha National Park is a restricted zone, accessible only to licensed Namibian tour operators and their clients. Much of it is a featureless scrubland of mopane and acacia-terminalia bush. In the far west, however, the landscape changes radically: toward Otjovasandu, dolomite reefs and granite rock outcrops pierce the scrub, and sand-filled streambeds meander between rolling ridges. Klipspringer and hyrax live among the rocky hills, and there are even baboons at Otjovasandu—the sole place they are found in the park. The dry west is the stronghold for Etosha's eland and the prime habitat for Hartmann's mountain zebra. Only there can Hartmann's zebra be seen alongside the common plains zebra. The two species sometimes mix at the western waterholes, which are also visited by elephant, giraffe, rhino, lion, eland, and other mammals, albeit in lesser numbers than in the east.

Etosha is an excellent birding area. When the rains are good, up to a million flamingos feed on the pan and it becomes a major breeding center. Fischer's Pan, a baylike appendage attached to the eastern end of the main pan, is particularly appealing to waterbirds. Here the rainy-season floods of the Omuramba Owambo River empty into Etosha, and water usually lasts well into the dry season. Etosha is on a major migratory flyway, so a wide variety of waders and waterfowl stop off at its rainy-season pools. Birds of prey and vultures abound, as do such conspicuous grassland species as korhaans, secretary birds, bustards, and ostriches. Etosha is home to the rare and beautiful blue crane, a fashionably elegant bird with a long, streaming tail. Other attractive specialties include the rosy-faced lovebird, violet wood hoopoe, and bare-cheeked babbler. Ruppell's parrot is found in the park's wild west.

Etosha was first proclaimed a protected game area by the Germans in 1906. It was then a part of a much larger system of reserves that stretched all the way through the Kaokoveld to the Skeleton Coast and included grassy savannas to the north of Etosha Pan. The reserve's boundaries went through several revisions before 1970, when two-thirds of its territory was turned over to tribal homelands. The shrunken park was still huge, but its 8,699 square miles no longer constituted a complete ecosystem. In 1973, the park was fenced, cutting off the northern plains that were used by migrating herds during their annual circuit of the pan. Fencing disrupted animal migration patterns and created the necessity for intensive management of game populations and park vegetation.

The change of migration routes ultimately had important effects upon Etosha's wildlife. Whereas the grazing animals had formerly performed an annual loop around the pan, the herds of wildebeest, zebra, and springbok now had to migrate in a pendulum movement back and forth on an arc along its southern perimeter. Relieved of the necessity to follow the herds on northward treks, lions were able to take up long-term residence at waterholes that offered good hunting. That led to the survival of more cubs. As the lion population grew, there was a large reduction in the number of wildebeest and zebra. Eland, once common, became scarce in the eastern half of the park. Under competitive pressure from lions, wild dogs virtually vanished from the park and the cheetah population went into decline.

The introduction of artificial waterholes to supplement natural sources had other major consequences. While beneficial for game viewing, waterholes tend to concentrate animals, with the result that surrounding vegetation takes a cumulative beating over the years. Gravel pits, excavated for the maintenance of park roads, turned into rain-fed pools that became the source for outbreaks of anthrax, a highly infectious disease spread by contaminated water. Anthrax remains a persistent problem in Etosha and must be combated by disinfection and vaccination.

Anthrax, wildlife populations, and other aspects of the environment are closely monitored by the Etosha Ecological Institute, and its findings help determine park management policies. But in the long term, major threats to a fenced "island" like Etosha may lie beyond the park's boundaries. A growing human population in neighboring Ovamboland has led to increased soil erosion and tree cutting, raising the specter of damage to the region's *oshana* system of waterways. This could eventually affect the amount and quality of water reaching Etosha Pan. It's only since independence that park authorities have begun to wake up to the importance of outreach programs that assist and educate the people living around the park.

Access and Accommodation

It's a five- to seven-hour drive from Windhoek to Etosha (333 miles to Namutoni rest camp; 272 miles to Okaukuejo). Air Namibia serves Mokuti (just outside Etosha's eastern gate), the town of Tsumeb (60 miles from the same gate), and Ongava, a private game reserve just to the south of Okaukuejo. A couple of flights a week also connect Tsumeb with Victoria Falls, Zimbabwe. Car rentals are available at Mokuti and Tsumeb. A number of Namibian tour operators run scheduled flying safaris to Etosha, and charter flights can be arranged directly to landing fields at any of the park's three rest camps.

Etosha's rest camps offer air-conditioned accommodation in furnished bungalows of various sizes. Cabins have kitchen facilities, but pots and dishware are not provided. Each camp has a restaurant, shop, gas station, and swimming pool, as well as a waterhole at which game can be observed. The standards of lodging and catering at the rest camps vary because of periodic lapses in management; services generally are adequate. Camping is allowed only at the rest camps' public sites; these are not particularly attractive and have been criticized in recent years for deteriorating bathroom facilities. All Etosha rest camps are fenced to prevent the larger wild animals from wandering around within.

Okaukuejo is the park headquarters and Etosha's best known rest camp. Located near the southwestern end of the pan, the camp is ideally suited for exploring the grassy plains favored by Etosha's big herds in both wet and dry seasons. Okaukuejo is celebrated for its floodlit waterhole, where game watching takes place round the clock from the benches of its "grandstand." Elephants and rhinos regularly visit, as do seldom-seen nocturnal animals such as brown hyenas. Huge flocks of sand grouse and doves descend every evening, creating an excellent arena in which to watch African wildcats as they hunt. When lions take up residence at the waterhole, it is a likely spot to witness a kill. The only thing to disturb the excellence of the wildlife viewing is the crowd, which is sometimes overly boisterous.

For many years, nighttime viewing was an Okaukuejo exclusive, but floodlit waterholes have now been installed at Etosha's other two rest camps: Namutoni and Halali. A whitewashed, foreign legion–like fort dominates *Namutoni* camp. The original German fort was destroyed in a battle with the Ovambo in 1904. Rebuilt and enlarged, the restored fort is now used to accommodate tourists (some rooms do not have private baths). Additional accommodation is provided outside the fort. Namutoni is located close to the park's eastern Von Lindequist gate. It is in a good game area with many productive waterholes nearby. The camp is close to Fischer's Pan, so birdwatching is particularly rewarding, especially during the wet season when great numbers of flamingos are present.

Halali is located midway between Okaukuejo and Namutoni rest camps and is an excellent base for visiting nearby game-rich plains during the dry season. Halali is set at the foot of a dolomite outcrop, one of the only hills in the eastern half of the park. A walking trail on the rocky knob is good for a leg stretch as well as an opportunity to discover unusual plants. The placement of the camp waterhole affords exceptionally close-up viewing from above as animals come to drink.

Etosha's busy rest camps provide comfortable accommodation, but are by no means luxurious or noted for personal service. For that, you will have to stay outside the park. *Mokuti Lodge* is the principal tourist hotel. It is located just outside the eastern Von Lindequist gate. This large, 96-room hotel has all the amenities and has won awards naming it Namibia's best for several years running. It offers game drives in the park, as well as night drives, walks, and horseback safaris on its own grounds. Nearby (6 miles from the park gate), the 20-bed *Etosha Aoba Lodge* offers a more intimate alternative. Guests stay in thatched cabins among tamboti trees. The property fronts Fischer's Pan, where the lodge has its own lookout point.

The private Ongava Game Reserve abuts Etosha's southern boundary, near the Andersson (Ombika) gate that leads to Okaukuejo. This huge, 1,200-square-mile property does not have game populations to match Etosha's, although it is getting stocked up: both white rhinos (which are not native to the area) and black rhinos (which are) have been introduced. It does offer luxury accommodation and the freedom to explore in open 4x4 vehicles or on foot; guided game drives are conducted into Etosha (the lodge is 12 miles from the park gate). Accommodation is provided in stylish thatched chalets at the 20-bed *Ongava Lodge*. There is also a tented bush camp on the reserve.

Hobatere Lodge is located just outside Etosha's remote western gate. From this small and comfortable lodge (11 chalets), you can explore (on night drives and escorted walks) a 1,250-square-mile concession or use it as a base for visiting Etosha's restricted western region. Hobatere is a favorite stop for safari tour groups passing from the Kaokoveld into Etosha. Until (and if) a proposed new rest camp is built at Otjovasandu, Hobatere offers the only accommodation west of Okaukuejo.

Touring the Park

Wet and dry seasons contrast sharply at Etosha National Park. The dry season is the best time for big game viewing, as animals concentrate at the waterholes around the pan. The rains usually start in November and continue into April. Etosha's thirsty landscape is then transformed: the pan holds sheets of water while the plains are covered with new grass and carpets of yellow flowers. It's a great time for birding (this is when the flamingo spectacle is on), but animals are widely dispersed and more easily hidden in dense woodland foliage.

Game movements continue to take place on a seasonal basis. The great herds of grazing animals — zebra, wildebeest, and springbok — tend to move in an arc along the southern edge of the pan. During the winter dry season, they congregate along the grassy Halali Plains between Okaukuejo and Halali rest camps, and can then be seen coming in massive numbers to the waterholes in that area. With the arrival of the rains, the herds quickly trek to plains west of Okaukuejo where they find the short, sweet grasses they most relish. Sometimes large concentrations also move into the neighborhood of Fischer's Pan, near Namutoni. Large numbers of animals also gather on the Andoni Plains, north of Namutoni, at the end of the dry season.

In Etosha's main visitor area, a good network of tracks connects waterholes and viewpoints strategically placed along the eastern and southern perimeter of the pan. These tracks extend west of Okaukuejo to a small pan bordering the plains of the Grootvlakte, the rainy-season stronghold for the herds of grazing animals. Game is sparse there during the dry season, and the main attraction is then the *Sprokieswoud*, or Haunted Forest. This is an unusually large grove of bizarrely gnarled moringa trees (*Moringa ovafolia*), a fat-trunked species that can indeed conjure up fairy-tale fantasies. The public sector of the park ends at Ozonjuitji m'Bari, a pumped waterhole that attracts a variety of animals including roan antelope, which are very rare in Etosha. Beyond, a single track goes on into the restricted western zone. There are several good waterholes on the way to Otjovasandu.

Etosha's population of some 300 black rhino makes it one of Africa's main strongholds for that endangered species. After 1970, the park's resident rhino population was supplemented with animals brought in from outlying areas threatened by poachers. Their numbers have since grown to the point where "excess" rhinos are being exported to other parks and private reserves. Because rhinos are creatures of habit that drink and wallow at favorite waterholes, these animals are often seen in Etosha. They can be found in all parts of the park.

Black-faced impala (*Aepyceros melampus petersi*) are peculiar to northwest Namibia and are essentially seen only in Etosha. As their name implies, these animals are marked with a beautiful black blaze down the center of the face. Etosha's impala population grew from animals originally translocated from their native Kaokoveld, where they were virtually exterminated by poaching. They have done sufficiently well that some are now being moved back to restock the Kunene region. Black-faced impala inhabit lightly wooded savanna; they are most likely to be seen at woodland waterholes between Halali and Namutoni.

The Damara dikdik (*Madoqua kirkii*) is another Namibian specialty that is most often viewed in Etosha. This bantam—it weighs 11 pounds and stands only 15 inches high—is the smallest antelope in *southern* Africa (there are also dikdiks in East Africa, and even smaller antelopes in central Africa's tropical rainforest). With its big eyes and long twitching nose, the delicate dikdik looks too innocent to survive in the African wilds. But this little inhabitant of thickets and wooded bush knows every inch of its territory and is a deft escape artist. Dikdiks live in pairs. They are extremely territorial and will only tolerate their own immature offspring on their property: any intruding dikdik will be quickly chased off. Namutoni is the best area to observe them, especially on a track called Dikdik Drive.

At Etosha, visibility for game viewing and photography are greatly enhanced by low-growing vegetation and the flatness of the countryside. Quite startling views can be had of giraffes dipping their heads to browse a low bush, or of rhinos nibbling in the middle of an open plain. But nothing beats the show presented at the waterholes, where almost every type of animal emerges into the open. Certain waterholes, notably Sueda and Salvadora, are located at the edge of the pan and offer panoramic shots of animals backdropped against the endless whiteness of the salt flats. Other waterholes, like Olifantsbad, Rietfontein, Kalkheuwel, and Goas, are situated inside woodlands. These attract a much wider variety of animals and are favored elephant bathing spots. There are many waterholes; the best ones to visit are determined by the season, the amount of water they hold, game presence, and the time of day (some are better in morning light, others in the afternoon). It's best to inquire at the rest camps about which waterholes are most active at the time of your visit.

Etosha's waterholes are frequently guarded by lions that patiently wait for thirsty animals to approach. If you are equally patient, you have a good chance to witness a kill. Even if no lions are around, waiting to see what turns up is often just as profitable, or more so, than covering a lot of ground on game drives. A tremendous variety of animals (and birds) are attracted to water, so there is seldom a time when there is nothing to see. The relative ease of finding game makes Etosha a good park to explore on your own, if you can do without the interpretation provided on guided safaris.

Etosha is a highly regulated park, not a wilderness area. It is very popular with both tourists and residents of southern Africa, so it can get fairly crowded, which can be an annoyance to those used to safaris in Africa's more wilderness regions. The park is run according to a stringent set of rules. Rest camp gates are open between sunrise and sunset, and woe to you if you are late (you'll get a lecture and a fine). Outside the rest camps, you can get out of your vehicle only at specific toilet sites. That's a tough rule, but one needed to prevent disturbance to animals as well as to protect careless visitors from accidents.

Although probably no more dangerous than lions elsewhere, Etosha's lions have a reputation for man-eating. This may be a holdover from an incident that occurred one night in 1950, when four Ovambo men were devoured at Okondeka, on the west side of Etosha Pan. More recently, in 1994, a German became the first tourist casualty: he was taken while sleeping in the open *inside* Okaukuejo Rest Camp. The culprits were a very old, broken-toothed lioness and a male consort. The incident will no doubt add to the Etosha mystique: it illustrates that, despite fences and regulations, lions will be lions, and the park's animals are truly wild.

The North: The Caprivi Strip, Bushmanland, and the Kaudom Game Reserve

The flat Ovambo country to the north of Etosha is the most densely inhabited part of Namibia. When the rainy-season floods fill the pans and channels of its *oshana* waterways, it has a pleasant green landscape peppered with makalani palms and the labyrinthine stockades of Ovambo homesteads. In the dry season, the only time it is easy to get around, it is an overgrazed dust bowl. For the most part, Ovamboland is avoided by tourists.

The primary areas of visitor interest in northeastern Namibia are the Caprivi Strip, Bushmanland, and the Kaudom Game Reserve.

The Caprivi Strip

The Caprivi Strip is a narrow finger of Namibian territory that juts deeply eastward into central Africa. The 250-mile-long corridor divides Angola and Zambia from Botswana and runs all the way to the Zambezi River just upstream from Victoria Falls. Two other major rivers slice through the Caprivi: the Okavango and the Kwando, a river that meanders through the Linyanti Swamps before metamorphosing into the Chobe. These permanent waterways and a relatively high annual rainfall (average 20 inches) give the Caprivi region a very different environment from the rest of Namibia. Underlain by Kalahari sands, its flat countryside is dominated by deciduous savanna woodlands and seasonally flooded plains. In contrast to Namibia's deserts, this is the abode of hippopotamus and crocodiles, floodplain antelopes and waterbirds, as well as the game typical of wooded savannas. It's big game country, but most of the animals are migratory and shy.

The Caprivi's geographic isolation from the rest of Namibia makes it primarily a destination for visitors on flying safaris or for those traveling overland to Victoria Falls on the Trans-Caprivi Highway. Scheduled Air Namibia flights to Katima Mulilo make it convenient to stop off in the parks of East Caprivi while flying between Victoria Falls and Etosha or Windhoek.

Bounded by the Kwando-Linyanti-Chobe river system and the Zambezi, East Caprivi is Namibia's real swamp country: when the rivers come up in the rainy season, over 30 percent of its territory goes under water. Two national parks are located along the Kwando River: Mudumu National Park (390 square miles) fronts the river's floodplain, and just down river, Mamili National Park (1,250 square miles) fills the triangle where the Kwando takes a sharp northeastward turn and spreads out in the Linyanti Swamps. Both parks hold the gamut of bush country game and are on elephant migration routes between Zambia and Botswana's Chobe National Park. They offer much the same ambiance and environment as the Okavango Delta, with game viewing focused mostly on hippos, crocs, sitatunga, red lechwe, and aquatic birds. Mamili National Park has no tourist facilities. Inside Mudumu National Park, *Lianshulu Lodge* is a well-run, up-market safari camp with 10 thatched bungalows. In addition to game drives, it features a double-decker barge, as well as smaller boats for cruising the river. The lodge also encourages visits to the nearby Lizauli Traditional Village, a community-run project that opens a window on the crafts and culture of the Caprivian people. Upriver and outside Mudumu, but only minutes by boat from Caprivi Game Park, the 20-bed *Namushasha Lodge* offers much the same experience. Both lodges have private airstrips for charters and pick up clients coming in on Air Namibia's scheduled flights to Mpacha (about 90 miles from Mudumu). Mpacha is the airport for the district's administrative center, Katima Mulilo. Pickups are also made there for *Kalizo Fishing Camp* on the Zambezi. In addition to fishing, the camp offers mobile camping and canoe safaris in Mamili National Park. The *Impalila Island Lodge* is nicely situated at the confluence of the Chobe and Zambezi rivers, so it is convenient to overland travelers coming from Chobe in Botswana or from Victoria Falls. Its specialty is fly fishing, but the lodge also features game viewing cruises and *mokoro* (dugout canoe) explorations on the backwaters of the Chobe floodplains.

The Caprivi Game Park occupies most of the 25-mile-wide waist of the strip's 150-mile-long western portion. This mopane and Kalahari woodlands country is ranged by such animals as elephant and roan antelope, but visibility is restricted by thick vegetation and visitors are not allowed to leave the main road.

The Mahango Game Reserve is located on the west bank of the Okavango River. This 1,200-square-mile park was created to protect a portion of the riverfront environment, most of which has been severely
affected by human activities. A wide variety of aquatic and savanna
wildlife is found in the reserve, which consists of a ribbon of forest along
the riverbank, extensive reedbeds on its floodplain, and Kalahari woodlands or grassy flats further back. There are few game tracks, however,
so wildlife viewing is pretty much restricted to the riverine area. No facilities for accommodation exist in the park, but there are some at
nearby Popa Falls, and the *Ndhovu Safari Lodge* is only a mile from the
reserve gate. This tented camp is set on the banks of the river where
hippo and elephant are often seen. Ndhovu runs guided boat and vehicle excursions into the park.

Popa Falls is one of the Caprivi's better known attractions, and a
main stop-off point for overland travelers. The falls itself is merely a
rapids with a 13-foot drop, and it is completely washed out in the wet
season. But its shady riverine forest makes it a very pleasant spot. The
small *Popa Falls Rest Camp* is a popular, self-catering government
campsite offering accommodation in thatched wooden cabins. Huts and
campsites are also available at the nearby *Suclabo Lodge*.

Bushmanland

Bushmanland was originally set aside as a "homeland" for the aboriginal hunter-gatherers of the Kalahari. Their uncanny mastery of the bush
and their primordial culture have long made the San Bushmen the object
of considerable interest. (For more information about Bushmen, see the
Bushmen section of the Botswana chapter.) Bushmen can easily be encountered at farms and settlements, most notably at Tsumkwe, around
which several thousand have adopted a more sedentary lifestyle. It has
always been difficult to meet San engaged in traditional activities, but
some tour operators are now arranging safaris to meet the Bushmen. If
handled with sensitivity, such ventures enable local San to gain some income out of tourism at the same time as they preserve and enhance the
prestige of their native skills and culture. The best program is operated
by !Ha N!ore Safaris, which is a partnership with Tsumkwe's Ju'Hoan
community. Run by a former Etosha head warden, the safaris offer an
unparalleled opportunity to experience the Bushman way of life; participants learn about tool making and survival techniques as they forage
for plants and track animals with the Ju'Hoan people. The Bushmanland
portion of the Kalahari is vast, flat, featureless, and underlain with deep
sand. Roads are bad and amenities few, so visitors must put up with
some hard travel to get there (or fly in by charter) and be prepared to

camp if they want to explore. Accommodation is available in Tsumkwe at the little *Tsumkwe Lodge*.

Kaudom Game Reserve

Kaudom Game Reserve protects 1,500 square miles of Kalahari bushland. Remote and undeveloped, it is a park for the wilderness connoisseur. It has the full range of wildlife suited to the seasonally dry woodland savannas of the northern Kalahari; this includes buffalo, elephant, giraffe, tsessebe, roan antelope, kudu, eland, and red hartebeest. All the predators are present and Kaudom is notable as the only park in Namibia that has wild dogs. Game is most abundant during the hot and uncomfortable rainy season, but a number of waterholes have been put in to attract animals during the dry months. There are no lodges or safari camps near the park. There are two campsites with four-bed huts: *Kaudom*, on the north side, and *Sikereti*, in the south toward Tsumkwe. Unlike Etosha, these camps are not fenced and animals can be expected to wander through. Camping parties must consist of at least two vehicles (four-wheel-drive is mandatory) and must carry in all food, gas, and a three-day supply of water.

Waterberg Plateau Park and Neighboring Private Reserves

Several game reserves are located in the cattle ranching country between Windhoek and Etosha. Their central location makes them popular stop-off points for travelers. Such animals as kudu, eland, steenbok, cheetah, and leopard range naturally over the area, while other species have been introduced or reintroduced.

Spectacular red-rock cliffs and unusual wildlife are the signal features of the 1,600-square-mile Waterberg Plateau Park. A dramatic 25-mile-long wall of sandstone rising abruptly from an immensity of flat bushland forms the park's southern boundary. Atop the plateau, wooded savannas are home to both species of rhinoceros (until recently, the Waterberg was the only Namibian park with white rhino), as well as buffalo, roan and sable antelope, and all the game typical of the region. Birdlife is quite good and includes such Namibian endemics as Monteiro's hornbill, Damara rockrunner, and Hartlaub's francolin. The cliffs themselves are the site of the country's only breeding colony of Cape vultures. The flora of the Waterberg is also very interesting: colorful lichens cling to the rocks of the cliff face, while figs, commiphoras, and red-flowering erythrina are just a few of the many varieties of trees that make up the densely wooded slopes at the base.

The Waterberg is named for the numerous springs that emerge at the foot of the park's long wall of sandstone cliffs. It was here the Herero made their last stand against the Germans, and a small cemetery remains as a relic of the battle. The *Barnabe de la Bat Rest Camp* is set among the tangled woods beneath the cliffs. This new camp blends well with the landscape, and all its facilities are very nice. Its restaurant is located in the rebuilt Rasthaus that once served as a German police post. Tours of the plateau are conducted daily by park rangers in open vehicles; otherwise, only licensed Namibian tour operators are allowed to drive up to the plateau. Visitors can also take advantage of walking trails that loop through the bush around the rest camp. These are a boon to the birder and the botanist. One trail leads to a cliff-top viewpoint, an ascent of about 400 feet.

Backpackers can tackle the Waterberg on multiday treks. The Okarakuvisa (or Waterberg Wilderness) Hiking Trail requires a park conservator escort, while the Waterberg Hiking Trail can be taken unguided. This is rhino country, so walkers must be prepared to climb trees quickly and accept all risks. These four-day hiking excursions must be prebooked with the Reservations Office in Windhoek.

The Cheetah Conservation Fund headquarters is located at *Elandsvreugde* ("Eland's Joy"), an 18,000-acre ranch just west of the Waterberg. Guests can visit (and may be able to stay at) this research and education center, where captured cheetahs are kept until suitable locales are found for their release.

Further conservation efforts take place at *Okonjima Guest Farm*, a homey 10-cabin lodge just south of the Waterberg and the town of Otjiwarongo. The owners of this working cattle farm run the Africat Foundation and are trying to develop techniques that allow ranchers to coexist with predators. Guests can walk in the bush with tame cheetahs, or sit in a blind to watch leopards drawn to a bait. Birding is excellent.

Mount Etjo Safari Lodge is the biggest private game reserve in the area. It has been stocked with elephant, both black and white rhinos, and a variety of other game. In fact, it has gone over the top with stocking, bringing in animals such as nyala, blesbok, and waterbuck that do not even remotely belong in this habitat. Game drives at the 27-room luxury lodge are conducted in open vehicles.

The South: Red Dunes, Karakul Country, and the Fish River Canyon

The country to the south of Windhoek is primarily settled farmland in which no great tracts of wilderness were ever set aside as game parks.

The *Hardap Recreation Resort*, near Mariental, hosts a variety of plains game around the reservoir of the Hardap Dam. There is not much to interest overseas visitors there, but the rest camp is commonly used as an overnight stop by overland camping safaris.

The red dune country of the southwestern Kalahari begins just east of Mariental. The best place to appreciate the wildlife of this region is just over the border, at South Africa's Kalahari-Gemsbok National Park. (For more information about that park, see the South Africa chapter and the Kalahari section of the Botswana chapter.) That park is too far out of the way to be included on Namibian tour itineraries, so the principal alternative is *Intu Africa Game Lodge*, a private reserve near Mariental. The place is stocked with game (including leopards) and, in a new twist, with Bushmen, several families of whom have been resettled on the reserve. Game drives in open vehicles, bush walks, and demonstrations by Bushmen are the featured activities. Luxury accommodation is available in the main lodge or in two satellite tented camps. A campsite serves as the base for walking expeditions led by Bushman guides.

Duwisib Castle is just that — a stone castle painstakingly constructed in the desert for a German nobleman and his American wife. After completion in 1909, it was furnished royally with European artwork and antiques, then abandoned after the husband's death in the First World War. Now government-owned, the castle is open to the public. A small campsite is located there, and guest farm accommodation can be found nearby at the *Haruchas Guest Farm*. Duwisib is near the town of Maltahohe and can be visited by those traveling southward from the Sesriem-Sossusvlei area to Luderitz or the Fish River Canyon. There is excellent arid-country scenery along the way, but all the land is in private hands. Some of the farms on the eastern edge of Namib-Naukluft Park have facilities for campers; accommodation is available at *Namtib Desert Lodge* and *Sinclair Guest Farm*.

The vast and barren plains of southern Namibia are karakul sheep country, where the lambs are raised to produce the expensive Nakara leather. Some of the towns here have historic interest: Bethanie is the site of the Schmelen House that belonged to the first German missionary. The house is a national monument that dates back to 1814. Keetmanshoop, now the center of the karakul industry, was also a German colonial town and has a stone church built in 1895. This is the land of the Nama tribe, and many of the people working its farms and villages belong to that distinctive group. The chief places of natural history interest in the area are the Quiver Tree Forest and the crater of Brukkaros Mountain. Few visit the zone of desolation around the crater, but the massive remains of this once-violent volcano are visible along the main road between Mariental and Keetmanshoop. The quiver tree, or *koker-boom* (*Aloe dichotoma*), is the largest and most distinctive of Africa's aloes. Its branches are hollowed out to make the container in which San carry poisoned arrows. Tree-sized and multibranched, the quiver tree is widespread in the semideserts of central and southern Namibia, where specimens are normally found as isolated individuals or in small groups. In the Quiver Tree Forest, an unusually large grove has been declared a national monument. It's on private land, and the owners have put up the *Quiver Tree Rest Camp* to serve campers.

The most famous attraction in southern Namibia is the Fish River Canyon. Although comparisons with the Grand Canyon are exaggerated (it lacks the vibrant colors), the scenery provided by the chasm is certainly splendid. Here, the river has carved a series of U-bends that wind through magnificent, steep-walled buttes and gorges. In places, the canyon is 16 miles wide from rim to rim and up to 1,800 feet deep. Furthermore, the chasm is encountered unexpectedly, for it is cut into a flat and stoney-surfaced plateau. The setting is harsh and bare, relieved only by the sparse greenery of quiver trees, smaller aloes, and succulent euphorbias. The river flows only in rainy-season spate, but pools hold water throughout the year.

Although the canyon is 100 miles long, only about half its length is included in Fish River Canyon Park. A 36-mile road along its eastern rim provides access to a couple of scenic overlooks. The road ends by winding down to the floor of the lower canyon, where accommodation and camping are available at the *Ai-Ais Hot Springs Resort*. At this popular rest camp and spa, mineral-rich scalding water is piped to both indoor and outdoor pools. Camping is permitted at the main canyon viewpoint, where there are shelters and toilets. *Hobas*, which is about 6 miles from that lookout, is the preferred campsite because it has proper cooking and washing facilities. Campers can also find secluded sites (each with its own toilet and bathroom) outside the park at the *Canyon Restaurant and Campsite*, a privately owned complex 15 miles from the main viewpoint. It is part of a coalescing private reserve (to be called Gondwana Canyon Nature Park). Regular tourist-class lodging near the Fish River Canyon is found on the Gondwana reserve at *Canyon House* and at *Canyon Lodge*. The 10-bed Canyon House is located on a branch canyon about 35 miles north of Fish River Canyon's main viewpoint. The 40-bed Canyon Lodge is closer to the main road and only 12 miles from the viewpoint. Set among granite boulders, its modern chalets have natural rock walls and thatched roofs, while its restaurant is a restored 1910 farmhouse. The modern *Canyon Hotel* and the *Pension Gessert* (a bed-and-breakfast) are in Keetmanshoop, which is about 90 miles from the main viewpoint. A shuttle bus runs daily between Keetmanshoop and the Fish River Canyon.

While most visitors have to be content with views from the top, fit walkers can trek the canyon floor. Indeed, the Fish River Canyon is one of southern Africa's classic walking trails. The route runs from the main viewpoint to Ai-Ais, a distance of over 50 miles. Along the way, there are great views, the Sulphur Hot Springs, and pools that give sanctuary to barbel and yellow fish. Birdlife is good and there are mountain zebra and leopard around, but the most likely mammals to be seen are klipspringer, hyrax, and baboon. The trail is open from May through September. It is very popular and difficult to book, which must be done well in advance with the Reservations Office in Windhoek. Hikers must present their credentials (and a recent doctor's certificate of fitness) at Hobas before starting out. Hikes can also be undertaken on private land in the upper part of the canyon. The Canyon House is a good base for hikes, and Gondwana Tours offers guided trekking or backpacking expeditions.

The southernmost part of Namibia is botanically interesting but difficult to explore. It has many weird and wonderful desert-adapted plants that are related to those of Namaqualand in South Africa. These include various aloes, *Lithops* ("living stones" that hide themselves in pebbly areas), mesembryanthemums ("ice plants" that form huge masses of flowers), and stapilias (which have star-shaped, foul-smelling flowers that attract flies for pollination). Among the most conspicuous are the *halfmens* ("half-human") or *Pachypodium namaquanum*. These have a tall unbranched stem with a little "head" of greenery at the very top. They can be seen in the rocky mountains that flank the Orange River.

Canoe and rafting trips on the Orange River are beginning to become popular. Most are arranged by South African tour operators and start at the border at Vioolsdrif (Noordoewer on the Namibian side). They tour the river that bounds one of South Africa's newest sanctuaries, the Richtersveld National Park. (For more information on that park, see the South Africa chapter.)

CHAPTER NINE

South Africa:
The Fairest Cape

S ET BETWEEN THE CLEMENT SHORES of the Indian Ocean and
the cold waves of the Atlantic, South Africa is possessed of a stunning
variety of landscapes and climates. Indeed, it has long been promoted as
"a world in one country," and many consider it the most beautiful part
of the continent. Yet for all its natural attractions, South Africa's notorious heritage of racial discrimination has kept it a pariah nation for
most of the last 50 years. Now, with the birth of its new multiracial
democracy, the country looms as a giant among African travel destinations.

South Africa's size and placement at the tip of the continent give it a
geographical diversity unmatched in southern Africa. It is divided into
starkly different climatic zones, each with its own natural habitats. Although mostly outside the zone of the tropics (the Tropic of Capricorn
passes through the Northern Transvaal), the warm waters of the Indian
Ocean influence the climate of the eastern part of the country. Wooded
savannas dominate lower elevations and reach down the coast all the
way to the Eastern Cape. South Africa's premier big game sanctuaries
are found in the Lowveld of the eastern Transvaal and the savannas of
northern KwaZulu-Natal. A subtropical climate prevails along the eastern seaboard, where hot summer temperatures are balanced by a delightfully balmy winter season. These conditions make the coast of
KwaZulu-Natal and the Eastern Cape a seaside vacation paradise.

A great arc of mountain escarpment divides the lowlands of the Transvaal and Natal regions from the inland plateau known as the Highveld. The grassy prairies of the Highveld once supported vast herds of game, but those have vanished: the region was long ago converted into South Africa's agricultural and industrial heartland. With elevations above 5,000 feet, the Highveld is subject to bitterly cold winter weather. Snow can fall on the Highveld, and it regularly carpets the heights of the escarpment mountain ranges. The flat-topped mountain giants of the Natal Drakensberg often carry a mantle of winter snow. Snow also whitens the Maluti Mountains of the Lesotho highlands, a region of montane grassland that forms the headwaters of South Africa's largest river, the Orange. The Drakensberg thus forms the country's great divide of watersheds: to the north and west, streams eventually join the Vaal-Orange river system that runs into the Atlantic, while streams spawned on the steeper eastern flanks of the mountains tumble down toward the Indian Ocean.

The climate grows progressively drier to the west of the Highveld plains. The Kalahari Desert reaches down into the Northern Cape Province along the Botswana border. Further south, Kalahari sands merge into the stony vastness of the Karoo, a region of arid scrubland that dominates the interior heartland of the western half of the country. Winters in the Kalahari and Karoo are bitterly cold and dry, while summers are brutally hot and marked by scattered thunderstorms. Dry conditions prevail all the way to the Atlantic coast, where the deserts of Namaqualand and the Richtersveld are renowned for their spectacular displays of springtime wildflowers.

At the southwestern tip of the continent, the Western Cape is strongly influenced by its position as the meeting place of the Atlantic and Indian oceans. The waters of the South Atlantic are chilled by the Benguela Current as it rushes northward from Antarctica. This cold stream brushes against Africa's west coast and is responsible for its dry climate. Unlike the rest of southern Africa, the southwestern Cape has a pattern of winter rainfall; its rains come between April and September, the reverse of all the territories to the north. Winters in the southwestern Cape are cold and rainy, while summers are only moderately warm. This temperate climate has produced the Cape's unique zone of fynbos vegetation. Fynbos habitat is superficially similar to the scrubby *maquis* of the Mediterranean and to California's chaparral. Yet it is so botanically distinct, and so rich in species, that it is considered one of the world's six "floral kingdoms." For all its interest to botanists, however, the Cape is most celebrated for a nonnative species: its grapes produce some of the world's finest wines. Rugged mountains and fertile valleys characterize the Cape's wine country and extend eastward to the hinterlands backing

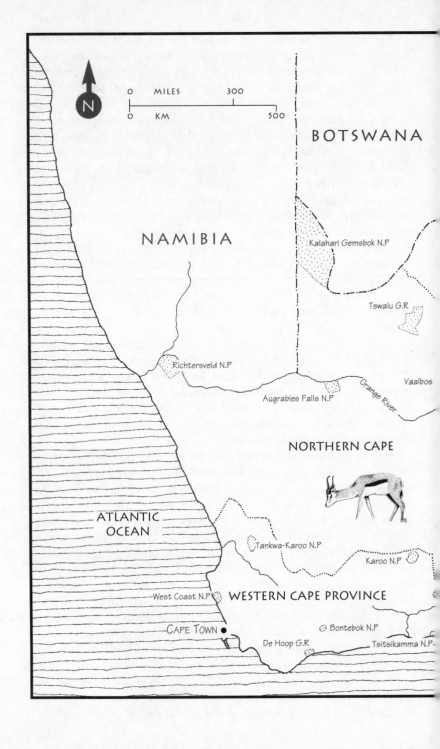

N

0   MILES   300

0   KM   500

BOTSWANA

NAMIBIA

Kalahari Gemsbok N.P

Tswalu G.R

Richtersveld N.P

Augrabies Falls N.P

Orange River

Vaalbos

NORTHERN CAPE

ATLANTIC
OCEAN

Tankwa-Karoo N.P

Karoo N.P

West Coast N.P

WESTERN CAPE PROVINCE

CAPE TOWN

Bontebok N.P

De Hoop G.R

Tsitsikamma N.P

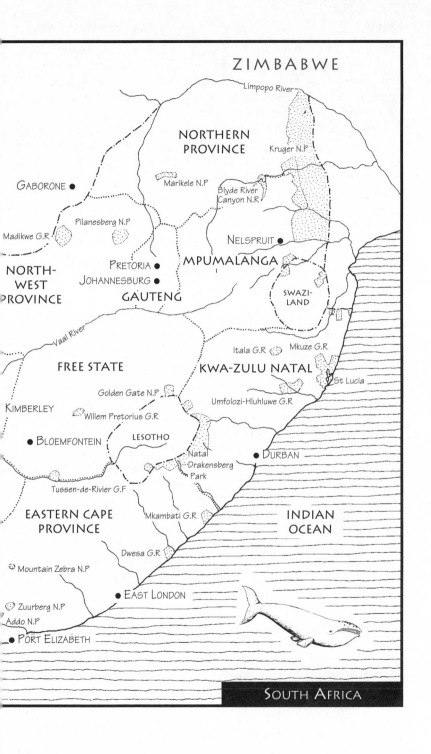

ZIMBABWE

Limpopo River

NORTHERN
PROVINCE

Kruger N.P

Marikele N.P

GABORONE ●

Blyde River
Canyon N.R

Pilanesberg N.P

Madikwe G.R

NELSPRUIT ●

NORTH-
WEST
PROVINCE

MPUMALANGA

PRETORIA ●
JOHANNESBURG ●

GAUTENG

SWAZI-
LAND

Vaal River

Itala G.R   Mkuze G.R

FREE STATE

KWA-ZULU NATAL

St Lucia

Golden Gate N.P

Umfolozi-Hluhluwe G.R

KIMBERLEY

Willem Pretorius G.R

● BLOEMFONTEIN

LESOTHO

Natal
Drakensberg
Park

● DURBAN

Tussen-de-Rivier G.F

EASTERN CAPE
PROVINCE

Mkambati G.R

INDIAN
OCEAN

Dwesa G.R

◌ Mountain Zebra N.P

◌ Zuurberg N.P
Addo N.P

● EAST LONDON

● PORT ELIZABETH

SOUTH AFRICA

the lovely stretch of Indian Ocean coastline known as the Garden Route. The beauty of the Cape of Good Hope earned it the famous sobriquet, "the fairest Cape of them all." Certainly Cape Town, nestled between the cliffs of Table Mountain and the rocky bays of the Atlantic, is one of the most beautiful cities in the world.

South Africa's history has been troubled by racial strife and prejudice. Colonization began there more than 200 years before it seized hold on the rest of the continent, and extended for a generation after it ended elsewhere. South Africa is the only sub-Saharan country where a large European population took root. One white community, the Afrikaners, goes back a very long time.

The Dutch first settled at Cape Town in 1652, about 30 years after they established their North American colony on Manhattan Island. Cape Town was founded by the Dutch East India Company as a refitting station for ships plying the route to and from their colonies in the spice islands of Indonesia. The site was chosen because of the landmark shape of Table Mountain and the availability of the fresh water that tumbled from its springs. When the Dutch arrived, they encountered two groups of click-speaking Khoisan people living in the western Cape: the Khoi, who the Dutch called Hottentots, and the San, who became known as Bushmen. The Khoi already kept cattle and were easily drawn into trade. Most soon found themselves forced to work as servants. The San hunter-gatherers never accepted the concepts of domestic animals or private property and readily hunted the Dutchmen's cattle: from the beginning, they were despised as much as any predatory wild animal, although their poison arrows were more feared. Extermination proved their lot. The Hottentots were enslaved, and their culture collapsed. Through sexual exploitation, their racial traits became increasingly mixed with white blood, and they eventually came to be known as Cape Coloureds.

Although the Dutch East India Company showed little interest in set-tling the hinterlands, a steady stream of colonists escaped the confines of Cape Town to establish farms in the region's fertile river valleys. In the 1690s, an influx of French Huguenots escaping religious civil war in France arrived to augment the tiny Dutch population. The Huguenots quickly blended with the Dutch, but left an enduring legacy: they brought a knowledge of viticulture and started the wineries that were to make the Cape one of the premier wine-making districts in the world. As the white population grew, young men were constantly going off to es-tablish their own farms in the wilderness, with the result that the fron-tier of the colony was always growing to the east. Hottentot slaves were taken to work the new farms. For several generations, this expansion went on unhindered; when the Dutch encountered the Bantu-speaking

Xhosa people of the eastern Cape, they met their first serious resistance. The frontier thereafter became a place of almost continual racial warfare, just as it did on the fringes of the European colonies in North America.

By 1800, Dutch farms were spread all over the southwestern Cape region. During the Napoleonic wars, a Dutch alliance with the French led the British to seize Cape Town to protect their sea route to India. After Waterloo, the British decided to stay. The Cape Dutch had by that time evolved a way of life and a language quite different from those of their European forebears: rooted in their experiences on the southern continent, they had become Afrikaners. The settlers, especially the ultraindependent frontier *Boers* (farmers), didn't like British authority. They grew especially restive after 1834, when slavery was prohibited in the British Empire. Grumbling led first to a small and unsuccessful revolt, then to a major exodus. In 1835, bands of Boers spanned their ox wagons and marched northeastward into the wilderness: the Great Trek had begun.

The *voortrekkers* (pioneers) encountered only scattered bands of Hottentots and San in the thirstlands of the Karoo. As they climbed onto the prairies of the Highveld, they found those grasslands uninhabited, too: the resident tribes had been annihilated or uprooted in the carnage of the *mfecane,* the regional tribal warfare of the 1820s. The exact degree of depopulation is a controversial topic, as it may have been exaggerated later to justify occupation of the land. The territory had certainly been ravaged in the *mfecane* wars, but it's likely that its Basotho and Tswana survivors stayed well hidden from the white strangers. It's also well documented that the trekkers met King Mzilikaze and his Matabele tribe when they reached the Transvaal, and sent them fleeing into what is now Zimbabwe. Whatever the truth of the matter, it became an article of Afrikaner lore that the Highveld was uninhabited at the time of their arrival.

There is no dispute that the trekkers found the land well occupied when their columns spilled down the escarpment into Natal: that was the territory of the Zulu nation built by the Zulu warrior-founder Shaka. The dramatic events that followed ultimately became the core of the Afrikaner mythos. A peace parley at the kraal of Dingane (the Zulu king), at which Piet Retief and his men were massacred, was immediately followed by bloody Zulu assaults on the Boer wagon trains. The Boers rallied and went on to defeat the Zulus at the Battle of Blood River in 1838. That lopsided victory has ever after been commemorated on the Day of the Covenant, thus fulfilling the Boer leader Andries Pretorius's prebattle vow that the Afrikaner people would hold the day eternally sacred if God granted *voortrekker* victory. All this had the spiritual effect of confirming the Afrikaners' belief in divine backing for their occupation of the land and convincing them of their own invincibility in their struggles with the blacks. Images of embattled pioneers, their wagons circled in the defensive *laager* to repel the onslaughts of multitudes of warlike savages, were thereafter deeply inscribed in the collective memory of Afrikaner culture.

The trekkers went on to establish a Boer republic in Natal. If the impetus for the trek had been to escape the British, however, it didn't work. In 1824, British traders had founded a settlement at Port Natal (which would later become Durban). After defeating the Zulus, the *voortrekkers* tried and failed to dislodge the British by force of arms. By 1843, the British formally laid claim to Natal. A few Afrikaner settlers accepted British authority; the rest joined new trek columns that rolled on to settle further north, in the Transvaal.

The trekkers ultimately set up two Boer republics, the Orange Free State and the Transvaal. Although a certain amount of tension with the British was caused by the trekkers' endless seizures of African land, the Boer republics were pretty much left to go their own way: the British recognized their independence in 1852. The discovery of diamonds near Kimberley in 1867 led to the arrival of tens of thousands of English prospectors. Fortunes were made, most notably by the new immigrant Cecil Rhodes, and the Cape Colony suddenly assumed great importance in British eyes. Newly rich, it was granted self-government in 1872. A few years later, the British began to push for a federation in South Africa, one that would unite the Cape and Natal colonies with the Boer republics.

The Boers didn't want anything to do with plans for a South African union, but the British had another obstacle to deal with first: the Zulus. Although Cetshwayo, the Zulu king at that time, had lived peaceably with the British in Natal, his army was large and it was deemed necessary to the politics of federation that he should be disarmed. The resulting war in 1879 was a disaster: the first British invasion force was wiped out at the famous battle of Isandlwana; a second, and more cautious, military expedition thereafter succeeded in laying waste to Zululand and its army. Cetshwayo was sent into exile, but a figurehead Zulu monarchy was kept in place.

Attention then refocused on the Boer republics. The British officially annexed the Transvaal, but the Boers wouldn't submit: led by Boer leader Paul Kruger, independence was secured in 1881 by Boer victories in a lightning war. British interest never really waned, however, and was soon greatly inflamed by the gold rush to the Transvaal that began in 1886. Almost overnight, the new city of Johannesburg sprang up around the gold-rich Witwatersrand (the "Rand") discovery site, and railroads, riches, and British colonists soon flooded into the country. Political and diplomatic machinations between the British and Boers led to increasing bitterness, especially after Cecil Rhodes became the prime minister of the Cape Colony. Ever the empire builder, Rhodes sponsored the 1896 Jameson Raid on the Transvaal, a failed attempt to launch a coup d'état and a British takeover.

Ultimate catastrophe was realized in the Anglo-Boer War of 1899–1902. After an initial string of victories, the Boers set about besieging the strongholds of Kimberley and Ladysmith, only to be crushed by overwhelming numbers of British reinforcements. The occupation of Johannesburg and Pretoria soon followed. But the Boers wouldn't give up: their commandos took to the veld to wage guerrilla warfare. The British reacted by rounding up the civilian Afrikaner population and putting them in concentration camps, a military innovation that led to the deaths of thousands of women and children. This tragedy left a legacy of bitterness that was to inform the policies of Afrikaner nationalists for several generations.

At war's end, the country was wrecked but the British and moderate Boer leaders worked rapidly toward reconciliation. By 1910, the Transvaal and the Orange Free State (renamed the Orange River Colony) had been given parliamentary self-government, and all the colonies were combined in the Union of South Africa. Although the Afrikaners formed the bulk of the European population (the black Africans were, of course, unrepresented), the former Boer generals Louis Botha and Jan Smuts ran a conciliatory pro-British government and were able to block hard-line Afrikaner nationalists from revolting and allying with the Germans during the two world wars. (During the Second World War, many of the leaders of the National Party were openly pro-Nazi.)

What were the black Africans doing while all this was going on? In the 19th century, they were buffeted by land seizures and military defeat. Later, the boom in mining for diamonds and gold created a demand for black labor, but they had no means of organization. For a long time, blacks had to depend on their traditional chiefs to petition for grievances with the various white governments. It was not until the creation of the Union of South Africa that blacks began to form nationwide political groups. In 1912, the Union government passed the first law designed to foster the legal separation of the races: it limited where blacks could own land and restricted the movements of Indians, who had immigrated in large numbers to the Natal coast. In response, a young lawyer named Mohandas Gandhi organized mass protest demonstrations in Natal (a warm-up for his more celebrated exploits in India), while a handful of educated Africans banded together to form the African National Congress. The ANC pressed the government for protection of black rights, but the movement remained small until the advent of apartheid.

The policy of apartheid, the complete separation of society according to race, came into effect in 1948 after the National Party's victory in the elections. The National Party was dominated by conservative Afrikaners who were ideologically racist and deeply resentful of the British, whom they regarded as having stolen their country. The Nationalists set about establishing apartheid as the law of the land. The Group Areas Act absolutely segregated land ownership according to race, while the Population Registration Act ensured that race was certified at birth. The whole machinery of white domination — passbooks, pseudo-independent tribal homelands, repression — was loosed upon a black population already lacking political rights or workplace equality. The Nationalists also reorganized the electoral process to ensure that the English population, and any liberal parties opposed to apartheid, had no chance of getting into power. As a final snub to the English, the Nationalists left the British Commonwealth and declared the Republic of South Africa in 1961.

As repression increased after 1948, so, too, did the activities of the African National Congress. The postwar economy boomed, drawing black workers to the cities where they were more amenable to unionization and political action. The ANC was closely allied with the Communist Party; both organizations supported armed insurrection and were subsequently outlawed. ANC leaders Nelson Mandela and Walter Sisulu were imprisoned for life in 1964, while Oliver Tambo and Joe Slovo escaped to exile in Zambia.

Needless to say, the struggle for black rights didn't end there. Both political and armed resistance increased even as the government unrolled new schemes to support the racist state. "Independent homelands" for blacks were created within South Africa. These lands — KwaZulu, Ciskei, Transkei, Bophuthatswana, and a few smaller ones — were supposed to be internally self-governing countries, but they were never recognized by any foreign nations. In 1974, Chief Mangosuthu Buthelezi started his Inkatha Freedom Party, a legal antiapartheid organization with widespread support among the powerful Zulus of Natal. Demonstrations in South Africa periodically turned into bloody scenes that led to international condemnation. As long as the South African economy held strong, the government was able to snub its nose at world opinion. In the 1980s, that economy went into a dive and international pressure was stepped up. United States sanctions against trade with South Africa went into effect in 1986, hurting an already teetering economy. Voices cried out worldwide for the release of Nelson Mandela.

The story of Mandela's passage from prison inmate to resident of the president's mansion is as inspiring as it is unbelievable. Few people imagined that the talks begun from prison in 1988 would lead to his victory in the country's first democratic all-races election in 1994. A number of background factors contributed, not the least of which were the end of the Cold War and the tacit agreement of the corporate leaders of the South African business community that the time for change had come. Nonetheless, full marks go to Mandela and to the former president, Frederick "F. W." de Klerk. They managed to negotiate and deliver on a peaceful transition that few would have thought possible. Walking a dangerous path between right-wing Afrikaners and militant black revolutionaries and stepping around tribal as well as racial divisions, Mandela and de Klerk succeeded in cobbling together a constitutional formula for a multiracial democratic state. Even if this experiment in democracy should ultimately fail, Mandela's place in history is certainly assured.

Yet fail it might, for despite the euphoria surrounding Mandela's accession to power, the problems faced by the reborn South Africa are legion. Throughout the 1970s and 1980s, many kids in the sprawling African townships spent more time in the streets than going to school. Those youths now form a poorly educated and not-too-employable underclass. Their expectations for a better life have been considerably raised, however, as have those of all black South Africans. The future prosperity of the country depends on stability and economic growth that can keep the whites secure in their lifestyle while improving the lot of the black majority. As the civil rights movement showed in America, getting political rights is easier than attaining economic equality. Even with the best intentions in the world, the next years will be difficult for South Africa. Many observers fear the passing of Mandela, though his heir apparent, Deputy President Thabo Mbeki, appears to be equally committed to economic moderation and racial reconciliation. As South Africa grapples with its social problems, it remains to be seen if it will decline into the bureaucratic chaos and corruption that has bedeviled so many African nations or be forged into a working economic powerhouse that will light a beacon for the continent. In the meanwhile, the country has ratified a constitution that is the envy of civil libertarians around the world.

Under the new constitution, the huge Cape and Transvaal provinces have been broken up. The old Cape Province was divided into three new provinces: the Eastern Cape Province, which is subtropical in climate and includes the reabsorbed Xhosa "homelands" of Ciskei and Transkei; the Western Cape Province, the heart of the original Dutch colony around Cape Town; and the Northern Cape Province, which is a vast and lightly inhabited semidesert country. The old Transvaal was similarly reapportioned into the eastern Mpumalanga ("the place where the sun rises"), Northern, and North-West provinces, while the Johannesburg-Pretoria metropolitan area became the province of Gauteng. The Orange Free State and Natal were rechristened the Free State and KwaZulu-Natal provinces, but kept their original borders. The seat of the national government remains divided between Cape Town (where parliament meets), Pretoria (the administrative center), and Bloemfontein (the location of the Supreme Court).

South Africa is a large and ethnically diverse country: more than 40 million people share its land mass, which is about three times the size of California. Some 60 percent of the population lives in urbanized areas. The black population is broken into a number of major ethnic groups; although they are now well mixed in the country's big cities, each still has its traditional geographic stronghold. The Zulu and the Xhosa are the largest groups. Each numbers about 7 million, and their political rivalry is one of the country's major arenas of potential trouble. The Zulu home territory is in KwaZulu-Natal. The Xhosa have their stronghold in the Eastern Cape Province. The Tswana (about 3.5 million), whose "homeland" was the archipelago of tiny enclaves known as Bophuthatswana, are concentrated in the North-West Province. The South Sotho or Basotho (2.5 million), kin to the people of Lesotho, live primarily in the Free State Province. The North Sotho group (3.4 million) is composed of the Pedi and Lobedu peoples who inhabit the Northern Province along with the Ndebele and Venda (each less than a million), while the Shangaan or Tsonga (over a million) live in the Lowveld of the eastern Transvaal (Mpumalanga Province). South Africa also has about a million Swazis living on its side of the border with Swaziland. The Western and Northern Cape provinces are home to some 3.5 million Cape Coloured people, as well as a small population of Cape Malays who are the descendants of servants imported from Indonesia by the Dutch. Most of South Africa's Indians (about 1.2 million) live in Natal, to which they emigrated in the last century to work in the sugarcane fields. The white population (5.5 million) is mixed between people of Dutch and English heritage, along with a good admixture of Portuguese (who flooded into the country after the collapse of the colonies of Angola and Mozambique). There are also other Europeans who emigrated to South Africa after the Second World War. Afrikaners make up about 60 percent of the total white population.

South Africa is an anomaly among African nations in that it is a highly developed country with a thoroughly modern economic infrastructure. Diamonds and gold were the original engines for producing the country's wealth, and mining continues to be a crucial and productive industry. Yet farming and manufacturing of all sorts make South Africa the colossus of African economies. Even during the years of official boycott and confrontation with black-ruled Africa, it remained the breadbasket, supermarket, and employer to its neighbors. Its domination of the economies of the region was and is near complete. The apartheid state's quest for independence and security in the face of international isolation actually spurred the development of important industries — notably the production of synthetic fuels and armaments. A sophisticated power grid, a network of excellent roads, modern domestic rail and air systems, and the ready availability of motor vehicles make transportation in South Africa a breeze.

For all its wealth and modernity, however, South's Africa's split of the economic pie is badly divided along racial lines. Most of the white population (although by no means all) live a middle-class consumer life analogous to that of their counterparts in the United States: they live in lovely private homes (often with spacious gardens and swimming pools), and they possess cars, CD players, computers and all the other accouterments of consumer society. They also have the income to enjoy sports, travel, and the outdoors. The contrast between the good life of Johannesburg's swank northern suburbs and that of the nearby townships of Soweto and Alexandra could hardly be more complete. Although there are wealthy and middle-class black Africans living in the townships, life within the townships is overall pretty grim — housing is monotonous and transportation is crowded. Never mind that black South Africans enjoy greater prosperity than citizens in other African countries: it is against their white neighbors that they weigh their circumstances, and they have found them wanting.

South Africa has had a profound influence in the field of African conservation. Alone among African nations, it harbors an array of protected nature reserves within the boundaries of a highly modern industrialized society. Its conservation efforts go back a long time and are instructive — perhaps crucial — for pointing the way to the future of wild Africa.

When the first Europeans reached its shores, South Africa was a wildlife paradise. Elephants wandered right down to the southern Cape, where there were also enough herds of antelope and quagga (a curious half-striped zebra) to support the big-maned subspecies of Cape lion. As the Dutch penetrated deeper into the interior, they continually discovered new types of animals: black rhino, mountain zebra, bluebuck, and bontebok were all common. They found great concentrations of game on the plains of the Karoo. Quaggas were plentiful there, and springbok lived in such numbers that they indulged in migrations in which untold thousands poured past the same point for days on end. Vast herds of

Burchell's zebra, blesbok, and black wildebeest inhabited the grasslands of the Highveld. The wooded savannas of Natal and the bushveld of the Transvaal teemed with game of every description. Herds of elephants, both white and black rhinos, hippos, giraffes, and the whole panoply of African big game were found in South Africa in great abundance. Everywhere, wild animals lived in such profusion that few settlers or explorers imagined that the wildlife could ever be eliminated. Probably fewer cared: unregulated mass slaughter was the rule and, region by region, South Africa's wildlife vanished as European civilization advanced. By the end of the last century, South Africa's wildlife was mostly gone. The fauna of the Cape was hardest hit: there the Cape lion, bluebuck, and quagga had been driven to total extinction. Elsewhere, the devastation wrought by rifles was abetted by the great rinderpest epidemic of the 1890s, and the destruction of wildlife was near complete. The massive herds of the Karoo and the Highveld had vanished. Elephants, too, had virtually disappeared: in the eastern Cape, a mere handful held out in the dark of the Knysna Forest and the impenetrable thickets of the Addo bush, while a few odd survivors roamed the Transvaal's Lowveld bush country. Elephants had been completely wiped out in Natal, where a last score of white rhino were known to be holding out.

Just in the nick of time, a few visionaries began to repent the destruction and took steps to save what little wildlife remained for future generations. In 1895, Africa's first game reserves were created when the province of Natal set aside refuges for its beleaguered white rhinos. In 1898, the Transvaal's president, Paul Kruger, proclaimed the Sabie Game Reserve. These sanctuaries turned out to be the kernels that would grow into South Africa's splendid collection of parks and nature reserves. Despite fierce opposition from ranchers and developers, the game reserves gradually gained public support. The Sabie Game Reserve eventually was expanded and became Kruger National Park in 1926, while Natal's Hluhluwe and Umfolozi game reserves — which actually did save the white rhino from extinction — were only the first in an extraordinary system of provincial parks.

Over the years, many additional areas were set aside to preserve the remnants of South Africa's natural heritage. Both the national parks and parks in Natal grew in number, and those reserves were supplemented by other government-run and private sanctuaries. With so much of its wilderness already fenced or plowed, however, the tracts devoted to wildlife protection were generally small. Among the national parks, only Kruger and the Kalahari-Gemsbok were large enough to support the full range of wildlife natural to their ecosystems. Elsewhere, small pockets of wilderness habitat were turned into nature reserves. Several refuges —

Once near extinction, the white rhino is now commonly seen in the parks of South Africa. Mkuzi Game Reserve, South Africa. Photo: Allen Bechky.

notably Mountain Zebra, Bontebok, and Addo Elephant national parks — were created primarily for the benefit of individual endangered species. Others were designed to protect sites of special scenic or botanical value. Whatever their original purpose, each sanctuary preserved whole communities of plants and animals. Here a wetland was preserved, there a small tract of mountain fynbos or a relict indigenous forest was protected. In recent years, a number of new national parks have been established and there has been a tremendous surge in the development of private game reserves. Today, several hundred nature reserves are spread across the breadth of South Africa.

South Africa not only led the way with the establishment of the continent's first fully protected game reserves, it also pioneered the creation of parks where wildlife could be appreciated by the public. A park has to serve double-duty by providing a home for wild animals while allowing people to enjoy the wilderness in safety. Much of the ground-breaking work in the previously unknown science of park building was done at Kruger National Park. Poaching had to be quashed and waterholes built to serve the needs of animals that could no longer migrate to their old dry-season ranges. Rest camps were designed to offer guest accommodation. Roads were cut and rules were developed to allow visitors to explore in vehicles. As time went on, new concepts of game management came increasingly into play. Species that had become locally scarce or absent were restocked from areas where they could still be found. Culling was introduced. At first, culling was meant to encourage the growth of animal populations by eliminating predators. Later, as game populations grew large, it was determined that the numbers of some species — particularly elephant — had to be regularly trimmed. The policies and management techniques worked out at Kruger were later extended to other game parks in South Africa and served as models elsewhere in southern Africa, especially in Zimbabwe and Namibia.

Today, South Africa can boast with some justification that its wildlife and parks are the "best managed" on the continent. Both the national park and Natal park systems maintain research facilities to guide senior wardens in management decisions. These official research bodies are backed up by the large cadre of independent scientists and game managers turned out by South Africa's universities. The result is a highly technical approach to wildlife and range management. Animal populations are intensively monitored and controlled by translocation and culling. The success of the Natal parks in translocation has been second to none: white rhinos have been moved from Natal to game reserves all over southern Africa. The national parks also translocate animals; most notably, they have recently been moving Kruger National Park elephants to suitable parks and private game reserves in Natal and other areas from which they long ago disappeared. Both systems use wildlife to generate income to sustain overall operations. The Natal Parks Board holds an annual auction that supplies excess animals to a ready market of overseas buyers and private African game reserves. In the larger South African parks, overstocked species are routinely culled and their products used to bring in revenue. Skins, skulls, and horns taken from culled animals are sold in park shops or wholesaled to private emporiums, while meat is dried and sold as *biltong* (jerky). The ivory harvested from the Kruger elephant cull has long been a key source of income for South Africa's national park system.

If South Africa's wildlife establishment has a fault, it is probably arrogance: its officials tend to be dead sure in their policies and have little regard for outside opinions, a trait that has never endeared them to East African conservationists, who take a more laissez-faire approach to wildlife management and generally oppose culling. Under the old apartheid regime, the taint of racism kept South African authorities from making their case at international conservation forums. It also soured relations between park administrators and their black neighbors.

What does the future hold for conservation in South Africa? It looks bright so long as the political situation remains stable. Both the South African government and the private sector are anxious to see tourism grow into a major industry. The national parks and Natal parks are modernizing their accommodations and activities to attract overseas visitors. The success of luxurious private game reserves around Kruger has spurred interest in such ventures all over the country. Increasing numbers of landowners are stocking their properties with game and building lodges to accommodate tourists. While many of these projects are relatively small or overly contrived, game animals are becoming welcome in areas where they were formerly exterminated. The general trend is definitely toward better stewardship of wildlife on private land.

Yet the politics of the new South Africa could spell trouble for wildlife conservation. In the days when parks and nature reserves were first created, land was sometimes taken from black residents who were forced to move. While the various park authorities are now trying to take account of the interests of neighboring people, voices have been raised calling for the return of traditional tribal lands. Boundaries and leases for parts of Kruger and other parks may have to be renegotiated, and it will be hard to please all parties. Wildlife could well be held hostage in such land disputes. This has already occurred at Augrabies National Park in the Western Cape Province, where some local people want to repossess land leased to the park and have threatened to kill its newly reintroduced black rhinos if their demands are not met. While this is an extreme case, it illustrates how tough a task park managers face in balancing the desires of black communities with the goals of conservation in the new South Africa. The Natal parks have taken the lead in building bridges to their black neighbors through community-development projects: they are already expanding employment opportunities and allowing local people to harvest renewable resources such as thatching grass and other plant materials. Even so, incidents of rhino poaching have sharply increased in the Natal parks since the changeover to majority government. However, this may be more symptomatic of a general increase in crime than of local hostility to the parks.

Another potential hazard could come with the inevitable Africanization of South Africa's various park systems. Under the old regime, black Africans served the parks as foot soldiers or laborers: on foot or bicycles, they performed antipoaching patrols as game scouts while other employees carried on with all the gritty labor necessary to keep the parks running. Entry to top-level jobs as game rangers, conservation officers, or wardens was restricted to whites. Even while black Africans could ordinarily advance only as far as the level of senior game scout (the equivalent of a noncommissioned officer), desk jobs in the national park system, like many other departments of the national government, were largely perceived as sinecures for Afrikaner constituents. That obviously is going to change. Although the transition agreement negotiated by Mandela and de Klerk envisages a gradual process for increasing black enrollment and responsibilities in government jobs, they must soon begin to take positions that were formerly reserved for whites. It would be very surprising if blacks were not put on a fast track to promotion. That will be all to the good as long as they are deemed qualified by their peers. The history of other African park systems is not encouraging, however. In many countries, white rangers and wardens became disillusioned after they judged that they were being passed over for promotion by black officers with lesser qualifications. Too often, the result was a rapid exodus of highly qualified managerial personnel, who were replaced with inexperienced or even unqualified job-seekers. Such was the fate of park systems in Kenya, Tanzania, Zambia, and Zimbabwe, all with dire results for morale and efficiency. The South African parks must find a way to promote black citizens to positions of leadership without losing their experienced staff.

Money will prove a key factor in the future of South African conservation: funding must be maintained at a high level if parks are to pull their weight in bringing tourism up to its full potential. Yet such funding is not likely to be a top government priority at a time when black communities are hungry for better housing, transportation, electricity, and all sorts of basic services. It is hoped that South African authorities will learn from experiences elsewhere. In most African countries, park revenues go into the national treasury and little is returned to support park operations, even if the parks produce hefty profits. The result has been chronic underfunding, with attendant inefficiency and decay. If South Africa's parks are permitted to keep revenues for their own support, as they have in the past, they are likely to continue to do very well. Parks might also receive a financial boost from the private sector. The country's biggest corporations, some of which take an active caretaker role on their own extensive land holdings, have contributed generously to park conservation projects in the past and it is likely that they will continue to do so. The public, too, has a role to play: the popularity of the parks among white South Africans has given birth to a large constituency of concerned citizens. Many belong to environmental groups that serve as watchdogs on government policies regarding wildlife and conservation. Such foundations also raise money to support innumerable nature reserves, educational campaigns, and conservation projects. Grassroots environmental organizations can be counted on to provide a strong voice for conservation in the new South Africa.

Whatever the future may bring, South Africa's parks are certainly in good shape today. The country is a treasure house of natural habitats. It presents an extraordinarily diverse collection of parks and nature reserves that offer such unexpected African experiences as whale watching, wildflower displays, beachcombing, and mountain hiking — in addition to big game safaris. South Africa actually has some limitations as a classic big game safari destination, yet it is particularly appealing to travelers who want to go on their own, especially real nature aficionados who take pleasure from all the flora and fauna they see.

South Africa's major safari venues — where the so-called big five are found — are largely limited to Kruger and its bordering private reserves, and to Natal's Hluhluwe-Umfolozi Park. But for the real nature enthusiast, there is much more to see. Several fascinating parks are clustered in northern KwaZulu-Natal Province, close to Hluhluwe-Umfolozi. Greater St. Lucia Wetlands Park, for example, encompasses a coastal ecosystem of ocean beaches, dune forests, and freshwater swamps surrounding the largest lake in the country, while the nearby Mkuzi, Phinda, Ndumo, and Tembe reserves provide key refuges for the rhinos, elephants, and other threatened species of Natal's unique Maputaland region. A visit to KwaZulu-Natal Province's Drakensberg Mountains to explore the Afro-montane habitat would be a must for nature enthusiasts. So, too, would be a visit to a sanctuary in the Karoo, such as Karoo National Park or the scenic Karoo Nature Reserve, where relict herds of rare species such as black wildebeest, mountain zebra, and blesbok can still be seen in their natural habitats. It would be a shame to miss the lovely forests and beaches of Tsitsikamma National Park on the Eastern Cape Province's coastal Garden Route. In the Western Cape Province, it would be worth visiting some of the lesser known sanctuaries such as De Hoop Nature Reserve (for rare bontebok antelopes and possible viewing of southern right whales) or West Coast National Park, not to mention Cape Town's famous Table Mountain and the nearby Cape of Good Hope Nature Reserve. The Northern Cape Province's Kalahari-Gemsbok National Park is very little visited by foreign tourists, but if you want to see the wildlife of the Kalahari, this is the place. The full list of South African parks and habitats is practically endless: for the dedicated naturalist, time and money are the only limitations to enjoyment.

Paradoxically, for all its natural attractions, South Africa does not really measure up as a top big game safari destination. To some visitors, especially those seasoned by previous safaris elsewhere, Kruger and the major Natal parks are likely to prove disappointing. This has nothing to do with the quality of those parks, which are superb wildlife sanctuaries: they simply lack the feeling of unfettered wilderness that one gets in the reserves of Botswana or Tanzania. Safaris in South Africa have a very different character than those in the countries to the north.

Modernity is both the glory and the bane of South Africa's parks. Like the country itself, the parks possess a modern infrastructure. They generally have a well-marked network of excellent roads and provide fenced rest camps that offer comfortable (and very affordable) accommodations, as well as campsites with all the amenities. Museums and interpretive displays help visitors understand the environment, as do nature trails, arboretums, and name tags on trees in rest camps and picnic sites. Animals are drawn to strategic human-made waterholes, where they are easily viewed in the open (albeit often at a distance). All this makes South African parks highly conducive to self-touring by car. Indeed, unlike other African countries, South Africa's parks are used primarily by its own citizens, not by overseas visitors. White South Africans are crazy about the outdoors and flood into their parks at every opportunity. During weekends and holiday seasons, the parks are likely to be full to capacity. In the course of a year, Kruger alone receives over a half-million visitors. Crowding is sometimes inevitable. Perhaps worse than any actual inconvenience is the damage to the park's image: troops of family-filled RVs patrolling paved roads hardly jive with the overseas visitor's concept of an African safari.

To handle large numbers of people, regulations in Kruger and other parks where there are dangerous animals must be strictly enforced, and these, too, detract from the feel of a wilderness experience. Some rules (such as speed limits or bans on off-road driving) are essential. Other rules feel overly confining, even though necessary to protect visitors from possible risk. Walking is, of course, prohibited except on special multiday Wilderness Trails (foot safaris led by park rangers), but no matter how safe the circumstances, visitors are rarely even allowed out of their vehicles anywhere outside fenced areas (such as picnic sites). A long-standing ban on open-roofed tour vehicles has recently been lifted, removing a major source of complaint by foreign visitors accustomed to roof hatches by previous safaris in East Africa. But even with the improved visibility offered by open vehicles, some visitors are still disappointed by the photographic opportunities presented in Kruger, where animals are usually seen at a distance.

The South Africans are making changes that should make their parks more appealing to foreign tourists. At many national park rest camps, for example, night drives in open vehicles are now conducted by park rangers and most parks have given the green light to roof-hatched or open tour vehicles. More luxury-style cabins are being built, especially at the new "bush camps." These are much smaller than the main rest camps, and many of them are rented exclusively to one party at a time. The national parks have also taken a cue from the Natal parks, which long ago pioneered the concept of Wilderness Trails. These ranger-led foot safaris through remote and roadless sections of the parks have proved immensely popular. A maximum of eight participants are accommodated in simple camps hidden deep in the bush. These multiday adventures are very reasonably priced: they are probably the cheapest big-game-country foot safaris in Africa. Consequently, they are heavily booked and must be reserved over a year in advance, so few overseas visitors get a chance to participate.

Many of the drawbacks of safaris in South Africa's public parks can be remedied by visiting its private game reserves. In the private sanctuaries, open vehicles, off-road driving, and night viewing are the routine, and vehicles are regularly dispatched by radio to zero in on specific animals. Some of the private reserves adjacent to Kruger National Park offer unbelievably good game watching: probably nowhere else can so much be seen in a short time. Certainly there is no better place to view leopards than at the famous Londolozi or MalaMala reserves, where the spotted cats are completely habituated to vehicles and can be followed as they make their nightly rounds. Yet, to experienced safari hands, the viewing seems almost *too* good. Are these animals wild or not? They *are* wild, but the private reserves have been stocked up to their carrying capacity with translocated animals and the veld environment has been manipulated to keep them around (by burning or bulldozing bush and creating waterholes). The size of the various private reserves is also relatively small compared to that of Kruger National Park, and their safari vehicles are linked by radio. The guides know the animals' regular haunts; once the animals are found, all the lodge's vehicles are called in to see the leopard in its tree, the lions on their kill, the buffalo herd, or the white rhinos. Sightings are so good that some lodges almost guarantee that even casual visitors spending a single night will see the "big five." Although the viewing is incomparable, the experience seems somewhat contrived: it lacks the sense of discovery that is such a part of a real safari. Without question, however, the top private reserves in South Africa deliver terrific up-close wildlife observation. They also have impeccably charming and knowledgeable young guides who double as attentive hosts at beautifully appointed luxury lodges. The fact is, a visit to a good private reserve should be included on any South African safari. Purists may grouse at the methods, but they will probably see some amazing things and are not likely to complain about their photos when they get home. For many people on tour in South Africa, a two- or three-night stay at a private reserve will satisfy all their expectations for game viewing and will be all the safari they need.

If other African countries offer more wilderness-type safari experiences, none can combine those safaris with South Africa's array of non-safari attractions. Indeed, few visitors go to South Africa solely for its game parks. Most spend only a few days on safari before hitting the Garden Route on the Indian Ocean, then wind up with explorations around Cape Town and its nearby wine country. Style and comfort are very much a part of South Africa's appeal. Charming country hotels abound, especially in the Western Cape, where numerous old Dutch homesteads have been converted into picturesque lodges furnished with period antiques. Such establishments take pride in setting a gourmet table at which fine meals are always accompanied by even finer wines. Luxury travel aboard the famous Blue Train or on the antique Rovos Rail is a South African specialty and an attraction in itself. The sumptuous Lost City is a fantasy casino-entertainment resort and theme park of world class. The country is a sports paradise: from professional rugby and soccer to golf, horseback riding, surfing, diving, and bungee jumping, it's all there to be enjoyed. So, too, are museums of every type, while well-preserved historical sites are found all over the country. No matter what your interests, South Africa can more than meet your needs.

South Africa is receiving lots of media attention at the same time as it is being advertised in a flood of glittery brochures. If the news tends to overemphasize crime and political strife, the advertisements put a happy face on everything. In reality, a visitor is no more likely to be a crime victim in South Africa than at home, but the country's deep social and economic divisions have not disappeared overnight. South Africa is alive with problems and potential. That's part of what makes it such a fascinating place to travel.

Safari Facts

ENTRY: No visas or vaccinations are required for US citizens.

CURRENCY: The currency is the South African rand (1997 rate: R4.5 = US$1). US currency and traveler's checks are easily exchanged at banks. Major credit cards are accepted throughout the country.

AIR TRAVEL: The principal international gateway cities are Johannesburg and Cape Town. South African Airways flies directly from New York and Miami. British Air and KLM have daily flights into Johannesburg from Europe. South African Airways also has an extensive network of flights within the country. Domestic air routes are also flown by Flitestar, British Airways/Conair, Sun Air, and other local airlines.

DRIVING: US drivers' licenses are accepted in South Africa. You must drive on the left side of the road. Car rentals are readily available everywhere. Avis, Budget, Imperial (Hertz), Tempest, and Dolphin are the major rental companies. Credit card deposits for insurance (including hefty deductibles) are mandatory.

BUSES: Translux and Greyhound operate intercity coaches throughout the country. Translux has passes that allow unlimited travel for up to 30 days. The passes are sold at any Translux office in South Africa and are also available from local travel agencies.

TRAINS: Train travel is well developed on South Africa's Spoornet system. Main Line long-distance trains have sleeping berths in first- and second-class compartments (you purchase a separate ticket for bedding). Reservations and information can be made by contacting: Main Line Trains, P.O. Box 2671, Joubert Park 2044. Tel: (11) 773-2944 (Joburg). Fax: (11) 773-7643.

The famous Blue Train is a luxurious 25-hour service between Pretoria and Cape Town. It also runs on weekends between Pretoria and Nelspruit, in the Lowveld outside Kruger National Park. It's quite elegant and has cruise-ship prices that *start* at over US$500 for the Cape Town–Pretoria journey and go way up from there. Despite the price, the Blue Train is very popular and bookings can be difficult to get. For reservations and information on the Blue Train: Tel: (11) 774-4469. Fax: (11) 773-7643.

The Blue Train now has a competitor: Rovos Rail operates luxury journeys aboard old beautifully furnished steam- or diesel-powered trains. It operates on the Cape Town–Pretoria run and offers trips to the Lowveld that combine with safaris in the more exclusive private game reserves. Rovos Rail also has service between Pretoria and Victoria Falls. For reservations and information, contact Rovos Rail, P.O. Box 2837, Pretoria 0001. Tel: (12) 323-6052. Fax: (12) 323-0843.

A variety of tours aboard vintage 1930s and 1940s steam trains are offered by Union Limited Steam Railtours, which is a division of the official Transnet Museum. Information and bookings are available from their Cape Town offices: Tel: (21) 405-4391. Fax: (21) 405-4395.

HOTELS: South Africa offers a tremendous variety of accommodation, ranging from luxury hotels and game lodges to simple guest houses and backpackers' hostels. Although booking a complete safari with small game lodges and country hotels could be a complicated and tedious business, making direct reservations with city hotels is easy. Many accept a

reservation by credit card. Several hotel chains offer reliable countrywide accommodation. These include Southern Sun/Holiday Inn, Protea,
and Karos. An annual guide to accommodation that lists a great number
of hotels along with prices and contact information is available from the
South African Tourism Board (SATOUR). SATOUR has an official hotel
rating system with grades from one to five stars, but many fine lodges go
ungraded and many of the lower grades merely indicate that a particular hotel meets certain standards (that is, that it has an elevator, en suite
bathroom, or carpeting) and are not an indication of charm. The SA-
TOUR offices US addresses are listed later in this section.

TOURS: There are many safari tour operators offering countrywide or
regional tours. See the list of safari tour operators in the Appendix of
this book.

SOUTH AFRICAN NATIONAL AND PROVINCIAL PARK BOOKINGS:
South Africa's parks are heavily traveled, so reservations for accommodation or trails should be secured in advance when possible. Rates for
various types of accommodation vary widely, even within a single park
or rest camp, but parks are always cheap compared with private lodges.
The national and provincial parks described in the text have different
administrations, so be sure to apply to the right agency for reservations.
Get current rates and rush your deposit as directed.

National Parks. National Parks Board, P.O. Box 787, Pretoria 0001.
Tel: (12) 343-1991. Fax: (12) 343-0905. You *may* get better service if
you call the National Park Board's Foreign Desk at (12) 343-2006 or
fax (12) 343-2007. Bookings can also be made on the Internet at:
http://Africa.com/~venture (click on National Parks Board). Preference is given to applications received 13 months in advance of the
date requested and processed at 11 or 12 months in advance.

Natal Parks. Natal Parks Board, Reservations Officer, P.O. Box 1750,
Pietermaritzburg 3200. Tel: (331) 471981. Fax: (331) 471980 or
473137. Applications are accepted nine months in advance, but accommodation is allocated six months in advance.

KwaZulu Department of Nature Conservation: For Ndumo and
other Maputaland parks: tel: (331) 946698. Fax: (331) 421948.

Western Cape Nature Reserves: Cape Native Conservation, Private
Bag X9086, Cape Town 8000. Tel: (21) 203-4093.

Free State Nature Reserves: The Directorate of Environmental and Nature Conservation, P.O. Box 577, Bloemfontein 9300. Tel: (51) 405-5245.

SAFCOL Hiking Trails: SAFCOL Ecotourism, P.O. Box 428, Pretoria 0001. Tel: (12) 804-1230. Fax: (12) 804-5101. These include the Hogsback, Magoebaskloof, Fannie Botha, and Tsitsikamma trails.

Eastern Cape Nature Reserves: Eastern Cape Tourism Board, P.O. Box 186, Bisho 5605. For booking the Amatola Hiking Trail, fax Keishamma Eco-Tourism at (433) 22571.

North-West Parks: Golden Leopard Resorts, Central Reservations, P.O. Box 937, Lonehills Sandton 2062. Tel: (11) 465-5423. Fax: (11) 465-1228.

FOR FURTHER INFORMATION: The South African Tourism Board prints and distributes a number of informative brochures about the country. They are a useful source of both general and specific information. There are two offices in the United States: SATOUR, 500 Fifth Avenue, Suite 2040, New York, NY 10110. Tel: (800) 822-5368 or (212) 730-2929. Fax: (212) 764-1980; SATOUR, 9841 Airport Boulevard, Suite 1524, Los Angeles, CA 90045. Tel: (800) 782-9772 or (310) 641-5812. Fax: (310) 641-5812.

Gauteng Province

Gauteng is the new name for the province that includes the Johannesburg-Pretoria metropolitan area. The region is South Africa's industrial powerhouse, a complex of modern cities, black townships, and white suburbs linked by a maze of freeways. Although not a dazzling tour destination, most visitors enter the country at Johannesburg International Airport and some stay on for a look around.

Johannesburg is the nation's business capital. Never a major tourist draw, it has acquired a reputation as a high-crime area, so most visitors avoid the city center. That district does have a couple of things worth seeing, however. The newly rebuilt Africana Museum has a fascinating architectural design and exhibits that illuminate the human experience in South Africa from times long past right up to contemporary township life. The nearby Market Theatre is renowned for its excellent productions and is at the center of a lively multiracial entertainment district where a weekly flea market takes place. Joburg's gold mines have long been the engine of the nation's wealth, earning the city its African nickname, *egoli*, "the city of gold." A tour of Gold Reef City, where you descend into an underground mine, watch liquid gold being poured into ingots, and wander through a replica of 1890s Johannnesburg, is a traditional tourist attraction. In the last few years, tours of the famous black township of Soweto have become increasingly popular. These are usually run by black entrepreneurs and include quite a bit of interaction with local people. Given the sanitized nature of tourism and the realities of economic and social segregation that still exist in South Africa, Soweto tours offer a pretty good opportunity for overseas visitors to have some contact with urban black African life. Various theme parks near Johannesburg present the more traditional aspects of African culture, notably dancing. Also outside of town are the Sterkfontein Caves, one of Africa's most important sites for fossils of early hominids.

Pretoria, which is only 36 miles north of Johannesburg, has more to offer in terms of sightseeing. The city is especially attractive in October, when its tree-lined streets burst with the purple-blue colors of flowering jacarandas (which are native to South America). As the administrative capital of South Africa, Pretoria houses the government in the Union Buildings, which are surrounded by terraced gardens and monuments. Old historical buildings are clustered around Church Square, and Paul Kruger's modest cottage is only one of many Pretoria museums. The monumentally strange Voortrekker Monument is well worth a visit. Its sculptured reliefs, which depict wagon trains of determined pioneers in the process of conquering a continent, lend important insights into the Afrikaner view of history. The Premier Diamond Mine is another popular attraction often included on Pretoria tours.

Although there are many hotels in central Johannesburg (including the five-star *Carlton*), most visitors prefer to stay in the fashionable northern suburbs around Sandton. Shuttle buses (notably the Magic Bus) regularly ferry between the airport and the major Sandton hotels. These include the five-star *Sandton Sun and Towers* (which is next to a huge shopping mall) and the cheaper *Balalaika Hotel*, which has a garden atmosphere. The *Michelangelo* is the newest luxury hotel in Sandton. A *Hyatt* recently opened in nearby Rosebank, and a *Hilton* is on the way. Backpackers will more easily find accommodation in downtown Joburg at places like *Zoo Lodge* or the *International Traveller's Hostel*. Outside the city (to the northwest), the *Heia Safari Ranch* and the *Aloe Ridge Hotel* are popular with tour groups. They offer country atmosphere and game on their properties, and both feature Zulu cultural villages. The *Lesedi Cultural Village* features a more intimate "homestay" in huts (modernized to Western standards) in Basotho, Xhosa, Pedi, or Zulu kraals.

Kruger National Park
and Neighboring Private Reserves

Let there be no mistake: Kruger is one of Africa's great wildlife parks. Covering 7,600 square miles of Lowveld bush country, it is by far the largest chunk of wild gameland left in South Africa. Kruger's wildlife population statistics alone are breathtaking: a recent census showed that the park was inhabited by over 7,600 elephants, 22,000 buffaloes, 14,000 wildebeest, 31,000 zebras, 4,600 giraffes, 1,800 white rhinos, over 100,000 impalas, and more than 2,000 lions.* To these can be added some 2,000 each of hippo and waterbuck, a sprinkling of rarer antelopes such as eland, tsessebe, and sable, a thriving population of leopards and other predators, more than a hundred black rhinos, and countless other species as diverse as baboons, warthogs, and crocodiles. Over 500 species of birds have been recorded in the park.

Kruger's wild animals are far more numerous now than they were at the time of the park's birth. When the original Sabie Game Reserve (the territory between the Sabie and Crocodile rivers, which today forms only the southernmost section of the park) was proclaimed in 1898, the wildlife of the Lowveld was in desperate shape. Gold miners had already flooded the hills of the Drakensberg, while land-hungry white settlers were pushing ranches deep into the bush country below. Unrestricted hunting and a lethal rinderpest epidemic had devastated the Lowveld's wild herds, leaving starving lions a menace to humans and their livestock alike. Poachers had reduced the region's elephants to a mere handful.

Although the original impetus for creating a wildlife reserve is usually attributed to President Kruger, most of the credit for actually building a park goes to its first warden, Colonel James Stevenson-Hamilton. Arriving in the Sabie reserve just after the Boer War, Stevenson-Hamilton worked tirelessly to suppress hunting, increase wildlife populations, and expand the boundaries of conservation. He was remarkably successful on all fronts. In 1903, he was given control of a second territory, the new Shingwedzi Game Reserve, in the north country between the Letaba and Limpopo rivers. To his trained corps of Shangaan game scouts, Stevenson-Hamilton became known as *skukuza* ("the man who sweeps clean"), a tribute to his vigor in pushing poachers out of the reserves. To

---

*These figures are from the 1992 game count, which was taken after drought had significantly reduced the populations of impala, buffalo, and other species. There were 137,000 impala in 1984; buffalo can number as high as 27,000, which is deemed the park's maximum capacity. Exact game populations could well be much higher or lower today.

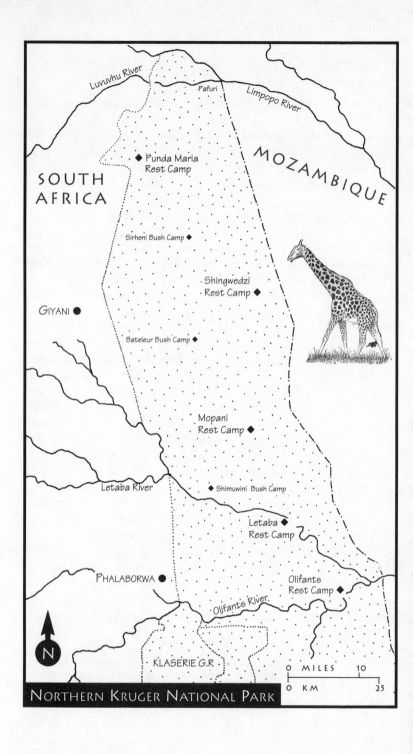

Luvuvhu River

Pafuri

Limpopo River

MOZAMBIQUE

SOUTH
AFRICA

◆ Punda Maria
Rest Camp

Sirheni Bush Camp ◆

Shingwedzi
Rest Camp ◆

GIYANI ●

Bateleur Bush Camp ◆

Mopani
Rest Camp ◆

Letaba River

◆ Shimuwini Bush Camp

Letaba ◆
Rest Camp

PHALABORWA ●

Olifants
Rest Camp ◆

Olifants River

N

KLASERIE G.R

0   MILES   10
0   KM   25

NORTHERN KRUGER NATIONAL PARK

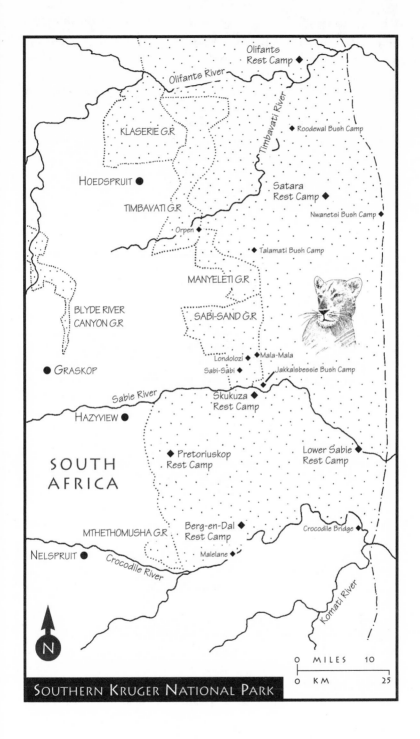

Olifants
Rest Camp ◆

Olifants River

Timbavati River

KLASERIE G.R

◆ Roodewal Bush Camp

HOEDSPRUIT ●

Satara
Rest Camp ◆

TIMBAVATI G.R

Nwanetsi Bush Camp ◆

Orpen ◆

◆ Talamati Bush Camp

MANYELETI G.R

BLYDE RIVER
CANYON G.R

SABI-SAND G.R

● GRASKOP

Londolozi ◆ ◆ Mala-Mala
Sabi-Sabi ◆
Jakkalsbessie Bush Camp ◆

Sabie River

Skukuza
Rest Camp ◆

HAZYVIEW ●

SOUTH
AFRICA

◆ Pretoriuskop
Rest Camp

Lower Sabie
Rest Camp ◆

MTHETHOMUSHA G.R

Berg-en-Dal ◆
Rest Camp

Crocodile Bridge ◆

NELSPRUIT ●

Crocodile River

Malelane ◆

Komati River

N

O   MILES   10

O   K M   25

SOUTHERN KRUGER NATIONAL PARK

hasten the recovery of the wild herds, Stevenson-Hamilton initially waged war against predators as well as poachers. Lions and other carnivores were killed to give the herbivores a respite from predation. (Although such predator control was carried out intermittently as late as the 1960s — with wild dogs particularly persecuted — modern wildlife biologists consider the practice misguided. Predator populations are now thought self-adjusting as they rise and fall in response to the abundance of prey.)

As game populations rose, Stevenson-Hamilton began to experiment with the reintroduction of species that had already disappeared. He also built dams and windmills to provide dry-season waterholes for the animals. A deft politician as well as a pioneering administrator, Stevenson-Hamilton succeeded in garnering enough public support to get the Sabie and Shingwedzi reserves, as well as the rich game country in between, included in Kruger National Park when it was officially declared in 1926. Stevenson-Hamilton built the first park roads and rest camps. More than anyone else, he was responsible for opening up the park to the public.

Running almost 220 miles from north to south and averaging about 40 miles wide, Kruger National Park forms a long, semirectangular strip along South Africa's border with Mozambique. As large as it is, however, the park's vast territory does not form a complete ecological unit. In the past, the region's animals were free to wander over a much bigger area. They migrated annually into the foothills of the Drakensberg Mountains to find water during the dry winter months. As the escarpment country was settled, it became highly dangerous for wildlife, which were at risk of being hunted there even after the creation of Kruger National Park. Conflicts with farmers led to the fencing of Kruger's western boundary in the 1960s, and the border with Mozambique was fenced in 1975. Although they weren't impermeable to game, the fences made Kruger an ecological island. With the animals cut off from their dry-season range, water became an ever more crucial issue in park management.

Average annual rainfall in Kruger generally decreases from south to north (going from 26 to 16 inches), although hilly areas around Punda Maria (in the northwest) and Pretoriuskop (in the southwest) receive higher precipitation (about 30 inches). Even during normal years, the Lowveld has a seven-month dry season (from May through October), and the region is often afflicted with long-term drought. Rivers are the primary natural source of Kruger's dry-season water supply. With their headwaters atop the Drakensberg Escarpment, Kruger's principal rivers run generally from west to east. Although they largely disappear during the dry season, the major streams remain vital lifelines that thread right across the park. Elephants and other animals dig for water in the sands of the riverbeds, where natural pools have been augmented with man-made dams. The dams — and the park's ubiquitous windmill-powered waterholes — have become essential for the survival of Kruger's large wild animal population. Rivers also serve as corridors of moister habitat that support species of plants and animals that cannot survive in the drier surrounding bushlands.

Kruger is primarily plains country at an altitude of less than 1,000 feet above sea level. Here and there, isolated hills rise above the plains, but overall, the park's topography is rather flat. Pockets of hill country are found around Punda Maria in the north and particularly in the southwestern corner of the park around the Pretoriuskop and Berg-en-Dal rest camps, where one granite outcrop reaches 2,753 feet, the highest elevation in the park. Kruger's eastern edge is marked by the long scarp of the Lebombo Mountains, which divide South Africa from Mozambique. Each of these higher areas hosts a distinctive community of plants and animals.

Kruger is more or less heavily wooded country. It is the sort of environment that South Africans generically call "bushveld." Although the casual observer might see Kruger's wooded bushveld as fairly uniform, scientists describe 16 different ecozones within the park, each with its own associations of geology, vegetation, and wildlife.

Vast tracts of Kruger's north are dominated by mopane vegetation (*Colophospermum mopane*). Low-growing mopane scrub (also called mopane shrubveld) blankets the northeastern plains. The scrub is replaced by taller woodlands of mopane and red bushwillow (*Combretum apiculatum*) toward the west, and this type of vegetation is dominant in the neighboring Timbavati Game Reserve. Most of Kruger's elephants live in the northern mopane country. Kruger's scrublands are also good places to see herds of buffalo and small groups of sable antelope, eland, and tsessebe. The mopane-bushwillow zone is good habitat for those animals, too, and is particularly well suited for white rhinos. The Olifants River runs through the middle of the park and marks a major vegetational divide. To the south, mopane is replaced by open grasslands peppered with knobthorn acacia (*Acacia nigrescens*) and marula (*Sclerocarya birrea*) trees. These grassy savannas attract large herds of wildebeest and zebra and are consequently home to numerous prides of lions. A narrow band of this savanna country continues right through the southeastern sector of the park. Most of the southland, however, is covered by woodlands and thorn thickets. The wide variety of ecozones in the mixed woodlands between the Sabi and Crocodile rivers give this southernmost section of the park the richest assortment of vegetation and animal life. Acacia thickets in this area are the haunt of most of Kruger's black rhinos. White rhinos are also plentiful in the south, particularly in the grassy hill country of the southwest.

With its diversity of ecozones and large animal populations, Kruger is a terrific place to see a tremendous variety of wildlife. While some animals are confined to specific habitats within the park, others range through many ecozones. Lions and elephants can be found in virtually every part of the park, and species such as giraffe, buffalo, kudu, and impala are similarly widespread. Certain unusual species are restricted to particular habitats: the mountain reedbuck is found only in the hilly savannas of the southwestern Pretoriuskop and Malelane mountain bushveld zones, while the grysbok, a small and mostly nocturnal antelope, lives primarily in the wooded sandveld and mopane savanna zones of the north and occurs as far south as the alluvial plains along the Shingwedzi River. The beautiful striped nyala antelope can be found in riverine forests throughout the park, but these antelopes are really only common along the Luvuvhu River in the far north. Although the roan antelope is well adapted to Kruger's widespread mopane-covered plains, its susceptibility to anthrax puts it among the rarest of Kruger animals.

Kruger is a great place for predators. Lions are common throughout the park, and there are plenty of spotted hyenas and leopards. Wild dogs and cheetahs are both considered rare, but Kruger is a good place to see them. Although there are only about 250–300 cheetahs, these diurnal cats are often seen on both scrub mopane plains and knobthorn-marula savannas. Wild dogs are supposed to number almost 400, but their population is subject to rapid fluctuations. These wide-ranging predators are closely monitored by Kruger scientists, and park authorities encourage visitors to report any sightings. Packs of wild dogs are often seen lying down during the day near waterholes. Black-backed jackals are quite common, as are a large variety of other small carnivores.

Kruger is no doubt Africa's most closely managed national park. Annual game counts keep track of game populations, and the park's vegetation is carefully monitored. Selective burning is used to maintain various plant communities and keep grasslands in top production. Certain species, most notably elephant and buffalo, are controlled by culling. Kruger is a heavily wooded park and could possibly support far more elephants than it now has, but the authorities aim to keep elephants at their current population to prevent excessive tree damage. (As of 1996, the culling of elephants has been suspended on a trial basis.) Buffalo, too, are culled to prevent them from overgrazing the range. On the other end of the management spectrum, some species are nurtured by extraordinary means to keep their populations viable. Whereas a sick or injured lion might be left to recover (or not) on its own, a cheetah or wild dog would likely receive veterinary attention. The park's scarce roan antelopes are regularly vaccinated against anthrax. Both black and white rhinos are now thriving in the park as a result of their reintroduction in the 1960s and 1970s. Translocation of animals still takes place. Most recently, Lichtenstein's hartebeest have been reintroduced to Kruger, while elephants are being taken from the park for reestablishment in other parts of South Africa.

Park policies have always reflected a certain tension between the goals of conservation and the need for public access. In recent years, Kruger's accommodation facilities have been greatly expanded to meet increasing demand, but this has only tended to increase congestion in the park. As visitation to Kruger has skyrocketed, however, so has the growth of neighboring private game reserves. The largest of these are located in the bulge that pushes against the narrow waist of Kruger's central region. They include the Sabi Sand, Timbavati, Umbabat, and Klaserie private reserves, as well as the government-run Manyeleti Game Reserve. Altogether, these reserves total almost 900 square miles of wildlands that border directly on Kruger National Park. In 1993, the fences separating Kruger from the neighboring reserves were taken down, effectively making them all one conservation unit. This remarkable development is good for both the private reserves and the park, as it expands the range freely available to wildlife.

Kruger's future holds both threat and promise. Assuming that the high quality of its management is maintained, the most pressing problems will lie beyond the park's boundaries. In the past, the impoverished inhabitants of nearby African "homelands" tended to look on the park as a white man's resort that would be better used for grazing or as a meat larder. Increased economic rewards will somehow have to be steered to neighboring rural communities if African attitudes are to be changed from indifference or hostility to support. Water will also be a major headache. Aside from the increasing demands of agriculture and a growing human population, the proliferation of exotic timber plantations in the Drakensberg has potentially dire consequences for Kruger. Atop the escarpment, tracts of pine and eucalyptus have largely replaced native grasslands. Whereas the natural vegetation sustained the watershed, commercial timber farms deplete the water table and decrease flow to the rivers that nurture Kruger.

Kruger's greatest promise could well be fulfilled by vastly expanding wildlife habitat in the greater region outside the park. With fences already down between Kruger and the neighboring private reserves in South Africa, proposals are afloat to extend the zone of conservation into Mozambique. The idea is to get Mozambique to declare much of its thinly populated border territory a conservation area, which would then be leased for management and development. South Africa would provide the capital and expertise (the South African national parks would help manage the new reserve and provide animals for restocking), Mozambique would get desperately needed cash from tourism (and a first-rate game reserve), and wildlife would thrive in an unbroken tract of wilderness that could stretch all the way from Kruger through Mozambique to Zimbabwe's contiguous Gonarezhou National Park. Kruger would then be the core of a vast international park that would forever protect the remaining wildlands of the Lowveld. Many details must be worked out before such a superpark can be brought into being. It may prove only a dream. Yet if it can be made to work, this dream park would be fitting reconfirmation of Kruger's pride of place in the annals of African conservation.

Access and Accommodation

Kruger is easily reached by air. Commuter airlines connect Johannesburg with multiple daily flights to the park's four gateway airports: Phalaborwa, Hoedspruit, Skukuza, and Nelspruit. Phalaborwa provides quick access to the central and northern regions of the park (particularly the popular Letaba and Olifants rest camps), while Hoedspruit is convenient to Kruger's Orpen Gate, as well as to the Timbavati and Klaserie private reserves. Skukuza airport is the best gateway to the southern sector and the lodges in the Sabi Sand Game Reserve. Nelspruit airport has good access to Kruger's southwestern rest camps (Pretoriuskop and Berg-en-Dal) as well as to the attractions of the Drakensberg. Tour operators and lodges make their pickups from the appropriate airports, and rental cars are available at each location.

Depending on the route selected, it takes roughly five to six hours to drive directly to Kruger from Johannesburg. This estimate does not leave time to tour the scenic hill country of the Drakensberg, where a stop for a night or two would be well worthwhile on either end of a Kruger safari. (For more information on the Drakensberg region, see the Mpumalanga Drakensberg section of this chapter.)

Camps operated by the national park are spread throughout Kruger. They provide comfortable and cheap accommodation. Different types of accommodations are available at each camp. Facilities range from simple, twin-bedded rondavels (round cottages built to resemble African huts) without kitchens to large three- or four-bedroom guest houses. Most have air-conditioning or an overhead fan and all are cleaned daily and provided with fresh towels, soap, and bedding. Most units also have private bathrooms and cooking facilities (or at least a place to barbecue). Visitors in units without kitchens must bring their own cooking utensils and use communal kitchen areas or eat at rest camp restaurants. Units can be occupied any time after 12 noon; checkout time is 9:00 A.M.

There are three types of national park camps: rest camps, bushveld camps, and private camps. Main rest camps have shops, gas stations, and restaurants in addition to resident rangers. Many have museums, herbariums, and other interpretive facilities. The bigger rest camps have the capacity to accommodate hundreds of people in both huts and campsites. Big does not mean bad, however; rest camps are usually suitably quiet and pleasant, and many are quite beautiful. True, the larger camps can get crowded, but they are also the easiest to book. Bushveld camps are much more restrictive. Set in remote locations, access to these small camps (which have a maximum of 15 cottages) is limited to visitors lucky enough to secure reservations. Bushveld camps are solar-powered (units have lights and fans), and there are no restaurants, shops, or campsites. Some have small networks of restricted roads that allow fairly private game viewing, and most offer night drives. Private camps are similar to bushveld camps but must be booked entirely by a single party. They do not have a resident ranger or offer night drives. Although guests must cater for themselves, both the private camps and bushveld camps are smaller and have a tranquil character that makes them rival private game lodges in bush ambiance. They can be hard to book, however: many chalets in bushveld camps and private camps (as well as some of the newer units in main rest camps) have been built with funds from individual or corporate donors, and these are reserved for donor use some of the time. Some bushveld camps are also heavily monopolized by vacationing National Parks Board staff. Many of Kruger's main rest camps have campsites, and there are also a couple of special camps in the park exclusively for campers and caravans (trailers). Each individual campsite allows a maximum of six persons. Kruger campsites have communal toilet and kitchen facilities.

All Kruger camps are fenced to keep out dangerous game. Animals are often seen just beyond the perimeter fences, so game viewing from platforms, walkways, or blinds is often rewarding. Many camps have short nature trails, and conspicuous trees or plants are usually labeled to aid identification. Most camps are well shaded by large trees, so birding is always interesting. So, too, are night walks: within the safety of the fence, you can see many small nocturnal animals. If your flashlight is strong enough, you may spot any of the bigger stuff beyond the perimeter. Most rest camps and bushveld camps now offer ranger-led night drives in special open vehicles. These popular excursions have limited space, so they can be hard to get on, especially in large rest camps. It's first-come, first-served, so book excursions early upon arrival into camp.

Although accommodation has been vastly expanded in recent years, Kruger is nonetheless filled to capacity during holidays and weekends. Although it is possible to get reservations on short notice (due to cancellations), it is best to book all your Kruger accommodation before your trip. (For more information about reservations in South African national parks, see the Safari Facts section of this chapter.) The southern half of the park gets the brunt of visitor pressure; aside from offering excellent game viewing, it is the closest area to Johannesburg (it's a straight shot on the N4 national highway). Consequently, its rest camps are often full and its roads crowded with cruising vehicles.

Four main rest camps are located in Kruger's southernmost sector. *Skukuza Rest Camp* is by far the largest camp in the park (with about 488 beds in 188 huts, plus 100 campsites) and is also park headquarters. In addition to all the normal facilities, Skukuza has a car repair workshop and a bank. Although overlarge and busy, the camp is set along the banks of the Sabie River and is well located for touring diverse habitats and directions. Further downstream, the smaller but very popular *Lower Sabie Rest Camp* (153 beds in 67 cottages plus 30 campsites) has an ideal location. Set among great trees overlooking the placid Sabie River, this camp offers a combination of riverine forest and open savanna that makes the surrounding area prime game country. *Pretoriuskop Rest Camp* (326 beds in 115 huts plus 60 campsites) is a large camp located among rolling hills with granite outcrops. The area's unique sourveld ecozone is dominated by unpalatable silver terminalia trees, sicklebush, and tall grasses. Game is relatively sparse around Pretoriuskop, but it's a good area for white rhino, wild dog, and mountain reedbuck. So, too, is the country further south, where high rocky hills surround *Berg-en-Dal Rest Camp* (359 beds in 94 units plus 70 campsites). Although it is a large camp, Berg-en-Dal's mountain scenery and modern design give it a pleasant atmosphere. Both Pretoriuskop and Berg-en-Dal have swimming pools. A fifth rest camp, *Malelane* (19 beds in 5 rondavels plus 15 campsites) is set on the Crocodile River, which marks the park's southern boundary. Formerly a private camp, Malelane is now open to individual bookings; it is a very small camp without a restaurant or shop, although it has a campsite. Its atmosphere is somewhat marred by noise coming from the railroad, pulp mills, and cane plantations on the south bank of the river. Downstream from Malelane, and located near a well-known hippo pool, is the small *Crocodile Bridge Rest Camp*. It offers chalets, a dozen campsites, and a shop, but has no restaurant.

Jock of the Bushveld is the southern sector's private camp. It is named for South Africa's most celebrated canine hero. During the gold rush days, Jock's owner, Sir Percy FitzPatrick, ran ox wagons on an historic freight transport route that went through Kruger. The book he later wrote about his hunting exploits with Jock became a classic of South African safari literature. By all accounts, this private camp, built with donations from the FitzPatrick family (Percy went on to make a fortune on the Rand as a close associate of Cecil Rhodes), is one of the nicest in the park. It accommodates only 12 people in six double rooms and is filled with memorabilia of Jock and relics of the ox wagon era.

Biyamiti Bushveld Camp is situated on the tiny Mbyamiti River, about midway between Malelane and Crocodile Bridge. It has its own 14-mile stretch of private road. Its 15 cabins, which each have four or five beds, are often booked by National Parks Board employees. Another small bushveld camp, *Jakkalsbessie*, is located just outside Skukuza Rest Camp. Jakkalsbessie's ambiance, however, suffers from its proximity to the larger rest camp, as well as from the buzz of aircraft using the nearby Skukuza airport.

Kruger's central region extends northward from the Sabie River up to Letaba, in the center of the park. This excellent game country has a great variety of habitats. Accessible from the Orpen and Phalaborwa gates, the central sector has some of Kruger's most popular rest camps. *Satara Rest Camp* (about 440 beds in 165 units plus 60 campsites) is one of the largest in the park. Although the camp itself is not especially scenic, it is located in one of Kruger's most game-rich areas. The open savannas that surround it are particularly good lion country. *Olifants Rest Camp* is a gem. It is perched atop a bluff overlooking rugged bush country and the Olifants River. The view is magnificent, and the deep roars of distant lions are often carried up to camp. There is no camping at this medium-sized camp (about 250 beds in 106 units), but the riverside *Balule campsite* is located nearby. The Olifants River marks an abrupt transition between the open savannas to the south and the mopane country of the north. *Letaba Rest Camp* is in the mopane zone. This large but attractive camp (about 360 beds in 103 units plus a campsite) is set among tall shade trees on a bank of the Letaba River. The wide riverbed is choked with reeds, among which herds of elephant and buffalo are often seen grazing. *Orpen* (which has 44 beds in its 15 units) is a very small rest camp located just inside the Orpen Gate. Unlike the other main rest camps, Orpen has no restaurant, so all visitors have to cater for themselves. There is a shop, however, and the camp is the administrative center for the nearby *Maroela campsite*. The 90-bed *Tamboti Tented Camp* is also close by. At this unusual national park–operated camp, visitors stay in 3-bed safari tents and use communal kitchen and washing facilities.

Talamati is a remote bushveld camp to the southeast of Orpen Gate.

Situated along a seasonal stream that meanders through mopane-bushwillow country, Talamati (with 15 chalets that each take four to six people) has 19 miles of private road in an area noted for sightings of sable antelope, white rhino, cheetah, and lion. Elevated viewing hides overlook Talamati's two waterholes, and the whole gamut of game can be seen from the hides without leaving camp.

Nwanetsi Private Camp is located east of Satara and quite close to the Mozambique border. It is set next to a lily-covered river at the foot of the Lebombo Mountains. Built in the 1920s, Nwanetsi, which takes up to 16 people in its six chalets, does not have electricity (hence, no fans during the hot summer), but the nearby savannas toward Satara provide visitors with exceptional game spotting. *Roodewal Private Camp* (19 beds in four chalets) is on the Timbavati River between Olifants and Satara. It's in an area where Kruger's savanna and mopane-bushwillow zones intersect, so there is a wide variety of animals and vegetation.

Kruger's northern region has far less accommodation than the south, although more camps have recently been put up there. *Mopani* is the newest of Kruger's main rest camps. It was built entirely with donor money, so its cottages are all very nice and modern. There is no campsite. Mopani is large (384 beds in 103 units) but its design incorporates baobab trees and other vegetation to preserve a bush atmosphere. A large waterhole attracts animals, and there is a swimming pool for the refreshment of humans.

Shimuwini Bushveld Camp (71 beds in 15 units) is located on an isolated stretch of the Letaba River. Crocs and hippos can be seen in camp from a blind on the Shimuwini Dam, and the camp has about 7 miles of private road along the river. Night drives are conducted at Shimuwini. *Boulders Private Camp* (with a capacity of 12 beds) occupies a rocky hillside with fine views over the surrounding mopane-covered plains. Its cottages are linked to a central living area by walkways and the entire complex is built on stilts, allowing this luxurious little camp to go unfenced.

Shingwedzi is one of the older main rest camps and one of the nicest. This midsized camp (about 300 beds in 80 units plus 50 campsites) offers cottage accommodation, a campsite, a swimming pool, and night drives. Its older, thatched chalets are more charming than the new brick models. The camp is beautifully laid out among shade trees, groves of mopane, clusters of lala palms, and beds of pink and white impala lilies (which flower from May to August). The camp hugs the bank of the Shingwedzi River. Lined with impressive sycamore figs and other riverine trees, the river is an oasis in the northern mopane country and provides good habitat for leopard, waterbuck, hippo, and crocs. The

Shingwedzi area was the haunt of four of the celebrated "Magnificent Seven," Kruger's biggest tuskers. Although all those famous bulls are now gone, many still consider the Shingwedzi area the best elephant country in the park.

With only seven chalets, *Bateleur* (25 beds) is the smallest of Kruger's bushveld camps. It is hidden in a remote spot near Silwervis Dam on the upper Shingwedzi River. Bateleur has a waterhole on its periphery, as well as a small network of private roads that include lookout points on two major dams. With so much water to draw animals out of the surrounding mopane-bushwillow woodlands, game viewing around Bateleur is quite good. In addition to the usual big game animals, local specialties include eland and Sharpe's grysbok.

Sirheni is Kruger's northernmost bushveld camp. It is located about midway between Shingwedzi and Punda Maria rest camps. Sirheni (76 beds in 14 cabins) is set among big trees and overlooks its own dam, so game viewing is good even in camp. It is in excellent elephant country and is a prime area for encountering Lichtenstein's hartebeest. Like Punda Maria, Sirheni is well situated for making a day trip up to Pafuri in Kruger's far north.

Small size, remote location, and unique habitat give *Punda Maria rest camp* its special charm. Punda Maria is located among the hills of Kruger's northwestern corner, where higher rainfall and sandy soils produce a unique sandveld vegetation. The camp is small: it has only 56 beds in 24 cottages, although it also has 50 campsites. Punda Maria's thatched huts are laid out on a wooded hillside in two parallel lines. This unusual arrangement does not allow much privacy but it does have architectural charm. As elevations rise from Kruger's northern plains into the hills around Punda Maria, vegetation changes first from scrub mopane to tall mopane forest, then to the mixed woodlands associated with the sandveld community. Game in the area includes buffalo and zebra (the camp's name is a corruption of the Swahili word for zebra), as well as lion and wild dog. Punda Maria is the usual northern gateway or exit point to the park and is the most convenient place to overnight if you want to visit the unique Pafuri area near Kruger's northern boundary. Pafuri is noted for luxuriant riverine forest along the Luvuvhu River. It is the best area in the park to see the beautiful nyala antelope and is especially rich with unusual forest birds.

Around southern Kruger, there are plenty of places to stay outside the park. Hotels include *Karos Lodge*, which is located just outside the Paul Kruger Gate (near Skukuza), *Kruger Park Lodge* in Hazyview (about 28 miles from Kruger Gate and 10 miles from Numbi Gate), and the *Malelane Sun Lodge* (on the Crocodile River near Malelane Gate). There is much less choice around northern Kruger, although a couple of cheaper lodges and campsites are found just outside the Phalaborwa Gate. These include the *Impala Inn* and *Sefapane Lodge*. The nearby *Tulani Safari Lodge* runs game drives into Kruger and the Timbavati reserve. Many charming lodges are located in the foothills of the Drakensberg around Hazyview and White River. These can be used as a stopping point before or after a Kruger visit. So, too, can any of the private game reserves bordering Kruger.

Touring the Park

Kruger is an ideal park for touring on your own. A fine network of roads crisscrosses the park. Main roads are paved and gravel roads scrupulously maintained. All are well marked, so it is easy to get around with the help of a park map (on sale at all gates and rest camps). Speed limits are 30 mph (50 kph) on tar roads and 25 mph (40 kph) on dirt. These limits are enforced: you can be fined and booted out of the park for speeding. Distances between points of interest may not seem far, but it's hard to estimate travel time including stops for animal viewing (the rule of thumb is 15 mph). Be conservative in planning your daily itineraries.

Rest camps post the hours when you are allowed to tour the park. The time varies seasonally, but more or less coincides with sunrise and sunset. You will likely be fined if you get into camp late. Because checkout time from cabins is 9:00 A.M., it's best to be all packed up and underway at first light if you are moving camp. That way, you can get out early and stop off at another rest camp for breakfast or lunch after a good morning's drive. Always travel with some food and drink in your car: you may get delayed by interesting observations or just want to stake out an active waterhole and wait for animals to turn up. Kruger's waterholes, where animals are drawn out into the open, are often rewarding places to see game. Fenced picnic sites (with toilets) are spread around the park. With the exception of a few viewpoints, picnic sites and rest camps are the only places where you are allowed out of your car.

Kruger is open year-round and its network of all-weather roads and rest camps certainly make it possible to visit at any time. Every season has its charms. April and May have great weather with pleasant temperatures, clear skies, and colorful fall foliage. June through August (Kruger's winter) is the season when trees are bare and nights are chilly, but game viewing is good. September and October warm up, and as spring showers start (in October or November), the country turns green and many animals give birth to their young. The summer (December to March) is hot, with (it is hoped) heavy rain showers. Great electrical storms usually light up the night sky, and the park is alive with greenery and insects (so precautions against malaria must be assiduously maintained). Rest camp cabins have screens and most have air-conditioning or fans, so the discomforts of summer do not keep visitors away. In fact, summer is South Africa's vacation time and Kruger's busiest season of the year.

Because the park is so large and has such a diversity of habitats, an ideal Kruger tour would require four or five nights; a comprehensive tour requires even longer. Group tour itineraries usually stay for only a night or two, which allows only a taste of what the park has to offer. Most tours focus on Kruger's southern and central sections, which are the most accessible areas.

Kruger's southern half possesses the greatest variety of ecozones and wildlife. The southernmost sector, between the Crocodile and Sabie rivers, has a terrific variety of flora and fauna. Habitats vary from the hilly Pretoriuskop sourveld and Malelane mountain bushveld zones to mixed bushwillow woodlands and various types of thornveld. Most of these ecozones are densely vegetated, so game spotting is not always easy, although this is the best part of the park for seeing both white and black rhinos. Game viewing gets better around Lower Sabie Rest Camp, where more open knobthorn-marula savannas allow better visibility. The southern sector of the park is also very rich in historic mementos of the *voortrekker* pioneers and gold rush ox wagons that once passed through the region on the way to the port of Delgoa Bay (now Maputo, the capital of Mozambique).

A favored game drive route in the southern part of Kruger follows the course of the Sabie River, which is one of the biggest in the park. Like many Kruger rivers, the Sabie is fringed with riverine forest that offers food and shelter to a wide assortment of species that could not survive in the surrounding bush country. Roadside turnouts invite the possibility to glimpse hippos, crocodiles, and waterbirds, or animals coming down to the water to drink. The forest is always invitingly cool and alive with birds, and it may harbor bushbuck, monkeys, or baboons. Much of the Sabie's riverbed is filled with thickets of tall *Phragmites* reeds. These reedbeds obscure game viewing, and although they are much frequented by grazing elephants and buffalo, even those giants can be difficult to see among the head-high vegetation. Riverside viewpoints are always worth a good leisurely look around — you could even be rewarded with a sighting of a leopard.

Excellent visibility and rich habitat combine to give the grassy savannas around Satara the best game viewing in the park. Herds of buffalo, zebra, and wildebeest thrive on its nutritious grasslands, and these in turn attract the full array of predators. Although lions can be found anywhere in the park, they are commonly encountered on the savanna plains between Lower Sabie and Satara.

ADVENTURING IN SOUTHERN AFRICA

ADVENTURING IN SOUTHERN AFRICA

Few roads climb into the Lebombo Mountains, which form a back-drop along the eastern edge of the park. Several tracks skirt the foothills, and a couple of these — notably Nwanetsi — rise to viewpoints that over-look the vastness of the Kruger plains. The heights of the Lebombo Mountains are the haunts of klipspringer and leopard. Although there is always a chance to glimpse those animals, the vegetation of the Lebombo bushveld will be much more conspicuous. Huge baobabs (to the north of the Olifants River), giant candelabra euphorbias, spiny red-flowering aloes, and white-barked *Kirkia accumulata* trees are typical of the slopes and rhyolite outcrops of the Lebombo ridge.

Northern Kruger has plenty of game, but viewing is made more diffi-cult where roads are enclosed by dense tracts of mopane or bushwillow. The difficulty of viewing is more than offset, however, by the relative scarcity of tourists to the north of Letaba. The north preserves much more of a wilderness feel; here the patient visitor will be rewarded with uncrowded game encounters. Whole herds of buffalo or elephant can emerge quite unexpectedly from obscuring bush, perhaps to disappear just as suddenly, leaving only a dust cloud and fresh scat on the roadway to mark their passing. Areas of particular interest in northern Kruger in-clude the alluvial plains and riverine forests along the Shingwedzi River and the woodlands around Punda Maria. The Luvuvhu River in the far northern Pafuri area is really special. Aside from nyala antelope, its lush fringe of forest harbors special birds such as trumpeter hornbills, crested guinea fowl, and Pel's fishing owl. There is also an impressive forest of yellow-barked fever trees. The Pafuri picnic site is only a few miles from the infamous Crooks' Corner, which marks the three-way border be-tween Zimbabwe, South Africa, and Mozambique. As the name implies, the place was once a notorious hideout for a collection of nefarious smug-glers and ivory poachers who took advantage of the convenient avail-ability of borders to slip away from any approaching forces of the law. Although there is a police post nearby today, no road leads to Crooks' Corner or to the nearby Limpopo River, which is more often a wide bed of dry sand than the "great gray-green, greasy" river of Kipling fame.

One of the best ways to explore Kruger is on a ranger-led foot safari. On these guided foot safaris (which are known as Wilderness Trails), guests are accommodated for three nights in tiny camps set in remote lo-cales. Although rough by safari standards, the camps are comfortable. Guests sleep in simple two-person huts (no singles are available). Bed-ding and meals are supplied (as are a daypack and water bottle for each participant). Showers are solar powered, and the camp cook brings hot water to fill guests' basins in the morning. One of the beauties of these "trails" is that there is no trail. Rather, the walks are footloose rambles through the wilds in the company of a naturalist-ranger and an armed game scout. Although you might walk up to 10 miles a day, the idea is to savor the wilderness and learn about the bush rather than cover ground. Age limits restrict participation to persons between 12 and 60. Since each trail takes a maximum of eight people, these very popular adventures are very difficult to book. Wilderness Trails foot safaris commence on Mondays and Fridays, and use a designated rest camp as a jumping-off place.

There are currently six Wilderness Trails in Kruger National Park. The Bushman Trail and the Wolhuter Trail are both in the craggy granitic hills near Berg-en-Dal (which is the starting point for both). The hilly savannas of this distinctive Malelane mountain ecozone are excellent for white rhino, mountain reedbuck, and lion. The Bushman Trail is the more mountainous and features numerous rock paintings. The Wolhuter Trail is named for a pioneering ranger who used to patrol the area. Wolhuter is celebrated for having killed a lion with his knife after it had ambushed him and was carrying him away in its jaws — something to think about as you trek through lion country! The Napi Trail camp is set alongside the small and seasonal Mbiyamiti River, about midway between the Pretoriuskop and Skukuza rest camps. Walks take place in mixed bushwillow woodlands — good country for lion, white rhino, giraffe, kudu, and impala.

Metsimetsi Trail camp is located at the foot of Nwamuriwa Mountain, an outlier of the Lebombo range. Black rhinos are a specialty in a trail area that combines undulating knobthorn-marula savannas with the unique rhyolite rock formations and vegetation of the Lebombo Mountains ecozone. The trail begins at Skukuza Rest Camp.

Sweni Trail is in the game-rich savannas to the southeast of Satara, which is the assembly point for the foot safari. The camp overlooks the Sweni River, where the surrounding country is renowned for large herds of grazing animals and attendant predators.

Olifants Trail camp is located near the confluence of the Olifants and Letaba rivers. The camp is sited over a beautiful stretch of the Olifants River, where hippos and crocodiles are usually in view. Walks take you into the foothills of the Lebombos or rambling through the water-cut gorges and riverine vegetation along the riverbeds. It's good country for waterbuck, lion, and klipspringer. The assembly point is Letaba.

Nyalaland Wilderness Trail is located in Kruger's far northern sandveld country, so the rendezvous is at Punda Maria. The camp is surrounded by rocky, baobab-studded hills. Walks take you into the lush riverine forests fringing the Luvuvhu River or eastward into scrub mopane plains where you are more likely to see buffalo and elephant.

If you are lucky enough to secure a reservation for a Wilderness Trail, you can plan the rest of your Kruger itinerary around it. A trail experience makes an ideal combination with a road tour of the park. Another fine way to expand your familiarity with the Kruger ecosystem is to combine your park tour with a visit to one of the adjoining private reserves.

The Neighboring Private Reserves

In recent years, the private reserves outside Kruger National Park have become extremely popular. They offer a much more freewheeling experience than you can get in the park. Off-road driving in open, radio-controlled vehicles allows terrific, up-close game viewing in a relatively uncrowded environment, and night drives are a routine attraction. Although the safari atmosphere is often overly contrived, the quality of the game viewing can be phenomenal. At the best reserves, game drives are punchy, with sightings of the "big five" frequently racked up in a short stay. Visitors on tight schedules often choose a safari in a private reserve as an alternative to Kruger. People with more time will find such a visit a rewarding complement to a tour of the park.

The private reserves owe their origins to Lowveld farmers who ran professional hunting safaris on their properties to supplement the meager returns they got from cattle ranching in marginal, lion-infested country. Eventually, the landowners began to join together to form good-sized private sanctuaries, of which the largest became the Sabi Sand, Timbavati, and Klaserie game reserves. All of these border on Kruger National Park, and there are many smaller reserves scattered in the Lowveld between Kruger and the Drakensberg. Hunting still takes place on some properties within the private reserves, but most have been converted for the exclusive use of photographic safaris.

The larger private reserves are official conservation areas managed by professional game wardens. The various owners can opt whether or not to allow hunting on their properties, but the warden establishes quotas for any species that may be taken. The warden is also in charge of stocking and decides where newly introduced animals are to be released. Over time, the bigger game reserves, like Sabi Sand, have been able to build up a good population and variety of wild animals. Resident species (including the various antelopes as well as predators like lion or leopard) were augmented by stocking animals that were rare or had previously disappeared. Price and habitat are major considerations in determining which animals to stock: white rhinos are now quite common on private reserves because they could be bought cheaply and are well suited to the area; black rhinos were not stocked because of the expense (they used to cost US$100,000 each, but in recent years, the price for a black rhino has dropped to US$30,000). The removal of fences between the private reserves and Kruger makes game stocking more problematic, as costly translocated animals can simply move elsewhere. The private reserves probably will come out ahead, however. Although bull elephants are no respecters of game fences, females with calves rarely pass through, so breeding herds of elephants were always uncommon in the private reserves. Now, breeding herds are sure to move in, adding an exciting element to game viewing, while the reserves' resident white rhinos and big cats are likely to stay on their territories. Black rhinos are already finding their way across the Sabie River to recolonize suitable habitat in the Sabi Sand Game Reserve.

The last decade has seen a boom in the development of game lodges in the private reserves. The most successful have become bywords for luxury and excellent game viewing. They tend to be exorbitantly priced, but appeal to affluent overseas tourists. Less pricey lodges are mainly used by South Africans.

Although lodges on the private reserves vary in size and luxury, all have much the same game viewing routine. Drives in open vehicles are conducted by a naturalist-ranger with a Shangaan game spotter seated out front. Radios direct lodge vehicles to any special animals discovered. Afternoon drives tend to get started late (at about 4:30 P.M.), but they inevitably include a stop for sundowners in the bush, then continue into the night. The night drives often produce the most startling game viewing: once found, lions or leopards are followed on the prowl. Most lodges offer short, midmorning, leg-stretcher walks; a few specialize in real bush walking or game tracking on foot.

Landowners of private reserves regulate traversing rights on their properties. The size of each lodge's traversing rights is important, as it determines the amount of land available for game drives. Too small an area is a severe and often frustrating limitation; it's especially exasperating when an animal being followed wanders into forbidden territory! Generally, the larger a lodge's traversing rights, the better its game viewing.

The Sabie Sand Game Reserve is probably the best of the private reserves. It abuts Kruger on two sides. Named for the Sabie River that forms its southern boundary with Kruger and for the Sand River that runs through its middle, Sabi Sand is well endowed with water. Its mixed woodlands provide good game habitat. Over the years, land damaged by the effects of overgrazing cattle has been restored and the reserve has been well stocked with wild animals. Within its 226 square miles are two of South Africa's most famous private reserves: Londolozi and Mala-Mala. Commanding prices in the range of US$600 a day (per person), these polished operations have become the prototype for all up-market safari lodges. Most of the lodges in the Sabie Sand Game Reserve are strung out along the Sand River.

MalaMala is the flagship lodge of the Rattray Reserves, which is by far the largest property in Sabi Sand (over 70 square miles). Ten years ago, MalaMala was the ultimate in bush luxury, although it is hard to say that it now provides more comfort than rival top-rated lodges. Its roomy brick-and-thatch rondavels do feature such niceties as dual "his and her" bathrooms. MalaMala is a fairly large camp, but is divided into two separate sections: *Buffalo,* which accommodates 34 guests, and *Sable,* which takes only 16. The lounge and bar areas have a nice hunting lodge atmosphere generated by trophies and wildlife art. Mala-Mala's outdoor patio commands a delightful view over the Sand River. Service and guides are impeccable. Game viewing is excellent, although there is definitely an emphasis on going after sightings of the "big five," which are practically guaranteed. *Kirkman's Camp* has equally fine game viewing. This 20-bed lodge is a gem. It was originally an old farm complex and retains a charming 1920s period atmosphere. So does the 8-bed annex at *Kirkman's Cottage. Harry's* is the smallest (seven rooms) and cheapest of the Rattray camps. All three camps have access to the entire game-rich property.

In recent years, Londolozi has eclipsed MalaMala's pride of place as South Africa's top private reserve. Londo's reputation was originally built on the strength of fantastic leopard viewing, which was accomplished with the aid of several very well habituated cats. The management also played the ecotourism card hard and early; Londolozi is now the flagship of the Conservation Corporation, a leading multinational developer of African game lodges, whose advertising stresses its commitment to wildlife and community benefits. Although it's hard to assess how much of this is marketing hype, ConsCorp and Londolozi are certainly doing well while they are doing good. Londolozi does produce excellent game viewing on its 55-square-mile property and its staff stresses the virtues of their style of conservation. The lodges are superb. *Londolozi Main Camp* takes its theme from the original 1921 farmhouse. Set in dense woods above the Sand River, it accommodates up to 24 guests. The neighboring 16-bed *Bush Camp* features larger and truly luxurious rock chalets with huge picture windows and private decks that look right into the bush. Unusual for luxury lodges, neither Londolozi Main Camp nor Bush Camp have air-conditioning. Instead, big overhead fans and generous screen doors and windows provide all the ventilation that's needed. The 8-bed *Tree Camp* is the pride of Londolozi. Its luxury chalets are set around a central dining area and deck raised 70 feet into the trees. *Singita Lodge* is the latest ConsCorp-managed property in the Sabi Sand Game Reserve. This 16-bed luxury lodge (with air-conditioning) offers sweeping views over an open plain beyond the Sand River.

Sabi Sabi has a prime game location at the south end of the Sabi Sand Game Reserve. Its River Lodge is set right on the Sabie River, opposite Kruger National Park, where hippos and other riverine animals are constantly in view. *River Lodge* has 20 chalets and 3 suites; *Bush Lodge* has 22 chalets and 5 suites. Both are nicely designed to afford views of the river or waterholes, but they are a little on the large side. Sabi Sabi also features *Selati Lodge*, a 7-chalet camp with an antique, turn-of-the-century theme. The *Nkombe Tented Camp* (7 beds) is used by small groups who want a "Ranger Training Experience." Because Sabi Sabi has a relatively high number of guests for the size of its property (about 30 square miles), there can be some vehicle congestion at game sightings. Opportunities for viewing are top-notch, however.

A number of less well known lodges are located in the northwestern part of the Sabi Sand Game Reserve. *Exeter Game Lodge* is a 12-bed luxury lodge with 12 chalets. Exeter also runs *Hunter's* and *Leadwood* lodges, which are for small, self-catering parties. The 9-chalet *Inyati Game Lodge* stresses luxury. Food is excellent, but instead of the traditional dinner in the *boma* (an African-style open-air enclosure), meals are taken in a variety of locations (such as surprise champagne breakfasts in the bush). A nice luxury lodge on the neighboring Idube Game Reserve also has 18 beds: *Ulusaba Safari Lodge* is set on a small watercourse among fig trees. Its 6 thatched chalets are built on elevated platforms. Ulusaba's sister camp is the 22-bed *Rocklodge*. Built high on a boulder-strewn outcrop, its guests enjoy commanding views of the bushveld even while lounging in the swimming pool. All these lodges have fairly small properties but share traversing rights and offer good game viewing. *Djuma Bush Camp*, *Chitwa Chitwa Lodge* (both in the northern sector), *Gomo Gomo Lodge*, and *Notten's Bush Camp* (in the south) are the most affordable lodges in the Sabi Sand Game Reserve. These camps are small (12 beds), but have very limited properties for game drives.

Located between the Sabie Sand and Timbavati reserves, the Manyeleti Game Reserve (90 square miles) was originally set up during the apartheid years as a place where black South Africans could go on safari. As such, it was administered by the "homeland" of Gazankulu and did not have the funding to stock game to the extent of its neighbors. However, it does have all the game native to the area (including white rhinos, elephants, and all the big cats) and visitors are very scarce.

There are two small private camps in the park: *Honeyguide* is a lovely 16-bed tented safari camp, while *Khoka Moya* has simple log cabins. Both camps feature bush walking in addition to game drives.

The Timbavati Game Reserve is famous for its white lions. The "white" color phase is caused by a recessive gene and is very rare. Unfortunately, the last of Timbavati's white lions died a few years ago. But the genes are still floating around in the local population, and there should be new white lions coming along in due course. Timbavati has much more to offer than freak lions, however. It is located in the mopane-bushwillow zone, which is good elephant country.

Timbavati was never as stocked up with game as the Sabi Sand Game Reserve and has more of the cheaper camps that appeal to cost-conscious South Africans. The simple *Umlani Bush Camp* puts guests up in six reed-and-thatch huts, or they can choose to sleep out in a hide. The camp is on a 40-square-mile property with plenty of game. Nearby *Kambaku Private Nature Reserve* has nice accommodations but the property is pretty small (15 square miles). *Sandringham Private Nature Reserve* is slightly larger but this property still allows hunting. Consequently, it is fenced and has no elephants. It has a lovely setting over a dam on the Timbavati River. *Timbavati Wilderness Trails* has a very simple camp that much resembles the setup on trails within Kruger National Park. Wood cabins are without electricity, en suite toilets, or hot water (basins are brought to guests so they can fill their own bush showers). Bush walking is the main activity, although the camp runs game drives, too. It's possible to do a three-night foot safari on a walking trail that connects Umlani and Kambaku with Tanda Tula Game Lodge.

Timbavati Game Reserve also has its up-market luxury lodges. The Motswari and M'Bali game lodges share the same large property. *Motswari*'s thatched bungalows accommodate up to 26 guests. *M'Bali* is a 15-bed tented camp. Both overlook dams where elephants or even hippos (which are scarce in the Timbavati) can be seen. *Tanda Tula Game Lodge* is a small camp with 12 luxury safari tents. *Kings Camp*'s luxurious cabins will accommodate up to 24 people, but adventurous guests can opt to sleep out under the stars in the traditional hunter's style: you must help prepare a thornbush *boma* and take your turn standing watch for prowling predators.

Ngala Game Reserve has the swankiest lodge in the Timbavati area. This 55-square-mile property was recently incorporated into Kruger National Park, but has been leased to the Conservation Corporation, which built and runs *Ngala Lodge* in "unashamed luxury." Ngala's chalets accommodate 40 guests; another 2 guests can stay in a totally private Safari Suite complete with its own pool, staff, and vehicle. Some guests may choose to spend the night at a special sleep-out *boma*, watching game at a waterhole. Visitors are flown to Ngala by charter aircraft from Londolozi. Game viewing (especially of elephants) is excellent.

The 234-square-mile Klaserie Game Reserve is not as appealing to overseas tourists as the Timbavati and Sabi Sand reserves, although it does harbor big game. Klaserie is divided into many small properties and has lots of little lodges with patchy traversing rights. These are mostly patronized by South Africans looking for budget safaris. A couple of outfits are worth mentioning. *Gary Freeman Safaris* operates an 8-bed tented camp as the base for educational, five-day foot safaris that emphasize bush walking. The upscale *Buffalo Lodge* accommodates 8 guests in stone-and-thatch chalets that overlook a floodlit waterhole. The neighboring Umbabat Game Reserve (59 square miles), which is surrounded by the Klaserie and Timbavati reserves and Kruger National Park, is characterized by small properties and time-share developments. It is popular with Afrikaner hunters.

A number of small private reserves are clustered just west of the Klaserie and Timbavati reserves. These sanctuaries cater primarily to a South African clientele, so they are moderately priced. Although plenty of animals are about, big game viewing does not generally compare to that in the larger reserves. Thornybush Game Reserve is nestled along the Timbavati boundary. The *Thornybush Game Lodge* (40 beds) and its two 8-bed satellite camps (*Monwana* and *n'Kaya*) are luxury standard, while the small *Mbili Game Lodge* is a much more budget operation offering accommodation in tents or cabins. Thornybush Lodge has the better game viewing, while Mbili features mountain bicycling in the bush. Elephants from Kruger have recently been relocated to Thornybush as well as to the nearby Kapama Game Reserve.

Kapama Game Reserve is unusual in that it offers tours to day visitors, who can also go on conducted night drives. Kapama's owners run the adjoining Hoedspruit Cheetah Project, where the lithe cats are bred and can be seen in compounds. This place offers an opportunity to see a king cheetah, an exceptionally rare and beautifully colored cheetah with black stripes on its back. Overnight visitors to Kapama are accommodated in 12 luxury tents at *Buffalo Camp*, or in the regal 4-bedroom *Guest House*. *Tshukudu Game Lodge* is famous for its menagerie of tame animals; guests get to hang out with young elephants, as well as lions, warthogs, and wildebeest, or whatever pets the owners have taken a fancy to hand raising. Lions are also bred for sale (and trophy hunting) on the property. The family-run lodge can take up to 40 guests in its cottages, and there is also a small bush camp located in a forest of sycamore figs along the Blyde River. Of the many other small private game reserves in the area, *Moholoholo Forest Camp* stands out because of its unique setting and habitat. Located right beneath the sheer cliffs of the Drakensberg Escarpment, Moholoholo combines mountain views with a mix of Lowveld bushlands and montane forest. Samango monkey, bushpig, bushbuck, nyala, eland, and sable antelope can all be seen from blinds or vehicles (guests can drive their own cars here). The 14-bed lodge, which accommodates visitors in comfortable log chalets, has a nice bush atmosphere and is very popular with birders.

The *Makalali Reserve* occupies some 40 square miles of bushland below the escarpment. This ConsCorp-managed property has three separate 12-bed lodges. Each features stone-and-thatch chalets built with an odd "deconstructed ethnic feel" that makes them resemble African hobbit houses. They are packed with locally made artwork. Makalali is relatively game-poor (elephants have been introduced), but more emphasis is put on walking, artwork, and stylish living in a bush setting than on classic wildlife viewing.

Bongani Mountain Lodge is located on the Mthethomusha Game Reserve, which occupies some 30 square miles of mountainous country adjoining the southwestern Berg-en-Dal area of Kruger National Park. The cabins of this luxurious 60-bed hotel are set among boulders and offer fine views of the surrounding hill country. The reserve (which is tribal-owned land) has been stocked with big game from Kruger. Nice walks offer the opportunity to see klipspringer or examine odd plants such as coral trees (*Erythrina*) and candelabra euphorbias. Bongani has one special claim to fame: Nelson Mandela is a regular visitor.

The Mpumalanga Drakensberg Region

The great escarpment mountains of the eastern Transvaal, known as the Mpumalanga Drakensberg, mark an abrupt transition between the South African Highveld and the subtropical bushlands of the Lowveld. Although not nearly as high as the mountains of the Natal Drakensberg (with which they are sometimes confused), the Mpumalanga Drakensberg region (formerly known as the Transvaal Drakensberg) overflows with historic and scenic attractions. Beautiful waterfalls leap into deep chasms, while scenic roads wind over mountain passes that offer mementos of gold rush days and Boer War skirmishes. The region has long been a magnet for tourism and is convenient to visit if you are traveling to Kruger National Park by road.

Blyde River Canyon Nature Reserve is the prime scenic attraction in the Mpumalanga Drakensberg region. Extending for over 25 miles along the lip of the Drakensberg Escarpment, the park offers splendid mountain vistas. Famous viewpoints such as God's Window (a dramatic drop-off) and the Three Rondavels (sheer-walled, conical outcrops resembling

African huts) overlook cliffs that plunge into the Lowveld country below. Another well-known geological marvel in Blyde Canyon Nature Reserve is the river-carved gorge known as Bourke's Luck Potholes. The reserve is extremely interesting from a natural history point of view. Here montane grasslands mix with patches of evergreen forest. Both are vestiges of the Drakensberg's native vegetation. Hidden in clefts along the escarpment, proteas, cycads, and tree ferns grow in cloud-moistened profusion, combining elements of Cape mountain fynbos habitat with those of more tropical climes. Large animals are scarce atop the Drakensberg Escarpment, although you might be lucky enough to spot gray rhebok, bushbuck, or klipspringer, and its birdlife is interesting. The reserve also includes the Swadini sector at the foot of the canyon, where a large lake has been created by the Blydepoort Dam. This Lowveld area harbors such animals as hippo, bushpig, leopard, and samango monkey.

Roads connect the park's major viewpoints and most visitors are content to tour by car, although there are a number of short nature walks and hiking trails. Serious hikers can tackle the four-day Blyde Canyon Hiking Trail (or two shorter trails), on which simple huts provide shelter to hikers. Accommodation in the park is otherwise limited to *Belvedere Lodge*, an old farmhouse available to self-catering parties, or at two privately run rest camps: the *Aventura Blydepoort* camp is located atop the escarpment overlooking the Three Rondavels and the dam-filled lake in the Blyde River Canyon, and the setting is spectacular; the *Aventura Swadini* camp is found in the canyon below. Both camps appeal to the budget-oriented South African family market.

The little town of Pilgrim's Rest is especially interesting. A turn-of-the-century gold miners' boom town, its ramshackle wooden buildings have been well preserved and the entire village is a national monument. Some of the old miners' cabins and larger houses have been converted into funny (and funky) hotels. The best is the restored *Royal Hotel*. Much of the countryside in this part of the Drakensberg is covered with pine forests planted by giant wood-products corporations. Although scenic enough (except where timber has been clear-cut), the plantations do not have any natural history value. Pockets of natural forest have been preserved, however, and these are interesting to explore. The *Mount Sheba Hotel and Nature Reserve*, in the mountains above Pilgrim's Rest, preserves one such tract of native forest. It's a good place to walk among ancient yellowwood trees and look for bushbuck and red duiker or birds such as Knysna lourie and Narina trogon. The *Mount Anderson Ranch* preserves 27 square miles of montane grasslands in a key water-cachement area atop the 7,500-foot escarpment crest. An exclusive six-guest lodge (which is owned by the private MalaMala reserve) features trout fishing and walking in the nature reserve, which has been stocked with high-altitude species such as black wildebeest, bles-bok, rhebok, and mountain reedbuck.

The whole Drakensberg region is very popular with South African tourists, so hotels of all categories abound. *Cybele Lodge* is one of the most elegant country hotels and therefore very appealing to overseas vis-itors. Other nice places include the *Blue Mountain Lodge*, *Hulala Lake-side Lodge*, and *Farmhouse Country Lodge,* all in the foothills between the escarpment and Kruger National Park's southern sector. The *Coach House*, another superb up-market hotel, is located near Tzaneen on the northern route to Kruger National Park. Although technically outside the Drakensberg (and within the Northern Province), Tzaneen is in a high-altitude tea-growing region and the greenery of its plantations is simply gorgeous. The nearby Grootbosch Nature Reserve (in Woodbush State Forest) is the largest tract of native evergreen forest in the entire eastern region, but is only accessible to hikers on the Magoebaskloof Hiking Trail. The Modjadji Cycad Reserve, which protects a rich grove of those ancient plants, is much more accessible. Its grounds are sacred to the local Lobedu people's much-revered Rain Queen.

KwaZulu-Natal and the Natal Parks

With its delightful climate and tropical beaches, KwaZulu-Natal Province is South Africa's vacation playground. The province also holds plenty of interest for the overseas safari traveler. Its north is the tradi-tional stronghold of the Zulu people, and it remains an area rich in cul-tural and historic attractions. The superb system of provincial parks and nature sanctuaries in KwaZulu-Natal ranks among the best run in Africa. The Natal parks system also boasts an amazing diversity of nat-ural environments that encompasses major big game reserves in Zulu-land, the pristine Indian Ocean coast of Maputaland, and the mountain parks of the Drakensberg.

KwaZulu-Natal's reserves are administered by the Natal Parks Board. The Natal Parks Board takes the white rhino as its logo with justifiable pride, thus proclaiming its role in saving that species from extinction. Snatched from the brink by the creation of the Umfolozi and Hluhluwe game reserves in 1895, the white rhinos' numbers were nurtured to the point that over 3,500 of them have been relocated from Natal to other parts of Africa since the 1960s. The Natal Parks Board can boast of many other achievements in African conservation. It was the first to in-troduce Wilderness Trails (ranger-led walking safaris) in African game parks and remains the leader in developing techniques for translocating wild animals. The Natal Parks Board annually auctions rhinos (both black and white) and other species to restock game reserves all over the

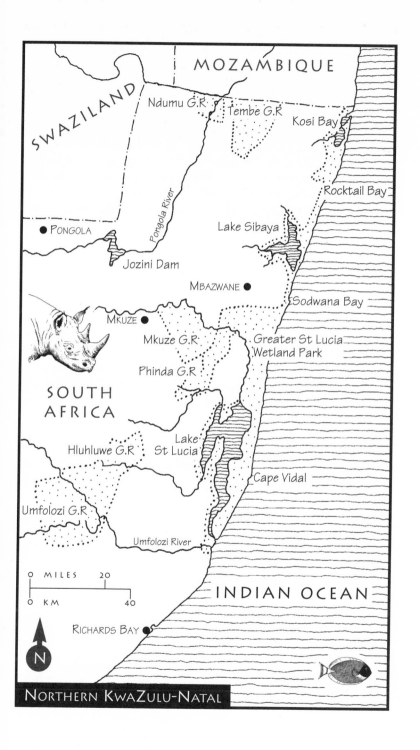

MOZAMBIQUE

SWAZILAND

Ndumu G.R.

Tembe G.R.

Kosi Bay

Rocktail Bay

Pongola River

PONGOLA

Lake Sibaya

Jozini Dam

MBAZWANE

Sodwana Bay

MKUZE

Mkuze G.R.

Greater St Lucia
Wetland Park

Phinda G.R.

SOUTH
AFRICA

Lake
St Lucia

Hluhluwe G.R.

Cape Vidal

Umfolozi G.R.

Umfolozi River

O   MILES   20

O   K M   40

INDIAN OCEAN

N

RICHARDS BAY

NORTHERN KwaZulu-Natal

continent. Aside from working on the salvation of individual species, the Natal Parks Board's efforts are geared toward the conservation of entire habitats. It administers over 75 reserves in the province. Among them are large game parks, like the now-combined Hluhluwe-Umfolozi Park, which are home to a full range of large African animals. Others are tiny sanctuaries designed to preserve pockets of unique and threatened habitat. The Natal parks system is still growing. New reserves are being established, their damaged habitats restored and once-vanished wildlife restocked. To its credit, the Natal Parks Board leads the way with innovative community outreach programs. Through education and economic partnerships, the Natal parks are striving to involve local communities in conservation.

Several interesting parks in Maputaland (KwaZulu-Natal Province's far north) are separately administered by the KwaZulu Department of Nature Conservation, an organization that is likely to merge with the Natal Parks Board. There are also a growing number of private game reserves and conservancies developing in northern Natal.

The Natal parks offer an extraordinary range of activities. Although Natal's game parks are small by African standards (the biggest, Hluhluwe-Umfolozi, is only a twentieth the size of Kruger), they provide a satisfying contact with nature. They tend to attract keen visitors who do not measure the quality of a wilderness experience solely by tallying the quantity of animals seen. The parks of the Natal Drakensberg region are the realm of mountain hikers as well as avid naturalists, while the province's coastal parks are very popular with sports fishermen and divers. The various reserves offer a very wide array of accommodation. Lodging runs the gamut from simple mountain huts (or even caves in the Drakensberg) to luxurious modern chalets in spanking new rest camps and private bush lodges. Natal's old-style rest camps are traditionally oriented to self-catering visitors; guests bring their own provisions, and staff are on hand to do the cooking. Although some of the newest rest camps do have public restaurant facilities, self-catering is still the rule at most Natal Parks Board camps and lodges.

In 1959, the Natal Parks Board first pioneered ranger-led walking safaris in Umfolozi. These excursions proved so popular that they are now also featured at Itala, St. Lucia, and Mkuzi parks. Ranger-conducted game drives and night drives are a more recent innovation. Game viewing hides are a specialty in the Natal parks; some of the hides are legendary for stupendously close-up wildlife observation.

Natal possesses much fauna and flora of special interest. Although its major game reserves are not huge, they support the full range of African megafauna. The parks are particularly good places to observe rhinos of both the black and white species. Another Natal specialty is the nyala (*Tragelaphus angasii*), which is one of the most beautiful African antelopes. A smaller relative of the kudu, the reddish female nyalas have boldly striped, tigerlike coats. Male nyalas are a rich chocolate brown and have a shaggy fringe of long hair running down their undersides. They also sport heavy, spiraled horns and have a mane down the center of the back that can be erected in a startling display. Although nyala are not unique to Natal, it is the only place where they are really common and can easily be seen or photographed. Red duiker (*Cephalophus natalensis*) are small and secretive antelopes that inhabit bush and forest on Natal's coastal plain. They are most often seen at night, when they emerge from dense cover to feed in forest glades.

Natal's tropical coast offers a wealth of interconnected ecosystems that range from sandy beaches and coral reefs to tidal estuaries and dune forests. Each hosts a unique community of flora and fauna. The warm coastal lowlands are particularly good for reptiles, so northern Natal is famed for its crocodiles and the variety of its snakes. Its beaches are also a haven for nesting sea turtles. One hundred miles inland, it's a completely different world. There, the heights of the Drakensberg Mountains beckon with the opportunity to investigate Africa's montane environments.

Durban is KwaZulu-Natal Province's major city and the gateway to the province. Although it hosts a big port and industrial area, Durban is a clean city, famous for its beaches. Its hotel-lined Marine Parade district is reminiscent of Miami Beach, and ocean-front resorts continue northward through Umhlanga and the Dolphin Coast. Durban has hotels to suit every taste and pocketbook. Among the best are the *Elangeni Sun* on Marine Parade and the *Beverly Hills* at Umhlanga.

One of South Africa's best dive sites is located 30 miles south of Durban, off the village of Umkomaas. The Aliwal Shoal is renowned for sharks, especially the scary-looking (but generally mild-mannered) ragged-tooth shark. Aside from "raggies," the more dangerous Zambezi shark is also present, as are manta rays, whale sharks, schools of yellowfin tuna, and other pelagic fish. The *Aliwal Cove Hotel* makes a good base for diving expeditions.

Multiple daily flights connect Durban with Cape Town, Johannesburg, and all parts of South Africa. The excellent N2 highway leads north along the coast, through lush sugarcane plantations toward the game parks of Zululand. The N3 rapidly climbs inland to the lovely farming districts of the Natal Midlands, passing through the province's charming capital, Pietermaritzburg, before continuing on to Johannesburg (365 miles from Durban). Roads diverging from the N3 connect to the various parks and resorts of the Drakensberg.

Hluhluwe-Umfolozi Park

Hluhluwe-Umfolozi Park is one of the most interesting game reserves in South Africa. The Hluhluwe and Umfolozi reserves, which are now joined as a single conservation unit, are the oldest on the continent. Celebrated for their historic role in saving the white rhino from extinction, they remain models for wilderness and game management. The combined park possesses a wonderful variety of plants and animals, including all the big game species.

In 1895, the government of Natal proclaimed three small reserves to protect the dwindling wildlife of Zululand: Umfolozi, Hluhluwe (pronounced shlu-shlu-way), and St. Lucia. Umfolozi had been the traditional hunting ground of the great Zulu kings and was known to harbor the last of South Africa's white rhinos. The nearby hills of Hluhluwe, which were separated from Umfolozi by a corridor of unprotected state land, and the great coastal estuary at St. Lucia, were declared sanctuaries at the same time.

Although rhinos were thereafter safeguarded from hunting, the early years saw little protection for the other animals of the Umfolozi and Hluhluwe reserves. In the 1920s, an outbreak of cattle-killing *nagana* disease led to demands by local ranchers for the elimination of tsetse flies. The putative remedy was to starve the flies by removing their food source in the game reserves. Toward that end, all wild animals except rhinos were shot on sight. The anti-*nagana* campaign lasted 30 years. Although tens of thousands of wild animals were killed, the tsetse held on until the advent of mass spraying of DDT. By 1952, the tsetses were gone and rhinos were abundant, but all the other large mammals in the reserves were locally extinct. The land itself had suffered tremendous devastation, as miles of bush had been clear-cut in a vain attempt to destroy the tsetse's breeding grounds.

The three reserves' fortunes have turned dramatically since the dark days of the tsetse wars. Although even normally common animals like impala, giraffe, and nyala had to be reintroduced, game populations ultimately bounced back under the careful management of the Natal Parks Board. Buffalo, lion, cheetah, wild dog, and elephant were eventually brought in, restoring the full range of species native to northern Natal. Game has since thrived to the point where, as an alternative to culling, excess animals are captured for transfer to other sanctuaries. Umfolozi has long been the world's nursery for white rhinos; a population of some 1,700 allows those that move into "sink holes" of marginal habitat to be sold at an annual game auction. By using the natural processes of dispersal, this method lets the rhinos self-select the individuals to be removed. Black rhinos are also doing well at Hluhluwe-Umfolozi Park. The park has some 350 black rhinos, making it one of the most important strongholds in Africa for that highly threatened species. Elephants began to be introduced in 1981, and now number over 170. Hluhluwe-Umfolozi Park suffers from an ongoing problem in maintaining its shrinking grasslands from invasion by woody vegetation. Whereas elephants in other parks are culled to prevent the destruction of woodlands, at Hluhluwe-Umfolozi it is hoped that elephants will help control bush encroachment. The park's elephants are breeding well. Their population will be allowed to expand until it reaches about 320.

Although originally separated by a neck of unprotected land, Hluhluwe and Umfolozi have been officially connected by the Corridor Reserve since 1989. Covering 375 square miles, the combined Hluhluwe-Umfolozi Park complex is the third largest in South Africa. Although that is still relatively small, Hluhluwe-Umfolozi has an extraordinarily rich flora: it contains over two-thirds of the total number of plants found in Kruger National Park, which is 20 times its size. Climate and geography account for this diversity. The park is located at the edge of Natal's tropical coastal plain. Elevations range from 148 to 1,899 feet. Its hills are composed of a complex assortment of rocks, which weather into a wide variety of soils. These each support different communities of plants. Rainfall varies considerably, with the mist-shrouded hills of Hluhluwe receiving over 12 inches more annual rainfall than the driest parts of Umfolozi. All this creates numerous different niches for plants, which in turn lead to a great variety of animal life.

The two sectors of Hluhluwe-Umfolozi Park are quite different. In the north, Hluhluwe is heavily wooded and dominated by high hills. The heights of these gently rounded hills are often veiled with mountain mists, especially during late winter and early summer. The mist helps sustain moist upland forests. Toward their crests, the densely forested hills are topped with grassy balds. After the rains, buffalo and white rhino take to the freshly green hill pastures. But most of the year, game is much more plentiful in the deep valleys below, where the gently flowing Hluhluwe River and its tributary stream, the Nzimane, wind through lush riverine forests of sycamore fig, weeping Boer-bean (also known as tree fuchsia), and tamboti trees. These forests are the haunt of trumpeter hornbills, green pigeons, and purple-crested louries, as well as good habitat for black rhino and nyala. The lower reaches of the Hluhluwe area always hold water and are thickly vegetated, so it's a good area for elephant and nyala as well as hippo, crocodile, and the gamut of waterbirds. A hide at Hluhluwe's Thiyeni waterhole is a great spot for game watching. To the south, and in the Corridor Reserve, Hluhluwe opens up into drier acacia savanna country.

Umfolozi has a more expansive landscape in which undulating savannas roll down to the banks of the wide Black Umfolozi and White Umfolozi rivers. Although these two big rivers shrink to little more than ankle depth in the dry season, they can rage. They were once known for their lovely fringing forests, but most of the riverine vegetation was swept away by devastating floods in the wake of Cyclone Demoina in 1984 (a cyclone is what we call a hurricane). Only a few patches of mature riverine forest remain, although the process of regeneration is going on. The rivers' broad sandy beds and fringing woodlands are excellent places to find game. Umfolozi's mixture of woodlands, tree savannas, and grasslands provides ideal conditions for a wide variety of animal life. Plains animals such as zebra, wildebeest, and giraffe, woodland species such as kudu and elephant, and riverine animals like waterbuck and nyala are all around in good numbers. The open country makes game spotting easier, too, so lions and other predators are more likely to be seen in Umfolozi than Hluhluwe. The best game tracks wind along the Black Umfolozi River and below the high Zintunzini Hills on the park's western boundary. The hide at the Mphafa waterhole is usually very active.

The southern part of Umfolozi is designated a Wilderness Area in which there are absolutely no roads or vehicles. The entire course of the White Umfolozi River is within this restricted zone and the only way to explore it is on a foot safari. These ranger-escorted walking safaris (Wilderness Trails) take place between March and November. They are limited to eight participants (minimum age is 14 years old). Hikers spend the first and fourth nights at Mnindini Base Camp, with another two nights at satellite camps (shorter, two-night foot safaris based solely at Mnindini are run on weekends). Amenities are fairly basic: accommodation is in simple tents, but a cook prepares your meals. All camps are located along the White Umfolozi. Each day, you walk about 10 miles, tracking game and enjoying the spirit of the wilderness. Baggage is transported between camps by donkeys. These adventures, which are very cheap, are the best way to experience Umfolozi. Needless to say, they are extraordinarily popular, so you must persevere to get a booking accepted.

Hluhluwe-Umfolozi Park is a very pleasant place to enjoy a relaxed, low-key safari. There is plenty of game, but you cannot expect to see huge numbers of animals. Encounters with the big predators, and even elephants, must be considered as bonuses. One thing you will see, however, are white rhinos. These big pachyderms are extremely common throughout the park. Their huge dung middens seem to be everywhere, advertising their presence even where the animals themselves remain hidden. Black rhinos are less likely to be encountered but are also present. Those timid beasts tend to keep to denser bush and are less prone to visit waterholes during the daylight hours.

During the winter dry season, blinds at waterholes provide the best opportunities for game viewing at Hluhluwe-Umfolozi Park. Most action usually takes place between 9:00 A.M. and noon, although animals can arrive at any time of day. The blinds are built right over the waterholes, so you are often extremely close to the animals as they drink and wallow. Visitors approach the blinds through long enclosed pathways. Blinds have comfortable bench seating and are large enough for quite a few people to use at one time. Visitors are supposed to be quiet, so as not to disturb the animals. The overwhelming majority of blind users do observe excellent etiquette.

The ideal visit to Hluhluwe-Umfolozi would call for a two-night stay in each sector of the park. This would allow enough time to explore by car and still have adequate leisure for viewing at blinds. A game track through the Corridor Reserve connects the park's two main sectors.

Access and Accommodation

Most visitors to this area travel by car from Durban. Hluhluwe-Umfolozi Park is 175 miles north of Durban on the N2 motorway. Daily flights from Johannesburg go into the town of Richards Bay (about 50 miles from the park), where cars can also be rented; flights are irregularly scheduled to the closer town of Hluhluwe. Local tour operators and lodges will pick up at either airport.

Hilltop Camp is the park's principal rest camp. This lovely camp is perched atop Hluhluwe's range of forested hills, so it is relatively cool and has wonderful views. It has recently been completely rebuilt to provide accommodation for up to 180 visitors. The newest section has beautifully designed modern chalets and a full-service restaurant. The original double row of quaint rondavels, which have been upgraded and modernized, have facilities for self-catering. The colonial-style *Mtwazi Lodge* was the home of the park's first ranger. Set apart from the main camp, it affords privacy for up to 6 guests and comes with the services of a cook. At Hilltop Camp, the Mbhombe self-guiding nature trail affords an excellent opportunity to look for birds and examine the unique flora of the moist upland forest. Here you can see the ropelike *umHluhluwe* vine (*Dalbergia armata*), after which the river and the park are named, as well as a variety of trees, orchids, lichens, and ferns. Escorted game drives by day and night are available at Hilltop Camp.

Two-hour bush walks in the hill country are conducted by armed game scouts.

Montulu Bush Lodge is a new self-catering camp available to private parties of up to 10 people. Located in a secluded spot in the hills overhanging the Hluhluwe River, it is beautifully designed to afford comfort while preserving intimacy with the bush. A game scout is attached to the lodge to take guests on bush walks. Even newer, the *Munyawaneni Bush Lodge* is set on the Hluhluwe River in a remote area much favored by elephants and both black and white rhinos.

Several camps are scattered around the Umfolozi sector of the park. *Mpila* is the main rest camp and can accommodate a maximum of 80 visitors in various types of rustic thatched huts and chalets. Set atop a hill in the middle of the park, this old-style camp has great views over the surrounding savanna. Its smaller huts are pretty rudimentary and share communal bathroom and toilet blocks. Although slated to be upgraded and given a restaurant, Mpila Camp is currently is set up only for self-catering parties (as are all the other camps and lodges in Umfolozi). Cooks are available to prepare the food that visitors bring. Escorted game drives and night drives are run out of Mpila, and game scouts conduct two-hour bush walks twice daily. Night drives and short bush walks are also run at *Masinda Camp*. Masinda consists of only six simple rest huts with communal kitchen and toilet facilities. Part of Masinda Camp, yet secluded, *Masinda Lodge* is much more lavishly appointed, as it was built to accommodate visiting dignitaries. It takes 6 people. *Nselweni* and *Sontuli* bush camps are in secluded locations along the Black Umfolozi River. These rustic yet comfortable private camps (for parties of up to 8 people) each come with a cook and game guard (for bush walking). Sontuli is in one of the park's most game-rich areas and guests there can arrange night drives. The nearby *Gqoyeni Bush Lodge* is Umfolozi's newest and most comfortable private camp (for up to 8 guests). Set in one of the park's only remaining pockets of fig forest, Gqoyeni overlooks a deep, crocodile-infested pool on the Black Umfolozi. It makes an ideal base for explorations on foot in the company of a resident game scout.

Several lodges outside the park make excellent bases for touring Hluhluwe-Umfolozi Park and the nearby Greater St. Lucia Wetlands Park. Zululand Safari Lodge and Bonamanzi Game Park are both located close to Hluhluwe's Memorial Gate. The *Zululand Safari Lodge* is a comfortable 41-room hotel. *Bonamanzi* is a smaller hotel and has more bush atmosphere. It features accommodation in tree houses, as well as bush walking and game viewing from hides. *Bushlands Game Lodge* is midway between Hluhluwe and St. Lucia. This charming little lodge has its rooms set on stilts and connected on elevated walkways that wind through sand forest, a good place to spot bushpigs, small antelopes, and birds. The lodge arranges guided tours to Hluhluwe and Umfolozi, as well as the St. Lucia and Mkuzi parks.

Greater St. Lucia Wetlands Park

The Greater St. Lucia Wetlands Park is one of South Africa's most unusual conservation areas. In 1895, Lake St. Lucia was proclaimed a reserve to protect its hippos. That original sanctuary has since expanded into a 464-square-mile complex of parks that surround the lake and form a long stretch of coastal wilderness. St. Lucia's system of wetlands is so unique that it has been nominated as a UNESCO World Heritage Site. Although the park is particularly popular with South African sports fishermen, it is a fascinating destination for serious naturalists.

St. Lucia is South Africa's largest lake and estuarine ecosystem. The lake is fed by numerous rivers, but is attached to the ocean by a long channel called the Narrows. The salinity of the lake varies widely. In times of good rains, flooding rivers fill the lake and fresh water flows to the sea. During seasons of drought, ocean water backs up the Narrows and subsequent evaporation makes portions of the lake extremely salty. At each stage, the lake becomes attractive to different species of birds and fish. Except for the Narrows, most of the lake is less than a meter deep, but it is very rich in nutrients. When its shallow waters are fresh, tilapia and catfish thrive, as do ducks and coots. As salinity rises, many varieties of fish and shrimp come in from the sea. Schools of mullet and other species then attract flocks of pelicans and Caspian terns. When the lake becomes overly saline, most of the fish return to the sea or die, but algae blooms draw thousands of flamingos.

The estuary ecosystem is in almost constant flux and provides a wonderful variety of habitats and creatures. Much of the lakeshore is fringed with reedbeds or short lawns of salt-resistant grasses. These areas and exposed mudflats are always thronged with wading birds. Mangroves thrive along the Narrows channel, creating habitat for fiddler crabs and the mud skipper — a bug-eyed little fish that can live out of water at low tide. Goliath herons and fish eagles are always somewhere to be found. Lake St. Lucia and the Narrows channel shelter about 700 hippos and over 1,500 crocodiles. The crocs are the top predator in the lake's food chain. When the mullet are running, big crocs concentrate in the Narrows to catch their fill. When the lake is salty, they congregate at the mouths of incoming rivers where there is more fresh water.

St. Lucia's Eastern Shores separate the lake from the ocean, and this sector of the park is the best wildlife area. Grasslands along the lakeshore teem with herds of reedbuck and provide grazing for St. Lucia's hippos. Water-lily-covered pans punctuate the grasslands, and there are patches of flooded swamp forest and reedy wetlands. The most conspicuous feature of the Eastern Shores is the huge sand dunes that have become stabilized and crowned with dense forest. Heavy rainfall on the sand ridges supports the luxuriant forest and makes the dunes the chief catchment area for water flowing into the lake. The tall dune forest is home to samango monkeys, bushbabies, rusty-spotted genets, and a wide variety of birds and reptiles. The forest floor is the habitat for the beautifully camouflaged but deadly poisonous Gaboon viper. On the seaward side of the dunes, salt-laden winds sculpt the trees into stunted, hedgelike shapes. In some areas, dry grasslands and woody bush replace forest. Such bushy areas shelter the Eastern Shores' population of black rhinos, which have been successfully reintroduced.

The dunes of the Eastern Shores are rich in titanium. They were the center of a bitter seven-year battle between mining interests and South African environmentalists. A 1996 government decision to forbid mining in the dunes was a great victory for conservation in the new South Africa.

Beyond the dunes, Greater St. Lucia Wetlands Park fronts some 60 miles of coast between the mouth of the St. Lucia estuary and Sodwana Bay. Here, endless beaches face the onslaught of the open ocean. Big waves make swimming hazardous for humans, but that does not stop both loggerhead and leatherback sea turtles from coming ashore to lay eggs on summer nights. Rocky points such as Mission Rocks are excellent for tide pooling, and surf fishermen come in droves to try their luck at the St. Lucia Mouth, Cape Vidal, and Sodwana Bay. Sheltered waters at Cape Vidal are safe for swimming and snorkeling. North of Cape Vidal, the open sea is all within protected marine reserves. Rocky offshore reefs are graced with a veneer of corals. These are Africa's southernmost coral reefs and home to a colorful community of invertebrates and tropical fish. Sodwana Bay is a very popular diving site. Further out, the sea is the realm of big billfish, manta rays, and whale sharks. Humpback whales also ply the coast and are often seen off Cape Vidal in October.

The Mkuze Swamps are on the north end of Lake St. Lucia. Here the Mkuze River forms a delta before it enters the lake, and the area is a mosaic of flooded pans, reedbeds, and riverine forests. There are also extensive areas of swamp forest and papyrus. Access to the swamps is limited, but they are of special interest to visiting birders. Like other marshy areas in the park, the swamps are used by local Zulu people, who annually harvest stands of tall *ncema* grass (*Juncus kraussii*), a salt-marsh plant that is used to make sleeping mats.

St. Lucia's Western Shores are characterized by dry acacia bushlands and sand forests peppered with termite mounds. It's a good area for red duiker and termite-eating animals such as aardvarks. Pangolins were once common but have apparently become locally extinct due to being hunted for the traditional medicine market. The demand for such medicines is also taking its toll on rare plants such as the pepper-bark tree (*Warburgia salutaris*), which is found on the Western Shores.

The park's main area of activity centers on the St. Lucia Mouth. Here a comfortable double-decked, 80-passenger launch is used to carry visitors on a two-hour cruise up the Narrows. Hippos, crocs, and waterbirds are the stars of the show, and a guide gives an informative lecture on St. Lucia's ecology. The nearby Crocodile Center has interesting interpretive displays and an impressive collection of captive crocs, including rare West African species. The estuary mouth is very popular with beachgoers and fishermen. Relatively few visitors take advantage of a good network of trails that permit exploration in this most accessible section of the Eastern Shores. One trail leads through grassland and patches of forest to a lakeshore hippo pool. Plenty of reedbuck will be seen on the way. Another traverses the dunes, passing through high-canopy dune forest before emerging on the beach.

Several small self-catering rest camps are scattered around the park and there are a number of large campsites that are very popular with fishermen. One such campsite is located at the St. Lucia Mouth, close to the bustling little resort village of St. Lucia, where the modern *Boma Hotel and Cabanas* offers air-conditioned comfort and tranquillity. Hutted rest camps are located at *Charters Creek* and *Fanies Island* on the Western Shores. Only camping and rustic huts are available in *False Bay Park*, which is also on the western side of the lake. All three camps have hiking trails, and at False Bay, lake cruises on a 20-passenger launch are available. *Mapelane* is a popular fishermen's rest camp, but it is on the south side of the estuary mouth, so access to the rest of the park is poor. A hutted camp and large campsite are located at *Sodwana Bay National Park*, on the northern end of the St. Lucia complex, where nocturnal turtle nesting tours are run during December and January. For fully catered accommodation at Sodwana, there is the nearby *Sodwana Bay Lodge*, a rustic but comfortable private hotel that features a complete dive center and deep-sea fishing charters. Another large rest camp and campsite is located at *Cape Vidal*. It has a great location on the Eastern Shores where sheltered waters permit safe swimming and snorkeling. Both Sodwana Bay and Cape Vidal are extremely popular campsites with fishermen. The new *Bhangazi Bush Camp* is the best accommodation within the Greater St. Lucia Wetlands Park. Restricted to private parties of up to eight, this secluded little private lodge overlooks beautiful Lake

Bhangazi South, which is hidden in the dunes near Cape Vidal. The lodge is a simple, rustic hut located high in the dunes on Mount Tabor (which reaches 426 feet). It is used by hikers walking the self-guided Mziki Trail that connects the St. Lucia Mouth with Cape Vidal.

A hike on the St. Lucia Wilderness Trail is probably the superlative St. Lucia experience. A comfortable tented base camp high in a dune forest above Lake Bhangazi South provides accommodation for two nights, with two additional nights spent in rougher tent camps (guests return to base camp for the fourth night). Participants on these foot safaris get to enjoy a wide range of activities: hiking through dune forest and grasslands, camping next to a hippo pool, canoeing the lake, trekking over big bare dunes to reach the sea, snorkeling, and tracking black rhinos, all in the company of a park naturalist. Donkeys transport baggage and a cook prepares all meals. These guided excursions operate from April to September.

Mkuzi Game Reserve

Mkuzi is a beautiful little park. Set against the Lebombo Mountains at the western edge of Natal's coastal plain, it is a transition area with a nice mix of ecozones and animals. The Lebombos are not huge, but they rise over 1,000 feet above Mkuzi's plains. Most of the Mkuzi Game Reserve is covered by wooded acacia savannas that roll down from the hills to the floodplain of the meandering Mkuze River. The river fills Nsumo Pan, a wetland of extraordinary beauty, before flowing on to Lake St. Lucia. A corridor of reserve land along the river connects Mkuzi with Greater St. Lucia Wetlands Park.

Although only 135 square miles, the variety of species present at Mkuzi Game Reserve is impressive. It has a good population of both white and black rhinos. Elephants have recently been reintroduced, making lions the only nonresident member of the "big five." Smaller animals are exceedingly diverse: Mkuzi boasts 31 species of amphibians (it has more frogs than Kruger National Park), over 60 types of reptiles, and an astonishing 413 varieties of birds. Game viewing at Mkuzi is facilitated by its superb blinds, from which photographers routinely collect trophy photos of nyalas and white rhinos.

Nsumo Pan and its neighboring Fig Forest are the reserve's twin highlights. Covered with water lilies and circled by fever trees, Nsumo is a delight to the eye. Aside from its resident hippos and crocodiles, it teems with waterbirds. Huge flocks of spur-winged geese and white-faced ducks are seasonally present, as are pelicans, cormorants, pygmy geese, and waders. Birders will enjoy spending time at the Nsumo bird blinds.

The Fig Forest is a woodland of exceptional loveliness. Composed of huge sycamore figs and giant fever trees, this type of alluvial forest is now very rare in South Africa. It is the haunt of splendid but hard-to-see birds like Pel's fishing owl and green coucal, although active fruit eaters such as crowned or trumpeter hornbills and white-eared barbets are easier to find. The self-guiding Fig Forest Trail makes a wonderful yet challenging bird walk.

Mkuzi Game Reserve also has a belt of sand forest, which is another rare South African ecozone. The woody thickets in this dry, semideciduous type of woodland are excellent habitat for black rhino and suni antelope. Sand-forest bird specialties include African broadbill, yellow-spotted nicator, and pink-throated twinspot. The Lebombo Mountains are also distinctive. There are no loop roads for game viewing in the hills, but the park entrance road follows a narrow valley that pierces the Lebombos. Acacia-combretum savanna is the dominant vegetation, although spiky aloes are very conspicuous. Mountain reedbuck, klipspringer, and black rhino live in the hills, but are only likely to be seen by bush walking.

For a park of its size, Mkuzi has an ample number of self-catering camps. The main rest camp at *Emantuma* offers a variety of huts, cottages, and bungalows, while a new tented camp has recently opened in the vicinity. A nice campsite is located at the park's entrance gate, which is set in a valley among the Lebombo hills. There are two private bush camps. The reed-and-thatch chalets of *Nhlonhlela* overlook a lovely, forest-fringed pan. *Umkumbi* is a tented bush camp in a remote area used for controlled hunting. It is only available to nonhunters from October to March. Game scouts are on hand at the bush camps to escort walking safaris.

Night drives are conducted in Mkuzi Game Reserve, and game guards are available at Emantuma to guide walks at Nsumo Pan. More extensive bush walking takes place on the four-day Mkuzi Wilderness Trail, which operates from a secluded tented camp. All three nights on the foot safari are spent at the base camp, from which daily forays are made. Visitors to Mkuzi can also visit a cultural village within the reserve. It commemorates the sacred burial site of the local Jobe tribe's chiefs, and revenues go to that neighboring community.

Phinda and Private Reserves

Private game reserves are beginning to flourish in the country adjoining Mkuzi Game Reserve's southern boundary, where landowners are converting their overgrazed cattle ranches into wildlife havens. A number have joined together to create the 117-square-mile Mun-ya-Wana Game Reserve as an official conservation area.

The largest and best known property in the region is the Phinda Private Game Reserve. Phinda is run by the Conservation Corporation, which also operates the upscale Londolozi and Ngala lodges in the Kruger National Park region. Like its sister lodges, Phinda is designed to provide a top-notch wildlife experience for an affluent clientele. Toward that end, Phinda has been clearing bush and restocking game as well as developing income-earning projects with local communities to make them receptive to having wild animals as neighbors. There are two superb lodges. *Phinda Mountain Lodge* crowns a hill with a view over surrounding bushlands. It is tastefully modern and accommodates 42 guests in suitable luxury. The 32-bed *Phinda Forest Lodge* is built on platforms in the midst of a sand forest. Its glass-walled chalets give unobscured views into the woods.

Phinda Private Game Reserve occupies over 60 square miles of land and has extensive traversing rights on neighboring territories. The country is similar to that found in Mkuzi Game Reserve, with landscapes running from the bush-covered slopes of the Lebombo hills to the riverine forests and marshes along the Mzinene and Munyawana rivers that flow into Lake St. Lucia. Most of the reserve is fairly bushy, but its grasslands are being restored from the ravages of overgrazing cattle. Thorny acacia savanna, ilala palm grassland, open plains country, and sand forest mingle with wetland areas to yield a good variety of habitats. Lion, cheetah, white rhino, and elephant have all been reintroduced. The release of lions caused some controversy after one of the big cats (which may have been semihabituated to humans) killed a guest near the lodge swimming pool, but that incident has to be regarded as an unfortunate accident. Resident species at Phinda Private Game Reserve include nyala, impala, wildebeest, zebra, hippo, red duiker, and suni. It will take some time to build up animal populations, but there is definitely game to be seen at Phinda.

Phinda complements its game viewing (which is not yet up to the standard of its sister lodges at Kruger) by offering a tremendous range of activities. In addition to game viewing (day drives and night drives in open, four-wheel-drive vehicles), guests can take a sunset cruise down the Mzinene River between forests of golden fever trees, or paddle their own canoes. They can go off the reserve to track black rhinos on foot in Mkuzi Game Reserve, take a private boat on Lake St. Lucia, or fly down to the coast for beachcombing, snorkeling, or scuba diving.

Zulu Nyala is another private reserve and lodge in the area. It features day and night drives on its property, as well as horseback riding and fishing trips to Sodwana Bay or St. Lucia. Guests are accommodated in a comfortable 35-room lodge.

Maputaland Parks

Maputaland in northernmost Natal (KwaZulu-Natal Province) is currently an area of intense interest to South African conservationists. Bounded by the hills of the Lebombo Mountains, the Mozambique border, and the waters of the Indian Ocean, this semitropical region possesses a pristine coastline and some fascinating wildlife reserves. It has tremendous potential for tourism.

Although it once teemed with great herds of wild animals, Maputaland is now well populated by Zulu and Thonga clans (the Thonga, sometimes called Tsonga, are the dominant tribe in southern Mozambique), and the vestiges of its wildlife are confined to its game reserves. Yet its people depend heavily on natural ecosystems for resources crucial to everyday life. Wetland areas are particularly important sources of food and plant materials, and also serve as key repositories for wildlife. Several important Maputaland reserves are administered by the KwaZulu Department of Nature Conservation (KDNC), which has a mandate to promote conservation for the tangible benefit of local people. Toward that end, 25 percent of KDNC park revenues are returned to neighboring communities, whose residents retain rights to harvest certain plant materials (such as thatching grass) and to fish in the reserves on a sustainable basis. The KDNC may soon be joined with the Natal Parks Board, but the principles of sustainable community benefits will be maintained. It's also likely that the various KDNC reserves will be knit together with Mkuzi Game Reserve and the Greater St. Lucia Wetlands Park to form a huge, L-shaped park running across the whole length of the Mozambique border and down the coast all the way to the mouth of the St. Lucia estuary. If plans to create a contiguous reserve in Mozambique come to pass, this Maputaland park will have international significance.

The most important KDNC wildlife areas are the Ndumo Game Reserve and Tembe Elephant Park, which both abut the Mozambique border. Ndumo is a great little park. Although only 40 square miles in area, it is one of South Africa's hottest birding spots, with 420 species recorded. Tucked between the Usutu and Pongola rivers, Ndumo Game Reserve has plenty of riverine habitat and is particularly celebrated for the beauty of its water-filled pans, such as Nyamithi, which is surrounded by magnificent, yellow-barked fever trees. Crocodiles haul out everywhere on the shores of the pan, where a fringing grass lawn is cropped short by resident hippos. It's much the same story on the larger Banzi Pan, and both lakes are thronged with water dikkops, spoonbills, open-billed storks, fish eagles, and myriad other birds. Giraffe and white rhinos are often seen along the lakeshore, too. Black rhinos also inhabit the reserve, part of which is covered with *mahemane* bush, a dense thicket of spiny euphorbias that is all but impenetrable to everything except rhinos. Other animals in Ndumo Game Reserve include red duiker, suni, kudu, and nyala. Elephants roam the dry sand forests of nearby Tembe Elephant Park, which is more than triple Ndumo's size. The elephants would no doubt enjoy wandering over to Ndumo's watery pans, but they are prevented from doing so by a stout fence because a 3-mile gap of inhabited community land separates Ndumo from Tembe Elephant Park. Negotiations are going forward with the residents to persuade them to move their kraals (settlements) so the two reserves can be united.

Both parks have accommodation for self-catering parties: Ndumo has a nice but simple seven-chalet, hutted camp run by the KDNC, while Tembe has a no-frills KDNC tented camp. Ranger-led walks and guided drives are available at Ndumo, but visitors must have their own four-wheel-drive vehicle to tour Tembe. *Ndumo Wilderness Camp* is a superb 16-bed luxury tented lodge within the Ndumo Game Reserve. As a partnership between the local community and an accomplished private safari operator, this camp is a model ecotourism project. With its lavishly furnished tents raised on stilts, Ndumo Wilderness Camp has wonderful views over the waters and forests of Banzi Pan. A beautifully designed open lounge and deck area enhances its relaxed bush atmosphere, while professional naturalist guides accompany all game or "bird" drives and walking excursions.

The entire coast of Maputaland is protected within various conservation areas. The Kosi Bay Nature Reserve is located just below the Mozambique border. The "bay" is actually the mouth of a pristine, 11-mile-long waterway consisting of four interconnecting lakes that are separated from the ocean by a narrow ridge of forested dunes. Each lake is different. The first is a tidal estuary crisscrossed by an elaborate network of wooden fish traps. The last and largest is a freshwater lake lined by a forest of tall raffia palms (*Raphia australis*). Raffia fronds can reach 60 feet in length, making them the longest leaves in the entire plant kingdom. These magnificent trees are the nesting sites for the odd palm-nut vulture, which is another Maputaland specialty. Cabins and campsites are located at a small self-catering KDNC rest camp on the third lake, from which there are excursions to visit the Kosi Mouth or view sea turtles nesting at night. There is also a four-day guided walking trail at Kosi Bay.

The Coastal Forest Reserve extends south from Kosi Bay to Sodwana Bay, at the north end of Greater St. Lucia Wetlands Park. The Coastal Forest Reserve protects over 60 square miles of coastal dune forest, grassland, and beach. From the high-tide line, the beach strand and sea fall within the Maputaland Marine Reserve, so the entire coast is free from commercial exploitation. Lake Sibaya is another of Maputaland's coastal lakes, but this one is without an exit to the sea. Sibaya is the largest and deepest freshwater lake in South Africa and is completely devoid of development. *Baya Camp* is a small self-catering KDNC rest camp on its eastern shore. The only catered accommodations on this whole section of deserted coastline are found at the 20-bed *Rocktail Bay Lodge*. The lodge's A-frame tree houses are hidden in a dune forest, through which a boardwalk runs down to the beach. Birding and butterfly watching are terrific, while bush babies and Natal robins are among the many creatures to be seen and heard around camp. Lodge activities include snorkeling or diving expeditions, nocturnal turtle-nesting observations (in season), and walks on endless miles of untouched beach. Guided four-wheel-drive tours are also undertaken to Lake Sibaya and Black Rock, a scenic headland noted for its own endemic species: Bouton's skink.

Itala Game Reserve

Unlike the other game reserves of northern Natal, Itala is far from the low-lying plains of the coast. Located about 100 miles inland, it is nestled among rugged hills and valleys that run down to the Pongola River. Since its creation in 1972, this 116-square-mile reserve has been very well restocked with game. In addition to the animals typical of the other Natal parks (of the larger species, only lion and hippo are absent here), Itala hosts several species that do not occur on the coastal plain. These include tsessebe, roan antelope, and brown hyena. Reintroductions are still taking place: most recently, red-billed oxpeckers were returned to Itala and found the reserve's many giraffes (which host innumerable ticks) much to their liking.

Although it is usually overlooked by international tourists, Itala's scenery and bush ambiance makes it a popular destination for South Africans. The reserve's *Ntshondwe Camp* is the pride of the Natal Parks Board. Camouflaged among sandstone cliffs, this brand-new 40-chalet, 220-bed facility offers comfortable accommodation and commanding views toward the Pongola Valley. The camp features a restaurant and a swimming pool set among massive boulders. Game drives in open vehicles and bush walks are offered at Ntshondwe Camp. The camp is large, however, so if you want more privacy you can book its adjacent *Ntshondwe Lodge* (6 beds), which comes with its own pool as well as a cook and a maid. There are also three secluded bush camps in Itala, each with a game scout for escorted walking safaris. *Thalu* is the smallest (4 beds).

Mbizo (8 beds) is celebrated for its lovely swimming hole in a bilharzia-free river. *Mhlangeni* (10 beds) overlooks a stream and has an excellent observation area for wildlife viewing.

Zululand and the Battlefields Route

When traveling to the game parks of northern Natal, or between those parks and the Drakensberg Mountains, you can't help but pass through Zululand and the districts in which some of the most dramatic events of South African history took place.

Although "Zululand" encompasses roughly half the province of KwaZulu-Natal, the historic heartland of the old Zulu kingdom was in the rolling hill country to the south and west of present-day Hluhluwe-Umfolozi Park. This area is still rife with historic and cultural interest. Monuments mark the kraals and graves of the great Zulu kings and record their struggles with European invaders. Zulu culture is very much alive among the country people, but the more picturesque aspects of traditional tribal life are only easily observed at commercial mock-ups of old-time villages. Such establishments may be touristy, but they do give you an opportunity to marvel at the architecture of thatchwork beehive huts and the functional beauty of Zulu crafts and dress, as well as to learn about tribal life and customs. Although having your fortune told by a *sangoma* (a diviner) or consulting a *nyanga* (a healer) is a contrived experience, no one can fail to be moved by the furious energy of Zulu dancing. Depending on your point of view, cultural villages are either "infotainment" theme parks or educational living museums.

Although new cultural villages seem to be popping up everywhere (even far from Zululand), a couple are worth noting. The most famous is *Shakaland*. Built as the set for the film *Shaka Zulu*, this complex of beehive huts and royal enclosures now houses a charming hotel. Overnight guests stay in comfortable huts and are treated to spectacular torch-lit dancing, a sampling of traditional foods (as well as conventional Western meals), and demonstrations of beer-making and the sport of stick-fighting. *KwaBhekithunga* is another intimate kraal that offers an overnight immersion in Zulu culture to private parties. Both are located outside the town of Eshowe, near Shaka's original kraal. *Dumazulu Traditional Village* is near the Hluhluwe-Umfolozi and St. Lucia parks. Although it is mostly used by day visitors, it also offers overnight accommodations in ethnic-style huts. *Simunye Pioneer Settlement* (north of Eshowe) combines an experience of traditional and contemporary Zulu culture with that of the early white settlers. Guests get to ride on ox wagons and stay in a lodge lit by old-style lanterns and candles.

Natal's historic Battlefields Route includes the sites of many fierce struggles of the Zulu and Boer wars. Of them all, none compare in atmosphere with the austere battlefield at Isandlwana. Here, white marble plaques are scattered on a lonely plain beneath the brooding Isandlwana outcrop that the English called the Sphinx. They mark the places where British soldiers fell when their column was wiped out by a Zulu army. Although primarily of interest to history buffs, any visitor will enjoy an overnight at nearby *Fugitive's Drift Lodge*. Located above the ford on the Buffalo River where a handful of survivors crossed to safety, the owner of this antique-packed lodge makes the events of Isandlwana live through vivid on-site lectures. *Babanango Valley Lodge* also makes an excellent base for touring the Zulu battlefields area. Further toward the Drakensberg, the Siege Museum in Ladysmith is well worth a visit for insights into the Anglo-Boer War.

The Natal Drakensberg Parks

The Zulu call the Drakensberg *Quathlamba*, "the barrier of spears." It is an apt name for the sheer mountain wall of cliffs, buttes, and buttresses that divides the bucolic farmlands of Natal from the wind-swept Lesotho plateau. For well over 100 miles, the Drakensberg Escarpment presents a near-continuous front of towering, flat-topped mountains. Although peaks reach as high as 11,424 feet (at Thabana-Ntlenyana in Lesotho), for most of their length, the palisades run at a roughly uniform height of about 10,000 feet. This imposing mountain range is the highest in Africa south of Kilimanjaro. The palisades of the Drakensberg tower above the 5,000-foot-high country below.

At lower elevations, the Drakensberg is composed of several strata of ancient sedimentary rocks. These are capped by a colossal layer of volcanic basalts that form the precipitous cliffs of the escarpment. In the foothills, which are known as the Little Berg, an exposed band of sandstone accounts for the many caves in which galleries of San paintings are found.

The Drakensberg vegetation is dominated by open grasslands. In the foothills, patches of montane forest nestle into protected north-facing valleys, while river bottoms and sandstone slopes harbor protea savannas, fynbos, and various other types of scrubby brushland. Many interesting plants occur. Aside from the beautiful flowering proteas, there are colorful bottlebrushes (*Greyia*), conspicuous cabbage trees (*Cussonia*), the rare Berg cycad, and the fire-sensitive Berg cypress. Grasses carpet the hills and sweep up the mountainsides wherever they can get a foothold on the basalt cliffs. Atop the escarpment, grasslands mix with the woody heaths and everlasting *Helichrysum* flowers typical of the Afro-alpine environment.

Game is not abundant in the Drakensberg, but there is interesting wildlife. Eland are the largest animals and are still relatively common in some districts. Mountain reedbuck and oribi are also locally abundant, while klipspringer and bushbuck occur in suitable habitats. The graceful gray rhebok (*Pelea capreolus*) is a small antelope of the mountain grasslands. Although it looks much like a reedbuck (it can be distinguished by its very straight upright horns and ears), this unusual animal is entirely restricted to South Africa and Lesotho and has no close relatives. Blackbacked jackals are the most common of the predators, but caracal, serval, and African wildcat do occur. So, too, do baboons, which fare quite well in the mountains. Rock hyrax are common and an odd rodent called the ice rat (*Otomys sloggetti*) is endemic to the Drakensberg, where it can be seen sunning itself on rocks at the top of the escarpment. Birdlife is varied and includes such unusual species as bald ibis and orange-breasted rockjumper. The black eagle, Cape vulture, and bearded vulture (or lammergeier) are the Drakensberg's most prized raptors, and the beautiful jackal buzzard is quite common.

Scenery is spectacular along the whole length of the Drakensberg. In winter, snow-covered cliffs rise above russet-toned grasslands into a clear blue sky. During the summer months, clouds and mists prevail. Skies are clear at dawn, but spectacular cloud formations soon obscure the mountain views, then give birth to violent afternoon lightning storms. When the mists lift, they reveal an escarpment wall sheathed in greenery. During this summer season, the lower grasslands blaze with wildflowers. Even more conspicuous is cosmos, which, although non-native, blooms in the autumn, when it forms impressive purple carpets in the farm country of the foothills.

A large part of the Drakensberg falls under the protection of the Natal Parks Board, which is charged with the mission of conserving the province's primary watershed. Many separate reserves compose what is now called the Natal Drakensberg Park.

Among the most famous sections is Royal Natal National Park, which many consider to have the most spectacular scenery in the entire Drakensberg. This park is located near the north end of the range. It possesses two of the Drakensberg's most impressive features. The Amphitheatre is an imposing, 5-mile-long, flat-topped wall of stupendous cliffs. Flanked by buttressing buttes, it dominates the park and constantly draws the eye. From its summit spills Tugela Falls, a ribbon of falling water that plunges 2,788 feet in five vertical drops, the longest of which is a sheer leap of 600 feet. The Tugela River finds its headwaters on Mont-aux-Sources (10,768 feet), a mountain that stands behind and is largely obscured by the Amphitheatre. After its plunge over the es-

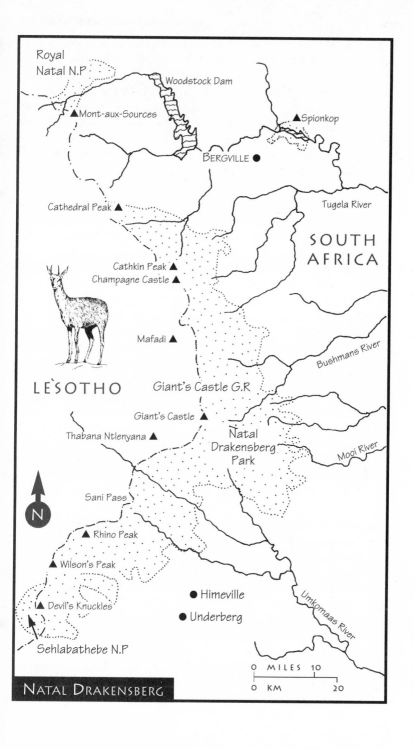

Royal
Natal N.P

Woodstock Dam

▲Mont-aux-Sources

▲Spionkop

BERGVILLE ●

Cathedral Peak ▲

Tugela River

SOUTH
AFRICA

Cathkin Peak ▲
Champagne Castle ▲

Mafadi ▲

Bushmans River

LESOTHO

Giant's Castle G.R

Giant's Castle ▲

Natal
Drakensberg
Park

Thabana Ntlenyana ▲

Mooi River

N

Sani Pass

▲ Rhino Peak

▲ Wilson's Peak

● Himeville

Umkomaas River

▲ Devil's Knuckles

● Underberg

Sehlabathebe N.P

O   MILES   10

O   KM   20

NATAL DRAKENSBERG

carpment, the Tugela runs through a rugged gorge as it flows through the park, picking up tributary streams that eventually make it the largest river in Natal.

A good variety of montane wildlife is found in Royal Natal National Park and hiking trails wind all over the park. It's even possible to ascend to the top of the Amphitheatre for startling views of the escarpment and Tugela Falls. This can be done as a day trip by driving a circuitous mountain road along the rim of the Drakensberg to a car park near the Amphitheatre's flanking Sentinel buttress. It's then only about a 2.5-mile hike to the head of Tugela Falls, but it is a steep trail involving many switchbacks and an ascent of a 100-rung chain ladder. Backpackers can undertake a strenuous two- or three-day trek (28 miles round-trip) to the head of the falls and Mont-aux-Source's summit, spending nights at a mountain hut atop the Amphitheatre.

Royal Natal National Park is a very popular destination for both South Africans and international visitors. Its *Tendele Camp* is one of the Natal Parks Board's nicest. Named for the redwing francolin whose cry resounds in the vicinity, Tendele offers great vistas and comfortable accommodations. The camp has recently been expanded to accommodate over 100 guests in a variety of furnished huts, including its exclusive *Tendele Lodge*. There are also two campsites in the park. Visitors to Tendele must bring their own food, but catered accommodation is available at two neighboring hotels. *Royal Natal National Park Hotel* is a private lodge within the park. This historic hotel (which, like the park, got its name after King George VI and his family paid a visit in 1947) has a modest charm and offers guided hikes and horseback rides. These activities are also on hand at the more modern *Mont-aux-Sources Hotel*, which is located just over the park boundary. Both hotels have superb views.

A number of prominent peaks are clustered in the central Drakensberg between Royal Natal National Park and Giant's Castle Game Reserve. This scenic area falls within the Cathedral Peak and Monk's Cowl state forests and harbors many popular resorts.

Cathedral Peak (9,856 feet) sticks out from the main escarpment wall. Along with neighboring pinnacles (known as the Bell and the Inner and Outer Horns), it dominates the Mlambonja River Valley. This tranquil vale is attractive to hikers and climbers and offers access to the remote Ndedema Gorge, which is renowned for its numerous Bushman paintings. The isolated *Cathedral Peak Hotel* is one of the oldest Drakensberg resorts. Although expanded and modernized, it offers spectacular vistas from a lovely garden setting and retains its appeal to both vacationing families and active outdoorspeople. Among the guided hikes

Hikers approaching the cliffs of the Drakensberg. Giant's Castle Game Reserve, South Africa. Photo: Allen Bechky.

run by the hotel is a day-long ascent of Cathedral Peak. Although it is considered an easy climb, it is strenuous and requires some rock scrambling. The Natal Parks Board's Cathedral Peak State Forest campground is located next to the hotel.

Monk's Cowl State Forest Station is the gateway to the trails of the Champagne Castle region. Although the summits of Champagne Castle (11,079 feet) and Monk's Cowl (10,610 feet) are the highest in this area, the imposing block of Cathkin Peak (10,328 feet) stands in front of them and dominates the view from below. These mountains beckon climbers, yet relatively few visitors venture into the wilderness high country. Most are content to enjoy the vista from one of the many resort hotels that dot the foothills in this part of the Drakensberg. The *Drakensberg Sun* is the largest and most luxurious of the modern leisure resorts. The *Champagne Castle Hotel* is one of the original Drakensberg lodges and retains much of its old-time charm. Once a magnet for the mountaineering crowd, it has now yielded that honor to the nearby *Inkosana Lodge*, a hotel with an atmosphere and prices that appeal to climbers and budget-conscious travelers. The Inkosana dishes out hearty, home-cooked food and accommodates guests in either private rooms or dormitories. It also offers a range of guided treks to suit varying abilities. The more family-oriented

Cayley Lodge also appeals to hikers by offering escorted walks. A Natal Parks Board campsite is located at the Monk's Cowl Forest Station.

The 346-square-mile Giant's Castle Game Reserve possesses magnificent scenery and numerous mementos of the Bushmen. It is also the best place to encounter the wildlife of the Drakensberg. This large park is divided into three sectors, each with its own rest camp and access road: Injasuti, Hillside, and Giant's Castle.

Injasuti Camp, in the north, has wonderful vistas of the Champagne Castle range, including an unobstructed view of Monk's Cowl's striking tower. The camp is located on the Injasuti River, which finds its sources on the summits of the Injasuti massif (11,185 feet). The dome of this mountain (like that of its neighbor Mafadi, which at 11,307 feet is the highest point in South Africa) is partly eclipsed from view by the Injasuti Buttresses (10,538 and 10,505 feet) and the needles of the Injasuti Triplets (10,456 feet) that line the wall of the Drakensberg Escarpment. In contrast to the cliffs and grasslands that surround it, the Injasuti Valley offers sanctuary to the lush greenery of montane forests. Berg hardpears, yellowwoods, tree ferns, and tree fuchsias dominate in these evergreen woods. Bushman paintings are also found in the Injasuti Valley. The most famous gallery is in Battle Cave, which depicts a clash between Bushman clans. Wildlife in the Injasuti area includes gray duiker, blesbok, bushbuck, and klipspringer. The combination of great mountain views with grassland and forest habitats makes Injasuti a great area to explore.

Along with its beautiful setting, the old-style *Injasuti Camp* provides accommodation in simply furnished bungalows. Cooks are available, but guests must bring all their own food. Injasuti also has a campsite nearby. Backpackers venturing onto the trails of the Injasuti sector of Giant's Castle Game Reserve can use designated caves as campsites. These make convenient stops when penetrating the Injasuti Valley, climbing Injasuti Dome (there is a cave campsite near the top), or connecting to the huts further south in the main Giant's Castle sector. Cave camping is strictly controlled: caves can be used by parties of up to eight people and must be booked in advance.

Hillside Camp is located in the northeastern sector of Giant's Castle Game Reserve. It is basically a campsite, but has one rustic eight-person hut. It is also the venue for the Natal Parks Board's guided Horse Trails at Giant's Castle. These ranger-led horseback expeditions are open to a maximum of eight experienced riders (with a minimum age of 14). Expeditions take place from September through May and last from two to four days. Nights are spent at a Hillside base camp and in caves. Guests must bring their own food, but the horses, saddlery, sleeping bags, and camping gear are all provided. Guided morning and afternoon rides also take place daily (weather permitting) at Hillside Camp. Visitors looking for hotel accommodation near Giant's Castle can stay at the *White Mountain Inn*, which is outside the park close to Hillside.

Giant's Castle Camp is the principal Natal Parks Board camp in the reserve. It has a magnificent location on the Bushman's River that looks toward the great table mountain of Giant's Castle (10,872). That spectacular, flat-topped basalt block is thrust forward from the Long Wall of the main escarpment. It looms above the southern sector of the park where vast tracts of rolling grasslands front the cliffs of the Drakensberg. This area is rich in wildlife. Herds of eland, mountain reedbuck, and gray rhebok are frequently encountered in the vicinity of Giant's Castle Camp. The celebrated Lammergeier Hide is also found nearby. This viewing blind allows photographers to get close-up shots of the rare bearded vulture (or lammergeier), as well as Cape vultures, black eagles, Lanner falcons, and other scavenging birds attracted to a nearby "vulture restaurant." The feeding station was set up to prevent the rare bone-breaking lammergeier from straying onto farmlands where it might take poisoned baits left out by ranchers. The hide operates on Saturdays and Sundays from May to September. It is extremely popular with birders and photographers, takes a maximum of 12 people, and must be booked in advance.

Another special feature near Giant's Castle Camp is the Main Caves Museum. Located on a sandstone block above the Bushman's River, the Main Cave contains several galleries of Bushman paintings. Glass-encased replicas help visitors interpret the faded yet graceful paintings of animals and hunters that adorn the cave walls, and a game scout plays a tape-recorded lecture. One section of the cave includes a life-size diorama of a Bushman family, a tableau that is accurate down to the last detail.

Giant's Castle is a good area for day hikes or longer treks. A network of trails fans out from Giant's Castle Camp. One leads up the Bushman's River to mount the escarpment at Langalibalele Pass. Another goes to the foot of Giant's Castle, where the Giant's Hut provides backpackers with shelter. From there, the Contour Path follows the base of the escarpment (at roughly 7,700 feet) below the Long Wall to Bannerman Hut, then continues north toward Injasuti.

At 5,830 feet, Giant's Castle Camp has stunning views and provides pleasant accommodation in an isolated wilderness setting. Cooks will prepare food for those who desire it. Otherwise, it is entirely a self-catering camp. Its thatched bungalows vary in size and accommodate up to 76 guests. The best is the seven-bed *Giant's Lodge*, a beautifully sited luxury chalet.

The Drakensberg continue for a long way to the south of Giant's Castle, but aside from a few resorts in the foothills, this section of the Drakensberg is little known or visited.

The Kamberg and Loteni Nature Reserves are both in the foothills of the Little Berg and have small self-catering rest camps. *Kamberg* is primarily for trout fishermen. *Loteni* also has trout in its streams, but is known for its seclusion and views of the southern Drakensberg. It is also a good area for wildlife.

Sani Pass is one of the southern Drakensberg's best known landmarks. A hazardous four-wheel-drive road snakes up to the top of the pass (at 9,429 feet) and the Lesotho border. To get across to visit Sani Top, the highest pub in southern Africa, a passport is necessary (but no visa for Americans). It's a popular 4x4 trail, but the many wrecks below the summit are a reminder not to linger too long at the bar. Visitors can stay overnight at *Sani Top*, which has self-catering lodging. The dawn vista from atop the escarpment is terrific (with views of Thaba Ntlenyana and Giant's Castle). Birders make the trip to look for mountain species such as Drakensberg prinia, yellow warbler, and Drakensberg siskin.

At the foot of the Sani Pass road is the *Sani Pass Hotel*, a large and popular modern resort. The *Drakensberg Gardens Hotel* and *Bushman's Nek Hotel* are its rivals in the southern area. There is also a Natal Parks Board camp at Cobham on the Pholela River.

Starting near the Sani Pass Hotel, the Giant's Cup Hiking Trail winds through the Cobham and Garden Castle state forests. The trail (which covers roughly 42 miles and can be done in two to five days) is relatively easy because it sticks to the foothills of the Little Berg. The area has good mountain wildlife, an abundance of Bushman art (including the Siphongweni Cave, where unusual paintings show mounted settlers with wagons), and excellent views of the peaks of the southern Drakensberg. These include Hodgson's Peaks (10,682 feet) which rim the Giant's Cup, the Rhino (10,010 feet), Wilson's Peak (10,531 feet), and the Devil's Knuckles (9,934 feet) at the south end of the Natal Drakensberg. The trail finishes near the Bushman's Nek Hotel.

From the Bushman's Nek area, the line of the Drakensberg turns westward where it eventually merges into the tangled mountain ranges of the Eastern Cape. The cliffs gradually lose altitude and cohesion, but not their mystique. It was in this little-visited sector that early Dutch settlers first heard the tales of dragons (which may owe their origins to fossil dinosaur footprints) that gave the Drakensberg Mountains their name.

The Garden Route, Tsitsikamma National Park, and Parks of the Eastern Cape

The Garden Route is one of South Africa's best known tourist attractions. Here rugged mountain ranges push close to the Indian Ocean, creating the country's most scenic stretch of coastline. Much of the 230-mile-long coast road between Port Elizabeth (in the Eastern Cape) and Mossel Bay (in the Western Cape) is well developed with beach resorts and holiday villages. Yet the combination of mountain views, forest greenery, and magnificent seascapes remains alluring, and there are still places of tremendous natural beauty. Chief among them is Tsitsikamma National Park.

The standard tourist trek through the Garden Route involves a two- or three-day drive between Port Elizabeth and Mossel Bay and includes a visit inland to Oudtshoorn in the nearby Little Karoo. Airports at Port Elizabeth and George (near Mossel Bay) are the usual gateways for one-way tours and car rentals. Hotels of every type abound. Among the most popular is the *Eight-Bells Mountain Inn* (in the hills above Mossel Bay). The antique-packed *Hunter's Country House* (between Knysna and Plettenberg Bay) is probably the most elegant small hotel in the area, while the *Plettenberg,* with its private beaches and hiking trails, is the most exclusive resort hotel. The region is very congested with South African visitors during their summer (December through February) and Easter holiday seasons.

Mossel Bay is more historic than scenic. A museum contains a fascinating replica of explorer Bartholomeu Dias's tiny Portuguese caravel, and there is a centuries-old Post Office Tree, which early sailors used to exchange messages. The town of George is at the foot of the Outeniqua Mountains that divide the coast from the Little Karoo. That valley's drier inland climate makes it ideal country for raising ostriches, and the ostrich farms around Oudtshoorn are a very popular tourist attraction. Oudtshoorn's many fine old mansions (known as "feather palaces") testify to a turn-of-the-century boom in ostrich plumes, but today the big birds are much more valued for their leather and meat. Although oddities like ostrich races and ostrich rides (be careful: riders are routinely thrown, and it's a long way down) are a bit hokey, a visit to an ostrich ranch is surprisingly interesting. Another Oudtshoorn attraction is the limestone formations in the extensive Cango Caves. Relatively few visitors venture beyond the caverns into the scenic passes over the Swartberg Mountains that lead into the great Karoo desert.

The Garden Route's main resort area extends from George to Plettenberg Bay. Within it are two small national parks that protect coastal lagoons and lakes. The tiny Wilderness National Park is no longer what its name would imply, although it has some tranquil lakes and there are wild ocean beaches nearby. Its reed-fringed lagoon is very pretty (and a boardwalk facilitates birdwatching along the lagoon's edge), but it is under heavy pressure by boaters and developers. So, too, is the larger Knysna National Park. Its beautiful lagoon is connected to the sea by a narrow strait that passes between two rocky portals called the Heads. The western head is part of the private Featherbed Nature Reserve, where milkwood forests and coastal fynbos can be explored. The Knysna area has some interesting dive sites; the lagoon is noted for its highly unusual seahorses and pipefish. Like Knysna, Plettenberg Bay is a highly developed resort. It is renowned for its diving and ocean beaches and is a good area for seeing southern right whales from July until October.

The waters of this part of the Indian Ocean are subject to seasonal (and even daily) fluctuations of heat and cold. It's a difficult environment for marine animals, yet life adapts and sea creatures thrive. While the warm waters of summer attract calving whales, sea snakes that come this far south can be killed by cold currents. Soft corals and other invertebrates add color to the undersea world, while big pelagic fish, including great white sharks, provide excitement for divers. Ocean beaches can be dangerous for swimming, but there are many protected bays.

High annual rainfall (over 45 inches, spread throughout the year) accounts for the Garden Route's luxuriant greenery. Fynbos vegetation carpets the sea cliffs and exposed coastal terraces as well as the rugged hills of the inland mountains. More protected areas shelter dense forests. Near the seashore, forest trees are stunted and sculpted by wind, and the gnarled white milkwood (*Sideroxylon inerme*) is a common and conspicuous species. Further inland, the forest grows tall. Giant Outeniqua yellowwood (*Podocarpus falcatus*), stinkwood (*Ocotea bullata*), and bastard ironwood (*Olea capensis*) form a high canopy well festooned with lichens and moss. Successive tiers of smaller trees filter the light that reaches the forest floor, where fungi and ferns grow in a rich but shallow layer of leaf litter. Tea-colored streams, stained by the tannins of decaying vegetation, meander through glades of overhanging trees, while climbing lianas and the buttressed roots of forest giants bestow a jungle-like atmosphere. It is a magical green world, cool and silent but for the croaking birdcalls of Knysna louries.

Until the middle of the last century, the coastal terraces of the Garden Route region were covered with great forests. But most of those aboriginal woodlands have succumbed to the ax or fire, and relatively little for-

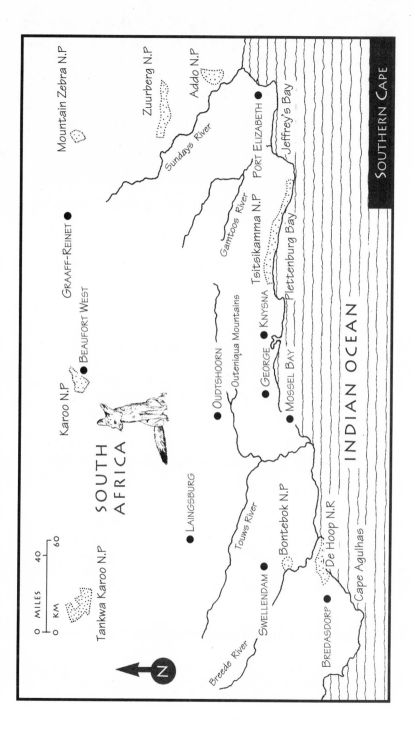

SOUTHERN CAPE

est now remains. Where it occurs, forest wildlife is mostly limited to birds and shy small mammals such as blue duiker, Cape grysbok, and bushpig. But one good-sized tract in the Knysna Forest still harbors elephants. The surviving handful of indigenous Knysna elephants have recently been reinforced by pachyderms moved down from Kruger. The newcomers are doing well and it looks as though elephants will continue to exist in this southernmost outpost of their range. They are still pretty unlikely to be encountered by casual visitors, but you can try your luck on a lonely, 11-mile circular forest trail called the Elephant Walk (starting at the Diepwalle Forest Station).

Some of the most pristine native forests, as well as the best scenery on the entire Garden Route, are found within Tsitsikamma National Park and the adjacent Tsitsikamma Forest Reserve. Tsitsikamma National Park occupies a narrow, 50-mile-long ribbon of coastline (there is also a mountain section, but it is not yet open to the public). Its scenery is dramatic: there are startling vistas of fynbos-covered cliffs plunging into a wave-wracked ocean, and deep gorges cut by tannin-colored rivers that empty into the sea. General access to the park is limited to the De Vasselot (Nature's Valley) and Storms River areas. *Storms River Rest Camp* has an incredible seaside setting at the mouth of the Storms River. Its comfortable wooden chalets and its scenery (as well as the presence of a restaurant) make it an ideal place to stay, but it is difficult to get a booking (it also has a campsite). From Storms River Rest Camp, easy hiking trails lead through deep forest glades or to a 260-foot suspension bridge that spans the Storms River. There are also unusual Underwater Trails for snorkelers and divers. Another fine network of hiking trails fans out from the *De Vasselot Camp Site* at Nature's Valley. Among them, the Kalanderkloof Trail is notable for its impressive groves of giant yellowwoods. A couple of short trails and a campsite are also found at the Tsitsikamma Forest Reserve Station, which is located where the main coast road crosses the Storms River Gorge. The bridge is a routine stop for motorists traveling the Garden Route, and a nearby 15-minute walk leads to the Big Tree, a 120-foot-tall yellowwood giant. Aside from the Storms River Rest Camp, hotel accommodation in the Tsitsikamma area is scarce. *Tsitsikamma Lodge* and *Tsitsikamma Forest Inn* are both nice places near Storms River, while the *Forest Lodge* is closer to Nature's Valley.

The 30-mile Otter Trail that connects Storms River Mouth with Nature's Valley is probably South Africa's most famous hiking trail. Only 12 people a day are allowed on the trek, which takes five days to complete. Backpackers are accommodated in nice huts, each in a dazzlingly wild setting. Many rivers must be negotiated on this coastal walk, including a couple that have to be crossed at low tide. The scenery is spectacular throughout. The Otter Trail is named for the Cape clawless otter, which forages here in both rivers and sea. It is very shy, however, and only likely to be seen by lucky visitors at dawn or dusk.

Backpackers can also explore the Tsitsikamma Trail. This tough five-day trek starts at Nature's Valley and winds inland into the Tsitsikamma Mountains before ending at the Storms River highway bridge. Unlike the Otter Trail, which must be reserved through the National Parks Board, this hike is booked through SAFCOL Ecotourism at the Forestry Department.

Not on the Garden Route proper but easily reached from Port Elizabeth (about 35 miles away) is Addo Elephant National Park. This little park is covered with thickets of speckboom (*Portulacaria afra*), a fleshy-leafed woody tree that grows to about 12 feet high. This dense "Addo bush" was the refuge for a herd of elephants that confounded numerous determined attempts at extermination. When the park was established in 1931, only 11 elephants remained, and they were understandably wary. Today, they number over 100 and are easily seen. Cape buffalo also managed to hold out in Addo, and black rhino have been reintroduced. *Addo Elephant Park Rest Camp* provides bungalow accommodation (and a restaurant) and has a waterhole that is floodlit for nighttime game viewing. The nearby Zuurberg National Park is one of the newest in South Africa. Proclaimed in 1985, this mountainous park has no roads or facilities, but hikers can get permits to enter. It is currently mostly of botanical interest (because of its forested valleys and odd mountain vegetation), but elephants, buffalo, and other animals may yet be restocked. Elephants, both species of rhino, and other game (including some antelopes that are not native to the area) have already been stocked at *Shamwari Game Reserve*, a private sanctuary with accommodation in the historic Settler Country between Addo and the old British colonial stronghold of Grahamstown. This 30-square-mile reserve features several luxury lodges, Xhosa cultural villages (including an unusual "African healing village" that focuses on traditional medicine), and tours to old settler sites.

Aside from the Settler Country and its portion of the Karoo, the rest of the Eastern Cape Province is largely ignored by tourism. Its eastern districts were formerly the Xhosa "homelands" of Ciskei and Transkei. Those areas remain poor and undeveloped and are not considered entirely safe for travel. Two areas are outstanding in interest, however. The Amatola Trail through the Hogsback Mountains is legendary for its beauty (and the area is deemed safe), while Transkei's Wild Coast is just that: 150 miles of undeveloped Indian Ocean seashore.

Karoo Parks

Although less than 100 miles distant from the inviting coastline of the Garden Route, the arid expanses of the Karoo seem a different world. Subject to the alternation of frigid winters and broiling summers, this thirstland receives a mere 10 inches of annual rainfall. The harsh Karoo environment is only softened when spring rains stimulate its hardy plants to leaf and flower. But for all its starkness, the Karoo landscape has a certain austere grandeur. Its vast, barren plains are punctuated with isolated koppies (rock outcrops) and flat-topped table mountains. The Karoo is home to unique communities of plants and animals. These can be investigated in several interesting parks.

Mountain Zebra National Park is located on the eastern edge of the Karoo, near the town of Cradock, about 125 miles to the north of Port Elizabeth. It was originally set aside as a refuge to protect the last of the Cape mountain zebra (*Equus zebra zebra*), an animal that was once widespread in the Karoo and western Cape. There are now about 200 mountain zebras in the park, and many others have been moved to restock other South African reserves. The park comprises a mere 25 square miles but has impressive mountain scenery. Its vegetation mixes the sparse scrub typical of the Karoo with the grasslands of the Eastern Cape's inland plateau. In addition to mountain zebra, the park supports such unusual species as blesbok and black wildebeest. Red hartebeest, mountain reedbuck, eland, and springbok are also resident. The caracal is common, and the park is reputed to be a good place to observe this elusive cat. *Mountain Zebra National Park Rest Camp* offers bungalow accommodations and has a restaurant.

The Karoo Nature Reserve surrounds the historic town of Graaff-Reinet in the Eastern Cape. The 62-square-mile park is run by a private conservation foundation. It has been stocked with mountain zebra, black wildebeest, blesbok, eland, and springbok, but is most celebrated for its mountain scenery. The Valley of Desolation is the scenic highlight. Here the dolerite cap so typical of many Karoo peaks has crumbled, leaving a spectacular landscape filled with rock pinnacles, giant boulders, and collapsed columns. The nearby, nipple-topped butte of Spandau Kop dominates the valley of the Sundays River, which flows through the park and forms a U-bend around the town of Graaff-Reinet. There is no accommodation in the park (other than hikers' huts), but lodging can be found in town. Graaff-Reinet dates from the 1700s and is a major attraction in its own right. Often called "the gem of the Karoo," this charming old town is known for its many beautiful Dutch colonial buildings.

Karoo National Park is the largest of the Karoo sanctuaries. Established in 1979, the 128-square-mile park consists of open plains dominated by the flat-topped tablelands of the Nuweveld Mountains. Their cliffs, canyons, and koppies lend a grand scale to the park's classic Karoo landscape. Dwarf scrub is the dominant vegetation of the plains, while sweet-thorn acacias (*Acacia Karoo*) grow along dry watercourses, and sparse grasslands appear atop the mountain plateaus. The park has been restocked with mountain zebra, black wildebeest, red hartebeest, gemsbok, and springbok. Black rhinos (of the "desert" subspecies) are now being reintroduced from Namibia. Leopards occur, but the smaller predators (which include caracal, Cape fox, and black-backed jackal) are much more likely to be seen. Rock hyrax abound, so their nemesis, the black eagle, is fairly common. The Karoo is known for its tortoises, and five different species inhabit the park. The region is also famous for its fossils. Among those discovered in the park are dicynodonts — short-legged, beaked reptiles that date back 240 million years.

Karoo National Park Rest Camp, with its charming, white, Cape Dutch–style chalets, is set in an austere valley enclosed by flat-topped peaks. The camp has a restaurant and a pool, as well as air-conditioning in its cabins. Night drives and guided 4x4 driving trails are conducted by park staff. The night drives provide a good opportunity to see Cape fox, striped polecat, bat-eared fox, and other nocturnal animals. A nice campsite is located near the main rest camp. The primitive *Mountain View Rest Camp* (where guests must bring their own bedding and lighting as well as food) is open during the summer. Hiking trails in Karoo National Park range from the mile-long Bossie Trail (with labeled plants) and the easy Fossil Trail to the backpacker's three-day Springbok Trail, which leads to the top of the Nuweveld Mountains. Karoo National Park is located just outside the town of Beaufort West, which is about 125 miles north of the town of George, at the western end of the Garden Route.

The newly proclaimed Tankwa Karoo National Park straddles the borders of the Western and Northern Cape provinces, at the western edge of the Karoo. The park is situated between the seasonal Tankwa River and the Roggeveld Mountains. It currently has no facilities for visitors.

Those interested more in flora than fauna will find a visit to the Karoo National Botanic Garden rewarding. Located near Worcester (which is only about 70 miles from Cape Town), the garden features the plants of the great thirstland and has an impressive collection of Karoo succulents.

Cape Town and the Western Cape

Africa's southwestern tip does not fit the continent's tropical stereotype. Here game-filled savannas are replaced by rocky mountain ranges and fertile valleys nestled against the pulsing shores of two oceans. Magic scenery, a mild climate, and a unique Cape Dutch ambiance give the Western Cape Province a special appeal and make it one of South Africa's most desirable travel destinations. Chief among its attractions are the cosmopolitan city of Cape Town and the delightful vales of its winelands.

Although it is not a major safari destination, the Western Cape Province holds tremendous interest for the nature-oriented traveler. Wedged at the meeting point of the Atlantic and Indian oceans, its coasts teem with animal life. Offshore islands are the breeding grounds for cormorants, gannets, penguins, and fur seals, while the great whales of the southern seas — the southern right whale, humpback, and Bryde's whale — are regular summer migrants to Cape waters. The southern right whales calve in protected bays, where they are often seen from shore.

On land, the Western Cape is distinguished as one of the great botanical regions of the world. Known as the Cape Floral Kingdom (one of only six such "kingdoms" that divide the entire planet), this relatively small area possesses an astonishing diversity of endemic plants. Over 80 percent of the Cape's 8,500 native species belong to a unique community of scrub vegetation called fynbos (or Cape Macchia). Fynbos is characterized by aromatic evergreen shrubs. Although fynbos-type vegetation occurs elsewhere in Africa's mountain regions, Cape fynbos is thought to be very ancient and that helps account for its extraordinary degree of speciation: more varieties of plants can be found in a square meter of Cape fynbos than in any other type of vegetation in the world, including tropical rainforest. Although restios (also called Cape reeds), which have a superficial resemblance to grasses, are the most unusual component of Cape fynbos (and of the entire Cape Floral Kingdom), it is the ericas (heaths), proteas, and geophytes (flowering bulbs) that are its most spectacular floral groups. There are some 450 varieties of erica, over 100 types of protea, and 1,400 species of flowering bulbs. Ericas are evergreen shrubs with tiny, often prickly, leaves; it is from this *fijnbosch*, or "fine bush," that the fynbos community derives its name. Proteas have big leathery leaves and their flowers are famous for an infinite variety of form. Among them are the giant king protea, which is the South African national flower, and the colorful pincushions of the genus *Leucospermum*. A profusion of smaller flowers appears seasonally amidst the dense fynbos shrubbery. There are literally thousands of varieties. The daisy, iris, amaryllis, and lily families are particularly dazzling in their abundance and diversity, and delicate ground-dwelling orchids are also well represented. Although sugar and cone bushes (both proteas) make whole hillsides blaze with winter color and many of the amaryllids

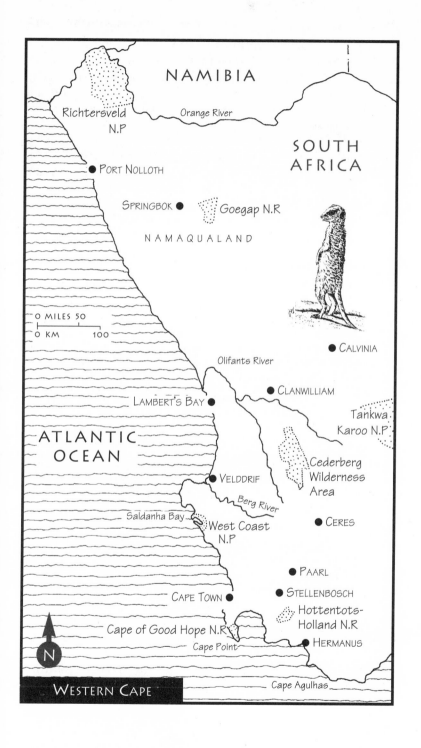

NAMIBIA

Richtersveld
N.P

Orange River

SOUTH
AFRICA

● PORT NOLLOTH

SPRINGBOK ●   ⋮ Goegap N.R

N A M A Q U A L A N D

● CALVINIA

Olifants River

● CLANWILLIAM

Tankwa
Karoo N.P

LAMBERT'S BAY ●

ATLANTIC
OCEAN

Cederberg
Wilderness
Area

● VELDDRIF

Berg River

Saldanha Bay   ● CERES
West Coast
N.P

● PAARL

● STELLENBOSCH

CAPE TOWN ●

Hottentots-
Holland N.R

Cape of Good Hope N.R

● HERMANUS

Cape Point

N

WESTERN CAPE

Cape Agulhas

O MILES 50
O KM   100

476 ADVENTURING IN SOUTHERN AFRICA
bloom in fall, it is in springtime that the Cape flora is in its full glory: the blossoms of wild gladiolas, watsonias, lilies, pelargoniums (geraniums), and daisies then light up the fynbos and form colorful carpets along South Africa's west coast. The entire region is a delight to botanists and gardeners, who will recognize innumerable common decorative plants that have their origins in the Cape Floral Kingdom.

Although the Western Cape does not support large numbers of big game animals, it does have interesting fauna. The smaller animals, such as the Cape grysbok and the Cape fox, were never wiped out, and many of the larger species that had formerly disappeared from the region, like Cape mountain zebra and eland, have been restocked in suitable parks. The most notable is the bontebok (*Damiliscus dorcas dorcas*), a beautiful antelope native to the Western Cape that has been brought back from the brink of extinction. Birdlife is varied and interesting. In addition to the birds of sea and shore, there are many varieties associated with fynbos. Some of the smaller birds make themselves prominent. The Cape sugarbird is a conspicuously long-tailed species associated with proteas, from atop which males launch an impressive aerial display. Colorful sunbirds of the malachite, orange-breasted, and double-collared varieties flit around fynbos flowers, while Cape bulbuls, which are also active birds, are easily recognized by their prominent white eye wattles. Skulking bush dwellers such as the Cape robin may take more effort to see, but their calls will advertise their presence.

With its glorious setting between Table Mountain and the Atlantic, Cape Town surely rates as one of the most beautiful cities in the world. The famous flat-topped mountain, with its characteristic "tablecloth" of cloud laid upon its summit, looms over the downtown area and the historic anchorages of Table Bay, while the outlying peaks and promontories that range all down the Cape Peninsula separate the city from its green suburbs. Aside from the appeal of such mountain scenery, Cape Town has much to tempt travelers of diverse tastes. There are innumerable historic buildings and monuments. Among them are the Castle, a star-shaped Dutch fort that goes back to 1666, and the Company's Garden, started in 1652, which is today a lovely central city park. Even as museums and picturesque Victorian neighborhoods attract culture mavens, a bevy of beaches, boutiques, fine restaurants, sport facilities, clubs, and galleries make Cape Town and its satellite communities delightful places for contemporary urban explorers. Fun seekers are attracted to the Victoria & Alfred Waterfront (yes, named for her second son, Prince Alfred, not for her better known royal consort, Albert), a working port that has been transformed by the addition of a lively entertainment complex of restaurants, shops, and pubs.

The Cape Town area has many fine parks and places of special interest to nature enthusiasts, including a couple that are located in the middle of town. The South African Museum has a number of fine collections. These include an assemblage of dinosaurs and other fossils from the Karoo and a hall devoted to whales. It also houses a magnificent collection of Bushman rock paintings carefully transported from their original sites. The world-class Two Oceans Aquarium vividly presents the undersea life of the Cape. Its huge tanks display the fauna of different ocean communities, such as rocky reefs and kelp beds. The Open Ocean tank features ragged-tooth sharks and other large pelagic fish, while the River Ecosystem display links the thread of life from mountain stream through marshland to the sea.

The cable car to the summit of Table Mountain is one of Cape Town's prime tourist attractions. From the top, there are fabulous vistas of sea and city. Most visitors are content to take in the view from the immediate vicinity of the cableway, but a network of foot trails beckons hikers to further explorations. The rocky tableland, which reaches 3,563 feet, is covered with mountain fynbos. Hyrax are the most commonly seen animals, especially around the cable car vista point, where they are exceedingly tame. Baboons, Cape grysboks, caracals, lizards, and snakes (including cobras and Berg adders) live on the mountain. So does the Himalayan tahr (*Hemitragus jemlahicus*), a goatlike animal introduced from Asia. Although the tahr does not by itself present major environmental problems, the same cannot be said for introduced plants. Indeed, invasive alien flora, together with vandalism and frequent fires, are degrading Table Mountain's natural vegetation. The same problems threaten all the peaks and nature sanctuaries on the Cape Peninsula, an area that is surely one of the world's botanical treasure troves: this small neck of land possesses 2,285 species of native plants—far more than the whole of the British Isles. To better protect this amazing natural heritage, the various nature reserves of the peninsula are being incorporated into a single entity, the new Table Mountain National Park.

The Cape Peninsula is a lovely place, and virtually every visitor takes the drive down. There are wonderful mountainscapes and seascapes where the Atlantic coast road winds beneath the mountainous Twelve Apostles and Chapman's Peak. On the peninsula's east side, pleasant little towns and beaches front the waters of False Bay. Jackass penguins can be seen at a beach called the Boulders, in Simon's Town. The Cape of Good Hope Nature Reserve occupies the tip of the peninsula. This 30-square-mile park has been stocked with eland, bontebok, Cape mountain zebra, and ostrich. Baboons are likely to be seen, as they have learned to beg at the side of the road. The reserve has great scenery and a good variety of both fynbos vegetation and marine life, which differ on its Atlantic and False Bay sides. The park can be explored on hiking trails as well as by car. The main tour destination is the cliff-top lighthouse that overlooks the thrashing waters of Cape Point. The actual Cape of Good Hope, which lies a mile and a half to the west, is much less visited.

Kirstenbosch National Botanic Gardens is a must-see destination for plant lovers. This scenic park covers 2 square miles on the eastern flanks of Table Mountain. Most of Kirstenbosch retains its natural vegetation, but there are 150 acres of cultivated gardens that grandly display the indigenous flora of South Africa. There is no better place to encounter the myriad plants of the fynbos, and there are great collections of cycads and succulents. The gardens are good for birding, and hiking trails lead right up the back side of Table Mountain. Kirstenbosch is located in Constantia, which is also the site of South Africa's oldest wine estate. Established in 1685, Groot Constantia's beautiful manor house is now a museum, but the estate is still producing fine wines.

The Cape is synonymous with excellent wine, and the heart of its beautiful winelands is only 30 miles to the east of Cape Town's city center. The interior Cape valleys have a gentle climate and provide a great setting for its centuries-old wineries. Here, thatched and whitewashed Cape Dutch farmhouses are placed among idyllic vineyards and surrounded by fynbos-covered mountains. Most of the old wine estates have gone to great lengths to maintain their historic buildings, and lovely little colonial towns add to the region's charm. The most famous is Stellenbosch, which is celebrated for its oak-lined streets and numerous old buildings. Although most visitors restrict their activities to the civilized pleasures of wine tasting and sightseeing, there is great hiking in the wine country. The gleaming-white granite dome above the town of Paarl ("the pearl") earned this wine-growing hamlet its name. The dome attracts day hikers, while the rugged mountains of the Hottentots-Holland Nature Reserve are renowned for the diversity of their fynbos vegetation.

Of Cape Town's many hotels, the *Mount Nelson* is the most prestigious. Set among its own luxuriant gardens at the foot of Table Mountain, the five-star "Nellie" is truly in a class of its own. The *Cape Sun* and *Capetonian Protea* are top-rated hotels in the central district, and the *Victoria & Alfred Hotel* is part of the waterfront complex. It is a good choice for those who wish to be in the thick of the city's night life. The *Breakwater Lodge* is just next door. A former prison, it has been converted into a clean and comfortable budget hotel. The attractive, up-market *Bay Hotel* is set on an Atlantic beach at Camps Bay. Other hotels and guest houses of every class and budget are found throughout the city and its environs. Some of the most charming are found in Constantia, a lovely green suburb to the east of Table Mountain and about a 20-minute drive from the city center. The luxurious *Cellars-Hohenort Country House* centers around a restored Dutch manor and its neighboring wine cellars. *Constantia Uitsig* is a 200-acre wine estate offering accommodation in cute Cape cottages, while the elegant, antique-filled manor house of the *Alphen Hotel* is a national monument placed in 16 acres of wooded parkland.

There are also many charming places to stay in the Cape wine country, which is less than an hour's drive from Cape Town. The *Grand Roche Hotel* in Paarl is the last word in luxury: its 18th-century manor house and outbuildings have been turned into a five-star hotel, and its Bosman's restaurant is rated one of the finest in the country. Many other old farmhouses have been converted into lovely little lodges. Included among them are the *Roggeland Country House* and *Mountain Shadows*, both near Paarl. The *Lanzerac Hotel* is a 300-year-old manor house on a wine estate just outside Stellenbosch. Within that historic old village, the *D'Ouwe Werf* is a country inn that dates back to 1802. It has Georgian-style architecture and is noted for the Cape Dutch specialties produced in its kitchen. The *Stellenbosch Hotel* (which dates to 1876) is also very quaint.

Many local tour companies offer day trips around Cape Town or to Cape Point and the wine country. But if you want to hike or spend any time in the local nature reserves, you will need to hire a car. Cape Town's airport is located about midway between the city and the winelands, so it is convenient to rent a car and divide your stay between town and country hotels.

The Western Cape is worth exploring beyond the immediate vicinity of Cape Town. The Overberg is the region to the east of the wine country. This rural farming district is not much visited by overseas tourists, although some do drive through on the way to the Garden Route. The main highway passes through Swellendam, an old town noted for its fine Cape Dutch architecture. Bontebok National Park is located just outside town on the banks of the Breede River. This little park (11 square miles) was originally created as a refuge for the last of the bontebok. Low-growing fynbos scrub permits good viewing of those animals, and the park is also a good place to see gray rhebok. There is a campsite on the wooded banks of the Breede, and the beautiful *Klippe Rivier Homestead*, which dates back to 1825, provides charming luxury accommodation on the outskirts of Swellendam.

The Overberg's coast is celebrated for its whale watching between

August and November. Although whales can be seen in many places, Walker Bay, near the little resort town of Hermanus, is a particularly favored calving area for southern right whales. Seaside cliffs facilitate viewing from shore, which is the only way whale watching is done in South Africa: strict regulations prohibit boats from venturing closer than 300 meters (about 1,000 feet), so there are no commercial whale watching cruises, but regulations could change in the future. Nearby Cape Agulhas is the southernmost point on the African continent.

The De Hoop Nature Reserve is one of the undiscovered gems of the Cape coast. The park protects 140 square miles of rich coastal fynbos. This community is much rarer than mountain fynbos because so much of the natural vegetation in low-lying areas has been destroyed by human activity. Aside from its botanical interest, the park hosts more bontebok than any other reserve, as well as Cape mountain zebra and all the small antelopes native to fynbos. De Hoop extends out to sea in a 90-square-mile marine reserve. Its 25 miles of undeveloped coastline are gaining a reputation as an excellent place to observe southern right whales. The park has loops for game drives, as well as hiking trails. It also possesses South Africa's first official mountain bike trail. Up to 12 bikers can be accommodated in a nice furnished hut (no bedding) and ride to various remote beaches. The reserve has a couple of other self-catering bungalows, but regular hotel accommodation can be found in Swellendam or at the tastefully modern *Arniston Hotel*, near the quaint old fishing village of Waenhuiskrans (also called Arniston).

There are also interesting nature reserves to the north of Cape Town. Several bays and salt pans along the Atlantic coast support large seasonal concentrations of birdlife. The most important is Langebaan Lagoon, which is within West Coast National Park. During the South African summer, thousands of migrant waders from the northern hemisphere make the lagoon their home, while the islands within the adjoining Saldanha Bay are inhabited year-round by cormorants, gannets, penguins, and gulls. The Postberg section of the 117-square-mile national park has been restocked with an interesting mix of game that was formerly native to the area. The most unusual species are black wildebeest and black rhino, although there are also gemsbok and springbok, as well as bontebok antelope and Cape mountain zebra. Vegetation consists of a unique floral community called West Coast sandveld, which is famous for its startling displays of ephemeral springtime wildflowers. *Langebaan Lodge* provides comfortable hotel-type accommodation within West Coast National Park. The *Farmhouse* is a nice private lodge in the vicinity.

Flamingos and waterbirds can be seen at the Velddrif salt ponds,

Rocher Pan, Verlorenvlei, and other West Coast reserves. Bird Island, which is connected to the mainland by a causeway from the fishing port of Lambert's Bay, is renowned for up-close viewing of Cape gannets and cormorants. Jackass penguins can sometimes be found there, too. Large numbers of penguins can be seen at a breeding colony on Robben Island, which is reached by boat from Cape Town. The island is the site of the infamous prison where Nelson Mandela and many other political prisoners were incarcerated; it is no longer a jail, and is now a popular tourist attraction.

The Cedarberg is a fascinating mountain range to the north of the Cape winelands. These craggy hills, which reach up to 6,654 feet, are celebrated for their eroded sandstone formations. The most famous are the 60-foot pillar known as the Maltese Cross, the Wolfberg Arch, and the Stadsaal, a weird rock labyrinth pitted with caves. The Cedarberg is also known for such rare and beautiful plants as the snow protea, which only grows at the highest elevations, and the Clanwilliam cedar (*Widdringtonia cedarbergensis*). The mountains take their name from the gnarled old cedar trees, some of which have been standing for 1,000 years. Game is scarce, but there are leopards, as well as the more common mountain animals like klipspringer. Over 320 square miles of the Cedarberg are protected within the Cedarberg Wilderness Area and the Matjiesrivier Nature Reserve. Huts are available to shelter serious trekkers, and there is a campground at the Algeria Forest Station, as well as small hotels in the nearby towns of Citrusdal and Clanwilliam.

Many excellent galleries of Bushman paintings are found in the Cedarberg, and this prompted the creation of an unusual tourist attraction. Several families of Bushmen were induced to move down from the Northern Cape Province, where they were eking out a rather miserable existence as laborers on cattle farms, to settle on the private Kagga Kamma Nature Reserve, where they now live by reenacting the traditional hunter-gatherer way of life for visiting tourists. Arguments rage as to whether this project is a good thing (the developers make a good case for it) or sheer exploitation. In addition to visiting the Bushmen, guests at *Kagga Kamma Lodge* can see authentic rock paintings, hike amidst Cedarberg scenery, and view game. The 22-square-mile reserve has been restocked with a good variety of Cape wildlife.

The West Coast is particularly appealing in the spring, when it is graced by amazing carpets of wildflowers. The wildflowers peak in August and September, but can continue into October. By their nature, the floral displays are brief and erratic, but there are many small reserves where they occur and up-to-date information on the best current locales is easily available in Cape Town. Springtime flower tours are regularly

run up the West Coast. These visit blooming areas of sandveld and fynbos and continue northward into Namaqualand, in the Northern Cape
Province. When conditions are right, this arid semidesert region flaunts
particularly extravagant wildflower exhibitions. Astounding masses of
blossoms can extend for miles. The colorful mats are composed mostly
of daisies, although lilies and succulent mesembryanthemums (also
called *vygies*, or ice plants) are also integral to Namaqualand's legendary
flower displays.

Kalahari-Gemsbok National Park and Parks of the Northern Cape

There is no better place to encounter the wildlife of the Kalahari than
South Africa's Kalahari-Gemsbok National Park. Located at the southwestern corner of the vast Kalahari thirstlands, the park showcases the
fauna and flora of that celebrated "desert." From ground squirrels and
suricates to the big Kalahari lions, the creatures of the waterless Kalahari
savannas are all here. A large population of migratory antelope — gemsbok, springbok, wildebeest, red hartebeest, and eland — supports good
numbers of lion, cheetah, leopard, and both brown and spotted hyenas.
By nature of the harsh environment, these animals are all highly mobile.
An unfenced boundary with Botswana's adjacent Gemsbok National
Park permits them to wander over more than 11,000 square miles of
wilderness habitat. Although the biggest herds of antelope ordinarily
congregate only during the rainy summer months, the South African
park's human-made waterholes attract and hold game year-round.

Kalahari-Gemsbok National Park is situated in the Kalahari's attractive red sand country. In places, there are bare, wind-blown dunes, but
mostly the low sand ridges are held in place by stabilizing desert grasses
and a scrub composed of driedoring bush, silver terminalia, gray camel-
thorn, and shade-giving shepherd's trees. Two major riverbeds traverse
the park, but water rarely flows in them. The Auob is the narrower and
deeper river valley, and it gets water more frequently. The larger Nossob
only floods two or three times a century. At its upper end, the Nossob is
a shallow valley, almost a half-mile wide, but it narrows as it moves to
its junction with the Auob at the south end of the park. Tall camel-thorn
acacias grow in the sandy riverbeds, where sweet grasses attract herds of
antelope when the rains come. The big acacias are often weighted with
the huge nests of social weaver birds, and make fine photographic subjects with the red dunes as a backdrop. (For more information on the
Kalahari environment and wildlife, see the Kalahari Ecology section in
the Botswana chapter.)

Rainfall is scarce and erratic in this part of the Kalahari, averaging only about 8 inches per year. The park is prettiest during the rainy season (if the rainy season comes), a time when greenery crowns the red dunes and wildflowers bloom. This is also the most prolific time for wildlife, but temperatures soar to over 100 degrees. In winter, game disperses more, but daytime temperatures are pleasant, with nights dipping below freezing. Windmill-powered waterholes allow for excellent game viewing, and a network of gravel roads makes the park accessible to visitors with ordinary two-wheel-drive vehicles. The number of game tracks is limited: one major route follows the Nossob (which forms the border with Botswana), another the Auob, and there is a 42-mile track that crosses the dune country in between.

The 3,746-square-mile Kalahari-Gemsbok National Park is the second largest in South Africa, but due to its remote location and the severe nature of its climate, it is not visited nearly to the same extent as Kruger or the KwaZulu-Natal reserves. The closest major town is Upington, from which the park is reached by 222 miles of gravel road. Upington is served daily by scheduled airlines, and car rentals are readily available there.

There are three rest camps in the park. *Twee Rivieren* is the principal camp, and the only one with air-conditioned cottages, a restaurant, and a swimming pool. It is located at the park's southern entrance, near the junction of the Nossob and Auob riverbeds. *Nossob Camp* is 105 miles to the north, on the banks of the riverbed, and *Mata Mata* (76 miles distant) is located on the Auob, right at the Namibian border. Both those rest camps are only for self-catering guests. All three have facilities for campers.

Augrabies National Park is also well worth visiting. Its prime attraction is the thundering waterfall, "the place of great noise," which gives the park its name. Here, the big Orange River plunges 184 feet into a spectacular, sheer-walled granite canyon. Augrabies is outside the sandy realm of the Kalahari. It is part of Africa's true southwestern desert, where a scant 4 inches of annual rainfall supports only the hardiest of plants and animals amidst a harsh granitic landscape. At Augrabies, jumbles of weathered granite dominate much of the terrain. It's ideal country for klipspringer and rock hyrax. Baboon, steenbok, and springbok are the other mammals most likely to be seen, while multicolored Cape flat lizards (*Platysaurus capensis*) are very conspicuous along the lip of the Augrabies gorge.

Augrabies National Park is located 75 miles west of Upington. *Augrabies Rest Camp* has air-conditioned chalets, a restaurant, swimming pools, and a campsite. Well-maintained gravel roads permit explorations and game drives in the park's southern sector, where there are several vista points along the 11-mile length of the Orange River gorge. Three short nature trails are open to all visitors, but the hutted three-day Klip-springer Hiking Trail is reserved for backpackers. Conducted night dri-ves can be booked at the park's rest camp.

The vast preponderance of Augrabies National Park's 314-square-mile territory lies on the north side of the Orange River and remains un-developed for tourism. Black rhinos of the "desert" subspecies have been reintroduced to this northern sector and can be seen on the specially conducted tour called the Black Rhino Adventure. A boat carries partic-ipants across the Orange, where an open Land Rover and rangers await. The rhinos are then tracked down by vehicle and on foot. Although the animals are thriving in their adopted home, a wrinkle has developed in the rhino conservation plan: the 17-square-mile riverfront sector where they live has been awarded to the Riemvasmaak community, which had been evicted during the apartheid era, and they want it back. The land is now leased by the park, but its final status as a conservation area is still unresolved.

Augrabies National Park is also a good place to discover the unusual vegetation of the southwestern desert. Quiver trees, or *kokerbooms*, are the most conspicuous of the region's many succulent plants. These tree-sized aloes grow in Augrabies and are very prominent in northern Na-maqualand. That area, which is especially famous for its springtime wildflower displays, possesses lots of botanical oddities. The Goegap (formerly Hester-Malan) Nature Reserve, near the town of Springbok, is often included on Namaqualand flower tours. Its worn granite land-scape supports lots of quiver trees and other succulents, as well as a sprinkling of desert animals. A new national park will soon be estab-lished on the coast to the west of Namaqualand.

Further north, the remote mountains of Richtersveld National Park are reputed to harbor the world's richest collection of succulents, in ad-dition to many other kinds of rare or endemic desert plants. The 634-square-mile Richtersveld National Park, which was only proclaimed in 1991, is brutally rugged and completely undeveloped, although it is open to exploration by self-sufficient, four-wheel-drive expeditions. A few overland tour operators run springtime trips to the Richtersveld. The area can also be explored by canoe along the Orange River, which loops along the park's northern boundary and divides it from Namibia.

Vaalbos National Park is located in the eastern part of the Northern Cape Province, near the historic diamond-mining city of Kimberley. The park's vegetation mixes elements of the Karoo and Kalahari and is dom-inated by grasslands with patches of *vaalbos*, or camphor bush (*Tar-chonanthus camphoratus*). The little 87-square-mile park was only established in 1986, but has since been restocked with black and white rhino, red hartebeest, zebra, buffalo, wildebeest, and giraffe. Vaalbos

National Park is not likely to become a major game destination, but might be worth a stop if you are visiting Kimberley, which is famous for the Big Hole at its original diamond works. The deep pit, which was dug by hand, is mind-boggling, and the adjacent Kimberley Mine Museum recreates the Victorian buildings and culture of the diamond-rush era.

A huge new private game reserve has recently opened in the Northern Cape Province. Located at the southern edge of the Kalahari, the 230-square-mile *Tswalu Private Desert Reserve* showcases the wildlife of South Africa's vast thirstlands. Lion and "desert" black rhino have been introduced, and various other species have been brought in to supplement native herds of springbok, gemsbok, and eland. The reserve's luxurious lodge at the foot of the Korannaberg Mountains accommodates 22 guests in air-conditioned comfort. Safaris are conducted in open vehicles and night drives increase the chances of finding predators like the brown hyena. Guests are transferred to Tswalu by air from either Upington or Kimberley.

Golden Gate Highlands National Park and Parks of the Free State

The vast Highveld plains of the Free State Province were long ago converted to farmland, so the province does not have much to offer in the way of game parks. However, it does have a couple of reserves where some remnants of the old wildlife community of the Highveld grasslands can still be seen. The big roaming herds are gone, of course, and the quagga is extinct, but black wildebeest, blesbok, red hartebeest, springbok, eland, and other plains animals are found on the Tussen-die-Riviere Game Farm and the Willem Pretorius Game Reserve. Neither of these small parks (82 and 45 square miles, respectively) host any large predators, but the Willem Pretorius reserve is known for its large population of black wildebeest (*Connochaetes gnou*). This animal, which is also known as the white-tailed gnu, looks quite different than the common or blue wildebeest (*Connochaetes taurinus*); it is smaller and has a white mane and tail, as well as dangerous-looking, forward-thrusting horns. Like its more plentiful cousin, the black wildebeest is prone to clownish bucking and cavorting displays. Tussen-die-Riviere has a splendid location at the junction of the Caledon and Orange rivers. Both parks are far from the normal tourist routes and offer only self-catering accommodations.

Golden Gate Highlands National Park hosts the same selection of Highveld herbivores, but the park's main attraction is its fine scenery. Located in the foothills of the Maluti Mountains, this 45-square-mile national park is characterized by grass-covered mountains and steep-cut sandstone cliffs. In morning and evening light, bands of yellow and red sandstone make the cliffs glow with soft color. Elevations in the park range from 6,207 to 9,088 feet. Its bracing montane climate produces snow in winter and dramatic thunderstorms in summer. There are numerous hiking trails to explore, and horses can be hired for riding. Bushman paintings and fossil sites are found in the cliffs, and the park is a good place to see lammergeier, black eagle, ground woodpecker, and bald ibis.

Golden Gate Highlands National Park is located 224 miles south of Johannesburg, and it is a popular holiday destination. Its *Brandwag Rest Camp* offers both self-catering chalets and a hotel complex, while the *Glen Reenen Rest Camp* has rustic huts and camping facilities. Night drives can be booked at Brandwag. A hut serves backpackers who are traveling the two-day Rhebok Hiking Trail.

Parks of the North-West and Northern Provinces

Several parks and private reserves are found to the north of the Gauteng Province's metropolitan area. Although they primarily attract South Africans, their proximity to Johannesburg and the resorts of Sun City appeals to tour planners, and they are starting to attract increasing numbers of overseas visitors. These reserves are all fairly recent phenomena; most are the result of conscious efforts to spin money out of ecotourism. Nevertheless, big game is rapidly being restored to places from which it has long been banished and the trend toward wildlife conservation is definitely positive. At least one locale, the Waterberg, has the potential to become a conservation area of major significance.

Pilanesberg National Park is the best developed of the northern nature reserves. The 226-square-mile park has a fascinating geological history. It is nestled into the eroded crater of a giant 1.3 billion-year-old volcano. Seventeen miles in diameter, the crater walls still rise 2,000 feet above the surrounding plains. On the crater floor, concentric rings of worn-down lava hills, each composed of different types of rock, pop up on the plains and account for a great diversity of vegetation. Since it was established in 1979, the park has been extensively restocked. Game viewing is quite good. The park is inhabited by all the big game species, as well as unusual animals like brown hyena, sable antelope, black-footed cat, and bushpig. It is one of the best reserves in the country for rhino watching.

Pilanesberg is already on the tourist map because it's located right next to the resort of Sun City. Its main rest camp, *Manyane*, is located on the park boundary and allows 24-hour access, so guests can come and go to the casinos at night. Manyane is a large camp offering accommodation in chalets or safari tents; it also has a restaurant and a campsite.

Several other self-catering camps are scattered around the park. The 12-bed *Metswedi Camp* is the only full-service tented safari camp. It features open vehicles, night drives, and walks. *Kwa Maritane* and *Bakubung* are both luxury lodges in the area.

Pilanesberg National Park is readily accessible to day visitors from Sun City. Long a popular gambling and entertainment center for South Africans, Sun City is poised to become an international destination. Its latest and greatest attraction is the *Palace of the Lost City*, a hotel and theme park based on a century-old legend about a "lost city" in the Kalahari. The Palace's lavish architecture is mostly Moghul, but there are plenty of elements borrowed from other cultures, and all are infused with a fantastical African motif. Animal sculptures and painted murals are everywhere. With its imaginative design, abundant recreational facilities, and luxurious ambiance, the Lost City is sure to succeed as a major tourist draw.

Pilanesberg is not actually a national park. It had that status when it was part of the "independent homeland" of Bophuthatswana, but it is now under the administration of the North-West Province. The provincial parks department also runs the small Borakalalo National Park, which is close to Johannesburg but has no large predators, and the 290-square-mile Madikwe Game Reserve. Madikwe is a new park on the border with Botswana that is being ambitiously restocked with game: some 10,000 animals have been moved into the reserve and it is already inhabited by all the "big five" species (including over 200 elephants). The park's two luxury lodges, *Madikwe River Lodge* and *Tau Lodge*, cater primarily to international visitors on fly-in safaris.

Mabula Game Lodge is a well-publicized private reserve only a two-hour drive from either Johannesburg or Sun City. Mabula is conveniently accessible to tourists who want a taste of the bush. The 47-square-mile reserve has been stocked with the "big five," and offers horseback riding in addition to open-vehicle safaris.

One hundred and twenty miles to the north of Johannesburg, a fractured wall of sandstone cliffs heralds the abrupt rise of the Waterberg Escarpment. Atop the mountain wall, a 6,000-square-mile plateau holds tremendous ecotourism potential. The Waterberg's wooded bushveld is good wildlife habitat, and its high elevation gives it a healthy, malaria-free climate. Several big blocks of territory have already been officially declared conservation areas and major wildlife restocking programs are under way.

Marakele National Park is South Africa's newest. Proclaimed in 1994, the park (which was previously called Kransberg in honor of the 6,840-foot peak that is the highest in the Waterberg), Marakele is barely open to the public; it has a single eight-tent rest camp that can only be reached by four-wheel-drive vehicles. Plans are in progress to establish hiking and 4x4 driving trails and to put in more tented camps. One of the largest remaining colonies of the threatened Cape vulture is protected within Marakele National Park. Rhino and elephant have already been reintroduced, while lion and roan antelope are on the way. The 131-square-mile park (which will ultimately double in size) bounds the Welgevonden Private Game Reserve, a 100-square-mile tract, and the fences between them are coming down. Welgevonden's wealthy landowners are funding extensive restocking and breeding projects, so the area's game population is rapidly growing.

To the east of the Marakele-Welgevonden area and separated by a belt of farmland is the Waterberg Conservancy, which protects another 293 square miles of scenic bushland. Its best known components are the Lapalala Wilderness and the Touchstone Game Ranch. Lapalala, renowned as an environmental education center and pioneer in the reintroduction of black rhinos, has two catered safari camps: the 16-bed *Kolobe Lodge* and the tented, 8-bed *Rhino Camp*. Walking trails and game drives are conducted on its extensive property. Equus Trails horseback safaris take place here, too. Riders can stay at a tented base camp or explore on longer-range mobile safaris. The neighboring *Touchstone Game Ranch* also has several small safari lodges that offer game drives and bush hikes.

There are many other game ranches and hunting lodges in the Waterberg and throughout the northern Transvaal region. The private Lesheba Wilderness reserve takes up an 11-mile stretch along the crest of the Soutpansberg, the northernmost of South Africa's numerous mountain ranges. It's good walking country where Bushman paintings, cycads, and a colony of Cape vultures come as bonuses to expansive views. Game is present (leopards are reputed to be particularly abundant and it is one of the best places to view bushpigs), but Lesheba and its camp are probably most appealing to hikers who are traveling by road to the northern Pafuri entrance of Kruger National Park. Greater Kuduland Game Lodges is a safari operator that has two large properties in the baobab country to the north of the Soutpansberg (these private reserves are primarily used for hunting safaris). Greater Kuduland may open a game-viewing camp on the beautiful Luvuvhu River, right on the Kruger boundary.

Two more official parks may be created in the Northern Province. The Madimbo Corridor, a strip of land on the Zimbabwe frontier to the west of Kruger National Park's Pafuri area, has been proposed as a new national park. Formerly a restricted army security zone, the area protects a large belt of riverine forest along the Limpopo River. Another park will be further upstream on the Limpopo, where the boundaries of South Africa, Zimbabwe, and Botswana meet. This area is expected to soon be proclaimed as Dongola National Park.

Swaziland: An African Kingdom

Swaziland is a tiny independent nation squeezed between South Africa and southernmost Mozambique. With a population of about a million, the New Jersey–sized kingdom of Swaziland is mostly a place of historic and cultural interest.

The Swazis first gained prominence during the early part of the 19th century. By a combination of skillful diplomacy and military might, the Swazi kings managed to fend off absorption by their powerful Zulu neighbors while extending their own control over a swathe of territory that stretched all the way north to the Limpopo River, which today forms South Africa's border with Zimbabwe. The kingdom later shrank under pressure from the Boers and British, but rivalry between those two European groups enabled it to avoid consolidation into the former Union of South Africa. In 1968, Swaziland obtained its independence from Britain and has since been governed solely by the Swazi royal family. Although there is a parliament, this African kingdom is one of the world's few true monarchies. The current ruler is King Mswati III, a young man born in the year of Swazi independence.

Swazi tribal culture remains quite traditional. Due pomp and circumstance surround the king, who is the head of state as well as spiritual leader, and the queen mother, who holds a position of key political and social significance. The paramountcy of the king is celebrated annually in the *ncwala* ceremony, which takes place in December or January and sanctifies the "first fruits" of the new year. Attendance at many of the *ncwala* rituals is largely restricted to Swazi participants. All visitors are welcome to attend the Reed Dance, or *umhlanga*, a festival that takes place in August or September. At this colorful event, thousands of unmarried Swazi girls, bare-breasted and colorfully attired in short, beaded skirts, pay homage to the queen mother with elaborate parades and dances. The major royal festivals are hard to plan for, however, as their exact dates depend on the calculations of court astrologers. But even the most casual visitors to Swaziland will encounter people clad in the traditional *emahiya*, a colorful red toga, and male troupes can often be seen performing their vigorous *sibhaca* dances.

Swaziland is a pretty country that is hemmed in by mountains. In the west, a belt of Highveld runs along the mountainous crest of the Transvaal Escarpment. Then follows the Middleveld, a pleasant region of hills and fertile valleys that drops into the hot Lowveld country. The

Lebombo Mountains form the eastern border with Mozambique. Most of the countryside has been put to intensive agricultural use. Huge timber plantations of pine and eucalyptus trees are found in the highlands, while fruits and vegetables are grown in the Middleveld, and sugar or cotton farms cover much of the Lowveld. Although there is little true wilderness in the country, several nature reserves have been established.

Swaziland became a hot getaway destination for South Africans during the apartheid years, when its resorts acquired a steamy reputation for sex shows, prostitution, and gambling. Although the casinos are still there, the sex trade has been toned down and the resorts are promoting a cleaner image. Even so, Swaziland is still primarily a vacation spot for South Africans. Most overseas tourists make only a brief overnight transit of the country as they travel by road between Kruger National Park and KwaZulu-Natal. The main overnight stops are Pigg's Peak, a country resort and casino in the mountains of the northwestern Highveld, and the casino-hotels of the Ezulwini Valley, a lovely area to the south of the Swazi capital, Mbabane. Although Swaziland has its own currency (the Lilangeni), its value is the same as the South African rand, which is equally acceptable throughout the country. Visitors must have a passport, but no visa is required. Royal Swazi Airways connects the country to Johannesburg, Durban, and several African capitals.

Although none of Swaziland's nature reserves are outstanding by African standards, local conservationists, with the support of the king, have done a remarkable job of reintroducing wildlife to a country from which large animals had been all but exterminated.

Mlilwane Wildlife Sanctuary is located in the hills that flank the Ezulwini Valley. A scenic reserve of grasslands and rocky outcrops, it has been stocked with a variety of game and serves as an environmental education center. Although it is somewhat zoolike in character, Mlilwane is close to the capital and the royal kraal at Lobamba, so it is the best known and most visited of the Swazi game reserves. *Mlilwane Rest Camp* is a convenient place to stop overnight in the Mbabane area. The rest camp (with a restaurant) provides accommodation in wooden cabins. Visitors can explore the park on hiking or horse trails as well as on game drives.

The scenic Malalotja Nature Reserve is Swaziland's most unusual park. It is an important sanctuary for the flora and fauna of the Transvaal Escarpment. Its 6,000-foot-high mountains and deep-cut gorges provide refuge to the species of montane grassland, fynbos, and forest habitats. Three rare types of cycad occur in the reserve, and it is a good place to see such mountain birds as bald ibis, blue swallow, and Gurney's sugarbird. The typical montane antelopes — mountain reedbuck, gray rhebok, oribi, and klipspringer — are all native, while blesbok, zebra, and both types of wildebeest have been reintroduced. The reserve has over 125 miles of hiking trails. It features the oldest known sedimentary rocks, as well as a Stone Age mining site that dates back 40,000 years. The 300-foot Malalotja Falls are its most popular scenic attraction. Only self-catering bungalows (no bedding provided) and campsites are available in the park, but *Pigg's Peak Hotel,* a large resort popular with South Africans, is close by. Nature lovers will feel more at home based at *Phophonyane*, a charming little lodge located near Pigg's Peak. Set amidst indigenous forest, this private reserve features its own hiking trails and beautiful swimming holes in bilharzia-free rivers.

Big game can be seen in the Mkhaya Nature Reserve and at Hlane National Park. Mkhaya is a small private reserve (only 24 square miles in area), but it is a good place to see black rhino. White rhino, elephant, roan antelope, giraffe, tsessebe, and other Lowveld species have also been reintroduced at Mkhaya, and the reserve possesses a herd of pure-bred Nguni cattle, a hardy African breed that is now extremely rare. A small tented camp provides comfortable accommodation, and game drives in open vehicles are available. Hlane is the largest park in Swaziland. Located in the northeast, its 117 square miles of Lowveld savanna are home to herds of zebra and antelope. White rhinos, elephants, and lions have also been reintroduced. The park has camping facilities and two small, self-catering hutted camps. Campsites and hiking trails are also found in the neighboring Mlawula Nature Reserve, which extends into the Lebombo Mountains on the Mozambique border. It supports a fascinating range of plant species and an extremely diverse avifauna. The Muti-Muti Private Reserve is also located in the Lebombos.

Lesotho: The Mountain Enclave

Lesotho is southern Africa's mountain country. Although it possesses considerable natural beauty and cultural interest, its isolated position as an enclave within South Africa and the inaccessibility of its mountains have left it well off the path of international tourism.

Lesotho's origins as a nation-state go back to the wake of the *mfecane* tribal wars of the 1820s, when successive rampages by Zulu and Matabele armies plunged the Sotho-speaking clans of the Highveld into a cyclone of destruction. War led to starvation and the collapse of traditional society; some clans were even reduced to cannibalism. Out of the chaos, Moshoeshoe, the founder-king of the Basotho nation, led his people to safety atop a flat-topped mountain fortress called Thaba Bosiu, "the mountain of night." From that refuge, he gathered scattered bands of frightened survivors and forged a domain centered on the valley of the

Caledon River. Throughout the 1850s and 1860s, the Basotho were embattled with the land-grabbing Boers of the Orange Free State. The Boers failed to conquer Moshoeshoe's stronghold, but they occupied all the rich agricultural lowlands to the west of the Caledon, which became the border with South Africa, and forced the old chief to seek the protection of the British. Left only with the harsh uplands of its mountainous heartland, "Basutoland" remained a colonial backwater of hardscrabble stock herders until given independence in 1966. Although politically distinct, the new nation of Lesotho was an economic vassalage of the apartheid state. As a geographic island surrounded by South African territory, its very survival depended on the money sent home by the Basotho men who labored in South Africa's mines.

Political change in South Africa has not done Lesotho much good. Foreign workers have become less welcome in South Africa, putting even more stress on Lesotho's ramshackle economy. Although it does have some diamonds, Lesotho's chief natural resource is water: its highlands are the spawning place of South Africa's great rivers: the Tugela, which pours off the eastern Drakensberg into Natal, and the Orange (or Senqu, as it is called in Lesotho), which drains the whole interior of the country and flows to the Atlantic. The immense Highlands Water Project is designed to dam the Senqu and divert its waters northward into the Vaal River system, where they will meet the needs of South Africa's industrial heartland. Water is thus destined to be Lesotho's most valuable export. Whether that will be enough to sustain a viable economy is open to debate. The country, which is a bit larger than the state of Maryland, is already hard pressed to support its nearly 2 million inhabitants. It is not inconceivable that Lesotho could one day be absorbed as a province of the new South Africa.

Although it has no glaciers, Lesotho's highlands possess an austere mountain grandeur. The great barrier range of the Drakensberg, which reaches up to 11,424 feet, delineates the eastern and southern borders, while the Maluti Mountains (which top out at 10,751 feet) form a northern chain. A third range, the Thaba Putsoa (10,157 feet), extends through Lesotho's west. Two-thirds of the country is between 6,500 and 9,500 feet in elevation. Afro-alpine grasslands cover the mountain ridges, sensuous rolling hills, and plunging river gorges of the high plateau country, creating an impression of vast open space. Snow commonly blankets the uplands in winter, while summers are characterized by mists and violent thunderstorms. The highlands are primarily suitable as pastures for sheep and goats, although cattle are also grazed and people eke out crops where they can. The best agricultural land is limited to the strips of "lowlands" (which are mostly above 5,000 feet) along

Lesotho's western and northern borders. In most places, the highlands are seriously overgrazed by domestic livestock.

Bushman paintings attest to the abundance of game that once roamed Lesotho (at least in its lower regions), but there is very little left today. There are no game parks, so the country's chief attractions are its mountains and its people. The Basotho are hardy mountain folk, well accustomed to a tough life in a cold climate. Both they and their villages are often very picturesque. Hamlets of thatch-roofed rondavels are clustered here and there throughout the mountains. Trees are virtually absent from the highlands, but the villages are studded with the spikes of spiny agaves (introduced from the Americas) that are planted to form cattle enclosures. Country people typically wrap themselves in colorfully patterned woolen blankets. Thus clad, the Basotho rider, mounted on his pony and wearing the traditional wide-brimmed conical straw hat, has become the country's photographic icon.

The horse first came to Lesotho in the middle of the last century and was quickly adopted as the favorite means of transport. It did not take long for a special breed suited to the mountain environment to emerge. The Basotho pony is somewhat smaller than a normal horse, but it is sturdy and extremely sure-footed.

Bridal paths extend all over the country and are still the primary network of travel in the highlands. All this makes Lesotho an ideal place for horseback riding, and pony trekking is acknowledged as the most unusual travel experience the country has to offer. Organized pony treks take place primarily in the western part of the country. The Basotho Pony Project, which keeps a stud herd to maintain the breed, organizes day rides and multiday treks from its base in the Maluti Mountains. Guests can stay at the nearby *Molimo Nthuse Lodge* (which has hotel accommodation and a restaurant) or trek to the village of Semonkong, from which they can return by a flight or a drive. The most popular trek, however, traverses the Thaba Putsoa from west to east, an undulating mountain route that begins at Quaba or Malealea, on the Makhaleng River, and ends at Semonkong. The 630-foot Maletsunyane Falls, near Semonkong, is one of the highlights of either trek route. The basalt gorge the waterfall drops into is itself quite spectacular and hosts a major colony of Cape vultures.

Pony treks are as much cultural as scenic experiences. Local guides accompany trekkers and take care of the logistics, horses, and cooking. Overnights are spent in real Basotho homes (some are specially built for trekkers, but local people sometimes move out of their own huts to accommodate larger parties). The houses are spare and clean, but don't expect luxury. The tradeoff is a genuine experience of village life, and one that actually does put tourist money into local communities. Treks are arranged through the Lesotho Tourist Board, the Basotho Pony Project, or *Malealea Lodge*. Malealea Lodge also runs day rides and four-wheel-drive excursions.

Paved roads in Lesotho are confined to the western edge of the country, although the Mountain Road that crosses the Malutis is tarred as far as Molimo Nthuse Pass. (There are plans to improve roads into the heart of the eastern mountains, where work on the Highlands Water Project is going on.) Places of interest can now be reached along the main paved routes. They include Bushman paintings, cannibal caves, dinosaur footprints, historic missions, and several mountain fortresses, the most famous of which, Thaba Bosiu, is located just outside Lesotho's capital, Maseru. To travel deeper into the mountainous high country requires a four-wheel-drive vehicle, although Lesotho Airlines has a network of scheduled flights that connect remote towns (like Semonkong) with Maseru. Small lodges are found in outlying areas, but they are mostly self-catering. Sehlabathebe National Park, which provides excellent scenery and hiking along the Drakensberg crest, has a self-catering lodge. Arrangements can be made with Lesotho Airways to fly in to the nearby Paulus airstrip, but most visitors are South Africans who drive 4x4 vehicles up from Natal.

Lesotho Airways has direct service between Johannesburg and Maseru, but there are many more flight options to Bloemfontein, which is only 97 miles away. Vehicles can be rented in either Bloemfontein or Maseru. US passport holders do not need visas to enter Lesotho. The local currency is the maloti, which exchanges at par with the South African rand (which is also universally accepted). Maseru is a modern capital with a variety of hotels including the *Lesotho Sun* and the *Maseru Sun Cabanas*. The city and its neighboring villages are excellent places to buy Basotho handicrafts. Tapestries or rugs woven from local mohair are particularly outstanding in quality.

Appendices

Appendix A: Safari Tour Companies

United States

Abercrombie & Kent International, 1520 Kensington Road #212, Oakbrook, IL 60521. Tel: (800) 323-7308; (312) 954-2944. One of largest companies operating scheduled safari tours.

Adventure Center, 1311 63rd Street #200, Emeryville, CA 94608. Specialists in overland expeditions all over the continent.

Africa Calls, 10 Lincoln Circle, Andover, MA 01801. Tel: (508) 470-8686. Fax: (508) 470-8687. Zambia specialists.

African Travel, 1000 East Broadway, Glendale, CA 91205. Tel: (800) 421-8907; (818) 507-7893. A well-known tour operator.

AfricaTours, 875 Avenue of the Americas #2108, New York, NY 10001. Tel: (800) 235-3692. Safari tours.

Allen Bechky Safaris, 1140 Washington Ave., Albany, CA 94706. Tel: (510) 524-7587. Fax: (510) 527-0187. E-mail: abechky@pacbell.net. Distinctive personally guided safaris. Consultations to arrange custom safaris or to book scheduled safaris all over Africa.

Baobab Safari Company, 210 Post Street, San Francisco, CA 94108. Tel: (415) 391-5788. Safari bookings.

Bicycle Africa, 4247 135th Place SE, Bellevue, WA 98006. Tel: (206) 746-1028. Bike tours.

Big Five Tours, 819 South Federal Highway #103, Stuart, FL 34994. Tel: (800) 345-2445. Lodge safaris.

Born Free Safaris, 12504 Riverside Drive, North Hollywood, CA 91607. Tel: (800) 372-3274; (213) 877-3553. Tours and custom safaris.

Bushtracks African Expeditions, P.O. Box 4163, Menlo Park, CA 64026. Tel: (415) 326-8689. Zimbabwe specialists.

Eco-Expeditions, 1414 Dexter Ave. N. #327, Seattle, WA 98109. Tel: (206) 285-4000. Nature tours.

Fun Safaris, P.O. Box 178, Bloomingdale, IL 60108. Tel: (800) 323-8020. Mostly zoo groups.

Geo Expeditions, Box 3656, Sonora, CA 95370. Tel: (800) 351-5041; (800) 826-9063 (in CA). Camping safari tours.

International Expeditions, One Environs Park, Helena, AL 35080. Tel: (800) 633-4734; (205) 633-4734. Nature tours.

Joseph Van Os Photo Safaris, P.O. Box 655, Vashon Island, WA 98070. Tel: (206) 463-5383. Specialty photography tours.

Ker & Downey, 2825 Wilcrest Drive #600, Houston, TX 77042. Tel: (800) 423-4236. Represent a reputable Botswana safari company.

Magical Holidays, 501 Madison Ave., New York, NY 10022. Tel: (212) 486-9600. African heritage and cultural tours. Mostly West Africa.

Maupintour, 1515 St. Andrew's Drive, Lawrence, KS 66047. Tel: (800) 655-0222. Large worldwide tour company; multi-country lodge safaris.

Micato Safaris, 15 West 26th Street, New York, NY 10010. Tel: (212) 545-7111. Mostly East African holiday lodge safaris.

Mountain Travel/Sobek, 6420 Fairmount Ave., El Cerrito, CA 94530. Tel: (800) 227-2384; (510) 527-8100. The oldest adventure travel company. Scheduled luxury camping safaris and walking safaris.

Nature Encounters, 9065 Nemo Street, West Hollywood, CA 90069. Tel: (213) 852-1100. Bookings and custom safaris.

Next Adventure, 575 The Alameda, Berkeley, CA 94707. Tel: (800) 562-7298; (510) 526-7027. Fax: (510) 527-0187. E-mail: safari@pacbell.net. Africa experts who arrange custom safaris with top guides; also book regularly departing safari tours offered by reliable local operators in Africa.

Park East Tours, 1841 Broadway, Suite 900, New York, NY 10023. Tel: (800) 223-6078; (212) 765-4870. Holiday lodge safaris.

Questers, 381 Park Ave., New York, NY 10016. Tel: (800) 468-8668; (212) 251-0444. Worldwide nature tours.

Safaricentre, 3201 North Sepulveda Blvd., Manhattan Beach, CA 90266. Tel: (800) 223-6046; (800) 624-5342 (in CA). Booking agents.

Safari Consultants, 4N211 Locust Ave., Chicago, IL 60185. Tel: (800) 762-4027. Booking agents.

Safari Consultants of London, 3535 Ridgelake Drive, Suite B, Metaire, LA 70002. Tel: (800) 648-6541. Custom safaris.

Travcoa, P.O. Box 2630, Newport Beach, CA 92660. Tel: (800) 992-2003. Scheduled lodge safaris.

Victor Emanuel Nature Tours, P.O. Box 33008, Austin, TX 78764. Tel: (800) 328-VENT. Worldwide birding tour specialists.

Voyagers, P.O. Box 915, Ithaca, NY 14851. Tel: (607) 257-3091. Safari tours.

United Touring International, One Bala Plaza #414, Bala Cynnyd, PA

19107. Tel: (800) 611-7500. One of the biggest companies in Africa. Mostly lodge safari tours.

Wilderness Travel, 801 Allston Way, Berkeley, CA 94710. Tel: (800) 247-6700; (510) 548-0420. Camping safari tours.

Wildlife Safari, 346 Rheem Blvd., Moraga, CA 94556. Tel: (800) 221-8118. Lodge safaris.

Botswana

(COUNTRY TELEPHONE CODE: 267)

Afro Ventures, P.O. Box 32, Kasane. Tel: 650 119. Fax: 650 456. Scheduled camping and flying safaris.

Capricorn Safaris, P/Bag 021, Maun. Tel/Fax: 660 647. Camping safaris.

Crocodile Camp Safaris, P.O. Box 46, Maun. Tel: 660 265. Fax: 660 793. Scheduled safaris.

Gametrackers, P.O. Box 786432, Sandton 2146, South Africa. Tel: (27-11) 884 2504. Fax: (27-11) 884 3159. String of safari camps in Delta, Moremi, and Chobe.

Ker & Downey, P.O. Box 27, Maun. Tel: 660 375. Fax: 661 282. Safari camps and custom luxury camping safaris.

Linyanti Explorations, P.O. Box 22, Kasane. Tel: 650 505. Fax: 650 352. Safari camps in Chobe National Park and Selinda Reserve.

Okavango Horse Safaris, P/Bag 23, Maun. Tel: 660 822. Fax: 660 493.

Okavango Tours & Safaris, P.O. Box 39, Maun. Tel: 660 220. Fax: 660 589. Books safari camps, including budget Oddball's.

Okavango Wilderness Safaris, P/Bag 14, Maun. Tel: 660 086. Fax: 660 632. Safari camps in Okavango Delta, Moremi, and Linyanti reserves, including Mombo and King's Pool; scheduled camping and flying safaris.

Penduka Safaris, P.O. Box 55413, Northlands 2116, South Africa. Tel/fax: (27-11) 883-4303. Camping safaris to remote areas of the western and central Kalahari.

The Legendary Safari Company, P.O. Box 40, Maun. Tel: 660 211. Fax: 660 379. Photographic safaris at Xudum Camp and horseback safaris (at Macateer's Camp). Also hunting with Safari South, the best-known hunting safari operator.

Lesotho

(COUNTRY TELEPHONE CODE: 266)

Basotho Pony Project, P.O. Box 1027, Maseru 100, Lesotho. Tel: 314165. Pony trekking.

Lesotho Tourist Board, P.O. Box 1378, Maseru 100, Lesotho. Tel: 322896. Fax: 310108. Pony trekking bookings.

Malealea Lodge, P.O. Makhakhe 922, Lesotho. Tel: 785336. Or P.O. Box 119, Wepener 9944, South Africa. Tel/fax: (27-51) 473-200. Pony treks and tours in Lesotho.

Overland Safaris, P.O. Box 81192, Parkhurst 2120, South Africa. Tel: (27-

11) 442-8007. Fax: (27-11) 442-8015. Land-Rover, camping safaris starting in Johannesburg.

Malawi

(COUNTRY TELEPHONE CODE: 265)

Central African Wilderness Safaris, P.O. Box 489, Lilongwe. Tel: 781393. Fax: 781397. E-mail: WildSaf@eo.wn.apc.org. Excellent operator of guided safaris, individual tours, Mvuu Lodge, and air charters.

Heart of Africa Safaris, P.O. Box 8, Lilongwe. Tel/fax: 740848. High-quality guided safaris; specialists in riding safaris on Nyika Plateau.

Hello Afrika, P.O. Box 187, Cape Maclear. Tel/fax: 587775 or (in South Africa) fax: (27-11) 463-3001. Diving and sailing safaris (and operators of Chembe Lodge) on Lake Malawi.

Kayak Africa, P.O. Box 48, Monkey Bay. Tel/fax: 584456 or (in South Africa) at (27-21) 689-8123. Paddling expeditions on Lake Malawi.

Lake Divers, P.O. Box 48, Monkey Bay. Tel: 584657. Fax: 587384. Diving courses and charters at Cape Maclear.

Rift Lake Charters, P.O. Box 284, Mangochi. Tel: 584473. Fax: 584576. Sailing and diving safaris on Lake Malawi.

Soche Tours & Travel, P.O. Box 2225, Blantyre. Tel: 620777. Fax: 620440. Tours, transport, and hotels.

Namibia

(COUNTRY TELEPHONE CODE: 264)

African Extravaganza, P.O. Box 22028, Windhoek. Tel: (61) 263086. Fax: (61) 215356.

Bonanza Car Hire, P.O. Box 4114, Swakopmund, Tel: (641) 4503. Fax: (641) 5273.

Byseewah Safaris, P.O. Box 495, Outjo. Tel: 6548 (ask for 4222). Fax: (651) 304294. Reputable hunting safari operator.

Canyon Travel Center, P.O. Box 80205, Windhoek. Tel/fax: (61) 251863. Bookings for Gondwana Tours and private lodges in Canyon Nature Park near Fish River Canyon.

Charley's Desert Tours, P.O. Box 1400, Swakopmund. Tel: (641) 4341. Fax: (641) 4821.

Desert Adventure Safaris, P.O. Box 339, Swakopmund. Tel: (64) 40-4459. Fax: (64) 40-4664. Runs special desert rhino tracking safaris in conjunction with Save the Rhino Trust.

Ecotour, P.O. Box 9511, Eros, Windhoek. Tel/fax: (61) 236157. Camping safaris in Kaokoveld.

!Ha N!Jore Safaris, P.O. Box 5703, Ausspannplatz, Windhoek. Tel/fax: (61) 220124. Camping safaris in northern Namibia; noted for excellent cultural encounters with Bushmen of the Ju'Hoan community run in conjunction with the Tsumkwe Conservation Trust.

Kalizo Fishing Safaris, P.O. Box 501, Ngwezi, Katima Mulilo, Caprivi. Tel/fax: 67352 (Ask for 86). Safaris in Caprivi Strip.

Kessler 4x4 Hire, P.O. Box 20271, Windhoek. Tel: (61) 233451. Fax: (61) 224551.

Kolmanskop Tour Company, P.O. Box 357, Luderitz. Tel: (6331) 2445. Fax: (6331) 2526. Tours into restricted Diamond Area.

Olympia Reisen, P.O. Box 5017, Windhoek. Tel: (61) 262395. Fax: (61) 217026. Flying safaris to Skeleton Coast Park.

Ondese Travel & Safaris, P.O. Box 6196, Ausspannplatz, Windhoek. Tel: (61) 220876. Fax: (61) 239700. Self drive or guided safaris.

Oryx Tours, P.O. Box 2058, Windhoek. Tel: (61) 217454. Fax: (61) 263417. A big company; bus tours.

Skeleton Coast Flying Safaris, P.O. Box 2195, Windhoek. Tel: (61) 224248. Fax: (61) 225713. The pioneer flying safari in Namibia. Excellent trips to Kaokoveld.

Springbok Atlas, P.O. Box 11165, Windhoek. Tel: (61) 215943. Fax: (61) 215932. A big company; bus tours.

S. W. A. Safaris, P.O. Box 20373, Windhoek. Tel: (61) 221193. Fax: (61) 225387. Big company; bus tours.

Trans-Namibia Tours, P.O. Box 20028, Windhoek. Tel: (61) 221549. Fax: (61) 230960. A good variety of scheduled tours.

Wilderness Safaris Namibia, P.O. Box 6850, Windhoek. Tel: (61) 225178. Fax: (61) 239455. Scheduled small group departures of lodge or camping safaris; also flying safaris.

South Africa

(COUNTRY TELEPHONE CODE: 27)

Adventure Runners, P.O. Box 31117, Braamfontein 2017. Tel: (11) 403-2512. Fax: (11) 339-1380. Canoe safaris on Orange River and camel safaris in Northern Cape.

African Routes, P.O. Box 201700, Durban North 4016. Tel: (31) 833348. Fax: (31) 837234. Budget safaris.

Afro Ventures, P.O. Box 1200, Paulshof 2056. Tel: (11) 807-3720. Fax: (11) 807-3480. Scheduled tours throughout southern Africa.

Aliwal Cove & Dive Resort, P.O. Box 24, Umkomaas 4170, Natal. Tel: (323) 31002. Fax: (323) 30733. One of top dive sites.

Andy Cobb Eco-Diving, P.O. Box 386, Winkelspruit 4145, Natal. Tel/fax: (31) 964239. Guided dives on Natal's Aliwal Shoal.

Battlefield Safaris, P.O. Box 4, Nottingham 3280. Tel/fax: (333) 32131/31129. Guided tours of Anglo-Boer and Zulu war sites of Natal.

Boleng Adventures, P.O. Box 75483, Lynwood Ridge 0040. Tel/fax: (12) 804-2392. Walking safaris in Timbavati.

Conservation Corporation, P/Bag X9, Sunninghill 2157. Tel: (11) 803-8421. Fax: (11) 803-1810. Londolozi, Phinda, Tswalu, and other deluxe lodges.

Dragonfly Travel, P.O. Box 1042, White River 1240. Tel: (13) 750-0511. Fax: (13) 751-2839. Helicopter tours.

Drifters Adventure Tours, P.O. Box 48434, Roosevelt Park 2129. Tel: (11) 888-1160. Fax: (11) 888-1020. Budget tours.

Equus Horse Safaris, 36 12th Ave., Parktown North 2193. Tel: (911) 788-3923. Fax: (11) 880-8401. Rides in the Waterberg.

Exodus Tours. Tel: (11) 706-1217. Fax: (11) 706-7608. Backpacking trips in the Natal Drakensberg.

Felix Unite River Adventures, P.O. Box 2603, Rivonia 2128. Tel: (11) 803-9775. Fax: (11) 803-9603. Canoe and rafting safaris.

Gary Freeman Safaris, P.O. Box 1885, Nigel 1490. Tel/fax: (11) 814-2855. Educational walking safaris in the Klaserie, Lapalala, and Mashatu reserves.

Gaylards Safaris, P.O. Box 15008, Port Elizabeth 6001. Tel: (41) 321935. Fax: (41) 383797. Safaris to lesser known parks.

Greater Kuduland Safaris, P.O. Box 1385, Louis Trichardt 0920. Tel: (15539) 720. Fax: (15539) 808. Hunting safaris in Northern Province.

Honeyguide. Tel: (911) 880-3912. Fax: (11) 447-4326. Tented safari camp in Manyeleti Game Reserve.

Idube, P.O. Box 2617, Northcliff 2115. Tel: (11) 888-3713. Fax: (11) 888-2181. Game lodge in Sabi Sand Game Reserve.

Inyati Game Lodge, P.O. Box 38838, Booysens 2016. Tel : (11) 493-0755. Fax: (11) 493-0837. Game lodge in Sabi Sand Reserve.

Jimmy's Face to Face Tours, Johannesburg. Tel: (11) 331-6109. Fax: (11) 331-5388. Tours of Soweto.

Kagga Kamma, P.O. Box 7143, North Paarl 7623. Tel: (21) 863-8334. Fax: (21) 863-8383. Private reserve in Cedarberg, Western Cape.

Karibu Safaris, P.O. Box 35196, Northway 4065, Durban. Tel: (31) 839774. Fax: (31) 831957. Budget camping safaris throughout southern Africa.

Lapalala Wilderness, P.O. Box 645, Bedfordview 2008. Tel: (11) 453-7645. Fax: (11) 453-7469. Camps in the Waterberg Mountains, Northern Province.

Lawson's, P.O. Box 507, Nelspruit 1200. Tel: (13) 755-2147. Fax: (13) 755-1793. Specialty birding tours.

Mabula Game Lodge, P/Bag X1665, Warmbaths 0480. Tel: (14734) 616. Fax: (14734) 733. Safari lodge close to Johannesburg.

MalaMala/Rattray Reserves, P.O. Box 2575, Randburg 2125. Tel: (11) 789-2677. Fax: (11) 886-4382. Deluxe MalaMala, Kirkman's, and Harry's camps in Sabi Sand Game Reserve.

Molepe Tours, Johannesburg. Tel/fax: (11) 982-2447. Soweto tours.

Motswari-M'Bali Game Lodges, P.O. Box 67865, Bryanston 2021. Tel: (11) 463-1990. Fax: (11) 463-1992. Camps in Timbavati reserve.

Mpila Adventures, 79 Woodhouse Road, Scottsville 3201. Tel: (33) 142-8023. Fax: (33) 194-2841. Biking, hiking, and rafting in Natal and Lesotho.

Papadi Tours, P.O. Box 3684, Honeydew 2040. Tel: (11) 985-1373. Fax: (11) 958-1042. Budget camping tours.

Richtersveld Challenge, Box 142, Springbok 8240. Tel: (251) 21905. Fax: (251) 81460. Desert hiking and vehicle tours.

Sabi Sabi, P.O. Box 52665, Saxonwold 2132. Tel: (11) 483-3939. Fax: (11) 483-3799. Private game reserve near Kruger.

Shamwari Game Reserves, P.O. Box 32017, Summerstrand, Port Elizabeth. Tel: (42) 851-1196. Fax: (42) 851-1224.

Specialized Tours, P.O. Box 14049, Green Point 8051. Tel: (21) 253259. Fax: (21) 253329. Specialized tours of Cape Town area.

Springbok Atlas, Cape Town. Tel: (21) 448-6545. Fax: (21) 447-3835. Large tour operator; countrywide bus tours.

Tailormade Tours, P.O. Box 5435, Cape Town 8000. Tel: (21) 729800. Fax: (21) 729001. Small group tours of Cape Town area and Garden Route.

The Richtersveld Experience, P.O. Box 229, Port Nolloth 8280. Tel/fax: (255) 8041. Northern Cape desert tours.

Trans Africa Safaris, P.O. Box 64, Constantia 7848. Tel: (21) 61-9104. Fax: (21) 683-2437. Large tour operator. Bus tours of South Africa.

Trout Adventures, 10 Dean Street, Cape Town 8001. Tel: (21) 26-1057. Fax: (21) 24-7526. Fly fishing.

Two Ocean Divers, Cape Town. Tel/fax: (21) 438-9317. Diving in the Western Cape, including great white shark cage dives.

Which Way Adventures, 34 Van der Merwe Street, Somerset West 7130. Tel: (24) 22364. Fax: (24) 21584. Unusual tours in western Cape.

Wilderness Safaris, P.O. Box 651171, Benmore 2010. Tel: (11) 884-1458. Fax: (11) 883-6255. Highly reputable operator of scheduled tours throughout southern Africa. Ndumo Wilderness Camp and Rocktail Bay Lodge in Maputaland.

Swaziland

(COUNTRY TELEPHONE CODE: 268)

Central Reservations, P.O. Box 234, Mbabane. Tel: 44541. Fax: 40957. Bookings for Mkhaya, Mlilwane, and Hlane parks.

Eco-Africa Safaris, P.O. Box 199, Pigg's Peak. Tel/fax: 71319 (fax also to: 44246). Operators of Phophonyane Lodge and Nature Reserve and Muti-Muti Nature Reserve.

Umhlanga Tours, P.O. Box 2197, Mbabane. Tel: 61431. Fax: 44246. Wildlife and cultural tours.

Zambia

(COUNTRY TELEPHONE CODE: 260)

Across Africa Overland, P.O. Box 60420, Livingstone. Tel: (3) 320823. Fax: (3) 320277. Luxury mobile safaris.

African Experience Limited, P.O. Box 30106, Lusaka. Tel/fax: (1) 262456.

Operates Lunga Cabins (safaris in northern Kafue National Park) and Lunga Air Shuttle.

Africa Tour Designers, P.O. Box 13802, Lusaka. Tel: (1) 273864. Fax: (1) 273865. Booking agent.

Andrews Travel and Safaris, P.O. Box 31993, Lusaka. Tel: (1) 223147. Booking agent.

Big Five Travel and Tours, P.O. Box 35317, Lusaka. Tel: (1) 229237. Fax: (1) 274264. Booking agent and chauffeured car rentals.

Busanga Trails, P.O. Box 30984, Lusaka. Tel: (1) 221197. Fax: (1) 222198. Safari camps in northern sector of Kafue National Park.

Bushwackers, P.O. Box 320172, Lusaka. Tel: (1) 253869. Fax: (1) 253869. Booking agent.

Chinzombo Safaris, P.O. Box 30106, Lusaka. Tel: (1) 211644. Fax: (1) 226736. Camps and walking safaris in South Luangwa National Park.

Chundukwa Adventure Trails, Livingstone. Tel: (3) 323235. Fax: (3) 323224. Canoe and horseback safaris at Victoria Falls; walking safaris in Kafue National Park.

Kapani Safari Lodge, P.O. Box 100, Mfuwe. Tel: (62) 45015. Fax: (62) 45025. Camps and walking safaris in South Luangwa National Park.

Kasanka Wildlife Corporation Ltd., P.O. Box 36657, Lusaka. Tel: (1) 228682. Fax: (1) 222906. Camps in Kasanka National Park and Bangweulu Swamps.

Makora Quest/ Raft Quest, P.O. Box 60420, Livingstone. Tel: (3) 321679. Fax: (3) 320732. Canoeing and rafting at Victoria Falls.

Maziba Bay River Safaris/ Tukuluho Wildlife Ltd., P.O. Box 1120, Ngweze, Katima Mulilo, Namibia. Tel: (27-11) 705-3201. Fax: (27-11) 705-3203. Safaris in Western Province: Sioma Falls and Liuwa Plain.

Remote Africa Safaris, P.O. Box 30751, Lusaka. Tel/fax: (1) 291764. Camps in both South and North Luangwa national parks.

Robin Pope Safaris, P.O. Box 80, Mfuwe. Tel: (62) 45090. Fax: (62) 45051. Camps in South Luangwa. Also mobile expeditions to Nyika and Liuwa Plain national parks.

Safari Par Excellence, P.O. Box 5920, Harare, Zimbabwe. Tel: (263-4) 720527. Fax: (263-4) 722872. Rafting at Victoria Falls and canoe safaris on lower Zambezi.

Shearwater Adventures, P.O. Box 3961, Harare, Zimbabwe. Tel: (263-4) 757831. Fax: (263-4) 757836. Rafting at Victoria Falls and canoe safaris on lower Zambezi.

Shiwa Safaris, P/Bag E395, Lusaka. Tel/fax: (1) 611171. Safaris to North Luangwa, Bangweulu, Shiwa Ngandu.

Sobek Expeditions Zambia, P.O. Box 60305, Livingstone. Tel: (3) 323672. Fax: (3) 324289. Rafting at Victoria Falls.

Tongabezi, P/Bag 31, Livingstone. Tel: (3) 323325. Fax: (3) 323224. Tongabezi Lodge at Victoria Falls and canoe safaris in lower Zambezi National Park. Charter air services.

Wilderness Trails, P.O. Box 35058, Lusaka. Tel: (1) 220112. Fax: (1) 220116. Chibembe Lodge and walking safaris in South Luangwa.

Wild Zambia Safaris, P.O. Box 100, Mfuwe. Tel: (62) 45015. Fax: (62) 45025. Mobile expeditions countrywide and traditional walking safaris in Luangwa Valley.

Zungulila Zambia, P.O. Box 31475, Lusaka. Tel/fax: (1) 227729. Chauffeured car rentals.

Zimbabwe

(COUNTRY TELEPHONE CODE: 263)

Abercrombie & Kent, P.O. Box 2997, Harare. Tel: (4) 759930. Fax: (4) 759940. Booking agent.

Backpackers Africa, P.O. Box 108, Victoria Falls. Tel: (13) 4424. Fax: (13) 4510. Low-cost backpacking or vehicle-supported walking safaris.

Biza Saddle Safaris, P.O. Box GD305, Greendale, Harare. Tel: (4) 45752. Fax: (4) 48265. Horseback trails in Zimbabwe's Lowveld.

Black Rhino Safaris, P.O. Box FM89, Famona, Bulawayo. Tel: (9) 41662. Fax: (9) 77300. Excursions into the Matobo Hills.

Bushlife Zimbabwe, P.O. Box GD305, Greendale, Harare. Tel: (4) 496113. Fax: (4) 498265. Foot safaris in Matusadona and canoe safaris at Mana Pools with pro-guide John Stevens.

Far and Wild, P.O. Box 14, Juliasdale. Tel: (29) 26329. Rafting, hiking, climbing, and mountain biking in Nyanga.

Frontiers, P.O. Box 4876, Harare. Tel: (4) 732911. Fax: (4) 732914. Rafting at Victoria Falls.

Garth Thompson Safari Consultants, P.O. Box 5826, Harare. Tel: (4) 756318. Fax: (4) 756602. A highly reputable booking office; also operates Natureways canoe and walking safaris in the wilderness area of Mana Pools National Park.

Kalembeza Safaris, 306 Parkway Drive, Victoria Falls. Tel: (13) 4480. Fax: (13) 4644. Canoeing and walking safaris at Victoria Falls.

Kariba Cruises, P.O. Box 186, Kariba. Tel: (61) 2839. Fax: (61) 2885. Houseboat and cruiser charters.

Landela Safaris, P.O. Box 66293, Harare. Tel: (4) 73404. Fax: (4) 708119. Operates a string of safari lodges around the country.

Londelmela Safaris, P.O. Box 130, Queens Park, Bulawayo. Tel: (9) 43954. Fax: (9) 46436. Mobile camping safaris.

Rail Safaris, P.O. Box 2536, Bulawayo. Tel/fax: (9) 75575. Train tours between Victoria Falls and Bulawayo.

Run Wild, P.O. Box 6485, Harare. Tel: (4) 795841. Fax: (4) 795845. Books a string of safari lodges around the country.

Safari Par Excellence, P.O. Box 5920, Harare, Zimbabwe. Tel: (4) 720527. Fax: (4) 722872. Rafting at Victoria Falls and canoe safaris on lower Zambezi.

Sail Safaris, 4 Cheshire Road, Mount Pleasant, Harare. Tel: (4) 339123. Fax: (4) 339045. Sailboat charters on Lake Kariba.

Shearwater Adventures, P.O. Box 3961, Harare. Tel: (4) 757831. Fax: (4) 757836. Rafting at Victoria Falls and canoe safaris on lower Zambezi.

Touch the Wild, P/Bag 6, Hillside, Bulawayo. Tel: (9) 74589. Fax: (9) 44696. Operates safari lodges at Hwange, Matobo, and Great Zimbabwe.

Wilderness Safaris Zimbabwe, P.O. Box 288, Victoria Falls. Tel: (13) 4527. Fax: (13) 4224. Excellent camping safari operators; also make bookings countrywide.

Appendix B: Southern African Embassies and Government Tour Offices

Note: The tour offices are the best sources of information for the traveler.

Embassy of Botswana, 3400 International Drive NW, Suite 7M, Washington, DC 20008; Tel: (202) 244-4990

Embassy of the Kingdom of Lesotho, 2511 Massachusetts Avenue NW, Washington, DC 20008; Tel: (202) 797-5533

Malawi Embassy, 2408 Massachusetts Avenue NW, Washington, DC 20008; Tel: (202) 797-1007

Embassy of the Republic of Namibia, 1605 New Hampshire Avenue NW, Washington, DC 20009; Tel: (202) 986-0540

Embassy of South Africa, 3051 Massachusetts Avenue NW, Washington, DC 20008; Tel: (202) 232-4400

South African Tourist Board (SATOUR), 500 Fifth Avenue, 20th Floor, Suite 2040, New York, NY 10110; Tel: (212) 730-2929; (800) 822-5368; Fax: (212) 764-1980

South African Tourist Board (SATOUR), 9841 Airport Boulevard, Suite 1524, Los Angeles, CA 90045; Tel: (310) 641-8444; ; (800) 782-9772; Fax: (310) 641-5812

Embassy of the Kingdom of Swaziland, 3400 International Drive NW, Washington, DC 20008; Tel: (202) 362-6683

Embassy of the Republic of Zambia, 2419 Massachusetts Avenue NW, Washington, DC 20008; Tel: (202) 265-9717

Zambia National Tourist Board, 800 Second Avenue, New York, NY 10017; Tel: (212) 972-7200; (800) 852-5998; Fax: (212) 972-7360

Embassy of the Republic of Zimbabwe, 1608 New Hampshire Avenue NW, Washington, DC 20009; Tel: (202) 332-7100

Zimbabwe Tourist Office, 1270 Avenue of the Americas, Suite 2315, New York, NY 10020; Tel: (212) 232-1090; (800) 621-2381; Fax: (212) 332-1092; E-mail: ztonyc@juno.com

Appendix C: Conservation Organizations Involved in Southern Africa

African Wildlife Foundation, 1717 Massachusetts Ave. NW, Washington, DC 20036. With a focus on Africa, this leading conservation group aims to involve local communities in sustainable projects that protect wild animals and their habitats.

Appendices

505

Africat Foundation, P.O. Box 793, Otjiwarongo, Namibia. Tel: (264-651) 4563. Fax: (264-651) 4565. Works on cheetah rehabilitation and conservation education for Namibian farmers.

Birdlife South Africa, P.O. Box 84394, Greenside 2034, South Africa. Tel: (27-11) 888-4147. Fax: (27-11) 782-7013. The successor to the Southern African Ornithological Society.

Cheetah Conservation Fund, P.O. Box 247, Windhoek, Namibia. Fax: (264-61) 34021. (They also have a US office: 25725 Basset Lane, Los Altos Hills, CA 94022. Tel/fax: [415] 949-4133.) This group does cheetah research and education in Namibia.

Endangered Wildlife Trust, P/Bag X11, Parkview 2122, South Africa. Tel: (27-11) 486-1102. Fax: (27-11) 486-1506. South Africa's leading wildlife conservation group.

Flora and Fauna Preservation Society, c/o London Zoological Society, Regents Park, London NW1 4R4, England.

Frankfurt Zoological Society, Alfred-Brehm-Platz 16, D-6000, Frankurt/Main, West Germany.

Kalahari Conservation Society, P.O. Box 859, Gaborone, Botswana.

Owens Foundation for Wildlife Conservation, P.O. Box 55396, Atlanta, GA 30355. They support the Owens's project in Zambia.

Save the Kalahari San, 29310 Seabiscuit Drive, Fair Oaks Ranch, TX 78006. Tel: (800)) SAVESAN. Fax: (210) 755-2227. Their object is to preserve the culture of the Bushmen and protect the Kalahari environment.

Save the Rhino Trust, P.O. Box 22691, Windhoek, Namibia. Tel: (264-61) 232154. Fax: (264-61) 223077. Works on community involvement in the conservation of desert rhinos.

The Wild Foundation, 2162 Baldwin Road, Ojai, CA 93023. Tel: (805) 649-3535. Fax: (805) 649-1757. They support the Wilderness Leadership School and the Magqubu Ntombela Foundation, two South African organizations that strive to expose young black Africans to the joys and importance of their wild heritage.

Wildlife Conservation International, New York Zoological Society, Bronx, NY 10460. This respected organization manages research projects crucial to species and ecosystems preservation.

Wildlife Conservation Society of Zambia, P.O. Box 30255, Lusaka, Zambia.

Wildlife Society of Zimbabwe, P.O. Box 3497, Harare, Zimbabwe.

World Wildlife Fund, 1250 Twenty-Fourth Street NW, Washington, DC 20037. Tel: (202) 293-4800. The American branch of the World Wide Fund for Nature (WWF); the largest wildlife conservation group.

WWF South Africa, P.O. Box 456, Stellenbosch 7599, South Africa. Tel: (27-21) 887-2801. Fax: (27-21) 887-9517.

Bibliography

General

Bull, Bartel. *Safari: A Chronicle of Adventure*. 1988. Reprint. New York: Penguin, 1992. A history of African big game hunting.

Haggard, H. Rider. *King Solomon's Mines*. The classic novel of African adventure and exploration.

Heminway, John. *No Man's Land: The Last of White Africa*. New York: Harcourt Brace Jovanovich, 1983. Fascinating portraits of white holdovers living in postcolonial Africa.

Hibbert, Christopher. *Africa Explored: Europeans in the Dark Continent, 1769–1889*. New York: W. W. Norton, 1982. The journeys of the famous explorers, based on their own records.

Huxley, Elspeth. *Livingstone and His African Journeys*. New York: Saturday Review Press, 1974.

Johanson, Donald; Johanson, Lenora; and Blake, Edgar. *Ancestors: In Search of Human Origins*. New York: Villard Books, 1994. The views of a leader in the field.

Lamb, David. *The Africans*. New York: Random House, 1983. An American journalist looks at Africa.

Leakey, Richard. *The Origin of Humankind*. New York: Basic Books, 1994. An update on human evolution by the celebrated anthropologist.

Leakey, Richard, and Lewin, Roger. *Origins Reconsidered: In Search of What Makes Us Human*. Garden City, NY: Doubleday, 1992.

Lessing, Doris. *The Grass Is Singing* (1950) and *African Stories* (1965). Fiction by a well-known writer raised in Rhodesia.

Marnham, Patrick. *Fantastic Invasion*. New York: Harcourt Brace Jovanovich, 1979. An unsettling view of foreign meddling in Africa: touches conservation, aid, economics, and politics.

Mazrui, Ali. *The Africans: A Triple Heritage.* Boston: Little, Brown, 1986. History and contemporary affairs from an African point of view; stimulating and controversial.

Miller, Charles. *Battle for the Bundu.* New York: Macmillan, 1974. The First World War in Africa.

Murray, John A. *Wild Africa: Three Centuries of Nature Writing from Africa.* England: Oxford University Press, 1996. A sampler from the works of early explorers (and from native oral traditions) to those of modern scientists and travel writers.

Pakenham, Thomas. *The Scramble for Africa: White Man's Conquest of the Dark Continent from 1876–1912.* New York: Avon Books, 1992. A definitive account of the colonial takeover.

Selous, Frederick Courtney. *African Nature Notes and Reminiscences.* Reprint. New York: St. Martin's Press, 1993.

Selous, Frederick Courtney. *Travel and Adventure in South-East Africa.* 1893. Reprint. New York: Hippocrene Books, 1984. Hunting and exploration tales, and an account of the British conquest of Rhodesia.

Severin, Timothy. *The African Adventure: Four Hundred Years of Exploration in the "Dangerous Continent."* New York: E. P. Dutton, 1973. Illustrated history of exploration from the search for Prestor John to the Boer's Great Trek.

Smith, Wilbur. *The Leopard Hunts in Darkness.* New York: Fawcett, Crest, 1984. Also *Elephant Song, When the Lion Feeds, The Burning Shore,* and many other popular action-adventure novels set in Africa. Formula fiction with a good sense of place and history.

Swain, Bob, and Snyder, Paula. *Africa by Road.* Old Saybrook, CT: Glove Pequot Press, 1996. A how-to guide for taking your own car.

Turnbull, Colin. *The Lonely African.* New York: Simon & Schuster, 1962. An anthropologist documents the West's cultural assault on native African beliefs and values and its sad consequences.

Natural History and Conservation

Adams, Johnathan S., and McShane, Thomas O. *The Myth of Wild Africa.* New York: W. W. Norton, 1992. Argues the role of economic benefit for Africans as key to the success of wildlife conservation.

Bonner, Raymond. *At the Hand of Man: Peril and Hope for Africa's Wildlife.* New York: Knopf, 1993. A brutal attack on the international conservation establishment that pleads the case for sustainable use of wildlife. Interesting but one-sided.

Bosman, Paul, and Hall-Martin, Anthony. *Elephants of Africa.* Safari Press, 1989. Paintings by Bosman and text by elephant expert Hall-Martin.

Calburn, Simon, and Kemp, Alan. *The Owls of Southern Africa.* Cape Town: Struik Winchester, 1987. Comprehensive life histories with large-format color plates.

Capstick, Peter Hathaway. *Death in the Long Grass.* New York: St. Martin's Press, 1977. Bloody but fascinating tales about the dangerous animals of Africa written by a professional hunter.

Child, Graham. *Wildlife and People: The Zimbabwean Success*. Washington DC: Wisdom Foundation, 1996. A Zimbabwean wildlife manager champions sustainable utilization of wildlife and examines Zimbabwe's flagship CAMPFIRE program.

Douglas-Hamilton, Ian and Oria. *Battle for the Elephants*. New York: Viking, 1992. Renowned elephant researchers describe the ivory wars of the 1980s.

Hes, Lex. *The Leopards of Londolozi*. Cape Town: Struik Winchester, 1991. Photos and text follow a long-term study of Africa's most secretive big cat.

Hockey, Phil, and Douie, Clare. *Waders of Southern Africa*. Cape Town: Struik, 1996. Beautiful, comprehensive bird monographs.

Kruuk, Hans. *Hyaena*. London: Oxford University Press, 1975. A highly informative text; with great black and white photos.

Lovegrove, Barry. *The Living Deserts of Southern Africa*. South Africa: Fernwood Press, 1993. Comprehensive text and pictures.

Martin, Esmond, and Bradley, Chrissee. *Run Rhino Run*. London: Chatto and Windus, 1982. Conservation and the poaching trade.

Matthiessen, Peter. *African Silences*. New York: Random House, 1991. A gloomy view of the prospects for conservation.

McNutt, John, and Boggs, Lesley. *Running Wild: Dispelling the Myths of the African Wild Dog*. Johannesburg: Southern Books, 1996. A beautiful and informative book with superb photos by Helene Heldring and Dave Hamman.

Mills, Gus, and Hes, Lex. *The Complete Book of Southern African Mammals*. Cape Town: Struik Winchester, 1997. Large-format book with excellent photos and scientific species descriptions by leading authorities.

Moss, Cynthia. *Elephant Memories: Thirteen Years in the Life of an Elephant Family*. New York: Morrow, 1988. Fascinating study.

Moss, Cynthia. *Portraits in the Wild*. Chicago: University of Chicago Press, 1982. A readable compendium of research projects documenting the life histories of a variety of African species.

Moss, Cynthia, and Colbeck, Martyn. *Echo of the Elephants*. New York: William Morrow, 1993. Text and photos chronicle 18 months with one elephant family.

Mundy, Peter; Butchart, Duncan; Ledger, John; and Piper, Steven. *The Vultures of Africa*. South Africa: Russel Friedman Books, 1992. Beautifully illustrated life histories.

Patterson, Rod, and Bannister, Anthony. *Reptiles of Southern Africa*. Cape Town: Struik, 1987. A comprehensive photographic guide.

Poole, Joyce. *Coming of Age with Elephants: A Memoir*. New York: Hyperion, 1996. The story of a leading elephant researcher and conservationist.

Potgieter, De Wet. *Contraband: South Africa and the International Trade in Ivory and Rhino Horn*. Cape Town: Queillerie Publishers, 1996. An indepth exposé of the poaching and smuggling industry in southern Africa.

Ross, Charles A., ed. *Crocodiles and Alligators*. London: Merehurst Press, 1989. Brilliant photos and natural histories of this group of reptiles; scientific yet comprehensible to laymen.

Sinclair, A. R. E. *The African Buffalo*. Chicago: University of Chicago Press, 1977.

Skaife, S. H. *African Insect Life*. Cape Town: Struik, 1995. A classic for laymen and specialists; with superb photos.

Smithers, Reay. *The Mammals of the Southern African Region*. South Africa: University of Pretoria. Scientific reference.

Steyn, Peter. *Nesting Birds: The Breeding Habits of Southern African Birds*. South Africa: Fernwood Press, 1996. Detailed, informative text and wonderful photos by one of Africa's most respected ornithologists and bird photographers.

Strum, Shirley C. *Almost Human: A Journey into the World of Baboons*. London: Elm Tree Books, 1987. Baboon behavior.

Stuart, Chris and Tilde. *Africa: A Natural History*. South Africa: Southern Book Publishers, 1995. Twelve major habitat types described in text and photos.

Tarboton, Warwick. *African Birds of Prey*. Ithaca: Cornell University Press, 1989. Excellent text with great photos by Peter and Beverly Pickford.

Field Guides

Alden, Peter; Estes, Richard; Schlitter, Duane; and McBride, Bunny. *National Audubon Society Field Guide to African Wildlife*. New York: Knopf, 1995. A nice all-in-one book that covers the continent and includes mammals, birds, and reptiles (much more comprehensive for mammals than the others). With photos.

Braack, L. E. O. *Insects of Kruger National Park*. Cape Town: Struik, 1994. A field guide with photos; useful elsewhere.

Branch, Bill. *Field Guide to the Snakes and Other Reptiles of Southern Africa*. Cape Town: Struik, 1988. Excellent and comprehensive, with photos of each species.

Branch, E. M.; Griffiths, C. L.; Branch, M. L.; and Beckley, L. E. *Two Oceans: A Guide to the Marine Life of Southern Africa*. Cape Town: David Philip Publishers, 1996. Excellent field guide including fish, seaweeds, and the gamut of invertebrates. Photos.

Carcasson, R. H. *Collins Handguide to the Butterflies of Africa*. London: Collins, 1981. Compact; with color plates.

Carruthers, Vincent, and Passmore, Neville. *Southern African Frogs: A Complete Guide*. rev. ed. South Africa: Southern Book Publishers, 1995. A keyed guide with photos and sonograms.

Estes, Richard D. *The Behavior Guide to African Mammals*. Chicago: University of Chicago Press, 1990. A large, comprehensive reference work for researchers and serious students of nature.

Estes, Richard D. *The Safari Companion: A Guide to Watching African Mammals Including Hoofed Mammals, Carnivores, and Primates*. Post

Mills, VT: Chelsea Green Publishing, 1993. A terrific field guide that will give you a better understanding of what is going on while you are observing wildlife.

Haltenorth, Theodor, and Diller, Helmut. *A Field Guide to the Mammals of Africa Including Madagascar.* London: Collins, 1980. Excellent and complete.

Heinzel, Hermann. *The Birds of Britain and Europe.* London: Collins, 1979. Useful for identifying migrants in Africa.

Holm, Eric. *Insects of Southern Africa.* Cape Town: Struik Pocket Guides, 1987. Compact with illustrations.

Liebenberg, Louis. *A Field Guide to the Animal Tracks of Southern Africa.* Cape Town: David Philip Publishers, 1990. Not as easy to use (or as comprehensive) as the Stuarts' guide (see below), but the author is an acknowledged expert. He has also a scaled-down version, *A Concise Guide to the Animal Tracks of Southern Africa.*

Mack, Peter. *Night Skies of Southern Africa.* Cape Town: Struik Pocket Guides, 1987. Sky charts and astronomical objects of the southern sky. Compact with illustrations.

Maclean, Gordon Lindsay. *Roberts' Birds of Southern Africa.* 6th rev. ed. Cape Town: John Voelcker Bird Book Fund, 1993. The experts' standard reference for the subcontinent.

Migdoll, Ivor. *Butterflies of Southern Africa.* Cape Town: Struik, 1990. Field guide with photos.

Newlands, Gerry. *Spiders of Southern Africa.* Cape Town: Struik Pocket Guides, 1986. Compact with illustrations.

Newman, Kenneth. *Birds of Malawi: A Supplement to Newman's Birds of Southern Africa.* South Africa: Southern Book Publishers, 1994.

Newman, Kenneth. *Newman's Birds of Southern Africa: Extensively Revised Edition.* South Africa: Southern Book Publishers, 1995. A great field guide with excellent layout, text, and illustrations.

Palgrave, Keith Coates. *Trees of Southern Africa.* rev ed. Cape Town: Struik, 1994. An authoritative, keyed, identification guide; heavy, but it is the standard reference book.

Patterson, Rod. *Snakes of Southern Africa.* Cape Town: Struik Pocket Guides, 1986. Also useful for East Africa. Compact; excellent text and color illustrations.

Rourke, J. P. *Wild Flowers of Southern Africa.* Cape Town: Struik, 1995. A photographic guide.

Sinclair, Ian. *Birds of Southern Africa.* Cape Town: Struik, 1987. A field guide with photos (often preferred by beginners).

Sinclair, Ian. *Southern African Birds: A Photographic Guide.* Cape Town: Struik, 1995. Acclaimed for its photos, which show various plumages and postures, as well as some birds in flight.

Sinclair, Iain; Hockey, Phil; and Tarboton, Warwick. *Sasol Birds of Southern Africa.* Cape Town: Struik, 1993. (Also published as *Birds of Southern Africa,* Princeton University Press, 1995). Superb illustrations and text make this field guide the choice of experienced birders. This volume has been revised and issued in a slightly bigger format, *The Larger Illustrated Sasol Birds of Southern Africa* (1996), which shows its color plates to better effect and is easier to read.

Skelton, Paul. *A Complete Guide to the Freshwater Fishes of Southern Africa*. South Africa: Southern Book Publishers, 1993.

Smithers, Reay. *Land Mammals of Southern Africa: A Field Guide*. rev. ed. South Africa: Southern Book Publishers, 1995. Written by a leading authority; with color plates.

Stuart, Chris and Tilde. *Field Guide to the Mammals of Southern Africa*. Cape Town: Struik, 1988. Excellent, comprehensive guide inclusive of rodents, bats, and marine mammals, as well as larger game animals. With photos (marine mammals are color drawings).

Stuart, Chris and Tilde. *A Field Guide to the Tracks and Signs of Southern and East African Wildlife*. South Africa: Southern Book Publishers, 1994. A terrific handbook; includes tracks and scats of birds, reptiles, and insects, as well as mammals large and small.

Van der Eist, Rudy. *Common Sea Fishes of Southern Africa*. Cape Town: Struik Pocket Guides, 1987. Compact with illustrations.

Van der Westhuizen, G. C. A., and Eiker, A. *Mushrooms of Southern Africa*. Cape Town: Struik, 1990. A field guide with photos.

Van Wyk, Piet and Braam. *Field Guide to Trees of Southern Africa*. Cape Town: Struik, 1990. With photos.

Walker, Clive. *Signs of the Wild: A Field Guide to the Spoor and Signs of the Mammals of Southern Africa*. 5th rev. ed. Cape Town: Struik, 1996. A well-known book but second best to the Stuarts'.

Williams, Mark. *Butterflies of Southern Africa: A Field Guide*. South Africa: Southern Book Publishers, 1994. A thorough guide for nonexperts, with color illustrations.

Regional

Brandon-Kirby, Robert. *Fly Fishing in Southern Africa*. Cape Town: Struik Winchester, 1993. Beautiful and informative book with excellent, atmospheric photos.

Bristow, David. *Mountains of Southern Africa*. Cape Town: Struik, 1985. With great photos by Clive Ward.

Chittenden, Hugh. *Top Birding Spots in Southern Africa*. South Africa: Southern Book Publishers, 1994.

Clarke, James. *The Roof of Africa*. New York: Holt, Rinehart & Winston, 1983. The mountains of southern Africa.

Duggan, Allan, ed. *Reader's Digest Illustrated Guide to the Game Parks and Nature Reserves of Southern Africa*. rev. ed. Cape Town: Reader's Digest, 1995. All nature reserves south of the Zambezi.

Levy, Jaynee. *The Complete Guide to Walks and Trails in Southern Africa*. rev ed. Cape Town: Struik, 1991. Comprehensive.

Mayhew, Vic, ed. *Reader's Digest Illustrated Guide to Southern Africa*. rev.

ed. Cape Town: Reader's Digest, 1996. Geography, history, and nature south of the Zambezi.

Olivier, Willie and Sandra. *Hiking Trails of Southern Africa*. South Africa: Southern Book Publishers, 1995. Guide to the best backpacking and wilderness trails of South Africa and Namibia.

Stuart, Chris and Tilde. *Guide to Southern African Game and Nature Reserves*. Cape Town: Struik, 1989. Brief summaries of parks, large and small, throughout the region.

Botswana

Bannister, Anthony, and Lewis-Williams, David. *Bushmen: A Changing Way of Life*. Cape Town: Struik, 1993. A paperback update on Bannister's earlier photographic book on the Bushmen.

Butchart, Duncan. *Wild About the Okavango*. South Africa: Southern Book Publishers, 1995. Nice compact all-in-one field guide that covers all the common plants and animals (includes mammals, birds, reptiles, and insects); with color photos.

Johnson, Peter, and Bannister, Anthony. *The Bushmen*. Cape Town: Struik, 1979. Excellent photo study with informative text by Alf Wannenburgh.

Johnson, Peter, and Bannister, Anthony. *Okavango: Sea of Land, Land of Water*. rev. ed. Cape Town: Struik, 1993. Excellent photo study with brief but informative text and captions by Creina Bond.

Lanting, Franz. *Okavango: Africa's Last Eden*. San Francisco: Chronicle Books, 1993. Superb images by a renowned photographer.

Main, Michael. *Kalahari: Life's Variety in Dune and Delta*. 2d ed. South Africa: Southern Book Publishers, 1990. An excellent work covering geology, natural and human history, conservation issues of the Kalahari and Okavango Delta.

Owens, Mark and Delia. *Cry of the Kalahari*. Boston: Houghton Mifflin, 1984. Story of research in central Kalahari.

Roodt, Veronica. *The Shell Field Guide to the Common Trees of the Okavango Delta and Moremi Game Reserve*. Botswana: Shell Oil Botswana. A terrific guide filled with natural history facts and relationships, as well as local folklore about and use for the trees. With color and black and white illustrations.

Ross, Karen. *Okavango: Jewel of the Kalahari*. New York: Macmillan, 1987. Excellent natural history text and photos.

Van der Post, Laurens. *The Lost World of the Kalahari*. New York: William Morrow, 1958. Account of his classic expedition in search of the Kalahari Bushmen.

Van der Post, Laurens, and Taylor, Jane. *Testament to the Bushmen*. New York: Viking Penguin, 1984. History and way of life of southern Africa's hunter-gatherers.

Walker, Clive. *Savuti: The Vanishing River*. South Africa: Southern Book Publishers, 1991. Natural history of the Savuti Channel.

Malawi

Carter, Judy. *Malawi: Wildlife, Parks, and Reserves.* London: Macmillan, 1987. A most definitive text with excellent photos.

Eastwood, Frank. *A Guide to the Mulanje Massif.* Johannesburg: Lorton Publications, 1979. Still the best reference.

Johnston, Frank, and Garland, Vera. *Malawi: Lake of Stars.* Blantyre: Central Africana Limited, 1994. Photos and text.

Maurel, Martine. *Visitor's Guide to Malawi.* rev. ed. South Africa: Southern Book Publishers, 1995.

Ransford, Oliver. *Livingstone's Lake: The Drama of Nyasa.* Blantyre: Central Bookshop, 1966. Lake Malawi.

Van der Post, Laurens. *Venture to the Interior.* 1951. Reprint. New York: Penguin, 1983. Explorations of Mulanje and the Nyika Plateau at the end of the colonial era.

Namibia

Balfour, Daryl and Sharna. *Etosha.* Cape Town: Struik, 1994. Beautiful coffee-table photo essay.

Bannister, Anthony, and Johnson, Peter. *Namibia, Africa's Harsh Paradise.* rev. ed. Cape Town: Struik, 1992. A beautiful and informative coffee-table format book.

Berry, Cornelia. *Trees and Shrubs of the Etosha National Park.* Namibia: Multi Services, 1982.

Craven, Patricia, and Marais, Christine. *Damaraland Flora.* Namibia: Gamberg, 1993. Another fine plant guide.

Craven, Patricia, and Marais, Christine. *Namib Flora.* Namibia: Gamberg, 1986. A lovely guide with paintings and drawings.

Craven, Patricia, and Marais, Christine. *Waterberg Flora.* Namibia: Gamberg, 1989. The interesting plants of north central Namibia.

Cubitt, Gerald. *Namibia, The Untamed Land.* Cape Town: Don Nelson, 1981. Another excellent photographic overview of the country.

Hall-Marten, Anthony; Walker, Clive; and Bothma, J. du P. *Kaokoveld, The Last Wilderness.* South Africa: Southern Book Publishers, 1988. Geology, fauna and flora, ethnology, and conservation of Namibia's northwestern region.

Jacobsohn, Margaret; Pickford, Peter and Beverly. *Himba, Nomads of Namibia.* Cape Town: Struik, 1991. Coffee-table photos along with informative text by an expert on Himba culture.

Jensen, R. A. C., and Clinning, C. F. *Birds of the Etosha National Park.* Windhoek: Meinert, 1980. Photos and descriptions of local species.

Namibia, Shell Tourist Guide. Windhoek: Shell Namibia, 1990. Road maps with brief descriptions of sites of interest.

Reardon, Mitch and Margot. *Etosha, Life and Death on an African Plain.* Cape Town: Struik, 1981. The annual life cycle described through informative text and excellent photos.

Rogers, David. *Etosha National Park*. Cape Town: Struik, 1994. Nicely illustrated guide to the park.

Schoeman, Amy. *Skeleton Coast*. rev. ed. South Africa: Southern Book Publishers, 1996. Photos and text cover everything from geology and climate
through natural history to explorations, shipwrecks, and legends. Highly
informative.

Seely, Mary. *The Namib, Natural History of an Ancient Desert*. Windhoek:
Shell Namibia, 1992. A desert expert presents a readable and informative
introduction to Namib ecology.

South Africa — General

Becker, Peter. *Hill of Destiny: The Life and Times of Moshesh, Founder of
the Basutho*. London: Penguin, 1982. Lesotho history.

Brink, Andre. *Imaginings of Sand*. Orlando, FL: Harcourt Brace & Co.,
1996. Fiction about several generations of women in a South African
family, by the author of *A Dry White Season*, *Rumors of Rain*, *On the
Contrary*, and other novels (both historical and contemporary) set in
South Africa.

Bulpin, T. V. *The Ivory Trail*. 1954. Reprint. South Africa: Southern Book
Publishers, 1988. Popular story of a famous elephant poacher in the
Lowveld of the early 20th century.

Elliott, Aubrey. *The Zulu: Heritage of a Nation*. Cape Town: Struik, 1993.
Photo book with good information. He has also done a couple of smaller
photo books, *The Zulu: Traditions and Culture* and *The Xhosa and
Their Traditional Way of Life*. Good pictures and some interesting information.

FitzPatrick, Sir Percy. *Jock of the Bushveld*. 1907. Reprint. England: Viking
Kestrel, 1985. A South African classic; tales of hunting and pioneering
days in the bushveld.

Gordimer, Nadine. *Lifetimes under Apartheid*. New York: Knopf, 1986. Ex-
tracts from the works of one of South Africa's best known writers, with
photos by David Goldblatt. Her novels about South Africa include *My
Son's Story*, *July's People*, and *Burger's Daughter*.

Mandela, Nelson. *Long Walk to Freedom: The Autobiography of Nelson
Mandela*. Boston: Little, Brown, 1994. Also available in an abridged illustrated version.

Mathabane, Mark. *Kaffir Boy: The True Story of a Black Youth's Coming of
Age in Apartheid South Africa*. New York: Macmillan, 1986.

Michener, James. *The Covenant*. New York: Random House, 1980. A readable novel that spans South African history.

Morris, Donald R. *The Washing of the Spears*. London: Johnathan Cape
Ltd, 1965. The rise of the Zulu nation and the dramatic events of the
1879 Anglo-Zulu War.

Pakenham, Thomas. *The Boer War*. New York: Random House, 1979. A
history of the conflict between British and Akrikaners.

Payton, Alan. *Cry, the Beloved Country*. New York: Scribner's, 1948. A celebrated novel about racial injustice in South Africa.

Reitz, Deneys. *Commando, A Boer Journal of the Boer War*. 1929. Reprint. Johannesburg: Jonathan Ball Publishers, 1990. An amazing memoir by a soldier who was there from start to finish.

Ritter, E. A. *Shaka Zulu*. London: Penguin, 1987.

Schreiner, Olive. *The Story of an African Farm*. 1883. Reprint. New York: Crown, 1982. A classic account of rural settler life.

Thompson, Leonard. *A History of South Africa*. New Haven, CT: Yale University Press, 1995. This text focuses on the black experience rather than the story of the whites.

Turco, Marco. *Visitor's Guide to Lesotho*. South Africa: Southern Book Publishers.

Turco, Marco. *Visitor's Guide to Swaziland*. South Africa: Southern Book Publishers, 1994.

West, Martin, and Morris, Jean. *Abantu: An Introduction to the Black People of South Africa*. Cape Town: Struik, 1979. Still a good overview of the various ethnic groups. Color and black and white photos.

South Africa — Nature

Braack, L. E. O. *Kruger National Park, A Visitor's Guide*. Cape Town: Struik, 1988.

Butchart, Duncan. *Wild About the Lowveld*. South Africa: Southern Book Publishers, 1996. Compact, informative photo guide to the flora and fauna of the country's richest wildlife area. In the same series, *Wild About Cape Town* (1996) covers the Cape region.

Cairncross, Bruce, and Dixon, Roger. *The Minerals of South Africa*. South Africa: The Geological Society of South Africa, 1996.

Carruthers, Jane. *The Kruger National Park: A Social and Political History*. Durban: University of Natal Press, 1996. An examination of myths about the creation of the park and its administration, as well as its uneasy relations with neighboring communities.

Courtney-Clarke, Margaret. *Ndebele*. Cape Town: Struik: 1992. Photo study of one of South Africa's most colorful ethnic groups.

Cowling, Richard, and Richardson, Dave. *Fynbos: South Africa's Unique Floral Kingdom*. Cape Town: Fernwood Press, 1995. A beautiful and informative book with photos by Colin Paterson-Jones.

Fraser, Michael, and McMahon, Liz. *Between Two Shores: Flora and Fauna of the Cape of Good Hope*. Cape Town: David Philip Publishers, 1994. The natural habitats and creatures of the Cape revealed in text and fine color drawings and paintings.

Kornhof, Anton. *Dive Sites of South Africa*. Cape Town: Struik, 1996. Comprehensive guide covering diving and snorkeling.

Kruger National Park. *Make the Most Out of Kruger*. Johannesburg: Jacana, 1993. An indispensable tool when visiting; color coded maps linked to descriptions of ecozones, plants, and animals.

Lundy, Mike. *Best Walks in the Cape Peninsula*. rev. ed. Cape Town: Struik, 1996. Hiking guide for this very scenic area.

MacRae, Colin. *Fossils of South Africa*. South Africa: Geology Society of South Africa, 1996. Photo and text descriptions cover the entire range of fossils found in one of the world's richest areas.

Paterson-Jones, Colin. *Table Mountain Walks*. Cape Town: Struik, 1994. Also *Garden Route Walks*. Hiking guides.

Pearse, R. O. *Barrier of Spears, Drama of the Drakensberg*. South Africa: Howard Timmons, 1980. A South African classic: the geography and lore of the Natal Drakensberg; with color photos.

Peterson, Wally, and Tripp, Mel. *Birds of the South Western Cape and Where to Find Them*. South Africa: South African Ornithological Society, 1996. An illustrated guide to 40 sites.

Pooley, Tony, and Player, Ian. *KwaZulu-Natal Wildlife Destinations*. South Africa: Southern Book Publishers, 1995. A guide to Natal's nature reserves by its leading conservationists.

Ryan, Brendan, and Bannister, Anthony. *National Parks of South Africa*. South Africa, 1993. Useful information and fine photos.

Taylor, Ricky. *The Greater St. Lucia Wetland Park*. South Africa: Natal Parks Board, 1991. Highly informative.

Wagner, Patrick. *The Otter Trail, and the Tsitsikamma Coastal National Park*. Cape Town: Struik, 1988.

Williamson, Graham. *Richtersveld National Park*. South Africa: National Parks Board, 1995. A useful guide to this unique park.

Zambia

Benson, C. W.; Brooke, R. K.; Dowsett, R. J.; and Irwin, M. P. S. *The Birds of Zambia*. London: Collins, 1971. An out-of-print field guide that is still a useful reference.

Carr, Norman. *A Guide to the Wildlife of the Luangwa Valley*. 2d rev. ed. Zambia: Save the Rhino Trust, 1987.

Carr, Norman. *Kakuli: A Story about Wild Animals, Their Struggle to Survive, and the People Who Live among Them*. 1996.

Carr, Norman. *Valley of the Elephants: The Story of the Luangwa Valley and Its Wildlife*. London: Collins, 1979. Excellent description of Luangwa's annual cycle, with many anecdotes.

Murphy, Iain. *Zambia*. London: CBC Publishing, 1992. A large-format photo portrait of Zambia.

Owens, Delia and Mark. *The Eye of the Elephant*. Boston: Houghton Mifflin, 1992. An adventure story about their research in North Luangwa. Informative but somewhat hyped-up.

Plewman, Nicholas, and Dooley, Brendan. *Visitor's Guide to Zambia*. South Africa: Southern Book Publishers, 1995.

Zimbabwe

Drummond, R. B., and Coates Palgrave, Keith. *Common Trees of the High-*

veld. Harare: Longman, 1973. A concise guide to Zimbawe's native species.

Garlake, Peter S. *Great Zimbabwe.* London: Thames and Hudson, 1973. A scholarly work on the ruins and their historical context.

Garlake, Peter S. *The Hunter's Vision: The Prehistoric Rock Art of Zimbabwe.* 1996. An examination of San society as revealed through their rock paintings.

Igoe, Mark and Hazel. *The Manicaland Guide.* Harare: Argosy Press, 1990. A local guide to the Eastern Highlands.

Joyce, Peter. *Zimbabwe the Beautiful.* Cape Town: Struik, 1996. Large-format photo book.

Lott, Catie, ed. *Spectrum Guide to Zimbabwe.* Edison, NJ: Hunter Publishing, 1991. Photos and text. Informative.

Ponter, Anthony and Laura. *Spirits in Stone.* Sebastapol, CA: Ukama Press, 1992. Celebrates Shona sculpture with photos and informative text.

Plowes, D. C. H., and Drummond, R. B. *Wild Flowers of Rhodesia.* Harare: Longman, 1976. Guide to common species; with photos.

Vaughn, Richard. *Zimbabwe: Africa's Paradise.* London: CBC Publishing, 1993. A photo book, with images taken by Ian Murphy.

The Zambezi River and Victoria Falls

Main, Michael. *Zambezi: Journey of a River.* South Africa: Southern Book Publishers, 1990. Superb coverage of human and natural history, geography, conservation, exploration.

Phillipson, D.W., ed. *Mosi-oa-Tunya, A Handbook to the Victoria Falls Region.* rev. ed. Harare: Longman, 1985. Geology, natural history, ethnology of the area.

Teede, Jan and Fiona. *African Thunder: The Victoria Falls.* South Africa: Russel Friedman Books, 1994. A beautiful hardcover book with photos and drawings.

Teede, Jan and Fiona. *The Zambezi, River of the Gods.* South Africa: Russel Friedman Books, 1990. Informative, with beautiful photos and line drawings.

African Wildlife Periodicals

Africa—Birds and Birding. P.O. Box 44223, Claremont 7735, South Africa. Tel: (27-21) 686-9001. Fax: (27-21) 686-4500. A magazine with solid articles on birds and their conservation; excellent photos.

Africa—Environment and Wildlife. P.O. Box 44223, Claremont 7735, South Africa. Tel: (27-21) 686-9001. Fax: (27-21) 868-4500. A journal about wildlife and conservation, with excellent articles and photography. Includes news from WWF South Africa.

African Wildlife Update. P.O. Box 546, Olympia, WA. Tel: (360) 459-8862. Fax: (360) 459-8771. E-mail: awnews@aol.com. A very informative newsletter on African wildlife and conservation issues.

Getaway. P.O. Box 180, Howard Place 7450, South Africa. Fax: (27-21)

531-7301. Devoted to adventure travel and ecotourism in southern Africa, this magazine is a great source of information on all types of destinations and travel. It features articles on parks and private reserves, luxury resorts and small lodges, hiking trails, 4x4 vehicles, photography, and camping equipment.

Sources for Books

Nature and travel specialty booksellers are the best sources for material on Africa. Any good bookstore can special order titles of books in print from publishers or distributors and get them quickly into your hands. Vendors of hard-to-find books include:

Adventurous Traveller's Bookstore, P.O. Box 14687, Williston, VT 05495. Tel: (800) 282-3963. Fax: (800) 677-1821.

Amazon.com Books. An on-line vendor that sells almost any book that is in print. E-mail: www.amazon.com.

Book Passage, 51 Tamal Vista Blvd., Corte Madera, CA 94925. Tel: (800) 999-7909 or (415) 927-0960.

Buteo Books, 3130 Laurel Rd., Shipman, VA 22971. Tel: (800) 722-2460. Birds, natural history, Africana.

Easy Going, 1385 Shattuck Ave., Berkeley, CA 94707. Tel: (800) 675-500 or (510) 843-3533.

Gerald Rilling Out of Print Books on Africa, 1315 Ryan St., Machesney Park, IL 61115. Tel: (815) 654-0389. Fax: (815) 633-2361. Africana: history, hunting, exploration, anthropology.

Literate Traveler, The, 8306 Wilshire Blvd., Suite 591, Beverly Hills, CA 90211. Tel: (800) 850-2665 or (310) 398-8781.

Los Angeles Audubon Society Bookstore, 7377 Santa Monica Blvd., West Hollywood, CA 90046-6694. Tel: (213) 876-0202. Fax: (213) 876-7609. E-mail: laas@ix.netcom.com.

Magellan Travel Books, 53 S. Main St., Suite 310, Hanover, NH 03755. Tel: (800) 303-0011.

Phileas Fogg's, #87 Stanford Shopping Center, Palo Alto, CA 94304. Tel: (415) 327-1754; (800) 533-FOGG; (800) 233-FOGG (in CA). Books and maps for the traveler.

Rafiki Books, 43 Rawson Ave., Camden, ME. Tel: (207) 236-4244. Fax: (207) 236-6253. Specialists in Africa books.

Russel Friedman Books, 4651 Glenshire Place, Atlanta, GA 30338. Tel: (770) 399-6777. E-mail: abrfb@aol.com. Importers of nature books from South Africa; almost every title published in South Africa is available. [Can also be ordered direct from: Russel Friedman Books, P.O. Box 73, Halfway House 1685, South Africa. Tel: (27-11) 702-2300. Fax: (27-11) 702-1403.]

Traveller's Bookstore, 22 W. 52nd St., New York, NY 10019. Tel: (800) 755-8728.

Index

(Note: italic page numbers indicate photos or maps.)

About the Author

Allen Bechky has been exploring the wilds of Africa for over 25 years, both on his own and as a safari guide in more than a dozen African countries. "Hooked on safari" after his first visit to Africa in 1971, he returned again and again on natural history journeys to the continent's major game parks and little-known wildlife havens. In two decades of safari life, Allen has developed an intimate knowledge of African wildlife and the African environment, and his boundless curiosity about the natural world of Africa has not waned—he is "never happier than when camped within earshot of the big herds." In 1990, he brought his considerable expertise into print in the guidebook *Adventuring in East Africa: The Sierra Club Guide to the Great Safaris of Kenya, Tanzania, Eastern Zaire, Rwanda, and Uganda.* As Director of Africa Operations for many years for Mountain Travel/Sobek (one of America's leading adventure travel companies), he has designed and guided safaris to all of Africa's great wildlife destinations, from Congo's gorilla country to the salt pans of the Kalahari. In 1997, he founded his own safari company. When not leading safaris, Allen resides in Berkeley, California.